Penguin Books

Ourselves and Our Children

About the British contributing editors

Michèle Cohen grew up in France and Canada, studying Psychology and Linguistics at McGill University, Montreal. Since 1966 she has lived and worked in London, and is now teaching a variety of subjects at Richmond College, the American International College of London, pursuing her involvement in the women's movement and raising her son. In 1975 she translated Claudia Broyelle's *Women's Liberation in China* into English (with Gary Herman).

Tina Reid entered motherhood and the women's liberation movement in the late sixties. After five years spent living and working communally in rural Scotland, she returned to London and a collective household. She makes her living as a community worker, writer and, on occasion, claimant. With a group of women writers, she is co-author of *Licking the Bed Clean* and *Smile Smile Smile Smile*, collections of poetry and fiction. She has a son and a daughter.

Some of the authors of this book also wrote
Our Bodies, Ourselves

Ourselves and Our Children

A Book By and For Parents

The Boston Women's Health Book Collective

Penguin Books

Penguin Books Ltd, Harmondsworth, Middlesex, England
Penguin Books, 625 Madison Avenue, New York, New York 10022, U.S.A.
Penguin Books Australia Ltd, Ringwood, Victoria, Australia
Penguin Books Canada Ltd, 2801 John Street, Markham, Ontario, Canada L3R 1B4
Penguin Books (N.Z.) Ltd, 182–190 Wairau Road, Auckland 10, New Zealand

First published in the U.S.A. by Random House, Inc. 1978
First published in Great Britain by Penguin Books 1981

'Food' from 45 Mercy Street by Anne Sexton is reprinted by permission of the publisher,
Houghton Mifflin Co. Copyright © Linda Gray Sexton and Loring Conant, Jr. 1976

'The Haunting' by Jeri Bain originally appeared in Stepparents Forum

Made and printed in Great Britain by William Clowes and Sons Ltd., Beccles
Phototypeset in Photina by Filmtype Services Limited, Scarborough

Acknowledgements

Special thanks go to:

CHARLOTTE MAYERSON, our editor at Random House, on whom we confer an honorary degree in psychology for her work with us. Over the three years she has wholeheartedly shared her impressive editing skills, her life experiences, her sense of humour, and her persistent faith in us and our book.

ROBERT FEIN, MARY HOWELL, JOSEPH PLECK, and MARY ROWE, who, from the earliest stages, recognized and affirmed what we sought to do. They waded cheerfully through lengthy unedited versions of many chapters, and spoke with us most helpfully out of both their professional and personal lives.

RONNIE KONNER, who kept us sane by handling the enormous job of coordinating all the typing. We thank her for her indefatigable organization and, as our first outside critic, for her strategic words of encouragement.

GINA PRENOWITZ, who edited the entire manuscript with care and clarity. We thank her for her loving objectivity, for her endless hours of work, and for the firmness with which she held to her instinctive grasp of our vision even when it became clouded for us.

ROZ GERSTEIN, whose skills as a graphic artist, generously shared photographic resources, honest criticism, and sheer creative energy helped us work towards an exciting visual design for our book.

FRANCES LITMAN, of the Wheelock Center for Parenting Studies, who read our manuscript under considerable time pressure and shared with us her experience, her wisdom, and her ability to discern significant details.

To the other members of the Boston Women's Health Book Collective, PAMELA BERGER, VILUNYA DISKIN, JUDY NORSIGIAN, ESTHER ROME, and NORMA SWENSON, who stuck with us lovingly even when they weren't quite sure of what we were doing.

And most special thanks of all to our families – husbands, children, lovers, parents – who laboured with us as we gave birth to this book, and believed us the three hundred and sixty-five times we said we were finally finished.

Doress; Joshua and Gina Hawley; Sami and Ben Pincus; Susan Moon; Francie Shaw; Nora Ausubel and Mitch Ryerson; Matthew Sanford; Howie, Linda, Sharlene and Ilene Speizer; Jesse and Marya Wegman; Lea and Alexi Wolf.

Thanks beyond measure go to our husbands and lovers –

David Alexander   Jeffrey McIntyre   David Wegman
Bruce Ditzion   Ed Pincus   Tom Wolf
Irvin Doress   Frank E. Speizer

Your love, your partnership, and your sheer endurance have much to do with our book coming out the way we hoped it would.

Contents

Introduction to the British Edition

Ourselves and Our Children is written by parents, rather than by students of parenthood, and the book has been made from their experience, feelings and insights: 'the stuff of our lives'. These lives are American and the book is an American book. Our purpose as editors has not been to alter the heart of it, but only to add, or occasionally substitute, information useful to a British reader. To be sure, there is a cultural divide, but it is not a hard one to leap. Any of us can empathize with the mother stuck between a miserable, screaming infant and hostile co-passengers during an inter-state flight, even if our equivalent experiences usually take place on the bus. Children create bother on both sides of the Atlantic.

The same can be said of late-twentieth-century capitalism, by which we mean a social system which is organized around work and the making of profit, rather than around people and caring for their needs. But while our two societies are geared in the same direction – and it is not towards happy childhood and happy parenthood – there are crucial differences in the detail of how each hinders or helps our parenting. So in the last two chapters, where the book moves away from the personal and subjective and towards social comment and information, we have made larger changes in this edition.

Possibly the major difference in bringing up children in Britain is made by the existence of a 'welfare state': interwoven systems of health care, education, social services and social security which are directed by central policy-making. The overall system is imperfect and inadequate. Resources for schools, hospitals, nurseries and other social services are unevenly distributed, and further inequalities result from the priorities and politics of local councils. Welfare benefits are a bewildering maze of contributory and non-contributory, means-tested and non-means-tested, but uniformly mean allowances. But however embryonic, or, worse, vestigial, we think it, the welfare state does exist and profoundly affects parents, both helping and interfering. The same local authority which provides a reasonable nursery for a toddler can insist, with legal muscle, that her elder sister attends a totally unsuitable school.

We have not attempted a comprehensive review and critique of state provision affecting parents; we have instead pointed to it piecemeal, where appropriate in the text, and directed readers to other literature for more information and to organizations working to maintain and improve services. Our chief concern has been to demonstrate that the state acknowledges a limited responsibility in caring for our children, whilst insisting on some authority over them, and that the voice of parents should be heard and should shape the exercise of that responsibility and authority.

Our working on this book coincided with the first years in office of a government which appears to favour the rapid dismantling of our welfare services, rather than the subtle erosion allowed by previous administrations. Vast cuts have been ordered and made in public spending which hit at and hurt parents and children. Already child-care facilities have been closed, maternity benefits cut, extra charges for school meals imposed. With fine disregard for working parents, a much shorter school-day has even been proposed. In the prevailing mood of enthusiasm for curtailing provision and liberties, the continued availability of legal abortion is still at risk, and the supplementary benefit service, on which most lone parents depend, is threatened. This organized assault on services and entitlements explains our concern, expressed in the text, to encourage parents to organize to defend them. Whilst we have grave criticisms of existing provisions, their disappearance would damage the quality of our lives, our childrens' lives and of our parenting.

Our sense of urgency about parents coming together to protest or campaign thus comes from our particularly British context and times. It is extra to the primary aim of the book, expressed by the Boston Collective, 'to urge readers to break through their isolation and seek out support and help from sources appropriate for them – neighbours, friends, relatives, agencies'. We wholeheart-edly endorse this aim. We know too, from experience, how hard it can be to break through. 'Motherhood is the best-kept secret in the world', quotes one of the women who talk about their lives in *Dutiful Daughters*,* and adds 'They're right, because no one really owns up to what it's like'. And fatherhood is barely whispered about. We hope that sharing the feelings and experiences of these American parents will be a first and positive step for readers to begin sharing their own.

Michèle Cohen
Tina Reid

---

*Edited by J. McCrindle and S. Rowbotham (London: Penguin, 1979).

To the Readers of the British Edition

Greetings to you from our Collective! We are glad that our book about parents' lives has come to your country. We wrote it from our experience as adults who are loving and working and raising our children in one part of the USA. We wonder what common themes you will find between your lives and ours.

We hope that our book will encourage you to look at your lives and your needs as mothers and fathers. You may be moved to talk with other parents about issues you haven't spoken openly about before, and find that you aren't alone in your worries, problems, satisfactions, angers, joys. We want the book to support you in looking more critically at the social institutions which shape your parenthood: your workplace, the economic structures of your society, its health and education institutions. We hope you will see institutional changes that you and other parents can get together to make, in order to make your society a more supportive one for parents. The book will also urge you to explore how you and other parents in your community can help each other in informal ways, building networks of personal support that we all need so badly.

Life may look quite different in the diverse cultures and nations around the globe, but at the heart of every society are parents caring for their children. We hope this book and others like it can open a dialogue among parents in different countries. As parents around the world understand each other more deeply, and affirm each other's life-sustaining role, we can help build a more humane and peaceful world community.

Please, if you have time, write to us with responses to our book and stories from your life as parents.

Warmly,

Ruth, Joan, Paula, Nancy, Jane, Alice, Wendy, Jeanne, Peggy, Dennie

Boston Women's Health Book Collective, PO Box 192, West Somerville, MA 02144, USA

Introduction

Wendy Coppedge Sanford

This book is an invitation to you as a parent, an about-to-be parent, or as someone who is wondering whether to have or adopt children. Our invitation is one that parents don't often hear: *Consider yourself.* Who and where are *you* in this lifelong process of being someone's child and, perhaps, someone's parent? How does being a parent interweave with your overall life, your work, your relationships, your social and political concerns, your own childhood, your sense of yourself? How does the society around you shape your experience for better or worse? What do you need? Where does your support come from?

When we who are writing this book first started talking about ourselves as parents, in an ongoing women's discussion group two years ago, we found these questions to be unfamiliar and stirring. *Ourselves and Our Children* represents our exploration of these questions about parents, which was carried on among ourselves and in interview-discussions with more than two hundred mothers and fathers. It has been a challenge to find a language for these new considerations, and we offer this book knowing that what we say will be much improved as readers discuss it among themselves and share their responses with us.

After looking at the crucial decision about whether and when to become parents, the first half of the book will follow parents' lives from the beginnings – pregnancy, adoption, or initial step-parenting – through the time when our children grow old enough to leave home and we become parents of 'grown-ups'. The last four chapters will consider more analytically some special dimensions of parents' experience and needs: shared parenthood, in which two parents share the primary daily care of their children; family and the different forms that families take; the social institutions and attitudes which affect parents, and ways that some parents have worked for change; and, finally, the kinds of help that parents need, ways they can help themselves and each other, and the various professional and lay resources to which parents can turn. We see the book as a resource to be picked up and read at different stages of your life – not necessarily from cover to cover.

The ten of us have chosen to write the book collectively, believing that an experience as varied and complex as parenthood might best be expressed by a number of voices. Each chapter has one or two primary authors; each writer brings the particular insights, preoccupations and emotional atmosphere of where she is in her own life as a parent-person. Each chapter has also been discussed and added to by everyone else in the group and a number of outside readers on its way to final form. While we share an underlying philosophy about parenthood, we have sometimes disagreed on what is important to write about; we have tried in our collective process to give the book unity while still respecting the integrity of what each woman has written. The book's unity, such as it is, comes not from a unified voice but from the belief that many voices together can come closer to telling the truth.

The original conception for the parenting book emerged from two years of exploratory meetings among Ruth Bell, Joan Ditzion, Paula Doress and Nancy Hawley, who pursued their vision of a book for and by parents until it took coherent shape. Before we began writing, Wendy Sanford joined as editor and coordinator, midwifing both ideas and words. Jane Pincus, who had taken part in some of the earliest discussions, contributed to the writing process, despite having moved away. The six of us had worked together before as co-authors of *Our Bodies, Ourselves*, a book on women's health, reproduction and sexuality. As the project became larger, we needed help, and were extremely lucky at getting the four people who joined. Alice Ryerson, from Chicago, not only urged that we have a chapter on being parents of grown-ups, but also offered to write it. Jeanne Speizer, Peggy Wegman and Dennie Wolf brought their particular skills and insights to their chapters and became invaluable members of our parenting group as they laboured with us. The parents we spoke with are mainly mothers and fathers in the greater Boston area who are friends or friends of friends. While they in no way represent a complete cross-section ethnically or economically, they are varied: mainly white, with a few minority parents, married, single, divorced, straight, gay, living in nuclear families and in communal situations, in suburbs and country and city. What most of them have in common is that whether or not they work outside the home, they take an active role in their children's daily life and have a desire to look reflectively at their lives as parents. Our 'interviews' were informal – we were looking not for statistics but for insights, feelings and experiences. We are deeply grateful to the people who gave us their time, energy and thoughtfulness as they told us the stories of their parenthood.

Before moving into the main body of the book, we want to address a few preliminary questions. Why focus on parents? What is our notion of a parent as a whole person? Who are we, the authors – through what lens are we looking?

Why Focus on Parents?

We have found in ourselves and others a hunger to talk and to hear about *being parents* – not about how to do it, but about what it's like. This, we suspect, is what women and men wondering whether to become parents need to hear about; and it is what parents themselves need a chance to explore. We need to discover that other parents worry as we do, grow as we do, feel inadequate as we do, feel joyous, exhilarated or angry as we do. We need to hear from all sides – from those who mostly delight in being a parent, from those who feel trapped, from those who love their kids but don't enjoy parenthood. We need to hear how others work out the crucial balance between their activities as parents, workers, lovers, friends. Quite simply, parents need to hear from each other. This book is an attempt to make space for the speaking and the listening which can help us feel better about ourselves as parents and as people.

Steve Smith/David Alexander Studio

As the ten of us spoke among ourselves, we found that we all grew up with certain assumptions about parenting: that everyone will of course have children and that everyone will of course be suited to it; that the ideal parent is a 'grown-up' before the kids arrive and doesn't go through unsettling or painful changes after that; that the ideal parent will give selflessly of herself or himself without conflict, ambivalence or resentment. A tall order, we have found! While each of us writing this book always assumed we would have children, we have not found ourselves immediately or equally suited to the task. And the mythical ideal parent has not fit our own experience: our parenting is both worse than this – more conflicted, more entrapping, more uncertain – and better – more engaging, more stimulating to our own growth. Yet until we talked honestly with other parents about the 'real' parenting experience, this mythical ideal parent wielded a powerful influence on us from without and within, silencing our protests and hampering our joys. Focusing on ourselves as parents has helped us shrug that superparent off our shoulders, to accept our imperfections, to accept with one father whom we interviewed that 'at certain stages of the game certain people do better.'

Further, we have found that talking about our own lives and needs as parents is a first step to looking more critically at institutions and attitudes in our society which unfairly distort the lives of parents and children today. For we discover that parenthood *can* be different from our culture's 'institutionalized' version of it.* In other words, certain structures of our society generated by sexism, racism or a preoccupation with technological production and profits create an 'institution' of parenthood which violates the potential of the parenting experience. In this book we will suggest changes in parental role and in social structure which can help us to reclaim our parenthood as an integrated, nourishing enterprise. We believe that the best social and political critique grows directly out of what parents say about themselves.

Is it selfish for parents to spend time considering themselves? The myth of the all-giving, selfless parent might have us think so. As one mother of four teenagers witnesses: 'I feel selfish talking about myself. Where I live, the accepted avenue for talking about yourself is through your kids.' The question of 'selfishness' subsides as we discover how creative it is for our own parenting and family life when we balance our concern for our children with attention to ourselves as full human beings who are parents. While benefiting our children was not necessarily our first motivation, we find that when we pay attention to ourselves it really does seem to help our kids. One mother of four puts it this way:

I believe that unless I, the parent, feel good about myself and comfortable with myself and my own identity, and have some way of getting myself validated – through work or committee activities or something – my kids become too important to me as extensions of myself. How many parties have we been to where everybody sits around and talks about their kids and what grades they made, and which kids are doing what? I think that as parents if we begin to sense that we are getting our feelings of identity and goodness about ourselves because our kids are succeeding, we had better take the time to really look at ourselves and say 'Now this isn't helping us and it certainly isn't helping our kids.' Because sooner or later it puts too heavy a load on the kids and it doesn't free them to be themselves.

Some fear that if parents start listening to their own wants and needs they will neglect their children. It is our belief that children are in fact far less likely to be neglected when their parents' needs – for support, for friendship, for decent work, for security, for health care, for learning, for play, for time alone – are being met.

Considering ourselves more fully as people has allowed us to see our children as people, as unique human beings who are separate from us and as worthy of respect as we are. It has allowed us to move away from interacting with them solely in terms of roles – the role of mother/child, or father/child, or, what's often even worse, of united-parental-front/child. We are their parents, with all the responsibility, the need for limit-setting, the hopes and pains and pleasures that parenthood carries. Yet we, as much as they, are in the process of growing. When we feel freer to reveal ourselves to them as developing, many-dimensioned,

---

*This distinction comes from Adrienne Rich, *Of Woman Born – Motherhood as Experience and Institution* (London: Virago, 1977).

imperfect human beings, we are able to give our children a more realistic picture of what being a person is all about.

Mothers and Fathers as Whole People

This notion of a parent being a whole person is central to our vision as we focus on parents. As we see it, becoming a whole person involves a different process for mothers and for fathers. Most women who are considering parenthood or who already have children think of themselves as the primary daily parent, whether or not they also work outside the home. Mothers who choose to stay home until their children grow up want a range of interests, sociability and creative activities beyond child care and housework. To get time for civic work, for exercise, for neighbourhood projects, reading meditation, or just plain time to themselves, mothers need to hold out against the fairly recent but surprisingly entrenched myth that 'good mothers' are constantly with their children. They will have to speak out at last about the demoralizing effect of spending day after day with small children, no matter how much they love them.

Burk Uzzle/Magnum

For the increasing numbers of mothers in paid employment, to become a whole person as a parent requires wrestling free of the guilt that the 'good mother' myth instils. It means negotiating family arrangements so mothers don't end up doing all the housework after they get home from their job; it means struggling to get time for themselves, to explore other dimensions in themselves – their hobbies, relationships, spiritual concerns and so on. This woman expresses it well:

I think that one of the most difficult things for me as a woman is.trying to put myself into all these different places, be a wife, and be a mother, and also have a job, and trying to look where that goes and what's important to me in my life, and to form a kind of balance so I am not all mother and not all wife, and I am not all worker. Somehow all of that is important to make me see myself as a whole person.

For fathers, being a whole person as a parent often means exploring far more of the child-oriented and nurturing sides of themselves than our culture has encouraged them to do. It means moving beyond the stereotypical notions that fathers best show their love by providing or struggling to provide financially, or that men are biologically less suited to be nurturing than women are. It means starting to participate more in the daily care of their kids, to open themselves to both the pettiness and wonder that such daily care brings.

Mothers and fathers who work outside the home need to struggle to get their workplaces to respect them as workers who are parents, rather than expecting them to drop their parent identity as they walk in the door. More flexible working hours, day care on the job and maternity and paternity leave are examples of what parents are pushing for. We can't work for personal change without also working to change our society, whose economic structures and parenthood myths make exploration of more varied roles next to impossible for so many parents.

We will talk a lot in this book about mothers and fathers expanding their roles and sharing the various tasks of parenthood, because in our experience this helps mothers, fathers and children to grow as whole people. If you are someone who believes that male and female parents should do strictly separate and complementary things, then you may find us suggesting changes that you would prefer to avoid. We must say here that we do not presume to speak for all parents in this book. When we talk about sharing parenthood, we offer a vision of parenthood that grows out of our own experience; we hope to hear from readers as to what parts of it make sense to you and what parts don't.

Who are we, the authors – through what lens do we look at parenthood?

The experience of being a parent varies tremendously from person to person and from culture to culture according to family form, financial status, geography, ethnic background and more. Since this book has grown out of our particular experience of ourselves as parents, out of our own history and way of looking at things, we need to tell you something of who we are. The rest of the introduction will take up a number of our characteristics as individuals and as a group. By exploring these, we hope to give you an idea of the perspective we bring, of our vision and our values, so that you can read the book in dialogue with us. In return, we invite you to look at some of the same categories for yourself: what particular history and perspective do you bring to this topic of 'being parents'?

We are all parents. It is important to say that we are writing not as professionals or experts but simply as parents. We write not about parenting 'out there' as an object of study, but about parenting 'in here' as the stuff of our lives. We write out of our daily involvement with our children – from the full mixture of repetitive work, arduous emotional struggles, moments of intimacy, picky irritation, sleepy kisses, boredom, panic, fascination, self-doubt and wonder. Out of this involvement comes what we think is the true expertise.

Among us we have twenty-three children ranging in age from one to thirty-five, so we bring to the book the various perspectives, perplexities and wisdoms that each different stage of children's growing brings. Since all but one of us has children still living at home, we write from the midst of the psychic and logistical 'balancing act' of parenthood, in which we struggle to live coherently as parent, worker, partner, lover, child to our own parents, friend to self and to others.

Writing as parents and not as professionals, we will emphasize wherever possible what parents can do for themselves and each other to help meet the stresses of parenthood. While we acknowledge the value of professional resources at certain times and talk about some of these in the Helping Ourselves chapter, we believe that first and foremost we can help each other – by listening, by taking each other's children, cooking a meal, keeping an eye out for kids on the street, giving a teenager a home away from home or forming a support group. We see the ability to ask others for help as one of the major skills that parents can develop. And we see parent-action groups, such as Action for Children's Television or Children in Hospitals or some local PTAs, as important instruments of the power parents must wield, working cooperatively, to make changes in the institutions which affect our parenting experience.

Several special aspects of the *way* we are parents have shaped our perspective in writing this book. In the first place, though at moments the glamorous child-free go-where-you-want-to-when-you-want-to mystique has its allure for us, we take the work of parenting seriously, believing that helping children grow is an important thing to do, and that we ourselves will develop in invaluable ways in the process of their growing. We may, in fact, perhaps take our parenting too seriously: like many parents in the United States, we probably worry too much about whether we are doing a 'good job'. But this preoccupation is not just a function of our perfectionism; it is a response to being a parent in a society which gives us too little support: we worry because we are alone on the job in certain important ways.

We are parents who work part or full time on non-parenting, non-householding work, more or less according to the age of our children. Although we work out of differing degrees of financial necessity, we all want to work. We are among the increasing number of mothers who, through necessity or inclination or both, are moving into the work force even when their children are very young. We are writers, therapists, teachers, administrators, education consultants, graduate students, artists. One in-depth series of interviews in California* showed that even the mothers who have tedious, low-paying jobs

*Lillian Breslow Rubin, *Worlds of Pain: Life in the Working-Class Family* (New York: Basic Books, Inc., 1976), pp. 169 ff.

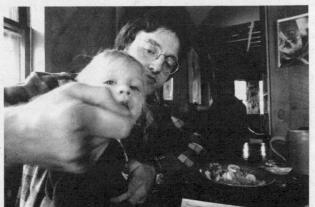

Antonio Mendoza

tended to be less depressed and to feel better about themselves than mothers in the same neighbourhood who were staying at home with young children full time. Many women who used to be full-time mothers are discovering that outside work gives them friends, challenges, variety, money, independence; it makes them feel better about themselves, and therefore lets them be better parents.

The flip side of this coin, however, is that many parents have to work so much outside the home that they can't have enough time with their kids. All of us in the group have been able to work less than full time until our children were in school, and most continue to do so, which allows us to spend the time we would like with our children and yet still have the challenges and satisfactions of other work. We are fortunate. Many working parents yearn for just such a balance between time 'inside' and time 'outside' the family and yet their jobs do not allow it. While there is no one way to be a parent and a work person at the same time, every parent should be able to shape this crucial balance; yet our society today is quite inflexible in this regard.

Several different chapters in the book will talk about work – about the ways that our workplaces could better respect us as parents, about the difficult shifting of focus in transition from one arena to the other, about the tugs back and forth that so many parents feel between the different calls on their time. In stressing the importance of the worker-parent balance, however, we want to be careful to leave space for the non-worker, non-parent parts of our lives. A working mother gives us a good warning:

I think the reason we focus all the time on work and parenting is that those are the two things that we are categorized with: you are a mother with or without a career, or you are a career person if you have no children. And people don't really take into account your hobbies, your church life, your friendships, your other interests. You are just looked upon as: she is a mother and she does this, or she does this and she is a mother.

Both mothers and fathers need to pay attention to ourselves as parents, as workers *and* as the whole rich variety of other things that we all are.

While the majority of us are married and live in nuclear families, a number of us in the group are divorced or separated, and bring to the book some of the special insights of single parenthood. We are no longer in the family unit so widely considered in this country to be 'normal': the unit of mother, father and children. We know the pain of feeling different, incomplete; we know the tendency to blame every problem our kids have on our not having a 'proper' family. Yet most single parents who stay single for a while come through this time of feeling bereft and apologetic to discover that while we are missing certain benefits of a two-parent family, we are in fact *still a family* with, even, certain strengths that are unique to single parenthood. In order to accept who we are as parents, we have had to work through the deeply internalized myth of 'normal' parenthood. Doing this has opened our eyes to the whole variety of ways that people can parent and that kids can get what they need. It keeps us from assuming in this book that the 'best' or only viable family form is the conventional one. Our perspective is a timely one, too, for the myth of normality is in fact way behind the actual situation. Nearly 40 per cent of families in this country do not conform to the norm in one way or another. It is estimated that over a third of American children alive today will at some point during their childhood live in a single-parent home. And these children will often, through remarriage, find themselves with a step-parent and stepbrothers and stepsisters: these families, too, will be harassed by the myth of normalcy. The single parents in our group help keep us from making assumptions about what is normal and what is not.

Those of us who have to work to support our kids – and especially those of us who are single – know well how incredibly stressful it is when earning money for and being with our family come into conflict; the push to bring the provider and parent roles more into harmony is one of the main themes of the book. Further, single parents (especially mothers) nearly always face a lower standard of living: being more economically precarious, we feel the full negative force of the absence of certain measures that society could and should take to support all parents. We bring this awareness to all sections of the book, particularly to the chapter on Society's Impact on Families.

Perhaps most creative of all is our new understanding of the value of reaching out to others for support and cooperation. Having been forced by our situation to look outside the traditional nuclear family for care for our children and ourselves, knowing so well that we cannot 'do it on our own', we bring to the book a sharpened sense of the many resources that all parents can turn to once they drop the constraints of our culture's pride in self-sufficiency. Family, friends, neighbours, church members, our children's teachers, women's groups, single parents' groups, our children themselves – each of us has found one or another of these a rich source of help once we asked for it. Some of the book's emphasis on networking with others – that is, on building links of cooperation and mutual help among friends and neighbours – comes from our experience as single parents.

Although the Families and Sharing chapters have sections which focus on single parents, we have also chosen to integrate their voices into the whole of the book. This is because so many issues are shared by all parents no matter what their family form, and because the special insights of single parents can bring new understanding to coupled parents as well.

Aside from divorce or separation, we have on the whole had fairly standard parenting experiences. We have not lived with special challenges such as adoption or special problems such as having a retarded or crippled or very sick child. While we have tried through interviews to bring these experiences into the book, they won't appear in nearly the amount or complexity that a parent living through such a situation might desire. We do not have the expertise of first-hand knowledge to do them justice, and we have chosen instead to explore most fully the things that all parents have in common. We suspect that in not hearing more from parents whose children have special needs, we have missed some important dimensions of what it can mean to be a parent. We hope that our focus on parents will encourage those mothers and fathers to consider in ways that will help them their own issues and needs, in a life which surely demands more sacrifice and single-focus parenting than ours does. In the Helping Ourselves chapter we list some resources, such as the various support groups which have been formed. Interestingly enough, there are far fewer organized resources for parents *without* special needs; there is an assumption in our society that unless there is some kind of crisis, parents won't or shouldn't need help. This book is witness to the need of all parents for support, companionship and understanding.

The fact that we are daily parents – that even though we work full or nearly full time we still spend considerable time with our children – has shaped our vision of the possibilities for parents. We have learned that being actively engaged in our children's lives from their infancy on is a satisfying and creative form of parenting for us and for our children. As long as there is a balance of time away from and time with our children, being a daily parent is a unique opportunity for learning, growing and loving. When we urge this daily involvement on fathers, it is partly because we as women, suffocated by the boring parts and exhausted by the arduous parts of our daily parenting, want to bring fathers back into the home to free us. Yet the truth is also larger: we want for fathers the growth that comes from living intimately with children, from being responsible for their daily care, and from opening up to the changes that children bring out in us. We want partners who share both the joy and the aggravation with us, who in learning to love their children and to be vulnerable to them may learn also to love us more fully. We as women-mothers would suggest that certain so-called feminine strengths, such as compassion, intuition, patience, endurance, humaneness, have over the centuries taken root in parent-soil – called forth, sometimes with great pain, by the daily parenting experience. We wonder whether the humbling, humanizing work of daily parenting might not be an effective antidote to the cruel efficiency of the 'best and the brightest', of those people, often men, who run our country from board rooms and offices, who tend too often to sacrifice human values to goals of profit, defence, competition and winning.

Yet not everyone is the better for having children. While most of us in our group have found it so, the parenting experience is not humanizing and growth-producing for everybody. For some, parenthood involves predominantly endurance, resentment, frustration, misery and pain.* On the whole we in the group affirm our parenthood, are glad that we are parents; many parents are not so glad, and they need to be heard. Being a parent is for many a remarkable way to grow up, to engage oneself with life, to be schooled in some universal human

---

*In a number of recent books, parents have spoken out more openly than ever before about the painful parts of being parents and about their negative feelings. See Shirley L. Radl's *Mother's Day Is Over* (New York: Warner Paperback Library, 1974), and *Of Woman Born* and *Worlds of Pain*, both cited above.

values. Yet for some, parenting is an obstacle rather than an opportunity. Both sides need to be spoken for.

In a society which expects every 'normal' person to have children, inevitably some will fall into parenthood when it isn't right for them. And just as important, in a society which then fails to ensure every family's right to decent shelter, food and health care, many who might flourish as parents do not. They may be so locked into the uphill struggle to make ends meet and to wrest nourishment for their children and themselves from an ungiving society that their parenthood is crippled. Or they may find themselves isolated in a house in a suburb away from family and old friends, trying to parent alone: the sheer isolation can change their parenting experience into a struggle. We want in this book to address these different situations: to encourage people to examine whether they want to become parents; to give voice to those who find themselves parents and feel caught; to help all parents live with more understanding and satisfaction and with more of a sense of their rights, possibilities and resources. We want to look at what in our society makes it hard even for those who are well suited for parenthood. If we focus on sex-role stereotyping, on a profit-motive economy, on our culture's values of rugged individualism and self-sufficiency, it is because so many parents report these as the source of their pain. If we focus on the proper balance of daily parenting and outside work, on growing to treat ourselves and our children as unique respect-worthy human beings, on learning to be open about our feelings, on networking with others, it is because so many parents report these as the source of their satisfaction and optimism.

A second primary characteristic of the ten of us is that *we are all women*. Since 'parents' includes both mothers and fathers, why are there no men in the group?

Although we interviewed many fathers and use their stories throughout the book, we did not include men in our core group, initially because we had worked together as a women's collective before and wanted to do so again. (Six of us have been in the same work-and-personal-support group since 1969.) Increasingly, the choice seemed appropriate, for the questions we were asking came out of our experience as women. We believe that as women, as mothers who have done most of the direct daily parenting in our families and who have been most directly parented by women as we grew up, at this point in history we *are* the most appropriate people to grind the lens for the focus of this exploration into parenthood.

Why did we write about 'being parents', instead of about 'mothering'? We didn't want to write simply on 'mothering' because of the very fact that in our society at present so much of the parenting is done by mothers only, and we want to see men and women share the role in a mutual way. To use 'mothering' as the key term would be to support the myth that only mothers can do the important parts of child raising; it would be to perpetuate just the role split that we want to dissolve.

As women raising our children in Boston in the 1960s and 1970s, most of us have been influenced in some way by the women's movement, be it through participation in a women's discussion group, through work for improved health care and equal rights or through reading newspapers and journals and talking with friends. This experience has shaped certain aspects of our book. One creative insight – not new to the women's movement but newly accessible to us – has been the recognition that the 'personal' and the 'political' are inseparably intertwined. When we as women began to speak more openly with each other about our lives, we discovered, for example, that many painful situations – on the job, with parents, in our relationships – which we had been suffering in isolation and blaming on ourselves were in fact shared by many. This discovery prompted us to look beyond ourselves to the social attitudes and political structures which contributed to the problem. If, for instance, we had considered ourselves 'frigid' and unresponsive in sex, we began to understand that poor sex education, the double standard and general societal power imbalances between men and women had far more to do with our sexual problems than did our own personal inadequacy. Understanding these things, we could stop blaming ourselves and

get together to work for change – both at home, where we could confront our situation with new understanding, and out in the world, where we could work for sex education courses, for better birth-control laws, for new attitudes toward sex and women's sexuality. We also saw that larger political movements had to be rooted in the realities of our personal lives: the public struggle for women's rights, for instance, must both reflect and be expressed in what happens in our very kitchens, in the domestic negotiations over who does the dishes or stays home with a sick child.

We bring to our exploration of parenting this growing awareness of the interconnection of the personal and the political. The Society chapter's analysis of social policy and possible social change is rooted in the earlier chapters' presentation of parents speaking from the midst of the very immediate personal experience. We believe that the daily life of parents all around the country has political significance. The negative parts of being parents – the frustrations, the isolation, the feeling of being powerless over how our children grow – are not our 'fault', as many would argue. Too often what goes on in families is looked at in terms of the four walls of the home. Yet in speaking with other parents we find that these problems are shared; so we begin to trace them to larger social causes – to the structures of work and profit, the condition of our neighbourhoods, inadequacies of the health care system, sexist and racist attitudes, the isolation of the nuclear family. The changes we work for will be both within our four walls and beyond.

For instance, many parents of young children will recognize themselves in this mother's 'confession'.

Some mornings when I wake up and realize I'm going to be with my kids all day, I have this sinking, suffocated, panicky feeling. It's as though I see my core self, the me I know myself to be, fading off out of reach. Yet I love my children and I mostly love being with them. I feel guilty about this panicky feeling, which makes it even worse.

So many parents speak of having this feeling from time to time that we begin to see that it's not a matter of individual parental inadequacy or unlovingness. In *Towards a New Psychology of Women*, Jean Baker Miller, M.D.,* looks from the individual parent to the larger social picture. Our culture, observes Miller, values the world of commerce and public life far more highly than that of home and child rearing. People who move in the former are therefore most often perceived by others and themselves as being 'in the action', while those who are at home or whose work is with small children are judged 'out of the action' – especially because that work has normally been assigned to women, and because it doesn't produce immediate economic results. The parent who feels suffocated at the prospect of a day with kids is responding not only to the nitty-gritty demanding reality of children's needs and play; s/he is responding also to the judgement implicit in our culture that s/he will be 'out of the action' all day. This deeply entrenched social attitude makes parents feel bad, and saps away the psychic energy we might bring to being with our children. Understanding it for what it is, we can stop blaming ourselves and begin to work to bring the personal and political together: in this case, we can begin to redefine where the 'action' is.

We can also begin to let the *positive* dimensions of being a parent shape our political and social vision. Consider the fact that often the most rewarding time spent with children is non-goal-oriented time, where no 'product' results and efficiency is not a priority; we could extend this value into our public life by

*Jean Baker Miller, *Towards a New Psychology of Women* (London: Penguin, 1978).

reorganizing our work structures to build in time for community experiences and celebrations. On a more immediate level, if policy makers, both male and female, were truly conscious of themselves and/or others as parents, instead of being encouraged to leave their parent-identity at home as secondary or 'out of the action', our country's laws and public policies would take parents into account far more than they do at present. So, in the same way that people's eyes need to be opened to the role that society plays in shaping our experience of parenthood, we need to make it possible for the flow of our insights as parents to enter into our larger society's ethos. The public and private worlds cry out to be reintegrated, for the split between them is a destructive one. Because family life is bearing the brunt of this split, parents can point to where it most needs healing.

Our very act of writing this book reflects an interweaving of the personal and the political, the private and the public. While in writing we direct our efforts outward, offering our thoughts as tools of understanding and change, at the same time we raise emotion-packed issues in our own parenthood. For example:

One day after writing a section on the resources people can turn to as newly single parents, I found myself quite unexpectedly exhausted, feeling curiously vulnerable and shaky. My topic for the morning had been no mere academic one but a highly charged chapter of my own history. The writing put me in touch with all those feelings I'd had when I first separated from my husband. No wonder I felt exhausted and vulnerable!

Writing this book has allowed each of us to reflect on our own parenthood, to consider ourselves as parent-people, to hold our own anxieties and pleasures up to the light of caring scrutiny. While we have tried to be careful not to write a book that is *just* us, we believe that the intensity of feeling, the pain and the love with which we are working toward an understanding for ourselves will give the book a life and feeling that no sociological study could have. Yet there are moments when we experience the height of irony: our group came together to think and write about being parents, yet on snow days or sick days or long weekend afternoons when we need to get work done to meet a deadline, being parents is just what gets in our way! The very fact that this book exists represents a long series of tugs and pulls and compromises between our public and private, work and parent selves.

Our familiarity with working collectively in women's groups, particularly in the *Our Bodies, Ourselves* group, led us to write this book as a collective. In consciousness-raising groups and work groups, women have discovered the creative potential of pondering and working together in a non-hierarchical fashion. Because we each gain personally from the sharing and the struggling that goes into working together, the project accomplishes more than its final 'product'. It has felt supportive at certain key moments to each of us to work in a group of people who are sensitive to our special needs and preoccupations as parents.

We in the group call ourselves *feminists*, a term which is used to mean so many different things that we want to say what we mean by it, and then to look at a few popular stereotypes of feminism which might lead to a misunderstanding of what we are about in this book. By feminism here, we mean, most simply, a way of looking at the world which takes women seriously as full human beings with a right to a full share in all kinds of work and creative enterprise. Feminism means affirming the particular insights and strengths of women which grow out of our cumulative history as the nurturers, the ones unaccustomed to exerting power over others, the ones who know the oppression of culture-bound roles from the inside. Feminism means carrying these special insights and strengths with us as we move into the world to take our share of responsibility and power, with the hope that the very structures of society and nature of power will be changed by our involvement. We are eager to find new ways of being, of working, of parenting, which are not circumscribed by stereotypical assumptions of what men and women 'should' do. We know men who are 'feminists' according to this definition – who, like us, are trying to break out of rigidly defined roles.

One popular stereotype of feminism sees it as opposed to parenthood and family life. Where did this impression come from? Most of us had our children just before the current wave of the women's movement brought its challenging and healing message that we are whole people with many roles to play in society. As our eyes were opened, we saw that the oppressive institution of motherhood in a sexist culture caged us, kept us from the promise of becoming full persons. The reaction of some feminists was to turn against motherhood altogether. Women's movement rhetoric, especially in the early years, often seemed to suggest that married women and mothers were somehow regressive, many crucial steps behind on the path to liberation. Many mothers and wives therefore felt excluded or put down by the feminist message.

The ten of us believe that feminism does not exclude family life and parenthood, but that it will and must change them. Feminism must change the old pattern in which a woman gives all of herself to her husband and children, only to be left empty and depressed at mid-life when her children leave home. Feminism must change the role of fathers, urging them back into their children's lives and into mutuality with their partners. Feminism must open up the forms of parenthood, pushing us to realize that single parents, gay parents and parents in communes can *be* parents in the way that children need. As we discover in women's support groups how much we need to be nurtured by each other and how much we can 'mother' each other, we understand that nurturing and good parenting can flow among all persons, and not just in hierarchical fashion from parent (usually mother) to child. Feminism must change the way we raise our children, pushing us to open the world of feelings and vulnerability to our sons and the possibilities of self-assertion and decisiveness to our daughters. Yes, our feminism makes us want changes in our family life. Although for a few of us the risk taken to push for change has resulted in marital conflict, separation or divorce, still what we most deeply want is 'change with connection'.

In the other direction, being parents has shaped our feminist awareness. Most immediately, it was motherhood that brought home to us the need for change in fundamental political and social structures. For many of us, motherhood has been our most radicalizing experience. But there's more. Being parents has taught us something perhaps best described as tolerance. Having vowed as teenagers never to do the awful things that our parents were doing to us, we catch ourselves now doing just those things: yelling, for instance, or not listening, or being arbitrary, or guilt-tripping. For each of us it may be a different particular, but many times in this book parents describe the sudden shock of realizing they sound or act just like their own parents. Or, having sworn to raise our kids in sexist-free ways, we find our own latent sexist programming creeping in to make us treat our daughters and sons differently. Or we watch a daughter reject her cars and trucks for party dresses, and a son drop his friendships with girls because that's 'sissy'. We learn that change comes slowly, that people are human, that our children are who they are and not who we would programme them to be. Learning these things, we are no less committed to change; we are no less vehement about certain issues; but we are almost inevitably more tolerant of differences.

This tolerance makes us wary of seeming to set up an ideal, a 'way' that parents should be. Perhaps the most hurtful aspect of the late sixties' rhetoric of feminism was that it was too programmatic. If you didn't fit the programme you were behind, unenlightened, unliberated, bad. While it is true that we want to encourage new possibilities in parenting – sharing roles, openness to non-traditional family forms, a certain kind of reflectiveness about what we are doing, a balance between home work and outside work – we do not intend to set these up as a new norm for parents to compare themselves to. We want readers whose experiences and opinions differ, as all will in some or many ways, to feel that they can be in dialogue with us and with one another, for this is a time of transition in parenting and we need to hear from each other.

A second possible misconception about feminism and parenting has to do with men. Will a group of feminists talk at all about fathers, and if so, will they do it fairly? Some of the more radical separatist women's movement voices rarely consider men except as part of the overall class of oppressors. It is true that, in trying to break through the limits of stereotypical motherhood, women have to struggle with employers, law-makers, judges, even psychiatrists, mostly male. And there are oppressive fathers: fathers who expect us to do all the child care and housework even if we work outside the home; fathers who after divorce give no money for the children or who rarely see them; fathers who unleash their anger in violence on their partner. Yet while we condemn such hurtful behaviour, we also see men as complicated fellow human beings, subject to many of the same stresses as we are. They are our children's parents too, whether or not we are living together. We are committed to the presence of loving, attentive men in the lives of our children – for us the most persuasive feminist vision is one of mutuality.

In part because of the women's movement, an increasing number of men are looking anew at their parenthood and asking the same kinds of questions as we are: how does the typical father-knows-best father image warp my parenting experience? What price do I pay for being the only provider in my family? What do I lose by being so distant from my kids' daily lives? What parts of myself might I reclaim? What do I learn about myself when I really open up to being a father? For our interviews we sought out men who are asking such questions. We read eagerly the books and articles that men are writing about their parenthood. We hope that you fathers who move through the book with us will hear the men's voices, even though there are certain sections that speak more of the experience of mothers. We hope you will find here a space within which to look at your own life as a parent, a space which perhaps you do not often get.

In the belief that understanding brings power, we in our group set a high value on awareness and self-consciousness. When we invite you to 'consider yourself as a parent' we assume that by being more self-conscious about the dynamics and issues of our parenthood we can gain more control over the factors both within our families and outside which are hurtful or destructive. There are parents of all backgrounds who would find it pointless to be so self-conscious and all kinds of parents, too, who spend time reflecting on their parenting experience.

We bring to this book who we are, not only as parents and as women, but also as people who are white, middle-class and from the Boston area. It has been important for us to look around – to take off our blinders, so to speak – and to realize that despite many common threads the experience of being a parent varies significantly both in our society and through history. Ours is not the only way that parenthood is or has been lived; ours are not the only resources, needs or strengths.

We are all white. The sheer fact of social and economic discrimination against racial minorities in this country gives race an inordinately large role in determining how different parents live. Although we interviewed some non-white parents, we and most of the parents we have spoken with are white. How different our view on being parents is from that of black and other minority parents only they can tell us, as we hope they will.

All but two of us *live in the city of Cambridge or dense suburbs of Boston* (and the other two moved away recently). The area in which we live is fairly open to experimentation in life styles; it is fairly safe physically; it has a wide range of helping services and some neighbourhoods in which a lot of sharing goes on between parents. Our location brings limits, too. We, like most people, tend to assume that others think and live as we do. It will be mind-stretching for us to find how our view of parenthood strikes parents in different kinds of communities from ours.

As you move on now into *Ourselves and Our Children*, we remind you once again of our invitation: consider yourself. Our aim in this book is to help some people feel freer to choose not to be parents, and to help those who choose parenthood to live with fewer crippling role stereotypes, with more community and social support, with more understanding and with more joy. And it seems to us that one thing that could help bring such a situation about is to let parents hear from one another about stresses, pleasures, conflicts and resources in this enterprise which is for so many years at the centre of our lives.

1. Considering Parenthood

Ruth Davidson Bell

The decision to have a baby has a permanent, irreversible effect on our lives, and yet up until quite recently it was not really even considered a decision. Most of us just grew up assuming that we would marry and have children. That's the way everyone else did it. The idea of parenthood was as natural as finding a place to live or a way to support ourselves.

I always assumed I would be a parent some day, and I really can't say why. It was so long ago that I decided, that it has just always been a fact. I think very early in my life I saw being a parent as one of the things that one was born to do, one of the purposes of life, and I never questioned it.

The woman quoted above is now a grandmother. She has three children, the first born a year and a half after her marriage. She speaks for most women of her generation, for whom marriage and motherhood were not only the norm but also the goal. She goes on to say:

I never thought that having children would interrupt the plans I had for myself, because that was my goal . . . to raise a family. At the time I felt it was about the most fulfilling thing in my life. Having a career was second to that. I didn't really start my other career until my littlest one was well into school.

Her husband's ideas about marriage and parenthood mirrored hers, but from a man's perspective. He was equally committed to the norm, but for him there was a difference. He explains:

I patterned my life, consciously or unconsciously, on my parents – and they got married and had children. I never considered anything else, but I always assumed that I would also have a career. There was no conflict: I never thought that having a career would interfere with my having kids. I would take care of the family from a monetary point of view and my wife would be the home person. I never thought having children would restrict my life – I always assumed that it would enhance my life.

These two people in their late fifties are like millions of others who had children because they wanted to have children, but also because they never gave the alternative a thought. As far as they were concerned, only people with a problem or people who remained single didn't become parents, and they were to be pitied, not emulated.

Thirty years later, things have begun to change. The improvement and availability of birth control and abortion have allowed many of us to think about pregnancy and childbirth as an option, not an inevitability. The women's movement has helped both women and men to explore choices for their lives that are different from traditional expectations. Popular culture, the media and increased personal mobility have also made settled family life with several children only one of the images we can aspire to. Now almost 5 per cent of the population has declared its intentions to remain child-free.* Many other people, although not questioning whether they will have children, spend time trying to decide when to have them.

In our discussion of parenthood as a choice, we will focus on both parts of the question: do I want to have children at all? When do I want to have them? Answering these questions means dealing with ill-defined and unquantifiable factors such as self-image, life goals, romantic ideals, spiritual beliefs and personal needs and expectations. Add to that our parents' dreams for us, society's programme for us, our friends' ideas about us and our own hidden agenda for ourselves, and we begin to see how complicated the problem can become. In this chapter lots of different people will speak about how they have made or are trying to make the decision about parenthood. Some of them have children, many of them don't.

Do I Want to Have a Child? Some Things to Consider

It takes only a simple yes or no to answer that question, and some of us feel sure enough to say either yes or no. For many others, however, 'Maybe' is an answer much closer to reality. Trying to turn 'Maybe' into a yes or a no may mean months or years imagining what parenthood would be like. Much of our thought is based more on memory and myth than on actual experience with babies and young children. We remember what our own childhood was like or at least we remember some things about our childhood. We have pictures or moods or sounds stored in our minds which represent our early family life. If those pictures are sad, scary or in some other ways negative, we might fear having children, not wanting to reproduce that time.

I never want to have children. Why should anyone have to go through what I went through?

On the other hand, positive childhood memories usually leave us open to the idea of parenthood for ourselves.

I came from a family in which children were everything. I don't know much about

*Zero Population Growth, Los Angeles chapter, May 1977.

what it was like for my parents, but for us kids life was pretty nice. I think I'd like to have children so that I could relive some of that fun.

There are a lot of people who say I don't want kids, I don't want to have to bring them up in this age of terrible disasters and no food and the whole deal, you get a lot of people opting for not having children. Like a lot of my friends say 'I wouldn't want to do that – that's terrible; I don't want kids – yuck!' But, ahhhhh, I do! I want one! I want one basically I think because I look at the relationship I have with my mother and the relationship that she has with her mother, and I want that with my kid. You know, I think I can really do something for that kid.

How we think about parenthood also comes from books, movies and television, which generally portray family life and parenthood in a romantic, idealistic way. The image of the white-picket-fenced life of children happily playing and grown-ups wisely and smoothly carrying on has strongly influenced our idea of what family life ought to be. When we held our own life up to the ideal and found it lacking we were sure there was something wrong with us – not with the romanticized image. Since neither myth nor memory tells us a great deal about reality, we ought not to base our decision about parenthood solely on either one.

There are other things which influence our feelings about being parents. Many of us do not want to miss the experience of being pregnant, undergoing childbirth and raising babies and helping them develop into adults. One twenty-one-year-old woman said:

I don't think I would want to live my life without ever having that experience – of being able to give to a child. I would feel like I'm missing out on something that's really important if I didn't have a child. And I'm very interested in childbirth and want to learn as much as I can about it. I want to have that experience for myself.

A man in his thirties:

I think kids are mind-expanding. That's one reason why I know I would have kids, because if I didn't there'd be a whole chunk missing. It's a very basic human experience that you've already experienced as a child and now you experience as a parent.

And a mother of two explained:

I don't think you have a full garden unless you have kids ... I can't imagine being without my kids. They're the most essential things in my life.

Along with the wish to experience childbirth and parenthood is a desire to leave something in the world that will live on after you – to have an effect on the world. For some people, children are their way of making a contribution to society, as well as a kind of leap into immortality. One man said 'There's a saying that a man hasn't really lived his life until he builds a house, writes a book, and has a son.' As traditional and sexist as that statement may sound, it expresses something that a lot of us feel, women as well as men: we want to leave an impression of ourselves in the world which will last after our own lives are over.

Other people argue that that imprint need not be our children, especially since there is no guarantee that our children will choose to represent us and stand for our goals and interests. There are other more direct ways to influence society. A thirty-year-old man who considers himself a social activist said:

I just don't want to put my energy into raising children for twenty years. I want to put my energies into the organizations I'm in. I want to make some difference in society, so that things might be a little bit different because I lived.

The sentiment is the same – having an effect on society – but this man's means are his own. In fact, if we count on our children to represent us, we are likely to be disappointed. By asking that of them we are type-casting them, putting pressure on them to perform according to our needs and expectations. It's a set-up for disappointment. Still, many people feel that simply having a child, however and whoever that child turns out to be, is like adding a link to the human chain. As one woman, now in her fifties, said:

If you think the world is a sorry place and you give up all hope, that is a very depressing way to live. But as long as you are bringing a new child into the world, there is hope with that new child, that new person. And it gives you a little step into the future.

This poet expresses another concern for many of us*:

How can you bring
a child into *this* world?
worries her:
there is no other.

Obviously, the decision to have children is not totally rational. There are elements of mystery and emotionality involved which go beyond the desire most of us have to keep everything well thought out and clearly planned. Those forces may exist in varying degrees for each of us, but some kind of wish for immortality, a feeling that with each child there is renewed hope for the future, and the sense that we want to participate in the human chain are three very basic, if not perfectly logical, reasons why people choose to have children.

Some might call those feelings about parenthood instinctual. However, given all the reinforcement in our society for having children, all the sugar-coated descriptions in ads, TV shows and magazines of what it's like to be parents, we ought to question what's instinct and what's simply propaganda. The pro-natalist forces, those which are *for* having children, are everywhere. Especially for little girls. As one man who has been very active in the Zero Population Growth movement explained:

*'This World', by Kathryn Van Spanckeren.

I don't know if there's an instinct involved. All I know is that from the day you're born all you're told is when *you have a child, not* if *you have a child, so you're bound to think of it just the same way you think about eating: 'Well, of course.'*

The woman quoted next had her first child before she turned twenty and her second soon afterwards. She speaks for countless women who were directed down a single road:

You know, by the time you are a young woman, you know . . . well, yes, I'm supposed to get married and be a mother. And how can anybody buck that? When I got out of high school my parents wanted me to go to college, not necessarily to study to be something for myself . . . they wanted me to go so that I could meet the 'right' kind of people and marry the 'right' kind of man, a doctor or lawyer or some such person. You're socialized from the time you're very young, to be a mother and a wife.

Yet, as this next woman explained:

Whether it was socially ingrained or not, I certainly felt some biological stirrings toward motherhood. This happens when you're younger and also seems to happen, according to my own experience and that of my contemporaries, when women get into their forties. I know there are obvious sociological reasons for feeling something like 'O.K., now's my last chance to have a baby . . .' However, all this is certainly perceived as some – almost physiological – longing, like what happens when you pick up a baby and have almost sexual feelings about wanting one.

Some Practical Considerations: Am I Ready for Parenthood?

Whether it is through myth or memory, romantic ideal or instinct, that we long for parenthood, we would do well to take a good look at what the experience is really like. Being a parent demands a lot of time and energy, and awareness of the weight of the responsibility has caused many of us to question whether we want to or are ready to take on that commitment. A thirty-year-old woman, married six years, said:

I think that having a child would be the biggest responsibility that I could ever take on in my life, and I think that it will require more of me than anything else I have ever done. It's not like you can decide or the child can decide to quit if it doesn't work out. I don't think I'm ready for that.

Of the many things people consider when deciding about parenthood, career is often one of the most important. How will having children affect my career? For women today this is a particularly thorny issue. Society accepts the fact that some women must work for economic reasons, but it still doesn't like the idea of women *wanting* to work. Either way, it is neither easy nor totally acceptable to have a full-time career and be a full-time mother. One young woman put it this way:

I feel like I got a double message from my parents. They wanted me to get married, but they also wanted me to be a successful career woman. And the work of mothering isn't respected – it isn't even thought of as work, certainly not important work. I think in many women's minds the decision to have a child means that ultimately that responsibility is going to be yours for about twenty years.

Another young woman in her mid-twenties who has been married for several years always wanted to have children. Now she and her husband are embarked on a serious career involving a large time and travel commitment, so she says:

I always imagined that having children would be an adventure that I would have in my life. It's actually taken me by surprise that I ever started to doubt that I wanted to be a parent. Now I think it could be a mistake for me to change my life drastically to accommodate a child. If I had a child now, I know I'd have to stop doing what I'm doing, because Joe and I travel a lot for the work we do together. Having a child would stand in the way of that, at least for the time being. There are other smaller life-style things that it would change too. I sort of have a schedule for myself these next few years, and I couldn't follow through with it if I had a kid.

The daily responsibilities of child care have traditionally fallen to the mother, and so far, at least, the attempt to have a career and to raise a family has been a struggle. Recently, however, men have begun to express their desire to participate more fully in child rearing and a number of young men we interviewed expressed concern about how parenthood might affect their career plans and vice versa. A man in his early twenties said:

I have to spend as much time as I can getting my career going. I want to establish myself as an artist, and that means long, long hours and an irregular schedule, which just wouldn't be fair to a woman or a child. If I have kids I don't want to just be a weekend or Sunday father. I really want to be able to devote myself to them.

The difference between his concern and that of the women we interviewed is that he assumes he has a choice. Most women don't see themselves as having that choice. Single mothers and working mothers feel that parenthood is their responsibility, and although they may put their kids in day care or have someone taking care of the children while they work, they wouldn't think of themselves as 'weekend mothers'.

Another point to consider is the other parent-to-be. Most of the single people interviewed agreed that they first wanted to be in a committed long-term relationship before considering parenthood. One middle-aged woman said:

I've always wanted to have a family, but I wasn't going to get married just to have children. I've never met a man who was a good friend and a good lover, as well as someone who loved to be with children. So now I'm fifty and still don't have children of my own. I feel sad about this sometimes, but since my work has been so fulfilling and involves working with children – I'm a teacher – I still feel that my life has been rich and complete.

A woman in her twenties explained:

It feels good to be clear about my priorities. Though I have a fine relationship with a man I love very much, I know I won't choose to live with him on a long-term basis if he doesn't want to share parenthood with me. I want very much to be a parent, though I don't want to take on that responsibility alone. I need space for myself – to work, to make music, to be alone, to be with friends – and this is pretty hard to do without sharing parental responsibilities. I also want someone else to be as important to and as involved with my children as I am – for their sake as well as my own.

It is not at all uncommon for one member of a couple to want children and the other to feel differently, or for one person to be ready now and the other to want to wait a while longer. This difference can lead to deep feelings of resentment, but having a baby before both parents-to-be are ready doesn't seem wise:

When I turned twenty-five and couldn't figure out about jobs and career, I decided that now was the time for us to have the baby we both always assumed we'd some day have. Subtle and not so subtle pressures from my mother and mother-in-law helped my decision. But notice that I say 'my' decision. Peter wasn't nearly so sure that he was ready to start a family, but somehow we were never able to discuss the whole thing clearly. He kind of assumed that since I was the woman and would do most of the child-raising work, I should get to decide. I went right ahead trying to 'get us pregnant'. Since then I have bitterly regretted this lack of mutuality in our decision, which I can now see as a step toward our eventual divorce.

A baby ought to be a shared experience unless one of the individuals is truly committed to single parenthood. A pregnant woman we spoke with does think of herself as a potential single mother:

I think that there's something weird about being as old as I am, thirty-nine, and not ever having had that kind of responsibility for another person. I often feel that all parents, no matter how young or old they are, are stronger because of that experience of really being responsible for another human being. I wanted that permanency of connection to another person which I'm much too jaded to think that marriage can ever provide. I really don't want to get married and Ronnie doesn't, either.

On the other hand, a young woman spoke to us about her feelings about wanting a child but not feeling comfortable with single parenthood:

Right now I'm living as a lesbian woman. I can't say that I would never have that kind of a relationship with a man, but I'm not sure that I ever would either. Some women I know have thought about artificial insemination and done a lot of research on that. I don't see my lesbianism as saying that I can't ever be a mother, but I do try and think practically about what that would mean, both to me and to the child.

Recently more and more women have begun to choose single motherhood. A few get pregnant on purpose just so they can have the baby they've always wanted. Most get pregnant by accident and then decide to have the baby rather than to have an abortion. Teenagers who find themselves pregnant sometimes fear going through an abortion or don't know where to go for help. Often they see their pregnancy as a way to leave home, a way to grow up. They might think the small welfare cheque which will come to them each month as Aid to Dependent Children means financial independence. Unfortunately, most find out, too late, that it's hard to live on what welfare pays and raise a baby without a lot of strain. Although we might get swept away with the romantic image of pregnancy and child raising the media have presented to us, that idealized view wears thin very quickly when we actually go through the experience, and all the more quickly if we have to handle it alone. Before you choose to raise a baby without a partner, make sure to talk to others who are doing it to find out what it's like for them.

A third point to consider is what having a baby might do to a relationship.

Right now Stuart and I are there for each other all the time. We have the energy to take care of each other whenever we need to. If we had a baby now, we wouldn't be able to devote so much attention to each other. I'm worried about how that might affect our marriage.

Another woman described how her friends' experience opened her eyes:

After we were married for about a year, our very closest friends had a baby and we thought, Well, maybe we should, too. But we waited. And we watched what happened to our friends. People we used to see at least three times a week, whom we felt really close to, all of a sudden couldn't go anywhere with us any more. And pretty soon Tommy would be going off without Jeannine. And she started feeling envious of his freedom because she just sat home all day with the baby, and he'd be going off to work. He was still active outside and she was beginning to feel resentful and like she wasn't important any more. Well, Brian and I watched this all happening and we said to ourselves, Hey, wait a minute. Maybe we don't want to have kids yet after all.

Young couples who see the divorce rate climbing also see that having children introduces extra responsibilities and pressures into married life. Reports show that many child-free couples generally feel very satisfied with their lives, and couples whose children have grown and left home have a level of contentment, companionship and mutual understanding that surpasses their pre-parenthood satisfaction. On the other hand, couples with young children readily acknowledged that there are 'both costs and rewards' to parenthood and 'during the years of raising small children, the costs appear to be substantial.' One woman we interviewed suggested:

So many couples break up after their first or second child comes. It's almost like that shift in attention is too much for them. Who knows, maybe it's because the man used to depend on his wife's mothering him and can't stand to share that with a child, or maybe they just can't cope with the added stress of children. But whatever it is, it scares me and makes me want to put off having kids until I feel more certain that Eric and I will really make it as a couple.

Another point uppermost in the minds of many couples trying to decide about parenthood is the effect a child will have on their life style. A lot of couples, especially but not only for those who have two careers, are content with their financial security, mobility and freedom to make plans spontaneously. They realize that not only does a baby increase the family budget, but usually one of the parents – in most cases the mother – will interrupt her paid work in order to take care of the child, at least for a year or two. That means more expenses with less income. Furthermore, the ability to go out or away on short notice is very important to many of the couples interviewed. Even though a lot of them freely admit that they don't necessarily go out all the time or take very many trips, they enjoy the knowledge that they could if they wanted to. They feel that having a baby would change that.

One man in his mid-thirties talked a little about this dilemma:

You have to decide what kind of life you want to have ... being a parent basically means that there are going to be a whole set of restrictions on your freedom and your mobility. You can't just take off, either on the short term, off to the movies in five minutes, or off for a year to bum around. Now, that kind of life, moving around a lot, is the sort of high-energy existence which would be much harder with a kid. If we had a child we would probably stay home and our pleasures would be centred around this child and other friends who had children. So that's trading freedom and mobility for another set of satisfactions ... which are more private and personal.

Another couple, in their thirties, have ambivalent feelings about parenthood for similar reasons. The woman explained:

If we had a child we wouldn't be able to be as free as we are now – able to decide at seven-thirty that we want to go out to the show or just sit around naked and make love in front of the fireplace. If we had kids we'd have to consider them first. After all, they didn't ask to be born. We'd have to be less irresponsible – not that we're irresponsible to each other or to our work – but we'd have to weigh more things in each decision we'd make.

One young man in his early twenties said:

All I know is that I don't want to have a child until I have an idea of who I am and what I'm going to do with my life. I don't think it's right for me to be flitting around, not knowing what I'm doing, and involving a child in that drifting.

And a working woman said:

I don't have children. Right now my life style is tremendously incompatible with children: I'm active, I'm travelling, I have a lot of commitments, I keep crazy hours, weekends and working nights. But if the time comes where my life style changes, I might be ready for a new life experience. And parenthood is an experience that I'm not afraid of. But I do consider the consequences, and I do consider the very serious responsibility of it. When I'm ready for that, when I'm ready to leave the city – I'm thinking of the country and a farm as a positive place to raise a child. When I'm ready to make that kind of life-style change, then I'll have a child.

There aren't any perfect circumstances for bringing up children. If we continue waiting for them to materialize, we probably won't ever have kids. However, one's style of life is certainly an important consideration to take into account before jumping into parenthood.

Another factor to consider is that parents need a supportive network of friends and/or relatives. So in the process of deciding, consider where you will get the help you need. Where are the baby-sitters, the paediatricians, the playmates for your children? Where are the friends and relatives who are willing to take over for you when you want some time away from your children? Go into parenthood assuming that you can't do it all alone and you'll find yourself much better prepared for the demands of the task. The rest of this book will emphasize that point over and over: parents need help. As one woman we know said:

I don't want to have a baby until I know who'll be around to share the work with me. My husband and I now spend a whole lot of time taking care of each other, but when that energy gets focused on a baby we'll have to get our parenting from somewhere else.

Age is another important element in deciding about parenthood. Not too long ago thirty-five was considered old for having a first baby. One woman we interviewed talked about how she feels her age is pushing her to change 'some day' into 'now or never'.

I feel like I'm under this incredible time pressure, like I'm in a pressure cooker. We've been married for eight years, and for at least four of those we've thought, Well, someday we'll have a baby. But now I'm thirty-two and, you know, I don't have the luxury of choice for too much longer. Time is catching up with us, but who wants to decide to have a baby just because the calendar says it's time. I'm just afraid that by waiting any longer we'll really be saying 'never' to parenthood.

In *Pregnancy After 35*, Carole Spearin McCauley* describes in detail the risks of late pregnancies. She carefully dispels many of the myths that have un- necessarily caused women to look with fear on a pregnancy after the age of thirty-five. With a history of good nutrition and health, as well as early and thorough prenatal care, women who become pregnant in their mid-thirties and even forties have an excellent chance of giving birth to normal, healthy babies.

The more time it takes us to decide about the right moment, however, the older we get and the more we get used to a child-free way of living. As one man said:

Here we are in our mid-thirties. I've finally got my musical career off the ground, and Susan is finally set up as a writer and we just don't have the time or energy to devote to having a baby now. So although Susie and I are emotionally and psychologically ready now – and we sure weren't before – we just don't feel we want to shift gears away from

---

*Carole Spearin McCauley, *Pregnancy After 35* (New York: Dutton, 1976).

our work now that it's going so well. I really wish sometimes that we had had a baby years ago, although that probably would have been a disaster and ended in our divorce or nervous breakdown.

Now at thirty-five and thirty-seven this couple doesn't have to make a final decision never to have children, but each of them agrees that it seems unlikely that they ever will.

People who are trying to decide if they want to be parents may sometimes feel as if they were on a seesaw. When one side is up they say 'Sure, let's have a baby now'; when the other side is up they say 'No, let's not have a baby – at least not now.' The actual decision may be based on very deep personal feelings and not on logical, well-formed reasons. But at least more individuals are weighing their options before having children.

A mother of five unplanned children was moved to tell us:

I think the most important thing is to want to have your children, not to have them willy-nilly like mine were, because you resent them and you resent the fact that you didn't have a choice. But, see, that's all cleared up now because of birth control. I wanted it, but in my day and in my circle it just wasn't acceptable. I wanted to have the privilege of saying 'Well, I am going to work for two years, then I would like to start a family.' That was taken out of my hands. I think it's so important to feel like you can be in some control of your life.

'No, Let's Not Have a Baby'

A small but increasing number of people are choosing non-parenthood for very concrete and positive reasons, and sticking to their decision. An organization which supports these people is called NON (National Organization for Non-Parents).* Since our society is overloaded with propaganda in favour of pregnancy, childbirth and parenthood, NON feels that support is a very important issue for non-parents. An active member of NON who has decided not to have children himself said:

The fact is we're severely overpopulated. So there's really no reason to have a child unless you know you really enjoy the process of raising one. Not because you have some tremendous expectations for it: it's going to do the things you never did; it's going to love you because it has to. No. The only reason to have one is because you really enjoy the process of raising a child.

The reasons for not wanting to have children are as varied and as personal as the reasons for wanting to have them. Some people don't want to have children because they know that they are carriers of hereditary diseases, such as Tay-Sachs disease or sickle cell anaemia. (In the UK many large hospitals have a

---

*Its British counterpart, the British Organization for Non-Parents (BON), is at 24b Avenue Road, London N6.

Someone Else's Children
for Miriam & Julia

I wait all afternoon. Finally a child comes banging up the stairs, yells *hello*, heads for the fridge.
She stands in front of the mirror, tugging on her
corduroys. *They're too short*, she whines.

From the apartment below, a flute recording. Up
here, piano practice. A woman said, *I feel complete
only when I'm pregnant.*

I am not a biological parent, another woman said. I
understand this statement. Neither am I. I borrow
other people's children to remind me of disasters I've
discarded: pants too short, lunch left behind, best
friends fighting, other people's rules.

– Robin G. Becker

genetic counselling department to give information on hereditary illness; ask
your GP.) Others feel worried because they have Rh-negative blood. Genetic
counsellors can help you discuss your chances of having a normal child before
you make the decision out of fear never to have children.

Still other people choose not to have children because they don't like the idea of
raising kids, as this twenty-eight-year-old woman indicated:

*When I see someone who's dragging along a child who's crying and screaming and
I'm on a date with a man who's saying 'You're not a whole woman if you can't have my
baby', then I say 'Why don't you go over to that child and listen to the screaming for a
few minutes?' The reality is that there's a lot of noise. There's a lot of mess. And it's not
just for a few days. It's for years. And the horror of pregnancy. You know, why anyone
would want to subject herself to that, I simply can't understand. And it's not that I don't
like children. It's just that I don't want to be with them twenty-four hours at a time. If
we had communal societies where people could trade off the child-care responsibilities, it
might be less overwhelming. But as it is now the woman is usually stuck with a
hundred per cent of the responsibility. All her time is devoted to it – all her money, all
her emotions. I'm sure not willing to do that.*

A single man in his thirties said:

*Parenthood is just simply not the kind of experience I would have any interest in. I do
not relate to children; I only relate to adults. I put a high value on my time. When
children are well behaved and very intelligent, I can enjoy them for short periods of time.
That's not parenthood, because for parenthood it's a long period of time and you have no
idea what that child's going to be like. And you are tied down for eighteen years both
psychologically and financially – for at least eighteen years. Motherhood is supposed to*

be an obsession and fatherhood is supposed to be a hobby. If I were a father I would want to share absolutely equally. I would spend half the time taking care of the child. Otherwise it isn't fair. And that's not the way I want to spend my time.

A middle-aged woman said:

It's too bad that young women think that they have to have children in order to be 'fulfilled'. I'm fifty-six, never had kids, and feel as 'fulfilled' as I could possibly be. Our lives can be rich with work, friends, other people's children and many other things. I don't think motherhood is the right choice for every woman.

In spite of the fact that deciding never to have children is a serious step and one for which there is usually little support and almost no commendation, it is easier to make that choice and to implement it now that it is not so unusual. Still, one of the problems remaining in the choice is that although birth control is readily available, there is as yet no ideal method in existence. The pill and the IUD have serious health complications; the diaphragm is messy and cumbersome; foam and condoms require preplanning. Many women and men feel unsatisfied with the available contraceptives and remain threatened by unwanted pregnancies. As a result, some who are sure they never want a child choose sterilization.* A single woman who got sterilized in her twenties explained her decision this way:

I've always known that I never wanted a child. I was twenty-four when I finally got sterilized. My choice came primarily out of being on the pill for nine years and facing another twenty years of saying 'Well, what abysmal form of birth control do I want to try now?' It's all hideous to me. It's all uncomfortable, foul-tasting, dangerous and nasty. Unless you really, really want a child, which I don't, I can't see subjecting my body and myself to more pain. I don't think that wanting a child is something you can reason about. You either want the responsibility, you want the intrusion into your life, or you don't.

For those people who are unwilling to undergo sterilization, abortion is at least legal now. The decision to abort a child is a difficult one to make, and for many people it is not really an alternative because of religious or personal convictions or lack of information. Nevertheless, the decision to have a baby or not is one of the most crucial in a person's life and it is a woman's right to decide whether or not she will bear a child. Whatever the philosophical or psychological complications of abortion may be for an individual, to give birth to an unwanted child is a tragedy for the child, for the parents – especially the mother – and for society.

Some women who become pregnant by accident and don't want to have a child give their baby over for adoption. A woman describes this traumatic decision:

*Sterilization is virtually 100-per-cent effective, but at this point it is irreversible. For detailed information about sterilization see *Our Bodies, Ourselves* (London: Allen Lane and Penguin, 1978, pp. 285–8).

I was living with a man and became pregnant. I was scared and not even twenty, and I didn't know where to turn. It was way before abortions were legal, and the doctor I went to gave me a hormone shot which he said would interrupt the pregnancy. It didn't, and by the fifth month I knew that I would have to go through with the pregnancy, but I also knew that our chances for making a real life would be impossible. So as soon as the baby was born I gave her up for adoption. Everything was arranged and I knew she was going to a good family. That's all I wanted to know. It was a harrowing experience and afterward I really felt sorry for myself. Sometimes when I've really wanted to have a child, I've thought it was to replace the daughter that I had to give up.

The sorrow of having to give up one's child at birth because of an unwanted pregnancy cannot be easily or quickly mitigated. Years later this woman, and others in a similar position, find themselves thinking about their child.

Rather than having to face the difficulties of abortion or adoption, it's best to avoid pregnancy by using birth control or to choose parenthood as a conscious and well-planned decision.

Phyllis Ewen

'Yes, I Want to Have a Baby Now'

A college teacher in her early thirties had been pretty sure she didn't want to have children, afraid that a baby would seriously interfere with her teaching career, but she explains:

A funny thing happened to me last year. Before that I didn't want to have children. I didn't really even like being around children. Then I read an article about working parents and their children and how they managed. After that I experienced a shift; I really felt different. It couldn't have been that article alone, but somehow after that I knew I was not only just ready, but wanting to get pregnant right away. Steve had always wanted children, so here we are, about to have our first baby in just a few months.

Many people have described their decision to have a baby as a feeling that just suddenly takes over. Sometimes it is based on a sense that it's time to share love and life with a new family member, as this man describes:

I want to have a baby. We want to have a baby together. It's the next stage in our relationship and we just feel like we're ready to share our love with a new person, one who's part of both of us.

Sometimes you aren't sure until it actually happens:

I had reached the point where I was looking at kids on the street and dreaming about babies and children. But I didn't know how I'd really feel until I went down to the Planned Parenthood clinic to have a pregnancy test. Sure enough, I was pregnant. They were worried that I might be upset, since it was an unplanned pregnancy, but I was so excited I couldn't sit down and drink the tea they offered. I found myself just sort of carousing through the room, telling everyone, congratulating myself. I was absolutely ecstatic. I wouldn't have known, I wouldn't have been able to be absolutely one-hundred-per-cent sure I would have responded that way, but finding out released joyous feelings I had which were tremendous. For if I had a hundred years to make up my mind – am I mature enough? financially stable? together enough with my man? – I might never have decided to do it.

Still others plan to have their babies when they do for very specific reasons.

We were going to be moving by the end of the next year, so we thought 'This is the perfect time to have a baby – while we're still here, while we know the doctor and the community.'

Or, as this professor explained:

We timed the pregnancy now so that I could have the baby between finishing my thesis and taking on a full teaching load next fall.

And this couple:

We talked a little bit off and on about having kids but my husband was in graduate school, so we decided to wait. And then he went for his draft physical – this was during the war – and he thought he would fail because of some minor disability, but he didn't – he came home with a 1A. We tried everything to avoid the army, and pregnancy was one way out. About two months after Ed was classified I did become pregnant. We had decided by then that we did want children, but we probably would have waited another year or two if it hadn't been for the draft. So our first child was a draft dodge.

Getting Pregnant

People say yes to parenthood for many reasons. Sometimes the decision is well thought out and planned to the day; sometimes the pregnancy just happens and the parents-to-be feel glad about their 'accident'. Sometimes outside factors, such as moving or work schedules or the draft board, influence the timing of a baby's birth. On occasion, however, our own calculations have very little to do with the time conception takes place, as couples who try for months and even years can attest.

Although even a year of trying without success to become pregnant does not necessarily constitute infertility, the waiting and trying and waiting and trying may make us very tense, make us feel the urgency of our desire to become parents. One woman told us:

I had two miscarriages and I had this feeling that I was never going to have a child . . . that it just wasn't part of what would happen to me. Maybe partly because of that, maybe just from childhood wishes or from the advertising industry or just everything, it became really important – like if I could somehow manage to have a baby I could complete this 'hole' feeling in myself or make up for what was lost. I would confirm my femaleness because I was feeling that I was failing at being a female.

As this woman suggests, the questions surrounding 'Why can't I conceive?' are multifaceted and pry deep into our sense of self-worth and competency. Moreover, sex can become a battleground for proving one's maleness or femaleness, as if parenthood were the prize for achieving sexual maturity. A young woman remembered how 'trying to get pregnant made us very tense. My husband thought it ruined our sex life and he was quite resentful.' Even for couples who are feeling the problem together and being understanding of each other, making love has a way of losing ground to trying to make babies. It's hard to maintain romance under those circumstances:

We began making love like crazy, with thermometers even. He'd go off to school and I'd take my temperature to see if I was ovulating, and I'd call him up at school and say 'Come home now, we've got to do it now!' It was the worst few months of love-making that I can remember in my life. Just absolutely mechanical to try and get pregnant.

Infertility

According to the most recent statistics, about 15 per cent of the people who are trying to have a baby will have some problem with infertility – the inability to conceive and give birth to a live baby after about one year of effort. That may seem like a very large percentage, and it is, but nearly 50 per cent of these people will eventually conceive and give birth. For individuals and couples who have continuing problems with infertility, there may be years of tense uncertainty. This is a time that calls for patience, although patience may feel like an impossible demand when you are eager to conceive. A couple who is experiencing infertility for longer than a year or eighteen months will often seek some kind of counselling from a gynaecologist specializing in fertility cases, and sometimes also from a psychotherapist or discussion group of people with fertility problems.* One man, who has been married ten years and now has a six-year-old son, explained:

Even though to each other and to the world we maintained a united front – our problem – to ourselves privately we each were blaming the other and just not believing that 'I' could be the one.

Infertility may feel like a tragedy. The hardest part is that most people don't find out about their infertility until after they have made the decision to have a baby. At that point the discovery is laced with irony and psychological pain.

We got married not only because we were in love, but because we each felt the other one would make a perfect parent. Johnny would make a terrific father and I would make a terrific mother. But I had a job and we were getting to know each other, so we used contraception for the first two years of our marriage. Now it makes me smile a wry smile at the trick fate played on us. The worst part is, I'm still not sure why I'm unable to get pregnant; it's not as though I can blame it on something specific. Johnny had tests which said he's O.K., and the doctors can't find a reason with me so they call it 'normal infertility'. But it's not normal. It makes me so angry! I just sort of vacillate between being grief-stricken and furious. I feel like the family part of our marriage contract hasn't been fulfilled, and so a lot of times a part of me could understand why Johnny would leave me. That might sound irrational ... but when I think about it, if the situation were reversed, that's how I would feel. I'd be resentful and angry. I feel that way now – angry at myself. I feel like I've been cheated.

Society does not help us, either. Just when understanding and acceptance are what's needed, we are offered pity and, at the same time, are censured. Coming to terms with infertility may mean delving into our fears and insecurities in other areas of life, as this woman explains:

The issues infertility hits are at the very core of my being – sexuality and my femaleness – but they're complicated with feelings that I'm ineffective, incompetent, a failure. I find myself thinking, How can I be successful in anything else if I'm unable to bear a child?

Almost everyone feels grief at being infertile. Allowing yourself a time of mourning for your child who will not be born is both emotionally helpful and psychologically strengthening.

Adoption is one possibility for infertile couples, but give yourself time to work through your feelings about infertility before you adopt. These days it is not as easy to do as it was in the past, and you may want to consider a child of a different

---

*In Britain the National Association for the Childless, 318 Summer Lane, Birmingham, gives support, help and information to people with fertility problems.

racial or ethnic background from your own. But first you ought to question how important the experience of pregnancy, childbirth and heredity are in your image of parenthood. An infertile woman asked:

> Can a child
> move in
> as easily
> as a cat...*

We are too limited by space to include more specific information about infertility, but if you need help we encourage you to read as much as you can about the subject, so you'll know what to ask your doctor or clinic and what to expect when you go to them. In the UK you can ask your GP to refer you to a clinic specializing in infertility. Family Planning Association clinics also run infertility sessions to which you can refer yourself – be prepared for a wait.

Adoption

Adoption is a different way of becoming a parent. It is an alternative for people who can't have their own biological children and for families who want to add to their number without adding to the world population.

Deciding whether to adopt a child involves most of the same deliberations that exist for people trying to decide about biological parenthood, but it also brings up other considerations. A mother of three adopted children explained:

There are a lot of bad reasons to have children. So I guess what was really good about the adoption procedure was that it made me examine my motivations. I really had to think about what my motivations were. And after thinking I was able to say 'It's a miracle to adopt children.' It's a miracle different from the miracle of birth because they come from different places at different ages and you get this feeling of fate entailed with the exact child who came to you. You can't imagine – I can't imagine not having the three children I have. Each was in need of a place at the same time that I was in need of having them, and we somehow got together, and the sense of there being a destiny or fate involved in this is very beautiful. Three children is three times the miracle.

Some people who have adopted think that the hardest thing about adoption is making the decision that you really want a child, and then to face the fact that an adopted child can really be *your* child even though he or she is not from your body. Part of the pleasure of adoption is developing that relationship in which the child becomes *your* child. As one mother said of her four-year-old son from biological parents who rejected him:

He's able to call me 'Mommy' now, and the other day he said 'You love me, Mommy.'

*From a poem by Judith Steinbergh.

A mother of four – two born to her and two adopted – said:

I wanted a girl very much, and we had two boys. We adopted a girl and then we adopted another boy . . . and I am really happy to have a female child to identify with in the certain ways that I would whether she was adopted or born to us. I find this kind of identification with my adopted daughter even though she's black and I'm white, because in a family of four other males I take pleasure in her femaleness – she's like me! *There are all kinds of things to identify with and ways to mother her in her growing that aren't true with the boys.*

The adoption procedure can be tedious or smooth, depending on the particular agency, part of the country and availability of children. It can involve time-consuming and emotionally intense meetings and discussions with social workers, administrators and other pre-adoptive parents. As many adoptive parents say, you really have to want to be parents to survive the waiting, wondering and soul-searching that can be part of the adoption experience. A book that may be helpful if you are considering adoption is *The Adoption Advisor*, by Joan MacNamara.*

One of the problems a lot of us face is that many of the agencies making the judgement about who 'deserves' a child are bound into the Establishment and have standards which reflect societal norms, rather than what may actually be good for a child.

People who live on communes, who are artists without a weekly salary, who are Buddhists rather than members of some 'regular' religious persuasion, who are gay or are single may be ruled out, although they would make warm, loving and competent parents.

Here is a description of the pre-adoption procedure by one woman who has since adopted three children:

There is something very unnatural about going and sitting with a person – however nice a worker it might be – who is going to discuss your suitability to become a parent. The only good thing about it is that it focuses a lot of time and attention on the idea of whether or not you do want to be parents. Maybe it would be a good thing if all people went through this – had a chance to review whether or not they should be parents. The only real difference is that if you had natural fertility and you went through a review process like that, nobody could take away your right at the end to have that baby. The feeling you have when you go to a social work agency is that they hold a baby and they have the right to give it to you or withhold that baby from you. There's always that fear that you might be rejected. And even though it's ludicrous – I mean, I knew we would be accepted – we were very careful to give very correct answers and to be very model – to be appropriate. And we were rewarded with a child.

The anxiety involved in adoption is sometimes severe. First of all there is the waiting: waiting to be 'accepted' by the agency as a suitable couple; next –

---

*New York: Hawthorne Books, Inc., 1975. *How to Adopt*, published by the Consumers' Association, is an informative alternative for the UK.

especially – the waiting to hear from the agency if there will be a child for you; and then the anxiety always associated with beginning parenthood. Couples who are able to discuss their feelings with each other or with their friends or social worker may be able to relieve some of this anxiety. Agencies provide post-adoptive group sessions for just such purposes, although sometimes, these groups don't delve into deeper, harder-to-express feelings. Furthermore, talking isn't the only solution. Time and experience are, for some of us, the most reliable helpers, and becoming effective parents is dependent on time and experience.*

Step-parenthood

Like adoption, step-parenthood is an alternative way of becoming a parent. With the divorce rate zooming, more and more adults are faced with the possibility of entering an already existing single-parent family.

I love Diane and want to live with her – and she happens to have a child. Now, I love Tommy too, don't get me wrong. But I'm choosing to live with Diane, and Tommy comes along with the package.

Since it is the relationship between the two adults which brings the new individual into the already existing family, accepting parenthood in this way is different from parenthood by choice: it is parenthood as a fact of life. (For a full discussion of step-parenthood, see the Families chapter.)

For some people, moving into an already existing parent-child relationship is like frosting on the cake. As one man said, 'I always wanted to have children, and we still might have our own together.' For others there are problems and ambivalent feelings to be worked through before the members of the new family can feel committed to each other. A mother of two discusses her choice to live with a father of two:

Initially Peter had a lot of difficulty with one of my children, with Evie. He didn't like her and she didn't like him, and she was very outspoken about it. And she didn't want to share with his children. At one point when we were deciding whether to get together, Peter felt he couldn't live with Evie. I was feeling very angry with her for interfering in my life, but I also knew that if he couldn't manage it and be O.K. with her, then I couldn't go through with it.

For adults who don't already have children of their own, the decision to live with another person's children has special complexities. When you haven't been involved in a child's life from the beginning, you're starting a few steps behind in terms of the depth and understanding possible in the parent-child relationship. All of a sudden you're faced with a semi-grown person with whom you have to live and share your life. In the beginning it is very hard to imagine ever having a

*The Parent to Parent Information on Adoption Society, 26 Belsize Grove, London NW3 (telephone 01-722 9996), is a mutual help group for adoptive parents in Britain.

real, loving relationship with a child who may seem more of a nuisance than a potential friend.

The dynamic between the child or children and the adult who is about to live with them is often fraught with jealousy, anger, insecurity and yearning on both sides. Working out that new relationship requires not only care and attention but maturity on the part of the step-parent. A lot of the energy that might have otherwise gone into the couple's relationship is spent on trying to establish a good feeling between step-parent and child. In that sense it is a lot like the adjustment to new parenthood, in which the couple has to learn to include the new baby.

Deciding Whether or Not to Have More Children

Once we become parents, whether through pregnancy and childbirth, adoption or step-parenthood, we have made a decision that will produce countless changes in our lives. And as each new child is added, the family dynamic changes and new adjustments have to be made. Just because we have made the decision to have one child doesn't necessarily mean we have said a blanket yes to more children. As one young woman said:

I certainly don't regret having Susie; I know that if I hadn't had her I would be really obsessed with wanting to have the experience of having a child. But I had my palm read and the reader said that I have another child in my palm. Well, all I can say is – not if I can help it.

Lots of experts have lots of expert opinions on the number of children in the 'ideal' family and the spacing of those ideal children, but it is up to each of us to make our own decision about how many children to have and when to have them. The issue of how many children to have is obscured by myths and social attitudes just like the issue of whether to be a parent at all. We have heard about the lonely only child and the spoiled only child and the high-strung only child. We've also heard about the mixed-up middle child and the forgotten fourth child. However, like the decision about parenthood, the decision to have or not to have more than one child has less to do with facts and figures or expert opinions than with deep inner feelings about how we want our lives to be, what we expect for ourselves, and what practical things we can do to arrange our lives in a way that suits us and our existing family. One woman who just had a second child said:

I was always sure that having a family was part of my ultimate happiest self, and having a family meant a husband and at least two children. As it turned out, I was right in a lot of ways because I feel happier with myself as a mother the second time around. It gave me a chance to do things differently. I have more tolerance with myself. I feel a kind of lightness about it that I didn't have with my first child.

And a mother of three children, now all in school, said:

I always assumed that I'd have kids, and I think I'd always assumed that I'd have three kids ... sometimes I think I'm the classic brainwashed woman. It was a choice when to have the children, but I never thought of not having children. I came from a family of three children and that's why I think I chose that. I had a girl and then a boy, so it wasn't like I was trying again to have an other-sex child. But to me a family is three kids because that's what I grew up with.

And a father described his feelings about having a second child:

There has never been a moment's doubt in my mind from the time I had my first child that I would have another and probably another after that, so that the idea of having more than one child has always been part of me.

The 'if' part of whether to have another child is based on many of the same considerations as the 'if' part of having a first child. Many people argue that two children are as easy as one (is one easy?), while others insist that a second child increases your load not two times but five times over. Space, finances, marital stability and the age of the other child or children can and do influence our decision about whether to have more children. Timing is particularly important if both parents are working. Many men are sharing more of the daily chores of parenthood, but still it is the woman who usually feels the stress of each new child most acutely. More often than not, however, it is the husband who earns more money, so for him to give up his job to raise the new baby is usually not practical or even possible. This poses a special problem for women who want to have other children but also don't want to give up their work. One woman, an artist, describes this dilemma:

I have gotten very professional about my work, meaning I am not willing to paint less than a set number of hours each day. So how do we do it so that I can keep painting as many hours a day as I am painting now, and Michael keeps doing what he is doing. Now, he would be willing to give up his job, but he couldn't because we couldn't live. So it's really not logical. I don't think that any of these questions are problems that arise because I am a woman and he is a man, and I have to do this if I had another baby and he has to do that if we had another baby. I think it's more because of our set-up. I need a lot of time, but as a painter I cannot make enough money for us to live on and that seems to be the problem. If I could envision having a baby and keeping my schedule, then I would have a baby.

When both parents work full or almost full time, it's easier to make arrangements for just one child. The years and the expense of being 'on duty' are greatly shortened with one child, because once she or he is in school most of the day, there isn't another child at home still needing attention.

For some people it's psychologically and emotionally easier to raise only one child. We can give more concentrated time and attention to one child, and we usually feel less harassed as a result. As long as we make sure that our child has ample opportunity to play with other children, then we are not doing our child any disservice by not having more.

On the other hand, many people we interviewed really wanted to have more than one child. One young mother said, 'I just didn't feel like a real mommy with only one child. It wasn't until Heather came along that I felt legitimate.' She explained that her deep-seated image of motherhood involved a bunch of children and so she felt more comfortable in her role once her second child was born.

There is another aspect to having more than one child. It establishes clear boundaries between parents and children in a family. One man said:

Well, I think as a matter of principle kids should have siblings. I think that instead of a family in which there's the king, the queen and the prince, it's much better to have the kids versus the parents. That way the kids have allies and have to learn to deal with their peers. There was sibling rivalry in my family, but there was also a lot of kids teaming up against the parents. The kids formed their own society. My brother and I, for instance, invented a special language and we could speak together and our parents didn't know what we were saying. We had long fantasies, worlds that we created that our parents weren't part of.

And from a mother's point of view:

One child felt too enmeshing. I was too over-identified with my first child; I felt like I was burdening him too much with my issues. Having our second child was good for him, an ally for him, and a way of helping me to disengage myself from over-involvement with Seth. Now there's a clearer sense of the separateness between my children and me.

When to have another child can be complicated – like when to have a first child. Again, theories about the proper spacing of children are abundant, but each of us should plan according to the specific circumstances that seem important to us. One mother said:

You know, I didn't think about it the first time, but I think I would even plan the time of year that I had another child. It really makes a big difference.

A young father, who lost his job after his first child was born, talked about wanting to have a good job before having his second child:

I was terribly depressed when she told me that she was pregnant. It had a lot to do with being a father who can provide financially at a time when I'm financially unable to provide for very much. That got very scary. I might be very good at parenting, but I haven't, at least recently, been able to provide a job.

One woman who with her husband finally decided to have a second child said:

It took us about two years to make the decision. And once I made it, and my daughter was born, I sort of said to myself, what was the problem? What essentially was the problem? Because what I discovered is that the first child is the one that had changed my life drastically. No, two doesn't necessarily, because you tackled all this new business once, and you don't have to go through that a second time.

Those of us who decide to have children have made a choice that affects all the other parts of our lives. When we are glad about our parenthood it can feel like a special gift, like a miracle, in fact. For some of us, the more children we have, the deeper is our sense of that miracle. For others of us, parenthood can feel like a burden that we would have avoided had we had the opportunity or the forethought. We hope that more people will think carefully before deciding either way.

2. Beginning Parenthood

Joan Sheingold Ditzion and Dennie Palmer Wolf

Entering Parenthood

As soon as we've decided to become parents through pregnancy, adoption or step-parenting, we find ourselves facing a balancing act. We want to develop a strong bond with our child and at the same time maintain our partnership, our adult friendships, as well as our involvements with the outside world. What we discover even before we have a baby is that our lives are thrown off balance once we become parents and we need time to establish a new equilibrium.

Traditionally, this life adjustment was left to women. The women's movement has changed women's expectations for themselves as mothers. We now think about finding a place for parenthood in the broader context of our lives. Traditionally, men rarely had to consciously face this problem. Fatherhood mostly meant having to provide more income. In the wake of the women's movement, men may want to share in active parenting from the beginning. So, historically, we are living in a time of transition in terms of both family roles and structure. In many situations women are still the primary caretakers in the beginning years, so much of what we say comes out of women's experience and is addressed to women. On the other hand, many new parents are trying to co-parent, and so some of what we say comes out of men's and women's shared experience.

This period of parenting is an intense one. Never will we know such responsibility, such productive and hard work, such potential for isolation in the caretaking role and such intimacy and close involvement in the growth and development of another human being.

We believe that these are primary years not only for building child-parent relations but for learning to balance all that matters to us. There is a certain realism in talking about parenting as balancing. It means saying out loud that there are very real difficulties in having children and maintaining adult lives. But there is optimism, too. If parenthood can be a relationship shared by mothers and fathers, then we can hope to become closer to our partners as a result of having children together. If it can be a relationship where we learn from children as well as their learning from us, then we can hope that having children will carry *us* into new places. What paediatrician John Davies said of birth we believe applies to the longer process of having children:

> *Nobody goes to sea only to be sick . . . I feel very strongly myself that there is no point in a child being conceived, born, and reared, unless birth has that positive side to it by which it is recognized as something adult human beings need and want to do in order to 'be themselves'.**

Me the Expectant Parent

We know a child is coming and, whether it is a first or a fourth child, it's impossible not to ask over and over 'What will life be like?'

> *I remember standing at the sink, doing dishes or riding on the subway, I was always trying to imagine what it would be like to have a child. I would try to walk myself through the rituals that everybody knows happen when you have a baby – feeding, washing, dressing, diapering [changing nappies], going for a walk. I wanted to be practised and ready before the actual moment. But it was funny, you can't do that – all I could imagine was this faceless, mild little baby out of an Ivory soap commercial. I think I was trying to get a picture of me as a mother, too. I wanted to know how it would feel to breast-feed, if I could be pleasant waked up in the middle of the night. But the baby and the parent-me were both still embryos.*

As this mother points out, we are really also asking 'What will I be like as a parent?' It makes us examine what we think we have for the job and what we are worried we lack. We re-examine our own childhood, our role models, our present selves:

> *My growing-up experience was like a lot of men's. Weekday mornings I waved good-bye to my father as he got on a commuter train. Sometime close to supper, we picked him up again. Somewhere going up the hill to the house he asked me 'How was school?' or 'How was Little League?' And when we turned into the driveway, I probably mumbled 'Fine' no matter what had happened for me that day. What this means is that I am walking into this experience wanting to have something more than that between me and my children – but if having seen it counts for anything I am a total cripple.*

Single mothers may worry about how they will provide for the child and whether they will be able to get through the childbirth experience alone.

> *The man I'd been living with panicked when I got pregnant. When I decided to keep the baby, he left. Every month I'd get on the bus to the doctor's office feeling big and brave about wanting the baby. Then I'd get there and sit reading* American Baby, *with all the mama, papa, baby pictures staring out at me from comfortable houses. Some time during the visit the doctor would always ask some simple, plain question like 'Who*

---

*Aidan Macfarlane, *The Psychology of Childbirth* (London: Fontana, 1978).

is going to be with you during labour?' I wouldn't know the answer right away. I'd ride the bus back home, hugging that baby but feeling not at all brave.

The questions flow the other way, too. Once we've asked 'What will I be like as a parent?' we also want to know 'How will having children change the life I'm used to leading?' This lets loose thousands of questions – what about work, what about the life I've shared with a partner, what about the times I used to dash out to movies with friends on three minutes' notice? In the course of all this wondering, we realize that children, even before they are physically present, have begun to touch us:

She wasn't even born yet, and already in her name I was taking a fine-tooth comb to my life – trying to decide things that I had skirted, until her coming forced my hand. Things like 'How much does it mean to me to have a career in addition to having a child?'

As we continue through the period of anticipation and preparation we find that some of these changes are exciting, even exhilarating, while others are just plain complicating and difficult. We think we're in the process of getting children and, in addition, we get a new picture of ourselves, a changed partnership, an altered relation with the world at large:

You think that it's all in your womb and then you find out that your whole life is pregnant.

As an expectant father put it:

The biological fact is that it's your wife who is pregnant. The psychological fact, if you admit it to yourself, is that you are too. Becoming a father isn't pocketing a birth certificate, it's moving to a whole new place in life.

In the absence of a child as the focus of attention, people approaching parenthood often experience considerable changes in their sense of who they are. They find their adulthood, their sexuality and their readiness for a new kind of caring affirmed. Parents speak of making a rite of passage out of adolescence into adulthood.

Up until then we lived minute to minute. With a baby coming we began – at least more than before – to think about tomorrow, about where to live, what we wanted to do.

This feeling has little to do with the purely physical process of conception, as adoptive parents and step-parents point out:

It is hard to explain – but knowing we were actually going to adopt a child was like having a mirror reflect back to me where I was in my own life.

Attached to this feeling of transition is the sense that we are approaching a tremendous change. We guess that having children is a watershed, a point in time that can be used to make changes. This is so whether it's a first or fifth child, whether the children are our own or not.

Peter and I had been seeing each other for maybe a year when we wanted to live together. But I had Sara, who was four then. He would be moving in with her too, becoming, if not exactly her father, the man who was going to hug her or not, pee in front of her or not. It made me think of it in a whole different light. It made me see that we had been dating like high school kids, him treating me and courting me. If it was going to work out, we had to sit down at the kitchen table to find out if we could be good to each other with a child yelling 'I want a drink of water' in the background.

Phyllis Ewen

Even though we may not share it out loud, parents feel that child rearing is a new venture that will ask a lot of them, let them express feelings and develop skills that are not called for in other parts of their adult lives:

I have work that is important to me, it's true. But it doesn't take all of me. There is a kind of deep joy, a belly laugh, a kind of deep feeling, too, that just isn't needed in an office.

Also there can be a sense of wanting to take on 'something big and lasting', something that will be demanding but satisfying:

I know a lot of women who are terrified of childbirth, but not me. I was afraid it would hurt and that I wouldn't be 'good' at it, but I wanted to go through something that big.

Finally, as other prospective parents point out, there is a way in which a child's coming reorganizes our network of relationships. We reconnect with our own parents, often more easily because we have become what they are – mothers and fathers. As one expectant father put it:

At last I feel the equal of my parents. Knowing you are going to have a child is like extending yourself in the world, setting up a tent and saying Here I am, I am important. Now that I'm going to have a child it's like the balance is even. My hand is as rich as theirs, maybe for the first time. I am no longer just a child.

At the very end of my pregnancy it was summer and we were outside, and remembering an old photograph I had seen in a family album of my mother right before I was born – a small face pushing an enormous belly, a little bit overwhelmed, a little scared-looking behind the clowning for the picture – I felt a kind of kinship with her that had been lost since childhood.

Still other parents speak of entering a new community of children and parents:

I remember – on the way home from the doctor's – the world made it plain that it was full of parents and children making their way together. In one city block I counted three huge bellies coming toward me – almost like a greeting. And on the subway going home I watched every child I could spot; I felt like I needed to drink in all they could tell me about what was coming. I needed to know what kinds of shoes kids wear, if they can ride the subways by themselves, what a baby sounds like, if they are frightened by crowds and subways. I needed to drink in the parents too – always asking 'Is that how I will be? Is that how I want to be? Is that how my parents were? Is it good? Is it hard?'

The Potential Mother in Me

As much as there is excitement over parenthood, there are also very real difficulties. For us as mothers some of these difficulties are clearly physical: morning sickness, loss of balance, fatigue, frequent urination.

I was in school then. That whole winter of being pregnant I kept checking the same book out of the library. I would take it to a desk, sit down, read a sentence or maybe two and fall dead asleep. When you have that little energy you can begin to panic – am I always going to be tired like this – is my mind just slowly going to melt away?

All too often we have been told that our reactions to these symptoms are signs of 'not accepting pregnancy'. This is simply not true – the hormonal and physical shifts of childbearing *are* enormous. And they do bring feelings of loss of self, of winding down, even in the course of the healthiest, most normal pregnancy. Of course, if our pregnancy was unplanned or unwanted, these changes can be somewhat frightening.

Another aspect of the physical side of pregnancy is that our appearance changes. Our role, as we begin to look pregnant, is suddenly public. Every morning, when you face your protruding stomach, you yourself also see the evidence of your changing life. You may not like some of these changes and they may bring you face to face with your physical self-image. Society has not given us a likeable picture of a maternal, mature woman. Either we are supposed to affect a kind of adolescent sexiness or else we are 'over the hill' or a 'mother' whose body is saggy and unattractive. When we are pregnant we are not supposed to 'show' until the last possible moment. After the child is born we are supposed to achieve instantaneously the body of a young girl again. What could be a profound rite of passage from girlhood to mature womanhood is denied us because of the conflicting messages we are getting: be maternal but look like a movie star. We're told that unless we're very well fed while we're pregnant the baby won't develop properly, but we're also told to stay thin.

How do we then make friends with our stretch marks, our varicose veins, our stomach in pregnancy or the pendulous breasts we're going to have when we nurse our babies? Our body is doing what it should: nurturing our unborn child. We also may worry about how we may look to our mate. Again, we've been taught that unless we're beautiful a man won't love us, and that image of beauty is defined as being slender and glamorous. Often, women want their own familiar bodies back:

There came a day when I couldn't fit into my own clothes any more. I realized that I didn't want to get out the box of maternity clothes because it signalled giving over my own familiar body to the process. It was like I was just the person behind the pregnancy.

And it went on like that. Later, when I couldn't see my feet or walk up to the counter close, I'd have this sensation of 'Wait a minute, where is how it used to be?' The baby was late, and every morning past the due date I'd wake up, look down at that mound and say 'Hey, kid, there is one too many of us in this body.'

Feelings of being invaded mix with whatever worries we have about our capacities to be parents, whether we will be for ever tied down, whether our partners will really support us and share in what's coming, whether our friends will really support us if we are alone. But it is often difficult to express these negative emotions. We are afraid of being judged as unfeminine or afraid that they mean we will not be good mothers.

The Potential Father in Me

It is all too easy to forget fathers and what they may experience at this time. They are not physically pregnant, and traditionally they have not been important in child rearing. An adoptive father points out what it is like to be ignored:

We were being interviewed by a social worker who was supposed to be finding out if we would make good parents. She turned her chair so that it faced Lil and asked all her questions to her. She came around to talking to me only when her list of questions got down to matters of income. I was furious. I felt like asking 'Should we set up another appointment for you to interview the father?'

Though fathers don't carry children, the process of a wife's pregnancy affects them. Even for the most loving partners there can be shock at the changes in a woman's body. These changes almost certainly affect his concept of what is beautiful and the place of traditional 'attractiveness' in relations between men and women:

She got to be perfectly pear-shaped. I'd see her standing that way in the bathroom. Sometimes it would be beautiful, sometimes ugly, and often just very funny.

What happens for fathers during pregnancy extends beyond bodily things. It can be a confusing, difficult time – in part, because he, unlike his partner, is not undergoing a rite of passage – he is just supposed to be there. There are very strong feelings and few traditional outlets. He may feel shy and locked out of the creative aspect and the direct involvement in the physical process. His partner may be very involved in herself, withdrawn or at least preoccupied.

I think I was terrified that there would be nothing left for me. She was absorbed in her diet and her rest and every moment of quickening and how many days there were left. I felt like a drone catering to the needs of a queen bee.

Fathers, too, question and wonder about their capacity to be parents:

There is not only the fear of not being able to support her and a baby economically but also a lot of worry about becoming a person a child could like and respect. There will be this person who will need a lot from me emotionally and be able to see how I am as a person.

This kind of questioning can be acute, particularly when fathers anticipate radically altering what they will do as fathers from what they saw their fathers doing:

When I thought of becoming a father, I thought right away of my own father. I thought about some stern, worldly, competent man in a suit, with a bank account, who knew about mortgages and carving a turkey. Beside that professional man who sat at the head of the table I felt dumb and young. I felt even 'greener' when I realized that those pictures weren't going to help – that I was going to be a man who diapered and fed and put to sleep. All of that – and I could not even remember having dressed a doll.

And all too often it is hard to get a handle on what is coming because he is excluded:

I wanted to be a part of the process, so when Diana made her first visit to the doctor's I went along. As I started to go down the hall with her to the examining room the nurse told me 'We'll be right with you, Mr W.' So I ended up sitting in the waiting room, looking through old copies of Vogue *and* Good Housekeeping, *not knowing how not to be cut out. When at last the nurse motioned me in, it was to discuss insurance, hospital payment plans and the doctor's billing policy.*

The Us of It: Parenthood and Partnership

Women are pregnant and men are not – at no other time do we face so fully the unerasable biology of sex differences or the way we have internalized sex roles. Previously in our adult lives we may have been able to ignore or blur these differences. In pregnancy it is possible to see openly physical and even psychological differences:

It is a time of female power and men have to learn how to deal with it, and women to

Roots and Stems

A field of
daisies
she walked thru to find
his tree
naked &
growing

He was shy. Loving
him was picking
wildflowers to set
illegal in a jar
by the window

When they married
it was daisies
on the dress
and she held them

and considers naming
the child daisy
if it's a girl

She thinks there may be
connections between events'
roots and stems

Under her daisy-print smock
the child tumbles,
her belly cupped
in her hands

She has him feel it.
When they make love it's
as if he were loving the child
thru her skin

— Kathryn Van Spanckeren

enjoy it. During it, there was a way in which I was alone, my body was pregnant with a child and his was not and could not be. At times I felt distant from him, at times close.

During this period of preparation these differences make for new forms of closeness and new forms of distance from one another.

There is the discovery of a different aspect to sexuality. The experience of making love without contraception is exhilarating:

It was wonderful to be making love with nothing between us. For once the anxiety of 'What if . . .' wasn't there. It was exciting to have made a baby together.

There can be a kind of awe and pleasure at the productivity and flexibility of our bodies:

I think that carrying a baby inside you is like running as fast as you can. It feels like finally letting go and filling yourself up to the widest limits.

All the time, after I knew Ellie was going to have a baby, I would be in the middle of something else and stop and say 'Hey, man, you made a baby.'

Expectant biological parents sometimes feel a shift in the feel of their sexuality:

Sometimes Maggie and I would go walking together when she was very pregnant. People would look at us in a way that said, Now, there's a couple. It had never been like that before she showed. It made us very aware of being seen as fertile, as having had intercourse, of having moved from sex for fun to sex for making babies.

The physical excitement of becoming parents is shared by people who haven't conceived, as this adopting mother makes clear:

I Just Gave Birth to a Son

I yell to the desk clerk
in Vermont, the birth
delivered by phone at 7 a.m.

a son, I call
through the door
to my husband
who is asleep

and we hold each other
like children
for the last time
childless

dress in shorts and boots
grin over waffles
fill ourselves with juice

and hike through the valley
where the men plant
their dark patches
with seed

we climb up through spring
up the granite mountain
just breaking water
giving life to what it bears
each year.

— Judith Steinbergh

The procreative aspects of sexuality momentarily set aside, there can be a renewed sense of love-making as a kind of communication between people. The fears, dangers and difficulties of birth control are temporarily not an issue, permitting a vacation from worry and responsibility. Moreover, as sexual appetites on both sides change, it is possible to draw attention away from climax to more tender forms of stimulation and communication:

Because I was pregnant and a little more clumsy, it took the edge off for me in terms of my expectations of my sexual performance. I felt freer to be playful, and there is something playful about sex. Towards the end, especially, sex became something of a production – especially if we tried to conduct it as usual. We became more aware of other forms of closeness – simple things like lying so that the baby lay between us.

Given the still predominantly different roles prescribed to men and women in pregnancy and, later, child care, the mutuality of these experiences is easily lost. The result can be a feeling of separation and isolation – the sense that the coming of parenthood has ruptured or buried a prior, vital commitment to one another.

After the nausea was over, I started feeling better but then went through a very-protective-of-my-body period. Sexually I was completely turned off. I didn't want to be touched. Intercourse seemed almost barbaric. This was followed by all kinds of feelings of anxiety and frustration toward my mate, feelings of guilt for putting him through such a rejection and feelings of distress at him putting me through so many changes.

Yes, I want this child; I hate my husband for making me pregnant . . . No, I don't really hate him, but I want to hate him. How wonderful how women were raped and they could blame men for what happened. I chose to be pregnant. Why? How could any rational creature permit an outside force to take over her body? I want to be mad at someone, but who? . . . I really enjoyed telling my husband that I didn't want to make love tonight because I feel lousy. I am locked into a game with him that I don't even know the name of.*

Where closeness is maintained, there can be a sense of profound growth.

Waiting for the baby to be born made us both think and, I guess, worry. We talked a lot about what we felt – Marc talked about feeling left out, I told him how I felt burdened and like a marked woman every day when I rode the subway taking up twice the space. Sometimes we would fall asleep talking, and later I would wake up to find Marc asleep with his hand on my belly.

But one thing is clear: we are not, during pregnancy and childbirth, dealing with just biology or sexuality. We are facing up to what our society has made biological sex differences into. We begin to have to deal with the expectation that as mothers and fathers our lives will be different and separate. This societal expectation involving stereotypes of who will do what begins in this anticipation period and lasts through the actual arrival of our children. It affects both mothers and fathers:

**Angela Barron McBride, The Growth and Development of Mothers (New York: Harper & Row, 1974; 1977 ed., p. 23).

It was impossible to see a family on an outing, the father lying in the sun on the picnic blanket, the mother serving lunch, wiping noses, tying shoes, and not feel angered.

God, it was one great gathering of the female clan – my mother, her mother, people she worked with – all sharing the mothering secrets of centuries. I could accept that it was the right time for female power but I think I resented being pushed into the distant, working father role – which was one that I didn't particularly want.

*Why do people keep reminding us that the baby will force us to change our life style, 'to settle down'? Who wants to be settled? It sounds like death . . . it sounds as if we are being punished for having a sex life.**

We See the World, the World Sees Us

Expecting children affects the way we see the world and the way the world sees us in enriching and complicating ways. We begin to watch and react to the lives of parents and families.

Carrying around this baby made me feel a new relatedness to the lives of women I had never known before. And a new interest in them. I wanted to watch them to learn from them skills I didn't have – how to play on a playground, how to talk with small children, how to settle fights over tricycles, how to hold tiny babies.

You find yourself reading about day care legislation, schooling, vaccine advances. You also find out that the world looks at you differently.

Our friends see us in a new light – possibly as unlike them, possibly as being in a place they are not quite ready for or sure about wanting:

We were coming out the door from work, a big crowd of us. One of us was talking about her mother – how she had spent a lot of life caring for children, not having time to care for herself, how no wonder she seemed old. She ended by saying that when her mother had been her age she was already married and with a kid on the way. They all stopped and looked at me – already as big as a barn. It was like they wanted to know what it was all about – part of it was wonder, part curiosity, part fear, I think.

We experience being seen and treated as mothers and fathers. For the first time we may meet, head-on, some of the stereotypes that surround parenthood:

I was buying baby furniture in the last weeks before Jamie was born. I was in one of those huge toy-and-baby-trappings stores. I wanted to buy the crib in parts, not assembled, because it was cheaper and I had put together plenty of things before. The salesman tried to talk me out of it. When I was stubborn, he said 'Well, tell your husband the directions are inside.'

This time was difficult for me as a single mother. I was constantly asked to justify my decision. I realized how many people think a parent ought to be married.

*McBride, op. cit., p. 25.

Readiness: On Your Mark, Get Set

Soon there will be another person smack in the middle of our lives. As we wait for the child there is a feeling of being stranded between two worlds, of no longer being 'just an adult' but being not quite admitted to parenthood.

I felt like an adolescent again. Expecting to prepare many hours for the person in my life I did not know – this baby – I did not want to get seduced into the processes of buying, practising, preparing for birth. I was somewhere between girlhood and womanhood when it came to parenting, though I was sophisticated in many other ways. I felt clumsy and inexperienced and I hated the feeling.

But we have the option of seeking both support and information if we are willing to admit our apprehensions and lack of knowledge:

For me, the women in my women's group provided the caring and the knowing that I needed. Most of them had one or two children. The women had loved being pregnant, had had positive birth experiences because they had prepared for an active role, had breast-fed, and believed in some kind of shared parenting. Becoming a parent was a complicated emotional experience for them and they were sensitive to the needs of beginning parents. It was really important for me at this time to feel part of a loving community of women who could share with me my anticipated fears and hopes around pregnancy.

As a to-be father you feel it's not kosher to be preoccupied with the baby's coming – but you are. I had nowhere in particular to turn to – few of my friends had kids, and the ones who did didn't take much part. But my brother was going to have a baby too. We spent a lot of time together – much more than usual. We didn't talk directly about it. We didn't have any information to share. But we talked about marriage and work – sort of putting everything in order as a way of getting ready.

Books and articles are available and offer us descriptions of the pregnancy period. But they cannot work out for you the ramifications of the changes that come over you in the way that other people can.

I faithfully read about the symptoms of early pregnancy – nausea, fatigue, temporary loss of balance, dulling of sexual appetites. Okay, I said to myself, we can live with that. But then a friend shared with me what that had meant in terms of her daily life. 'I spent the early morning hiding in the bathroom to escape the smell of Tom's bacon. Often as not, I threw up on the way to the car, having to rush back in to change clothes, threatening to make us both late to work. The rest of the day was lived on a five-year-old's schedule – nap in the late afternoon and in bed by eight or nine. Even on weekends when we could have made love in the middle of the day, I had no real interest – only the certain pressure that it had been a long time for Tom.' So I learned from her that I was not sick, crazy or strange . . . just pregnant.

Actually doing things in anticipation of the baby's arrival pushes our parenthood out into the open and deepens our sense of comfort:

One friend wisely advised me to spend time with infants and she was right. Especially since my fantasies of an infant were really of a much older baby. I visited two mothers with newborns. Both were extremely turned on and excited by the whole thing. I loved being in their presence holding their babies, feeling their enthusiasm and learning from them. We even wanted to do some daytime sitting for an infant. Unfortunately, we did not know anyone well who was receptive to the idea.

So much of my time and energy in the last trimester went into preparing a welcome for my baby by providing it with the space and clothing and equipment necessary for its care. I had a lot of anxiety about whether I could be a good mother, and one way of dealing with it was feeling well equipped. Clearly, being prepared is no substitute for an emotional relationship and day-to-day experience, but none of these was possible yet. We bought a carpet, a little dresser, a crib, changing table, clothes and some drapes. The colour scheme was all primary colours – as exciting and intense as the process was for us.

Maybe it was hard for Frank to feel involved in all those last-minute things. For him I think a lot of them were too womanly and made him feel embarrassed. At some point he just announced he was making a crib for the baby. He poured hours into it – even reading some stuff about infants so he could understand how to build the safest, most interesting place for the baby to spend its early years. It is a wonderful crib – sturdy posts at the corner, the edges all rounded, and Plexiglass sides so the baby could see everything.

The Event Itself

There is no way we can be totally prepared for any major change in our lives – only readier than we were before. The experience of childbirth is in many ways an illustration of this. Like other points in parenthood, we have never been there before, and so we are faced with trying to shape an event that is unfolding for the first time.

Childbirth, also like our parenting later, is a moment when all the different aspects of our lives compete for attention. Alive all at once is our own sense of not letting it be taken out of our hands, of wanting it to be a personal and not merely a medical experience, of wanting to do it well, of not getting isolated from our partners. It is not easy – doctors and nurses are trained to take over and not to assist. Hospitals value efficiency and standard medical practice over parents and children. But parents have found ways of coming to terms with the event of childbirth. Some do it by being active in their own behalf during hospital birth.

My water broke. 'Come to the hospital. I'll induce your labour,' my doctor said. I knew from childbirth classes that it was possible to wait twenty-four hours for the onset of labour before any induction was necessary. 'No,' I said, 'I'll wait to see if I go into labour.' Sixteen hours later I did.

Traditional hospital births have not allowed us to balance the medical and emotional sides of childbirth. Realizing this, parents have worked to have and make available to other families choices about how to give birth. In recent years the work of parents has made it possible to use the birthing process as a way of entering actual parenthood actively and thoughtfully.

As this woman describes her home delivery:

Most amazing had been how in touch with my body and its messages I had become. I knew the baby was coming. Awaking at midnight out of a deep sleep (my body had told me to go to bed at eight), finding myself in labour, my energies were totally directed. I knew the baby was coming and coming soon. The memory of her two-and-a-half-hour journey is filled with images, feelings, sounds. The long hot bath I took, the water soothing, relaxing, easing the intensity of the contractions. Peter, our two-year-old, resting his head on my lap as I laboured sitting on the rug while Tom fixed the bed, vacuumed the rug (or tried to – I protested at this point that a little lint wouldn't hurt anyone) and set up the stereo. And then the music, soft, beautiful in the background, totally concentrated on during contractions. And there was the support I felt in between contractions from the people who were with me.*

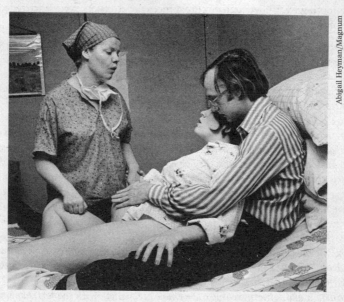

Abigail Heyman/Magnum

We often feel that if birth is not perfect we have failed or, worse yet, are already inadequate parents. It is crucial for us to know that there is no one perfect or right birth. There are as many human entries into the experience as there are parents. Moreover, we can reclaim or remake even difficult ones.

*Judith Dickson Luce, 'Damara's Birth' (privately circulated).

During the difficult period of transition my cervix wasn't dilated. An hour passed, and by that time transition is usually over, but mine was still as if it was just beginning. The doctor said 'We will let you go a half-hour more.' The half-hour passed and I was demoralized because I thought, oh, my God, nothing's happening. My motivation for breathing and just hanging in there was decreasing. So after another half-hour he gave me an internal exam and said 'It's not dilating any more – I'll have to do a C-section on you.' And I remember saying 'Oh, no, I don't want to have a C-section!' I was so emotionally involved in this whole process that it was like robbery. I felt cheated. Once a friend was talking about natural childbirth and I burst into tears – I had not been awake, Peter had been pushed out of the room, even though we had talked to the doctor about his being able to stay.

Several years after a second C-section, I started to work with parents who were going to have or had had section births. We worked on ways of preparing, getting spinals instead of general anaesthesia, getting fathers into the operating room. It was a little like getting back the experience I thought I'd lost.

Childbirth can be exhilarating when the events unfold in an uncomplicated and smooth way. Under such circumstances parents can experience a deepened sense of mutual effort and an enormous closeness to their child.

Barbara was doing great – in complete control; I was the coach; we had learned our Lamaze well. By 8.30, 5 cm dilated and the doctor was off to his other delivery, a C-section. We kept working, the nurses were great; we had practised and we were a team. The doctor returned about ten o'clock to see how we were doing. He did his last internal. 'Get dressed, Barbara, start pushing, you are ten centimetres – fully dilated.' We couldn't believe it – through transition, the hardest stage, and almost finished.

Through the hardest part I helped her by coaching her to remember places we had been together. Like floating together in the middle of a lake in the Berkshires. About fifteen pushing contractions later the baby's head was crowning and we were off to the delivery room. The nurse and the doctor got things ready, Barbara did some non-pushing breathing and I coached and watched. Then a couple of easy pushing breaths, and the head came out; the doctor unwrapped the cord from around the baby's neck. 'One, two,' one more push – 'It's a girl.'

'We got everything we wanted, Barb.'

'Give me my child!' She was so beautiful, six pounds, nine ounces, dark hair and lots of it, long limbs and fingers, crying with no stimulation, high Apgar (healthy) and wonderful, held in her mother's arms.

The labour and delivery went like the whole pregnancy, with comfort, happiness and ease. We are completely happy, and being together through the greatest experience of our lives brought us even closer than we had been before, and we had not thought that possible.

The First Year

The Initial Upheaval – Romance and Catastrophe

We feel joy and experience the miracle of life that people have been talking about for centuries when we take our tiny newborn into our arms for the first time. It's enormously touching, though sometimes frightening, to have this innocent, helpless infant totally dependent on us, and for most people it evokes an intense desire to nurture.

Where do these lullabies we seem to know come from? We're flooded with memories of the deepest attachments we've felt in childhood. What is this almost sexual feeling I have when I hold my baby? We sense our child will bring into our lives enormous joy and some of the highest moments of human happiness and excitement that we will share together in life as a couple. We anticipate our child's life unfolding before us as he smiles, sits and takes his first steps toward us. We know his life will intermingle with ours as we build together this central relationship which will influence in a major way our sense of who we are. Despite the problems we can anticipate, we feel happy – just because we have a baby.

But no matter how enthusiastic we are about welcoming our child into our lives, it's important to realize that it takes time and experience both to develop a strong bond with him/her and a strong sense of ourselves as parents. It takes time to work out ways we can cooperate in raising our child, and still maintain and lead fulfilling adult lives. For most new parents – and especially mothers, who tend to be primary caretakers – the demands of the initial days, months and, sometimes, first year of their baby's life feel overwhelming, and we as parents feel 'done in', somewhat out of control of our lives, panicked, lost in parenthood and immobilized by fatigue.

Take heart, relax, enjoy this precious time – it's shortlived, and with time you will find ways to handle your new baby and yourself in your new situation. But be prepared: your life changes when you have a baby, and most new parents, no matter how together and competent they might appear, feel shaky at first. As some new parents put it:

When I was pregnant I focused on my body and couldn't see beyond childbirth. I must confess the minute-by-minute demands of life with a baby came as a shock.

As men we have to deal with it, too, whether we talk about it or not. We have to watch our partner's body shifting – the rhythm of our sex life slows, even stops, we stand by while a woman becomes absorbed into her womb and later bonded to an infant. In this we sometimes feel shut out, angry, frankly ignored and jealous.

I think that obstetricians and hospital staff are very negligent about talking about post-partum [postnatal depression]. It can be a long process of recovery. And if you haven't been led to see it as normal or likely, you feel somewhat panicked that you are going crazy. You have lost your strength and your clothes size and your sexual self-image and maybe your job and your economic independence, your sense of adult community – and they call it the 'baby blues'. Instead, they should help you, talk about exercise and diet and finding household and child-care help, and sharing with your husband. They don't want to scare you, so instead they leave you stranded.

Feeling like a Zombie

In these early months the physical attachment and intimacy we feel with our baby is both satisfying and exhausting.

I really felt depleted. Every plant I owned had died. I didn't really cook – we had a lot of take-out food and sandwiches. I felt completely unable to nurture anybody other than my baby and self except in ways I totally had to.

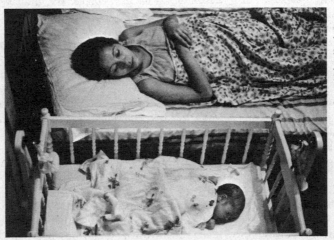

George Malave/Stock, Boston

Certain people have traditionally dismissed women's post-partum exhaustion, just as in recent years women have been told that menstrual cramps and menopause symptoms are neurotic adjustments to womanhood. In fact you really feel physically weaker than you usually do. You've done the very tough physical job of pregnancy and childbirth. You're most likely getting little sleep, and the nightly and daily demands of physical care of feeding, holding, rocking the baby *are* physically exhausting. So although there is a lot of emotional adjustment, you and your feelings do have a strong physical basis.

When I was pregnant I felt more tired than ever before in my life. Since my baby was born I am one-hundred-per-cent more tired. It's not just physical exhaustion from the stress of childbirth and subsequent days and nights of interrupted sleep, but I'm slowed down intellectually and emotionally as well. I'm too tired to make calls to find a baby-sitter. I see a scrap of paper on the floor and I'm too tired to pick it up. I want to be taken care of and have no demands made of me other than the baby's. Initially, I worried that I was so tired I couldn't function at all, but then I relaxed a bit, took each day as it came, and functioned as best I could.

The physical care of infants is demanding and time-consuming. As one woman describes it:

On one hand, I found the physical care immensely satisfying. I had to take over where my body left off – feed, hold, comfort, carry my baby. I was literally giving myself to my child and felt so valued, needed and important. On the other hand, I never felt so physically and emotionally taxed. The most simple of daily routines, going to buy some milk, became elaborate productions; gathering up snuggies, diapers, rattles, sweater, blankets – all for an hour's outing, and there was no guarantee that my baby wouldn't cry through most of it.

We have a desire to give all we can to our baby, yet have other conflicting wishes as well – to work, run the household, enjoy our partner, friends and family – not to mention our need for time alone. Parents directly responsible for the new infant suddenly have a new full-time occupation added on to other life activities. A lot of the things we are used to doing have to be speeded up, cut down or dropped altogether. This almost comes as a shock, no matter how much we've been 'prepared'.

In the traditional family it is the woman who bears the burden of this time-energy crunch, whether or not she works outside the home.

Time is an enormous issue – I do not have enough of it. I try to pack so much into a day. In addition to lovingly caring for my baby, I need a few hours to work, make baby-sitting arrangements and keep up with the household, not to mention shopping, grooming myself, making telephone calls. I feel so exhausted, sometimes 'crazy', but I do not want to slow down.

Although new mothers feel the physical stress more intensely, particularly if they are breast-feeding, new fathers, if they are actively involved in parenting to any degree, feel it as well:

I took over night feedings. Those moments of feeding and rocking my daughter in the quiet hours of night were extraordinarily precious to me. On the other hand, I woke up each morning to face a hard day at the office feeling wiped out, and slightly irritable as I anticipated facing my colleagues, who had no sympathy for my post-partum stress.

As a culture we need to include new fathers' needs in viewing the post-partum experience.

It's More than a Touch of the Baby Blues

In addition, society adds to new parents' post-partum burden because it expects that unless you constantly carry the high and the romance of parenthood with you, despite the fantastic new pressures you're under, you're a failure.

I was determined not to have a post-partum depression, and actively threw myself into parenting. One year later I found myself crying a lot and I didn't know why I felt so sad. I had thrown all my energy into successfully getting my feet on the ground, and it was only now that I felt strong enough to handle my sad feelings.

New mothers have been embarrassed out of openly sharing their feelings about the emotional complexity of taking on so enormous a responsibility and so intense a bond. We women have been left to think that if we have mixed feelings about accepting the consuming bond to our children, we are less than adequate women and mothers. For our well-being and adjustment we need to admit the many emotions we feel in becoming a parent.

I had a very difficult delivery and was furious at having been at the mercy of my body. I found the rage spilling over into my relationship with my son. 'How could you do this to me!'

Women's post-partum moodiness can be viewed as neurotic. But now, when new parents speak out honestly about it, what might at first seem like destructive or negative feelings have in fact their constructive aspects. We are entitled to give ourselves the psychic space for the growing pains of giving birth to ourselves as parents. Here is one woman's account about a difficult post-partum experience:

Since I didn't know about post-partum depression, I had no way of understanding what was happening to me for the nine or so months after Michael was born. I felt unexpectedly low-energy, uncertain about myself, fearful of not being able to cope, apprehensive about even the smallest tasks, and incredibly alone. On the surface I was a normal, happy new mother with a fine healthy son, a fine healthy husband, and a nice place to live. And these were true, but at the same time I felt terrible inside. Here are a few of the moments I remember:

— Lying in my bed toward the end of Michael's nap, with the butterflies in my stomach agitating in a crescendo at each little about-to-wake-up sound he made.

— Sitting one afternoon in the early spring sunshine with friends, deeply weary, my left breast large and sore, in the tentative, uneasy peacefulness of those first moments of Michael's nap. I asked Fred to go inside and get me a glass of water, and he shot me a look of sullen, hen-pecked resentment, a look that said, You bossy bitch – now that you have a kid you think you can make me wait on you in front of our friends. And he brought me a glass of water so tiny that though mortified by my neediness, I had to ask for more.

— The helpless amazement I felt one day when Michael was two months old and Fred started to complain that our life was so dull and what we needed to do was have a party. I lamely tried to get into giving a party, when all I wanted to do was curl up and be taken care of – so apologetic that our life was dull, so devastated by his boredom, so deeply angry, though I didn't know it, at his defection. And he angry at what seemed like my defection from him. I understand now that he got no help from our culture in comprehending what was going on: he didn't know about post-partum, he just knew that I had wanted a baby and now didn't seem to enjoy it; he needed my attention and got

my neediness, a change that he was totally unprepared for. I wish that during that time we had each been able to get the attention we needed without its having to be from each other.

– Sitting on the far side of my obstetrician's wide expanse of desk, telling him haltingly, not having easy words for it, how I had been feeling. And his fatherly advice: 'Don't want too much, that's what I like to tell my new mothers. Get to a library once in a while to keep your mind going, but basically you can feel good that you are raising a new generation and taking care of your husband when he comes home from a busy day – a fine fulfilment.' I believed him, felt worse but should have been furious.

The amazing thing is that through that whole murky time of self-doubting, emotional shakiness, and lack of support from those around me, the joy persisted – hand in hand with the depression, like its sister. The wonderful skin-closeness of nursing Michael and powdering his bottom; the high of strolling him down the street to the smiles of old ladies; lying on the rug in a quiet patch of sunshine watching Michael's eyes 'count molecules' in the air. I knew that I loved Michael and wanted to be his mother – why, then, did I feel so undone? Now I see the loneliness that existed before Michael, but didn't surface until his birth: the loneliness of an uncommunicative marriage, of friendships in which my true feelings were hidden, of an ethic which said: 'You do it by yourself.' I also see the little girl in me abruptly summoned to grow up, and I see my depression as the gestation period for my maturer self, psychic space for my new growing, and the labour pains as well. I emerged from it with strength and sadness.

Then when Michael was eight months old I went to a women's group for the first time, and heard mothers talking about post-partum depression as a phenomenon that happens. *It was a revelation to me: I felt relieved, released, forgiven. I wasn't crazy or lazy or ungrateful or unwomanly, after all – I was a mother. And I could talk about my feelings.*

New mothers are at least culturally given permission to have a touch of 'baby blues'. In contrast, men traditionally expected to have no responsibility for infant care and thus no symptoms of a post-partum recovery, are not permitted to have any emotional reaction to parenthood. Some men avoid active involvement – are solicitous and appreciative while at home, but leave their 'fatherhood on the doorstep' as they leave for work each morning. Other men feel embarrassed by their emotionality; both their intense feelings for their baby and their ambivalence in seeing all their partner's tenderness transferred to this new intruder or being shut out of a relationship with the baby, which implies 'It's been inside me all the time; it's mine, not yours.' If men try to do child care, it might be at the first blunder that they are excluded, or so they feel. It might be the first time in the history of the marriage that the men feel so inadequate in their performance. Some men don't acknowledge their feelings to themselves and 'act out' instead, having affairs or becoming accident-prone.

It's a time when both parents are under a lot of stress and need a lot of mothering themselves, but most of us tend to feel embarrassed by our own needy feelings. Although just caring for our child can be personally comforting, new

Food

I want mother's milk,
that good sour soup.
I want breasts singing like eggplants,
and a mouth above making kisses.
I want nipples like shy strawberries
for I need to suck the sky.
I need to bite also
as in a carrot stick.
I need arms that rock,
two clean clam shells singing *ocean*.
Further I need weeds to eat
for they are the spinach of the soul.
I am hungry and you give me
a dictionary to decipher.
I am a baby all wrapped up in its red howl
and you pour salt into my mouth.
Your nipples are stitched up like sutures
and although I suck
I suck air
and even the big fat sugar moves away.
Tell me! Tell me! Why is it?
I need food
and you walk away reading the paper.

                    – Anne Sexton

parents need appreciation and comfort from others. 'When I cry, if someone holds me I'll want to hold my baby when she cries.' In short, new parents need their own sources of nurturing to keep going.

One of the stresses of modern life is that those new parents who live far away from extended family networks and find themselves isolated have few loving adult relationships where there is a no-strings-attached give-and-take. We often find in the early months that we miss most the people who cared for us as children.

Often when I'm with my daughter, I think of my mother, aunts, grandmother. This adds such richness and depth to my relationship with her. It's important for us not to cut ourselves off from our emotional past and take time to miss people – memories of being nurtured sustain me.

We've Never Been Parents Before

We need emotional support from others, but we also need information. If we live in a community with a lot of new parents, we can compare notes with others and get information that is helpful in solving the small daily problems that come up.

'What is that horrible white growth on my child's mouth?' 'Relax,' a friend tells us, 'it's a harmless fungus that goes away.' 'My child at four months is not sleeping through the night.' 'Nor did mine,' a friend says. It takes time to build up a supportive network, and the isolation that comes from living apart from people in a similar life situation can emotionally burden new parents during this important first year.

At just the time when you need others for models and information the most, you are often isolated in your own little house with your own little kids and no institutional affiliation.

All we have to fall back on is our own experience, of which we have very little, since we've never been a parent before. In fact, many new parents are often surprised by newborns and realize they expected to give birth to a six-month-old baby. Some of us have had committed relationships with newborn siblings, cousins or neighbours, or have even been trained to work with children professionally, but many have not.

I had no contacts with children, and when Jim was born, I just didn't know what to do with this little creature that landed in my hands. What I discovered was comforting – if I just paid attention, I would probably find out.

With time and daily care we will come to understand our child's needs, but initially we feel somewhat panicked and insecure. As one mother put it, 'Up until now my body was doing all the caretaking, now it's all me!' This may hit new mothers harder than new fathers, because both society and new mothers themselves expect women to be automatically relaxed, comfortable and confident, since child rearing has traditionally been women's domain of life work.

I grew up with the idea that women have an instinctive way of knowing what a child's needs are and they do it wonderfully and they are always calm and happy and graceful about it all. When I discovered that I very often didn't know how to handle the baby, rather than relax and figure out what to do I felt that I was not a good mother.

I had just the right amount of help and support from my mother and mother-in-law that I needed. They really taught me a lot that I just wouldn't have known. Danny was really cranky and a real crier, and my mother would sit with him in the rocker and hold him close to her and rock him. I wouldn't have known that would make him happy. I also had to accept the fact that the baby just wasn't regular, like a little clock. Babies are totally demanding beings. You have to just give, give, give and be prepared. I think people who are educated, who have had careers for a while, done more things on their own and arranged their own lives feel a lot of that fatigue in the early months psychologically rather than physically. It was the tension of not knowing when he would get up and everything. With the second one it was so much easier to accept the fact that everything is topsy-turvy. The daily care I gave the baby made me see how important the process of loving and caring was. And the more skilful I got, the more excited I became. And I really began to feel like a mother when I could predict some things about him and help him get through different stages. With your first child you practically hold it under a microscope. There's nothing casual about it, you really question everything, physically and emotionally, because you feel the great weight of the responsibility.

Caring for a baby does not require magic powers. All it is, is the private, intimate relationship of paying close attention to another person's needs, which takes time, patience and commitment. Admittedly, though, some parents relate to newborns better than others.

I wonder if it would have helped me to know that parenting would become easier as the baby became older. Possibly some of the discomfort I felt as a mother in the early stages wasn't only career pulls, but rather that I relate better to verbal beings. Other people are wonderful with babies, I am not.

Fathers' changing attitudes toward the role of parent – partly in response to current feminist thinking or because of their own real desire – have resulted in new fathers wanting to share in the pleasures of active, committed parenting from the beginning, *but* both men and women as well as society still expect less of men in this respect. New fathers have traditionally excluded themselves from initial active caretaking because culturally it has been considered work that is inferior and unmanly. Men are expected merely to be providers and appreciators of their partner and children. But some men are delighted at the opportunity to be in from the beginning, as one new father puts it:

I have never thought of myself as a traditional father – whatever that is. Even during the first year I was pretty conscious of not falling into traditional ruts. My memory of that time is of having him around a lot – taking him to meetings. I also remember really enjoying that – it was neat to have my baby along with me. But then, I was lucky, too – the people working with me were not traditional, either. They never frowned – in fact, they welcomed his being around.

This father went on to say he was lucky in that his wife did not feel threatened that he was doing as much holding, diapering and rocking as she was, but at times they had to do a lot of sensitive communicating because it felt as if they were competing for the role of primary parent.

Another new father described how inexperienced he felt:

It's hard, the culture doesn't even think about what fathers may be feeling when they are first parents. Mothers of infants are isolated with their children and must reach out to find other people to share with – but there are at least informal ways for them to do that. Fathers are not supposed to feel uncertainty about their fatherhood.

New fathers need to be supported and not put down for nurturing babies. Some new fathers are skilled, but those who feel inept need encouragement from their wives and peers during their initial contact with their babies. Nonetheless, whether the caretaking is being done primarily by the mother or is being shared daily, new parents who don't have a lot of infant care experience are kept on their toes dealing for the first time with new situations that involve medical, psychological and household management. Let's face it, parenting is a kind of interdisciplinary work and a tricky act to get together.

When a baby cries and you change him and find he has diaper rash, you can put on ointment. But when he cries and cries and nothing seems to help – that's what is hard. You feel terrible that there is nothing you can do for him, but go berserk at the same time. It is hard but important to learn something about limits: when to take care of ourselves and ignore him, when to go on rocking and soothing. What is catering, what is caring, what is being indifferent.

I wish I had known to take things with a grain of salt – like the old saying that a child needs to be walked in the fresh air in a carriage every day, or a bath every day – these are not the most important things, it's true, but you do burden yourself with them and maybe you would trust yourself with your child a lot more if you didn't have to be the perfect mother.

At this point we hunger for folklore, tricks of the trade, humour and reassurance from experienced parents, a grandmother who says 'If he doesn't teethe by age two, *then* worry.'

I had this funny thing happen. I thought that to be a real family we all had to eat together. I said to myself, this is the right way, this is how I was brought up. I mentioned it to my mother, who said 'No, you always ate before us.' I had to laugh, I had had this totally screwy notion of what my past had been, I had been driven to making us eat at five-thirty. I relaxed, and began to more fully set up my own ways of doing things.

One thing you really have to realize – doctors, nurses, other parents will tell you bits about child care as if they were laws carved on stone. 'Meat has to be the last food you introduce into the baby's diet.' Then you go to Texas and find out that the going rule there is 'Introduce meat first.' It makes you realize that there are fads and opinions and old wives' tales, that you can collect opinions till doomsday, but in many cases you can do the choosing.

Also, we face scary situations like convulsions, severe diarrhoea or choking. Even in less dramatic situations we find ourselves not only worrying about the baby but about whom we should consult. Should we go to a paediatrician, nurse or social worker or to a neighbourhood clinic? How can we evaluate the advice we are getting? Who can we rely on, depend on? How can we develop a critical perspective on the advice we are getting – what is sound advice for one might not be so for another. We think we are not vulnerable to what other people say, but if even a stranger says 'Your child looks a bit pale', we panic. (See the chapters on Helping Ourselves and on Society's Impact on Families.)

Will We Measure Up?

All this throws us back to worrying about how we measure up – are we being good parents in the ways society has instructed us? Are we always loving and supportive to our children? Do we always feel good about them? Content? Fulfilled in the role of mother or father? It is important to have a trusted friend who can give us some perspective on ourselves. It is in this first year that we suffer first (though by no means last) from the conflict between the reality of parenthood and what we expect of ourselves as parents – the specific ideals we've inherited from our own family, as well as what society expects of us.

The message that we're getting is that there's an ideal we have to live up to, the ideal of the perfect parent. This isn't something that comes only from outside; it's also what we feel as we look at our baby and we say 'God! I don't want to mess her up physically or psychologically.'

We know that to our baby we loom large, because we provide her/his primary environment. On one hand we want to develop a strong bond and want our relationship to embody the most perfect form of love between mother or father. But we know there is built-in disappointment in that wish because we are people with human frailties as well as strengths; we are not omnipotent or all-powerful, even if our child might think so. We need not feel threatened because of that, but rather cope with our imperfections and weigh them against what we want of ourselves, rather than against the ideal of what mothers and fathers are supposed to be.

I wished to be an earth-mother type and demand-fed my son. As his demands escalated, my joy decreased and my fatigue and irritation rose. 'Listen,' my husband said, 'put him on a schedule of sorts or else you'll grow to resent him.' It was a sad moment for me to realize there were limits to my generosity.

If I spend a prolonged time with him, I don't enjoy his company after a while. But if I get bored or frustrated, I feel guilty. Frankly, I don't have such high expectations of any other relationship I have.

Hand in hand with our worries about whether we are the ideal parents is our concern over whether we have an ideal child. In the first year we discover ways our fantasy child meshes with our real child.

Children become this movie in which you see yourself. Sometimes it is very reassuring – you see your best self, but it's no fun to see your worst self.

My baby was colicky for eight months. During that time I couldn't help thinking, it's my fault – I'm just a bad mother.

Women have been led to think that if they have mixed feelings about accepting the huge responsibility of such intimacy, they are less than adequate mothers.

The first year was critical to my assessment of myself as a person. It forced me to realize that like being married, having children is not an end in itself. You don't at last arrive at being a parent and suddenly feel satisfied and joyful. It is a constantly reopening adventure. You know your child and you like him better, you like him better and you like yourself better. Like yourself as a mother better, and there is space to think about what else you want to be beyond a mother.

As much as our culture has locked women into a tight mother/child relationship which precludes stepping back from the relationship, it has locked fathers out. But men are beginning to more freely admit their mixed feelings about having total or near-total economic responsibility for the family, as well as being excluded from active parenting.

A friend of mine with a new baby said that he found himself wanting to talk to his child in baby talk, all those soft, teasing, cooing syllables mothers make to their children. But whenever he was around other adults, he felt himself holding back. He realized that he was thinking, men don't make noises like that – it's too childish. He was struggling with the injunctions most of us grew up with against being intimate with our children. That is something that takes a long time to work through.

Sometimes I find myself playing in public with a child in childlike ways. Then I become conscious of the people all around watching and the message that comes through is that you are weird to be down at that level. You should stand up and walk stiffly along, look after the children's welfare, but you don't play.

Mothers as well as fathers are expected to behave in 'adult' ways, and are often inhibited from unselfconscious playing with the baby or in dealing with situations in their own way. You should take issue with the cultural ideals of the perfect parent and inherited ideals from your family, and do what makes sense for you, realizing that some of what you do will mesh with ideals and some will not. Fortunately, since the women's movement began, parents feel more freedom in shaping their adult identities and are finding new ways of expanding parenting roles. But unfortunately, a new set of impossibly high expectations of being superpeople has developed along with this freedom.

When he was born I was determined to show all the people at work that it wouldn't take its toll on me. That I was different. I would stay up until morning, trying to prepare work for the next day, nursing betweentimes. It was a nightmare. Only two months into that period did I pause and say 'My God, I am trying to be a superwoman – it's insane.' What have I bargained for by saying that I would be better than normal? Looking back, I think that it would have been fine to ask a fellow worker to take some of the slack, to allow me to come back without killing myself. I think I bought the mentality that in order for a woman with a child not to be looked down upon, she has to be better than anyone else, to overcome other people's expectation that mothers' energies are being siphoned off. I think the society should support rather than penalize mothers for taking time off.

In a sense we have become pioneers, trying to chart new ways of being parents. Some of our peers won't like what we do. We have to find new ways both to be loyal to those of our sex and to tolerate differences among us. Men, now faced with the responsibility not only of active parenting, but of providing most of the income for the family, find themselves frightened of falling behind on their jobs and also of being cut off from their children.

Right now my career is more a means to an end – to be able to provide for my family – much more than to be a great this or a great that. Right now, having time with the family is much more important. Most of the time I feel confident of my priorities, but at times I have my doubts.

Also, men are struggling against society's expectations that men don't take care of babies.

I remember when my mother-in-law first heard that Tony shared in taking care of Sean. I was two rooms away, but I heard her voice saying to my father-in-law: 'Emasculation – that's what it is.'

When we become parents our past is reactivated, particularly our relationship with our parents. We tend to re-evaluate their parenting of us as well as what they are like as men and women. At times there is stress between new parents and their own parents. On one hand, we feel critical of them and what they did.

I grew up being taught, in quiet ways, that you never raised your voice. It was rude, next to crazy. I remember the first time that I let Laura cry herself to sleep. She screamed for almost an hour – loud, angry shrieks. The tension was so enormous that at last I screamed – not at her – alone in my room with the door closed and the pillow over my head so I wouldn't frighten her. I was the one who was frightened, as if letting my voice out like that proved some devil or sickness was in me. But it was more that I had pushed through some final outside boundary my own family had suggested marked the rim of sanity and decency. Once past the boundary I was in a new country – one I had always been taught was a desert.

On the other hand, we may feel a lot of admiration and empathy for what our parents accomplished. We want to say 'Thank you for giving so much of yourself to us.'

For the first time my vision of my mother changed totally. Instead of seeing her as selfish and angry, I realized what it must have been to care for my brother and me day in, day out. I wanted to phone her and say 'I know. I know.'

Suddenly the emotional distance that may have developed in adolescence and early adulthood collapses. We see our parents as other women and men who understand the demands of constant care, the pulls of total infant dependence. All at once we want to share what we have in common with our own fathers and mothers.

Last night after I put Terry to bed, my mother and I were sorting through old photographs, a collection of images spanning three generations. There was one picture of my grandmother as a new mother with her two babies: my mother, nine months, and her sister two and one half. The picture was taken sixty years ago. My grandmother had a young body, and I imaged her breasts full of milk and the pleasures she derived from the physical intimacy of holding, rocking and cuddling her babies. I felt a powerful identification with my mother and grandmother – realizing that we shared a common history of having and raising babies. Suddenly I felt an old familiar intimacy between my mother and me that I had not experienced in years, and I wished she could be a young mother again and I her baby. I looked down at our bodies and realized the impossibility of that wish. Since I became a mother I know the parent-child relationship from both sides now, which makes me feel both closer to my mother and more separate because I am not primarily her daughter now, but mother to my son.

We Are Now Co-Parents

In anticipating parenthood, whether natural or adoptive, we both eagerly awaited our child's arrival and worried about ways our life together would change. We are no longer simply 'lovers', 'friends', 'partners', but co-parents in another kind of venture altogether.

Up until then we had pretty much been two separate individuals, checking in with each other from two different lives, enjoying picking up where we had left off. Once we had Eric, the pattern reversed itself. It gave us something we really shared for the first time. It sounds phoney, but it gave us a piece of shared lifework.

With this change come new responsibilities and pleasures. How we are going to share the responsibilities is, in our opinion, the first question new parents have to answer:

We were just very lucky. The first year, Chuck was home most of the time. He was working at home. Because of that it has just never seemed that we got forced into the mould of his leaving for work and my staying home all day to do the child care. What that did for the politics of my doing work was very strong. It was like 'Hey, here we all are in the same space with a set of shared needs – let's share taking care of them.'

For many couples this is the first serious grappling to put issues of feminism into practice. We think that women and men are entitled to some life away from their baby and that men are also entitled to the pleasures of caring for the baby. (See the Sharing Parenthood chapter.) And whatever way couples decide to proportion time and responsibilities, it's important to feel you are doing the choosing together.

Up until now the question of who does what has not been too important. In most relationships both partners work, and if you are not too uptight about keeping clothes in the closet and so forth, the daily chores of living together can be coped with without too much stress.

When a baby comes along, the physical and psychological demands of child care are so enormous that new parents have to begin to divide up the responsibilities of work and householding. It's important to have anticipated this issue and done some planning before the arrival of the baby. These decisions are inevitably stressful to make and put into practice during the first year, when new parents feel conflicts of wanting to meet the baby's absolute needs, of their needs to be devoted parents, and their needs to work, particularly if they need to put a lot of time into work. You can't explain to an eight-month-old that even though she is feeling rotten her mother or father needs to go to work.

There is a range of ways couples can divide family responsibilities, depending on each person's personal satisfaction with parenting and work and on available work opportunities and the chances of finding trustworthy people to do child care.

I don't think that even though I am committed to working, I could take a job that requires total emotional and intellectual commitment. Just because I think that that would mean there were certain reserves unavailable to my family. My job at the hospital was like that – all my energy went into it. So having children does mean for me that besides needing a fairly flexible time schedule, I do need a job that does not require my emotional attention twenty-four hours a day. I am only ready and willing to give three, four or five hours. I think that is something men really have to consider before going ahead and having a family.

Luckily, we were both graduate students. We arranged our schedules so we could alternate periods of primary caretaking.

I was smack in the middle of my career and I knew if I gave up my work I'd resent my baby Sara. Also, practically speaking, I did not want to be like so many of my friends who gave up work during the early years in which they had small children and then had a difficult time getting back. I have delegated a lot of child care to a devoted and loving sitter. I trust Sara is in good hands, but I've come to realize that there is no easy way for a working mother. Yes, I love my work, but many days I feel I'm neither working nor mothering very well. The house is a mess, my child a bit of a stranger to me, I've lost the rhythm of daily child care, and I'm jealous of the intimacy between my child and her sitter.

Some parents want to be home the first year:

I worked for a couple of years before my children were born. But I hated every minute of the push and shove of it. I knew that the work I wanted to do was raising children. When mine came and at last it was 'all right' for me to be home with them – playing, sewing things for them, building a way of life for them – I was relieved and happy. Sure, there are hideous days and nights – times when Allie coughs for what seems like hours. I am cross-eyed from being up so much. Those are the days when I curse the fact that we live far away from our families and that Rob works all day nine to five. But they are not days when I curse having had children. Even a week like that does not subtract from my basic feeling that the most important thing I will ever do is raise children.

As a single mother, I had to go on welfare. I could not accept money from my parents, and to go back to work was unthinkable.

Although I would like my husband to do more of the caring, I have a lot of attachment to being the person to breast-feed and soothe and know her best.

It's important for mothers who are full-time active parents to find ways of balancing their baby's needs with their own without feeling guilty or selfish. New mothers need to leave baby with spouse, family, trusted neighbours or sitters, seek out the company of others and pursue their own interests.

When Eric was eight months old I started taking an art class evenings. I felt so energized and renewed returning home from class having done something just for me!

Some fathers really want to devote more energy to home life and have less economic responsibility. That is possible for some, but unfortunately, given the present economic realities and available work opportunities, most couples find it hard to divide work on a fifty-fifty basis. (For a more detailed discussion see the chapter on Society's Impact on Families.)

Whatever new arrangement a couple settles on brings changes in earlier ways of doing things and feelings about these changes. For women, who still more typically take on more of the child-care responsibilities, loss of both economic independence and a community of peers makes them fear loss of power in a relationship that might be intended to be egalitarian.

I felt so anxious that I'd never have another thought except what colour is her sheet today, how many times has she peed, etc. But the amount of money I could make on my job, three dollars an hour, is laughable, compared to the amount my husband could make. I couldn't support the family in the present way we're living. For me to say 'You work half time and I will' would substantially change what we could offer our children. A lot of women are in my position.

When our son was very young, I was earning more money than his father, but my job was a pressure cooker: long hours and a lot of hustling and competition. My husband could arrange more flexible hours, and very often it was he who would get home early to relieve the sitter.

That part was fine, but problems arose when somebody had to stay home because Ricky was too sick to leave with the sitter or, later, when someone had to go to a school meeting. Then, even though his job produced less family income and was more 'laid back', it was I who had to take off from work — because, whatever the practical reality, man's work was seen as more important than woman's. It made me feel angry but I had no way of forcing my husband to stay home.

If family roles are polarized, partners can feel a heightened sense of separateness and difference between themselves.

There were some hard things about those early times — I had to learn to do less and also to understand that my husband would not help. I had to discover that I may not, for several years to come, have the time I need to do work I want to do — that was the biggest sacrifice. Sometimes this feeling would creep in: maybe you will never be able to do everything you had hoped to.

It's important for couples to keep communication open, and to empathize with each other's new position. For couples who share responsibilities, this means new tolerance for partners' ways of doing things.

Before there were children, Mic was content to let me handle my career life the way I wanted. But when we moved to sharing earning and child care, he started to see me much more like half our annual income. He wanted me to push myself at work more, to be up on all the benefits. He was impatient because I didn't run my work life the way he ran his when he was the big breadwinner.

What I remember about the switch to our sharing work and child care was me having to bite my tongue a lot – when the baby's diapers would be on so loose they were falling off, when there were toys from one wall to the other, when he had let the older kids play cook and all the pots and pans were full of soap film, cinnamon and soggy noodles.

Interruptions

Another issue couples face in this first year after pregnancy and childbirth is getting back into a good sexual relationship. As a friend in desperation asked the other day, 'Tell me, do you ever make love again?' Having a child throws our intimate relationship off balance. We are now three instead of two people living together. Ironically, having a child together brings us close but creates new obstacles in our intimate relationship. A small baby sleeping way down the hall seems to act like a censor for many couples. People have speculated that babies have a built-in device for figuring out when their parents are making love.

We had just finished out the time waiting for the episiotomy to heal. We were looking to resume sexual relations and never thought to consider how totally a tiny child – two rooms away and presumably asleep – would thwart us. I remember really trying to focus our energy on relearning to touch each other. No sooner had we started active love-making than the baby woke howling. We tried to ignore it – imagine striking out to reach mutual climax with shrieks in your ear – all the while each of us thinking, he knows what we are doing; he is starving; soon he will throw himself out of his crib.

In the early weeks things were fine. It was settled that we had to fix our attention on the baby, developing some kind of routine for dealing with waking, feeding and sleeping for all three of us. It was the next month or so that was terrible. The baby still woke twice between ten and five. Rob was past the early nervous stage when he woke and helped. He was feeling pushed outside the charmed circle of those intense minutes in the dark and quiet. I would feed the baby, soothe her, lay her down to sleep – then go to bed with Rob where we would make love, or at least try to talk – then what seemed like only minutes later I would hear the baby cry. I would go to her, feed and soothe her, lay her down to sleep, return to bed – and it would be morning all over again. I began to feel like an orange slowly being pulled into separate sections – one for the baby, one for Rob, one for me, one for the baby . . .

A couple relation with our children has a lot of sexual focus to it. Particularly for a man there is a lot of strong feeling about this third person coming in and being very close to the mother. It's often deep-level jealousy. A baby can take away a partner in more ways than one: energy, attention, nurturance, sexuality, even how she looks. There is a significant male adjustment process following the birth of a child. And I think he has to work that out before the sexual relation can be anything but charged with jealousy. Most men deny it and it sneaks up on them.

This is true particularly if a woman is breast-feeding and doing much of the physical caretaking. She might need to take her time in resuming her sex life because maternal and sexual physical needs are not always compatible.

Weaning my son at eleven months was a bittersweet time. I wanted to get my body back as well as a more active sex life but it was with a sense of both joy and sadness. It marked the end of a tender intimacy with my baby.

Clearly, in the first year couples have less time together for sex or other pleasurable activities. With less time available, there is less time for talk, for going places together, and the bare essentials of sexual contact can become isolated from a fuller continuous relationship.

He was an easy baby – but even so, his coming worked profound changes in our relationship. There was a lot of tension between us because there was a third person.

On the other hand, caring for a child is a real awakening to our needs to be nurtured by our partner in a full way. We long for minute-by-minute intimacy – for someone in touch with our mood or fully putting himself (or herself) in our place. In short, we want to be taken care of in the way we care for our baby, to play with each other and enjoy new qualities that are brought out in ourselves and our partners as we parent our children.

Happy Birthday to Us

We can make a party for ourselves as the first year comes to an end – as parents we are one year old. Most of us feel like parents, and we find that people around us perceive us that way, too:

My friend Pauline gave me sweaters her grandmother had knit for her son John. It was as if she had held out her hand and said 'Join the circle of parents and children.'

The year has been very demanding (especially if we've been operating in a one-parent family), but we have come through it more mature. We have never been so needed before, never so responsible for a totally vulnerable being. But the joys have been tremendous, even unexpected.

If you had told me on the delivery table that grunts and squeals would make me love my child, I don't think I would have believed you. But just this week we started having these conversations – he makes a sound, I make one, he makes one. I get up from one of these exchanges and I feel two things – this incredible physical tie to him and adult amazement that I have been down on all fours, face-to-face with an infant, talking in clucks and groans.

Our baby's dependency on us is decreasing as our child becomes more and more him or her self.

He was sitting in his infant seat by the window, first squinting into the light, then lifting his hands up into the sunlight, then focusing on his moving hands. He was facing me, but had no idea that I was there. He was completely absorbed in what he was for himself. I felt a tremendous separateness – something I don't remember feeling when other people could comfort him or when I had to let him cry himself to sleep. In those times he still needed me – but playing like that, he was a closed perfect system of wants and needs. I felt it again when he learned to suck his thumb to comfort himself. I don't think that there is another kind of growth compared to this.

We have to find ways to let go, and at the same time find ways to love and relate.

I always loved the intimacy of nursing and never felt he was intruding upon my body – starting at nine months or so it began to be unwelcome to me. I wanted to find other ways of being with him. He was more mature now and I had to both let go a little and find new ways of being intimate with him.

I never would have believed that the simplest rituals of heating milk, adjusting the temperature in the room, in general creating a mood around feeding or night-time would give me such satisfaction. I do it with a sense of heritage. My parents, in caring for me, passed on these rituals, and I hope one day my son will pass them on to his children.

We have also discovered that as devoted as we are to our baby, we need and want to maintain other relationships and involvements as well. Having a child has altered these relationships and involvements by both enriching them and complicating them.

He got a hundred presents when he was born. It was as if his birth symbolized the affirmation of life. I was touched my friends and relatives welcomed him so wholeheartedly.

Though we have learned how to take our own and our child's needs into account as we plan our lives, we have also learned that no plans are possible!

Before Linda was born I spent hours planning 'how it would be'. I would return to work two months post-partum, she would be on a four-hour schedule, the sitter – a flawless replica of myself – would know exactly what to do, etc. A year later I look back and think how ridiculous I was to think I could predict and control things so much. First of all, I did not anticipate how attached I would feel to Linda. I did not want to go back to work so quickly and so fully. Second, her developmental pattern changes so that as soon as one pattern is established a new one begins. One morning she is up at six and the next day at eight, one day cranky and teething, the next day mellow. It was impossible to plan for anything more than a week in advance.

But the miracle that we have experienced is that suddenly into our lives has come this incredible, close, loving new relationship – with our child. Difficult? Yes. Time-consuming? Yes. Sometimes divisive and isolating? Yes. But joyful, full of meaning and worth it.

Parenting During the Early Years

No matter how much we have to grope or experiment, in our first year with children we cross from adulthood to parenthood. Our sense of ourselves as parents will continue to change, but we have accomplished much more than we sometimes realize. In the first months every day was a minute-to-minute experience. Through the first year we slowly built up predictable days and nights. Most of us began clumsy-awkward in how we diapered, bathed or fed and uncertain about how to open our lives to children. By the end of the first year, those of us who have been encouraged and helped have learned to care in both simple and deep ways for our children.

That process sometimes almost swallows us up, but in it we become parents. We share a history with our children, come to know our partner also as a parent, see how our society really treats families. Maybe more important, we get some handle on who we are as parents – different from our parents, from common stereotypes of fathers and mothers, from peers who were parents before us. Our parenthood is not at all finished – it's fragile, a 'work in progress' – but it's much more than we had before. As one father puts it:

In a week Paul is a year old as a person and I am a year old as a father. I really think of it as a double celebration.

But in the four years that connect infancy with the school years, our children change more rapidly than at any other time outside the womb. In these years they walk and run, talk, begin to spend time away from us, develop independent personalities. Suddenly there are many separate people, there are many demands – as parents, we want to love, play, teach, discipline. And somehow 'on the side' we want to remain individuals, lovers, workers. Any balance we achieve between adult and parental identities, between children's and our own needs, works only for a time – because, as one father says, 'It's a new ball game just about every week.' So we are always in the process of learning to be parents. Whether this constant demand to change stretches or breaks us depends not simply on our skill or on our children's health. It also depends on whether we can ask for help, work out ways of sharing parenting, are lucky enough to have or can create working and living situations which support us through all the changing that the early years ask.

The Pleasures of These Years

When she was a baby – I tried with her – standing by her basket, talking, making faces, winding up the mobile. But somehow I always felt I was making a long-distance phone call to nowhere. Now she is a constant feast for me. Something new is there and changing even as you look – new games in the mirror, a few steps, calling out new words all the time. You can't gobble it up fast enough.

Times like these feel like the right reward for the long, constant hours we put in during infancy. They feel like proof that our children are healthy and capable and we can have pride and gladness. Also, these moments promise we're not going to spend our lives feeding and changing and walking kids.

I want to tell you that each time he learned something new – to sit by himself, to drink from a cup, to point to things he wanted – it was like he was pushing open this big door that had swung shut. By inches, my life was coming back.

Our children become more adventurous, talkative and imaginative, and as their experience widens they are capable of sharing what they take in with us. Audience to their exploits, we are treated to insights, to the chance to pause and enjoy. Through our kids we hold an open ticket back to fantasy and wonder in ourselves.

If you didn't have kids how would you ever know that teakettles shout or that the sky cries rain or that boats don't sink because they used to be fish.

Children also give us a humorous perspective on the adult world:

At three a.m. Shauna is moaning. I go in and she's cowering in the corner, eyes wide open. 'Da bears are coming. I scared.' I crawl in bed with her and we snuggle up. In a while, she pulls the spread over her head. I do too, and find the light (she sleeps with all of them on) comes through making the space like a warm tent. 'This is nice,' I say. 'I hide here,' Shauna says. 'No ghosts come here.' 'Oh.' In the morning, she's afraid to go downstairs. She closes her bedroom door and when I try to dress her, she says, 'Dere's bears in dere.' 'Let's see,' I say. I open the door a crack and peer in. 'Oh,' I say, 'they're gone.' 'Dey must have gone to work,' she concludes.*

As their body skills increase children bring a rich, insisting physicalness into our 'hands to yourself' adult lives:

I grew up in a house where everyone dressed behind closed doors and you never peed until everyone was out of earshot. But Sara was one of those kids who are only comfortable naked and who shows you she loves you by poking and patting and drumming on every part of you that jiggles. When she was small we bathed together and she thought every flap and bump and crease was wonderful. Nobody – not even me – had ever taken that kind of pleasure from me. I think that whatever comfort I have about how I'm made comes a lot from those baths.

The physical freedom children introduce into our lives is matched by the directness of their feelings. Children's frank emotions unmask our adult reserve

---

*Judith Steinbergh's 'Journal' (privately circulated).

My Daughter's Morning

My daughter's morning streams
over me like a gang of butterflies
as I, sour-mouthed and not ready
for the accidents I expect

of my day, greet her early:
her sparkle is as the edge of new
ice on leafed pools, while I
am soggy, tepid; old toast.

Yet I am the first version
of later princes; for all my blear
and bluish jowl I am welcomed
as though the plastic bottle

I hold were a torch and
my robe not balding terry.
For her I bring the day; warm
milk, new diaper, escapades;

she lowers all bridges and
sings to me most beautifully
in her own language while
I fumble with safety pins.

I am not made young
by my daughter's mornings;
I age relentlessly.

Yet I am made to marvel
at the durability of newness
and the beauty of my new one.

— David Swanger

and open up, again, the possibility of saying honestly what we feel with them and with other people:

Over time in our family we have built up a way of venting our feelings that begins in fury and ends in laughing. We are all allowed to yell – 'You dummy, you stupid, you crazy' – whatever puts our feelings out on the table. The other can yell back. Then when the anger is spent, the insults get crazier and crazier – 'You watermelon head, you apple-eyes, you poo-poo nose' – until it is possible to hug each other all over again. It is really my kids' invention – and I consider they taught me not to simmer and brood but to show my feelings, to be in them fully, so I can be out of them.

Finally, young children give us affection that is hard to find elsewhere. Their love isn't conditional – it does not depend on sex or attractiveness or achievement. They see us and what we do for them as enormously important, as this child's story says:

Once upon a time there was a boy with no parents. One day he wanted to go to another place so off he started. After a long time he came to a big gate with a guard. Do you want to see the king? He said yes. The guard opened the gate and the boy went into the castle. When the king saw him and he asked him, if you kill the dragon outside you can have anything you want. So the boy did. What do you want? asked the king. Do you want gold? No, said the boy. Do you want my castle? asked the king. No, said the boy. I want parents. Then you can have them, said the king.

The Difficulties

The pleasures of these years are real – but so are the pains. Throughout early childhood we are always, as one parent puts it, 'in places we have never been before, not knowing how to watch out for things that tomorrow, when it's all over, we will know are dangerous or wrong.' Somewhere around nine months we may have found an even keel – our children are responsive and changing but predictable. But again everything turns topsy-turvy – it feels as if nothing that used to work still works:

I had always said yes to going out at night. I would just put her to sleep in a car bed and take her along, put her in a bedroom and pick her up along with my coat when it was time to leave. One time when she was just a little more than a year, I took her along with me to dinner. She wouldn't lie down – she stood up and screamed when I tried to close the door. I thought, she'll just cry a bit, but she shrieked. I tried getting her up, and sitting with her on my lap, but she kept fussing because she was exhausted, but wouldn't sleep.

We find ourselves having to change and it feels like sliding backwards. This brings us up hard against the realization that we will constantly have to be rebuilding how we are with our children, not because we're stupid or insensitive, but because our children are constantly changing.

You see this long line of changes out there in front of you and you ask yourself 'When won't I make it?'

A parent with several children makes it clear that even with her fourth child she finds herself still learning:

All the kids before Allie were easy – they ate, they slept, they did well in school, they were hardly ever sick. Allie was nothing like that – he cried, he never ate, he was constantly sick, he was always in trouble with kids or teachers. I had to learn a whole new way of being a parent – when I thought I knew it all.

These early years have darker sides, because our lives are still very much joined to our children's. Even when things as simple as their sleep or activity pattern change, our own lives feel dragged in the wake:

As a baby she took two huge naps – morning and afternoon. She slept so long that I would go in to see if she was still breathing. At around a year she became much more wakeful and active. She woke early, played hard and collapsed about noon, slept maybe an hour, woke, played and collapsed at five, screeching. It was as if she took the day and threw it against the wall. It was broken into useless bits.

Our children want and are increasingly ready to do simple things for themselves. We crave the free minutes and privacy that not having to feed, dress and change might give us. But a real surprise comes as we find out how much *more* time it takes to engineer these small steps toward independence.

You think to yourself, help her to eat with a spoon and then you can have the space to eat your own dinner. What you don't realize is what comes between – the banging on the metal tray with it, the constant putting it back into her hand, the food-filled spoon dropping to the floor.

It was walking that I hated. He and I would have a huge battle at every street corner, him wanting to walk by himself and me feeling, who knows what he will do once he gets out there? I would insist and he would say no and rush on ahead or sit down and refuse to cross holding my hand. But how can you let a two-year-old cross the street by himself? I tried saying that if he didn't take my hand, then we couldn't go on walks. But that was punishing myself. Who wants to be locked indoors all day? I would fall asleep thinking, how do I get him to cross the street?

Particularly during early childhood the new skills that children gain seem to have two edges – any new ability is not just a move toward independence but a deeper intrusion into parent lives:

For months the baby only crawls and you are either housebound or pushing a stroller. You dream of the day they take their first step. It comes – you are crazy with excitement. And then it dawns on you – now there is no place they can't get to. And you dream of the days when all they could do was crawl.

As many and as big as the steps are that young children take, each of them is only partial. Every step is fragile. A cold, a new baby, a strange sitter can destroy – at least temporarily – any move forward:

Training a little kid to use the john is really more like training yourself to ask every half-hour and after every cup of juice 'Do you need to use the bathroom?' You just get to the point where they tell you and something happens. The first snow comes and who can make it through the seventeen layers in time? Or they get diarrhoea and lose their sense of timing. Or there is a new baby and suddenly it's much better to be taken care of than to take care of yourself.

Maybe they can go find their shoes or climb the stairs, but realistically our children are still almost totally dependent on us. While they may insist on trying to do things themselves, any frustration or fear brings them flying back to us:

To survive it you have to be a human Yo-Yo. One minute you try and help them do the zipper on their jacket and they are shouting 'NO, NO – me do it.' So you leave them alone to wrestle with the zipper, and soon they are a thrashing heap of tears and frustration. They yank off the jacket, heave it across the room and it knocks over the milk glass. And at that moment you are magically supposed to be able to slide the zipper into place – but in no way cut in on their wanting to do it themselves – and then cheerfully go on to wipe up the pool of milk.

Even when they can walk and talk and use the toilet, they are still too little to pick up after themselves, to eat with forks, to stay out of the street, to control their anger, their yelling or running. Our lives, then, can't escape noise, confusion, mess, strong emotion. Even a simple phone call to talk with a friend about work is next to impossible to carry out:

The typical phone call: the children and I are in the kitchen. I have prepared dinner for them and David is sitting in his high chair mushing his food in his hand. Shauna is staring into her plate. They are deceptively quiet. I hesitate and figure I'll give it a try, although it's never worked before. I call Kate to discuss next week's workshop we are giving together in dance and poetry.

I dial the number. Just as she answers, Shauna falls off her chair and I have to say 'Hold on, Kate, one minute.' I put the phone down on the counter. Shauna is wailing and I put her on my lap trying to soothe her and pick up the phone. It falls off the counter, making a huge crash. I put Shauna down to pick up the phone, which sends her into apoplexy. She is nearly choking to death, a trick she has perfected to panic me. Instead of being smart and saying 'Kate, I'll call you back next year,' I put Shauna back in her chair letting her shriek, and move the phone and its long cord into the pantry, putting my hand over my other ear. It's been nearly five minutes since I left Kate holding on. She's still there muttering 'Maybe this isn't a good time to talk.' 'Oh, no,' I say. 'It's always like this.'

*Shauna is demonstrating her rage by flinging her plate and $1.50 worth of lamb chop across the floor. I move back into the kitchen with my long umbilical cord to the outside world and pick up the pieces of meat and put them on David's tray. He is saying NO, NO! as loudly as he can, which makes Shauna livid. YES, she screams back. YES and she goes over to his high chair to pinch him. I am waving at her to quit while Kate is responding, but the noise has gotten so loud, I can barely hear her. David is trying to bite Shauna's arm, while she screams DON'T BITE ME, and hits him over the head with a cup. The apple juice has run on to the floor long ago and I am standing in a puddle of it. Finally, I see the conversation is pointless. Kate hangs up in dismay and I am certain she will never have kids. There are a few sobs and whimpers and both kids settle back into their chairs. In a minute, it is perfectly peaceful.**

Ten minutes in a kitchen like this and what you feel is fury. These emotions – anger, resentment, disappointment – are a part of the range of feelings children provoke in us, especially when they are impulsive, dirty, loud, unpredictable and

*Judith Steinbergh's 'Journal'.

always there. Though no TV commercial or magazine ad shows how we feel, though these reactions are not part of our image of 'good parents', they are common, real, even appropriate. Rather than having to hide or deny such feelings, we need ways to deal with them – sometimes it's possible to laugh:

We were making pumpkin pie – you know, one of those educational projects where you do it from scratch and it only takes five hours and no one will eat it when it's done. We had already had one huge battle over who could hack the pumpkin to bits with what deadly weapon. Pumpkin slime everywhere. Then the doorbell rang and I had to leave them with the electric beaters up to their gills in orange glop. Just as I came back, Mark lifted the beaters high into the air, calling out 'Is this good, Mommy?' – throwing wads of pumpkin everywhere. I was covered with thick welts of dripping pumpkin. They were laughing so hard they were crying. For them it was wonderful, rich, crazy 'revenge' – to scold me, undress and wash me and warn me never to play in the pumpkin again.

Sometimes it is too serious or too constant to laugh off. There *are* times of wanting to shake or slap them or at least to walk out. We scream or name-call or hit – but we aren't 'bad'. Just angry, out of patience, too alone in child care.

The Explosion of Roles

If children change a mile a minute during early childhood, so does parenthood. Our babies aren't cute little sleeping bundles that people stop to admire in the supermarket any more. Active, curious, healthy two- and three-year-olds ask parents to be something more than holders, feeders and comforters.

We were visiting my mother's house – Jenny was about a year. My mother keeps a miniature fruit tree growing in her dining room. Jenny was very attracted by the bright little orange fruit and kept reaching up to pull them off by the handful. As children we were never allowed to touch that tree, and my immediate reaction to Jenny's interest in the fruit was a swift, strong, loud 'no'. For several days every time she went near it, she would reach up her hand and look back at me. One day she reached up her hand, turned around and very slowly formed the word 'no', then pulled off several fruit. At a time like that you say to yourself, now it begins – now there are two of us.

In these years there is something like an explosion in the sheer number of ways in which parents interact with children. Instead of sleeping bundles, our children are 'kids' who won't sit in the cart, want to choose food themselves, ask hard questions when we put back the candy and cereal they have taken down. Quickly we find ourselves filling the difficult new roles of limit-setter, authority, teacher, and guide.

The Role of Limit-Setter

Children's new skills and curiosities spill out into our lives. They try starting the car, cutting with knives, seeing what it takes to make you mad, what people do when you blow a bicycle horn in their ears. All at once, we are called on to set limits – 'You cannot bite or scratch or grab toys away, you have to take turns and use words instead of screams, you cannot run or yell at Grandma's.' It is as if all we know how to say is no no nonononononononononono. Every minute we find ourselves trying to control, to corral, to correct:

Everything – eating breakfast, getting dressed, using the toilet, putting on a jacket to go out, sitting in the car seat – seemed to spin itself out into a great tug of war – Laurie pulling one way, me the other. We had one bit of conversation all day – no yes, no yes, no no no, yes yes yes.

Though, clearly, parenting is going to be riddled with loving and limiting, the role of authority and limit-setter is difficult for some of us. Those of us who are uncomfortable with the role find ourselves asking: is this what being a parent is about – scolding, ordering, bossing? We may have promised ourselves that we will be understanding, fair or generous with our children – 'not authoritarian as my parents were' – and the sheer necessity of establishing limits to survive both physically and psychologically is hard to take. Another parent suggests that it is in limit-setting that we first begin to wrestle our way toward becoming a family unit – teaching children to think of others, learning to ask for or forgoing our own rights as parents:

There was something going through my head all through those years when they were little, like a broken record, 'How much, how much . . . how much do you bend them in order to grab a little peace, a little order, a little privacy?'

Becoming the people who set limits makes us examine our adult impulses to control our children. We have to ask which are selfish, which are fair, which are just old habits, which are appropriate:

Who knows how many times a day, maybe thirty, I have to decide how to wrestle with which of the limits I put on are right. I can choose the way my father did, the way the neighbours do it, the way the magazine article says, the way I think is right – but none of them comes with a guarantee.

Some decisions are clear – no walking in the street, no running with scissors, no playing with wires and sockets. But many are not.

When Edie was first old enough to go on walks outside with me, we would go up and down the block. A lot of the neighbours had little front gardens that were their pride and joy. She loved to climb over the little hedges and touch all the flowers. All at once the curtain in the window would pull aside and there'd be this angry adult face. I knew I was supposed to keep her out of other people's yards – but why, when I really felt they could stand sharing them with kids?

What this mother's story brings up is that there is another side to the business of limits and discipline. We're not only concerned that our children *don't* do all sorts of things. We want them to grow up able to think about limits, accepting decent ones, but not being docile or indifferent. That may be one of the binds and opportunities of being parents: how to help our children become their best selves within a framework that lets the people around them live well also:

Sometimes Mark orders me around: 'I want some apple juice', 'Get my mittens', 'Read to me'. On the one hand, I think, so, he's only four. On the other hand, I think, why let him have even five minutes' time learning to treat a woman who cares for him like that?

Clearly, then, choosing an appropriate limit is not easy. And living with it can be just as difficult. Two-year-olds want their way, and are capable of kicking and throwing to get it. Older children whine or bargain or ask hard questions. Sometimes, as this mother points out, you wonder why you ever tried to guide their behaviour:

One day I decided to write down the kinds of conversation Molly and I would end up having. I was folding laundry:
Molly: I want some milk.
Me: O.K., here is a cup, you can get it for yourself from the icebox.
Molly: No, you.
Me: Molly, you are four and big, you do it for yourself.
Molly: No, you are the mommy and you are supposed to do it.
Me: This way you can do it for yourself.
Molly: No, you HAVE to do it.
Me: Here is the cup. If you want it you can get it. I am working.
Molly: You get it, and if you don't you are very dumb. And I don't love you.

Occasionally we see how our effort to set sensible limits informs our children about danger, about looking out for others, about living effectively within a family:

We were always 'emotionally strict' with the children. I mean that in our house the 'crimes' were hurting people's feelings, not helping out or not sharing. It feels right inside – but sometimes you wonder, maybe I should be teaching them to get along in a world that couldn't care less. Then one night on the highway the transmission in the car quit. We were stranded for hours in the rain. It could have been a nightmare. But the oldest one made a bed for the little one with her parka. She told her stories and answered all her scared little questions. All the while I was trying to get someone to stop I could hear her voice, and in the pouring rain with no transmission I felt blessed.

Being Teachers

Since birth we have been teaching our children, or helping them to teach themselves, how to eat, how to walk, how to communicate. However, during the toddler years, our role as teacher becomes more explicit and more difficult, as we teach them to use the toilet, to play with other children, to talk. This kind of

Austin deBesche

teaching involves a great deal of patience – we have to accept the individual pace of our children, let them learn from their mistakes, take on the role of assistant instead of director. A parent recalls toilet training:

You finish breakfast and before you touch anything else, it's into the bathroom. It's hard to get in, between the bath toys and all the new books near the potty chair to make it an attractive place. You sit down on the edge of the tub and pick out one of them. You read and you wait, and you read and you wait. And then, giving up hope, you start making encouraging noises and realize that you yourself would like to use the john. But it would be foolish to interrupt. You read some more and then begin to notice that the sink needs washing and the towels are greyish. You give up for today, stack the books, and go out grocery shopping. It takes longer than usual because along about the dairy case you have to find the assistant manager and ask to use the bathroom. Because out of the cart comes a small voice saying 'Mommy, I GOTTA.'

All of us know that we do more than teach words or manners or skills. All the time, in thousands of small daily messages, we transmit attitudes and values subtly but powerfully:

He had a play phone, which he used a lot. One day he was dialling it while I was cooking supper. He put it to his ear and pretended he was talking to Dan – in just the surface-pleasant, underneath-angry way I do when Dan is very late coming home and hasn't called to say anything. It was like watching myself in a two-year-old mirror.

As we catch children reflecting 'not what we say but what we do' it can feel, as a father suggests, 'like you are never off-duty, you're always passing things on.'

When she was about four or five, she became very fussy about what she would wear, very into clothes for so little a kid. I kept asking myself, where did this come from? I have tried to be so non-sexist with her – why does she want to dress like a little princess? So I began to watch myself and, sure enough, she comes downstairs in plaid shorts and a polka-dotted shirt and I hear myself saying 'Take off that shirt and go put on your nice red one.'

The way in which our own mixtures of values 'leak' through to our children often points out how fragile certain new attitudes are in ourselves and how we're less finished as people than we might like to believe.

As we become aware of how much we transmit, many of us have to wrestle with just what beliefs and values we want to pass on to our children. A father recalls realizing this:

One Sunday night I called my parents, as I often do. My father asked 'Are you taking the kids to see the Memorial Day parade?' I tried sliding past giving an answer. I didn't want my boys standing on some street corner seeing lines of men in uniforms, marching to loud music, with drums and guns. Especially not when they were turning every stick into a pistol or cannon or knife. But it made me realize how alive my own relation to my father was, how shy I was of saying no outright, when I could still remember him telling stories of playing a trumpet in an army band behind Nat King Cole. If I said no, it seemed like it would be putting down the excitement and closeness I used to feel when he would take me on his shoulders down to the parades when I was growing up. But it made me think that as a parent I was 'the introducer of institutions' and that I couldn't side-step armies, or schools, police or robbers or Santa Claus. It pinned that role on me, my father reminding me of it this way. It also made me realize something about the sifting that goes on between parents and children. He gave me parades, but I only wanted to take part of what he offered. I wanted to share what mattered to me with my kids. But I wasn't so sure what that was. But I had to be able to take their putting what I offered back on the shelf.

But, like teaching, the sharing of values is no easy task. For one thing, what do we share? Even our partners may have values different from ours:

Gail wants him to be independent and self-sufficient. If another kid hits or bites, she says 'Hit back.' I feel just the opposite, like that is no solution at all. He comes in from outside to say that so-and-so punched him, and Gail is in there saying 'You go back and tell him if he hits you you'll hit him back', and at the same time here I am saying 'Let's go talk to him about it.' Who's he going to believe?

In many homes, women, whether they like it or not, end up doing most of the work of child rearing. They worry about what seeing this – day in, day out – tells their children. One mother said:

I'd fight with Jack about who would do the dishes, then worry about the effect of all that hopeless bickering on the kids. So, to keep the peace, I'd stop fighting and do the damn dishes myself and worry about whether five-year-old Alice and three-year-old Jacob thought I accepted that role or whether it was being transmitted to them as 'natural' woman's work.

The values we put forward may be slightly or radically different from the attitudes our children will meet when playing outside, being with friends, going to school. When kids question why we do what we do, as adults and parents we are up against finding out and holding firm for what we continue to believe:

I think TV deadens kids. I won't have one in the house. We both work, and why do I want the few hours we are together to be spent fighting to turn off mesmerizing junk? But every time my kids come back from visiting where there is a TV, we go round and round – 'Why can't we have a TV?'

It's fairly easy, if annoying, to deal with things like TV-watching. But what about more complicated problems? If we ourselves are gay, for example, how do we bring up our children to respect our way of life and yet not feel forcibly alienated from their playmates?

Most of us, during these years, begin to come up against some of the refrains of modern childhood: 'We don't do that', 'We don't believe in that', 'We don't behave that way toward others'.

When we're talking about things like not discriminating against other races, we feel pretty comfortable in transmitting our values. But there are shady areas when we have to first examine what we're laying on to our kids out of our own lives, and then examine the consequences for our children in *their* lives.

As adults, we conform to or set ourselves apart from the rules of society in our own lives. We try to live the way we think we should. But it may be hard on our children. We remember this perhaps from our own childhood, and it makes us sensitive to what our children may experience if our values make them 'strangers' among their friends or the community:

When I was about three or four we moved to this country. My father was very religious. I remember having to wear a yarmulke all the time – no excuses – feeling it go flap-flap when we played running games outside. I felt marked.

Increasingly, as our children near school age they meet up with things that perplex or frighten or bewilder them. They ask us to help them make sense of what they encounter – a dead bird, us making love, a crippled person. The explanation can be very difficult, and we become intensely aware of how little we understand and how far we are from the all-knowing, all-competent teacher we're supposed to be:

We were coming home from the store and there was a drunk a few yards in front of us. I hung back, hoping the kids wouldn't notice. I knew if they saw him weaving and staggering they would notice and want me to explain to them what was the matter. But the problem was that we had to pass him in order to get to the corner and then turn into our house. I remember wanting to hurry away and wanting to do something, but not wanting to have to answer the thousand questions – What is the matter? Was he sick? Why were you upset?

But as parents point out, children's questions can provide the basis for coming to terms with issues that otherwise we might shy away or hide from:

We were at the dock and my father took off his shirt to go swimming. Right out loud, Ben asked 'Why is Papa so white and skinny, does it mean he is going to die soon?' It meant I had to start dealing with death, my father's and my own.

Recently, and with louder and louder voices, early-childhood 'experts' have been telling us that it is during these years that our children become either competent individuals or failures. They insist that it is the parents' (and especially the mothers') capacity to act as teachers that makes the crucial difference. The teaching load feels enormous – it extends to language, imagination, manners, self-concept, numbers and letters. We *are* influential with our children – we cannot side-step that. But the image of all-powerful, all-shaping parents has been made a burden. Throughout early childhood, as our children move out of the house into backyards, neighbourhoods and pre-schools, we see that we are only one of the many, many influences on them:

From the living room windows I could see him up there on the front porch trying to break into a bunch of older boys. They were playing pirates, waving sticks for swords and guns and jumping off the top step shouting 'Bombs over Tokyo'. He didn't know what pirates were or what he was shouting but he did everything they did, just a few steps out of time. We had tried to keep violence out of his life – you know, no gruesome TV, no toy guns, talking instead of fighting. But now it was up for grabs.

Our ability to accept our children as separate people is often tested as they try out attitudes or activities that go counter to what we value or like. We begin to face their right, as separate people, to choose from a range of experience wider than what we're willing to give them. Possibly we have to acknowledge that beliefs we have barely learned to hang on to will be as confining to them as our parents' views were to us.

I spent years of my life trying to become comfortable with a small-breasted, big-hipped body and all she wants for her birthday is a Barbie doll. I felt strangled by one woman-image and here I am, locking her away in one that may be just a different prison.

We don't have to be alone in our teaching. Particularly during these years our children's lives open up – they reach beyond the affections of the parent who is with them most. They may develop warm relations with baby-sitters, older kids, day care teachers. They may seek out the parent they know less well, who may not have been sharing equally in their care. For the first time they have friends of their own. Letting in these other people lightens our work as teachers and provides our children with many people to learn from:

I am very clumsy and pretty uncomfortable doing things like riding a bike or swimming. I had a sister who drowned and my own parents were always worried that I would have an accident, and I guess I caught their worry. Being a single parent meant that all Michelle had at home was me. So when she first went to day care, she wouldn't even swing unless you held on to the chains the whole time. That year she had a terrific man teacher who taught the kids tumbling. I came one evening to pick her up and there she was going across the top bars of the jungle gym like a little monkey. You see that and you say 'Single doesn't have to be all alone.'

Letting others 'in' means moments of jealousy or conflict over what exactly we want our children to learn.

One time when Maria was about four I was working on a deadline for some illustrations. I hired a baby-sitter for the afternoon when she wasn't in nursery school. After lunch I went to my study and tried to shut out everything but the work. But voices kept floating upstairs: 'I told you if you carried all that it would spill ... Yes, you are going outside ... Did you lose those mittens again? ... That's naughty.' They weren't terrible things – but they weren't what I would have said. And I think that the hardest thing was that Maria liked the woman. All through lunch she would ask 'When is Sophie coming?' It was a terrible mix of feelings for me. I wanted and needed to do the work, I felt uncomfortable in little ways about the woman, and I was jealous. In some way I wanted Maria to miss me, and not to like this other way of doing things. But I wanted her to be happy and for me to be able to work.

We may not always like what others teach, or finding out that now we are one among many influences on our children. But in the end the fact that our children have other teachers means that we are not alone in our efforts to teach all we think they need to know. For our children it means they are not confined to our version of 'what they need to know'.

It can be a relief to parents to realize that the success or failure of their teaching efforts is not limited to those early years. Adoptive parents who have taken on older children tell us that we have time:

We had two kids of our own and we bought the idea that if you didn't pump them full of skills and love in those first three years, you were going to have wrecks on your hands. When they were eight and ten, we adopted two more kids. They were not the usual three-day-old infants but kids who had been around. They were tough and suspicious at first. We lived through running away and stealing and acting out while they tested that we cared. But now, after almost two years, they are really no different than our own, which leads me to think that as parents you have lots of time.

As parents we are encouraged and rewarded by society for making better, brighter kids sooner – in a way which seems to look at human growth as if it were economic success. Children are 'rated' by when they walked and talked. Parents gain credits if their children sit up, build towers, read books before the normal ages. This intensely competitive and individualistic way of thinking about growth is foolish, and it is harsh on both parents and children. It is especially cruel to families where children don't happen to match the 'norms' laid down in baby books:

He was twenty-seven months old and not talking. And he was big for his age. When people would realize that he didn't talk, they'd look at him funny and then ask 'How old is he?' I'd tell them and they'd say something like 'Doesn't he say anything?' I was worried and so I took him to the paediatrician. He took out a chart and showed me that Donny was 'over a year late'. It was all I could do then to ask 'Do you think he's retarded?' Now he is almost four and fine, and I wish I had known then that the doctor was only comparing Donny to an average age for talking, and that lots of normal kids don't talk at fifteen months on the button.

And That's Not All

We also can get caught in thinking that the roles of care giver and teacher sum up what we are – either as people or for our children. But as this mother comments, so child-centred a picture of a parent is incomplete and particularly imprisoning, harmful to both the parents and their kids.

My brother and I practically ignored my mother once we were five or six. After all, all she did was 'take care of us and the house'. When I look back to that, it shocks me that she accepted so one-dimensional a picture of all she did.

Yes, it's true that as a mother now I do all those traditional 'mothering' things – like love and talk to and teach. But it makes me angry how other things never make their way into the definition of what a mother does. I am a woman; I am a sexual being trying to work out a relation with another adult; I am a worker; I am a person with a political outlook. Why aren't these important? When Mara grows up she might never be a mother, but she is bound to have a sex life, a work life, and a point of view.

At the same time that we are caretakers and teachers and models, we are also adults, lovers, workers. Not only are all these roles in the air above us all at once, but each one of them seems to demand attention – lots of it – right away during these years. One father with a commitment to both child care and career describes his day:

It starts at seven-thirty when the phone rings and a man's voice tells me that the children's swing set is arriving today, is there anywhere for the cement truck to park. Deb dresses the kids while I make breakfast. She sits with them while I step in and out of the shower and jump into my clothes. I drink a cup of coffee as I drive them, one to one school and one to the other. I work steadily until noon, when Deb and I have a conference call about the afternoon pick-ups. At four I pick up Alan at day care and drive on to get

Elizabeth Hamlin/Stock, Boston

Lee at a friend's. We have to stop on the way home for more sequins for the Hallowe'en costume they are making. At home I bathe them and Deb makes dinner. I clean up dinner, while Deb reads to them, then I practise recorder with Lee for a minute and tell Alan a funny story to make up for the time he resents my spending with Lee. Then after who knows how many drinks of water they are asleep and my father calls very upset about his will. And that doesn't mention all the milk that has to be mopped up, the lunches that have to be packed or the fights settled.

We are the middle generation caring for both our own children who change every minute and our parents who may be ill, ageing, retired. We feel the press of having to take hold of and shape our work lives. These pressures all seem to echo across our partnerships, widening the gap between what we want from them and what we can contribute to them.

Often we discover we cannot juggle it all – something is always being neglected or dropped:

Most days I feel like an acrobat high above a crowd out of which my own parents, my in-laws, potential employers, phantoms of 'other women who do it' and a thousand faceless eyes stare up. There is a murmur from 'the experts' – no woman should leave her children, these are the most vital years, a mother is the mainstay of a child's emotional life. But things matter too much not to climb up anyway. There are three things to be juggled – a sense of self, a relationship with a partner and the lives of two small children. All are bright, beautiful and fragile. When I make it across to the far side, the sense of exhilaration is tremendous. It feels a part of some huge play that all kinds of women are preparing to celebrate their potential. But there are also days when I barely make it, when the juggling is ugly, broken, dangerously out of whack. There is a trick to this particular high-wire act. The secret of balancing can never be entirely learned; the I, the we, the use of it shift dramatically as the children grow; I change, the partnership alters. I am surprised at the continuous depth of my commitment to that act.

The juggling act is particularly difficult because even what we are juggling is constantly changing during the early childhood years. In infancy we may have struggled to bond with our children, but now we are faced with the first steps of letting go, pushing them off from us. Our partnership, once the intimacy between two adults, has to survive the transition from lovers and colleagues to parents. Those of us who work and take care of our children have to learn to concentrate in the face of interruptions and the nagging sense that we ought to be with our children more – or that we're not giving enough attention to our work.

It is our conviction that, difficult as this juggling is, it is vital for both fathers and mothers to live out both their parenthood and their adulthood, i.e. to take an active part in nurturance and in carrying out their adult lives. This requires juggling two functions that up until recently our society has walled off from each other – nurturing and working, caring and achieving. To do this we have to learn how to manage it emotionally and build into our lives and the world things which will make it possible.

Being People and Parents

When I used to think about having children I imagined us all fitting together neatly – like the parts of a puzzle. Come to find out, often it's more like pieces competing for the same space. You want the last piece of cheese, so do they. You want to read and they want you to read to them. You need to work and they need you – they have fallen down, gotten scared, have something wonderful they have to show you right that minute.

For as long as women accepted their 'work' as raising children, it was rarely thought that the needs of parents and children might not mesh. But as mothers began to work outside the home and as fathers tried balancing work and child care, the undeniable conflict between working and taking care of children became obvious. Perhaps this challenge has helped us to see the more general problem of how we must balance the love and privacy we need ourselves with the responsibilities to our children.

There is no doubt that we face this conflict in the very first days home – as we drop our normal routines of sleep and activity in order to take children into our lives. It continues throughout infancy – as we 'babyproof' the house or work in a kitchen full of toys. But it takes on a new quality as children break out of infancy into the definiteness of an older child. Earlier it was possible, as one mother suggested, to side-step or deflect demands, substituting another interesting distraction. With two- and three-year-olds, that's not a possibility.

In the morning she would get out of bed and come in to see us. We snuggled awhile in bed but then she would be bored and go off to her room to play. If I tried to follow she would slam the door in my face and keep it closed. She wanted to have that room and her things to herself.

But as we move toward a new kind of child-adult balance, one which involves two separate individuals, we often realize that it is emotionally hard to let go of our children. They are important extensions of our lives. Throughout parenting it is difficult to establish the boundary between living through our children and letting our lives be filled out by theirs. Particularly when they are little and ready to drink everything in, it is tempting to think that we could, through them, start again, remaking our own lives. A father of a four-year-old speaks to this point:

I think that I always wanted to be a scientist and never got there. I really have to hold myself back every time he asks about dams or moths or electricity. I want to cram him full of knowledge so that he can be what I wasn't. I have to wait and let him do the question asking, the experimenting. Sometimes it breaks my heart when he's bored or confused.

Letting go may be especially hard for the parent who has the main responsibility for the child. We may feel that children 'are all we have', or we may worry that once our children are independent of us we will have to hang on emptily or move out into a work world which years of child care have left us unprepared for:

I went to visit a friend of mine who had almost disappeared since the birth of her first child. We sat at the edge of the child's sandbox to talk. The mother's every answer hugged the fact of the child – everything came back to 'Callie is very attached to me and she can't stand it when I leave her.' I was very angry at her for dissolving into her child in that way because it reminded me of the years when I shrank down behind my children, clinging to them and teaching them to cling to me so that I didn't have to go and do and be.

We have been taught by tradition and again by modern psychology that child care is a woman's most important work. We have been told over and over about the importance of bonding to our children. Rarely do we hear about the skill of letting go, or, as one parent said, 'that we raise our children to leave us.' Early childhood, as our kids gain skills and eagerly want some distance from us, is a time to build a kind of adult-child balance which permits both of us room:

I was at a meeting of people interested in childbirth. In the audience were several women with small children. I watched with particular interest one woman sitting close to me. She tried nursing, then cuddling her baby, hoping that he would go to sleep – much as I guess he had as an infant. But he was wakeful and full of energy. For the first hour the woman tried to force him to act like that old infant. Repeatedly she offered her breast and her lap and arms. But he wanted to race up and down the steps. He laughed and called out, disrupting the meeting. She floundered in her embarrassment, started to stuff the diapers and pins and cookies she had brought back into her bag. Then she realized she had other options – she showed the child how she and he could play toss with the diaper, how he could play peek-a-boo with it. Later when he tired of those games, she emptied the entire bag and let him pack it up again. I admired her – when her first tools for handling her infant ceased to work, she found other resources within herself, ones that permitted her son to be with her while she did something she wanted to do.

Partnership and Parenthood

The transition from being adult partners to partners who are also parents is not simple or smooth. Whoever is the primary caretaker experiences enormous emotional pulls between these two parts of life:

For me, it's captured by my image of Sunday morning. You pull the covers over your head, hoping that the day won't begin just yet. You can almost taste the hour of privacy and quiet after a week when the only place to be alone was a locked bathroom. You begin to settle in and you feel a hand on your breast and another moving over your thigh. He wants to make love – all the love that you put off every tired night last week. You turn to face him, not even sure whether you want him, and suddenly there is a sticky, wet little hand on your back and a voice saying 'I spilled the apple juice.'

In these years, whether couples feel that their partnership is welded or broken, it is at least reshaped by the pressures of juggling the many parts of their lives. For possibly the first time, our relationship has to compete, long term, with another deep and very attractive relationship, that between parent and child. There, as adults, we are dealing with growing, responsive individuals who need and love us hugely. By contrast, in our partnerships we are dealing with another adult who may be more set in ways, less willing to express affection, less emotionally available, open about how they need you.

But the stresses are not simply or strictly personal. They are rooted in what we have inherited and accepted as traditional roles for fathers and mothers in these years. Where mothers are concerned, we have taken on, from Freudian psychology, a very demanding definition of what it is to take 'good care' of children. This requires that mothers act constantly to fill out children's immature abilities – to provide food, movement, interaction, entertainment, humour, love, relief from distress and fear. This picture of mothers is complemented by what is customarily expected from young fathers – achievement in work. The result is an intense pairing between children and mothers, and a walling off of fathers from both their wives and their children. It gives children mothers who are available and fathers who are strangers or visitors. A mother and father talk about how they were pulled into different worlds and how it affected them:

Michelle: When we were both in school together, you couldn't have told our lives apart – same classes, same friends, same thoughts about where we'd be and what we'd be doing in ten years. We got married and I got pregnant and we decided it was as good a time as any to have our kids. Have them early, then they'll be in school and life will be like before.

David: But I went on to graduate school while Michelle stayed home with Matt. I got very involved in work – staying there late, or wanting to. I think she felt like she was getting lost in long days that had big events like going outside or taking a walk around the block. My friends and interests shifted and we began to move in different worlds.

Michelle: Yours seemed like a 'big-time' world and all I seemed to do was to 'front-stoop it' and talk with neighbour mothers about snowsuits. It made for a kind of electricity between us – there was no safe topic. And I think that maybe the worst of it was when I could go back to work, I had no training. All I could do was to go back as a typist.

Other parents, like these, speak about getting frozen into roles that they first took on. Each from his or her perspective feels locked in and locked out. Caretakers, most often mothers, feel locked into 'days of ring-around-the-rosy and Dr Seuss' and isolated from any adult community. Working parents feel tied to office hours and work pressures and locked out of the playfulness and intimacy they see growing up between their children and their partners. Partners' worlds split apart. Loneliness and resentment leak into their adult relationship. It is hard to break down established roles and routines – they are what we know:

Whenever we talked about having the baby we talked about sharing in the responsibility. We never imagined that there would be obstacles in doing that. But when she came, Carrie left to come to Boston to be with her doctor. I stayed in Toronto because of important work I wanted to finish. After that, the gap got bigger – the first months of the baby's life coincided with the first months in a new house, a new city and a new job for me. Also, Carrie was nursing. She and Lila spent hours together locked into a pair very close to one another. By the time the pressures had let up on me Carrie was almost drowning in Lila – Lila nursed continuously, it seemed, and cried and crawled after Carrie every time she left the room. I wanted to enter in but I was less knowing and Lila treated me as a threatening stranger. I wanted to relieve Carrie and be with Lila. I wanted to break in and I had to do it soon. So every night when I came home I would catch her up in my arms and then no matter how she pushed and bent backwards out of my arms, I would walk around the house, talking to her about all the things we could see and touch. Slowly she would wind down. And I would take her with me – just the two of us alone – even to get gas. Just to put us in situations where she had to ask me if she wanted to be lifted or had to talk to me if she wanted to share.

It was hard because I didn't really know how to do anything else but whisk her away from Carrie. And Carrie had spent all that infant time learning how to just be with Lila. I was O.K. while I was intruding myself, but once Lila at least accepted me it was hard to know what next. One thing we did was to begin spending time, all together, the three of us – tumbling on the bed, going for a walk around the reservoir. A kind of strain went out of my relationship with Lila as I became someone who was around, who loved her, who was available to her. The real proof of that is just now coming. I redid the attic over our apartment as a playroom for her. I partitioned a part of it off to be my office. In the playroom I can be totally relaxed with her – there is nothing that can hurt her or that she can hurt. When she plays there and I can be in the study, in a way I feel like I have an equivalent to nursing, a very important way of being side by side with her.

But simply sharing child care is not a substitute for continuing to maintain an adult relation.

I guess we shared – it was like a new religion. I took Monday and Wednesday and Friday, and Pete took Tuesday, Thursday and Saturday. We alternated having Sundays. We got to be nurses changing shifts – all we did was pass in the hall and exchange a few words about the health of our charges. We tried, about twice a year, to give our husband-wife selves a shot in the arm – you know, a trip to Vermont when the leaves were changing, or a weekend at a hotel downtown. The pressure of suddenly having to be lively, attractive, sexy people – bang at four on Friday, and not wasting our precious time together – it was awful. We finally decided what we needed was to steal little bits of time to ourselves any chance we got. We went ice-skating for a half-hour at lunch time, or went out to a coffee house at ten-thirty. Some Sundays, George would drive the kids out to buy doughnuts, drive back, set them up a picnic breakfast, and come back to bed.

The effort to maintain, and maybe even to find, a satisfying adult relation is even more complicated for single parents:

You work all week on the theory that the weekend belongs to the kids. You arrive at Friday night or Saturday night or Sunday morning always, always alone – or going to see the Wizard of Oz and there's a part of you that's crying, hey, who's gonna look after me, and be with me and show me the world?

There is an added stress beyond trying to balance child and partner obligations. As parents, we are two different adults dealing with the same child or children. Sometimes we agree about how to be with them, what to teach them, how we want them to be. Other times we find ourselves competing with one another about whose childhood is going to be revised, whose idea of how 'a boy or girl should be' is going to be lived up to. In this process we can discover very fundamental differences that as people without children we were able to side-step or ignore:

When she was about two, my husband began to pamper her. She flirted right back. He wouldn't let me discipline her. If I did, she would run to him. She was becoming a whining, spoiled little girl, and I felt he was making her into the toy I had refused to become.

Even if we don't uncover deep differences, our husband-wife relationship is often chequered with countless small disagreements about how to raise children:

One time last summer I was trying to load Mira into her car seat for a long ride back home. She refused to get into it or to use the seat belt. I sat down with her and tried to explain that I used a seat belt, that it was safer, that I didn't want anything to happen to her. Still she refused. I told her that she would have to do it, because it was dangerous not to. As I tried to lift her in she began kicking and crying. Tara came over and told her that if she sat in her seat all the way home, she would buy her some candy. She climbed into the seat without another word. But I felt like the ground had been cut away underneath me, and angry, too. I don't think we said more than three things all the way home.

On the *stronger* side, parents also point out that the experience of having children together has made them into adults and given them work together that was serious, important and good:

We looked out across our free, uncomplicated, childless life and thought, how boring. It has been terrifically hard having Matt. Sometimes we have lost each other for what feels like months – just passing each other in the living room. But the other day we met in the hallway of the building where we both work, totally unexpectedly. And I was excited, really excited, to have five minutes together with someone I quite literally had lifework with.

Working and Caring

Like balancing our own and our children's needs, our own and our partners' hopes for intimacy, we also face juggling these caring relationships with resuming or exploring whatever lives we want beyond our domestic ones. For most men and an increasing number of women this means learning to live two lives – one in a workplace, one at home:

My work matters to me. Without it I am lost, angry, depressed. But I have two children who are very important to me. I can't substitute them for my work – they will go away, write me on my birthday, and wonder why I have become such a bitchy old lady. This means that I am always leaning too far over in one direction. I will feel a wide gap forming between my kids and me – they are these little foreigners at the end of a hall when my attention has been intent on work. Then I have to shift my energies to intense time with them – to win back the lost undercurrent of understanding. But then my work begins to have the look of what someone else does. And I go back in the other direction.

The division is never clear and clean, as this father suggests:

It gets to be close to five at work and I start to think about going home. It's close to the time I give Josh a bath. I love that, and I am daydreaming about putting all the boats in and running the water so that it makes the boats go round. And I can't work. So I pack up and sometimes almost run home to those boats.

Once we have children the way in which we enter a work situation is not the same until they are grown up, and it's hard to make it the single major focus of our waking hours.

When Lee was about a year and a half, we were interviewed to share a headmaster's job at a school. Luckily, the school was not too far from where my in-laws lived. My mother-in-law had had six children, but I think that I still tried to school her in all the things she would have to do for Lee while we were gone. The whole way there we tried to talk over what we wanted to say to the interviewing committee, but the conversation was all disjointed – I saying 'How soon do you think we will be back?' then Ted saying 'Did you leave enough diapers?' At one point during the interview one of the women on the committee turned to me and asked 'How will you take an active role in the running of the school with a young child to take care of?' As I was trying to answer her, I could feel my breasts spurting milk. She continued to press me, and as we went back and forth on the issue I could feel my nursing pads getting soggy, then my slip getting wetter and wetter.

Although both mothers and fathers may feel their relationship to work shift as children come into their lives, returning to work is probably hardest for mothers. Just biologically, it is the mother who stops work to give birth. Chances are, it is a mother who stays home during the first year or first few months and builds up an intimate bond with the child. But then because of, rather than despite, the care she has poured into forming that bond, she receives the harshest criticism for returning to work. The criticism can come from many different sources – from our parents, who may have raised children when it was rarer for mothers to work:

It felt good to have decided that it was important for me to continue working, but it was very hard to go on feeling good. My parents kept wanting to know exactly what I would do with the baby. People at work were amazed to see me back; they would constantly ask 'How is your baby?' or say things like 'What will you do when he is sick? What does he do all day at the sitter's?' Part of it was curiosity, some was envy – but I took it all as criticism.

Resistance comes from our children who have to learn that though we go away, we come back, that working may permit us to be more fully alive to them than if we were there every minute of every day, or that we have no choice but to work:

When you are a single mother, you don't have the choice about whether to work. Even so, your kids don't know that, or at least they don't understand that when they are little. All around them are kids with mothers who bring them late to day care and pick them up early. They are old enough to see that not all mothers work. So they say to you while you are rushing them to get dressed, 'Please don't go to work.' Or worse, when they are angry they say 'You love your work more than me.'

The harshest voice of all may be the one we hear inside our own heads. Those of us who must work or for whom it is important to continue to work may feel guilty:

My daughter chants 'Bye-bye' to the sitter from the moment she comes. Clever kid, she knows I am leaving, and by the time I reach for my coat she is wailing. Separation problems, I figure, perfectly normal. But the heavy weight in my throat spreads through my chest until, by the time I have started the car, I can barely breathe. I read about this too: guilt, heavy as lead pipes, poisoning the system. Comes on like milk with the first child. Leaving my kids to buy food; a guilt worse than adultery.

To fight it off, or at least put guilt in its place, we need the perspective of other parents who have negotiated leaving their children to return to work. They have a great deal to tell us about how well their children 'survived'.

When she was about a year old, the scenes at my leaving were unbearable. I would bring her into the centre, play with her for a while until it seemed she was involved and happy. The moment I stood up there were screams and tears. I tried everything – staying longer, trading places with her favourite teacher, leaving her off quickly. The teacher would end up having to hold her while she kicked and cried and I hurried away. God, the feeling that leaves in the pit of your stomach! You imagine that they are crying and hating you all day long. The teachers would reassure me that she stopped as soon as I was out of sight, but I never believed that. One time I sidled along the building so I could look in a window and see that for myself. She saw me watching and it started all over again. But before she burst out crying again I had seen her quickly join another child and rush for the play house.

Part of the pain in leaving our children to go to work is that we miss them, wish we could be with them. We also hate to turn them over to someone who is not identical to us, who will do things, at best, differently – at worst, in ways we don't believe are good for children. We are up against this whenever we share the care of our children with others – even grandparents or trusted and loved sitters:

Michael was a terrific sitter for Eric. He was almost like a member of the family. Even so, there were small things I noticed – things that were not me – that I worried about. Like he swore a lot. He'd be changing Eric and the phone would ring and he'd say 'Shit'.

But our fears are stronger when we use institutions like day care centres. Our children come into contact with lots of different adults, none of whom we have hired; we are likely to be gone much of the working day; the care takes place in a centre rather than in our own homes. Some of these fears grow out of the guilt that working parents, especially mothers, are made to feel for 'abandoning' their children to the care of 'strangers'. Others of these fears come about because we know little about 'when it's O.K. to leave them' or 'what it will do to them'.

This is a situation where 'non-traditional' families have a great deal to teach traditional ones. Working mothers and single parents have had to explore alternatives – finding out what exists, how to make use of it, how to change it to fit their needs.†

---

*Judith Steinbergh's 'Journal'.

†Both the Sharing and the Helping Ourselves chapters contain information on the range of possible solutions which parents have built for themselves.

There wasn't any choice, I had to work. But there was no way I could survive as a single parent and pay for day care. Also, I didn't want to leave her all day. I hunted for work with kids, thinking that in that setting I could keep her with me, at least part of the day. Every school principal laughed, nursery schools paid nothing you could live on, so I ended up working in day care. It was sometimes very hard; being a kid's teacher and parent has its bad conflicts. But it gave me a lot of what I wanted in a way I could afford.

The early years are perhaps the most intense period of parenting. They are both crazy and wonderful. In the middle of them you constantly think, I'll never ever live through this. They are driving me nuts, draining me dry. Occasionally, something happens to let us know that we're different for having survived them – maybe better because of them. Having cared for our own kids through strained peaches and fevers and tantrums and nightmares, we may have grown a capacity to notice and respond:

I was shopping in the food co-op late one afternoon. There was a woman there with a child who was screaming with exhaustion. She was trying to weigh vegetables and tend the child all at once. The bag over the handles of the stroller was overloaded and threatened to tip the baby out on to the floor. All around her other adults went about their shopping as if nothing was happening. I don't know how they could ignore her. I'd been there before and could remember what I'd wanted. I went over, and began to get the groceries she still needed, while she picked up the baby and walked him round and round. In two minutes he was asleep and she could be at peace.

3. The Middle Years

Ruth Davidson Bell

In this chapter we'll discuss the period when our children are between about five and twelve. They are in transition during these years, making their passage from baby to teenager, from being fully reliant on us for all their needs to being quite independent from us in many ways. For us as parents, it is a passage from being full-time, twenty-four-hour-a-day protectors of the well-being of a young child to being the provider and sometime guide for a semi-autonomous young person.

Our children are changing and maturing in a myriad of subtle and not so subtle ways, developing better speech, longer periods of concentration, physical dexterity and more control over their emotions. They are capable now of asking deep and complex questions about the life they experience around them, and they seem to want deeper and more complex answers to their questions. Consequently, our role changes from one 'who knows everything' to one who may not know all the answers.

At the beginning of the middle years our children formally enter the school system, and with that they enter the public world. This is a giant step in their movement toward separating from us; throughout this period we'll watch more and more outsiders and outside ideas become part of our child's life.

We, of course, are going through our own developmental changes, some of which are influenced and affected by what's happening with our children, and many of which influence who we are as parents. It is likely that our parenthood has had an effect on every part of our lives – our relationships, our work, our sexuality, our self-image. Depending on how many children we have, and how many are still under school age, we may be seeing the light at the end of the tunnel, or we may feel that we'll be changing diapers and wiping up spilled food for ever.

Basically, the issues we will be discussing are those of dependence and independence, separation and joining, power, intimacy and honesty. Our concentration will be on the interaction between parent and child and the resulting changes that occur in us.

We've been Parents for a While Now

By the time we've been parents for five or six years we are well over the initiation period. Even though we may still have babies and toddlers at home, we are no longer brand-new parents, we are no longer so overwhelmed. A mother of two children who was divorced after just a few years of marriage said:

I was very young to start, and I felt very helpless about the whole thing and just beside myself about not being able to take care of young children all by myself. That's at least gotten better! I'm very much more on top of things now. Well, it's really a process of growth on my part ... going through therapy, some insights into myself ... and simply doing the job and realizing that I was doing it. That provides the most strength, when you look at yourself and see what you're doing. The fact that I've assumed responsibility in ways which I didn't think I could. And, of course, the children's own growth and understanding helps a lot too. It's been a gradual process, but now, six years after my divorce, I feel very much more like I'm parenting and not like I'm one of the kids trying to learn what to do.

After these early years we've faced up to some of the limits and restrictions of being a parent. We may not like the fact that having a young child or children means that we can't be as spontaneous about some of the things we used to take for granted, such as eating at irregular times, going out on a moment's notice or making love with abandon anywhere in the house, but we've probably worked out some manageable routines by now so that we know which of our needs we can expect to have met and which ones have to be shelved until our children get older.

The restrictions of parenthood are very real, yet we learn to work around them. For some parents, however, the never-ending commitment and responsibility, coupled with the loneliness many of us feel who are home with little ones still under school age, can become oppressive after six or seven years without let-up:

Two outlets I tried that didn't work were tranquillizers and drinking. For a while I thought, it's just my nerves. I'm nervous because I have so many little children and they're so close in age. I'll get a prescription. So I went to a psychiatrist for one session, and he said 'You need Brand X, an antidepressant.' I took Brand X and I felt no better because the problem wasn't just internal depression, it was because my situation was crazy. When things aren't working out, if we need drugs or liquor in order to be parents, something's wrong. I think mothers need mothering. I think that in order to nurture children, we have to be nurtured ourselves.

This feeling of frustration after years and years of not being able to have a quiet moment to ourselves or some free time in which to pursue a personal goal can let up now only if we've learned how to ask for support and how to share some of the load of parenthood with the people around us – our mate, our relatives, our friends, our children.

Some of the Pressure is Off Now: Our Children are More Capable

The older our children get, the more capable they are of being resources in the family – helping out with younger siblings, running small errands, taking care of setting the table or making their beds, getting their own snacks, earning some money doing odd jobs around the neighbourhood, and even taking care of us sometimes. A mother explained:

The awareness of the transition to having older, more capable children was dramatic for me. One Friday afternoon I decided to relax in a hot tub. I must have made the water way too hot, because when I got out, after soaking myself for a nice, long time, I became nauseated and dizzy. I called out for help rather feebly, and just as I passed out, Lois, my ten-year-old, came up. She splashed some water on me and helped me to my bed. Meanwhile Curtis put on his boots and went out to look for my husband, who had gone to mail a letter. I was really touched by their concern for me and struck by their competence and lack of panic in dealing with an unprecedented situation.

Our children's developing maturity and ability to care for themselves and others take some of the burden off our shoulders. Yet the awareness of this change in them may come as a bit of a shock to us: we may find ourselves still behaving as we did when our kids needed us all the time, as this father of a six-year-old describes:

I was still carrying Tommy upstairs to bed and putting him in his pyjamas without even realizing what I was doing. We had been in that routine for years, and so even though I noticed how heavy he was getting, I never questioned our act until one night when Tommy had a friend sleep over and they ran upstairs to put on their pyjamas and get ready for bed. They didn't need any help, and actually they didn't want any help – although I insisted on checking their teeth . . . had to maintain some role responsibilities! But, really, I think if that hadn't happened I'd still be carrying Tommy up to bed.

A major question we keep asking during the middle years is: how much do our children still need us and how much can they do without us? By the time our kids are in school, they can and do take care of themselves in many ways, so we have to make adjustments in how we function as parents. We can forget that an eight-year-old doesn't seek our constant attention the way a four-year-old does. A mother said:

Christopher is eight and spending more and more time with friends around the neighbourhood. Until now he's needed me so constantly that I've had to learn to be firm in holding on to 'my time' for work or for myself, both because I needed it and because I felt Christopher needed to be able to play self-sufficiently. The other day, after he'd been at a friend's house for two nights in a row, we were on a bus trip together, and Chris wanted me to play cards with him. In my old 'hold on to my time' mind-set, I said 'Not now, I'm reading. Why don't you get out your baseball book?' Which he did happily. Only later did I realize with a pang that this was one of the only moments in the past few days that he'd turned to me. I wished I had responded. I see now that as he gets older I'll

Nancy Scanlan

come to cherish those moments of contact that aren't just around food or rules. From 'holding out for my time' I need to switch to a new flexibility, to open myself to the special moments when they are there.

As our children develop more skills and find more ways to take care of and entertain themselves, the limits and rules which we have set for them and the ways we have of relating to them may no longer be valid.

While we might have felt all too connected to our children when they were younger, now we may begin to feel left out of their lives. So at the same time their growing independence frees us, it also means that our children may not always be there when we want them to be. A father of two complained:

Saturday used to be my day with the kids, and we all looked forward to spending time together. Now, more often than not, they're off with their friends or working on some project that doesn't include me.

And a mother who works away from home all day said:

When I come home and am ready to be with my kids and they are more interested in doing what they're doing than being with me, I feel resentful inside. Like when Aaron sits on the floor with the baseball scores for a half-hour before he even comes in to say hello to me, I get testy about it.

We have to cope increasingly during this period with how separate our children are. The notion that we are raising our kids to help them leave us is becoming more and more of a reality.

Helping Our Children Become Independent is Complicated

One of the most significant characteristics of this age period is that our children are constantly pushing us to see how much more they can get away with and testing themselves to see how much more they can do. They still want our guidance, but they don't want to be held back from taking legitimate steps forward. This can raise complex questions for us as parents, because there aren't any rules for us to follow about when it's O.K. to let your child cross the street alone, or how old your oldest should be before you let him or her baby-sit for the younger ones, or when it's all right to allow your son or daughter to ride a bike to the park with a friend. Each time we have to make a decision like that we may feel that we have no one to turn to, that we can only trust our own judgement and hope for the best. However, these are the times when it would be helpful to check with friends about what they have done in similar situations, and if we are not parenting alone, we have our partner to talk to. Sometimes parents disagree over how much independence to allow their children, as this mother explains:

One of the recurring arguments between Steve and me is over my leaving Jonathan alone in the house while I go food shopping or on some other short errand. Taking him along is always such a bother, since he never wants to go and fusses so much that it isn't worth it. So I tell him exactly how long I'll be gone and explain what he can do and what he can't do while I'm gone. He is six and a half, after all, and he knows how to use the telephone if there's an emergency. But Steve thinks it's totally negligent if I leave him alone in the house – even for fifteen minutes. We really fight over that. He makes me feel like I'm being a bad mother and I think he's acting like an overprotective granny.

Since there is no 'right' way to raise our children, disagreements like this come up often during active parenthood. Parents can have entirely different ideas about what is appropriate and what isn't; negotiating those differences can be both frustrating and enriching, depending on how willing each of us is to respect the other parent's opinion. Lots of these decisions involve potentially dangerous situations, and since the lives of our children are at stake, we aren't willing to take unnecessary chances. A mother said:

Mark has recently been pushing to get to cross a major street by himself. He says his friends do it. But I am, frankly, scared to let him. 'Come on, Mom,' he says. 'You don't trust kids enough.' I'm in a bind: I want to trust him where it's appropriate, but not beyond, and I want to be a good guy at the same time.

Examples of this dilemma come up over and over during the middle years. A parent said:

When Peggy came to me and said 'I want a bigger bike' – she kept telling me 'Lookit, I can do it, I want to try to do it.' But I wasn't so sure, especially since she'd just had that accident. I wanted to hold her back because I was afraid she'd fall off, but in fact I knew somewhere that she has to go out and experiment – and if she falls off, then she falls off, and she'll learn from that. I don't know absolutely that the bike is too big, but I don't know absolutely that it isn't too big, either.

And a mother of a ten-year-old:

We were swimming at someone's pool and Ruthie asked me 'Can I jump in off the diving board?' She doesn't know how to dive. And I decided to handle it by saying 'Do it if you feel ready to do it.' But then she decided not to do it . . . it was like I had the magic – she wanted me to say it was O.K. and that would mean she could do it and everything would be all right.

This mother explained that she felt confused. She wondered whether she should have said 'Go ahead and try to dive.' Maybe then her daughter would have felt confident enough to do it. But the woman didn't know how to dive herself, and in fact had only recently learned to swim, so she felt a little uneasy about encouraging her daughter.

At this age our children still look to us for guidance and approval, and although they may act fiercely independent, they do tend to base their actions on our opinion. Sometimes we want to encourage our kids to make their own decisions. But when we are feeling ambivalent ourselves about a particular skill or feat, it's hard to give our children straightforward answers. The ambivalence we feel usually comes from deep inside, as this mother describes:

I should tell you first that as a child I was never allowed to walk home from school alone until I was in the third or fourth grade, whereas a lot of my friends began doing it in kindergarten. My mother had had two children die, and I think that made her irrationally very, very fearful that something would happen to either my brother or me.

In my own childhood there was a tremendous pull between catching my mother's fear and having wild imaginings about the things that could happen to me, while at the same time being very embarrassed that I couldn't do the things my friends could do. So when the issue of going for walks by herself came up with Cheryl, my six-year-old, it sparked in me not only my own old fears, but also a strong recollection of how fiercely I had wanted to be able to do those things. One time last spring I sent Cheryl with some letters to a nearby mailbox. It was clearly something that she thought of as a very important event in her life and a real mark of my respect for her, so since then she kept asking back about it, 'When can I go to the mailbox again?' Yet, I was experiencing a hesitancy. Then one night I thought, oh, hell, she's incredibly responsible about other things, why can't she walk two blocks to the mailbox? It was about twilight time, and I said to her 'Why don't you take these letters to the mailbox for me?' This time she hesitated, and I realized that I had made too big an offer. She really didn't want to walk alone in the near dark. That stood for me as an example of the fact that we were going to need a lot of balancing to find a mutual level of comfort. I was not only going to have to learn to give up ... I mean give up in the sense of giving her space, but I was also going to have to learn what she experienced as the boundaries she wanted to have put on her new responsibilities and independence.

So the responsibilities of parenthood take on a more subtle cast during the middle years. We are adviser now, not simply rule-setter. Some of us may feel it was easier to parent little ones, when we were able to control almost every aspect of our child's environment and experience. As our kids become more able and independent, and as they begin to develop their own opinions about their limits and goals, we do have to give up, as the mother above began to say; we have to give up some of our absolute authority. Our child is becoming a more conscious partner in his or her growth. We can't, nor do we want to, watch them every minute, so we have to trust that they will take some responsibility for their own well-being.

Each time our children take a new step, each time we allow them to move ahead to try something they've never tried before, we go through a period of doubt and questioning and ambivalent feelings until the new skill is mastered or the new rules are established. It is one of the most common experiences of parenthood, and it is also one of the most challenging. Our fears for our child's health and safety, our pleasure at our child's growing skills, our ambivalence about watching our child grow up, our joy at our own new freedom, our own insecurity about doing something unfamiliar, the new adventures we share with the child – all work together to make these times either stressful for us or a time of growth.

Watching Our Children Develop Stirs Feelings in Us

The middle years are full of changes for our kids, and for us. As we watch them learn to read or ride a bike or play sports or experiment with making friends, we are watching budding adults try out their talents for the first time. As any parent will say, this can be a joyful experience. A mother of two boys at grade school [i.e. roughly at primary-school age] told us:

Both of my kids read avidly now. That was a great pleasure for me as a child and just to see them gives me pleasure. Paul just loves to read, and my oldest is an active kid but still likes to sit down and read a book. That gives me a real kick. So I feel that that's a positive thing about having raised kids. Just WOW! because when I look back and see how I didn't believe I could do it. That's some kind of real achievement for me!

Ben Achtenberg

And the father of an eight-year-old boy said:

I can't carry a tune for the life of me, and here's Adam able to sit down at the piano and play a song . . . and sing – he can really sing. What a trip! I get such pleasure from that, it's almost as if I were singing myself.

From our baby's first smile on through the years, we can derive great pleasure from our children, from who they are as people, as well as from what they do.

If we're honest about our feelings, however, it isn't always just pride and pleasure. A stepfather of a nine-year-old boy told us how his son's new successes affect him:

It's hardest for me when I feel envy, when I see David working through something in a better way than I did, given a chance that I never had to experience something – to develop a potential that I don't feel I developed very well in myself. Where I see him fulfilling some of my own hopes, but in him, not in me. Then I experience the strongest conflict of emotions, because he is so clear about the happiness he feels and deserves to feel, while I'm feeling a little sorry for myself.

Those feelings of envy are familiar to many of us. We see our children accomplishing things that we've always been afraid to try, or we give them opportunities that we never had, and we find ourselves feeling jealousy mixed with our pride, or we feel resentful when they take it all for granted.

Our children are learning so many new things in what seems to be such a short period of time that their feats may overwhelm us. We see their undeveloped talents and we might think, oh, Timmy should play basketball, or Bonnie needs swimming lessons. We can get carried away with all the things we want to do for our children to help them fulfil the potential we see in them. As parents, it's hard to balance what is legitimate encouragement and skill building and what is asking our children to fulfil some of our own undeveloped potential or unattained goals. A mother said:

Your child has an interest or a talent and you see it and recognize it, and you also recognize the things the child isn't interested in and doesn't do well. I suppose a time comes when you have to stop thinking about the child as an extension of yourself who's going to do and know all the things you didn't get around to doing or knowing.

That understanding happens during the middle years. When our children are younger, it is still possible for us to imagine that they can be or do anything. Now they begin to let us know just what their limits are.

Those of us who never would have touched a musical instrument if our parents hadn't forced us know the value of some healthy parental persuasion. Yet, as parents now ourselves, we may find it hard to figure out the difference between offering direction to our kids and browbeating them. In the process of finding that out, we have to respect our own sense of what is possible for us to manage and what we simply cannot do for our children. As one father said:

Before your kid starts school it seems like your responsibility is limited to a kind of psychological and physical nurturing. As long as we sort of loved the kid up, hugged her five times a day, everything was fine. It wasn't terribly complicated. But now we spend a lot of time worrying about creating a stimulating environment and whether we can afford things like summer camps and piano lessons.

As our children get older the financial pressures on us increase. Clothes, toys, equipment, lessons, even food can strain our budget severely. Though we can't expect to be able to give our children everything, nor even want to, we can help them to take advantage of the sports activities and lessons that are available through neighbourhood schools and community centres.

Aside from the financial limitations to our support, we may begin to notice some personal blocks as well. It's all too easy to fall into the old trap of finding dancing classes for Patty but not for John, or encouraging Billy to attend Little League games while asking Sherri to stay home and help with the housework. Our own feelings about what it means to be a man or a woman influence how we support our children's interests and activities and how enthusiastic we are in helping them develop their talents:

I can see now how I treat my daughter differently from my son. I would cuddle him and love him and laugh at him and really be curious about a lot of the things he would get into. He explores and takes things apart and I would appreciate that a lot, but I'd get annoyed at a lot of the stuff when my daughter was doing it. I want her to be an independent, strong person – her own self as she grows up – but I became aware of some vague difference in how I felt about her and how I felt about my son. That started me thinking about how my mother related to me. I was given a lot of traditional woman's work – expected to wait on my father, to set the table and cook. It was my responsibility because, like me, my mother had a part-time job. I was the oldest, and I was the daughter, and there was just a certain pattern I was expected to follow. And now I am becoming aware that I really had that expectation for my own daughter. Luckily, being aware of it helps me to begin to change it.

Sometimes, because we are so angry about the sex-role stereotyping with which we were raised, we make it a point to see that that doesn't happen to our children, as this mother did:

I told my daughter that she had to take woodworking in school, even though it had always been an all-boys class. If she never took it because none of the girls in her class had the nerve to, she'd never know if she liked it. So I said, 'This year you have to sign up for woodworking, or I'm going to scoot right down to the school and yell.'

Though some of us might not take so forceful an action, this mother obviously knew her daughter well, because it worked out happily:

It turns out there is a new woodworking teacher who all the kids really like, so Pam's been enjoying the class a lot. She came home last week and said 'I'm so glad you're my mother,' and I said 'Why is that?' And she said 'Because you made me take woodworking.'

Dealing with Our Children's Problems: Learning to Keep Emotional Distance

When things don't work out so well, when our children are having trouble adjusting or when they don't succeed in their attempts, we may find ourselves feeling guilty or angry or uncertain about what to do. It is not easy to be tolerant of our children's mistakes or defeats, especially if we see them as reflections of our child's future character or on our ability as parents. The fact that Elizabeth is having trouble learning to read may make us worry that she is slow, or that she is lazy. It's often the case that a strong negative reaction like that comes more from some unresolved conflict of our own than from Elizabeth's possible handicap. Did we have trouble learning? Were we afraid to get up in front of the class? Were our teachers or our parents too strict with us? Do we wish we had done better in school? Sometimes our kids' troubles are hard for us to deal with because we have difficulty separating ourselves emotionally from their problems. A mother of a ten-year-old who's having trouble making friends told us:

I had a very similar problem when I was in sixth grade, so it becomes hard to separate. I notice that I personalize the problem too much. When Cora comes to me and tells me about how so-and-so was mean to her or so-and-so didn't include her, the little girl inside me feels like saying to her, oh, those girls in your class are just drips! You know, I get childish myself.

Another mother described the frustration and ambivalence she feels when her children are having a difficult experience:

I think I went through a lot of the things that the children are going through, and my parents didn't understand, so I not only want the children to know that I understand, I also don't want them to suffer what I suffered. And yet, it isn't enough for me to just put my arms around them and say 'I know how you feel because I felt that way too.' But I don't know what else to do.

Maybe that is all we can do. It's a further reminder that our children are separate people and that their feelings and experiences are their own. A lot of the pain they experience is the stuff of growing up – part of the foundation on which their adult sensibilities will be secured. However, for us, watching them go through those difficult experiences can be excruciating. Their pain seems deeper now and more grown-up, and their failures and rejections are sometimes too close to home for us. A father discusses his feelings about his son's experience in the Little League:

It's a wound to me – I can't see my separateness. The whole experience didn't work out the way I had hoped: I thought he would have a chance to learn more baseball, but in fact he was hardly chosen to play at all. The kids who were better to start with got to play more and he began to feel worse and worse about himself. He was failing. The choices for me were hard: encouraging him to stick it out or helping him decide if he wanted to quit in mid-season. The best thing I could do when I got over personalizing the hurt was to be able to talk to one of the coaches about it. Even though that didn't change anything, at least Eric got to hear me say something about it and know that I was supporting him.

I could experience how painful the whole thing was for him because I was remembering parts of my childhood and adulthood when I just didn't feel adequate to the situation. Why did I have to have a kid who couldn't play baseball better? He should magically be able to play baseball better! And I put myself down for not having gone out every night to play catch with him, even though that was the last thing I wanted to do. I had to cope with a whole set of confusing feelings – painful feelings, rageful feelings. I wanted to go and punch out the coach and rant and rave. How dare he treat my kid (myself) unfairly? I felt murderous feelings creep up inside me, and although I knew they weren't exactly appropriate to the situation, I still felt them. It helped me to appreciate my son's rage and frustration.

One of the most difficult aspects of being a parent now, during the middle years, is feeling powerless to protect our children from hurt. However 'growthful' it may be for them to experience failure, disappointment and rejection, it is nearly impossible to maintain an intellectual perspective when our sobbing child or rageful child comes in to us for help. Most of the time his or her cry for help won't even be clear; we may not know at all what's going on, which makes the whole thing even more frustrating. And although we may be able to quiet or comfort our child, we can't turn the hurt around by kissing the sore spot to make it better. We are no longer the all-powerful parent. Our children's world has gone out of our control in many ways, and we can no longer monitor and/or restrict all the activity within the boundaries of their experience.

Separating: Our Children Enter the Public World

Throughout parenthood we are continually facing the fact that our children are separate from us and will separate from us. Entering school marks their first formal step in that direction. More and more significant others will now have a place in our children's lives and development, and our children themselves will begin to make independent decisions about their actions and behaviour. As a mother of three said about her youngest:

He was so excited about entering the first grade. He kept saying 'Now I can go to first grade; now I can walk to the store by myself; now I can do a lot of things I couldn't do before because now I'm in first grade.'

We might remember that feeling from our own childhood: the excitement that now, finally, we were going to be part of the grown-up world, going to school with all the big kids, leaving home and going somewhere on our own.

For us as parents the experience is more complex. Now an outside authority, in this case the government, has stepped in to tell us what we have to do: we have to send our children to school. Consequently, during the middle years we quite literally have to relinquish some of our parental authority. Strangers are now in charge of our children for a good part of the day.

We can't regulate the way the outside world perceives our children. Once they start school they are being compared with other children in both behaviour and performance. A father said:

I had no sense before of this insidious business of comparing or contrasting kids like I do now that Sandy's in the first grade. From my point of view as a father, there was this moment when I talked to my daughter's teacher and got a completely different analysis of my child. You know, you find out how competent your kid is in comparison with all the other kids in her class in language development, in numbers, in spelling, etc., etc. Now she's 6.5 on this scale and 5.6 on that scale and with it there's this escalation of my anxiety and concern. My identification, too, wondering, is this kid going to make it? School's the kind of place where judgement is made, and my relationship to Sandy has shifted because now school is forcing me to think about where she stands, how she rates.

Betsy Cole

It is not easy to step outside the system of competition and rating set up in schools. As parents we may see part of ourselves going off each morning, lunch box in hand. If the teacher tells us our child is bright, we feel proud; if the teacher tells us our child is slow, we feel disappointed and worried. The challenge of these experiences is to separate our emotional selves from our children's performance enough to support them as people, not as numbers on a rating scale. If our children are having problems in school, either with behaviour or with learning, we want to find the best way to help them through their difficulties. Sometimes that means working with the teachers; sometimes that means taking a stand against the institution. More often we are caught somewhere in the middle, as this mother describes:

When my oldest was in the fifth grade, he had a teacher who was getting kind of senile. She was very disorganized and had trouble remembering things, but she was a very nice person. My views are when you're with somebody like that you try to make things easy for them, help them out, try to understand them. But my son was in there tearing the room apart, making life hell for the teacher. I found myself caught between the realization that being in that classroom was an awful thing for the children – total chaos, the poor woman was having trouble remembering what time of day it was – and the feeling that my son was in his own way trying to get some order going in the class. I felt that by putting the screws on him to shape up in class I would have been telling him to adjust to a situation that I knew was horrible for him. I would be asking him to sell himself out. It was a terrible time and I ended up trying to ignore it for as long as I could. Finally, I sat him down and tried to explain that I understood how unhappy he was in school, but that he really had to get off the teacher's back — he had to try to have some compassion for her as a person. As it turned out, I think he may have been waiting for me to put the brakes on, to tell him that he simply couldn't act that way, you can't treat people that way.

For better or for worse, our children have stepped into the world outside their family, and there are hours at a time now when they have to be able to get along on their own. New experiences come fast and furious during the middle years, and each venture is a learning time for us and them, as this story illustrates:

I let my seven-year-old daughter go herself to the shoe store to buy the sandals she wanted. When I came back for her, she was still sitting there without the sandals. I was confused about what to do because she had very much wanted to negotiate the sale herself, and yet it looked to me as if she was being ignored by the salesmen. A lot of adults were coming into the store and being waited on before Jenny. They were actually saying that they were next, even though it was clear that Jenny had been there a lot longer. I wanted to get involved because the situation was going against her, but also I wanted to use this experience as a way of talking to her about the fact that the world is not always as fair and as kind as the kindergarten book says it is. Policemen aren't always good, shoe salesmen aren't always sweet to little children, just because you're first doesn't always mean you'll be served first. Finally I did speak up, telling one of the salesmen that my daughter had been waiting for a very long time, and Jenny was very upset with me. She had really wanted to buy those shoes herself, but I realized that she didn't have the necessary social skills to carry it off. I saw then that it's up to me as her parent to teach her about the proper balance between concerns for other people — being polite, on the one hand, and frankness and standing up for herself, on the other.

Our children are going to encounter many difficult situations during these years, more difficult than the one described above. Grown-ups may take advantage of them; other kids may be mean to them; they are going to be exposed to things that may frighten them or confuse their sense of justice. The same children who only yesterday believed in Santa Claus and the tooth fairy are today facing a much seedier reality. They see violence on television, and if they watch or read the news they are bound to have lots of questions about subjects we ourselves feel uncomfortable with — war, kidnapping, rape, murder. We may feel like explaining that there *are* things in their world which are unjust, arbitrary and downright evil. Yet simple explanations no longer suffice. A father told us:

My son heard about the hijacked school bus, where a whole busload of kids was kidnapped, and he started asking questions about why would anyone do that, and why weren't the police there, and what would we do if he was kidnapped. We tried to explain — but how can you explain to an eight-year-old about the sickness in the world? How can you explain that to yourself, even? Anyway, after that he refused to go to camp on the bus. He never came out and said it was because he was afraid of being kidnapped, but we knew that was the reason, so we didn't push it and arranged a car pool instead.

And a mother remembered:

We live across the street from a large park, and when Rob was about seven, he made his own adult 'friend' there. Obviously, talking to that man had real meaning for the child – you could see it in the way he'd walk up, very important and grown-up, to the man's bench, and the way he'd talk about his 'park friend' to us at home.

Wow! What a problem that raised for us. The guy was a merchant seaman who was sometimes drunk, sometimes with really low characters in the neighbourhood. Both Rob's father and I made it a point to talk to the man, to get to know him and – sort of – to make our presence felt, but the whole thing made us very uneasy. Could we allow Rob to go down to the park by himself any more? What were they talking about? Etc.

How long do we continue to try to preserve our children's innocent vision of the world – that good always wins out over evil, that fair is fair and justice prevails? It's not easy to talk about death or growing old or sickness to children when we may have trouble accepting them ourselves. We can let our children know that we are there to protect them as much as we can, but that we are not omnipotent. These are the years during which our kids will come to know that, and we will be faced again and again with our own fragility and loss of innocence. We have to teach them some rules for taking care of themselves – don't talk to strangers; don't accept rides from strangers; don't play with kids who have weapons, etc. At the same time, we can't let our own fears take over; we can't protect our children from all negative experience.

Value Clashes

As our children become more aware of the larger society around them, they are continually being exposed to new ideas. They are moving into a world full of lots of ways of doing things that are different from the way we do things in our individual family.

All our values are open to challenge now – something that can be upsetting and frustrating for us. The familiar chant 'So-and-so's mother lets him do it' brings responses ranging from anger and hurt to understanding and compromise, from being very firm about what we believe is right to being more wishy-washy than we'd like to be. For most of us, all of these reactions occur at one time or another. The point is that to be faced with what so-and-so's mother lets him do, or what the teacher said in class today or what all the kids are wearing is to be required to re-examine some part of our belief structure. Each time we rethink our values we can reaffirm them or begin to change them. Seen in this way, parenthood affords us an exceptional opportunity for growth. An example of this was given by a mother of two, aged ten and eight.

A few weeks ago we were visiting my in-laws and they took us out for brunch and then afterwards – it was about eleven-thirty – they bought the kids an ice cream cone. Then they took us to a zoo-park kind of place, where we sat and looked at the animals. At about four o'clock the ice cream truck came by, and my mother-in-law immediately got up with her pocketbook in hand and started walking toward the ice cream truck with the two kids. I said 'No – they're not having ice cream again.' And her face dropped because she doesn't see them that often and she knows that they love ice cream. My son put up a fight like he'd never put up before and I kept on saying No, No, No, and I put my foot down and said NO. Well, afterwards he came up to me and said 'Mommy, this was just the one time when Grandma really wanted us to have ice cream. We don't have it twice every day. You could have let us have it this one day; it wasn't such a big deal.' I felt terrible and I realized, sure, they wanted ice cream, but on some level they were understanding things much better than I was, which was their grandmother's need to just shower them with everything she could because she sees them so infrequently.

The Code of the West for Sylvia Katz

APOSTROPHE: Mother cop, wearer of the pants,
Mrs Softie with the short, short fuse,
prey of the thieving young bastard
   you live with,
listen. And shut up; I'm the author.

ARGUMENT: Children give us back ourselves.
They steal our made-up faces and
Return not only seed, but nervous
Gestures, rage, our greed. Not
As a mirror with the speed of light
But on another day (perhaps a day
Of intentional peace), come
To display our old mistakes.

Your son is Tokyo Rose in your ears,
And you, an enemy of the establish-
   ment,
A hater of injustice, think his insistent
Broadcast beamed at yourself. Do
   you see
Little Caesar, you subscribe
To the very notion that galls you:
People have no power in this country.

REPLY: Miriam, I read your poem after a
hard day. I had 3 political meetings,
the kids were sick—you know we're
neighbours. Why not use the phone?

– Miriam Goodman

And a father told of how he learned from his son's different sense of what was appropriate:

We were down at the beach and Paul had been swimming, and he came up in his wet bathing suit, and I snapped at him to get out of that wet suit and get some dry clothes on. He looked me straight in the eye, and he said 'But the sun is blazing. I'll be dry in five minutes.' He was dead right. And he said it strongly enough, so that I backed off and said 'By golly, you're right.' Then I thought, where was that anger coming from in me? It was coming from the way that I was treated – if I went into the water when I was a kid I had to go and change right away, or I got all that anger I let out on Paul. Even more, I felt a little bit blessed that this kid knew how to confront me on that, and that I knew how to say 'You're right.'

If we are open to them, our children can teach us many important lessons and help us work through issues from our own childhood which we may not yet have resolved.

They can also challenge us, test us, force us to ask ourselves why we do certain things, as in this example from a woman who is a vegetarian:

Stevie asked me one night at dinner 'How come if you eat fish you don't eat chicken?' And I couldn't think of a good reason. Then he just had the best time. He got more and more pleased with himself that I couldn't think of a reason . . . He said 'Well, it's pretty crazy then for you to eat fish and not to eat chicken.' He was just feeling so good. Later a friend reminded me of some of the reasons why as a vegetarian I still ate fish – that fish don't require grain, and don't take up land and resources, they just swim in the ocean. So I told Stevie that and he just said 'All the more reason to let them be.'

Our kids are at an age now when they don't take very much for granted, and they can help us see just how much we do take for granted.

Many times, however, the new ideas to which our children are being exposed or the new people they are meeting are not acceptable to us. Then we find ourselves having to be very firm about what we believe is right or wrong, harmful or unhealthy. A mother of a ten-year-old said:

My values are in many instances so different from the values Ethan gets every place else. Like about what's good to eat, and about violence, about television, about sexism. We have constant battles over those things and I wonder, is this quarrelling going to shape his whole childhood? Yet I also realize that children this age are always pushing and testing to get what they want – or pushing to see if they can get even more than that.

Being Firm with Our Children

For some of us parental authority is a given. We assume that as parents we make the rules and that our kids follow them without question, or at least without too much questioning. For many of us, however, the issue is not so simple. Like the mother who has just been quoted, we may feel that we are in a perpetual battle with our children, because at this age they do test us so constantly. Furthermore, they are physically bigger now, they talk back more, and they can reason so much more clearly. Consequently we may find ourselves being talked out of any stand we take. Learning how to be firm with our children, to be an authority without being authoritarian is a challenge parents face during these years.

A mother said 'I started out being too wishy-washy with my son. Now I'm realizing that being brave enough to be firm with him is a gift to him: my firmness nourishes him as much as food does.' Another mother explained:

I've been feeling much more comfortable these days with being firm with my kids. One of the big problems when my kids were toddlers was my not liking the part of parenting that meant being an authority figure. Over time I've started feeling much more comfortable with that, feeling that kids do need certain boundaries and structures. Like yesterday we were walking home from the bus and the kids started squabbling about something during the walk and then got into that long, all too familiar explanation about whose fault it was, and Sam said Vicki did this or that and Vicki said Sam did this or that. So I said 'Look, I don't want to hear any more of this. Sam, you said you wanted to be alone, so go upstairs and be alone.' I could almost feel him breathe a sigh of relief when I said that. And, you don't know, he went upstairs and he cleaned up his room!

As parents of children this age, we are daily having to ask for certain kinds of behaviour from them. Part of being a parent is teaching our children how to act responsibly and how to be respectful of others and themselves. The security they feel from knowing what is expected of them really is a gift we can give them. One father said:

We just don't allow Kevin to hit Laurie. There simply isn't any arguing about it. And she isn't allowed to hit him, either. That's always been the rule, ever since they were little. But now it's getting important since he's big – almost eleven – and he could really hurt her.

Rules exist whether spoken or not. Each individual family has its own set of bylaws which help things run smoothly, and our kids are old enough now to participate in some of the rule-setting. A number of families have instituted family meetings, times at which rules and grievances are openly discussed by everyone.

During these years our children's behaviour may become a matter of serious concern. As we watch them growing and developing we might think, oh no, if Gregg keeps this up, he'll turn out just like my brother Jerry. Or: Susie is so demanding, just like my mother. We think about who our child is becoming and wonder whether s/he will be able to make a good life for her/himself. Most of the time we worry more than is necessary, since Gregg isn't brother Jerry and Susie isn't your mother. We see our children developing habits which they will take with them into adulthood, and we want to help them eliminate their negative traits while we reinforce their positive ones. Sometimes we go overboard, as this mother admits:

I'm much more worried about letting up on Phillip than I am on Gloria, I guess for a lot of reasons. Because he is my first, and because he is male . . . that may be one of the wrong reasons. But because he's male and because he's black, he needs to know that there's no way in the world that he can afford not to be in control. It's an awful lot to put on a child and I know that, so I'm trying hard to loosen up a little now that he's eleven. I've been so hard on him up till now that he expects himself to be perfect and isn't satisfied with less. I'm easier on Gloria maybe because I already see what's happened to Phillip – how nervous he is and what a perfectionist he's become.

It's particularly hard for us when we see in our children traits that we recognize and dislike in ourselves. The mother in this anecdote may be seeing her own need to be perfect and her own exacting compulsiveness in her son, wanting him to be both like her and different, to be easier on himself so he won't be so nervous, so rigid, but disciplined enough to succeed.

How to discipline the children is an area in which many parents experience interpersonal disagreements. Arguments over who's being too lenient or who's being too hard on them occur all the time. Depending on our own upbringing we have certain attitudes about how children should behave, what we feel comfortable letting them do, and what we feel strongly they shouldn't be allowed to do. When these beliefs clash with our partner's, our negative sentiments may run very deep. We may feel that our mate is 'spoiling' our child – that is, spoiling our chance to 'make' a new human being in the best way possible. When the other adult in the house is not the child's natural parent, the conflict may become particularly touchy.

On the other hand, some parents put up a united front to the children no matter how they really feel. It's either the father saying 'Listen to your mother, she's right' or the mother saying 'Wait until your father gets home and he'll give it to you.' This way out may seem easier at the time, but it leaves the kids feeling that they have no court of appeal for legitimate grievances. It also may leave the one parent, on whose shoulders the burden of discipline lies, feeling like the bad guy all the time. Working together as a parental team, sometimes agreeing and other times trying to resolve disagreements, requires a lot of willingness to talk and negotiate ideas together. It is a way of getting closer to each other in the long run, but sometimes it feels like an uphill journey. A single parent said:

I think in the area of discipline it's easier to be a single parent because you just have one style and the children get only one set of messages. I'm not saying it's better for the child, but I think it is easier for the parent.

It is true that when we're raising children alone we have only our own rules to follow. However, having a husband or wife or another adult around can be a comfort; we can share authority and ask for each other's support when the going gets rough. When that works, it can make parenting much easier, as this mother describes:

I was having one of those all too typical 'bad days' and everything seemed to be piling up. Company was coming for dinner; nothing was ready and the house was a mess. My son was trying to keep out of my way – clever child – so he stayed in the other end of the house. When I walked in to talk to him, I realized that he was making a colossal mess, leaving unfinished projects everywhere. I started screaming and yelling, and felt like I was almost out of control when Andy, the man I live with, stepped in to save the day. He immediately smiled, put his hand to his head in a mock military salute and started pretending to order Jimmy around like a drill sergeant. Jimmy fell into step with a big smile on his face, and in no time at all the two of them had the bedrooms and the playroom cleaned up.

We're Not Just Parents: We're People, Too

Adults who are living together and sharing the responsibilities of parenthood have different issues to face now that the children are in the middle years. We no longer have to decide who will get up for the 2 a.m. feeding or who will dress the kids in the morning. Our children can take care of many of their own needs, and a lot of the time-consuming duties of early parenthood no longer exist. As a result, we can spend a little more time as adults living together, not just as parents. One mother of two said:

More and more now the kids are excusing themselves as soon as they're through eating, and Lou and I are having some nice, peaceful time for after-dinner conversation.

Of course, although our children are more independent, they still make it hard to forget their presence when they are around. They may need help with their homework or a ride to their friend's house, or they may just hang around close enough to make intimate conversation between the adults less than intimate. With a baby or toddler, if they are quiet you can at least talk about anything you want to, but with bigger children around who hear and understand everything, you have to be careful. 'What, Mom? What did you say? Oh, I didn't know *that*!' says the nine-year-old, who just overheard information she shouldn't have. A father of two admitted:

School-age kids make their own demands on parents. You know, I feel enormous conflicts between the kind of time I'd like to spend on myself, and with my wife, and the kind of time that I spend with the kids. This is in part the famous five p.m.-to-eight p.m. problem. You know, in the evening, all these conflicts of interest come up – you really feel that you'd like to be alone, and have a drink with your spouse, and be with the kids, and all of these have to be done simultaneously. I think this is an important problem for parents of kids this age: privacy.

If both mother and father are working outside the home – which is becoming the norm – coming home at night is the time to get dinner, to clean up a little, to play with the children or tell stories and to put the kids to bed. After that, when the children are all finally asleep, we're lucky if we have enough energy for a kiss or a hug, much less an important discussion. For many couples, that's the time when the television goes on and in a few minutes one or the other of us is sound asleep. By the time we've been going through that for five or six or ten years, our romance may be hard to maintain without a concerted effort. In fact, keeping alive the passion and romance in our love relationship is one of the key issues of the middle years.

To do this, we may have to pay special attention to carving out some time just for ourselves. Some of us feel the need for private time before dinner so we can relax with each other after work, making the transition from work to home a little easier. Joining can become a ceremony each night:

> In our house my man and I need some time to be alone together before we jump into the family. I'm usually home first and I try to get the kids interested in a project or homework, or even TV, so that when David comes in, he and I can just sit and talk for about fifteen or thirty minutes – sharing the day's events and saying hello again to each other. That gives us the extra boost we need to feel enthusiastic about spending the next two or three hours with the kids.

We have to remember to build in some time for unwinding. Even if we are parenting alone, our kids are old enough now to allow us some time to relax by ourselves.

Sometimes we have to stop and remind ourselves and our kids that we are people who have lives and needs outside the parenthood experience. We may not know how much to explain to our children about our other self: our life as a couple, our work, our relationships with friends and lovers. Adults living together may wonder how much to let the children in on and how much to keep to themselves. By this age they can understand so much. We want to be sensitive to our children's feelings, but we also have to consider ourselves. Our being angry, crying, wanting time to think, demanding quiet, may all affect our children. Yet if we don't take care of these emotional and psychological needs, the tension builds up and everyone suffers. A single parent expressed how difficult this dilemma is for her:

> Somehow I haven't figured out how to communicate to my kids what's going on in my life and in my head without feeling like I was burdening them. My wish now is that if there were another adult in the house, the children would be involved in hearing us work things out and we'd all be able to be more open.

However, even when parents are living together or other adults are living in the house, it isn't easy for everyone to be open about sadness or anger in front of the children. One woman said:

> I hate to argue in front of the kids, but Larry thinks that if he wants to get his point across and the kids are there, well, he does it anyway. I control myself when the kids are around and then lash out at him when we're alone. Larry wants to talk about his feelings right away, whether the kids are around or not.

Being Open and Honest about Our Feelings

Often our children are more open about their needs and their feelings than we allow ourselves to be. They have ways of letting us know when they are sleepy, angry, worried, happy or sad. We can learn from them that it's possible to feel something intensely one moment, act on our feelings, and then feel better and move on to something else. Our kids are experts at that.

It helps to try to understand why we're feeling the way we are. Very often our being upset is not due to something our children did but related to something in our personal lives – at work, with our mate, with a friend, or just a bad day. A mother of four describes what it's like to be honest with her children about this:

If I am really unhappy about something and I come home, there are two things I could do. I could either act angry and my kids will probably think, gee, I did something to make Mom mad; or I could go home and say 'I've just had the most horrible day, I had a fight with my supervisor and I'm just in a really bad mood, so if I act crazy and mad, it's not because of anything you've done, it's because of where my head is.'

Sometimes, in times of family crisis, everyone is upset and worried. It's often hardest at those times to let out our feelings. One mother explained her experience with her seven-year-old at the time of her divorce:

I knew my son was grief-stricken over our divorce, but every time I broached the subject he would say 'Let's not talk about it now.' For weeks I tried to talk about the divorce with him, but was secretly relieved that we didn't. Then, one day, we were sitting quietly and cosily in the living room, just the two of us, listening to a record. All of a sudden something in the lyrics to a song made him incredibly sad. He started sobbing and then getting angry and hitting things and trying to hit me. I knew his reaction must have something to do with his anger and sadness over our divorce, so I said to him as gently as I could 'I bet you're so angry with us that we're getting divorced.' Then he just fell apart and buried his face in his hands and cried and cried. After some minutes he started saying all the things that he had been holding in, about how unfair it all was, and why did it have to happen to him, and why couldn't we stay together for his sake. After he calmed down, we talked about how sad it really was for all of us, but how necessary it was, too. I'm not sure he understood exactly, but I do know that it felt like we had really accomplished something, and that from then on the subject wouldn't be taboo. And the hidden benefit was that it helped me to get in touch with the sadness and the anger and the disappointment I was feeling.

Getting to know what we are really feeling about something is hard enough for most of us. Getting in touch with those feelings and then letting other people know about them is even more difficult, especially since sometimes the depth of the feelings we experience surprises us. The love, the sadness, the compassion and the anger can all reach extreme levels where our family is concerned. And as our children challenge us more and separate from us more during the middle years, we may find ourselves getting furious with them.

Anger

Having violent, angry, hateful feelings is a complicated experience. It's helpful to know that these feelings occur in all of us. The problem is knowing when and how to act on them so as not to be destructive to the people around us, especially our children. A lot of us have felt the way this mother does:

Boy, I really would like to know about the negative emotions that other people feel about their children. I worry about how extreme my negative emotions are toward Mickey and LeRoy. Sometimes I just can't stand them and I wish they would disappear. And I would like to know that other people feel that way, too. In this culture, maybe in every culture, it isn't allowed to talk about the problems you have with your kids. People don't say I just can't stand this about my kid. How could you feel good about yourself and your relationship with your child if you allowed those emotions to come out too often?

All of us have to find some way to let out the feelings we keep bottled up inside. We don't want our emotions to explode all over our children, but we also don't have to hide our feelings or squelch our anger simply because we don't want to upset the children. Our anger doesn't have to be scary if we can get enough control over it to express it clearly and let go of it when it's over, the way kids so often do. But there are times when all of us lose control. A mother of four said:

There was a time that I remember I lost control with Henry. It turned out that it had such shock value that I was quickly able to recover. It was during his time of not being able to sleep, and he got up in the early evening, and he started to scream and yell and tried to run away. And I literally had to hold him by the arms so he wouldn't run out the back door. He said he was going to run away. He hadn't ever tried this before, but he was yelling and screaming and I started yelling and screaming. It just really put me over the edge. I didn't know how to react, and I started to shout louder than he did. I was hanging on to him and screaming at him. It so surprised him that he stopped, and when he stopped I said 'Here now, you see what you are doing to me. That's what it feels like.' And it worked, but I, in that split second, really was as out of control as he was. The minute he stopped I was back in control, and I never lost it again because I was so shocked by my own behaviour. And so was he. He never tried to run away again. That is the closest I've come to feeling totally inadequate as a parent.

And a mother of three, the oldest of whom is seven:

I have felt, several times in the recent past few years, so close to wanting to hurt my children that I went into therapy to deal with those feelings. I kept wondering why the therapist wasn't working with me on the subject of child abuse. She kept going back to me instead – where was I getting my ego support? She kept asking me 'What's going on with you in your life?' And I recognized some connections – that I was thoroughly depleted at the time when I began to have murderous thoughts about my children.

Not only do our children bring out our most loving self, they also tap our most rageful self as this mother has described. A lot of us have strong feelings one way or the other about whether or not to hit children. Yet it is a rare parent who hasn't at one time or another, and especially during the middle years, felt angry enough with his or her children to consider walloping them. Even the most non-violent of us has felt it. However, if we find ourselves losing control a good deal of the time, then we ought to seek help (see the Helping Ourselves chapter).

Family life is full of angry situations. That's especially true because of all the voices we have in the back of our heads telling us about the things we should be doing and should be feeling: spouses should love each other; parents should feel nothing but love for their children; children should be respectful of adults; our children shouldn't be acting the way they are; we shouldn't be feeling the way we do. The conflict each of us experiences between what we really feel and how we think we ought to feel is the cause of much guilt and frustration.

Of course, not all anger in the family is between parent and child. Our kids fight with each other a lot, a situation which creates tension in many families. Ideally we try to step into sibling arguments before they become battles, but we aren't always successful, as this mother relates:

One night my boys had a fight that was so horrible. I was in the room when it began, feeling more and more upset because I immediately think that their fighting represents some failure on my part as a mother. Anyway, that night one thing led to another and Steven started to cry, not because he'd been hit but because Peter hurt him on the inside by making nasty cracks. Ten minutes later I was in my room crying my eyes out, and they were in their bedroom playing with each other.

Although we do have to try to keep our children from hurting themselves and each other, we are not responsible for all their actions. We can't blame ourselves every time they fight. In fact, if we can muster enough emotional distance to get some perspective, we can learn from our children about fighting and anger: get out your anger and be done with it so you can love each other again.

Children can learn the same lesson from their parents, as this mother describes:

Pete and I used to suppress a lot of anger when we were with the kids, because Julie, our daughter, would feel like she had to be the one to calm everyone down. We appreciated her for being able to do that, but after a while we said 'Well, this is really between us. We are going to fight and raise our voices, but, really, it has nothing to do with you or your brother, and you should stay out of it.' It made her tense at first, but we would say 'We are in charge, and it's under control, so you don't have to worry about it.' Then she could stay in the same room and listen to it and she was all right. And she learned from that that issues are resolved. She also learned that as a woman I didn't have to give in all the time. I could give some back and raise my voice with the best of them. I can remember Julie turning to me during an argument once and saying 'Ah, Mom, do that again, do that again.' It was like she had never really seen me get angry or stand up for myself before.

By expressing our anger clearly, we are allowing those around us to see how we are really feeling and to hear what is upsetting us. That can be a very intimate experience. The more loving and supportive our family is, the easier it is for us to let go of our anger when we're through expressing it.

Intimacy and Sexuality

Ideally, our family is the place where we feel comfortable showing our raw spots, where people will love us and support us. Parenthood, especially, can help us to understand what it is to give and accept intimate love. The affection that comes to us from our children simply because we are their parents allows us to feel that we are worthy of love. A father said:

We have to give ourselves – men in particular – permission to really be with and get to know our children. The premise is that taking care of kids can be a pain in the ass, and it is frustrating and agonizing, but also gratifying and enjoyable. When a little kid says 'I love you, Daddy', or cries and you comfort her or him, life becomes a richer experience.

Our children at this age are still pretty open about wanting to be loved. We can learn from them about that. But there are definite limits to the parent-child love relationship, and sexual and emotional intimacy between us and the other adults in our lives is the area in which our children have little if any part to play. As adults, we require nurturance, intimacy and appreciation from our peers; being parents often increases that need, since we are continually putting out so much nurturance and affection for our kids.

Unfortunately, many of us find that being parents interferes with our close adult relationships. The children's needs and demands have a way of coming first. One mother, who has since divorced her husband, said:

I think that children basically have a divisive effect on the adults around them. Especially if it's only one child, they help to set up a triangle situation, like odd-man-out all the time. I think with two parents and one child it tends to be that way. In my marriage it suited my husband, because he just wanted to be off to do his own thing anyway, so it really intensified the connection between Erica, my daughter, and me while it weakened the relationship between Paul and me.

And a single father told us:

I have the feeling sometimes that I couldn't live with another person, because I would be taking something away from the kids. I can see what happens when I have someone come in just for a dinner or something, that the kids and the guest are competing for my attention.

However strongly they resist it, our kids have to learn that as adults we need the companionship and love of other adults. The more direct we are about our needs, the easier it may be for our children to accept those needs. Their jealousy may come from a fear that if we adults love each other we might not have any left for them. We have to let them know that it's a different kind of love, as this mother explains:

I try to explain to the kids that besides being their mother and loving and caring about them, I'm also a person that would like to have relationships with other adults. I have a lot of the same problems and needs that the kids have, even though it's hard for them to realize that. In a lot of ways they see me as only a mother, not as a person.

It's healthy for children to see their parents as loving adults. Some of us feel easier with being openly loving to each other in front of the children; others of us feel that sexual affection should be kept private. The particular limits regarding affectionateness, nudity, fondling, kissing, hugging, are different for each family. Most families do have their own rules about sexual behaviour, but they are often unspoken rules. A woman said:

When my husband and I are home and want to make love and the children are here too, we tell them we are taking a nap and want privacy. Then we close the door to our bedroom and prop a chair against it so we won't be unexpectedly interrupted. Sometimes I wonder if it wouldn't be more honest to say 'Kids, we're going to make love and we want privacy.' But still, we don't say that. Maybe the pictures that would put in their minds would be confusing to them. It feels clearer not to be totally honest. Sometimes afterward, when we really are just resting, they might come in and see or feel us being very close and happy with each other. Now that can only be good and enriching to them.

Sometimes there is tension between the adults in the family because each has a different view about what is all right to do or say when the children are around, as this woman relates:

We just aren't spontaneous about our affection any more – my husband hardly ever comes in just to hug me or kiss me. For one reason, because the kids always want to get into the act, but for another reason, because that used to end up with us making love, and now with the kids running around and seeming always to be there, we just can't do that when we want to. But I don't think that should mean no tenderness at all. I need hugging – hugging that doesn't have to end up in bed. And Jim has a different idea, I think. To him hugging and kissing mean sex, and that's that. So I feel rejected a lot of the time. And then, after the kids are asleep, when I'm exhausted, Jim is ready for sex, and I'm always turning him down.

Lots of us recognize this problem. Being parents of children this age puts a tremendous strain on our sex life. However, it is a problem that has to be dealt with, or else the tension between partners keeps building and infects other areas of our relationship. Talking with each other about our different attitudes about displays of affection or simply loving attention is a first step toward easing the situation. We might not want to make love on the living room couch while the children are home, even if they are asleep, since children have a funny way of waking up just at the wrong moment. However, short of that, we can find ways of pleasing each other and taking care of each other. Perhaps we can make a little time once in a while for a hug and a little petting even when the children are up.

Some parents use the children as a good excuse for not wanting to make love. Sexual conflicts that may have existed even before the couple became parents can be conveniently pushed aside while we have to tend to the children. A mother of three said:

I think the kids are a good protection ... like an obstacle. They keep Larry and me from dealing with our own lack of communication – sexual and otherwise. It's easier to say we can't do such and such or talk about such and such because of the kids.

If we are not taking care of each other's needs – sexually, emotionally, or in any other way – those issues will come back to haunt us later on when our children leave home. The marital difficulties that are kept under cover because the children are around will not go away by themselves. If we want to sustain it, we have to try to make private time for dealing with whatever is bothering us about our relationship with our love partner. Shipping the kids off to the grandparents or a friend's for the weekend is one way of making time for ourselves. Renting a hotel or motel room for a night is another.

It doesn't hurt to find some private time and space for ourselves just for the fun of it, too. We don't have to have a complaint to discuss to want to be alone together.

Single parents are well aware of how important it is to make space in their lives just to be lovers. Children of single parents may not understand why we would turn to an 'outsider' for love, and they may be very resentful of a stranger's pull on their parent's affection. A divorced mother said:

It's been very hard. I have had to completely stop having lovers come home. Louise would just freak out. It's like she would be asleep and she could sense if I came in the house with a man. She would wake up and have this scene. You know, she wouldn't even know consciously that they were there; she would just sense it, and try and stop it.

Having to deal with our children's jealousy is just about the last thing we want to do when we are in the midst of the beginnings of a new romance. However, the reality is that we are parents and, as such, are responsible for trying to help our children understand that our love for them is in no way diminished by our desire to be with another adult. It helps if we speak directly to our children's concern about our not being there for *them* if we bring a new person into our lives. It's actually a lot like having to explain a new baby in the family, and even a new baby takes some time to get used to.

Of course, it is a bit of a juggling act to include a lover in our lives, as this widowed mother explains:

It's really hard to be with my boyfriend whenever I want to be. So it's two in the morning and you have a baby-sitter at home who's willing to spend the night, so you

say to yourself, hey, do I spend the night here or do I get up and go home to my kids? You have to put yourself first or your kids first. And I end up feeling guilty or resentful no matter which way I go. Usually I'm trying to find my way back home at five in the morning before my kids wake up.

The game is worth the candle, however, and for the sake of our sexuality, it deserves our best effort.

Sexuality and Our Children

As our children approach puberty they are becoming more aware of their own sexuality and of ours. They see, hear and understand so much, very often more than we give them credit for. During the middle years our kids start to form their own ideas and acquire their own information about sex, and it is up to us as parents to help them understand what they're learning.

My eight-year-old daughter came in from school the other day and said 'Hey, Mom, do you know what this means?' as she pushed a finger in and out of a circle made by the thumb and index finger of her other hand. I said I thought so, but what did she think it meant. She then proceeded to tell me that it meant making love. At that point I thought it was time to tell her more about what making love really is, just to be sure she didn't go through life thinking it had to do with fingers.

Good sexual information, provided from the earliest years on, can help our kids go through their own sexual changes a little more smoothly. It's important for them to know, for example, that their penis won't fall off if they masturbate or that they don't urinate blood when they're having their period. The longer we put off having our 'facts of life' talk with them, the more misinformation they may be acquiring.

Our children will give us signals about their growing sexual awareness. A mother of an eleven-year-old boy told us:

When we walk down the street now, he'll hold hands with me just till we get to the corner where the playground is across the street and some friends might be. Then he quickly drops my hand and walks on alone.

All of a sudden, almost without warning, their growing sense of their own separate body and their own sexuality demands that our children set some rules about what is appropriate and what isn't. They are beginning to separate from us emotionally, too – the major theme of their teen years. Sometimes their comments or actions may hurt us, make us feel rejected, since we aren't always so clear and understanding of the changes they are going through, as this mother described:

My nine-year-old went away to camp for two weeks, and when I went to meet the bus on their return, Taylor wasn't there. I didn't see him anywhere, and I waited and waited and still didn't see him. All the other kids got off the bus. Finally, after everyone else had gone, he appeared and kind of said 'Oh, hi, Mom' and walked off. It turned out he was hiding because he was afraid I'd kiss him in front of all his friends. That was a really hard moment for me.

Lots of people told about how their children at this age resist parents' attempts at open affection. As one parent said, 'You need emotional flexibility now – to give them the distance when they want it, but you love it so much when they still want to be close.'

Another aspect of our children's approaching adolescence is that they become more critical of us, more interested in how we appear to their friends, and more embarrassed by the way we act and the things we do. A mother of a pre-adolescent girl told this story:

One night, when it was a little later than usual, I was going to take the kids to the pool we belong to and I said 'Oh, goody, maybe there won't be many people there and we can go skinny-dipping.' Janie, my ten-year-old, looked at me and said 'Oh, Mother, please don't!' She was so embarrassed – how could I even think of such a thing!

As our children begin to differentiate themselves from us in the many ways they will, we may end up feeling like cast-off luggage. All this may begin to happen before we notice any real physical changes in our kids. But once we notice the hair on their legs or watch their shoulders or hips broaden, we'll start to recognize them for the budding men and women they are. Whether we like it or not, they and we can't ignore their sexuality. A mother of a ten-year-old shared this story with us:

When Neal came home from overnight camp last summer, he no longer wanted to share a room with his younger sister, and he was much more private about his body. It wasn't quite as clear as that makes it sound; it wasn't like he came out and said 'Now I want the door closed and to be private', but there was a feeling that I picked up that I really respected. And I had to change my behaviour – instead of walking around naked I had to really be careful to put something on, because for the first time I felt like I was being provocative to him in a way that was not responsible as a parent. It was subtle – I think it gets clearer in adolescence, but it begins now – our kids letting us know that they have their own sexual life.

There is a kind of underlying tension, sexual tension, that exists between parent and child once we begin to notice each other's sexuality. We might feel scared by the feelings we experience and try to ignore them or deny them. They are normal feelings, but to act on them is irresponsible and harmful to our children's growing sense of their own sexual development. Now is the time to respect our children's desire for privacy and separateness. The tension usually exists most strongly between father and daughter or mother and son. For single parents of children of the opposite sex, it's particularly important to respect our kids' boundaries, as this divorced mother says:

The other morning I was going to take Frankie to the station to go off to spend some time with his father. He had to get up and dress at the same time that I was in his room packing him up because we were a little late. I went in and we had a nice moment of greeting while I was waking him up. He acted a little embarrassed, but I couldn't quite read it, and he sort of hemmed and hawed, and I kept packing away and said 'Frankie, aren't you going to get up?' He started mumbling and stalling, and finally in the middle of the mumble I understood something like 'When you go into the kitchen.' And it suddenly dawned on me what was happening, so I said 'Are you feeling shy and a little sleepy?' I mean, I didn't say just baldly 'Are you feeling shy?' And he said 'Yes,' so I said 'Oh, I'm really sorry.' And I went out and closed the door – and he got up. That was a first for us. So now I know, he let me know, what our limits are.

Another facet of the middle years is learning how to respect our children's need for privacy without abandoning them when they come to us for holding or loving or for solid information about the changes they are experiencing. It's a time of seesawing up and down between the babies they were and the teenagers they are becoming.

The middle years of parenthood are characterized by ambiguity. Our kids are no longer helpless, but neither are they independent. We are still active parents, but we have more time now to concentrate on our personal needs. Our children's world has expanded; it is not enclosed within a kind of magic dotted line drawn by us. Although we are still the most important adults in their lives, we are no longer the only significant adults.

The whole process of letting go takes vivid shape during the middle parenting years. There are no rules to follow: we simply have to watch and learn and act in ways that feel right to us at the time. Lots of battles are fought during these years as we and our children try to negotiate our separateness and our connectedness. We are becoming more independent of each other, but the ties are deep – deeper perhaps than in any other human relationship.

4. The Teenage Years

Jeanne Jacobs Speizer

As with any other stage in our lives or in our child's life, there is rarely a precise moment when we are sure that we have entered a new period; no one arrives at our door and announces to us that our child's adolescence has begun. Sometimes it is signalled by the onset of the menstrual period, a voice changing, a new moodiness or a sense of fuller involvement in life outside the family.

Many of us begin to anticipate the teenage years long before our children have entered them. We hear comments like 'Enjoy them now because . . .' or 'These are the easy years, but . . .' Some parents' stories are certain to give us pause; a friend may tell us:

I wasn't prepared for how painful it is for my child to be a teenager. I know how I suffered when I was a teenager, I remember it was an agonizing time of my life when I thought I was horrible and unattractive, and nobody ever liked me – you know, all those awful things. Somehow I thought my children would escape a lot of this, but they haven't.

Other reports can make us eager to be there:

I like it better for me now. I'm not in a place where I want to be the mother of young children. I appreciate that my children are adolescents. There's a lot that I want to do for me, with me, or with the people I'm involved with.

I can see my kids turning into unique people whom I'm really glad to know. Part of who they are seems to come from what we've been in their lives, and part of it is completely original. For example, my son's sense of humour is something he gets from neither me nor his father, and I find myself surprised to be living with this very funny, nearly grown person.

For some of us there may be an extended waiting period for the arrival of adolescence, as the mother of a fifteen-year-old son describes:

It feels like we are hanging on the edge of a cliff. John and I have a great many fears about what the teenage years will be like, but so far they are fears unrelated to the real situation. Sometimes I think it will be a relief to be actually dealing with teenage issues rather than this unsettling period of waiting.

For others of us, teenage issues may begin even before our children are in their teens. In either case we know from other parents that these years will be tough, but that they will also bring great joys; that there will be a whole mix of feelings during this strenuous, humbling, exasperating, revealing and joyous time of growth for us and our children.

As our children explore further from us, we see them completing a major phase in their lifelong process of becoming themselves. Sometimes we swell with pride to see the development of a strong, capable, independent person. We begin to enjoy the addition to our household of a near adult who shares many of our ideas and values. At other times we find our children challenging all our assumptions or behaving in ways we find intolerable. We are never absolutely sure which part of our teenagers we will see at a given moment, and in fact they will probably change unpredictably back and forth. We may feel that our children are exploring too far and too dangerously. On the other hand, if they do not test the limits at all, we are concerned that they won't be ready for independence. There are genuine causes for worry during these years – such as drugs, alcohol, sexual experimentation, violence in school, fast cars – and thus it is not surprising that we spend a great deal of time thinking of our children.

As parents we may feel that we should be able to clear-sightedly guide our child toward independence. We think there must be a right way, if only we could find it. But parents who have been through these years seem to have learned that there is no right way. Experts can't give any solutions; although they can offer knowledge and advice, we and our child must explore together our way to independence.

This chapter will begin at the point when our child, and perhaps we ourselves, are changing at a very fast pace and exploring, sometimes simultaneously, the edges of freedom and control. We will end at the point when our children have taken the jump toward independence and to a life of their own. In between, we will look at the ways in which we try to establish an adult relationship with them, in which we share love and interdependence while living separate lives.

Living with Teenagers

The first sign that a child is entering adolescence might come as it did for this mother:

The other day Danny came home from school looking despondent. When I asked him what was going on, he said 'I feel totally worthless – have you ever felt that way?' I said 'Of course.' Then he asked me what I did when I felt that way. I said I may go jogging, or take a hot bath. Even though he said those particular suggestions wouldn't help, I could tell that just having the conversation made him feel better. Later on I told him how proud I was that he was able to talk so openly with me about his feelings. To me, that kind of conversation is a welcome sign that he's entering his teenage years.

This father's sign was less pleasurable:

My first awareness of the arrival of adolescence was when my daughter became very silent around the house and stopped sharing any of her outside life with me. When I asked her questions about what she was involved in, she was often sharp and hostile in her answers. She seemed to be saying, It's my life and none of your business.

This mother was forced rather abruptly to recognize that adolescence had arrived:

In our family, the teenage period was heralded dramatically by our oldest son running away at thirteen because we forced him to go to a school graduation. He ran away for two weeks, and this crisis made me really examine what I was doing.

Frequently, unexpected behaviour and a lack of sharing are signs that our child is working hard to develop an identity separate from ours. Although we may recognize this change as an important stage, it may be difficult to find a comfortable way of living with it:

The pain for me is that from being told everything, I was suddenly shut off totally and told nothing – and rejected for even wanting to know.

Some children continue to confide in us. Some seem to want to stake out their territories very clearly as their own. Learning how to respect this need for privacy, while remaining in touch with our children and their needs, is not an easy job. It requires tact and patience and a sense of humour – which are not always easy to come by. When we are faced with what seems like a real lack of information from our children, we may find ourselves asking more and more questions, which may be met with evasions or, sometimes, even outright hostility. We learn to pick our times carefully for talking about important things. At the same time that our teenagers may provide us with less direct information about their lives, we ourselves have less contact with the school and their other activities. Ironically, we often feel excluded from our children's school life unless they get into trouble. During these years we have fewer chances to see how well our children are doing in the outside world. We also have fewer opportunities to meet parents who are sharing similar experiences.

One of the reasons it's sometimes hard to communicate with teenage children is that this is a moody period of life for many of them:

I never know in what mood my teenagers will return from school. The mood in which they left in the morning is no predictor for the afternoon. So as each child enters the house, I say hello and go on about my business.

Parents who do not live with their teenage children often find the mood swings even more difficult because they see their children only at arranged times. This father of two teenagers talked about how he has handled what feels like the possibility of losing communication with his teenage daughter at a crucial period in her growth:

Wendy is often withdrawn and silent on our visits. Many times I fill in these moments by talking about my life and sharing with her stories from my younger years. Last week in the middle of one of my stories, she interrupted me and began to share a similar story from her own life. By the end of that visit we had both shared a lot about ourselves and felt very close.

As parents of teenagers, we try to be tolerant of a wide range of behaviour, parts of which we are not always comfortable with – but we try not to do this at the price of our own self-respect and the whole family's need for peace. Sometimes it feels as though the teenagers themselves, through their shifting moods, are controlling the emotional tone of the family – not a constructive situation for us or for them. Rules of mutual tolerance need to be and can be developed, sometimes by talking it out as a family and sometimes by getting help from someone else (see the Families chapter on the family as a system). For many of us, developing these modes of mutual tolerance and respect is one of the chief enterprises of family life during these years.

Sepp Seitz/Magnum

When our teenagers are uncommunicative or surly or even derisive, it hurts. We may respond by choosing for a while not to try to talk to them at all, or we may shout in anger and frustration. There are also occasions when we are cool, concise and clear about what we want our children to hear and know. However we respond at any given time, we have to remind ourselves that our children are people separate from us and that we cannot allow their interactions with us to interfere with how we feel about ourselves – though this is often easier said than done.

Underlying many of our feelings about the unevenness of communication with our teenagers is our concern about the serious issues which they may be confronting in their lives. Well-founded or not, there are those moments when all our worries come to the fore, as the mother of a sixteen-year-old daughter says:

I expected Agnes home from the party at twelve. She finally arrived at one-fifteen and explained that the car had broken down. During the long waiting time many questions and worries raced through my mind. Had she been in a car accident? Had she been assaulted trying to get home? Should I call her at the party? What if she didn't tell me the right place, or they tell me the party was over hours ago, or they say to me 'You mean you don't know where your daughter is?' Should I call the police? Is it too soon to be upset? Why does she do this to me – what am I doing up at this hour when I have to go to work tomorrow? Perhaps I'm over-reacting – but then, could I be under-reacting? Have I talked to her about the dangers of drinking and driving, of drugs, of rape? Does she know about contraception? She's too young to be out this late – have I been lax in my job as a parent? When she gets home, should I be pacing the floor in front of the door, in my room with the light on or in my room with the light off? What am I doing worrying so much? She is certainly sensible and if there was trouble, she would have called me. What if she can't call? What should I be doing?

Daily we see our children doing things or responding to us in ways which if carried to extremes would be a signal of trouble. Our child has a few drinks, cuts some classes, is evasive about where s/he has been, or gets home late, and we try to decide if these actions are stages through which all teenagers pass and therefore do not need a response from us, or if the child is in trouble and we should step in and try to help. We ask ourselves if we are hiding our heads and ignoring obvious indications of problems because we find it too painful to face the possiblity that our child is in trouble. When we are unsure of how to respond or even if we should, it is helpful to turn to other adults whom we trust and share with them our dilemmas. There may be friends, or a group of parents who have gotten together to talk, let's say, about children and drugs; sometimes a therapist or family counsellor will be more what we need (see the Helping chapter).

This form of sharing can sometimes be very difficult during the teen years, as this mother of three sons describes:

A strange thing happened when the children became pre-adolescent. I experienced a dramatic breaking away from the old custom of sharing experiences and advice with my friends . . . a reluctance, a shyness, an embarrassment almost to talk about these new, more psychological, less developmental problems. It was the beginning of the Great Silence. Except with very intimate friends, and then in an offhand way, we stopped communicating except in mock despair over our experiences. Somehow this silence is linked to pride – of hoping our children will make it. Suddenly we became competitive about our kids, and while we may talk and exult about the tangible successes our children garner, there is a big, deep silence about the problems these youngsters have and our problems of dealing with them in the family. I wish we could help each other not to be alone in feeling perplexed and upset with our puzzling, ego-bristling, ego-bruising creatures known as teenagers.

Perhaps it is pride or competitiveness which keeps us from reaching out to each other to gain a better perspective. Or perhaps we do not reach out to other adults because we are embarrassed or we feel we are betraying our children if we discuss their problems or our problems with them 'in public'. We need, however, to overcome our hesitancy about sharing with other parents so that we can lessen our feelings of isolation during these years.

As we search for ways to communicate with and provide care and nurturance for our often unpredictable teenagers, we find that our approach has to be flexible and to change as our child changes. One mother had to share something about herself if she wanted to hear from her son:

I felt a little bit closer with my seventeen-year-old son when I began to share with him about what it was like for me at his age – about dating and how hard it was sometimes. When I began to talk about those things, about myself when I was a kid, he began to talk about different things about himself.

A father found:

Accepting my sixteen-year-old daughter where she is with very little preaching and judgement is how I am able to communicate with her. To be sensitive and available – just to be there for her when she wants to talk to me as a father.

We may find that there are times when our offer to help is received with hostility and rejection. Some parents, like this father, have chosen to stand back and wait for their children to approach them:

I try to be available and flexible and let my sixteen-year-old son signal when he wants to talk to me. Of course, days can go by without any interaction except about the weather, and then when I least expect it he starts to talk, and we might spend hours talking about issues of great importance to us both.

There are periods of time during the teenage years when we cannot seem to talk to our children. At these moments our children sometimes find they can turn more easily to other adults:

The other night at supper, our nineteen-year-old was talking about where he's going to live next year and suddenly he exclaimed that we, his parents, kept him a prisoner. He thrust the table on its side so that the dishes landed on my lap, and stormed out of the house. Anna and I sat there stunned by his rage. I found out next day that he had stormed out to a neighbour's house and mowed their lawn while the woman, a family friend, walked about with him and listened to the whole story.

The patterns of communication that our family falls into during the teenage years will help determine both how comfortably we make it through this time and how we will interact later on as adults. As with most aspects of parenting teenagers, there are moments when we find ourselves talking to sensible, responsible near-adults who feel like new friends who share our values and beliefs. These wonderful times are followed, sometimes instantly, by confrontations with sullen, shouting children who act as if we were the enemy from whom they must escape. Our own feelings grow confused, we feel sympathetic, then resentful, wanting to help them and yet wishing sometimes they would go off somewhere and leave us alone.

Living with Ourselves

One of the things which makes these years both difficult and interesting is that even as our children are searching for an identity separate from ours, we may at the same time be looking more closely at who *we* are and where we are going. A feeling of unrest, unsureness and curiosity may pervade us as we try to chart the years to come. Our household begins to feel like an arena in which two generations are simultaneously exploring their identities. Perhaps some of the foreboding we feel about the arrival of the teenage years is grounded in our recognition that we, as well as our children, will be looking inward at ourselves during this time. This search for a refreshed sense of our identity can feel like a sudden crisis or it can come on slowly as it did for this man:

Around my fortieth birthday I began to feel that my life was ending. My work was no longer exciting, my children were preparing to leave me, I felt old, and I couldn't think of anything to look forward to but retirement.

It can also feel quite exciting, as it did for this woman:

All of a sudden I realized that a great deal of ferment was happening inside me. I felt like I was an adolescent again. I wasn't sure who I was or where I was going, but I felt happy to be exploring these new parts of myself.

Age is not really the crucial factor in this mid-life search: how we feel about ourselves and how open we are to new thoughts seem to be more pertinent. Yet we often focus on our age and how old we feel. What we don't talk about and what is frequently hidden under our conversation about age is that, as one woman said, 'I am thirty-eight but I feel thirteen!' We often remark that we would not like to have to go through adolescence again. Perhaps what we are really saying is that in fact we are experiencing a similar period and it is very painful.

A re-examination seems to happen for most people, whether or not they are parents of teenagers. But having teenagers prompts the search in its own way. As one mother observes:

My teenagers are really having a painful time trying to figure out who they are and what they are and how they fit into the world, and is life worth living or is the whole thing just incomprehensible and meaningless. A lot of questions they are asking are ones I once kidded myself I had the answers to, but now I see that I really don't, and it's a touchy time for me.

As parents, we may find our identity search intensified by the presence of young, vibrant people who have most of their lives ahead of them; who are planning for new careers when we may have reached a plateau in ours; who have available to them new and different life styles and relationships; who are not tied down and can travel and explore; who are perhaps stronger, sexier and more capable than ever before; and who are making plans to leave the household and us behind. As parents of teenagers, we may be made to face daily, by the sheer presence of our children, a reminder that our years of active parenting are nearly finished and we need to re-examine our past and search for a path or goal which we can pursue with energy in our new life.

Anonymous

Fifteen years later

The presence of teenagers in our household can stimulate creative changes in us. Our children are open to experimentation and they welcome new ideas and thoughts. Their excitement and enthusiasm may re-awaken for us our own joy at exploring new ways to do things and new ideas to embrace. A mother asserts:

I give Laura a lot of credit for starting growth processes in me which I don't think would have happened in quite the same way if she hadn't been trying herself to be a really open kind of person, urging people around her to do the same.

Sometimes our near-grown children become our teachers as they introduce us to new approaches to old problems and as they help us, or force us, to explore our long-held values and beliefs about such things as politics, religion, life styles and sexuality.

We stand at the midpoint in our lives, looking both forward and backward. We look forward as we plan for a time when our children will no longer be living with us; at the same time we look backward because our children's experiences make us relive many of our own adolescent issues and transitions. As we try to help our children figure things out, we may be helping ourselves re-examine those issues and perhaps have new insights about ourselves.

Being in our own period of ferment, perhaps self-doubt, opens us at times to feeling competitive with our teenage children. We may experience some jealousy as we see them with freedoms and options that were not available to us in our youth. If we have worked hard to make our children's lives better than ours were, we are upset when they seem to be misusing their opportunities or taking them too much for granted. Our feelings of competition might appear in the intellectual or emotional realm, as it did for this father:

I found that my daughter was ahead of me in many areas of intellectual life and some areas of emotional life. My response was to be overbearing in an intellectual discussion, and I tended to shut her out. I would discourage and anger her and then she wouldn't pursue conversations with me.

Or we may find ourselves feeling competitive in the sexual arena, as this mother and father report:

I've noticed that I want to be considered attractive by boys who are there to see my daughter. I don't want to attract them in a heavy sexual kind of way, but I do want them to see me as attractive.

As a single, male parent, some of the women I'm drawn to are close to my daughter's age – closer to her age than mine. She sometimes feels threatened by that, but I'm a social person and I won't stop dating because of her feelings.

One of the nagging questions in this period is: just how old or young are we anyway?

Sometimes I find myself wondering how someone as young as I could possibly be the mother of children who seem so old.

In becoming young adults, our children seem to nudge us over into middle age when our self-image might not be ready for that – and our competitive feelings, if we have them, may be a sign of our resistance. The fact that we have teenage children does not mean that we must change our image of ourselves, and yet we often do. One mother realized that her image had changed when she went to an old movie she had seen as an adolescent and found herself, this time, identifying not with the adolescent heroine but with the middle-aged parents of the heroine.

Other parents report a sense of shock at the moment when they realize that their image has changed:

Is it possible that I am one of 'those parents'? I remember all the conversations I had with my friends about 'parents', and now my children are having those types of conversations. Overnight I feel like the villain in the piece.

As our children become more grown up, and as we begin to open our minds and listen to new ideas, some of which our children may have introduced us to, we may find ourselves wondering at some point how to balance being their friend with being their parent:

I try to be friends with my children and understand what it is the youth of today are saying. My friends often say to me 'Act your age', and I wonder what age they think I am – seventy-six?

Sometimes when I buy clothes, I find myself wondering if they will be the same type which my daughter might buy. I want to be attractive and dress well, but I don't want to be seen as trying to look like my daughter.

How do we find the time to pay attention to our own searching? We are still actively responsible for our teenagers, and though they need less physical attention from us, they need an increasing amount of emotional attention as they experience the highs and lows of adolescence. As one father said, 'The accent is on youth, but the stress is on parents.' We can feel angry at the little time we have for contemplating our own issues. It is crucial for us to take time for ourselves and stick firmly to it so that we, as well as our teenagers, can explore our lives and make new decisions for ourselves.

The search for our new identity often entails a changing relationship with our own parents. During our children's adolescence, we often become even more aware of our middle position between our parents and our children. We may want to delve deeper into our past as we try to plan for our future. Our parents shared our past, and we often want to talk to them and re-examine what really happened to us when we were younger. A woman whose mother died when she was young lamented when she reached middle age that she had lost that opportunity: 'My mother took my childhood with her when she died and now I feel rootless and unsure how to proceed.' As we see our parents getting older, we may begin to try to develop a new, more adult relationship which might be similar to the relationship we are trying to establish with our children. The moments of sharing might be very beneficial, as this man found:

I called my mother on my fortieth birthday to tell her how old I was feeling, and she laughed and said 'That's young. Wait until you're my age to feel old.' Hers was the first helpful comment I had heard all day.

During the time when we are parenting teenagers we may begin to notice a subtle shift in our responsibilities as the middle generation. Our parents may begin to lean on us more and to shift the balance to one where we begin to parent them as well as our children:

When my father was ill, I found myself in a role reversal with him at the same time that I had to give my mother the support she had always gotten from my father. I felt overwhelmed, as I had to add a new role to my roles as wife and mother of three daughters.

Sometimes our teenage children gain new insights from their grandparents which help us in our interaction with them. A mother recounts:

After visiting her grandmother's house, my daughter developed a real compassion for my growing up. She seems to understand how difficult life must have been for me and she sees me in a new perspective.

Or our parents help us with our teenagers:

My mother said to me 'Don't worry. If it doesn't interfere with her health, let it be.' I have always remembered her comment, and it gives me a guide to live by through the teenage years.

Sometimes the interactions aren't so helpful. Our parents may still be unwilling to give up the 'right' to look over our shoulders and correct or instruct us:

My sick mother, who can't even remember her own phone number, still manages to berate me for my son's long hair and for my kids' having 'no religion'.

Whether we feel strengthened or overwhelmed by our key position in the generation cycle of our family, the feeling of being in the middle heightens for us our need to find space for ourselves so that we can also sort out who we are and where we are going.

The mid-life exploration of new dimensions in ourselves varies somewhat for women and men who have performed more traditional family roles. Although these roles are currently in flux, enough parents of teenagers today started out in fairly traditional roles so that it is worth giving some space here to their particular transitions. We will first explore the position of the many women who have stayed home to be the primary parent or who worked but still maintained primary responsibility for the family, and then the position of men who have had their work as a primary focus and their family as a secondary one. For the women, we consider the chief new movement is away from the home; for the men, it is toward it.

Women

With tears streaming down her face, a woman whose youngest child will be leaving for college in a year said 'I am experiencing what my friends said they experienced, but I have decided not to be what is commonly labelled a "depressed, empty-nest mother".' Another woman briskly stated 'I am busier than usual keeping up with the needs and problems of my adolescents and I don't have time to stop and think about myself.' A third woman said 'I feel that when the time comes, I will be really young and have a whole lot left to do with my life.' These three women are nearing the end of parenting teenagers, and they are responding in different ways to how they think their lives will be when their children have left their home – a time when they must shift their primary focus from their role as parent to something else.

The first realization that our life pattern is changing often comes with the recognition that the children are more independent and need less parenting:

I suddenly realized that my youngest child does not need me so much any more and I am unsure of what to do. So much of my identity is involved in being needed by my children that I have trouble imagining myself in another role.

Or, perhaps, the realization that we need a new focus for our lives comes as a result of a time of big emotional upheaval, as it did for this mother of three sons:

This past summer was a nightmare of pain over the letting-go syndrome with my teenaged sons plus the newer pain of moving my newly widowed mother to Florida, the week after my son was in surgery. I felt I would be consumed – there would be nothing left inside me but ashes, because all my energies were directed toward worrying about them. One day my friend stopped me short with her observation: 'Betty, what worries me is you. You aren't thinking about yourself. What about doing something for you?'

Once we realize that we must do something for ourselves and find a new focus for our lives, we may discover that we do not know who we are besides being a mother and housewife:

I said to my family that I want to find out who I am. I've been so much of them for so long that I really don't know who 'me' is any more. I made plans to go away for a couple of days in order to have some talks with myself. I wanted to find me, and I knew that when I came back they would know me better, too.

When a woman who has not worked outside the home begins to explore who she is as a first step toward deciding who she will be, she may think of herself as having been 'only a housewife'. What makes this image so poignant and painful for a woman in mid-life is that she especially feels the weight of her years and the length of the time she has been out of the 'big world':

I knew I had to do something, but I didn't know what I was good for. I was not equipped for a decent job that would be satisfying; I was not trained in any capacity that's recognized and rewarded by the work world. That was when I decided to go back to school.

It is really tough for a woman to get a decent job after being out of the job market for a long time. We have to learn to muster and value the many talents we have been using in our families and our community and use these to help us get a job. Even when we do find satisfying work, however, the transition is one to be reckoned with. We may worry that if we become too involved with other things our children will fare badly without our constant attention. A woman who took a job she liked very much talks about the first year of her job in this way:

Around four each day I began to watch the clock and wonder and worry how my children were doing. I felt guilty not being there when they got home from junior high and high school. Approximately once a week I would finish work early and come dashing home. I would run up the stairs, throw open the door and announce in a loud voice that I was home. Frequently I didn't find anyone home because they had after-school activities. On those times when there was a child home, s/he would say hello and continue doing homework. Toward the end of the year I realized that my children really didn't need me home when they arrived, and, in fact, I was rushing home because of a feeling of guilt or need on my part rather than for their need.

Teenage children often relish their independence, and we, as parents, frequently find that we are clinging to them more than they are clinging to us.

Outside interests and responsibilities can provide us with a sense of affirmation and independence:

I found my relationship with my children became much better as I began to feel better about myself. I have been very busy with my work activities and that seems to make my children feel better about me and our relationship. My son jokingly says that he knows now that when he leaves I won't feel abandoned, and I think he's right.

This woman approached her children's decreasing dependence with another strategy:

When I was forty, we adopted a child. It was another chance to start over again. We thought we'd do it differently this time. I had the need to still be a mother, and adopting met that need.

The mid-life identity search for women who have spent many years with a primary focus on their role as mother is a chance to develop and grow in previously unexplored ways. When her children are in their early teens, a woman has an opportunity to lay the groundwork for the later years when they will no longer be home. She can choose to go to a school, learn a new trade, develop new interests or take many other options which might not have been available to her mother a generation ago. Exploring these options and making decisions for ourselves during the years when we are parenting teenagers will give us the opportunity to find other facets of ourselves.

Men

When a man who has had to focus his time and energy primarily on his job reaches the midpoint of his life and begins to reassess his priorities, he may begin to question the balance between his work life, his home life and his leisure life. He might find that he is unhappy with the way he is spending his time: 'On occasion I have said "My God, I only have so many years left in my life and there are things I want to do for myself and by myself."' Some men look closely at their time at home and their relationship with their teenage children and discover that they are not satisfied:

I found that I was always pulled somewhere else. I was home a lot, but my mind and thoughts were elsewhere. I realized that my wife had the daily caring relationship with the children. I was the special parent. I'm the one who came in on crises only.

Fathers of teenagers in more traditionally oriented families are likely to have begun their parenting years with the assumption that they would not be the primary parent. However, when the children turn teenagers and become involved with issues and decisions which the man can remember from his own teen years, he may reconsider:

I am more involved with my children than I've been in a long time. They are more like people now whom I can relate to. They are at a place which is more familiar to me.

Some men find that re-entering their children's lives at this late date is not as easy as they may have anticipated:

The most important thing I ever did was to have children. Now that they're older, I want to develop a closer relationship with them, but when I'm around them I find that I don't know how to talk to them or to get them to talk to me. I have trouble making contact with them.

The problem for men who have not been actively involved with parenting their children until the teen years is that they need to enter an environment which up until that time has been considered a traditionally female place. A man may have to learn how to 'hang out', as this father of four teenagers describes:

I was feeling very isolated from my teenagers because I just didn't know what was going on in their lives. I began coming home earlier and spending more time in the house, but my teenagers still didn't share with me – they left me alone. Finally I talked with my wife about my feelings of loneliness, and she was able to point out to me that though I was home I always appeared to be busy. I didn't know how to 'hang around' and appear approachable. I began to spend more time in the kitchen and den and soon I found my children with me. After a while they began to tell me more about their day, and at the same time I began to tell them more about my day.

When a man decides to try to become closer to his children during their adolescent years, he might want more family times together. Yet teenagers tend to be drawn more and more out of the family toward friends, and this can make a father feel rejected:

My teenagers seem not to want to spend time with me. They prefer to be with their friends or alone. I remember all those years they would beg me to play with them or to do something and I was too busy – now I wish I had said yes.

This father discovered some surprising new ways of being with his children:

I found to my amazement that my adolescents began to find me an interesting person the more I got involved in household responsibilities. They seemed to think I was now a real part of the family rather than just a nightly visitor. Now I realize we don't have to go on family gatherings to share. We can share while making dinner or cleaning house.

Like the adolescent years, the years of our mid-life identity search seem difficult, unsettling and full of important, even painful, decisions for us. Often in talking about them we tend to emphasize the more distressing aspects of how we are feeling. Yet there is also excitement and the opportunity to look back over our lives and decide how we will live the second half. When we were adolescents, we lacked the maturity and experience to anticipate where our decisions would lead us. Now we have a clearer vision of who we are, and we know our own strengths and weaknesses better. Our children need us less and we have more time to concentrate on ourselves. This new-found free time without children allows us to focus more attention on who we are, to centre on learning more about our relationships, and to begin to engage in activities which fill our needs. It is a time of new learning and incredible growth, and though such times can be unsettling, they are also exhilarating.

Couple Relationship

If we are parenting teenagers as a couple, we may find that maintaining our balance during these unsettled years is at times complicated by the need to negotiate with our partner. At other times we are likely to feel ourselves strengthened by the presence of another adult who is as caring and as involved as we are.

Before the teen years, as we have seen, we may have been so busy with our children and so focused on their problems and growth that we postponed exploring our own relationship as a couple. Now that we are parenting teenagers, there seem to be even more issues on which to focus. The shared anxiety of parenting teenagers can lead to increased communication and closeness for a couple, as this father points out:

My wife and I have always been able to communicate about the kids. As they became adolescents, there was even more we needed to talk about. Our problems with them – the not knowing what to do or if what we were doing was the right thing – has brought us closer.

Joint parenting can also bring disagreements that can drive couples apart:

Barnard and I always found it easy to agree on what our children should and shouldn't do when they were younger. However, since they have become teenagers we are in constant disagreement – especially over our daughter. Every time she leaves the house he thinks she is running wild and defying him. He questions her before she leaves, waits up for her, and then questions her extensively when she returns. He accuses me of being lax and not caring enough about her to become involved. I accuse him of driving her to being wild because he so obviously expects it and can't trust her. His fights with me over her, and with her over her every action, are a constant source of friction in our house.

As we argue, discuss and worry about our teenagers, we may forget that there are other facets to our relationship unrelated to our roles as parents. If we are focusing exclusively on the children, we may be avoiding other important issues for us as adults and as partners. Perhaps we have always – up till now – ignored these issues, as this woman tells us:

When the children were smaller, problems with our relationship would crop up that we needed to deal with. But we didn't. We just submerged them. Now the children are changing dramatically, and we find that we have to face things in our married life that we had taken for granted or smoothed over while the children were small.

We may wonder if our relationship contains enough strong, independent aspects unrelated to our roles as parents. Our differences may seem far greater than our similarities when we first begin to re-explore our relationship, as this woman describes:

I want Lucas to fill more of my needs which, somehow, when we were very busy bringing up the children, I allowed him not to fulfil. Now I won't let that happen any more – I have needs for intimacy, for communication, for support and for encouragement.

As we look to our partners to fill more of our needs, we may find that they are unable or unwilling to change. Our asking for such changes may scare or upset them, and we may have to look outside the relationship to find people who can better fill our needs. Alternatively, our partner may welcome the chance to explore more deeply our ties. The years of shared experiences and common memories may prove to be a solid foundation on which to develop a more intimate, sharing partnership. A man who has been married twenty years recounts:

We are trying to build a new relationship between the two of us. It's almost as if we are newly married – doing things we never did when we were newly married.

If we decide to explore our couple relationship and to build new ties and bonds, we often find that our need to spend more time together is hindered by our teenagers. If we want to explore sexual intimacy, the presence of teenagers in the household does not leave many moments for being alone or intimate. 'There never seems to be a romantic evening at home,' sighed the mother of three teenagers. In fact there may be many more evenings at home without our teenagers actually in the house, or many quiet moments while they are busy doing their homework, but the problem is that we can never be sure when they will come home or come out of their rooms.

As we set up boundaries around times when we are to be left alone and not bothered, we may find that the only place where we can be sure to be alone is our bedroom, and sometimes we feel like prisoners huddled together and excluded from the rest of the house which has become our children's territory. Our strivings for more privacy – which often means more time in our bedroom – may cause us to feel embarrassed by so obvious a gesture of sexuality. We may try to wait until our children have gone to bed, a plan which requires more stamina than most of us have, since our teenagers often stay up later than we do, as this couple reports:

Our privacy is gone! 'They' are everywhere, and 'they' never seem to need any sleep. How can we continue to be intimately involved and exploring new ways to relate when 'they' never go to bed and are always home – at unexpected times.

The first and most difficult step seems to be to convey to our children and ourselves that we want and deserve privacy for intimate relations. One couple talked about spending weekends away so that they could have uninterrupted time together. Couples at all stages of parenting have the same need for privacy, but parents of teenagers may have to take more assertive steps to gain that privacy.

Our teenagers are acutely aware of our interactions as a couple. They become skilled at manipulating us – sometimes smoothing the way and other times hindering all our attempts at communication. For example, a teenager may jump into a discussion or argument and align herself with her father as she insists he is obviously correct in his view. As she adds her comments and ideas, the mother may feel isolated or ganged up on and either withdraw from the interaction or continue to argue, though recognizing the futility of continuing. On another day or another issue the teenager may join her mother or point out a middle ground and help the adults reach a compromise. In either case, the partners need to seek time to talk to each other without their teenagers present, so that they can listen better to each other without an extra person interrupting.

Our children also tend to be very critical and judgemental about us as adults and as a couple, as this father illustrates:

My children are always watching us. They never fail to point out when we do something they disapprove of. They keep suggesting how my wife and I could improve our relationship.

We may need to sort out how we really feel about the way we relate and to try to keep our children's opinions in the right perspective. In the end it will be our decision as to whether we will continue together, and we must be clear about our own views, separate from how our teenagers feel. As we struggle to better understand ourselves and our partners we may find moments of sharing which justify all our struggling:

One night after a big disagreement about how to handle our teenagers, we stayed up all night talking to each other. It was very rich — and beautiful and painful. We began to discuss how we perceive things and where we were different. We were dealing with some of those issues for the first time.

During the teen years a man may want or be forced to become more involved with parenting his children. What may immediately surface is that he and his wife have basic differences in style and approach to parenting which have not been disruptive as long as one person was making the majority of the decisions. Or even if such differences have arisen in the past, they often seemed easier to resolve through some sort of compromise because they were on issues which were fairly distant from the adults' memories. Compromises become more difficult during the teen years not only because the parents are trying to negotiate their own differences, but also because the teenagers are actively campaigning for what they want:

My husband responds with anger when he feels himself being pushed too hard by our fourteen-year-old daughter or when he feels out of control in a situation. I tend to retreat from the scene and try to smooth things over. At the end of an argument with her, we fight, sometimes for hours, over how we both handled the situation. I am furious with him for losing his temper and he is furious with me for retreating. One day we recognized how lonely and isolated we were feeling and how often our daughter was getting her way as a result of our disagreements. We decided to try and support each other and to try and understand better why we responded so differently.

Sometimes we find that we are not able to support each other as parents. Then we may feel that our children, and we ourselves, are the losers:

My children are much freer than I want them to be. My wife and I disagree about the boundaries and the rules and that seems to put a minimum of constraints on our teenagers because if one of us won't let them do something, inevitably the other one will.

The years when we are parenting teenagers may be full of moments when we feel incredibly good about our ability to solve our differences and work harmoniously as a couple, as well as moments when we feel discouraged and disheartened to find ourselves disagreeing so profoundly over seemingly insoluble issues. However, there may be times when we are grateful to the other person:

Sometimes when my son or daughter has done or said something outrageous, my husband and I will look at each other and one of us will make an obscene gesture. Then we'll laugh because it means we both feel the same way, and when we laugh about it we gain proper perspective.

Sexuality

Our children's sexual development may come long before we expect it, or long afterward. In either case we recognize that we are no longer dealing with a young child but with a budding adult. The sheer size of teenage children brings this point home to us, as this mother describes:

During a few short months, both my sons passed me in height and my daughter started wearing platform shoes. I had suddenly been transformed from the second tallest person in my family to the shortest. I literally felt that I must be shrinking!

We may find ourselves living with sons whose voices sound like men's, or a daughter whose sexual development causes us to say to ourselves:

Am I hearing right? Are the men I know saying to me 'Who's that woman? She's such a beauty!' Yes, I guess they do mean my daughter and she's no longer my 'little baby'. But what a relief that I am no longer the only woman who lives in my house! I feel less alone now, because I can talk to her about women's issues.

Watching our children develop sexually, we may be proud of their growth, anxious about their uncertainty and experimentation, sad at the reminder of our own 'lost youth', jealous of their sexual blossoming – or some of each of these. Whatever we are feeling at any one moment, we are brought up against our own feelings about sexuality – for ourselves and for our children. Living with teenagers makes us confront every day our own sexual questions, practices, beliefs and values.

Many of us have tried to be open in telling our children about sex since they were small. We did not flinch when they asked intricate and even what felt like embarrassing questions; we gave them as honest answers as possible. Now our children are facing these questions first-hand in their lives, and it's important that we be there for them still. Our child may be trying to make sense of menstruation or wet dreams, deciding whether to sleep with someone or 'how far to go', or figuring out what kind of birth control to use. Chances are, they aren't getting reliable information in school in a form that's emotionally accessible to them. We know that teenagers these days are experimenting more with sex at an earlier age, and are having to deal earlier with the related problems of contraception, VD, pregnancy, abortion and all the inevitable emotional ups and downs of sexual relationships. It's a crucial time for us to offer them the information and emotional support they need, or to make sure that these are available to them in some way. Yet there may be hesitation and resistance on both sides.

For our part, we may feel shy – we are no longer talking of future experiences, but about present or fast-approaching events in our teenagers' and our own lives. As we try to find a level of sharing which will put them at their ease without violating our own or their sense of privacy, we have few models: most of our parents didn't talk with us in this way. We may want to discourage our children from jumping casually into bed with their boyfriends and girlfriends, but we've learned from our own growing-up experience that interdictions don't work so well. And sex *is* a private experience – we want to respect our children's sense of privacy while signalling to them we are willing and available to help. With such an intensely charged topic, chances are we're not going to do it without some bumbling!

Our teenagers themselves may not be easily approachable. Since they are a lot more private than they used to be, with a healthy resistance to too many questions, we may not know what they are doing or thinking about sex. Often they prefer to talk to their friends, although there they may be getting questionable information. They may be unwilling to talk to us because, as the mother of two sons said,

My children think their own experiences are absolutely unique to them and that I couldn't possibly relate to, or be competent to deal with, their special problems.

A response such as this mother got may make us want to shout at them that we aren't so old and that we've coped with many different sexual situations in our lives and would like to be able to help them.

On the other hand, our children's unwillingness to talk to us about sex because they see us as 'too old', or 'out of it', may tap our own underlying fears that at 'our age' we are not as sexual as they are. In fact, how we talk with our teenagers about sex may have a lot to do with where we are in our own sex life. Many of us may feel we have put our sexuality aside, so to speak, for the demanding years of parenting; or we may have avoided doing something about a long-time sexual dissatisfaction in our relationships. Sex for this reason might be an extra tough topic for us. If our own sexual life feels alive and rewarding to us, we may talk more easily and affirmingly with our children about their emerging sexuality.

Despite possible hesitations and resistances on both sides, however, we have to keep trying. Sometimes we find ourselves in conversations about sex and relationships that we wouldn't have imagined when our children were younger, and which seem to get easier and more open each time after the initial ice-breaking. In other cases, we see that we aren't the best person to talk to our child and try to make sure s/he gets the information and support some other way.

Some of us assume that if we have been factual and direct with our children about sex, they, and we, will be able to handle rationally the issues which might arise as they progress through their teen years. However, sexuality rarely lends itself to rational consideration, as this father found the first time his fourteen-year-old daughter told him she had a boyfriend:

When I heard Stephanie was dating a twenty-year-old boy I was alarmed and concerned. Did she know enough to have such an old boyfriend? Was she sleeping with him? Alice and I began to fight about appropriate contraception for a girl her age; about what we should say to her; about our reactions to her dating. All our worries, prejudices and unexplored ideas came to our minds, and the more we talked, the more we became furious with each other. We had always prided ourselves on how open we were about sex and had assumed that we would easily accept our children's sexual development. Now, here was the first time when we had to think about Stephanie having intercourse, and Alice and I were fighting.

As our children begin to explore their sexuality, we face issues which may be new to us. For example, what if our child is exploring homosexual feelings or has decided s/he is gay? How does this affect us and our feelings about ourselves and our children? What if our child is sleeping with a different person every night? Or is pregnant? Have we failed them? What are their actions telling us? Is there something we should be doing to help them? Sexuality is frequently a prime area in which teenagers test out their autonomy and their emerging identity. It may be that our children will in fact rebel against us through sexual actions which we aren't comfortable with and which we fear will hurt them. Sometimes it is our very tendency to worry which signals for our children the way they can most effectively push out against us.

Whether we see ourselves as traditional or progressive in our views about sexuality, we may not, in the end, have very much of a say over how our children will handle this aspect of their lives. They are near adults and we can't, as we did with younger children, absolutely prevent their doing what they want. Many of us learned in our own youth that when parents 'forbid' sexual activity it rarely stops children from experimenting anyway; but it does leave them unable to turn to us with middle-ground questions that they need to talk about. We can talk with them, reason with them; we can try to examine together our sense of the possible alternatives and consequences. But in the end they choose.

We live in a society marked by a sexual double standard. Women have traditionally been expected to be careful and chaste, men to be aggressive and sexually active. Although in the past few years we have seen some change, as parents we may find ourselves caught between the old double standard in which we were raised and the new emerging single standard. We may instinctively be more tolerant of our son's sexual experimentation and more protective or restrictive with a daughter. (Unfortunately, the possibilities of pregnancy and rape do make our daughters more vulnerable.) Some of us have enjoyed taking a part in helping along the new single standard, by talking carefully with our sons about their responsibility for birth control.

As our children develop, we may find ourselves responding to their new attractiveness with sexual feelings. A mother said:

Now and then I'll feel a surge of attraction to one of my teenage kids. I certainly wouldn't act on it, but I experience it as a nice, lively responding to their emerging sexuality.

A mother of an eighteen-year-old son says:

Sometimes I find myself close to flirting with Sam's eighteen-year-old friends. They are so attractive and sure of themselves that they are often hard to resist.

These feelings may make us vaguely uneasy until we find out how common they are among parents of teenagers. However, there are times when some unspoken limit is passed and we are truly uneasy, as this father attests:

My daughter has become sexually attractive. Until recently she kept sitting on my lap, or walking around almost naked, or cuddling up to me a lot. I found myself very aroused. I restrained myself, but often got angry with myself for responding to her this way. Now I've told her that she has to wear clothes around the house, out of respect for my limits.

We sense that it is important for our children to know that we think they are attractive people, and usually find we can do this best when our sexual interest is invested in other adults, creating an appropriate space between us and our children. A mother put it well:

When I found myself getting somewhat turned on by seeing my sixteen-year-old naked in the hallway, I took that as a signal that it was time to widen the space between us so that he could do his growing.

Our teenagers tend to be preoccupied with their bodily changes. They seem to be constantly involved with whether they are too tall or too short, attractive or not attractive, too fat or too skinny – the list is never ending. Their anxieties may remind us of that image-conscious period in our own lives. Meanwhile they spend their time combing their hair, shopping, going on eating fads, excessively showering, exercising and generally being concerned about their physical selves. As adults approaching middle age, we may find that we ourselves are again becoming more preoccupied with our physical selves or the changes occurring in our bodies. It could be that these concerns of our children accentuate for us the vigour and youth which our culture tells us is ours no longer. Yet the attention they pay to their bodies may in fact spur us on to get more exercise, eat better, take better care of ourselves and feel better than we have in years.

As sexual beings ourselves, we find that our children's blossoming sexuality opens us to our own sexual consciousness. They may, in fact, be showing the same sexual drive, even wildness, which we experienced at their age, or they may be acting out some of our own sexual fantasies. Seeing the uncertainty and agonizing social self-consciousness that so many teenagers suffer from, we may think, thank heavens, I'm not there any more, and savour the richness of a couple of decades of learning about our bodies and getting comfortable with our sexuality. On the other hand, if we have been sexually monogamous but not happily so, we may see our older teenagers moving in and out of sexual involvements with an ease which piques our own yearning and even makes us feel jealous. If sex is a problem for us, perhaps one that's been swept aside for years, it becomes less possible now to avoid the issue, and we may be prompted finally to talk about it or to get some help. Of course, for some of us the problems continue to get pushed aside as we focus on our children or work or other activities and not on our own relationships.

Our own needs and desires, together with the changing standards in our society, free many of us to experiment more with our own wishes and fantasies than we have ever done before. However, living with teenagers can put some roadblocks in the path of adult experimentation. A separated mother of two teenage sons tells us what happened late one evening as she entered the house:

Tom and I had just walked into the entrance hall when I heard my thirteen-year-old son at the top of the stairs calling down to me 'Mom, do you know what time it is?' I felt like a teenager caught out misbehaving by a strict parent.

Many single parents of adolescents talk about making a conscious effort to decide what they want their children to know and what they want to keep to themselves. As teenagers do not allow for much privacy within the house, the logistics of a private life for a single parent can become very complicated. Yet there can be some nice interactions around a single parent's sexual activity. A single father shares with us an episode which helped him and his daughter feel easier:

I invited a friend to come to dinner and she stayed after the children went to bed. About two in the morning we were hugging in the kitchen and my thirteen-year-old daughter walked in. Without breaking her stride, she got a glass of water, waved at us and left the room. Since that time she seems more comfortable with me. Perhaps seeing me hugging my friend signalled to her that she did not have to be my wife – she could be my daughter, my little girl.

This newly separated woman talked about what happened the first time a man telephoned her; her story ends our examination of sexuality because it catches so much of the mixture of things that are going on in this lively period for parents and children alike:

There I was, a thirty-eight-year-old woman with eighteen-year-old dating skills. When I got off the phone after having nervously accepted a dinner appointment, my fourteen-year-old son, who had been sitting in the kitchen during the call, asked me three questions in rapid-fire order: 'Are you going to marry him? Do I have to call him Father? Are you going to sleep with him?' I answered no to all the questions and then I said to him 'By the way, when you ask someone out I won't ask you "Are you going to marry her? Should I call her Daughter? or Are you going to sleep with her?"' We both burst out laughing. Afterward I realized that his questions had cleared the air between us. He was just young enough to verbalize what we were both thinking about, and now that he has brought the questions out in the open, we can discuss them.

Setting Limits

'It is eleven p.m. Do you know where your children are now?' queries the television announcer. We may respond to that question with an uneasy feeling. We know that we cannot, nor do we want to, watch or direct our teenagers at every moment. We are aware that teenage children are constantly exploring the limits of freedom and control. They are old enough to decide more and more where they want to go and what they want to do. In setting the limits for them that we do, we are trying to balance between letting go and guiding. We hope that we will allow our children the space to explore and develop independent lives while we maintain enough control so that they will be safe during that exploration time. And it's very difficult to do!

We have been involved in limit-setting since our children were small, when somehow it seemed easier. A mother recounts:

When the children were young was the golden years. The children thought independently only in minor ways and they tended to accept my judgement. I thought that we could coast easily out of that period into giving the children more freedom. They would begin to think for themselves and grow up as well-adjusted adults.

Most of us find that we don't 'coast easily out of that period'. As one father said, 'The stakes are so much higher now because the children are beginning to make life decisions and I can see the impact of those decisions.' The stakes are higher – our teenagers may be experimenting with drugs, alcohol, sex, fast cars – and as we try to talk to them, we find ourselves intimidated like this mother confronting a six-foot, sixteen-year-old boy:

It was easy to tell a four-year-old or an eight-year-old what to do. It was appropriate because he was so much smaller than I, obviously a child, and also. frankly, he had little recourse. Now the situation is so much more intimidating, both psychologically and physically, even when what I have to say seems sensible to me.

As with everything else during the teenage years, our children are changing and we are changing. As we find ourselves facing decisions about limits and rules in nearly every area of our children's lives, sometimes we think it would be easy if we could just decide on certain guidelines for all situations and stick to them, but in fact these will change from situation to situation and from child to child.

Remember when we had two-year-olds who said no to everything? We had to decide on what was absolutely essential to their health and safety and enforce those rules stringently while letting up on others, so that we didn't have to have running battles with our young ones all day long. Now, in another shape and form, the same problem arises. Our teenagers need to test all of our rules and limits and we are often surprised to find out how many we have set! As they test limits – often several limits simultaneously – we again have to decide which ones are essential and which ones need to be renegotiated. Finding the balance between protection and freedom is sometimes a more complex task with our teenage daughters than with our sons, as this mother asserts:

My parents were always warning me about being careful and watching where I was going. I began to imagine rapists everywhere and avoided any activity which involved feeling unprotected. I don't want my daughters to have to curb their activities as I did, and yet I find myself thinking about the worst possibilities every time they come home after dark or are involved in an activity which seems adventuresome. I try to protect them only as much or as little as I protect my sons, but often that is hard for me to do.

Although we don't want to treat our girls differently than our boys, the realities of violent assault and rape in our society may make us consider different limits for our daughters.

Our children are more visible to the public now. Our self-image and self-esteem are often very involved with them, and we may feel that what they do reflects on us as parents and as community members. So in addition to being concerned for their health and safety, we naturally feel identified with their behaviour. Sometimes it feels difficult for us to separate our image from our children's and to realize that what they do or say reflects primarily on them as developing adults, rather than on us. At times we may even find ourselves confused about the point at which our identity ends and our children's identity begins – especially after so many years when a great deal of our life encompassed our role as parent. During the teen years we are trying to find a clear line between ourselves and our children and to learn to accept the person whom our child is becoming.

We cannot be with our children all the time, nor do we want to be, but we are unavoidably aware that they are living in an often more dangerous and complicated world than the one we knew. We, and they, are aware of daily pressures from their peers to drink too much, for instance, or to take drugs. They may be the victims of violence at school or on the way to school, as the mother of a son who attends a suburban school points out:

> Peter, who is fifteen, was standing in front of his school waiting for a ride when three boys whom he had seen in school but didn't know came up to him and began to hit and kick him. They took his watch and wallet and left him lying on the sidewalk. Finally, someone came from school to help him and they called me to come get him. As I railed and ranted that such an incident could happen in school, Peter said that students are assaulted frequently but no one seems to do anything about it. Peter then begged me also to not do anything about it because he thought the boys didn't know who he was – they chose him because he was alone. He was afraid that if I made a public complaint they would go out of their way to assault him again. I feel caught between his need to feel safe and his solution as to how that safety can be gotten – by doing nothing. And yet, how can I, and parents like me, try to make the school safer if we don't take any steps?

When incidents like this take place even in school, we begin to wonder if there is anywhere our children can go or anything they can do which is safe. Yet we know that they must learn to live in this potentially dangerous world and that with our help the teenage years could be the best time to gain confidence in their ability to handle what comes up.

'With our help' is unfortunately easier said than done, though it is the 'should' that we hear in our heads when we think to ourselves, A good parent should . . . We often feel uncertain about how to provide help. Do we forbid our children to drink, use drugs, cut too many classes or sleep around? Do we try to enforce rules which will inhibit their actions? Do we make very few rules and assume that our teenagers will be able to make good decisions for themselves? Do we try to find some middle ground, even if it is usually unclear and ill-defined for us all? Most of us do a little of each. Sometimes we set very strict rules and feel furious if we find our children have broken them. Other times we ignore hints that our rules have been overlooked, and hope that our children will be careful and learn from their experimentation how to be independent adults. We may worry a lot that our children are in danger or are harming themselves, but feel uncertain about what we should be doing. We often feel powerless to direct or even influence our teenagers' behaviour and decisions. As the father of three teenagers said, 'The older my children get, the narrower is my authority.' Another father described his feelings succinctly: 'I can guide my children when they ask my advice, but if they don't ask, there's nothing I can do. I don't seem to have control.' Not only do we not have control but we often feel as this mother does: 'Knowledge is power. But with *my* teenagers, *my* knowledge is often powerless.'

As we try to establish limits which allow our children to explore and make independent judgements while giving them boundaries within which they can be safe, we may find that our perceptions of what is dangerous may be very different from theirs. For example, our children are going to a party where they will be drinking. We may remember drinking as teenagers ourselves. Now we are the parents and we are aware of the alarming rise in teenage drinking and the problems which arise from excessive drinking. Our children, meanwhile, see themselves as well able to drink when they choose and have no fears about what might happen. They don't seem to even understand our worry. An acceptable compromise – even a procedure for obtaining one – is often difficult to come by. Should we outline for our children all our worries, or are we concerned that such a list might push them into actions they never thought of or might signal for them a way they can defy us? Do we not say anything about our worries so that they will learn to test their own judgement, or do we risk their thinking we don't care about them and have them do something to try to get our attention? As we weigh all our possible responses and options, we sometimes feel overwhelmed with the burden of parenting teenagers. The minute we seem to reach a compromise on one issue we find ourselves facing yet another dilemma. We feel a lot less clear about what rules are applicable to our own lives and those of our children than our parents seemed to be. We are constantly searching for a way to live together humanly during this time.

Implicit within our setting limits and rules for our children is our awareness that they need to begin to set their own expectations and rules by which they will live as independent adults. They need to take on more responsibility for their lives, and the first place where they can begin to assume a sense of responsibility is within the family. When they were younger, they probably shared certain family tasks such as drying the dishes or caring for their rooms, but as they enter the teen years we may expect them to take on household responsibilities that require more independent thought and action. A single mother of two teenage sons explains:

Last spring when I got home from work I saw that, once again, Ben had not begun to prepare dinner. Every Thursday he is expected to cook dinner, and yet he always seems to forget or to be too involved in his activities to plan a meal. I stood for a long time in the living room trying to decide what to do. I thought about my alternatives: I could make dinner for him; remind him, yet again, that Thursday night was his night to cook; or I could try a new strategy and say nothing. I chose the last alternative. I called upstairs and said 'I'm hungry.' My other son, Bob, said 'So am I.' Ben didn't answer. Then I went about my business around the house. An hour later Ben came dashing down the stairs and said 'I think I forgot to make dinner.' I agreed with him and said I hoped he would find something to make. He worked hard and came up with a fine dinner of leftovers.

As our children set out by trial and error to take responsibility for their own lives we may have to learn how to respond flexibly, as did this mother of five children:

I have learned that I must not try to respond to my children's grandiose schemes. If I ranted and raved over the things they say they are going to do – such as stand out in twenty-degree weather all night to get tickets to a ball game – they might feel cornered into doing it. When I just listen and don't respond, they often follow their own good judgement and call off the wild schemes. In most situations my plan is to wait a few days and then respond if I must. Usually a few days is all they need to rethink their plans and ideas and make sound ones.

What of those times when they make what we consider to be dangerous decisions? What can we do when we find ourselves in a predicament like this one:

I wasn't feeling well, so I left work early. When I got home, I saw that the car was gone and called the police in alarm because it had been stolen. When my ten-year-old came home, he told me that Mary, my fourteen-year-old daughter, probably had the car. 'She often takes it,' he told me casually. By now it was almost dark, there were a lot of cars on the road, and the road was icy. I didn't even know Mary could drive – or could she? I decided to tell the police I had found the car, and then begin to see if I could locate Mary at a friend's. She was nowhere. I paced and yelled and peered out the window and waited. Finally she drove up and calmly came in the house. She was unable or unwilling to understand why her driving was so dangerous – besides being illegal. She needed the car, someone had taught her how to drive, so she took it.

The challenge for someone in Mary's mother's position is to respond in a way which is firm and at the same time attentive to what the teenager's actions are saying indirectly about what's going on in her life – while also dealing with her own feelings of panic, disappointment, inadequacy or perhaps even guilt. When our children take such actions or make decisions which can harm them, our options often seem very limited. We can try to talk through our concerns with them at a moment that is not so highly charged; we may want to think about who else can help them work it out better than we can; we may need to examine once again the usefulness of the rules we've made; we can explore ways of getting help for them or ourselves from other parents, relatives or professionals. (See the Helping chapter.)

Just about every parent of grown-ups remembers moments of sheer despair during the teen years, when there seemed to be no clear, sensible, sane way out of a conflict or dilemma. As we do the best we can do, it is some consolation to us to know that many parents and teenagers alike have come out on the other side pretty much whole and feeling good about themselves, and that the chances are pretty high that we will do the same.

When there are two adults in the household sharing concern and responsibility for teenage children, the burden on either parent is generally lighter, but, as we've discussed, the decisions about limits can get more complicated. What worries one adult may not worry the other; what seems outrageous behaviour to one can seem like important signs of independence to the other. Sometimes the limits that are being set need to be worked out as much between the adults as between the adults and the teenagers. When one of the adults is a step-parent, then the decisions can be even more difficult because the children may be dealing with three or four adults, not all of whom were involved when the child was young. Of course, teenagers are well aware of the differences that arise between the adults. They may use these differences to get what they want themselves or they may be hurt and confused by the lack of clear-cut decisions.

Every time we read a magazine or watch television or talk to friends and neighbours, we hear about teenagers in trouble – and we worry. However, there is a point at which worry becomes debilitating to both us and our children. We begin to recognize that just because we worry about something is not a good reason to say no, as this mother realized:

My son had saved some money and wanted to take a course in skydiving. When I told him that I didn't want him to do it because skydiving is so dangerous, he said 'Mother, I can't live my life by what you're afraid of.' I stuck to my point about the skydiving, but about a lot of other stuff, he is probably right.

There are good reasons for setting limits, and yet there are limits to the limits we can set. We are in the odd position of having once (it seems like only yesterday) been the people who saved our toddlers from certain death at least once an hour, except when they were asleep. It is hard, even now – or perhaps especially now, when our children are doing things that are potentially dangerous to themselves and others – to give up that power of absolute protectiveness. We are getting close to the end of our function as limit-setter and, for some of us, letting go of that role is difficult.

At any rate, in the continual enterprise of trying to guide appropriately, renegotiate with, listen to and just generally coexist with our teenage children, we ourselves are changed. We learn even more clearly what our base-line values are. We listen to our teenagers and change our minds about some things, stretching our own limits. We learn our own capacity for flexibility, firmness and endurance. We experience the relief and pleasure of seeing our children make more and more judgements for themselves – judgements that may be different from ours but based on the foundation which we have helped them build.

Separation

When we reach the teenage years, we may begin to experience a feeling of freedom as we need less and less time for direct child care. We may also feel a twinge of sadness, as the mother of three sons says:

I remember thinking that last golden summer when the oldest were twelve and thirteen and came rushing to share all their dreams: this is the closest we'll ever be because this is the last of their boyhood. It was so vivid – they were so open and caring. I knew then the whole poignant wrenching sadness of what my husband had warned me on the day the first baby was born – 'Raising kids, hon, is one long letting go.'

Separation looms large in our minds from the start of the teenage years – not because our children are actually moving out of the house, but because they are spending more and more time in their own separate lives and because we and our children are working so hard to prepare ourselves for the time when we will actually separate. There are times when we lose sight of the joys of these years as we think and prepare for separation, and times when we are so involved with the teen years that we forget to prepare ourselves for separation.

Emotional Separation – Theirs and Ours

We need some emotional separateness from our teenagers, even as they need the same from us. The father of a teenage son discovered this:

Many times when my son is so distraught that I think he is going under, I worry, and talk and work on his problems. I am under great stress. I wait a few days and then bring up the painful matter again to try and help – often to find that my son has passed unscathed through whatever it was, and he is feeling that I'm a little nuts for taking it so seriously.

There may be many times when we need to keep our distance and not get swept up into the day-to-day ups and downs of our teenagers. For many of us, distance is more difficult than involvement because we may feel we are not doing our job unless we are involved. Yet we just aren't needed as much or as constantly during the teen years and, for many of us, this release from minute-to-minute being 'on duty' is a welcome relief. We are trying to find a balance between involvement and distance so that our children, and we ourselves, will emerge from these years as independent, whole human beings.

During the teen years, we are also vividly confronted with our expectations for our children. Some of our expectations were present at their birth, but these expectations were often made up of our wishes or dreams for ourselves and were not pertinent to our child. Our children need to separate their expectations for themselves from our expectations for them. They certainly need our help and support in developing realistic expectations for themselves, but they are in charge of where they will eventually go with their lives and the type of adult they will become. We are often not consulted as they proceed.

As they separate more from us, our children call into question many of our values and beliefs:

When my daughter was in high school, she announced one day that she would no longer bring her friends home because she was embarrassed by our lack of material objects in the home – we looked too poor. For days my wife and I wondered if we should change our house to better fit the pattern of our daughter's friends. After all, we didn't like her feeling that we didn't measure up. However, we realized that our house expressed our values and that we could not change to fit others' values. Our daughter ranted and raved, but we stood firm. Now she is in college and brings home her friends all the time because she says our home is so comfortable.

A father shares his feelings when his daughter challenged a value that he held dear:

Our small family has always done everything it could to maintain close ties. My daughter always seemed to agree with me that family ties were important, until the other evening when I announced that her cousin was coming to town for a few days and that I hoped she would take her to school with her. My daughter made a face and said 'Do I have to?' I was shocked and began to argue vehemently with her. How could she even suggest that her cousin's visit wouldn't be a complete joy for her? She saw my anger and consented to take her cousin to school. But on the evening when her cousin arrived, my daughter, who would usually be up until midnight, said she was tired and excused herself at eight-thirty from the family discussion to go to her room.

Neither of these incidents seems critical or crucial when we look at them from a distance. But for the parents who related them, there was an intense feeling of being questioned at a very deep level – in an area of long-held, frequently unexamined values and beliefs. We are often surprised by the heat and intensity which occurs in our discussions (sometimes fights) with our teenage children over what to us is so obviously the 'right' way to see or do things. We may see ourselves as only trying to help our children make good decisions – frequently in such presumably simple areas as length of hair or type of dress – but our children interpret our help as trying to force them to follow our path.

Then there are the times when our teenagers agree with our values and beliefs and act more fervently than we might, which may cause a dilemma for us similar to the one this father experienced:

To graduate, Marilyn had to take a senior civics course. The man teaching the course and Marilyn disagreed about many political issues. They often argued in class about their different views. Her papers and exams were graded very low and she was failing the class. The school officials wouldn't get involved because they said that Marilyn and the teacher had to work it out. I found myself caught between my complete agreement with Marilyn in her political views and my awareness that she had to pass that class to graduate. I didn't know whether I should stand behind her as she tried to get her views heard and accepted, or whether I should try to convince her to back off and write her papers and exams to fit with what her teacher expected.

Whether our children challenge our values and beliefs or vehemently defend them, we are put in the position of having to look at them more closely than we have ever done before. Our closer look may reinforce what we have always believed or assist us in making changes which are more in keeping with the person we are now, in mid-life, as this mother relates:

In my childhood I never saw my parents fight. I believed that a happy family was one in which all was quiet and calm. Whenever my children got angry, I suggested to them that they must be tired because I was sure they would never be so angry and hostile if they'd had enough sleep. When my son became a teenager, he began to express angry, hostile feelings. Every time he did so I tried to stop him and he just kept saying 'Why?' I didn't have an answer except I believed that a happy family didn't have people who expressed anger. The more he said 'Why', the more I realized that valuing peace and calm was not a value I wanted to continue. We all began experimenting with expressing angry as well as happy feelings, and we found that we became much closer than we'd ever been before.

In living with teenagers, we are constantly being challenged in areas that are close to our definition of ourselves. Up until the teen years, most of us have had a fairly good sense of ourselves as parents. It can be upsetting now to find our children making decisions according to what seem like different values. A teenage girl here gives her point of view:

I left home at sixteen to go live on my own. My parents were angry and upset and thought my leaving meant that they had failed. In fact my leaving showed they were good parents. They had raised me to be strong and independent enough to go off, get a job and a place to live.

Gaining in age and outside experience often makes our children feel qualified to criticize us. They begin to question our knowledge, look down on our way of doing things or look disparagingly at personal aspects of our life – our behaviour, dress, life style, speech:

My daughter has the idea that I can't be trusted to cross the street myself. Luckily, I have work outside the home which is going well, and I don't have to depend on my daughter's opinion of me for my self-esteem.

If we do not have satisfying work or accomplishments to turn to, it can be especially difficult to maintain a strong sense of self-worth when our children are being deprecating. Even if we do have outside reinforcement, we may still internalize our children's critical comments and find our self-image hurt, as this woman points out:

When my children are completely intolerant of me, I try to see the criticism as unreasonable and discount it. But no matter what I do, in the end what my kids think of me really does count. I feel deeply hurt when they disapprove of me and unreasonably happy when they cheer me on.

Separating our image and identity from what our children think of us is a necessary though difficult job. It may help to realize that they are often trying to get a distance 'from us so as to better see themselves. Yet although we may recognize that being the centre of our teenagers' anger and criticism is a stage which we and our children must pass through on the road to separation, such knowledge does not always make it easier for us to accept it. One father who described himself as feeling very philosophical this time around, as he tried to understand and guide his fourth and youngest adolescent, said:

I always keep in the forefront of my mind that she will suffer, test and then leave. It is a time we must get through, and I do everything I can to maintain a balance and a perspective on where she is and where I am in the process.

Physical Separation

With each passing teen year we seem to see less and less of our children. They become involved with their outside lives, and frequently we cannot keep track of their busy schedules; or because they begin to relish having the house to themselves, we find ourselves encouraged to go out more and leave them alone. Days – perhaps weeks – may pass before the entire family sits down for a meal or engages in a family activity. While we delight in our children's ability to develop independent, busy lives, we may at the same time wish we had more involvement with them. The ironic thing is that when they are home they take up so much space with their noise, activity and sheer physical bigness that we may long for moments of quiet and order even when we are excruciatingly aware that they'll soon be leaving home for good.

During the early teen years our children may go away for extended periods of time – perhaps to camp or to visit relatives or friends. Although we recognize that they need to be away from us more, and we from them, we may find it difficult to accept that there are times when they may prefer to be away from the family. The mother of a thirteen-year-old daughter describes one of those times:

My daughter had been away having a splendid time at camp for eight weeks. We planned a family vacation for the time when she returned, as we thought that would be a moment when we would all relish being together. The minute we got there she began complaining she didn't have enough space in the small vacation house. She was very unhappy with us all. She finally withdrew from us and read by herself for four days. I realize now that the fact that she had had all that distance made it all the more difficult for her to move back again into the family. She was clearly feeling threatened by dependency.

During the teen years we are always trying to decide when we should plan family activities and when we should allow our children to lead their separate, parallel lives. We can remember when, not so long ago, our children wanted to be with us most of the time and now, somehow, we are not such a big part of their lives. Again, we are involved in a balancing act because if we have more than one

child, they are at different ages and have different needs. We may plan family
activities for our younger children and find that our older children refuse to
attend. At other times, when they're not included, our teenagers are upset.

We find ourselves unsure not only about how our teenagers feel from moment
to moment, but also about how *we* feel, as this father expresses:

*There are times that I think, gee, it's going to be nice when I have enough spare time
for myself. On the other hand, I know that I gain a great deal by being able to give to my
children and having them give to me. The closeness of our relationship is very important
to me and I fear losing it.*

Separation is a key issue during the teen years, despite the fact that our
children are still living with us and we are still actively parenting. We seem to be
keenly aware that the teen years are the beginning of the end of our active
parenting and we think ahead to the years when we won't have children in the
house. We are often advised to relax and just enjoy these years while they are
here, but for many of us this advice is hard to follow. When our oldest begins to
make plans to move out, we are sometimes relieved to be finally facing an event
for which we have been preparing for so long. One mother describes her
preparation for separation in this way:

*I change jobs or start something new when a child is going to leave, so that I don't
have to experience the pain. Separation comes easier for me when I embark on a new
thing myself because I'm immersed in the excitement.*

It appears that no amount of preparation makes us totally ready for how we
feel when our first child leaves. As this father describes:

*After dropping my son off at college I drove home, and for the first time in my life I
cried for a prolonged period of time. I just cried and cried and cried.*

Many of us feel sad and lonely when our first child leaves our home, even if s/he is
only going a short distance and will be home frequently. We may also feel happy
to contemplate an extension of the time we will have to pursue our own thoughts
and activities. One father described his feelings of separation in this way:

*It's 'kicking out of the nest time', and I look on leaving for college as a positive time,
not like a death in the family. It's one hell of a growth experience for us all. Of course, I
get a lump in my throat, but I try not to choke on it.*

As parents we are often unsure how to handle temporary separation when
teenage children go to college or perhaps to an apartment of their own. Should
we consider our children grown up when they leave home for the first time, or
should we consider them children, who are temporarily away? If they move out
to start a long-term relationship with someone or if they move a great distance,
often the issue is resolved for us and we know we have moved into the stage of
having grown children. More often the lines are not clearly drawn, and we
remain for several years parents of 'almost' grown-ups. Our children often don't
know which stage they are in, either:

My daughter was very ambivalent about how she wanted us to treat her the first few times she came home from college. She was very eager to show us how independent and self-sufficient she had become while she was away. But she also wanted to be 'taken care of' again. Since it was difficult to tell which one of these feelings she was experiencing, we often coddled when we should have stepped back and ignored when we should have given extra attention.

We are forced to restructure our family life when our children leave – whether temporarily or not. Then when they return for a short period of time such as a school holiday, we may find, as one mother said, 'They seem to expect all their rights and privileges without any of the responsibilities.' As we may still be unclear whether we are dealing with grown children or teenage children, adjustments to their short stays can be difficult:

When my son came home from college, the dynamics within the family shifted. I hadn't realized how close my husband and I had become until he came home. All of a sudden all the stress was back again on our shoulders. The mess in the house, the noise, all the negotiations over who would do the washing and the marketing. We both felt so tired – we had forgotten what it was like.

It appears that from the start of the teenage years we are preparing ourselves for the time when our children will physically separate from us and then we are not quite sure when the actual moment arrives. As separation is such a crucial and sometimes painful issue for us, perhaps it is not surprising that we allow several years of indecision to pass while we and our children try on our new separate identities and try to reach out to each other as adults who will be interdependent, though separate, the rest of our lives.

Feminism

A chapter on parenting teenagers is not complete without exploring the effect the rise of feminism has had on those of us who now are mid-life adults and parents. When we first began talking with other women about our lives, many of us found ourselves questioning the standards and attitudes by which we had been living. We may have felt, as did this woman, that we didn't fit with the new changes:

In the sixties, when students said 'You can never trust people over thirty,' I was over thirty. When women began to talk about making choices, I had already made my life decisions, and there hadn't appeared to be many choices at that time. A woman succeeded by getting married and having children or she failed. Now I realize there were many possible alternatives and I feel like I'm too old and/or too late, again.

Many of us felt sad or angry that the women's movement had come at the wrong time for us – somehow we had been born too early or too late. Had we been born earlier we might not have been so aware of the lack of choices we had in our younger years, and had we been born later, we might have had the choices which are now available to younger women. The fact that we cannot go back and reopen our options from our youth does not stop us from responding to the new choices and attitudes now available to us.

As we see in the chapter on Families, one person changing in a family system affects all the members. In a household which has been established for a long time, resistance from other members can be extreme:

After twenty years, my wife is trying to change our original contract by insisting I share equally in the household chores. I have always helped around the house, but now she says that is not enough – I must share the responsibility. I have told her she can't possibly make money equal to what I make, so why should I share equally in the household chores?

Teenage children frequently resent their mothers' changing household expectations. Sometimes the resentment is extreme – and they seem to be speaking with the voice of our sexist culture. Hearing this voice coming from our own children can be very painful:

My son sees me as totally useless. I wouldn't be useless to him if I were cooking or baking. It feels awful to have a son who is a chauvinist. It's as though he takes what I believe and throws it back in my face.

My son asks my husband why he does the marketing or the dishes. He seems to feel that household chores put his father in a subservient role and he doesn't like that.

Whether we meet with this extreme resistance with a no less thorny passive aggression or with hesitant cooperation, we have to continue to press for changes so that we can live together in mutual freedom, responsibility and respect.

In a family with teenage children where household chores have never been shared, the changeover to sharing can be extremely difficult. As one sixteen-year-old girl told her mother, 'You cook so well and easily that it doesn't make sense for me to spend so much of my time trying to do something which you could do better in half the time.' Yes, the mother does do it faster and easier, but now she has begun to realize that family responsibilities should be borne by the entire family. Some feminist mothers may decide not to share the responsibilities with their daughters because they do not want to burden them with the stereotypic tasks. This sometimes leads to the 'superwoman' philosophy – the 'I can do it all myself' theory, which keeps some women working night and day at home and at their jobs. In any case, it is fair to neither mother nor daughter, father nor son. Women who have struggled to achieve equal sharing, inevitably report that the outcome is well worth the effort.

The influence of a feminist awareness can affect a mother's relationship with her daughter. A mid-life identity search, coupled with a new feminist awareness, may help a woman to look back on some of her life decisions and choices and see those times when being female limited her options. As she plans what she will now be doing she will probably be more willing to explore her strengths fully and not allow herself to be limited to stereotypic options. She may feel really happy that her teenage daughter has wider horizons and less limiting choices, but the gladness may at times be tinged with a kind of envy. The mother of a thirteen-year-old speaks:

There are times when I feel envious of my daughter. She wears her feminism and her freedom so easily. She doesn't see any barriers – she accepts her rights to any choices. I wish that I could be so confident and free, but I'm struggling with each step I take, each feminist decision I make.

On the other end of the spectrum are the women who see their daughters ignoring options that are open to them and who want to help them become more aware of their choices:

How do I get across to my daughters that I want to cancel the message I gave to them when they were small? I thought then that the main goal in life was 'to get married, have children and live happily ever after.' I now realize and I want to convey to them that they must also become strong, independent human beings – which I was not. I often worry that they will follow my path and they will also be forty before they realize that they should not have dropped their strong interests and talents along the way.

Although the first awareness of feminism is likely to come from women, men can develop into feminists, too. Many men see themselves as role models for their teenagers, and as they become more responsible for and responsive to the needs in the family, they may see themselves as setting an example which will help their teenage sons and daughters when they begin to develop lasting relationships with people outside the family. Yet feminist awareness is not always so welcome, says this father:

I became one man surrounded by three very assertive females. My wife and my daughters sided emotionally or intellectually one way and I sided another way. I found myself becoming more conservative as my daughters became more involved in their teenage years.

This man decided that the best solution for him was to withdraw from arguing with his wife and daughters. Other men may decide to try to seek a balance between their view and the view of the women in the family. In either case, attempting to change the accustomed household balance during the years when teens are in the house is never easy, but it is possible.

We do not have clear signposts for femininity and masculinity as our own parents felt they had, so as parents of teenagers we often question how we should advise our children. Often they, and we, are trying on new roles and behaviours to see what fits best. Sometimes we feel very strong and comfortable, and at other times awkward and shy as we undertake new tasks or actions that we have not tried before. We may envy the ease with which our children seem to try new, unexplored areas, but we also recognize that we have an opportunity to change and explore at mid-life which may not have been available to our parents when they were our age. We envision that the changing that we do will enrich and widen our world, and that vision makes the effort seem worthwhile.

Conclusion

Parenting adolescents is a strenuous, challenging time, full of highs and lows – perhaps at the precise time in our lives when we crave a peaceful interlude to contemplate our own lives' path. The exasperation that teenagers can cause prompted one father to say 'The problem with American families is that they live together!' Yet, as another father so aptly said, 'No one will ever love or hate me as much as my children do, and I cherish that thought.'

As parents we tend to report only the difficult and troubling times with our teenage children. Perhaps we are so programmed to expect trouble that we hesitate to speak up when life with our adolescents is relatively calm. We act as if we feel that merely admitting a lack of present problems will invite trouble.

Yet there are wonderful joys in being the parents of teenage children. When we stand back and look at the budding adults whom we have nurtured and encouraged for so many years, we may say with these parents in awe and amazement:

My kids are just nice people. They're fun to be with and they're good con-versationalists. They're fun to have around, and I enjoy them.

At this point I have a relationship with my kids that I don't have with anybody else – even with my closest friends and my husband. I wouldn't trade that for anything in the world.

After all these years we can begin to see emerging near adults who often have a perspective on the world similar to ours or views which we see as reasonable and thoughtful. Our children are insightful, caring people whom we like to be with. We also have the sense of having done our best, and can see that the rest is in their own hands:

I feel relief because I no longer feel responsible for developing a marvellous person. I have done all I can whatever happens – good, bad or indifferent.

We can and must trust our children to value themselves. We are aware, as one mother said, that 'They need to stumble and fall several times, so they will learn how to pick themselves up and continue.' We are prepared to see them fall, if they must, and we hope to be around if they need us to help them sort out the pieces.

Along with a sense of having done a good job of parenting, we can also feel good about ourselves and the stage we are in with our own lives:

I am changing every year. I am becoming more confident all the time, more aware of myself, more genuine. I am not trying any more to be someone I am not. I know who I am, and if you don't like it, it's too bad.

As we reach out to other adults who help us maintain a much needed perspective on our children and on how they, and we, are doing, we find ourselves helped in our parenting role. Our task is to keep in proper perspective the positive, invigorating parts of being a parent. Other parents are often able to provide us with the support we need in times of stress and to remind us of which things are going right during the teen years.

We may feel best about our parenting role when we finally let ourselves off the hook of trying to be perfect parents of teenagers, and recognize some of the tough aspects of the job we've been undertaking. A man who has three teenagers observed:

Here I am struggling to make connections with my children as human being to human being with the handicap of feeling responsible; being of a different generation; being seen as an authority who must be rejected; and at the same time, trying to decide who I am now.

It is helpful to recognize that there are many forces acting on us as we try our best to parent our children. The years when we are parenting teenagers are the high point, the crest when everything seems to be in bright colours and in ten-foot letters – as in the words of a father of four adolescents:

No one ever promised me it would be easy and it's not. But I also get many rewards from seeing my children grow, make strong decisions for themselves, and set out on their own as independent, strong, likeable human beings. And I like who I am becoming, too. Having teenagers has made me more human, more flexible, more humble, more questioning – and, finally, it's given me a better sense of humour!

5. Being Parents of Grown-Ups

Alice Judson Ryerson and Wendy Coppedge Sanford

Our child gets a job and moves into an apartment with some room-mates, joins the Peace Corps or the Army, or marries and moves across the street. It's hard to say when precisely one becomes a parent of grown-ups, but there is a period extending to the end of our lives when that's what we are. Our children are on their own, and active parenting is no longer central to our daily lives – yet we are still parents. This chapter will talk about what it's like to be a parent of grown-ups.*

Here we are concerned with this more final separation from our children, and the different meanings it can have to parents. We will talk about the different kinds of distance between parents and grown children, the various bridges that we and our children build. We will be concerned with the ways parents use any time, energy, money and psychic space released when children leave. We will look at the relationship of couples and some of the concerns of single parents at this time, and end with a look at being grandparents.

Separation

One parent's journey:

I keep trying to remember when I first felt that my children were grown-ups and how I knew. First I remember the dramatic moments when I realized that they could make important decisions in their lives without my hovering presence to steer by. Of course, this happened even before I was aware of it, and although it was the goal I'd been aiming for all along, still my children's first irrevocable plunges into life were painful to me. There was the telephone call saying 'I'm getting married, but it would be really better if you didn't come. I hope you won't mind', or the letter saying 'I'm trying to figure things

---

*For the purposes of this chapter, a definition of a grown-up would be anyone who is physically mature and who controls most of her or his own life, or who shares that control by choice with contemporaries rather than with parents. As the previous chapter pointed out, there is a period of years in which it is often unclear just how grown-up or independent our children actually are. These days, with advanced training, graduate study, and substantial uncertainty on the part of many young adults as to what work they are going to do, a period of prolonged semi-dependency goes on into the twenties for more and more young people. Are these children grown-ups? This question is one of the challenges of the transition period, as we shall discuss below.

*out, so please don't write to me or try to communicate at all', or 'I'm going to sea
tomorrow in a twenty-foot open boat. If there aren't any storms I should arrive in a
couple of weeks.'*

*As I riffle through these particular pictures, I realize that while they show my
children's independence from me, they don't represent my independence from my
children. I can tell by the way the communications I've described made my stomach feel
at the time. Even though I had let them choose their own socks since babyhood, I was
only beginning to learn to trust their adult judgement. My children's decisions to get
married or to go to sea in an open boat were possible only after years of learning to make
decisions, and although my first reaction was fear, it was followed by pride, not only in
them but in myself for having helped to produce four autonomous human beings. I had a
sensation very much like the moment in an airplane when you realize that even if you
stop holding the plane up by gripping the arms of your seat until your knuckles show
white, the plane will stay up by itself.*

*But I had to take another step, to detach myself from my children still more. For my
own sake, I had to achieve a condition which might be called loving objectivity.*

*I see myself standing in my backyard waving good-bye to one of my daughters and
her husband as they drive off in a camper of their own construction to live and work in a
loft in California. I care very much what's going to happen in their lives; I wish them
well; I know they'll let me know what's happening. As they drive off, my eyes fill with
tears because I'll miss them. But I have finally learned to let them have their own
anxieties about their own lives. I don't have to do that, as though by worrying I could
magically keep them safe. But as a kind of reward for letting them go, I have acquired a
new control over my own life. I can go back into my house as they drive off and return to
my own pursuits with a sigh of relief – without further interruption at a day-to-day
level but with a continued connection with them which nothing can destroy.*

Separation: The Context

There has been a recurrent theme through these chapters: that we as parents, for
our children's sake and for our own, need to let go. Parents learn gradually to
encourage and to allow children to be independent of us. In the teenage years in
particular, we have often struggled with the push and pull of their growing
independence. As we become parents of grown-ups our children move out on
their own more completely than ever before. We no longer have daily
responsibility for them. Even in rare cases where they continue to live at home,
they are and must be making their own decisions. Parents of adults vary as much
as any other kind of parent: some find it hard coming to terms with what they
experience as the disintegration of their family; others happily embrace the
condition of having grown-ups for children; many of us veer dizzily from one
extreme to the other. Here we want to look at parents' many different responses
to having their children 'leave', be it to get married, to join a religious sect, to
move across the continent or around the corner. First we will look at some things
in our own lives and in our society which shape this transition for us.

Leaving

Music comes up through the floor
rising from the strung wires
of that crouched black heart
and I hear, between the rush
of the piano's stroke and the resonance,
our daughter's voice
singing.

Frail, almost childlike,
her voice rising
only when the hammers of the piano
are soothed by the pedal,
are muted by a touch more gentle.

Now the piano surges, sounding
and we cannot hear her singing.

What have we made, you and I,
out of our coupling and loving
out of our trying and failing:

these children
who are now men and women

making music   poems   babies?

Hewing and cutting themselves
out of the block of family.

Though gritted and rubbed down
though spitted and strung
on the steel of days —

how beautiful are the children
breaking off   floating off!
Like jellyfish budding,
like seeds from a milkweed pod

blowing   and sailing
away

— Margery Cavanagh

We are influenced in this experience of separation by where we are in the life cycle, by the nourishment and intensity of our adult relationships, by our level of satisfaction at work, by the state of our marriage, by our physical health and by our own parents' situation. All of these will come up later in the chapter. We are influenced also by the pervasive youth orientation of our society, which pushes fathers and mothers to believe that we have handed everything over to our children, that their departure marks the end of the most active part of our lives, and that our own lives need only dwindle from there on. While many voices in this chapter will bear witness to just the opposite view – saying, in effect, that despite some sadness at separation our lives grow and change after our children go – still, the internalized echoes of the youth-culture message can conspire to make our children's departure more painful for us.

Some of our difficulties are increased because we are losing the ceremonies of separation. Like all rituals, these helped to make transitions easier by defining roles before and after an event. It used to be expected that a child would either finish high school or go to college or get some other form of job training and then would go to work. Everybody attended the ceremony of graduation; all the family congratulated him or her on landing a job; and finally, the family all gathered at the wedding. The young person was launched; a bottle of champagne had been cracked. Now these steps are often interrupted or not taken at all, or they occur in a different order and without reference to traditional procedures.

Marriage, for instance, used to be a rite of passage with a clearly marked before and after. But now it often occurs so gradually that the change of status is imperceptible. Two parents asked how they felt when their daughters married might say 'Well, Mary and Joe lived together for so long that there's hardly a change', or 'She left home years before she was married and we had entirely finished the job of becoming independent of each other.' A far cry these from the bride in white tulle kissing her weeping parents good-bye as she leaves to 'belong' to somebody else (though this still does happen). A mother of two and stepmother of three grown children comments:

Expectations also play a part in our attitude about the moment when children get married, or at any rate get mated. There is relief at the idea that the grown child's emotional weight has shifted to somebody else – that now that 'spouse' is the next of kin, the one who has to take the burden of responsibility – traditionally in money terms, too. Thus when people don't really marry, that shift isn't official, and the parent can't feel that the child is 'settled', one of the goals we all still secretly hold.

The separation is often further confused by money, particularly in more affluent families. For example, many parents continue to support a child who is getting graduate training, although this child may be married and even have children. Parents who disapprove of couples living together without being married may support this arrangement in order to keep a child in college. All sorts of confusions arise from these commonly encountered patterns. They are confusing because the people involved sometimes lose track of how to relate to each other. One mother confesses:

Neither party knows from moment to moment what the rules are. How long shall I go on supporting my grown child? Shall I support her only if she's going to college or doing stuff I approve of? Or is this blackmail? And I imagine she's wondering how much support she can accept without feeling there are strings attached, or without feeling that she's sponging.

Today, then, there is no single dramatic moment of loss which the parent can live through to come out on the other side. There are so many stages of a child's leaving home that it's difficult to get through a clear period of mourning, and to arrive at the important realization that certain attachments last for ever but in muted form. This mother queries whether the old ceremonies ever helped, and hopes for some creative alternatives:

The public ceremonies were and always are so formal and rigid. I feel challenged to replace these with smaller ceremonies with chosen friends and family at points that my daughter or I feel like marking.

Feelings about Separation

Letting our children go is something that has to happen inside us. Although most parents have been doing it little by little all along, for many of us the final separation is a shock no matter how well prepared we are by earlier ones. One mother said simply: 'I was just so happy to see her go and so sad at the same time.' Another mother expressed with a lot of clarity what many parents have said:

Even though I have had a full-time, satisfying professional career, I am experiencing the loss of parent-identity to be nearly as significant as the actual absence of my grown children. In their young childhood, and continuing in attenuated form for nearly twenty years, two people needed me in order to survive. The actual and symbolic end of parenthood is requiring me to accommodate to the total absence of being needed by anyone. To be needed, in survival terms, solved for me the existential question – the purpose of my existence was to maintain the existence of others. To no longer be needed has raised again all those old questions of the purpose or meaning of life.

Society provides no solace, no rituals, no real acknowledgement for this existential crisis – only a few joking comments about the empty-nest syndrome or advice to get a job or find a hobby.

Perhaps the truth is that most of us feel some grief when our children go – missing the companionship or feeling a nostalgia for the past eighteen or twenty years. Few of us, men or women, get stuck in the grief, and having other work and interests helps us put the sad feelings in their proper place. The mother who has spent most of her energy for twenty years in caring for her children might continue to grieve for a while, but perhaps she is mourning the loss of her mother-identity fully as much as the departure of her children. Even mothers and fathers who are engrossed in full-time work and have not (at least not recently) made their children their principal reason for being find they must learn to deal in some way with the emotional vacuum left by the absence of children. Both parents are apt to miss their children even if the children had become shadowy figures passing on the stairs. There may be a few routine occasions when a woman in a traditional family is reminded of their absence: the empty room, the empty laundry hamper, the full refrigerator. But the 'family times' when the children were present are now most poignantly full of the children's absence: the dinner table, the country picnic, holidays, the vacation in the summer.

Some of us feel more pain than others. One mother found it especially difficult, having been a single parent for a year:

My husband's job took him to another city for a year when our youngest child was a senior in high school. I stayed with Helen so that she could finish in the school she'd been in all along. During the year when we lived alone we became extraordinarily good companions, so when my daughter went away to college and I rejoined my husband the inevitable separation was terrible for me, much harder than it was for him. He had done it earlier and without the period of such closeness first.

Also, this husband had been the one who went away, and the leavers often feel less grief than the left. Preoccupied with a new environment, new people, new interests, they have less time to indulge in wistfulness about the past. This applies to departing children as well as to parents.

Some, like this woman who is fifty, works full time and has two grown children, feel the sadness even as time passes.

The spasms of letting go, the grieving, go on repeatedly. Each time a child comes home to visit and re-establishes familiar patterns, the pain and loss repeat themselves when she goes, though less intensely each time.

Despite the stereotypic view that fathers feel the loss less acutely, often the father suffers just as much. This father speaks of the day that his oldest daughter left to take a job several states away:

As we drove home from the airport I began to cry, and my wife turned to me sort of concerned and asked me why I was crying. Looking back at it now, I think it should have been pretty obvious to her why I was crying. And I guess I resented her asking me why I was crying, because in no way did I have to ask her at the airplane why she was crying. I dropped her off at work, and for the first time in my life I just cried and cried and cried. When I got to work I fully shared it with the people there – what had happened. They saw my eyes were red and I cried a little bit more. They were sensitive to what I had gone through; they were really sensitive, because I guess as social workers and psychologists they know what separation provokes.

This man was fortunate that even though he didn't feel that his wife was particularly open to his grief, he had a chance to express his feelings in the accepting environment of his colleagues.

For many of us there is a curious embarrassment about feeling grief at our children's departure. What makes it more difficult is that our society, because of its worship of independence, constantly rejects our grief. We are supposed to be so glad that these children of ours can lead their own lives that any expression of disappointment lays us open to the charge that we are trying to 'hang on' to them. If the child leaves to embark on any acceptable adult activity, the parents are supposed to be proud and supportive. And we are. Yet although most of us feel real pleasure in the knowledge that our children are equipped to lead their own lives, and although we have lives of our own that are ongoing, we can still feel real pain at the separation. And it is natural and necessary that we should be sad. Mourning prepares us to regroup our inner forces for a new phase of life. For all of us the opportunity to mourn without being misunderstood is important.

Here is a single mother who has been divorced for many years and works full time. She identifies the function of a period of grief in a helpful way. In fact, her grieving achieved its liberating effect too quickly, before her daughter actually left.

My daughter and her boyfriend were living in a second-floor room beneath my third-floor apartment. They promised that they would leave by the end of last summer. I had rented their room in the expectation that they would be leaving, and the person came in September and they moved up into the third floor with me – and it was very tight living with four people using the kitchen and the bathroom, and my daughter and her boyfriend, who still had no jobs, using the living room, and I had absolutely no place to hide . . . so I was being pushed out of my own house and finally said 'Well, it's really time to go' – after two weeks of this . . . so her boyfriend left and my daughter was still there, and it was clear that they were beginning to break up, too, and I had gone through a sort of realization that the last child would be leaving home – a small period of grief for that. It was a milestone, as I'd always lived in a house with people around, including my children – so that was sort of a grief period – and when she stayed on, I went through a period of anger that they were still there because I'd really gotten myself ready for the fact that they would be leaving.

Like the woman who just spoke, many parents feel predominantly positive feelings of anticipation, relief, pride and continuing connection when their children leave.

I remember when my daughter got married, people offered me sympathy, and I thought, how little do they know what we have been to each other. I don't have to be with her all the time to be with her. Perhaps because my husband and I both had our own occupations, we were able to see our children as independent people even when they were teenagers. When my daughter married I felt not bereft but enriched.

One woman expressed relief and pleasure that she now has time for her own creative work. In fact, she doesn't want this time encroached on:

I think if my daughter lived near me she would force me into the role of typical grandparent. But luckily she doesn't, because I feel my maternal instincts are spent.

And another woman, in the same vein:

I'm not going to suffer from the empty-nest syndrome. I have my own life. I'm busy and I go to school. I like the freedom of not having to come home at a certain time. Sometimes when I leave the house and I get on the subway, I realize I can do anything I

even as she runs: mother/daughter

black steam
on the tracks
compartments
windows
wheels
speed
listen
yes
listen
yes
how it is
straining
even
as they
stoke
up coal
cruel
oh cruel
how it is
held
back

Do you have everything
Yes
Your little bag
Yes
the black trunk
cornered
strapped
gone with a porter

And the ticket
Yes
The box of cake
Yes

sisters
clustered
speaking
their language
one hundred twenty
fingers
waving air
out

And your visa
Yes
And extra cash
Yes

daylight nearly
filtered
away
narrow walls
the aisle
between

And Uncle's picture
Yes
And address in New Jersey
Yes

ticket punched
dusted
seat

And paper to write back
Yes
And sewing
Yes

windows open
(she's covering her
eyes)

Mother

Anna you
must not leave
Anna you must
not leave
Anna you must not
leave
Anna you must not leave
Anna you must not leave

do you have do you have do
you have do you have do you
have do you have do you have
do you have do you do you do
you

shshshshshshshshshshshshshsh
— Marcie Hershman

damn well please today and no one's waiting to have their dinner cooked or their diapers changed. I love it. It's just a wonderful, wonderful feeling.

We get a similar message with a different twist from this father of two sons in their twenties:

I don't feel like hanging on to them at all, hanging on to the past. I am more interested in them as individuals than as children. There are certain sentimental things: I'd like for them to be able to have the toys in the attic for their children. But as I keep on evolving myself, they are part of the past and I'm not so interested in the past.

And a father of a twenty-one-year-old daughter who has left home:

I had the 'I have a life of my own' strategy built in because I always had to be at work, so it was pretty easy to let her know that life would go on for me one way or another ... I feel as though I am holding a place open which she may or may not choose to occupy at a particular time.

This father speaks for many of us in pointing to the place in our lives that we hold open for our grown children. For some that place is easily held, for others differences in values or life styles make it harder; for many of us for a period of time that place aches with our children's absence.

Distances and Bridges

Our grown children may move away from us geographically or in life style or in both ways. In this section we want to talk about some of the different kinds of distance, and about the challenge of bridging the distance, of maintaining a connection that affirms autonomy and caring concern on both sides.

Sometimes a son marries and moves across the country because, let's say (to be progressive), his wife has a new job. This person whom we knew daily for eighteen years and on weekends and vacations for several more will now be physically out of our lives except for rare visits, letters, phone calls. But even a move across town can create a huge distance if our child chooses to see us seldom or lives and works in ways very different from ours.

So many changes have taken place since we, now the parents of grown-ups, started out to be adults ourselves. To many of us it seems that our own children have been the ones to enact almost all these changes. One mother writes:

I have to force myself to realize that my oldest son is twenty-nine. When his father and I were twenty-nine, we had two children under five and his father was climbing the academic ladder. John is now separated from a close relationship of six years' duration, and the child he parented during that time he is now forbidden to see. That's a heavy thing to live through, yet I still have trouble consciously realizing that he is as old as he is.

When a daughter writes that she has accepted a job in a different city and will commute to be with her husband and children on weekends, or a son leaves a 'good' job to move to the country, when a child comes out as gay, or gets divorced, or even adopts an inter-racial child, it can take a tremendous amount of readjusting of our expectations and fears to be able to live comfortably with their decision. It can stretch our limits beyond what we've ever imagined.

Many of us wrestle with anxiety and uneasiness about our children's lives when they are out of our households. Sometimes behind this worry is the issue of trust. As the first woman who spoke in this chapter observed, 'Even though I had let them choose their own socks since babyhood, I was only beginning to learn to trust their adult judgement.' A friend, mother of three grown children, reports:

Joan Albert

My next-door neighbours talk in what I think is a naïvely proud way of how their twenty-year-old daughter is living with her boyfriend several blocks away. The mother, in particular, talks about how this will be an experience which will teach her daughter about taking care of her own home and responsibility and so forth. But in fact the mother sends Care packages to the daughter every day of whatever food the nuclear family happens to be eating, and when she goes shopping she stocks up on food for the 'children'.

This mother doesn't trust her daughter to take care of herself. Trusting our kids as adults is an indispensable factor in being able to let them go, as it has been throughout their growing up. In fact, the ways we have let our trust in them grow, through the teenage years especially, stand by to help us when they move away as adults. Even though we have had a good deal of practice during their teenage years, it can be hard to trust our grown children to do for themselves what we once, even a long time ago, did for them. And perhaps it's often not a matter of trust so much as of old patterns of protectiveness and guidance that parents have trouble letting go of. A fifty-five-year-old father of three grown-ups says:

My son has worked in South America for two years completely on his own, but when he came back last month to set up an apartment in our city, his mother and I were suddenly chock-full of advice, too much advice, about neighbourhood, rentals, furniture, etc. We couldn't just let him be – which he told us angrily!

Even when it's not just a matter of rentals and furniture but concern over our children's life choices, our ability to trust them certainly makes things easier for us. As one father put it:

It's like sending off a rocket. You get messages back but you can't do anything about it. What it comes down to is giving your child sympathy and love. What more can you do? You've done what you've done. They are what they are – partly you and partly themselves.

Another father remarks:

It's been fifteen years since Dan left home, and now at last I am feeling a kind of detachment. There he is out in the world, and I don't have to worry about him. He is a separate person from me like other close friends are. Of course I want my friends to care about me, and I want him to care. But I seem to be over the parental worries of 'How's he doing, is his apartment big enough, is his woman the right one for him?' I gained this new detachment at the time of a big change in my life – when I got divorced. I grew up a lot when my marriage ended, and I could see him with more clarity once we were no longer in the tight little tremendously complex emotional network of our nuclear family. It is a great relief to be rid of the parental habit of anxiety. There he is, a separate individual living his life on his own terms, never turning to me to ask how: he just gets on with it.

In assessing our children's choice of life style or work, there's a part of us that can't help seeing what they do as a reflection on us. Even when we are pleased by what our adult children are doing, we sometimes find ourselves accused of taking their success too much as a reflection of our own. A young lawyer complains that he cannot go to a social occasion where his mother is present without the most acute embarrassment.

She introduces me to strangers saying 'This is my son Freddy. He works in a storefront law office, after graduating at the top of his class in Columbia Law School. I'm so proud of him! Freddy, tell Mr Davis about the extraordinary man you defended in court last week. What a case! And of course we won.' I feel like a prize pig at a country fair.

Reading this story, a parent might feel, of course I feel proud of my children! Can't I boast a bit? We and our children sometimes differ on the fine line between rightful pride and suffocating over-identification.

On the other hand, when we are uncomfortable with what our adult children choose to do, and still see them or want to see them as reflections of ourselves, then we may feel insulted, outraged, embarrassed, threatened or rejected by what they do. A father recalls:

When my thirty-year-old daughter told us she had stopped eating meat for political reasons, I felt attacked and angry. Partly this was because she was somewhat self-righteous about it. But I realized later that I at first took her being a vegetarian as a rejection of how her mother and I live.

A mother who feels less threatened than she used to examines the source of her acceptance of her daughter's choices:

Mary makes very original choices in her life. She lives with a black man who doesn't seem to want to get married and she doesn't either. She likes kids but doesn't seem to want any, which is O.K. by me except for a small lingering wish for a chance to have a grandchild. I feel strongly that it's her life, and I admire her choices. I think I can do this because of my own feeling of being strongly identified with myself. I feel pretty clear about who I am. I don't need her to fill up the holes. Of course, like every life, mine is full of doubts and troubles, but it's my own life. I don't need her to compensate for what I haven't done, I don't ask her to justify or redeem me, so I can leave her alone.

The father quoted below manages not to feel attacked by his daughter's differences. He has been able to stretch in such a way that he can affirm her life and feel that her life affirms his:

In many ways Phoebe has acted out the suppressed fantasies that I had to forgo in order to pursue an academic career, so there is considerable mutual pride in being complements to one another and not as conflicts. In the foot-loose quality, the sexual indulgence, the lack of professional responsibility, are the opposite side of the discipline that has kept me at work. And from what her friends say, she talks about me in their presence with a similar respect. I feel that our values are similar, though our life styles differ. Phoebe may think of herself at times as a bourgeois suburban housewife, and I think of myself as a foot-loose, carefree traveller. I show the one side and she shows the other side, but if you could somehow see the whole breadth of each of us, we might not be that different.

Sometimes in the attempt to reconcile ourselves to these divergent life styles we find that our own lives are altered. Some of us have embraced views inconceivable to our younger selves, views learned from our grown-up children as they struggle to invent new ways to deal with old problems. We watch our children being the innovators, heroes and sometimes the casualties of these experiments, and as we struggle to understand we are often changed ourselves. For instance, our children have taught us to deal more naturally with sex. This does not mean that all of us accept the standards of our children. But we are learning to be less secretive, less prudish and more realistic about sex; we are learning to accept our children's sexuality, and they, in turn, become more willing to accept ours. Again, it is impossible to speak for everyone; there are still parents who feel that their children have met with the final catastrophe if they are 'living in sin', just as there are those who feel that the ultimate disaster is having them be 'saved'. But there are certainly an increasing number of parents who stretch to try and understand the ways their children deal with those old sources of conflict; sex, money and religion.

Some people attempt to take on the life styles of their children in toto, either because they want to get closer to their children or because they dream that acting young will make them younger. Other people consider these issues carefully, and change their life styles because they have actually changed their beliefs.

One bridge that can surprise and delight us is the sharing of a common cause, an acting out of agreement between the generations on basic values. A father says:

I think one of the most moving events in my life happened on the day after the invasion of Cambodia. Each of my sons was living with a girl someplace in this community, and there was a big get-together over on the other side of the stadium and we all six met that day and were together at that demonstration. I found that very moving ... you know, you feel that what really matters most, the values that matter most, are carried out. We were all together.

Another such moment happened for a middle-aged woman friend at an antiwar demonstration a few years ago. The crowd was chanting 'One, two, three, four. Nixon, stop this fucking war' over and over. She wasn't saying anything, but finally she turned to the stranger standing beside her and said 'I just can't say that word, but I'm with you all the way!' The young woman put her arm around my friend and said 'That's all right. My mother can't, either.'

Yet sometimes no amount of imagination, flexibility or acceptance can bridge the distance. One father whose daughter joined a fundamentalist religious sect writes:

I can't forgive her for writing me a letter saying 'I forgive you, Dad.' Who is she to forgive me, for Christ's sake!

A mother writes:

The problem with changes in extreme life styles is that we all have some limits – something we can't tolerate. I think of the feelings of one friend when her daughter wrote that she had become gay. I think of my own feelings about what is or isn't promiscuity, or – as we used to call it – 'sleeping around'. We all have these limits, and the conflicts that arise when they're crossed are not easily resolved.

A father we quoted earlier saves himself mental anguish by seeing his daughter's choices as complementary to his own; yet even he has his limits.

Her lack of any professional training and sense of disciplined application of effort weighs heavily on me ... that's the closest thing I come to nagging about. I can't see what she's going to do without it other than revert back to her looks and charm.

Even when we are clear of the common tendency to want our children to be reflections of ourselves, we have our fears for them. We deeply don't want them to be hurt. One woman writes:

If you're lucky, you've brought your child up to be an adult who makes her own decisions, who is adventurous and independent. But how about when, now that she's grown, she is using those very characteristics to move into situations which you, out of your own experience, see as dangerous or unwise?

Ironically, I hear myself saying things I would have scorned in my own parents, when I try to convince my child that the man she seems bent on marrying is somebody whom everybody else in the world perceives as a cruel and exploitative person who will negate her personality completely.

Perhaps one of the most excruciating struggles to us as parents of grown-ups is that of figuring out how much we can say, suggest or do to influence children who we feel are making hurtful decisions.

One parent of grown-ups remembers her own mother's efforts as totally inappropriate:

When I was divorcing my husband because I deeply believed it was the only thing to do for myself and for the children, my mother was always badgering me, 'Why leave such a wonderful husband, who provides so much?' That was the last thing I needed.

Yet a mother queries:

I would hope that parents and grown children could be friends. When a friend confides in you that she's going to do something that you think is most inappropriate, foolhardy or even dangerous, wouldn't you as a friend say so – in a calm, supportive way? Yet I have to be so careful what I say to my children. I have to walk on eggs to be sure I'm not hurting their feelings or interfering in their lives.

Advice, badgering, complaints, warnings – these seem to turn our children away. Yet there are times when in self-respect we do have to take a stand.

When Carla and Steve decided to get married I was extremely upset. It seemed a wrong, wrong, step, but I suspected that my saying so would just make her angry. Finally I couldn't keep quiet; I told Carla what I thought, as non-accusingly as I could, with the painful knowledge that I was speaking for my own sake only. Nothing I said would have changed her mind.

Even when the situation isn't extreme, we face the dilemma of how much support or input to offer and how much we can ask to know of what is going on with our children. One man with two sons in their late twenties says:

The biggest problem I know is to what degree you should become involved: too much support and you get in their way; too little, and they must feel unloved.

At 57, Not Sleeping

Like a top spinning down I tip and wobble
my high humming is slowing   my tense singing
will not vibrate the air
because I have
slowed to a
stop

I lie on my side   my bones ram
through my skin   the oldwords slat
around in my head like a loose sail
they do not slam taut to a dream
and slide   as in the past they have
out to sea   with low cloud   and the waves
rocking

No.   I lie here in bed   rattling the children
like dice in a box   all coming up wrong numbers
and I   now   only to stand   and watch
impassive   pretending not to see   not to know
until told

while my gut twists like to double me up

We smile and press cheeks together
and depart
depart
depart

— Margery Cavanagh

And a mother of five children ranging from twenty-two to thirty-six expresses her views about this:

I think a parent's opinion, at any stage, has weight and is 'fraught' no matter what. This also raises the question of questions, by which I mean the longing one has to ask 'Well, what are you going to do about graduate school? How long do you think you'll stay with the far left?' Part of one's children's growing up is a subtle shift in what you as a parent feel entitled to ask. I remember my mother's idiotic and intrusive questions when I was in my twenties – now I look back and realize she wanted to be in touch but didn't know how. I feel, often, that I'm sitting on all sorts of heavy questions I'd better not ask, but I'm dying to know what my children are thinking, or doing, or planning to do. Sometimes some blundering friend asks them, and I'm so grateful, because that way I get to know the answers without the burden of having to ask the question myself!

The mother just quoted has a full-time professional job, yet still has to struggle not to interfere inappropriately, whereas the following mother finds that her job helps in this effort:

I am happy that I've been able to live up to my philosophy and not interfere. But if I hadn't had a career I might have been tempted to.

And a father describes his dilemma:

The older one is very independent. We turned out to be, though we didn't really plan or want to be, in the same field, and he doesn't have a job. And perhaps I could help him but he won't tell me what his situation is. He needs that distance. I know that he respects me. Is he waiting for me to write to him? I am sure that if I wrote him every month and said 'Have you got a job yet? How are things going? Can I help?' he'd freeze up.

Like so many parents, this father is trying to give his son the psychic distance which is one of the essential stages of growing independently out and up. Also, like many of us, he has learned to let his son give him his cues as to how much distance is necessary; but the signs aren't nearly clear enough, and this can be a persisting problem for parents of grown-ups.

Sometimes we suffer because there is so little we *can* do to help when our grown children are in trouble of any kind. In the society we live in, adults are often defined as people who can get along without help from their parents. There have been many societies which were differently organized but not here in the United States, not now. One mother writes:

Near the beginning of a second marriage for me, I made a visit to my son and his family. He and his wife were in the process of having to decide upon high-risk major surgery for their elder child, in the face of disagreement among doctors. I felt keenly my isolation from them in the face of this decision, and finally said something about how I would like to help if there was anything I could do. My son replied 'It must be hard to be an outsider, unable to help.' The word 'outsider' hit me like a blow, and the bruise is still there a year later.

Sons

These tall sons
whose names I cannot distinguish –
to call one, I rattle them all off:

                    Tom, Charles, Nick, Will, George –

What my mind sees:
is little boys – to break your heart
with the growing they have to do –

not these men. No wonder
I don't know their names –
lounging about bent-kneed
and hairy; making love to their wives
or the girls that they live with,
acting out cruelties
on these women who threaten
to control them.

No wonder I cannot call out
the names of these men!
My sons were boys.
I number them over:

                    George, Will, Nick, Charles, Tom

sensitive, gentle, understanding.
Needing shelter and protection.
These giants, gone over
to the other side – I do not remember
which is which – the one with the moustache
laughing, the tall dark one, they are all
strangers to me – their own small sons seem closer.

And yet:
seeing one snubbed and hurt,
one defeated, my blood shouts
he is mine! go easy!
be gentle with him. Remember
how he was afraid of the dark
and he, of thunder, of how the blood
gushed out of his foot,
and of how that tall one used
to bring home bullfrogs
to sing under his window.

                                – Margery Cavanagh

This father has had to make his peace with his limited ability to help:

It's not that I don't care what happens to them and am not involved. I would do anything I could for either, of course – but there gets to be a point where you've done what you can and it's in the lap of the gods.

Parents of grown children, in addition to feeling helpless, often feel guilty for the problems their children have as adults. One mother of a son of forty who has serious neurotic problems said:

I would look at Tom's suffering and say, in all sorts of variations, 'Where did I go wrong? What did we do to make him turn out this way?' It took me years to get over this, to realize I'd done a good, conscientious job under often difficult circumstances. But one day I said to myself, hey, Tom's not my client any more.

Parents who see in their children what they perceive as serious problems – whether they are or not – have really painful feelings that they themselves are failures. After all, you've spent twenty years of time, effort and love and, it appears, you've done a rotten job. Your child can't support herself, he's gay in a non-supportive society, she's an addict. Not only are you heartbroken at your child's suffering, you feel you yourself have failed at your primary lifework. People get over this, learn that not just they are responsible for the adult child's life, that they are separate people – but it is very, very tough to accommodate.

Visits

When children move away, we exchange visits and that becomes a new way for the generations to communicate. One woman's daughter married and became a missionary for an evangelical group in the Northwest. The married daughter and her husband live in a small town, where the young woman works in a local laundry to help support the work of their religious group. Not long ago this mother came back from a visit to her daughter; although they had had some difficult visits during the past few years, this time the mother looked relaxed and happy. She said that when she arrived she'd found that her daughter was busy working extra shifts for extra pay. There was going to be little or no time for them to talk. But determined to see her daughter even if they could not talk, this woman had taken advantage of the rush of work in the laundry and had worked for three days folding cattle shrouds (*sic*) with her child. Afterwards, they talked more freely than they had been able to do for several years, and affectionate contact became possible again. Of course, not everyone has the determination and stamina or perhaps the money to take this course; and not everyone can find cattle shrouds to fold.

A mother of five grown-ups comments:

One way of bridging is not by intellectualizing, but by trying to communicate through working side by side. I feel this is part of what goes on when you visit your grown children at their place and help cook, diaper, garden, etc. It has deep meaning: seeing (and approving of) their house, their furniture, friends, children, climate, etc.

And a father observes: 'Visits on his ground are more successful because then he isn't the "child" coming "home". I visit as a friend and appreciator.' Certainly, it helps if parents and children can find ways like this of acceptingly entering each other's worlds from time to time.

Helping our children in their daily tasks can be a deeply felt pleasure, but it doesn't always work. A mother told of visiting her stepdaughter just after the birth of her second baby:

It wasn't very successful. Debby would agree to let me cook but she wouldn't let me clean, and the two-year-old wouldn't have anything to do with me!

A friend whose children are only eight and eleven offered this piece of wisdom about visits:

Help can feel like criticism – if your mother offers to clean a floor that you had no intention of cleaning. If my parents offer to do something I'd be doing anyway, it's companionable; if they offer to do something I wouldn't do myself, it's interference.

Many of us have experienced going home for a visit when we felt we were mature adults and then found ourselves slipping easily back into acting and being treated like a child again. This is a dynamic we need to watch out for when our children visit us. And manners! According to a mother of several grown-ups:

The hardest things about having grown kids home for a visit are their eating habits, their housekeeping styles. Is it my house or is it ours? Who makes the rules now? The same in reverse when one visits grown children's families: treading on eggs lest one give offence, feeling a bit cross that there's no toilet paper in the john and that the grandchildren are allowed to eat everything with their hands – and that the hands aren't washed.

Visits can be full of feelings on both sides:

The need for approval is profound, and it goes both ways! My children want me to see and validate how they're 'making it'. But I also yearn to be told that I'm still good, still valued. Our grown children do a lot of scrutinizing of us when they come home – reshaping their opinions of the past and what it did or didn't do to them. This can be a painful but exhilarating exercise.

Just as we want to be careful not to impose ourselves on our grown children by descending on them at inappropriate moments, we need to be able to be honest with ourselves and them about the times we *don't* want to visit or be visited. Sometimes it's hard to be so honest. One father admits:

I see my son and his family once or twice a year. I could see them much more. They keep saying 'Why don't you come up and see us, why don't you come up and see us?' I don't because I feel embarrassed, bored, and more interested in what I am doing. I feel embarrassed at their respect and warmth. If I could be around and invisible and see what they're doing, that would give me a great deal of satisfaction. I don't want them to do things for me, wait on me, I'm interested in what I'm doing here. I don't want to take the weekend off to go – maybe feel in the way with their friends. They're having a good time, I'm having a good time, why can't we just go on separately and talk over the phone, and see each other at Christmas?

Sometimes as we try to bridge these different kinds of distances, we feel that the confrontations will never end.

Recently a friend rushed up to me on the street brandishing a book in great excitement: 'Look what I found!' she said. 'See, it says in the subtitle, "How parents and grown children can comfort *each other." What a wonderful book it must be!' But when we looked together at the subtitle, we found that it said 'How parents and grown children can* confront *each other.' My friend had not been wearing her glasses in the store. Crestfallen, she went off to return the book, realizing that the one which will tell us about comforting has yet to be written.*

This desire for a comforting, comfortable relationship with our grown children is strong for many of us. Ironically, the eventual development of such a bond probably depends more than anything else on how well we *can* confront each other, and on how well we can let each other go, communicating with respect across whatever distance exists.

Children as Resources

We have spoken at length about the ins and outs of letting our children go and of trying to establish a connection with them which respects their autonomy and our own. The reward can be that once a kind of interdependence is no longer so threatening, we can treat each other as equals and friends. For some this point comes quickly, for others it takes years. The man who went to the antiwar demonstration with his grown children experienced this kind of mutuality. A woman speaks of the recent weekend when her grown daughter called and wanted to visit: 'I was delighted that it was her idea. I was going to be looking for an apartment that weekend, and I thought, she can help me do that.' This woman will be having a grown friend for the weekend, one with whom the bonds of history and love are especially strong.

A father remarks:

I think of Mark as one of the people who know something about me. He's someone I've known all his life and he's known me a lot of mine, and there just aren't many such people in your life.

And a mother:

I had been on a business trip in the area where my twenty-two-year-old was working, and we had arranged to meet for lunch. Well, by some miracle of perfect planning I found myself walking toward our meeting place just on time. It was a clear, sunlit day, and there on the corner stood this fine human being, bright and funny and attractive and interesting. I couldn't wait to hear what we would talk about and I felt really lucky to be having lunch with him. How great it was to recognize that this wonderful person was my son!

Alex Webb/Magnum

Another mother, whose husband died many years ago:

Right now I'm living near or with four of my five children, who range from twenty-one to thirty years old. I like having their frequent company, particularly sharing mealtimes. It's great not having to be so responsible for their physical and emotional needs any more – and I don't have to be on 'guard duty' now, always concerned about their physical safety. My children are supportive of my activities, and it's nice to get their approval on such a regular basis. My own relatives tend to be critical of me for my interest in yoga and meditation and health, so this support is especially important. Also, my children share material things with me, like cars, so we're all more able to save extra money for that occasional 'extravagant pleasure'. In our household, solitude and quietude are highly prized interludes, largely because of the feminist activities of my daughter, but it's still comfortable. I do think I would benefit from having more time and space to myself, but it's always been my instinct to share.

Here is a woman whose children were resources to her at a critical time:

My husband and I decided to live in separate places two years after our youngest child left home. When we told our four adult children about this, all four did unexpected things. Two, who had not felt ready for marriage or in need of it before, telephoned me on the same day from opposite ends of the country and unknown to each other, to say that they were getting married. For me this was an important reinforcement and support because, although they didn't say so in so many words, they seemed to be saying, don't be disheartened. Marriage is good. Yours was too, even if it isn't working any more. It's given us something which we value and want to try and live by. The other two did something else: they temporarily moved closer to home after living far away for several years. They didn't say it in words, either, but they seemed to be saying, don't worry. We can all still give each other comfort and reassurance – in times of stress we are still available to each other.

Even here, however, there are limits to what our children can be for us, and for many there is the fear that we may need them too much. One younger friend in her twenties says of her parents:

My father's mother wants to be called every night and insists on visits all the time. I think because she's so dependent on them, they try to be extra careful not to ask for much from me. As a result they almost never ask me over, and when I drop by they act glad but not overjoyed. I sometimes wish they'd turn to me more often.

A recently remarried mother writes:

One special, but not rare, situation in this period of life is the one in which one partner in a happy marriage dies at the time when the children are becoming adults. This was my experience. My husband and I were unusually close, in that for each of us the other was the most important personal and emotional resource. Within a month of his death I recognized that in the future, possibly for the rest of my life, I would need my children far more than they needed me. Recognizing this intellectually did not really enable me to keep from burdening them with my needs, even when geographical distance separated us.

Needing our children more than they need us, either for emotional support or for sheer physical assistance in times of sickness, can be an uncomfortable position for both sides.

Among parents and grown children, then, the crucial balance between dependence and autonomy shifts from one side to the other throughout the rest of our lives. Each at times is a burden to the other, each tries to handle the burden as well as possible.

Parents' Lives After the Children Leave

Freedoms and Responsibilities

After that symbolic though rarely specific moment when the last child 'leaves home', how do parents' lives change? How do we use the time, money or energy opened up by the diminishment of our daily responsibilities? As one mother queried, 'What will the dailiness of my life feel like?'

It used to be assumed in popular literature that mothers would need new interests and new hobbies when their children left. For the increasing number of women who work outside their homes the problem of using empty time is rare indeed. For those women whose reason for being continues to be their children even when those children are nearly grown, hobbies may have some relevance, but these days most women have adopted new interests and activities long before the last child goes away. The woman who wants to go back to work at this point can face many obstacles in a sexist and ageist job market in which her skills and experience as a parent are rarely taken seriously as marks of her employability. On the other hand, a woman may find that new possibilities for using her creative energies open around her like flowers. A man may feel that his only option is to work longer and harder at something he's been doing all along, or to face retirement with as good grace as possible. Or, no longer faced with the heavy burden of supporting children, many men are looking around them for new career options that may be less lucrative but more spiritually rewarding. For all working parents the departure of the last child (or the graduation of the last child from college) can bring a financial relief which opens up a chance to work less or to spend more money on themselves. One of the glories of having grown-up children is the sense of having accomplished at least part of one's basic purpose in life and of being given the bonus of free time to experiment and explore.

As we reassess our priorities at this time, some may wonder whether to move to smaller quarters. Often the house or apartment they lived in with their children is too big or, as they near retirement, too expensive. Should they or can they move in the same neighbourhood? Should they or can they keep some space for their children's visits? A father remarks:

The married one wanted her room at home kept ready for her and nothing about it changed unless absolutely necessary. We only added a new long bed for her husband. Most of her wedding presents (this was an old-style church wedding) stayed in our attic for years.

Moving from the old family home can cause an uproar from children even though they are in fact there only in their memories. It can be an uprooting for all, and add to the parents' sense that an era is over. Yet it can also symbolize the beginning of a new phase.

Our life after children go is profoundly influenced by where we are in the life cycle. While a parent who had an only child at twenty will be about forty when the child leaves, most of us whose youngest children are leaving are likely to be in our late forties or early fifties. Very often a woman reaches the menopause at about the same time her last child leaves home. If she is not engaged in a fairly active life of work and relationships, and often even if she is, the arrival of menopause may feel to her like an unnecessary underlining of the statement 'No more children for you, old girl!' In a culture which pigeonholes women as child bearers and child raisers, it is difficult to resist the sense that one's function is over when children go and menstrual cycles stop. Yet for many or most women menopause brings a sense of relief, of release into another phase of one's work and sexuality.

Very often our children leave just as we are beginning to feel our age. Our health and the level of our physical energies certainly shape our experience as parents of grown-ups. After our child-raising era is past, according to the actuarial tables we can look forward to a good many active years before we die or become incapacitated by illness. And yet statistics don't always apply, and often the freedom which we feel we've earned is spoiled by chronic physical problems or by sudden unexpected illness. Having said good-bye to children, a father or mother may find him/herself caring for a sick or disabled spouse who in some ways becomes like another child. The uncertainty is there. A father of two grown sons speaks:

I have a lot of learning and adventure to look forward to, but it depends on my health, doesn't it, which is so much more precarious now.

Often at the same time that our children grow up, our parents grow old and need care and attention. The dependency of an old parent may provide a welcome substitute for absent children, or it may mean that our anticipated freedom from responsibility doesn't materialize at all because there is an older generation to care for.

Caring for old parents may be prompted by a mixture of love and duty. Their dependence can move us, but it can be irritating as well. And when we care for them, self-interest may also be served. Foreseeing that in time we, too, will come to lean on our children, we may be good to our own old parents partly in order to set an example to our children. If you put grandma out on an ice floe to freeze as the Eskimos used to do, you can be pretty sure that your turn on the ice floe will come around in time. 'I'm trying to be nice to my mother,' says a friend (who really does care about her mother), 'so that my children will *see* how nice I'm being.'

Whether or not they are needing us in new ways, our parents continue to play a role in our relationship with our (now grown) children. In fact, sometimes they expect us to exercise the very control that we are trying to give up. For instance, great-grandmother says to grandmother 'You must *make* your daughter dress her baby more warmly!' and sets a whole series of rebellions bouncing down from generation to generation. One woman was intensely annoyed by her mother, who disliked her grown grandson's long hair but would only say to her daughter 'Dear me, what will people think?' A mother remarks:

Here I am, in mid-life, the middle person in a series of adults: my mother, me, my child, my grandchildren. The relationships and interdependencies when one is in the middle are fascinating.

Sometimes we would say 'demanding' or 'exhausting' as well as 'fascinating'. The truth is: here we are woven into the life cycle in both directions. According to the suggestion of one woman whose grown child has left home and whose parents are still healthy and active: 'If you are lucky enough to have this experience, enjoy it. It can't last very long.'

Parents' Intimacy and Conflict

The need for intimacy, for shared experience, does not diminish with age. People may become resigned to isolation because they have no choice; they may even choose it in preference to the pain of rejection in its many forms; people do become less resilient as they get older. But almost everybody wants some sort of companionship. Although they may compromise and settle for some less risky condition, most people would like to have somebody around who loves them and is willing to be loved in return. Yet, as one mother pointed out, 'For many of us, our children are the only people we've been intimate with.' This is true for married parents and single parents alike.

The way married couples develop through the long phase after their children have gone is usually an outgrowth of the way they have lived their marriage all along. Some couples have grown closer to each other through their children; they have learned to share their lives by sharing the raising of children and have forged a strong and enduring intimacy in this way. For those who have learned to be companionable, to enjoy sharing their lives, their joint freedom from the worry of children can feel wonderful, and the returning of children may simply feel like an interruption:

Why can't our son leave us old folks alone. He's thirty years old but he keeps coming home, looking in the refrigerator, and saying 'What, no blueberry yogurt?'

For many couples the child-raising years have strained the initial bond, bringing tension and difficulty. The children's departure may bring relief. A father says:

Jonathan left home when he was quite young. His mother and I were both artists and preoccupied with our work. Since we didn't have a lot of money, we both worked at home, so we felt the difficulty of having a child in the house. He was an intense kid, and we had a lot of conflicts both with him and with each other about how to raise him. When he left, we felt a certain regret but more relief. It just felt right. We had a better marriage after he left, for a long time.

This father's relief at his children's departure also comes from marital stress:

Separation from our children has been a great relief – partly because it meant less immediate confrontation with my wife, less conflict with her, and it meant more quiet at home, and less raising of questions over the breakfast table.

But the outcome for his marriage was different; he goes on to say:

Their moving away from home eliminated a source of conflict between us, but on the other hand it made even clearer the distance we had grown from each other. She couldn't complain to me every morning about what they were going to do, whether they were going to get a haircut or clean up their clothes or something like that. And so what were we going to talk about then? We found there wasn't much of anything. Their leaving gave us a chance to be together if we'd wanted to be together. But it only made the conflict between us even clearer.

Most of us fall somewhere between the two extremes of togetherness and estrangement, between the comfortable couple revelling in their time together and the unhappy couple who discover there's nothing left to say.

Many people remember longing for their little children to be grown up so that the harassed parents could have some privacy, and yet, often, when the free space opens up they find that they have lost the knack of enjoying it. Even nearly independent teenage children provided a distraction, a buffer, a prop for the relationship between the parents. One mother called these children, 'hand-tailored companions'. So there is naturally a time of readjustment when they go, and parents find themselves face to face without buffers and diversions.

What has happened to the old kinds of communication between partners? Sometimes young children are used as a language: we speak to each other through them by the way we touch them or talk to them. We may have learned to express our feelings most easily to the children, and this may have served to keep open a channel of expression to each other. There is, for example, a world of difference between a woman at the dinner table saying 'Johnnie, Daddy's tired; don't bug him' and a woman alone at the dinner table with her husband, not talking to him because she thinks he's tired. Silence can communicate a lot, and by long experience people can learn great skill in interpreting the body language which fills a silence, but they make mistakes and have no means of checking their interpretations except in words. The mother who has Johnnie to talk through can indicate love, sympathy, impatience or anger by the tone of her voice. But whichever she expresses, her words also tell her husband that she has noticed something about him and that she has responded to it in some way. The old couple who call each other Mother and Dad are relics of this mode of communication. They have addressed each other through their children for so long ('Let's help Mother with these dishes' or 'Daddy will lift that end and we'll take this one', etc.) that for the rest of their lives they can speak to each other only in the third person.

Thus for many couples the ability to express emotions directly has atrophied, either because the presence of children for many years has put a damper on the expression of certain feelings, or because the children have provided an indirect means of expressing them. Sometimes couples who find themselves in this predicament buy a dog to talk through. Many parents find themselves longing to renew their powers of direct communication, to learn to live without an intermediary.

With the children gone, some couples begin to treat each other as children. Everyone is familiar with the over-protective spouse and the bickering which makes both members of a couple seem equally childish:

'Put on your coat, honey, it's cold out.'
'I know if I'm cold or not. If you keep telling me to wear it I never will.'

One of this pair is attempting in a groping way to express feelings of concern and caring, but the exchange rapidly degenerates into a battle over autonomy. The caring-controller part of one partner is being inappropriately applied, and the other person is turning into a rebellious child as a result. So both are confused in the end.

This conversation can take other forms. Parents who have learned to give a lot of autonomy to their children may end up in a bind like this:

'Would you like to go camping on our vacation?'
'Not really, but you go. You should do what you want to on your vacation. I don't mind.'
'But I want you to mind.'
'Well, it's your vacation. You have to decide what you want to do with it.'

Betsy Cole

One person is trying to support the individuality of the other in such a way that the other feels rejected, like an unwanted child. In these moments's/he wants to share a vacation, not to be given autonomy.

The vacation dilemma brings up the whole question of recreation and how it is shared in a family. Some of us find that joint recreation has depended on the presence of our children and that we don't enjoy going on picnics or to ball games only with each other. It may be that one of us really does like the country or really is a baseball fan; but for the other parent, ants in the sandwiches or popcorn in the bleachers may have been acceptable in order to be with the children, but no longer, and we may be surprised to discover that there is little or nothing that we want to do together for fun. If we throw ourselves into our jobs, we need to leave time for some shared activity, or we may soon find ourselves living in a marriage which has become shadowy and unreal from lack of use.

Sometimes the estrangement is intensified when one member of a couple begins to fight the ageing process in an unrealistic manner. When the responsibilities of child rearing end, either spouse may suddenly act in a way that seems bizarre to the other. They may take up jogging to the point of heart attack; meditation to the point of remoteness; gestalt therapy to the point of saying 'I love you!' every day to the mailman. People who used to dress in a conventionally sober manner may take to wearing bib overalls or red suspenders on their jeans at directors' meetings and church suppers. One woman wrote of her husband's 'spectacular flirtation with the younger generation'. Sincere efforts to identify with another generation are worth making as long as the parent doesn't lose touch with reality altogether. But when the fifty-year-old begins to relate to the world as though s/he were actually twenty, the husband or wife of this middle-of-life adventurer is usually left far behind, sputtering in the distance. Actually, this may be exactly the right course of action for that individual, but it is another one of the strains on such relationships.

Sometimes a couple will find that without either work or play in common and with the shared bond of child rearing reduced to a minimum, they have nothing left of mutual interest except the past; if they have strong desires to do diverging things the marriage may collapse. It has been provocatively suggested that all marriages should automatically dissolve when the youngest child leaves home; in order to continue the marriage both partners would have to take positive action. This rather drastic idea reflects a strong element of common sense: in fact, many marriages today end in separation or divorce when the children leave home, and this is a period of reassessment for even the healthiest marriage.

Single Parents and Intimacy

For a single parent who isn't living intimately with another person, the potential for freedom and the potential for loneliness are both accentuated when children leave home. With no mate to take into consideration, the possibilities for change and adventure are perhaps greater. A long-time single woman exulted:

> I've raised my three kids by myself since my husband died. I've done it with a lot of loving and persistence, and now it's over. I've given them the house and I'm on my way to a great new research job across the country. A new life starting to unfold, at fifty!

And a father:

> I feel like I'm beginning over again. Within a few years after my children left home, I retired and became divorced. This means a curious feeling of a new start. I'm learning a lot of things I should have learned in adolescence.

A single mother who has worked full time for years:

At just about the time my son left home I was going through a wonderfully heady period of having come out of a very long marriage and feeling somehow 'out of prison'. The fact that I no longer had daily child-rearing responsibilities only added to this absolute sense of freedom. It was very exhilarating, for the first time in my life, to be able to say 'What do I want to do on Sunday afternoon?' The question had never come up before, and I found the answers were giving me wonderful experiences and all sorts of ways of exploring myself. Looking back on it, I can see that I was a little selfish. My son who was leaving home needed extra support and felt a certain amount of isolation. We finally talked about it, at his instigation, and were able to work it out.

Having children leave home can open up new possibilities for sexual relationships, for although many single parents do find sexual companionship while the kids are home, many others find that life with children gets in the way of developing bonds with another adult. This gay father expresses the feelings of many single parents, gay and straight, as he looks forward to being a parent of grown-ups:

I can't get the intimacy and loving I need until my youngest son leaves home, because although I do have lovers now, I know that in this neighbourhood there's no way I could have a lover live here with me. Deeply as I love my kids and glad as I am to have them, I find myself counting the years.

Although once those years do go by there *can* be a new freedom to explore sexual relationships, the cruel fact for many is that we are now getting older, in a society which views sexuality among older people, especially women, as inappropriate if not downright unattractive. And so the underside of this new freedom is loneliness. A woman writes:

For me as a single mother of fourteen years the loss of intimacy is striking. My children were the only people with whom I have had continuous sharing intimacy, and with whom I have always been able to be unselfconsciously myself. Losing them to their own autonomous adulthood has thus been a loss of emotional closeness in my life, a kind of closeness for which I haven't easily found substitutes.

(Ironically, many a married parent who has lost the easy marital intimacy of the early years would resonate with these feelings.) A parent living alone when children leave may or may not have an extra burden of loneliness to cope with: it depends partly on how long s/he has been living without a partner, and on how well s/he has learned to let other friendships and occupations fill her/his life.

So, where and how we live, and with whom, become especially pressing questions for single parents whose children are grown and gone. A single-family house or apartment can feel unbearably empty or refreshingly peaceful, depending on the person's moods and needs. Carefully considering her needs for intimacy and/or companionship, this mother ponders what the best living situation would be:

I anticipate having them all gone with great pleasure, but since I like having people around I'll probably rent rooms. I don't think I want a communal type of life because I'm used to my own space. Yet I remember one summer when both my roomers and my children were gone for six weeks and even my landlady was gone, and it was very weird for me – just because I'm so unused to being entirely alone. I don't think I want people around in order to feel needed – that has never been an issue at least in my conscious level of thinking. It's not that I want a job to perform for them – what I like is people around to talk to.

If a divorced or widowed parent of grown-ups does remarry, it may be easier for a grown-up child to deal with than for a teenager living at home. But it may not be possible or appropriate for the step-parent to form a close relationship with a grown child; they don't need each other so much, so they may not make the same effort to overcome any initial doubts they may feel about each other. It may require a special effort by the real parent to keep a continuing close contact with a son or daughter who is unsympathetic to, or distant from, this new marriage.

Being Grandparents

In the old days it was in the order of things that parents sooner or later became grandparents. As one friend puts it, in her generation everyone 'gotmarriedandhadchildren'. Today becoming a grandparent is not something we can expect quite so automatically. Yet enough of us do have grandchildren that it seems relevant to include in this chapter something about wanting or not wanting them; about the new relationship they cause us to have with our own children; about some of the dilemmas and pleasures that grandparenting brings.

Although we may try to respect a careful decision to remain child-free, it may be very difficult for us to accept it when our children don't want children of their own. A mother of five grown-ups recognizes:

When our children decide not to have children, it is a violation of deeply held expectations, and in a sense it's a slap at the parents, since it says being a parent isn't worthwhile. I think this cuts deep. For me, if my children were to decide not to have kids, it would be a great grief and disappointment. I would feel I'd failed in some essential way. I realize this is excessive.

One mother speaks of her gay son:

I told him I felt sad at first because I realized he would never marry and never have children and that part of the joy of being a parent is to anticipate grandchildren. Other than that, I'm very happy that he has found a relationship that's good.

Many people feel that they are *owed* grandchildren. We may want them as a sign of our own continuity; we may be looking for the son or daughter we never had or we may even look to a grandchild as a substitute for a child who died. It is not uncommon for a young mother or father to feel that his or her baby is in some sense a gift to its grandparents.

I gave my child a name similar to the name of my brother who died in infancy, and then I was horrified when I heard my parents inadvertently using my dead brother's name when speaking to my baby. I realized that I had unconsciously set up this situation – it was as though I was offering my baby to my mother and father as a substitute for their lost son.

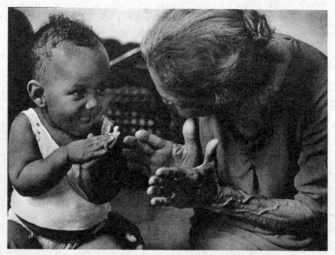

Jodi Cobb

Not all young mothers are so aware of what they are doing, but many will recognize the feeling, and many grandparents will recognize the baby as the fulfilment of the fantasy of having one more baby of their own. One divorced man lived out this fantasy in this way: his three adult daughters were childless and had resolved to stay that way. This rather dynastically oriented man was very unhappy not to have grandchildren of his own flesh and blood, but he solved the problem when he married a young woman and had several more children, whom he referred to as his 'do-it-yourself' grandchildren. In fact, he spends much more time with this set of children than he did with his first, participating in their daily care in ways that are new for him.

Another father copes with the situation differently:

I don't seem to have a strong need to be a grandfather in order to see my family carried on. I would like to see them have kids but it's not very important. I have a close relationship with two other sets of children now which gives me a grandfatherly feeling.

If we have ways of getting close with other young children, then perhaps we can make our peace with not having grandchildren of our own.

Not everyone welcomes the role of grandparent. Some of us worry that our children will expect us to be parents again and ask us to watch *their* children at a time when we're glad of our new freedom. Other people feel prematurely thrust into old age by the birth of grandchildren and don't want to have anything to do with them. This rejection may also have to do with a refusal to come to terms with one's children's sexuality. In any case, grandparents can be hurtfully distant:

My father was a doctor and never went as far as the corner drugstore without leaving several telephone numbers where he could be reached. But a week before my first baby was born he left for Europe leaving no forwarding address and it took us a week to find him and to tell him that the baby had been born.

This grandfather must have been feeling a terrible dismay over his new role. The reason there are witches in fairy tales is that they correspond to something in the real world. They perhaps represent the acting out of anger at not being young any more, and of jealousy that someone who used to love us best loves somebody else better now.

For mothers the birth of a daughter's first baby can establish a whole new relationship between daughter and mother, in which they have the sense of becoming equals for the first time.

The birth of my first grandchild made me feel accepted by my daughter. She was saying, I too want to be a mother. I also felt approving of my daughter and expressed satisfaction with her as an adult. I was saying, you are a complete and successful grown-up, and since the baby is the product of her sexuality, this means that I was accepting that as well.

These deep recognitions of mutual experience can really bring mothers and daughters close, although, as usual, there is another side to the question. Before real friendship can begin, the grandmother's fantasy of being a new mother again may have to be cleared up. When this first grandchild is born, a kind of symbolic struggle for possession of the baby can take place. The grandmother usually loses, of course, but sometimes it seems necessary that she act out her feelings of being the mother before she can quite admit that it isn't her child.

When my first child was born, my mother, pale and perspiring, stayed with me in the hospital through all the preliminary stages of a perfectly normal labour. In those days women stayed in bed for a debilitating two weeks after delivery. So after my baby was born my mother went home and stayed in bed for two weeks, utterly exhausted by the birth.

More and more young mothers are speaking up about their need to be 'mothered' during the days and weeks after they have a baby. It is a very special kind of sharing when we have separated clearly enough from each other for a mother to be able to be with her daughter in a nurturing and helpful way at this time, and for the daughter to want her mother to be there.

Of course, the challenges of proper communication and the dilemmas about advice-giving discussed above are especially important between grandparents and their grown children.

When my first grandchild was born, I was bitterly disappointed in not being allowed to come to the hospital to have another baby at second hand. Instead, the symbolic moment came a little later at home when the baby screamed for twenty-four hours but wouldn't nurse. My daughter had, of course, talked to the paediatrician on the telephone, who told her to relax before nursing, have a little beer and lie down, etc., but this hadn't helped, and after twenty-four hours of screaming, relaxing was obviously impossible. The interesting part of this story is the difference between my daughter's memory of what happened next and mine:

Daughter's version: The paediatrician, a good reliable man, carefully selected and totally trusted, came to see the baby and said 'This baby has thrush', gave him an antibiotic which cured the thrush in a day and said 'Meanwhile you'll have to feed him with an eyedropper.'

My version: I arrived to call on my daughter and the baby and found the baby screaming. 'This baby is getting dehydrated,' I said. 'That dumb paediatrican must be wrong that you need to relax. I think I should go get some milk and an eyedropper.' I got milk and an eyedropper, and later the paediatrician came, diagnosed thrush, and said 'Your mother was right.'

It's clear what an investment each had in her own version of the story. The grandmother's unconscious wish to be the mother of this baby stands out in all its naked splendour. At the same time, it is easy to see why the daughter finds this put-down of her role as competent mother intensely irritating.

Questions of communication and control can suddenly spring up again around life-style issues. Sometimes parents who were previously willing to accept a change in their children's life styles may find themselves feeling that a poor helpless baby is being imposed on, and it may be enormously difficult for them not to 'intercede on the child's behalf'.

Then there is the sometimes touchy question of how much the grandparents are going to help. Most grandparents learn how much they can volunteer to do without being sorry, and although it may take some trial and error to find out how good they still are at taking care of little children, a balance is gradually reached. Reaching a balance involves being *honest* about our limits, even though some part of us may feel uneasy that we're not being supergrandparents. One grandmother I know has told her daughter that she must never *ask* her to baby-sit. She will volunteer if she feels like it. Others are glad to be asked but want to feel free to refuse. One grandmother took two very little grandchildren for a month with no one to help and ended up exhausted and angry. But even when a grandparent willingly undertakes the less agreeable aspects of child care and doesn't simply hand the child with a tantrum back to its parents, this grandparent has one great advantage over the parents: whatever ultimately may go wrong in the child's life, the grandparent doesn't have to feel that it's his or her fault. This may be why there is often so little tension between grandparents and grandchildren and so much tolerance on both sides.

This warm identification which skips a generation is common:

When I was thirty-five years old, my widowed mother, then in her sixties, was being courted by a man almost seventy years old. One day I got a letter from my grandmother (then ninety) saying that my mother who had business in the South was being driven there by this man. My grandmother's letter was sputtering with indignation: 'Unmarried couples do not go on motor trips together!' So I found myself writing her a reassuring letter saying 'It's all right. The younger generation have different standards from ours and for them things like this are really O.K.'

In this case thirty-five and ninety were identifying with each other as distinct from those mavericks in their sixties.

. The sharing of attention can be a problem, too, when it is divided among generations. A grown child may feel left out: the grandparents only want to see the baby. Or a grandparent may feel that only the baby is the focus, like the grandfather whose grown children were all concentrating on a new grandchild on the floor of his living room. Finally he said 'I can't see why you're making such a fuss over Mary [the baby]. It's *easy* to be a baby, but it's taken me eighty years of hard work to get to be me.' Or there's the mother who goes to see her daughter but finds herself always left with the grandchildren when she turns up, and begins to feel that her daughter doesn't really want to see her but only to use her. In these generational relationships it's often hard to know who is thinking of themselves as child and who, at a given moment, is the parent. Again, clear communication seems to be the key.

One of the most valuable qualities of grandparents is their ability to provide a sense of continuity and rootedness. By making the past vivid for grandchildren through stories or through sharing places they have lived in for a long time, they can give them a sense of location in a larger family context. Stories of a grandparent's childhood reach back into a time so remote that it's hard to conceive of. Even young grandparents seem enormously old to a small child, although the child may politely deny it. One small girl, feeling proud of reaching the monumental age of four, turned to her young-looking grandmother and asked 'How come I'm so old if you're so new?'

My grandson used to say 'Mrs Jones is very old, isn't she? But you're just a little tiny bit old.' I appreciated this tactful effort on his part, but it really is O.K. with me if I seem old to him, as I'm sure I do. I like having a chance to relive parts of my childhood with children who are entranced by hearing about it. It reinforces my sense of continuity with the past as well as theirs, and it gives me the kind of mini-immortality which will carry me a short distance into the future in these grandchildren's memories. I find this a reassuring feeling as I approach the time when I really will be old.

Getting Old: The Conclusion

One of the final challenges for human beings is to get old with as much verve and gumption as possible. Old parents who keep on being interested in life give a subtle kind of sustenance to their children: they are givers of hope and affirmers of life. One older father speaks of where being a parent fits into his life now:

I want to do something that will make them proud. It does help keep me honest. I may be more interested in their being proud of me than in me being proud of me. I want to be the sort of guy they wouldn't mind being like.

And a mother of four adults speaks of her own mother:

Two weeks before her eightieth birthday my mother came home for a rest from the incessant round of activities at the retirement colony where she had chosen to live. She was tired from the Jung class, the Shakespeare reading group, managing the sculpture studio and doing portrait heads of several of the other residents. She needed a vacation. But she hadn't been home twenty-four hours when she began work on a new statue and set herself a schedule of daily work. This made me feel wonderful. She had shown me that I might have at least twenty-five more years of total involvement to look forward to – with enthusiasm.

Yet not everyone will be so healthy in old age. Many parents will provide the confirmation we speak of by the way they face the disabilities of age, and death itself.

The parents of grown children are a varied group. Because of the extraordinary position of the present generation of middle-aged people – midway between such differing customs – you will find every kind of character in the cast. You may come upon them rocking on front porches; devoted old couples who live near their children and grandchildren and make birthday cakes and Sunday dinner; or you may find them unmarried but middle-aged, living in geodesic domes while naked grandchildren dance around them to the music of a sitar and the young adults hunt for berries in the forest. It has not been a simple matter to compress this range of relationships into one short summarizing chapter, but the one clear fact is that there has been an enormous change in life styles in the American middle class since World War II, and especially in mores relating to marriage and the family. When the infants of today have grown up, it is impossible to know what their parents' relationships will be and what the local customs will be like. It is possible that a new generation of parents will bend more easily and crack less often, and it may be that the changes they deal with will be less extreme. They may devise better ways to find companionship in their lives. But the biological facts will remain the same, the children will become adults, and the adults will grow old and die. You can confidently count on these things happening, and everyone will have a turn at figuring out how to deal with them. If they are lucky and also wise, the next generation may discover better ways to be parents of children and to be children of parents while passing through the inevitable stages of being human.

6. Sharing Parenthood

Nancy Press Hawley

We all share the care and raising of our children with others. This chapter will focus on a particular kind of shared parenthood: sharing with one or a few others who are intimately connected with our children's lives and with ours, whose self-concept includes a primary sense of connection to the children. For many parents this means sharing with the other parent of their children; for single parents it may be with close friends, relatives or lovers; for remarried parents it's with the step-parent.* In this kind of 'shared parenting', mothers and fathers seek to share the primary caretaking part of parenthood in ways which move beyond the stereotypical notion that mothers should just take care of children and fathers should just earn money.

We who are authors of this book are excited by the possibilities of shared parenting, for mothers, fathers and children. We believe from our experience that such sharing opens up important new options – for men to nurture, for women to create beyond the sphere of the home, for children to grow up knowing daily love from more than one care giver and with a wider range of adult models. Several assumptions and values underlie our advocacy of shared parenting: we believe that being a parent is a very important job; it stimulates people to mature; it is a job for both men and women; men can be nurturing, gentle, tender, patient, playful, humorous – all qualities needed in caring for small children; women are capable of interests and activity and creative work beyond what child care and householding alone can provide; and family life can be a richer experience for all when parenting is shared. We recognize, too, that sharing parenting is not the only way of showing love to a child or partner. There are many very loving families in which parents play quite traditional roles. We want to affirm both those women who choose child rearing and householding as their primary work and those who do not: the 'ideal' of shared parenthood is not for everyone, and should not be seen as yet another pressure on parents to perform. We realize that not all relationships – especially ones that started with a traditional arrangement

---

*The emphasis in this chapter is on shared parenting for women and men in heterosexual couples, although many of the issues we discuss will be similar for a gay parent seeking to share children with a partner.

for child care – can handle the changes that shared parenting may entail. This is a risk we can be sensitive to as we think about shared parenting for ourselves or suggest it to others.

Sharing parenting has its problems, too. The social context in which we live is not supportive of shared parenting: we stumble over cultural expectations of what mothers do and what fathers do, and over the inflexibility of work schedules. Within the family, problems can arise when two parents become so

Peter Simon.

busy trading the caretaking function back and forth that they forget to spend time together as a couple or as a family. These and other problems with shared parenting will be addressed in the pages that follow. The problems, like the pleasures, are an integral part of the process of shared parenting as we have experienced it; when we look at them they can teach us about ourselves and allow us to grow as parents.

The Personal Context for Shared Parenting: Our Histories

Most of us who are writing this book have memories of a number of parenting people in our early lives. We were aware that our fathers, grandparents, aunts, uncles and people our families may have hired often shared responsibility with our mothers for our care.

One woman recalls how important her grandmother was to her:

My grandmother, my grandfather and an uncle lived with us. Actually it was my grandmother that I have the fondest memories of. I used to have very bad nightmares as a child and my parents' door was always shut. I would knock on the door but my mother would never get out of bed or say 'Come in.' I would have to talk to her through a closed door: 'What's the matter?' 'I had a bad dream.' 'Don't be afraid, just go back to sleep – nothing's wrong.' I would really be terrified and I would climb up to the third floor and my grandmother. She had this big soft bed and I'd climb right in with her. She was more of a mother to me than my mother was.

Another woman lived with an aunt and uncle as well as her parents:

Growing up with four caring adults around us was very pleasant. My sister and I got lots of attention and felt valued and secure. We had resources that we wouldn't have had if we lived with just our parents. For instance, during the years that my mother stayed at home with us, my aunt provided a role model of a woman with an uninterrupted work life. When my mother went back to work, her main commitment was still to the nurturing role, while my aunt's was to work. Also, while my father worked long hours, my uncle was around before dinner and would play games with us. When we were little, my sister and I were resistant to being disciplined by my aunt and uncle. My sister, especially, rebelled if my mother left us with my aunt. So our tendency was to take all the goodies that came from having four caring adults around but to be pretty clear that two people were enough to be bossing us around.

Traditionally, women have wanted to be good mothers, and have often assumed this meant that they, like their own mothers, should take primary responsibility for their children. 'Mother' and 'care-giving parent' seemed to be synonymous. Yet, those of us who became parents in the 1960s and 1970s quickly found that we wanted the fathers of our children as well as other adults to provide us with help and relief from the twenty-four-hour responsibilities of children. We found that we wanted our children to know loving care from their fathers, relatives and friends. Further, coming to maturity, having and raising kids at the height of the women's movement confronted us with questions about how we could raise our children and lead fulfilling adult lives at the same time. One solution that seemed workable – to us and to many of the men we knew – was to share parenting. Gradually men's voices began to be heard, too:

Ten years ago most men walked around with a pocketful of cigars in a sterile hospital waiting room, while their children were being born in some far-off, fantasy-filled delivery room. Today increasing numbers are with their wives during delivery. Many participate in the delivery, coaching their wives during labor, providing emotional support, even delivering the baby as a midwife in their own homes. Fathers have become participants in the unveiling of new life. We have box seats at the premiere showing. Never again should we, as fathers, settle for the pathetic role of sitting passively in the lobby as the show goes on. Why, then, should we settle for less than full participation in the raising of our infants? Surely, if we can be midwives, we can be mothers.*

So we started the slow job of integrating shared parenthood into our marriage partnerships – anger mounted, resolutions emerged, understanding often grew

*Rev. Peter Monkres, 'Mothering for Men as Well as for Women', Mothering, Vol. 2 (Winter 1976), p. 16 (Box 184, Ridgway College, Ridgway, Colo. 81432, USA). Monkres uses the word 'mothering'. We call this caring for children 'parenting' – a more general term which includes fathers as well as mothers and doesn't suggest that fathers are doing mothers' work by caring for children.

and sometimes didn't – as we pushed toward sharing. We are, each of us in our own way, still working at it.

Social Context for Shared Parenting

The social context in which we live has an enormous effect upon us as we attempt to share parenting.* In particular, the sexism of the society makes it difficult for both women and men to make shared parenting work. Social institutions and professionals resist recognizing the father as a primary day-to-day parent.

Gina, a working mother of two elementary school kids, speaks:

Diane had a stomach ache in school one day. And I was out doing a workshop and couldn't be reached. The school had Lou's telephone number at work, and he doesn't work very far away. He could have been there in ten or fifteen minutes. The third person on that list of emergency numbers was my sister-in-law, who is a music teacher and works out of her home in another town. The school nurse just took it upon herself to say 'Well, your Daddy is probably busy at work so I'll call your aunt.' So my sister-in-law had to interrupt her lessons and drive all the way to the school and all the way back home again.

Then there was the paediatrician who, when a father called to ask about his daughter's ear infection, said 'Have your wife call me.' The father happened to be separated from his wife and had full charge of his child that day. The stories go on and on and on.

It is clear that men who share child care more equally with women run up against the society's ingrained sex-role stereotypes. Social scientist Joseph Pleck discusses this:

... we should note a deep paradox in the way the social sciences have regarded men's relationships to children. On the one hand, it has been widely believed that men, compared to women, are biologically disposed to be relatively indifferent to infants and children. On the other hand, paradoxically, one of the leading hypotheses about the male role has been the notion that men envy women's capacity to create life through giving birth. To paraphrase [Margaret] Mead's 1949 famous formulation, it has been argued that it has been a recurrent problem in all cultures to create a social role for men that will give men the social valuation and importance that child-bearing gives women. What is intriguing in this paradox is that while so many different behaviours have been seen as a compensation for or consequence of men's envy of women's capacity to give birth, there has been so little consideration or encouragement of the most obvious and pro-social way for men to deal with this presumed envy; by taking more direct care of their children.†

*See the Society chapter for more details.

†Joseph H. Pleck, *Men's New Roles in the Family: Housework and Childcare* (Ann Arbor, Mich.: Institute for Social Research, 1976), pp. 41–2.

Rochelle Paul Wortis, a child care resource counsellor, talks about children:

What an underestimation this is of the importance of children to deprive them of the opportunity of interacting with men as with women; what an underestimation of the importance of children's early experiences, of early socialization and education!

What are the social realities that support these traditional stereotypes and make it difficult for many men and women to be equal partners in child rearing? A major external obstacle is economic. Many of the women we have spoken with find that their husbands can earn twice as much as they can because of greater education and because of discrimination against women in employment, especially because of occupational segregation. There are families that just can't afford having the husband work fewer hours. Work structures, too, often hamper shared parenting, though for many working-class families where the father may work the night shift and the mother during the day, it is taken for granted that the father cares for the children. It is difficult for both men and women to find part-time and/or flexible-time jobs, and schedule them in such a way as to be able to share the care of small children.

Although these are facts, economics do not fully explain why men on the whole do so little in the home. According to a review of past research by Joseph Pleck, men don't necessarily do more family work when they work less, and they don't necessarily choose to work less outside the home when they have the opportunity to do so.† Sex-role ideology is an internal influence on men and women both: most men don't jump to do more family work and most of the women surveyed don't push for men to do more. Joseph Pleck says:

The margins of difference between the sexes in attitudes about men's housework are, of course, not great ... But they do suggest a need for future research into the reasons why women, often more than men themselves, resist an expansion of men's family role. It may be that women have considerable psychological investment in their relative monopolization of family roles, and, at least in some cases, become psychologically threatened if their husbands move into this area.‡

In a sexist society, women have reasons to feel threatened at sharing their authority over the home. Though they may have power in the sphere of the family, they are excluded from an equal share of the power in the world of work and politics.

There are also potential complications of shared parenting in the legal tangles of the divorce courts. In our legal conventions fathers have an almost guaranteed right of access to their children, on the basis of economic *obligation* (fulfilled or not) to support – a kind of property right of the male parent. A mother's legal

---

*Rochelle P. Wortis, *Childrearing and Women's Liberation*, in Wandor, M. (ed.), *The Body Politic* (London: Stage I Press, 1972, 1978).

†Pleck, op. cit., pp. 46–7.

‡ibid., pp. 57–8.

right of access to her children, on the other hand, rests on the quality of her relationship with them, a quality that can be challenged and judged. In instances when fathers have made any significant contributions to child care, ex-husbands have often been successful in contesting and gaining custody of children. His property claim is, in effect, enhanced, and her relational claim diminished by the history of shared parenting. Anna Demeter, in *Legal Kidnapping*, has suggested that every child should have, from birth, a permanent guardian – who would ordinarily be the mother but who could be, by mutual parental agreement, the father – so that in the event of a divorce no contest over the child's custody is possible.

Austin deBesche

Social realities, then, make sharing parenthood more difficult than it should be. We need to work for the kinds of social changes which will make it a real possibility for more parents. Until then the many separate families that are struggling to integrate shared parenting into their lives do add up and contribute to change by what they are doing.

Starting to Share Parenting

When shared parenting begins varies for different people. Some couples start sharing with the decision to have a child together.

Stan: We decided we wanted to have a baby.

Sharon: In retrospect it doesn't feel as clear and pure a decision as it did at the time. I was in touch with feelings of being a woman in love with a man and wanted to have his child.

Stan: I felt initially afraid to have a baby. I didn't have one in my first marriage (of seven years) and that was an indication to me that I had some concern about having children. It was clear to me that Sharon wanted a baby and it would be an experience we would share. Then I decided I didn't want to miss having a child for myself . . . So we went ahead.

Gene has shared housekeeping with his wife and is starting early to share the care of his son:

As we try to work out a fair balance of care for Elliott, we have a precedent for sharing equally. For most of our time together as a couple we have shared cooking almost fifty-fifty; outside of that I may have done more housework, but she has been working full time and I haven't. We still have separate bank accounts, which is important to us, and, for instance, we each pay half the rent.

Amy and I began to share caring for Elliott when both of them came home from the hospital. We arranged to sleep in separate bedrooms, and I took him the first half of the night. When he woke and started to cry I would change him and take him in to Amy to be fed. Then she took him for the second half. So it really has been fifty-fifty most nights, except just before I have to get up early to teach. And we intend to reverse that on the nights just before she teaches.

This story is told by a mother:

My husband Joe is the kind of man who grew up knowing nothing about babies and who didn't intend to learn. He assumed that I would handle Peter's daily care. Yet I was always hoping and pushing for more sharing, and even though Joe resisted the 'idea' of it, he started to move in little by little – in his lunch hours sometimes, in the late afternoon, on weekends. I remember the moment when I felt that he moved out of the 'helping my wife in her duties' mind set into true sharing. It was a simple moment, yet so symbolic. I was sitting holding eight-month-old Peter on the stairs and Joe said casually 'I'm thinking he'd better eat now. He seems hungry.' Whether or not he then went to get the cereal and fruit ready is a matter of a different aspect of sharing: what pleased me so much then was that he noticed an intimate domestic detail and in that simple way took Peter more deeply into his life. Now, eight years later, they have a close and special relationship, and I think it came in part from the daily role that Joe grew to play in Peter's life early on.

Daniel was living with a group of people and slowly became involved with a woman and her child:

I started feeling like a stepfather when we all lived in the commune. The child that I felt closest to was Gregory, because when I first joined the group and was feeling nervous about it he adopted me – grabbed my hand and said 'Let's skip.' Our relationship grew in many ways. For instance, one time at about five he started wetting his bed again. Margaret, his mother, was angry and wanted to put him back in diapers. The situation was very emotional for both of them – he was expressing his emotions by peeing in bed and she by getting angry and resorting to diapers. I asked him what he wanted and he was clear about no diapers. I suggested maybe waking him at night and taking him to the bathroom. I did that for several months and eventually he didn't do it any more . . .

I don't think there was any moment of revelation but I felt more like a parent over the past couple of years we lived here (in an apartment as a family) and especially the past two years when I've gotten involved in the PTA. I have been recognized as his stepfather in the community.

As we've seen, separation and divorce introduce shared parenting in some families, for a father who has his children by himself all weekend may find himself playing a more down-to-earth daily role with them than he had been before.

The women's movement has had an impact on many families; some who had more traditional arrangements have attempted to renegotiate in midstream. A mother of teenagers speaks about how she and her husband share parenting differently now:

About the time I returned to work, my husband, Arthur, left industry and started teaching at college. He'd spend hours writing at home. So as I was going away more, he was at home more. He was there when the children came home from school. He would spend time with them and be the person who told them to clean up the kitchen after meals. I once was the person they went to if they wanted money or a ride. Now that Arthur's been around more and gotten to know them better, he wanted to do more of these things with them. When I take over he sort of reminds me that he would be glad to do that. He's taken a lot of initiative – and it's nice for them and for me. And yet it's hard to give up being the central person in their lives …

Josie with four teenagers ranging in age from twelve to seventeen discusses a similar change:

My attempts to restructure the work responsibilities of the household have led to a very important change in the family structure. For years Ernie said he did not feel an important person in the upbringing of the children. His example was that if he and I were sitting in a room with him closest to the door, a child would pass by him and go on to me to ask a question, to share an exciting story or to show a new cut or bruise. Neither of us could find a satisfactory way to increase his involvement. The children would have nothing to do with him. This situation probably came about because he was home less often and also because for many years the children were my only arena and thus my main base of power. At some level I probably did not want Ernie to be equally important in the lives of the children.

The solution came from an unexpected source. With the example and help of our couples group, we devised a scheme in which all jobs were listed on two lists. Each month we switched lists. Immediately Ernie reported that he had less to do than before. He was no longer 'helping' me – he had his responsibilities, and when he did them he was finished. Previously he had never felt finished, as he felt he should help me whenever I had something to do. Now he knew what to do and could relax when he chose.

The offshoot of this scheme was that the children now saw Ernie's role in the family differently. They no longer thought I had all the answers. They couldn't discuss with me dinner, money, washing, etc., if I was not the responsible person that month. They began to trust Ernie's answers because he had the final word for that month. Soon they began to share many things with Ernie which they had never shared before. They seemed to feel that they had his full attention now and that he really cared. This sharing with Ernie has been most evident with our two older adolescents. They seem to have different things they want to discuss with Ernie and me. In addition, our son Dave now does his share of all chores without any reference to what boys 'should' be doing. We are hoping that the children will see us as not fitting stereotypically anymore into the pattern of what a mother and father should do.

The Elements of Shared Parenting

People often assume that since they shared in the conception or adoption of a child, they share parenting, or that because they provide financial support for the family they share parenting. While these are certainly crucial aspects of being parents, they do not alone meet our definition of shared parenting. Naming some of the key elements in our group's concept of shared parenting may help both to define what it is and to distinguish it from what it is not.

Intimacy is perhaps the crucial element – closeness between parents or sharing adults and closeness between parents and children. 'Without attachments, bonds, desires, fears and repugnancies human life would hardly be possible. The unemotional life is not worth living.'[*]

A father speaks of his attachment to his six-year-old son:

There is a bond between me and Luke which transcends our being together. I feel this bond especially when I'm not with him. It's been so important for me to discover that I can love someone so deeply.

This kind of intimacy distinguishes someone who shares parenting from a babysitter who comes and goes.

Another important element in shared parenting is time spent with the children. To share parenting, a person must take care of a child in a regular, daily way. The father who spends only Saturday morning with his kids is perhaps doing what he can, given his job situation, and he may share much of the emotional responsibility with his partner, but he is not sharing parenting in the way being discussed here. The amount of time for daily child care is not won easily, either from the workplace or often from one's own self-concept, but it is crucial for shared parenting as we view it. Sam, a father of two girls, discusses the value for him of spending unstructured time with his daughters:

You need intimate contact with a child, not understanding from a distance. If there is any lesson I've learned, it is that I have to spend time with Mary Ann and Lena. Time, that's what I have needed. Not going to the museum and making little journeys to the park, but just kind of hanging out. And through this hanging out, I've become responsible. I've gotten to learn what I'm like and what they are like as people.

[*]Sidney Cornelia Callahan, *Parenting: Principles and Politics of Parenthood* (New York, 1973; Baltimore, Md: Penguin, 1974, p. 172).

A third element is your state of mind: an awareness that you are a primary caretaker or parent to the children. You aren't sharing if you feel your main purpose is to do the other parent a favour, as this mother of three explains:

My ex-husband had done occasional baby-sitting and that was it. And he even called it baby-sitting. I mean, it's such a dumb word for a father to use. Towards the end of our marriage when he'd say that he wanted to go out and see so-and-so, I would say 'Well, I'll be home, I'll baby-sit . . .' just to try and raise his consciousness a little bit.

Peter Simon

Being a parent can be a central part of your definition of yourself whether or not you are doing 50 per cent of the child care and whether or not you are legally the parent of the children.

Here is a father named Les who works at a nine-to-five job:

Being a father is very important and positive for me. My first son was born when I was twenty-one. Suddenly I went from the role of college student to the role of father. While I couldn't go to graduate school because I had to support the family, having a child provided a focus for my life at a time I felt very uncertain.

I've always enjoyed children. I had a lot of responsibility for raising my younger sister. In fact, I had more experience caring for an infant than my wife, Karen, did when our son was born. Nevertheless, I started out expecting Karen to be more like my mother than she is. Her major role would be taking care of my children while I worked. In the evening she would present them to me in fine spirits when I was ready to deal with them. It didn't take long for me to realize I was on the wrong track; my vision had to be revised. By the time our second son was born, I could take complete responsibility while my wife went away for a weekend, as well as the traditional financial responsibility for the family that I wanted.

Whatever the differences between me and Karen have been, I've always had a big emotional investment in my kids. I played with them when they were babies – even though I didn't have the daily hassles – but it's been easier for me to relate to them as they have grown older and can do more things I'm interested in. At the same time, as they've grown older I have a better idea of what I'm expecting from their mother, and my expectations of what a mother should be have changed.

Whatever the actual time division turns out to be, your state of mind as a parent is perhaps most significant. The fact that Karen can leave for a weekend speaks of shared parenthood.

Sonya, who lives with a man who has an eight-year-old daughter, finds herself taking on a parental state of mind – and struggles to define her parenting role:

Is anybody responsible for this child? My feelings are way overboard sometimes. Yet when Wendy needs clothes for school and it's the day before school begins, I find myself taking her shopping. I love her and think, wouldn't it be nice if she had a new dress or pants to wear? Still, I'm not sure I want this responsibility – but somebody has to take it and I do. This is an example of a conflict I've had all my life. Simply – I want Wendy to have the experience of going to school with new clothes like other children and I can help her have that. The complicated part for me is seeing an old pattern I want to break – of expecting myself to take responsibility just because other people (her father or mother in this case) don't.

Ongoing commitment is another element in shared parenting: you plan to be an important person in a child's life over time. Step-parents, lovers and friends as well as biological or adoptive parents can have this feeling. A sharing parent is responsible for doing or arranging for daily care of the children. Who stays home when the child is sick? Who brings the child to her/his job when the sitter doesn't come? Who goes to school to check how the child is doing? Who attends to the child's hurt feelings when s/he comes home having fought with a friend? It is in this day-to-day way that children most need care. Claudia tells of how she and her husband wrestled out an arrangement of who's responsible when:

Once we had two children and two jobs we could no longer think, come what may, we'll figure out a way to handle it. We worked out a sharing system. The basic agreement is that I take the early-morning shift – breakfast, dressing, kids waking up very early. We share taking car pools. Herb is responsible for times when children come home early, and then I take over when I come home about four. But there were still too many days when both of us needed to be somewhere doing something and one of the children was sick, had a doctor's appointment or a vacation day from school. We had to extend the sharing system still further. We worked out 'your days and my days' for those things. There are days when I could potentially be home and those disasters, special needs, are mine to deal with. This has removed the bitterness of early-morning, frantic arguments about which of us sacrifices more in order to care for children. This schedule has provided a consistent background of agreed-upon sharing that makes both of us more generous or flexible when sudden changes or unexpected needs arise.

The beauty of shared parenting is that parents can have more flexibility while the children are cared for by people who know and love them. But if flexibility is not part of the sharing arrangement, the relationships between partners and between parents and children can become severely strained. Parents need to be able to change plans if, for instance, they feel emotionally distracted or if they have time pressures in other areas of their lives. Here is a mother with a ten-year-old daughter:

I am a weaver and want as much free time as I can have during the daylight to weave. I'd rather not go out and teach and earn money, whereas if I was happy to teach and wanted to teach a lot of the time, Mark would be happy to take a part-time job and care for Leah totally or as much as I do now. I feel the decisions we make now come from a much greater flexibility even though it looks very traditional from the outside.

A rigid sharing arrangement may be necessary for a period of time. For instance, a woman who has been asking her husband to help with the children for a long time may insist that the sharing arrangement they finally work out be non-negotiable for a fixed period of time. In this way she knows it's serious sharing. Or, two people's work demands may make it essential to have a regular weekly child-care schedule with little room for adjustments. But the rigidity of sharing arrangements can put couples in difficult binds, as this mother tells us:

My husband and I from the beginning shared care of the children equally. When they were still very young – two and five – I took a half-time job expecting that my husband would be caring for Ben and Max when I was working. Well, in the middle of the year his work schedule changed. Neither of us could easily change our work schedules and we also didn't want to get a sitter and change the way we shared the children.

A final and key element in successfully shared parenting is attention paid to the adult relationship. When a couple shares child care they can wind up seeing each other only in passing from one shift to the next. Sue and Michael evolved a sharing arrangement like that. Sue speaks:

For the first couple of years after David was born I felt like a single parent. We lived far from the city, and each day, when Michael would go off in our only car, I would be left at home alone with the baby. I was bored and depressed a lot. I began to feel like I'd never be my happy old self again. Our marriage was floundering, too: Michael was too busy working to be a husband and I was too busy mothering to be a wife. Finally, when David was about one and a half, I began demanding that Michael stay home one day a week to care for him while I returned to work at a part-time research job I had found.

As the years passed and David grew older, we ended up sharing more and more responsibilities for his care. For example, we'd alternate waking up with David and we'd take turns making dinner or putting him to bed. We really shared tasks and I was able to work more outside the home and feel less isolated as Michael worked more inside the home and felt more connected to his son. We got along better as a couple because we had worked out a lot of resentments when we looked at how to both care for David and meet our needs apart from our child. But what was happening also was that we had divided our lives up so that if we weren't working outside the house, we were working inside and that meant two things: we didn't spend much time relaxing or just being with each other as a couple. Michael doesn't easily relax and play, but our sharing-of-tasks arrangement didn't help the situation either. One of us was always on duty while the other was off duty. We didn't find ways for both of us to be off duty enough to forget everything else but each other.

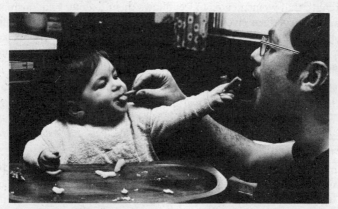

One way to avoid this is to make certain that when we share parenting we will have time for each other – time to do things as a couple and as a family. It also helps to keep a continuing dialogue about our couple relationship as much as about the joys, sorrows and assorted dilemmas of parenting. Such a dialogue is crucial, though not always easy.

Sharing parenthood brings up inevitable conflicts between partners – over differences in child-raising styles, hassles over who's going to do what, disagreements over values. All these come up in a more traditional arrangement, but they are accentuated daily when parents try to share equally in caring for their children. Some parents shy away from the opening up of such conflicts. But facing the conflicts can offer a chance at real communication and growth in their relationship.

Mothers and Shared Parenting

Some of the gains of shared parenting for women are obvious. Mothers have been doing the work of raising children and want some assistance or relief. They also want the opportunity to explore other interests and to grow and develop further. Or, they work full time and find it exhausting to come home and be fully responsible for the children. Leaving her children with another loving, fully committed person frees a mother psychologically in a way that few other day care situations can do. And having another person who knows and can talk about the daily life of her child can relieve her of the loneliness that so many mothers experience. Sharing is not just a matter of getting free time, though other gains are less specific and immediate. Women need time to feel, think and breathe separate from their children; they need time to know themselves as creative individuals, as friends, as partners distinct from their work as mothers. Women who are freed by sharing to bring outside experiences into their homes are richer people. They can be better parents and have more vital love relationships when they are caring for their own needs as well as their families. The strength that women come to feel allows them to enter relationships with their own sense of themselves. When they no longer depend on men or children for their self-definition, then more mutuality between the sexes is possible. One woman speaks of how the benefits of shared parenting can spill over and improve the relationships women have with men:

The ideal of men and women sharing equally in parenting and working is a vision still. What would it be like if women and men were less different from each other, if our worlds were not so foreign? A male friend who shares daily parenting told me that he knows at his very core what his wife's loving for their daughter feels like, and that this knowing creates a stronger bond between them.

Women can offer exciting role models to their daughters and sons alike. Children who see their mothers earning money, working outside their homes at jobs they enjoy, taking time to be by themselves or with friends, are often proud of their accomplishments. When this son was at a bookstore with his mother, he enthusiastically said 'Mom, I'm very happy every time I see the book you and your group wrote in the bookstore.' Then he turned to the store owner and continued with pride: 'You know my Mom's new book will be out in a few months, don't you?' And his sister loved it when her friends found her picture in the book 'my Mommy wrote'.

Special Issues for Mothers Who Share Parenting

Mothers are usually the ones who push for shared parenting, and yet sometimes when someone else is more or less willing to help, they either resist the assistance or experience it as a mixed blessing. What is women's resistance to shared parenting about? Here are some thoughts.

The expectation that women are supposed to be nurturers and the fact that women are models of nurturance for one another give growing girls and women both impetus and opportunity to learn about caring for others. Because we are taught, in fact and by rewards, that you are a 'good person' if you do so, most women learn fast how to nurture others. Just as most women have seen themselves as primarily responsible for the care and nurture of children, so men have seen women in a similar way. Having inherited the belief that women care for children, mothers move into pioneer territory when they consider shared parenting. A mother may feel she *ought* to be getting the kids up and giving them breakfast, even though it fits her partner's schedule better to do so. Or she may have a hard time believing that the father, or any man, is capable of doing what she does or of learning to be sensitive in ways that she is. Having been brought up with the notion that men aren't good with babies, mothers sometimes have to stretch their minds open – because you'll have trouble sharing if, for instance, you are both learning to care for a child from its birth and the mother assumes that men aren't good with infants. One mother tells of her encounter with another mother at work:

My friend, Molly, came into work looking worried and she was distracted at the staff meeting. Afterwards I went up to her. 'What's bothering you?' I asked. 'Well, Jason is responsible for the children today. I don't know if he took the chicken out of the freezer for dinner, if he arranged for the baby-sitter to get Jesse at school, if he'll be back home in time to pick Linda up at her piano lesson. You know all those details that we're used to, but Jason I don't think fully understands.'

Many a mother in Molly's situation has called home to make sure everything was all right. In fact, having a job at home and a job outside is very stressful, and it is particularly so for women who, as we've seen, have been traditionally assigned the basic responsibility for the children. Even when the reality is changing, the women still feel the pressure.

Angela works halfway across the state from her husband and four children, spending two nights away each week:

One snowy day I worried about how Ralph was managing, so I called him up, kind of just to check in. 'I hope it isn't too much trouble getting the twins to their Boy Scout troop in the snow,' I said. 'Look, Angela,' Ralph said in some exasperation, 'if I'm going to do this you've got to let me do it. You're at work, so be there. I really can take care of what's going on at home, and I want to.' I got the message.

And there's also the matter of style. Sharing mothers need, within reason, to let go of having things done their way. Clara told this story:

When Barbara was one, Jerry took over the job of dressing her in the morning, and the first few mornings she came out in clashing colours and stripes and plaids and all sorts of combinations I wouldn't have chosen. A tiny detail, but symbolic. That man doesn't know how to dress a kid! I thought. But I held my tongue: if I wanted him to share, I had to let him. If I tried to control what he did, in a few weeks there'd be no sharing.

Mothers who want to share parenthood often need to hold their tongues. Letting a partner in can be particularly difficult in a step-parenting situation. In this instance the mother has been the primary caretaker for several years and has trouble allowing the new stepfather to share the responsibility. Will speaks of his frustrations:

I felt like an apprentice to Beverly, but I wasn't very often treated as one – which was confusing to me. At times I could take charge of the particular situation – for instance, choosing a summer camp for our son, Nathan. After much looking around I finally decided on a camp. Nathan liked the camp, too. Yet when we encountered some problems with how the camp stereotyped kids, Beverly jumped in and took over. I ended up feeling terrible: angry and incompetent.

The fact is that as they move into sharing parenting, men often are apprentices to women because they are not yet as skilled in child care. Mothers have to be willing to teach fathers – both by stepping in and showing and by stepping back and letting them learn. Men have to learn to value what used to be 'women's work' and to accept instruction in an area where they are probably less prepared. Just as women have been taught by their male partners to work with tools or, even, to throw a ball, so men have to concede a lack of training in child rearing and nurturing in general. Women must be willing to take the time and expend the energy to teach. Yet it is also true that some men act out their unconscious resistance to sharing parenthood by accentuating their ignorance, asking a lot of questions that they could figure out for themselves. Sometimes it's not so much a matter of letting the father share in his own way as of urging him to share in a way that really helps. It can seem easier to do it yourself:

As a new mother learning how to care for Abe, I was at the same time teaching Ethan what I had just discovered and encouraging him to be a different kind of father than his father had been. By the end of the day I was exhausted. There was no one supporting me, and sometimes I thought, enough of this sharing . . . it would be simpler to care for Abe myself.

Relinquishing some of their power as they share child care with men, even their husbands, is difficult for many mothers. Seeing children who have turned to them for their primary needs also turn to someone else may stir up ambivalence in many. Pam, the mother of a four-year-old girl, describes these feelings:

The first day that Joshua put Sara to bed was a painful one for me. I was glad to be able to sit and rest after a long day home with her. And yet I felt very sad to be losing a singular tie. He even knew which was the special corner of the blanket which, once you gave her, would let her drift off to sleep.

As we mentioned earlier, the home is often the only arena where women have some power, and mothering the only role which gives them public recognition. Sharing parenthood allows a woman to look for some of her feelings of self-worth outside the family – but will she find them? She can no longer hold on to a tidy role-definition as mother when there is a father who can also change diapers, put a child to bed, prepare meals, intervene in a squabble and so on. There are now two or more people who can perform the mother role, and, moreover, no set role to perform. Yet job discrimination in the work world often means that a woman doesn't easily gain the coherent (though restrictive) self-image she might have had as a mother. Sharing parenthood, then, is not *the* answer to women's problems of inequality. But it's a start. 'Sharing is risky for me,' said one woman, 'but it's been a risk I'm willing to take. I want to try to live out that sense of what's possible between me and my husband, and for me separate from my family.'

Fathers and Shared Parenting

These days a growing number of fathers share in the daily care of their children. Whether they do it out of principle or practicality, in response to outright pressure from their partner or out of a loving desire to know their children and themselves better – or, as for many, out of a combination of all these – fathers are beginning to give voice to the special issues, incentives, hazards and wonders of being a sharing father.

Why are some fathers no longer content with the traditional pattern of spending only limited time with their children after work or among other activities on weekends? Why is it no longer so acceptable to some parents for a father to fulfil his family role by spending most of his time out of the house as the economic provider? Why are fathers starting to push for the kinds of changes in their work situations which would give them more time with their children? Joseph Pleck expresses this new attitude:

The 'men's two roles' perspective views men as appropriately doing the same kinds of things in the family that women do, for the same reasons, and with the same effects. They do this not to 'help out' their spouses, or to fill certain gaps left by their wives, but because it is one of their fundamental roles and responsibilities. Their participation takes the same form and fills the same needs that women's family participation does.*

Some of the reasons why men are moving into the home are financial. Today, as we've seen earlier, in the majority of families in this country, men are no longer the sole breadwinners. The role of breadwinner, then, is not so unusual in the family, and men begin to look to other aspects of their father role. Many men see shared parenthood as a way of getting out from under the burden of being the only provider. Ken speaks:

I remember one of the main forces behind our change to shared parenting was that I didn't want total responsibility for providing financially for the family. When Delia was about a year old, I realized I no longer wanted the family picture to be that I supported everyone while my wife took care of Delia and painted. I think this was unacceptable to me partly because of my awareness of my father's life: he always had the sole responsibility, and I think he paid a tremendous price for having so much of his self-esteem rest on that. The thought of having to do it for a whole lifetime got to me.

*Pleck, op. cit., pp. 2–3.

Also, the fact that more and more mothers are going to work, and wanting to go to work, relieves some fathers of just enough financial pressure so that they can begin to consider more flexible hours, part-time work and the like. As the mother moves more out of the home the father can move in: this, not full-time day care, is the aim of shared parenthood.

The emotional benefits of consistently spending daily time with their children are as compelling to many fathers as the financial ones. Many men who share have the chance to be more expressive and playful than they usually allow themselves to be.

Ted is very playful with his children:

I can dance. I can sing. I'm not very proficient in either area, yet my kids love it. And I love that they love it. I can't always be that way with my wife – there is still some awkwardness with her that there isn't with the kids. Kids won't say 'Doctors don't do that' – they may say 'That's my Dad and he's a nut', but that's okay. I feel very safe with them.

Jay, a stepfather, prizes the emotional growth he has experienced by becoming close to his new ten-year-old stepson:

Having been brought up as a pretty typical man, I rarely risked saying what my feelings really were. Getting to know Keith, especially during those first few months when his mother was sick a lot, forced me – painfully at the beginning – to bring my emotions up to the surface and put them into words so that we could find our way to a good relationship with each other. Now I am deeply grateful that his persistent asking, pushing, testing, opened up the world of my feelings to me.

Sharing parenting can expand the love that two partners feel for each other. Ed describes how his and Elizabeth's marriage has improved:

This sense of sharing strengthens our relationship and transcends our individual troubles with each other many times. It doesn't make us blind to our problems, but somehow there is Ruthie, and her existence reactivates some kind of life in us that's blocked. Don't get me wrong – it's not our duty to Ruthie that holds us together but our love for her and for each other.

For these men, sharing parenthood has expanded the dimensions of their feeling and loving. Harry Finkelstein Keshet, co-director of the Brandeis University Fathering Study, comments on this possibility:

The positives of parenting for men are that it is a rare place – probably one of the few places that men can learn to create in themselves, and experience in themselves how it is to care for another human being who can't give you anything tangible. Men are socialized to give and expect in return, but to give in this way can lead to poor moral development. When you have a man willing to give because someone needs you to give or they'll die or won't develop – that's a rare experience and it's in parenting that men can have that experience.

*It's a humanizing experience – a deepening and moving experience that can open up men to more loving. If you follow that through, it can't help but change society. For example, some men are lining up with women to change the structure of work so they can spend more time with their children. I can see the time when industry is going to be asked to meet the needs of the family rather than the family being asked to meet the needs of industry.**

Mark Nelson

A final benefit derived from shared parenthood mentioned by some fathers is the satisfaction of knowing that they are providing a different role model for their children. Andrew speaks feelingly:

I believe that I am letting my kids see that a man can be tender, sensitive, warm, attentive to feelings, and present, just plain there. That's important to me, because I didn't get any of that from my own father, and I am realizing now how much I missed it.

In a conversation with us, Robert Fein, a step-parent and psychologist, pointed out that in the past there was the notion of the patriarchal father – a very stern disciplinarian. During the 1950s the image was, on the one hand, the 'good guy', the pal or buddy, and on the other, the stereotype of the bumbling ineffectual Dagwood Bumstead father. Today, particularly in sharing parenthood, fathers are pushing toward a more whole and human notion of what being a father is.

Since his divorce Richard has had a lot more one-to-one contact with his children even though he sees them less. He describes his movement away from one kind of role model toward another:

*From an interview with Harry Finkelstein Keshet.

I was raised by a father who was a very strict disciplinarian. The most important thing to me in being a parent is breaking out of the Father-knows-best, very strict role where there is always a fixed response to every situation. You don't eat your dinner, you go to bed. You hit your sister and you get the strap. Responsiveness is the key for me. Just being emotionally available to my children in terms of what is happening at the moment and what they really need and want. Responding to what is going on instead of being angry at being challenged and dishing out pat solutions or the usual threats. I'm learning all this now that I'm responsible for them for longer stretches of time.

Anthony comments on his sons' emerging sexual identity:

I know that having a warm, affectionate, consistent relationship with me will be an important part of my three sons' growing up feeling comfortable with their bodies and their sexuality.

It's valuable for girls and boys to be nurtured by their fathers as well as their mothers. Seeing their fathers taking care of them will enrich and expand their view of what men do, and will help them become nurturing people themselves.

Resistance and Difficulties

Given these benefits for fathers in shared parenting, what are the obstacles and sources of resistance? The fact is that a majority of fathers do very little child care.*

A man who wants to go beyond the traditional definition of the father role encounters resistance because the society he lives in doesn't make either the idea familiar or the practice easy. We've talked about how the inflexibility of the workplace is an external obstacle, as is the tendency of schools, paediatricians and other professionals to assume that the mother is the primary parent. But perhaps the most potent source of resistance is the widespread attitude that men don't know how to take care of children. When men receive critical comments about how they take care of their children and are subjected to negative attitudes about their ability to parent, their enthusiasm about shared parenting is dampened.

One of the hurdles that men encounter in becoming fathers is that society offers them a limited definition of fatherhood – as provider, disciplinarian – which is instilled in them early in life. Jim declares:

There are those guys who have never had the chance to care for anything . . . can't care for plants . . . can't really care for themselves . . . it's terribly hard to care for other males because it's a violation of male norms. One guy said to me 'To be nice to somebody is like being weak.' What a locked-in life that is!

---

*Results of a recent UK survey conducted by Social Surveys (Gallup Poll) Ltd for *Woman's Own* magazine reveal that one in six husbands has never looked after his child on his own; one quarter have never put their children to bed, and one in three never reads to his children. In families where the mother works full time, three quarters of fathers never take time off work to care for sick children or collect them from school.

Jim goes on to tell how he once used to hide his interest in children:

As a teenager I was an in-the-closet baby-sitter. The lady next door had a baby and a five-year-old and I used to sneak over there to baby-sit at night. I can't remember ever telling a friend I did that. I used to wait until the family went out and then I would rock the baby.

The stories that little boys read don't often show them how to be fathers.[†] Andrea laments the lack of fatherly role models for her son:

I was reading to my son from the Greek myths, tiring somewhat as male hero after male hero strode across the scene. At last we came to the part where Hercules fights the women warriors called Amazons, and I thought, Good, an alternative! But things here were no better, for the Amazon women had just switched places with the men. While the larger-than-life women were depicted in the drawings as embroiled in battle, way in the background with silly looks on their faces were 'the little Amazon husbands . . . spinning and cooking and tending the babies.' I yearn for stories and images which will point for Mark the ways that he can be a strong and nurturing man, caring for others without lapsing into the mewling weakness of the little Amazon husbands.

Anne K. Moon/Stock, Boston

What underlies this prejudice against nurturing in men? Why are men in our culture afraid of being seen as weak, and why is caring for children seen as weakness? Many concerned people today are pondering just these questions. The fear of effeminacy, of being like a woman, seems to be related to the fear of homosexuality; as one mother put it, 'What is gay, after all, but being like a woman?' As long as our society fears homosexuality, it will be afraid of signs of femininity in men. And until men are freed to be human instead of 'masculine',

†One exception we know about is *William's Doll*, a children's book, by Charlotte Zolotov (New York: Harper & Row, 1972).

there will probably be a bias against men doing the so-called womanly work of diapering, cuddling, lullabying, soothing small children. The fathers who are sharing parenthood today are helping to break this myth of the distant father/manly man.

A number of studies have shown, in fact, that men are and can be nurturing persons. Joseph Pleck questions the assumption that men are not biologically fit to nurture young children. The research he quotes confirms that the assumption is wrong:

An important recent study by Greenberg and Morris (1974) found that fathers of newborns showed 'engrossment' in their infants, a sense of bonding, absorption and preoccupation in their child, which Greenberg and Morris interpreted as an innate potential in fathers which was 'released' by exposure to the infant. Both fathers who participated in the delivery and fathers who did not reported feeling that they could easily distinguish their baby from others, and that their child was perfect, that they were strongly attracted to their infant and focused their attention on him or her, that they could distinguish their child's cry from others' and that they felt extreme elation and increased self-esteem because of their child. Greenberg and Morris suggested that current hospital practices may interfere with the 'release' of this paternal engrossment response, and that fathers' visual and physical contact with the child should be encouraged as soon after birth as possible.*

But the myth of the non-nurturing male is a real stumbling block for men trying to share parenthood.

A further obstacle for some fathers is, quite simply, that sharing parenthood brings changes that they are not sure they want. Bruce gives an example:

One of my favourite things to do at home used to be to sit in my big chair and read a book. When I started taking Gordon and Helene three afternoons a week, I began by sitting in my chair to read and getting up only if they needed me. But they needed me so often that my afternoons were one long frustration. Now I've given up on 'getting things done' on my afternoons with the kids which makes the time more peaceful, but I wonder when I'll get to read a book again.

Women's patterns of getting together with friends have, through long experience, developed to accommodate children. Dropping in to have tea and bringing the kids along to play, for instance, is a common event which, with all its frustrations, manages to combine adult contact with caring for children. Most men are not so familiar with this way of socializing, and it can take some getting used to. Being one of the only fathers in your neighbourhood to take your kids to the park isn't exactly like 'hanging out with the guys'. Also, men who have been used to being able to leave the house whenever they wanted to, back when their partner arranged all the baby-sitters, find their mobility surprisingly curtailed.

*Pleck, op. cit., pp. 38–9.

Joseph Pleck explains his view on why the change to shared parenting is less appealing for some men than for women:

We have been able to have both careers and families simultaneously without having to choose between them or balance each off against the other, the way women have to, precisely because we have had women to do all the work in the family. When women ask men to do more in the family, men often say they are losing something ~ as if we have sex equality now, and would be dropping below it if we did more in the family. It's so easy for men to not really understand the privilege they have had by having wives do all the work in the family.*

But when men are ready to make changes, they can learn from women. Switching from the teacher to the taught for men, and from the taught to the teacher for women, is like walking down a bumpy road blindfolded. Our sexist views about what is appropriate for men and women don't disappear overnight, and we can't make up for all those years of inexperience quickly. Larry's efforts to decorate his son's bedroom point both to the inexperience that many men carry into parenthood and to the potential for learning:

The struggle was clear the day I went shopping for a rug for Bill's room. First I went to a large department store. The rugs were too expensive, so I went to a discount store in Danvers. Women were all around buying these rugs. I thought, God, what am I gonna do? But I had to get a rug. So I went up to one lady. I said 'Look, I feel very silly; honestly, I don't know how to buy a rug.' She said 'What is the rug for?' I said 'For my son's room.' Then she said 'And how old is your son?' 'He's three,' I answered. She explained everything to me. 'You don't want to have it too thin or this way ...' This experience taught me that while I have a lot of interest in being a good father, I don't have much skill yet. I left Danvers determined to get more information about how to create a role for myself out of nothing.

A stepfather tells of his discomforts and successes as he begins to share:

Lydia's attitude was to let me build my own relationship with Tom. Yet I often didn't know what to do, and I ended up feeling angry and unsupported by Lydia. I both wanted and didn't want her guidance, and I also didn't know when or how to ask for help. I expected Lydia would magically come in at the right moment ... Sometimes she and I worked well together. I remember an incident when Tom was upset about something at school. He came to me and I tried to talk with him, listening to get his sense of what was happening. I wasn't clear and left him to go consult with Lydia. Eventually she spoke with Tom and was able to zero in on the particular problem he was having. Later we discussed what had happened and I felt good about how we shared.

Children and Shared Parenting

We believe that the mother-child relationship is essential. Without it, children are in severe trouble. At the same time, we believe that children benefit from

*In conversation, December 1976.

shared parenting at least as much as their parents do. Much anthropological research shows that parenting is shared in other cultures and that the sharing is positive for children. Mary Howell puts it simply:

In most societies, child care has been and is a shared responsibility: mothers, fathers, grandparents, uncles, aunts, kin, friends, neighbors, adolescent and preadolescent children, take regular and willing part in the responsibility of caring for young children.[*]

Our society's norm of the at-home mother who is indispensable to the healthy development of young children is relatively new by historical standards – an important thing to keep in mind, for much of the social resistance to the idea of shared parenting for young children is based on the notion that a young child needs one and only one caretaker. Margaret Mead brings a cross-cultural perspective to this question:

At present . . . the continuing relationship of the child to its biological mother and its need for care by human beings are being hopelessly confused in the growing insistence that child and biological mother, or mother surrogate, must never be separated, that all separation even for a few days is inevitably damaging and that if long enough it does irreversible damage. This . . . is a new and subtle form of antifeminism in which men – under the guise of exalting the importance of maternity – are tying women more tightly to their children . . . Actually anthropological evidence gives no support at present to the value of such an accentuation of the tie between mother and child . . . On the contrary, cross-cultural studies suggest that adjustment is most facilitated if the child is cared for by many warm friendly people.[†]

Here is a story of a child in our society who has clearly attached herself to more than one adult. Both parents speak about what Joanna gains in the sharing:

Lynn: Joanna is a year old and I don't know what sense she has of parenting.
Ron: Sometimes I suspect she sees four parents – the two of us and her two sisters (aged twelve and fifteen). There is no specific mother role in this family or, rather, no mother function. That is, there is mothering going on, but there is no one person or one sex who is doing more mothering than another.
Lynn: In fact, that's not true, because if I really add up the hours, Ron has done more child care than I have. When Joanna was an infant I had an operation and couldn't lift her for six weeks. I didn't take her out of her crib, dress her or bathe her during that time. So that overall in this year Ron has done more of the physical work involved in child care.

---

[*]Mary Howell, *Helping Ourselves: Families and the Human Network* (Boston: Beacon Press, 1975), pp. 132–3.

[†]Margaret Mead, 'Some Theoretical Considerations on the Problem of Mother-Child Separation', *American Journal of Orthopsychiatry*, 24 (1954). Quoted in Wortis, op. cit., p. 3.

Ron: When our fifteen-year-old daughter is home, she spends a lot of time with the baby. When there are three or four of us in the room, she is just as apt to go to the twelve-year-old as to anybody else.

Lynn: I've always felt slight variations and I'm starting to know when she goes to whom for what. Judy, the twelve-year-old, is strictly the excitement, the silliness, the where-are-you-you-are-hiding person. She'll come to me when she is in pain or tired. Somehow she knows I am the person who takes care of these needs. I think she knows each of us and what she can get from the different people in the family. I question whether she knows the difference between Ron and me, but I think she responds to my voice and rhythm in a special way, since she was in my body. Something that happens when I pick her up relaxes her, and that doesn't happen with anyone else.

When there are several adults available, as Joanna has learned, children have more sources of love and nurturance. Mary Howell comments:

Children with only one caretaker have 'all of their eggs in one basket.' If the child knows only one person to be trustworthy, and if that person is tired, worried, angry, or irritable, the child has no other resource and must suffer the consequences of the adult's temporary and quite normal inability to provide appropriate care.[*]

Having more care givers diffuses the intensity of the exclusive mother-child relationship, which can be restrictive to both mothers and children. 'Caretaking that borders on servitude or tyranny is out of fashion for good reason. It is harmful for both mother and child when an isolated adult, without support and without relief, is the exclusive day-time contact of the child.'[†] This is not to say that children don't experience any difficulty from shared parenting. The most serious problems can arise when the tension, anger and frustration caused by the conflict of parents' values concerning sharing are played out through the kids. A father tells a mother: 'I am not going to pick up Jeremy from school because I am furious at you.' Or a mother screams at Miriam but she is really upset that her husband isn't home in time to fix dinner as he was supposed to. As parents become aware of the source of such behaviour, they can learn to deal directly with the other parent and minimize this problem for their children.

Sharing Parenting for Single Parents

A single parent is a person who is rearing a child or children without help from another parent who lives in the home. Single parents are people who are separated, divorced or widowed, or who have never been married or simply take care of children without legal arrangements. There is a small but growing group of women who are choosing to have babies without a partner, as well as single women and men who are adopting children. Many mothers and a few fathers

---

*Howell, op. cit., p. 132.

†Linda Weltner, 'The Family Under the Microscope', *Boston Sunday Globe*, 27 February 1977, p. 11.

who are not single parents are essentially raising their children alone, either because the partner is ill or because s/he is away most of the time. Today, however, single parenthood is usually the result of separation or divorce.

Even though some single parents share parenthood with an ex-spouse, many more, especially women, parent without any or with only minimal assistance from another parent. Since most single parents work outside the home, the pressure of full responsibility for both jobs and care of children is great. When they must provide all of the financial, physical and emotional resources for themselves and their children, the need to share parenting centres on finding what help is available to them.

Single parents need several different kinds of help: help measured in hours of child caretaking time, help sharing the emotional enterprise of raising the children and, often, financial support of some kind. If you have money it is usually less complicated to find child care – either by hiring baby-sitters or housekeepers, or through using institutions like a day care centre or school – than to find the ongoing emotional sharing some parents desperately need. Many single parents go from day to day without this basic support for themselves and their children: they survive, but the stress on both children and parents can be enormous. The economic realities are harsh for single parents (see Helping Ourselves and Families chapters). Even though some parents manage with working at part-time jobs, receiving child support or getting welfare payments, the financial situation is rarely easy or stable. Child-support payments tend to be less than adequate in meeting families' needs. They are not paid at all or paid irregularly and in inadequate amounts. For example, when they are paid – for only one-half of all separated and divorced mothers – the average payments are about $2,000, so that the major income for these mothers tends to come from welfare or their employment. Female-headed families have an average annual income that is about one third of the average two-parent family income, and it's estimated that about half of them fall below the poverty line.* For many single parents even a full-time job does not provide an adequate income for the family to have necessary child-care help. After divorce women lose most of the family income but retain most of the responsibility. Studies on child support and alimony show that for families that formerly lived on the man's income after divorce, women and children typically are awarded 35 per cent of his income.†
After ten years, only 13 per cent of husbands are in full compliance with child-support orders, according to a Wisconsin study referred to in the *Boston Sunday Globe* article cited above. Undoubtedly, men find it difficult to support two homes

---

*A Preliminary Review of Research and Selected Bibliography Related to Separated and Divorced Mothers (1976), by Dorothy Burlage (research associate in psychiatry (psychology) at the Laboratory for Community Psychiatry, Harvard Medical School), p. 18.

†1972 study by the Citizens' Advisory Council on the Status of Women (and reported in the *Boston Sunday Globe*, 6 February 1977, p. B2).

on one salary, but it is the women and children who suffer the financial deprivation and the greater anxiety.*

Getting the Help You Need

There is a more comprehensive discussion of where to find support in the Helping Ourselves chapter. Here we look into the special problems for single parents in finding people with whom to share child care.

For most people there is no one place or person – support is gathered from relatives, friends, lovers, neighbours, baby-sitters, teachers, mental health professionals.

Lucy, the mother of two school-age children, tells how she obtained help:

I got support from my family. When I was feeling depressed right after separating from my husband, I didn't think to turn to family. They were in another city and seemed so far away. But in the past couple of years I've either sent or taken the children there during school vacations. They spend a week there with their two grandparents and my sister, and I have that time for myself.

Andrew, a single father, talks about how supportive his community, especially his neighbourhood, is:

The school my daughter attends is very responsive to the needs of single parents in the community. There is a diversity of life styles that is supported in the school and a sensitivity to the fact that kids live in different kinds of families. Also, the community is aware that most of us work and has an extensive after-school programme. And I can also exchange child care with other single parents who live nearby.

Most single parents also have to learn who is appropriate to ask and under what circumstances. Sometimes parents do get support in child raising from a baby-sitter, from a family, another parent or a teacher who takes an interest in the child and shares her/his observations with the parent.

Janet found help in the apartment building she moved into after she and her husband separated.

I'd been in a single-family house, gaining privacy at the price of isolation. Providentially, I found an apartment in a building with four families, two of whose kids Tommy had been in a play group with for more than three years. Although we all live a fairly nuclear life style, we take care of each other's kids both formally and informally; we car-pool; we visit at odd hours to rejoice or consult or commiserate; we share snowstorms and blackouts. When I am emotionally or physically worn out, Tommy has other kids and adults to turn to. And though he is an only child, he knows some of

*Some UK figures: in 1976, lone parents (usually mothers) received benefit to the value of £402 million, against £47½ million received by DHSS or claimants themselves from 'liable relatives' (usually fathers): *Supplementary Benefit Commission Annual Report*. In 1977, some 370,000 lone mothers lived in poverty.

the hilarity, anger and cosiness of intimacy with peers. I really can't imagine living in a better place as a single parent.

Getting help is a mixed bag – essentially often positive, as the two stories above show, but also complicated. A mother speaks of her experience in turning to old friends for guidance:

Help from my old married friends was a mixed blessing – they cared for me and their help was invaluable. Yet my dependence on them kept me tied in with a part of my life that I was moving away from.

Many single parents, especially at first, turn to the most familiar people – close friends and family – for assistance. Sometimes they are helpful and other times they can't give us what we need. This single mother turned to a therapist:

My therapist's caring listening, her objectivity, her experience, and the work I have done for myself with her, have added to my strength and self-confidence in these years of new singleness. As I feel better about myself, I am a better mother – it's as simple as that. And at a turbulent time when my son was suffering both from his father's moving away and from our confusion about which parent he should be living with, a carefully chosen child therapist gave Dylan an ally and helped us see more clearly what needed to be done.

Single parents come face to face with the discomfort of approaching people they don't know well. They may find themselves asking other single parents in their child's school or neighbours, for example. Part of the problem is that being open about their need for help makes them vulnerable to the possibility of reciprocal demands that they may not be able to meet. 'I don't want to ask my neighbour,' one mother said, 'because if she said "No" I'd feel hurt and if she said "Yes" I don't know how I could reciprocate. I am so pinched for time and energy.' Many single parents are afraid they need more than they can give in return, and that makes them feel unequal. Sometimes it feels more comfortable for single parents to exchange with other single parents. But children don't always choose their friends on the basis of their also having single parents. This single working mother tells about a conversation with the mother of her child's best friend:

There was a period when I was frequently asking Terry, who was married and home most afternoons, if my daughter could spend Wednesdays after school at her house. I felt uneasy; she didn't really need to exchange child care and I didn't know how to reciprocate. Terry knew I was uncomfortable and brought the subject up. She acknowledged that she didn't need help from me in the same way I did from her. She also reassured me that it was fine for my daughter to visit and said if it wasn't she'd let me know. Also she told me that it was a special treat for both her and her daughter when we invited her daughter to our house. The relief for me was that our differences were out in the open and that I learned that there was some way that I could reciprocate.

Another mother, who has thought about how to reciprocate with a family that has her son over for dinner a lot, says 'Even when I can't "pay them back" directly, things do even out as I give where I can to someone else.'

When you first become a single parent, you often must find new people with whom you can share concerns and child care. The isolation and desperation can impel single parents to take risks in ways they wouldn't have tried before. Some people look for groups of other single parents. Here the leader of such a group, who is herself a single parent, describes the first meeting:

Everyone had a turn to share why they chose this group. All the people in the room, men and women alike, told in their own ways how they felt alone and unsupported. During that first discussion there was a visible change in the room – almost a group sigh of relief and sense of relaxation that came from understanding they were no longer as isolated as before they walked in the room.

Single parents may try different living arrangements. For instance, some single mothers choose to live with other single parents and children. This can be an opportunity to have other supportive adults to share parenting with and to give your child the benefit of having other adults and kids to be with.

Having other people important in their lives also provides special relationships for their children, as this father explains:

Maria spends several weekends a month with my mother. My needing my mother to take care of Maria means that Maria gets to be with her grandmother regularly and has developed a really important ongoing relationship with her that many kids living in nuclear families do not get.

Sharing with the Ex-spouse*

Most divorced or separated parents don't share child care with their ex-spouse. Usually the mother has custody and the father has visitation rights. Problems arise over child support and visiting arrangements.

However, some parents who have shared child care before separation or divorce continue to do so afterwards in two different homes. Some of these separated families have joint legal custody of the children; in others one parent, usually the mother, has legal custody. Whether or not they have joint legal custody, these parents see themselves as jointly raising their children.

How can you share parenting with someone you can't live with and probably no longer love? How can you remain a co-parent while striving to become an ex-spouse? How can two people who are at least for a time angry and estranged from each other cope with some of the difficulties and challenges inherent in a shared parenting situation? These are central questions for parents who share parenting after a marriage has ended. Without a doubt, a rocky path awaits them. But for some it seems to be the only way to proceed with parenting.

*Many of the ideas in this section evolved in discussion with Harry Finkelstein Keshet, director of the Divorce Resource and Mediation Center.

Parents who share parenting after separation or divorce usually do so in the belief that it is important for children to have both parents in their daily life. For these divorced people the hope is that many of the good things that children get from having parents who share parenting can continue despite the separation. So often a child of divorce effectively loses one or the other parent. With continued sharing, although there is no longer a joint couple life, at least the children can have a substantial ongoing relationship with each parent.

Sharing parenthood after separation can be beneficial for parents too. Divorce may leave one parent limping under the weight of having the children all the time without relief, and the other parent filled with sadness and yearning for the children. With continued sharing, neither parent gives up the satisfaction and challenge of regular parenting. There is, too, the ease of knowing that you can do whatever else you want and need to be doing and feel confident that your children are with someone who loves them as much as you do. And parents who share after separation may have the benefit of totally child-free time – each week, each month, each summer – time perhaps to spend with a new lover or partner, a luxury which married couples in nuclear families can rarely enjoy with each other. Having dependable blocks of time in which they are totally free of active parenting gives parents (particularly mothers) a chance to learn about themselves as people separate from their children. This is painful sometimes, and is sometimes resisted, but it is an important way for parents to learn to adjust as children grow toward leaving home.

Custody and visitation arrangements are not simple matters. Many kinds of arrangements have been used at different points in time and in various parts of the world. There are no easy answers. The arrangements that people make vary a lot, and they are often arrived at with great pain and much careful thought. Here are a few examples we're familiar with:

● The mother has the child during the week, and the father on weekends – most traditional arrangement.

● One parent has the child during the beginning of the week (Sunday–Wednesday), and the other parent at the end (Thursday–Saturday) – with flexibility on some weekends and during school vacations and vacations for parents.

● Parents alternate every week or ten days or month. Occasionally it is the parents who change homes rather than the children.

● During the school year the mother has the children during the week, and the father on alternate weekends; in the summer the father has them during the week, and the mother on alternate weekends.

● The child spends the school year with the father, and visits her/his grandmother three weekends a month; then s/he is with the mother for summers and school vacations.

● Parents each have the children for a year or two years at a time. They are committed to live in the same city until the children complete grammar school.

- One child lives with one parent, the other child with the other parent, on a permanent basis. The children visit with the parent they don't live with.

While simple enough on paper, these arrangements can be excruciatingly difficult to arrive at. For instance, parents may struggle and struggle over who will have the children for the school week because the school-week home may feel more like home base than the other. The arrangements are based on a combination of the children's school schedules, parents' work schedules and other needs of the parents and children. For parents the big question is: how do we meet both our own needs to be with our children in an ongoing way and our children's needs for a stable living situation? If parents commit themselves to living in the same town or neighbourhood, then they can divide the time spent with children more equally. Yet children who move back and forth too frequently may begin feeling like a 'bouncing ball', as one little girl told her mother. Will a good ongoing relationship with both parents offset this feeling? There are no set answers as to what arrangements are best. The parents who share after separation are pioneers on new soil: they learn from themselves and their children as they break the ground.

Issues Faced by Parents Who Share Parenting after Divorce

Trusting. No matter how sure you are intellectually that it's a good idea to share parenting with your ex-spouse, or no matter how desperate you are for the relief, trusting your children with this other person may be problematic. Even in the most amicable of separations, sharing parenthood means entrusting your children with someone whom you yourself cannot live with and love, with whom you have irreconcilable differences and a probable history of a great deal of struggle and anger. Any sharing parent has to let go of having things done his/her way; when you send your kids off, let's say, for the second half of each week to your ex-spouse, the letting go is an even bigger task. Questions persist. Will s/he pay attention to how they're feeling? Will s/he care tenderly for them even though s/he no longer cares for me? Will s/he let anger at me seep into how s/he is with the kids? Will s/he play up the differences in life style which divide us? Will s/he use the power of daily influence to turn the kids against me?

Clearly, if these questions are too compelling and too numerous, it's not an appropriate situation for sharing parenthood. A grounding of basic trust and respect has to exist between the ex-partners, as well as considerable maturity, self-restraint and psychological clarity, for parents to be able to put their concern for their children above their differences with each other. There's no point in shared parenting if it's going to turn into a continuation of the marriage struggles, with politics rather than child raising as the major dynamic.

The issue of trust gets raised again when a parent remarries or starts living with someone, for the new partner indirectly becomes a sharing parent. (See the Families chapter's section on step-parents.)

Communication. Separated parents who are sharing find themselves having to communicate often – about arrangements, about how the kids are feeling and so on. For some it is a real challenge to put hostility aside. Others find that they now communicate more thoughtfully and sensitively about the children than they ever did in their marriage. One woman remarked 'If we talked this well before, we would never have gotten divorced.' When communication is problematic, some parents call upon professionals to arbitrate. Two parents worked out this solution: they asked a child psychiatrist they knew if he would be willing to be included in their divorce agreement as a person who would consult with them on any child-care problems they encountered. He agreed. The arrangement has operated well for the family six years now; the children are protected from becoming pawns in their parents' old arguments, and the parents are saved from expending a lot of energy engaging in fights that go nowhere and interfere with their present lives.

Boundaries between co-parent and ex-spouse. There is now an ex-officio member in each of the re-formed households. 'I thought I got divorced but s/he is still there' and 'I wish s/he would disappear' are common sentiments for women and men alike. The shadow presence of the ex-spouse often is uncomfortable. It is

Phyllis Ewen

troublesome for many parents to figure out how to stay involved and yet no more involved than is necessary for the smooth sharing of children. Parents have to work out their limits – for example, when we can or can't call an ex-spouse and for what. While it is important to establish boundaries, it is as necessary to be flexible and realize that boundaries may need to change over time; for example, as children get older, parents may need to be less in contact with each other; or as time heals some of the animosities, parents are able to be more open with each other; or in the early separation period it's all right for the father to care for the child in the mother's home, but later on it's less appropriate. Boundaries vary from couple to couple; what is acceptable to one is horrifying to the other. For example, one woman told us how shocked she was to hear that a separated couple shared a two-family house. Yet when interviewed, this couple said that the arrangement was fine for them.

Living structured and scheduled lives. When they separate, the structure of life changes for men and for women in somewhat opposite ways. Living scheduled lives is stressful for all parents – how do I fit my child's dentist appointment between work and marketing and get home in time to prepare dinner so I can be at my meeting by eight? For parents who jointly share, the schedule is even tighter. For instance, now one has to fit in everything in three days that used to extend over an entire week. A mother feels the pressures: 'I have to pick the children up early from their friends because they have to be home to meet their father at a specific time.'

Men tend to be familiar with structured work lives, but not so much with having to arrange their lives around children. Women, in contrast, are more often experienced in structuring their lives around the family, and now must fit paid employment in.

Transitions. When children go back and forth from home to home, the times around their arrivals and departures can be unsettling for both children and parents. Kids may be tense, wound up, sad, disoriented – the act of going from one home to another underlies the separation in their family, and it can be exhausting to continually change their environment and style of living. Everyone, including parents, needs special attention. Living with children is very different from living alone or with other adults, as Laura illustrates:

I spend much more time around the house when the children are with me. When they go to their father's I am out more – either working or having a good time with my friends. I lead two lives: the settled and organized life of a mother who is responsible for two young children and the freewheeling life of a single woman who can work hard and party late.

Each transition time is unique and complex. Each person involved has his or her own feelings, and these feelings are never the same from one time to the next. For instance, one day a parent may feel relieved to have the children leave or return but another time feel equally sad. Parents' expectations may not mesh with those of the kids; for example, a parent may be eagerly waiting for the children to return but the children are unhappy about leaving their friends. After many disastrous scenes at these times of transition, some of us have learned to approach one another more slowly and with fewer expectations. As parents we can assume some responsibility for the atmosphere that surrounds these emotionally loaded transition times. We can appreciate these times for their special qualities: they teach us to be open and pay attention to what is happening at the moment. They are times of stretching for us as we reach out to meet other people and situations without preconceptions of what ought to be.

As separated parents wrestle with some of these issues there are no certainties as to whether what they are doing is 'right'. 'Is it worth it?' they ask at the hard moments. It seems fitting to end this discussion with the pronouncement of the little girl who told her mother she felt like a bouncing ball going from one home to another: 'But you know I feel very lucky. Most kids have only two parents and I have two parents and two friends.'

7 Families: The Context for Our Parenting

Nancy Press Hawley

As parents we live in families, and families are the context in which we raise our children. Many of us live in traditional nuclear families of father, mother and children or in an increasing number of varied family forms – single-parent families, communal families, families with step-parents, families with gay parents. The authors of this book believe that being more self-conscious about ourselves as parents can make the experience more satisfying. We also believe that family life can be richer, happier, more nourishing for parents and children when we understand some of the dynamics of how families work. In this chapter we will give some definitions of family and look at some of the tools that psychology offers us for understanding it. We will present the variety of families people are living in during this time of changing forms, the peculiar stresses of each and the special insights each offers us for our own family life.

Here some parents explore what family means to them:

Samuel: I can be my best and worst selves with my family. They accept me even when I sing out of tune!

Barry: Family is my flesh and blood. No matter how much I don't like certain relatives, they are still family and provide important connections for me. Friends can come and go, but my child is my child, my mother is my mother and my cousin is my cousin. I used to get so upset with my father. He would do anything for anybody who was a relative, and I'd say 'I don't like them and I won't see them.' Over the years I've gained some respect for these permanent ties that come out of traditional kinship – and a sense that I don't pick and choose and discard people simply because they don't meet my standards of what's right and proper.

Eva: Family has been a mixed blessing for me. On every Jewish holiday, for instance, as many families as were around got together to eat and celebrate. I loved the excitement of doing things together, eating good food and singing in a large group. On the other hand, people would hurt each other – they would stand around eating knishes, complaining about my mother who had prepared the food, or gossiping about Aunt Sadie who was standing across the room.

Family

What are we doing here jumbled
smelling of dust in a potato
sack? What is this dance we perform
sitting down? Tell me what are our faces
meant to declare, mashed together nose
against nose in friendly terror?

What is that word stamped faintly
on your forehead? – reversed blue ink
of an A & P melon? Oh in this crowd
it's a chore to breathe   to thrust a fist
through the bag to the dark
quiet cupboard –

Do we need so many elbows? so many
eyes crossing? Names leaping from mouths?

Why is it necessary to embrace
to make room? necessary to flatten the face
of stubborn signs? Why is the dance a jumble
of buttocks and calves
fingertips and eyelashes and stinging molecules
of sweat?

What are we doing here jumbled
for decades sharing the ache
of our dark back teeth? What is
the purpose of the dance? How does this
cupboard door unlock? Who has tied us
in here together and walked away?

– Joyce Carol Oates

The poem is a powerful statement about our often unclear perspective on our families. What is the point of being in a family? Is it an example of claustrophobia or one of nuclear bliss?

My family left me with a desire for connection and celebrating with other people but hesitancy to do so with them because of the suffering that came too. Most of the important celebrating I do now is with friends.

Carol: I grew up in a family with an alcoholic father and a severely depressed mother. I remember being asleep as a child and being suddenly woken up by my father staggering into the house drunk, getting into a fight with my mother and smacking her around. I still cringe as I recall her screaming 'Don't hit me, please don't hit me!' The next morning when I asked her about her black eye she would tell me that she fell down and hit her head on a chair, but I knew that she was lying and she knew I knew. Eventually I stopped asking and turned inward. The older I got, the less time I spent around the house. I feel angry and sick inside when I think of the violence of my family. Who needs family if that's what it's all about.

The control we as parents have over family life is a mixed blessing: it is exciting to know we can give shape to the ways our family works. For those who had painful family experiences growing up, it's important to know that we as parents can and do shape family life – it doesn't have to be the way we knew it as children.

Yet the responsibility can also be seen as another pressure on parents who already pressure themselves to 'perform' more perfectly. We know that society tends to blame parents exclusively for all their children's problems. Given the lack of social support (discussed in the Society chapter), the opportunity to shape our family is weighty. Still, what we do matters – how we choose to celebrate a holiday; whether or not we hit our children; whether we choose to live in a city or the country, house or apartment, nuclear family or commune; whether we listen to our children with respect; how we arrive at decisions; how we play, do chores, show affection. Through many small choices on our part, a family style emerges – an ambience, a dynamic, an environment in which we and our children move. It will become the stuff of our children's memories and the structure of their expectations as they move on into adult lives of their own. It will also provide the form of our own lives during these years.

In viewing our own family with an eye to our unique family style, Mary Howell, who is a parent, author and physician, has suggested several questions which may be useful in helping us define our family style:

What is the quality of the day for the family and its members?
Who feels supported, cared for, in control?
Who feels put upon, intruded on, out of control, neglected?
What are the sorrows – are they necessary, could they have been avoided, can they be dealt with in a growth-promoting manner?
What are the joys – are they noticed, savored, celebrated, can they be repeated or increased?
... What can we predict about the outcomes of days like this?
*How is each family member being shaped by living through this process of family function?**

This chapter will look at the choices parents can make about family life and the tools they can use to help them.

Here 'family' is defined as at least two generations of adults and children living together. This and Mary Howell's definition of family can provide a groundwork for further discussion. To her, the basic defining characteristics of family[†] are joint occupation of a household, with sharing of time and space; an exchange of

*Mary Howell, 'The New Families' (paper presented to the Conference on Separation and Divorce, Wheelock College, Boston, Mass., 19 March 1977), p. 11.
†See Mary Howell's *Helping Ourselves*, Chapters 1 and 2, for detailed discussion of these points.

unpaid services between family members; a commitment to stay together over time; and bonds of ritual, tradition and family history.

As we will discover later in this chapter, families of many different forms can meet these definitions.

Parents in the Family: as Parents, as Children, as Adults

Parents operate within the family on three levels:

● We are parents to our children, attempting to create a space that gives them nourishment and opportunities to grow and learn about living with other people. This is the level that parents are most familiar with.

● We are children of our own parents with all the memories, expectations, patterns, hurts and hopes that our family history generates in us. Our own parents have impact on our parenting in ways we may have never considered before.

● We are adults with our own interests and needs that we seek to meet or have met by others within this intimate group with whom we share experiences of daily living.

Our first opportunities to learn about being parents came as we watched our parents parenting us. We saw how they cared for us. We learned what they valued and what they didn't. We observed how they took care of themselves. As adults we can recall childhood vows – 'When I have children I'll never do that' – and then wind up doing just that with our own children or at least having to struggle hard to do something different. Here are illustrations – first from a mother and then from a father:

Lizzie: From the time I was five years old I fixed my own breakfast. I remember enjoying feeling grown up enough to get a bowl down from the closet and to select my own cereal. By the time I was seven I resented my mother for not getting up with me. During one of those impatient times I swore when I had children, I would not only get up early, but I would fix their breakfast as well. You can probably guess the rest. I have children of my own and I, like my mother, enjoy sleeping late. For a long time being a mother meant sleeping late and having children angry at me; but I no longer choose that for myself. I worked out a compromise where I get up four mornings a week and sleep the other mornings. The children know when I'll be up with them and when I won't. So they get both me making breakfast for them and a chance to enjoy the space and independence to prepare their own breakfasts.

Alan: In my family my parents kept their feelings hidden from me and my brother. So I felt nervous the day I cried in front of my son Caleb, who is six. I didn't know what would happen – how he would react to my tears and how I would react to him seeing me so sad. He broke the ice – 'What's wrong, Daddy?' he said. And I felt natural responding to him, telling him that I was sad because Bonnie wasn't going to be my girlfriend any more. Instead of being upset, he seemed relieved to see that fathers can get sad just like kids. What this experience did was to create a new openness between us.

As parents we also feel pressured as we attempt to sort out which comes first – taking care of children or doing for ourselves. Especially with young children and particularly for the primary caretaker, there seems to be more asked of us than there is time or energy to do it. So we often give first priority to others – children, our own parents – and last to ourselves and our own special interests. Miriam shared: 'At the end of the day I feel like an orange sucked dry.' Liza told us:

I need nurturance if I am going to have any to give anyone else. Some of the most nurturing times for me are when I play music with friends, write in my journal or just sit and meditate. Fortunately, in my family, I have my mother who is a model for me. She set aside time for herself each week. She would hire a sitter and go off by herself. She also felt entitled to spend time alone with my father after he returned from work. I used to resent being excluded, but now I can appreciate how she cared for herself and her relationship with her husband.

Bringing all these diverse elements together into something that works is like gathering a bouquet of flowers. Included in that bouquet are flowers that represent skills for parenting you learned from your parents, several afternoons for yourself to do whatever you wish, a weekend a month alone with your partner, a neighbourhood school that runs an after-school programme during the hours you work, a reliable day care centre or baby-sitting arrangement for your second child, jobs for you and your partner that allow for personal days when a child is ill. You may say that no such bouquet yet exists. But this suggests some of what parents need to fulfil their complex family roles.

Family as a System

Considering the family as a social system – knowing that what one person does affects every other person – can make us more conscious of how our family works. Sidney Callahan, author of a book on parenting, states:

*In most parental how-to books there's but minimal recognition of the whole family as a system. The 'family-point-of-view' is missing, that is an understanding of the family as a whole unit greater than the sum of its parts ... A family unit can be seen as a dynamic system in which each member has interpersonal interactions with every other individual in the family system.**

In the late 1950s articles began to appear about the family as a system and about family therapy based on that concept. Since then the literature has been growing, and courses and training institutes have been organized to present their particular viewpoint.

*Sidney Cornelia Callahan, *Parenting: Principles and Politics of Parenthood* (New York, 1973; Baltimore, Md: Penguin, 1974, p. 95).

What Is Meant by Family as a System

Recognizing the interrelationships in our families allows us to see the effect we have on each other. It encourages us to look at the mutuality that exists between us, to pay attention to the connection between and among family members, and to view what happens in our families from a more helpful perspective. When Johnny has trouble in school, for example, rather than perceiving him as 'the problem', we as parents can enlarge our view and notice the family stresses that Johnny may be expressing.

Ben Achtenberg

An analogy can be made to the human body, a system composed of organs, muscles, tissues, nerves, bones, fluids. All parts of the body are interconnected to compose a whole being. We can identify separate elements – a heart or specific muscles for instance – but no part exists in isolation. Our bodies are in constant motion – taking in air, digesting food, healing themselves – and are routinely negotiating exchanges between the inner environment and the outside world. Just as our bodies function because of the interrelationships of the different parts and the exchanges with the outside, so do our families.

The patterns that develop when people live together – whether related to feeding, loving, communicating, visiting, cleaning house – regulate and make relationships. Try to think of your own family as if you were an outside observer. Watch the variety of movements, activities and changes when you are all together, perhaps for meals or in the evening. Also watch the simultaneous events that occur outside the family, as members are at work, school, playing with friends, shopping at the grocery store, walking the dog, etc. Look for patterns – who tends to do what? What kind of space does an absent member leave? Is there a cluster of members who are close and one or two who tend to be on the periphery? Who contributes to that configuration? When you've finished this, you have a collage of your family as a social system.

Some Insights into Family Life

Far more is taught in the family than what is said in words. As parents we teach children primarily by how we act and what we do, rather than by what we say. Children are perceptive observers: they watch how we treat the neighbour next door, what we do when someone pulls into a parking space in front of us, how we act when an old friend calls on the phone, what happens when a sibling breaks a dish or when one parent arrives home late.

Kathleen recognizes that she sometimes gives her son Tony mixed messages:

I tell him not to steal, but I encourage him to slip under the subway turnstile even though he's old enough to have to pay. These values are fed back to me as he gets angry when I reprimand him for taking a candy bar from our local drugstore. In frustration Tony says 'The candy bar and the subway cost the same, so why does this bother you when you encourage me to sneak past the man at the subway?' Having a smart son who imitates me can be burdensome.

Rhea reacts to her daughter:

I can hear from upstairs Deborah using tactics on Naomi and I know where she's learned them. As she's trying to coerce her into doing something – 'If you don't let me play with that game, then you can't go outside' – she is repeating me. Hearing her makes me feel there I am up on a podium and these little eyes are all around all the time and I am responsible for what they see. 'Oh, God, is there no time I can get off this teaching channel?!'

Perceiving how much members of our families affect each other can open us to a more circular exchange with our children, and help relieve us of the intense pressure we often feel. The learning does not go just one way, 'from the top down', as Rhea was seeing it. We learn from our children as they learn from us. On one level we can learn very practical things from them: sports they enjoy; card games they pick up from friends; arts and craft skills or knowledge about car repairs. But perhaps more important is the emotional learning. Being able to express emotions can be a tool for improving family life – one we learn together:

Tara was angry that I asked her to take her games out of the living room. She started to yell at me and I said she couldn't yell. She got even angrier and said 'You are so unfair. You yell when you're angry and tell me it makes you feel better, and when I yell you tell me to shut up!' I realized I was telling her to express her anger but not to do it in an angry way – especially when it had to do with me. She was teaching me how to teach her.

It is also a relief to learn how much we can trust our children to teach one another and themselves. A father speaks:

My wife and I were cross-country skiing for a weekend with our children and some friends. When the children started to fall down a lot, we made suggestions that would help them learn to balance better. They heard our comments as criticism. Yet when the daughter of our friends began to ski without poles, our children followed and learned from her example and their own experience how to balance themselves and go up and down hills easily.

In each of these instances the children have had an impact on their family life. Seeing our family as a system allows us to let them know that what they do and think matters. When children see the ways that what we learn from them helps us and the family, they can experience their own impact. They also benefit from getting a realistic rather than a false sense of their own power. For example, children can leave home with a false sense of power ('I caused my parents' divorce because I fought with my sister a lot') or with the feeling that they had no impact at all.

Bruce Ditzion

David Wegman

Certain kinds of communication enhance the interaction of family members, encourage respect for the impact each person has in the family, and make it possible for the family to come to decisions that are satisfying to each person. Such an exchange between people involves speaking out loud the feelings, rules and customs that many of us are accustomed to expressing only in unspoken, indirect ways. Open communication also requires a willingness to find out what you need and a willingness to hear about the other person's needs that are different from yours. This is often a difficult process and one that takes time. Sometimes it's hard to really understand another person when you're feeling upset. You want all the attention, yet you need to carefully listen to the other if there is going to be any communication. Some families have found creative ways to deal with inevitable differences. This mother elaborates:

Our family was always fighting around dinner time. Steve, my husband, wouldn't come to dinner and Ian and Kristen wouldn't clean the dishes. Finally, out of desperation, we decided to talk about this. We gave each person a chance to say exactly how they felt and how they wanted to eat dinner and handle the clean-up. Other family members could ask questions if they were unclear but no one could argue. We decided to make a schedule which included three different kinds of meals – some special with candlelight, some everyone-grab-for-yourself and some we just called ordinary. The children also devised a specific clean-up schedule.

As illustrated above, one possible arena for this type of interaction is special family meetings at which parents and children can get together and air family matters, thoughts and feelings. One single father of two, Aaron, recounts:

I hung a bell over the kitchen door. Vivian, Martin and I could ring the bell to let each other know we wanted to meet and talk – about something that was bothering us or share a happy time or new ideas. For the first week Martin, who is eight, rang the bell frequently; he loved the power it gave him to get us all together and have an audience to listen to him. After a week or so, his bell ringing slowed down.

Whether they are prearranged or spontaneous, meetings offer us a chance to name family rules and to change the ones that aren't functional any more. There are often unspoken rules and family patterns for everything that happens in the family. For example, how do we decide where to go on vacation? Who washes the dishes? Can you eat in the living room while you watch TV or not? Do you knock on closed doors or just walk in? Do you talk to your parents about bringing a friend home or just invite the friend in? The clearer and more explicit the communication about rules in a family, the less likely there will be the kind of mixed messages that cause frustration and confusion for family members.

One area that benefits from clear communication is the whole knotty question of individual versus family needs. Think, for instance, of the struggles when a fifteen-year-old girl no longer wants to go on family vacations and yet her parents are still attached to the idea that family vacations include everyone and don't want to let her stay home. When the parents insist, she reluctantly goes with them to the beach and proceeds to make life miserable for everyone. 'Next year,' her parents say, 'you can't come.'

The binds on the family might be fewer if they could discuss their different feelings. The parents might say, honestly, 'It's the one time we can all be together without the pressure of work and school.' The daughter might say 'I can't be myself with you two, so vacation feels like pressure, not relaxation, to me.' Whatever the resolution, it's likely to be more satisfactory if it's talked about openly in this way.

Women today may experience some new aspects of this tension between group and individual. Many women grew up in families where mothers put themselves after everyone else, and as women try to redress this imbalance, they often work so hard not to fall back into the traps that were familiar to their mothers that they wind up in new ones. Instead of 'Me last', for instance, we may say 'Me first', and end up in painful struggles with our children – as if we were in competition with our children for their own time and our maternal attention. It is tricky for women to reach a balance between their needs separate from their family, their needs to be with their family and their family's need for them. There are parallel struggles for men as well, and communicating honestly, talking openly from the level of our feelings and expectations, seems to be a way of easing these struggles.

Neal Slavin

Change

A sign of a healthy family system is that it can adapt to changes – allowing space for resistance and time to make the transition. A new step by one member affects all the others in a way that makes clear our interdependence, as well as the family system. Erica states:

In my family, I'm going to change just a little, that is, not make breakfast any more. That means Mel and I are going to change because he's going to make breakfast for our two pre-schoolers. Then the first morning he's planning to fix the meal he forgets, and I get angry. Mel and I are fighting and the kids come running into the kitchen crying – they are hungry and they are also trying to get between us and stop our fighting. All this over a little change about breakfast!

Some changes occur as parents and children grow older, pass through different developmental stages and predictable life changes: a child learns to walk, a child reaches puberty, an adult becomes a parent. There are also voluntary changes: we may decide to move, for instance, or to institute family meetings, or to alter the division of labour in the family or the roles that family members play. While we choose to make the change, the change may not feel voluntary to us.

Changes are not always positive. Death, sickness, depression or the loss of a job brings painful change that in the short run may not seem positive, but that we can learn from in the long run. Some changes may look good, but have hidden difficulties: when a parent gets a better job, for example, the effect on the family may be that they have to move to another city, give up their friends and lose the parent to the demands of a new work situation.

Even moving into a new house can send a family into a tailspin. This family had thought only about how wonderful it would be to have additional space, and not about the hassles that might come with their new living quarters. The mother, Gretchen, says:

In our apartment we lived on one floor and could easily see or hear each other. After we moved, the kids' rooms were on the third floor and I spent most of my time on the first floor. Sandy would yell something and I would yell back 'What?' And that happened again and again. We both emerged from our foggy communication very frustrated. Being as little as he is, I think he interpreted my not hearing across distance as my not caring or wanting to hear. I interpreted his not coming down not just as a kid too tired or uneasy to go up and down but as stubbornness. These insights came when I realized that the move was shaking up familiar boundaries, all of us were reacting to those changes and we needed to discuss them as a group.

That each person in a family system resists change is as inevitable as change itself. The complexion of the resistance changes as families change. Often it's more than one member of a family who resists change. This mother, Evelyn, offers one instance:

We have a set of twin boys who are ten. It isn't only my husband and I but our two older children as well who encourage and applaud Justin and Jacob's childishness. It is very hard for all four of us to let them grow up.

Families can find themselves in trouble when some members resist changes that are necessary for other members. Olivia describes how her husband resisted changes she wanted to make:

Before I got married I was a teacher. I loved my work and left when our son was born because I wanted to stay home with him. I always planned to return to work when Kenny entered first grade and expected no opposition from Frank. When Kenny began kindergarten, I applied for teaching jobs. I talked with my husband about it and he got furious — 'You can't go back to work. I won't let you ... no wife of mine ...' I was stunned and angry. 'I was working when we got married,' I said. 'But that was different,' Frank replied. 'We didn't have a child then and now that we do I believe you should be at home.' It's a year later and we still haven't resolved our differences. I'm not sure how we will.

Overcoming the fear of change that this man and most people experience at one time or another can make change easier. Joel, now in his early forties, tells us:

When I was first married I didn't know how to deal with changes I wanted. I wasn't sure change was even a good thing. So anything that smacked of change I pushed aside. I hesitated when my wife suggested something as small as a different kind of family vacation. That would break my routines and I liked to keep everything on an even keel.

The mother of two young children is uneasy every time a new developmental stage approaches:

Just as Rochelle was about to eat solid food or start to crawl or take her first steps I would freak out. I found myself holding back and not readily able to help her make the transitions because I was so nervous that as she changed, so our relationship would change, and I wouldn't know how to act. It felt like I would just become comfortable being the mother of an infant, and she would turn into a baby; or I adjusted to her babyness and then she was a little girl.

Change usually comes slowly, which can reassure us if we fear it and frustrate us if we want it more quickly. Joan expresses her impatience:

I was a single mother for many years and was glad when Gary moved in with us. I loved him and also was eager for some help with the kids. Well, his timetable and mine were different. I needed immediate relief from the pressures of being a sole parent for many years, and he needed time to establish his own relationships with my kids. And the children's pacing was somewhere in the middle. Now, three years later, finally, we all live together as a family quite easily.

Times of change can present opportunities to family members to re-examine their relationships with one another. This can be both exciting and scary: until the family comes to some new balance, family members often feel on edge, tense, not certain of what will happen. Sometimes when couples elect to shift roles in the family, the change works better for one partner than for the other. And when one person calls a halt, the other may be so invested in the changes in how, for example, household chores are divided, child care shared or extramarital relationships tolerated that he or she does not want to slow down or return to a previous arrangement. Marriages can break up as a result of such imbalances. Yet it is equally possible for people to use the opportunity to grow further.

Other families have used temporary shifts in the family to make some long-term changes. A father, Neal, discusses what happened when his wife attended a two-week-long conference:

I had encouraged Tanya to go and loved it when she left. It was easier caring for the children than I expected. They really pitched in helping with meals and the house. I never really enjoyed being a father more than during the time she was gone. I got to know my four children better. Tanya had always been a buffer between them and me, which was something I had wanted but after these two weeks don't any more. I was not completely happy when she returned: in fact, I was quite angry and had a hard time admitting it. I was afraid family relationships would automatically return to what they were before and I would feel more left out than I wanted to be. I have been trying to keep my changed relationship to the children by spending special time with each of them regularly. I also think about whether I could arrange to come home from work earlier at least one day a week, but I haven't pursued that yet.

A mother, Ruth, shares the changes that took place when her daughter went to camp:

I experienced many feelings when Judy told me at ten she wanted to go to overnight camp. I was glad for her to have the chance to spend a summer in the country and sad that she would be leaving for all those weeks.

I didn't realize then how important an impact her leaving would have on the whole family. As time passed I got more distance from the intensity of her and my relationship and more time to be with my husband alone. It was a special summer for my son, Danny, who is younger and has struggled to keep up with his older sister – to be as strong and tough as she. With her out of the house, he was freer to express the more vulnerable parts of himself; he cried more easily, asked for help doing things that he would have insisted on doing alone when Judy was home.

When Judy returned there were more changes. She wanted privacy and moved further away from Danny; he was upset. What we learned during the summer helped us both find more time for ourselves as a couple, to listen to Danny's feelings more carefully, and to help Judy and Danny, where necessary, to work out their relationship.

Family as Training Ground

In our families we learn about living with other people. This experience has ramifications for how we are in other groups. How many times in school, in a social group or at work have you found yourself reacting to someone just as you would to your mother, your father, your sister, your brother? We may find ourselves depending upon a woman in the same way we depended upon an older sister. We get into the same arguments with a man at work that we had at home with our fathers. Or if we saw ourselves as the victim or the strong, active person at home, we're likely to feel that way in other group situations.

Not only our real families but other groups we are part of can become like families to us in the experiences and feelings they offer. Think of a work group (such as a food cooperative) or a social group (a bridge club, for example) or even a class or a therapy group: insights we gain in these groups may benefit us elsewhere. Learning to explain ourselves clearly in other groups can carry over and help us to communicate more clearly in our real families.

A family can also be seen as society in miniature, and our experience in this one unit gives us a way of perceiving how we fit into the larger system. The skills that we gain to help our families function well may be useful when we move beyond the family. On the other side, the larger social tensions can be played out in the family: for example, unemployed parents may take out their frustrations about the state of the economy and lack of work on their children; or single parents, suffering from lack of social supports for their families, may react angrily to requests for attention that children make.

Peter Simon

Conclusion

Family members are not as separate and isolated from one another as they sometimes feel: they have tremendous impact upon one another. Sometimes we need to create some distance from the family if its impact is destructive to us – as for a teenage child in an alcoholic family or a woman who is being battered by her husband. Often we can choose to use our connections to help each other. No system exists without the strains of daily life, of crises, of ordinary life changes – jobs being changed or children growing and leaving home. Our insights into the family as a system can aid us with both the stresses and pleasures of family life as they touch and change us.

Family Myths and Realities

People often carry around many myths about the family. These ideal notions of what family 'should be' are fine for storybooks but not for living with the complexity and confusion of daily life. These myths are often in direct conflict with the reality of family life, and may interfere with parents' individual ways of creating a nurturing environment.

Myths and Realities about Family Structure

There is a constellation of closely related myths about what a family should look like: in all of them 'the family' means nuclear family. That is the 'ideal' form which traditionally indicated not only who is included – father, mother and their children – but also how they live together – usually in some private, often isolated dwelling unit – and what roles the adults are expected to play – father earns the money, mother raises the children.

This ideal may expand to take in a mother who works in paid employment if the father still is seen as the head of the household, 'the provider', 'the chief executive'. The facts tell a different story:

● The traditional nuclear family is now in the minority: in only 34 per cent the man is the sole breadwinner; in 50 per cent both parents work; for 3 per cent of married couples, the woman alone is the provider; and the rest have no breadwinner.*

● The number of one-parent families is increasing faster than the number of two-parent families.†

● One out of six children (about ten million) live in a single-parent family; 87 per cent of such families are headed by women and 13 per cent by men. Between 35 and 40 per cent of children growing up in the 1970s will live in a single-parent family for an average of six years.‡

Even though the traditional nuclear family is less common now, we may match ourselves against various aspects of this ideal and feel inadequate. For instance, a working mother might compare herself unfavourably to the traditional mother who stays at home, and feel guilty even though she is glad to be working outside her home. An unemployed husband whose wife is working to support the family, or a husband whose wife is also contributing to family income, might contrast himself negatively with the 'ideal' man who is sole breadwinner. A single parent might get bogged down in missing the 'absent' parent instead of recognizing that s/he and the children are in fact a family.

Surprisingly, two-parent families also suffer from this feeling of inadequacy. In the mythology two-parent units are supposed to function easily and independently; after all, they don't face the problems of the single parent, who has all the responsibilities on her or his shoulders. Yet two-parent families don't always function smoothly. This conversation between two women illustrates how this mythical 'ideal' family oppresses them:

---

*Trends in the UK are similar: in 1971 at least one in six of all households were completely or substantially dependent on a woman's earnings or benefits; and between 1971 and 1976 the number of one-parent families increased by a third to one in nine of all families.

†From an interview with Mary Rowe, special assistant to the president and chancellor of MIT for Women and Work.

‡Susan Byrne, 'Nobody Home: The Erosion of the American Family', a conversation with Urie Bronfenbrenner, *Psychology Today* (May 1977), pp. 41–7; and Howell, op. cit.

Michelle: My family includes me and my children. Although we work well together as a family, there is some part of me that yearns to be that ideal nuclear unit. My fantasy is, if only we were more like that, all our problems would disappear.

Harriet: It's funny. My family fits the form, but the fact that we look so much like the 'ideal' has caused us problems. We appear to the outside world to be identical with the family I grew up in, while to the inside we are very different. Yet it's often impossible for people to see us for who we are because we seem to match the form so well. For instance, I am not the traditional housewife and mother. My husband and I both work full time and share equally in child care. I got furious at my mother when she criticized me for going off on a business trip and leaving the children with Greg. She never questions me staying home when Greg leaves for a week-long conference.

We distort our own experiences when we try to create the mythical family or when we see ourselves as the myth would have us be rather than as we are. We may let problems slide for too long because we're pretending they aren't there – for, after all, the 'ideal' family doesn't have real day-to-day hassles to contend with. Roberta tells of such a situation:

Until our daughter Kathie was born we ignored a lot of conflicts. We believed we had an 'ideal' marriage because we didn't fight. Jack and I never knew that fighting was a normal part of being married. He hadn't seen his parents fight, and in my family there were so many arguments that I swore I would never let that happen in my marriage. Well, both of us didn't let our angry feelings come to the surface, and the result was worse than if we had fought a lot. We had no way of dealing with the ups and downs of living together.

When Kathie arrived everything changed. Having a baby made it impossible to pretend we could live together and not face our negative feelings. What might have been normal emotions of new parents were distorted out of proportion by the years of build-up. Eventually we separated. We didn't know how to handle what was happening to us, and didn't know how to reach out to others for help before it was too late.

But even complete nuclear families do not always have enough people with sufficient time and physical and emotional energy to do all the tasks to keep the family running well. When each person in the family wants individual attention at the same time and has none available for anyone else, you need to call in extra help. As one little boy, Ezra, suggested to his divorced mother: 'If you get married again, Mommy, there should be three people: one for you, one for me and one for Ricky [his brother].'

One important nuclear-family myth is that the 'good' or 'successful' family can take care of everything by itself. This myth extends the American ideal of the totally independent individual to the small family group.

The ideas are related to another myth which says that women can and ought to ensure the smooth functioning of the family. Generations of women, responding to expectations of the society and their families, have struggled single-handedly to make their families function smoothly not only by doing all the maintenance and child-rearing tasks but by watching, tending and nourishing the family's emotional life as well. The fact is that, whether women are at home or employed outside, this is an impossible task to do alone. Both men and women need to accept that we and other people – friends, family, neighbours – are mutually dependent and need to learn to ask for assistance when necessary.*

Some parents who acknowledge the stresses of the nuclear family turn to another myth: wouldn't it be terrific if we still lived with our extended family? We miss familiar people. We yearn for the help with child care that relatives could provide. But in idealizing the possibilities of multigenerational family living, we tend to over-romanticize a complicated situation.

When we are with our own parents, we may find it difficult to change the patterns of giving and receiving that existed when we were children. Although we are parents ourselves, we are still also their children. The old lines of authority and power can make cooperation in child rearing difficult. We may ask for help with child care and get a lot of unasked-for advice; we go 'home' and want to be cared for, but our parents lavish that care on their grandchildren; or we want them to act grandparently and they would rather be with us.† Or we expect attention for ourselves and our children and, instead, our parents need the care they once gave us.

At a distance we tend to forget the family soap operas that make life both rich and interesting but also less rosy than we remember it. Here is Joyce's story, which refers to these points:

When my husband's parents retired, they decided to purchase a two-family house and invited us to move into the first floor. Their offer was wonderful – it gave us the chance to live in a house (which we couldn't afford on our own) and made it possible for me to work (which I couldn't have done because of lack of child-care facilities in our area).

There are several hitches in the arrangement. My in-laws don't approve of my working and take care of Rosemary only because they feel it would be worse if she stayed with a stranger. Also in accepting their help, I've had to open up my parenting to them and their disapproval of my ways of caring for their granddaughter. Don't get me wrong – I feel extremely lucky. When they care for Rosie they are wonderful; no day care centre could have ensured the caring they give. Yet they have different values about child rearing – for instance, put a child to bed when she has a cold, give her a sweet to comfort her when she cries. Another thing is that I'm the only person in the system who is not blood kin – the only one born with a different last name. And when I disagree with them, say, about restricting Rosie if she's ill, I have no ally. Sean, my husband, whom you might expect would support me, is their son and doesn't want any commotion. If we lived further away from them, I suspect that he might act somewhat differently.

*See the Helping Ourselves chapter for issues requiring asking for and receiving help.
†See the Parents of Grown-ups chapter.

The yearning for an extended family points to our need for community. While we may not live with our actual extended families, we can create communities of neighbours and friends or groups of families including two-parent and single-parent families that can provide similar kinds of caring and support that we associate with family.* Because these people are not blood relations, we sometimes feel freer to experiment with how to care for each other. However, it is also true that living near or with blood relatives can be a good experience for some people.†

Myths and Realities about Family Process

As parents we carry around mythical ideas not only about what our families are supposed to look like, but also about how they are supposed to function. These myths interfere with our families' ability to work as well as they might. Once we recognize them as myths, they cease to have the same power over our families' functioning. This section presents a few familiar myths. You will probably be able to name others.

One myth about family process is that everyone in a family is expected to like everyone else or, short of that, to act as if they do. The truth is that people related to one another sometimes don't like each other. Our response to other family members can range from passive resentment to overt hostility. Many parents try to actualize this myth of everyone liking everyone else by squelching family members' feelings of dislike, antagonism or anger toward each other, with the long-range result that children grow up not trusting their feelings and the more immediate result that family life becomes stilted, tense and punctuated by blow-ups. As an example, take competition between siblings. Letting children express their jealous feelings doesn't make the feelings go away, but perhaps it prevents them from being acted out in more destructive ways or locked away inside the person. This is equally true for fights between partners.

Another myth of family process is that the family will work effectively without any special effort. In other words, we don't have to pay attention to what happens in the family because some natural, spontaneous, unconscious process will take care of everything. The truth is that everyone who lives in the family has to assume some responsibility for keeping it going; no one can be passive if the family is going to be stable and secure for all its members.

Here a mother expresses what happened in her family when her husband became more involved with their children:

I've put effort into Julian taking over some of the emotional nurturing – as hard as it is, we're trying to shift the balance. As he's been able to sit down with Anita and let go of his extensive musical training to help her with her jumpy playing on the recorder, that

*See the Helping Ourselves chapter.
‡See Mark Jury and Dan Jury, *Gramp* (New York: Grossman Publishers, 1976), one book that illustrates this point.

*takes tremendous strain off me. And nobody feels cheated. I can feel the great freedom
and looseness and privacy that comes back to me and feel it doubly. Not only do I have
the time and permission but my kids appreciate that there is someone else who is slowly
becoming more and more willing to take on part of the emotional nurturance in the
family. In turn I also feel closer to Julian.*

Ann Popkin

A Variety of Family Experiences: Forms Families Take

The many ways people live in families today are exciting. As Mary Howell says,
'People are bravely and hopefully living out in their own lives some experiments
of relationship that could help bring us all to a more decent, respectful and caring
society.'*

In this section we will name some of these kinds of families and indicate the
strengths as well as the key problem areas for each. These experiences are
opportunities for growth – for people living them and for people who are open to
learning from the experiences of others. Your family is your own to create and
enjoy no matter how you name it.

A Prelude: Some Thoughts on Stigma

All families that look different from our imagined norm, the complete,
heterosexual nuclear family, have to deal with a sense of stigma – of being
marked by defect or disgrace for not being the 'ideal' family. In isolation from
others who share our experiences, we often internalize the social values and
come to feel that our family is abnormal. Here is a story of a single parent who let
herself feel judged:

*Howell, Wheelock paper, p. 11.

I was sitting in a staff meeting which included a group of mental health professionals. One woman was giving a presentation of a group she had been leading for many months. During her description of each of the group members, she mentioned a divorced mother of three who had 'failed in marriage'. The phrase stunned me. I was a divorced single parent and felt angered by her words. I wanted to strike out and tell her what an idiot I thought she was and stopped myself. Part of the struggle for me was knowing I had battled those feelings of failure for months after I separated from my husband. She said out loud what I had thought about myself for a long time and didn't like.

It helps to find other people who share our experiences.

As a lesbian mother, when you are doing something really different and not 'acceptable', it's very hard to do it by yourself or even with one other person – that's just not enough people.

Without some system of support, it can be extremely difficult to live at variance with the social conventions with which we grew up. Many single parents, step-parents and gay parents have all found or actively sought out other parents in the same situation to be with, to talk over common issues. Support groups of parents with similar experiences have been organized as these family forms have become more common.* There are books, newsletters and periodicals that are beginning to meet the same need for sharing with other people who have compassion for you.

Single Parents†

As we have seen, the ranks of single parents are rapidly growing, and these days they are more visible to the society and more able to find people like themselves. Yet many single parents still feel branded by the stigma: others judge them and they judge themselves for being less than the complete family. One single mother, Delores, shared this insight:

It's ironic. Here I am feeling guilty, ashamed and judged by society that as a working single parent I can't be there for my kids as much as I'd like to be. Yet many fathers in nuclear families work so hard outside their homes that they spend less time with their children than I do. For them there isn't the stigma attached because they're in a 'normal' family.

The central tasks for single parents are to believe that they and their children are real and acceptable families, and to build a network of friends who accept and support their families as they are. (See the chapters on Shared Parenting and on Helping Ourselves.) As they work toward these goals, single parents find their feelings of inadequacy fading and changing into a new perception of themselves

*See the Helping Ourselves chapter for a description of support groups.

†We are going to talk about single parents who are separated and divorced, not those who are unmarried or widowed. However, many of the issues apply to them, too.

as strong, competent and creative people. Both this self-acceptance and the helping network that single parents must of necessity build help to challenge the social bias which stigmatizes single parents today.

This section will focus primarily on parents who have custody of their children. To date most of these are mothers.

Families in the Process of Separating: Feelings

The first step for single parents is weathering the storm of the separation. This mother, Connie, poignantly describes her inner turmoil shortly after she separated from her husband:

If I am so strong, why can't I work it out this time? Something took my strength Thursday and won't give it back. I am lost without it. I can't work or eat or move or sleep. No one in the whole fucking world gives a shit. It's like a plane crash. Big news for a day and then everyone forgets by the end of the week. The worst is that I will be alone. And I am alone. And alone and alone. And the worst is terrible. In the middle of the night when your child is sick, there is no one else to help or worry with you or give love and support, and when you've changed the sheets for your child for the third time, there is no warm person in bed to soothe you back to sleep . . . Who else is there to love you but your husband, and who else is there to worry with you about your children but their father, and no one else in the world can do that. And where is he? Doing what he wants.

Separating parents sometimes focus all their worry on their children. Children do need attention at this time, yet to avoid facing their own hurt feelings, the adults may put all their concern into their children's reaction. Nina, a mother with a young daughter, speaks of this kind of experience:

Right after Matt left, Gwen ripped her toys apart for a week and kicked the dog when she thought I wasn't looking. So much of my attention went to Gwen that I forgot about myself. For a month I hovered over my daughter, trying to talk away all her angry, hurt and sad feelings. One morning I woke up and felt furious with her. I started to say something and suddenly I realized I was furious that Matt had gone and left me!

On the other hand, adults in the midst of a crisis sometimes forget about the children. Art remembers how he felt when he was surrounded by separating adults:

My parents separated when I was eleven years old. I was very sad. 'Why did this happen to me?' I remember asking again and again. But no one wanted to listen. My mother told me to be brave and not cry. What a crazy thing to tell a child whose parents have just separated. Years later in therapy someone finally paid attention and helped me with the loss of my father.

The truth is that parents in crisis have a hard time striking a balance between caring for themselves and for their children, and they need to have some tolerance for themselves because they aren't going to get this balance perfectly.

Separated adults often are surprised by their own mood swings – one minute they're delighted with the relief of a new-found freedom, the next they're depressed by the weight of the responsibility, by the loneliness and loss. Joy and grief flow together into a surge of emotional confusion, as Ellen, this mother of three, tells us:

It is four months after my separation and I am still warning friends and dates that I may cry in the middle of anything: talking, buying groceries, making love.

One weekend I go to Maine with a woman friend and we are walking along a ridge between two bodies of water, one rimmed with sand and one with rock ledges. I feel cleared and free. It is incredibly beautiful and serene and I breathe myself full of joy. Somehow it pushes me right over the edge into sorrow, sorrow over all the lost things in my life. This heightened emotional state is the ridge between joy and sorrow, and I never know what direction I'll be heading next.

Whether the separation is sudden or extended over a long time, there is one moment when kids must be told it's happening. The mix of feelings can be intense and hard to handle, as this mother describes:

The moment my husband and I chose to tell our two children that we weren't going to live together was excruciating for me. I was calm outside and shaking inside. My son was three and my daughter was six. As small as Ben was, he just shook his little head and said 'No, no, no' loudly while Naomi curled up into a sad little ball and didn't say anything.

'We both love you and will always love you and care for you, but we don't want to be married any more. This is not something either of you did but a grown-up decision.' Even as I said the words which I had to say, I knew no words were adequate for the moment. I felt only a deep anguish. I wanted to wash over their pain, my pain, even my husband's pain. I wanted what was happening to stop. I wanted to blame Ben and Naomi for causing the separation. I wanted to use them to try once more to hold the marriage together. And I couldn't do anything but keep the children close and get through the moment and go on living.

When parents finally do separate, even if they are very angry, they can never totally sever the connection to the other person because he or she is the child's parent. Often one parent will wish for more of a relationship. A mother shares a letter she wrote to her ex-husband.

I desperately miss having another adult come home (sometimes even if it's late at night) to report the day's details to. If you are raising kids and working, and trying to keep a household under control, and are under severe emotional stress, there is a lot to say, and no one to really say it to, thus these letters. Who cares if Melanie finds a huge carpenter ant in her bed? Who else cares if we plant a tree or build a teepee or if I take Melanie and some of her classmates to catch tadpoles and tent caterpillars? Who cares what I do with your children every day? Certainly you do not, and the fact that there is no sharing that goes along with my lack of family life is so sad to me, I could almost cry right now, right smack in the middle of the day. And it's even sunny out.

Other parents want less of a relationship. Some want none at all. The father of a ten-year-old son, recently separated from his alcoholic wife, confides that at times he wishes the earth would open up and she would just disappear:

Her comings and goings have been so erratic and upsetting to Ted and me that I imagine it would be easier living with the fact of her being dead than worrying about whether or not she was.

Here is a mother, Sally, who is struggling to get more distance from her ex-husband:

My husband and I were separated, planning on getting a divorce in the near future – and I wanted to move out of state with our daughter. He was, at first, very uncompromising, saying no, he wouldn't let me, he would fight all the way. And he had a good point, since we were both very close to Julie and both felt the need to have her with us. But the fact that I wanted desperately to move, to be with my own parents and start a new job, and that he wanted to stop me, made me feel trapped and powerless. I wanted to do something to release his grip on me. I had all sorts of violent visions about what could happen to him. And for the first time I had an inside understanding of why separated parents kidnap their children or murder each other. I really felt frantic until we finally reached an agreement that was acceptable to both of us.

Because of the intensity of the separation period, contacts between the ex-partners tend to be excruciating for both sides, yet this is the time when key negotiating goes on as to what is going to happen with the children. It is a time when it is very hard to keep from using the children as weapons of our anger or pawns in negotiating.

It sometimes takes every ounce of psychic stamina we have to keep on an even keel as our child's parent during this mixed period of anger, loss, loneliness, relief, hope, sadness, worry. Some separating parents have found the following helpful:

● good friends or a lover to be with.
● an objective person to talk with.
● someone special to take the kids for an afternoon – it's a time when kids are upset, too, and often just a baby-sitter won't do.
● support groups for separated or divorced persons or single-parent groups.
● a chance to be with people, to play and to relax.
● prayer, meditation, other methods of keeping centred.
● books, such as *Women's Survival Manual: A Feminist Handbook on Separation and Divorce* (Philadelphia: Women in Transition, Inc., 1977) or the British books *Women's Rights* by Anna Coote and Tess Gill (London: Penguin, 1977) and *The Directory of Social Change, Vol. 3: Women* (London: Wildwood House, 1978).

We can both ask for these or some of these ourselves when we need them or give them to friends who are separating and may need some of them from us.

Economics

The economics of moving apart are rarely simple, and it is hard to separate them from the feelings. Some people who want to separate cannot afford to do so. Women, who usually have less economic resources than men, have justifiable fears about how they will support themselves and their children once they decide to leave the marriage. The harshness of the economic realities, combined with the fears and feelings about leaving, often keep women living in psychologically unhealthy situations. This means that women who are physically abused by their husbands often don't have the financial resources to move out. And a man who wants to separate may feel held back by his economic inability to maintain two homes.

The economics of being a single parent are astoundingly difficult, especially for the parent who has custody of the children. Women who were primarily housewives lose their economic security, but still have the same job of maintaining a home and raising children. Women who work full time may be free from the greater economic insecurity of joblessness or part-time work, yet they must then struggle by themselves with the extreme pressures of juggling work and children. Too often the economic pressure forces single parents back into traditional family situations before they are ready, or into a relationship with an inappropriate person, as Holly tells us:

Six months to the day after my divorce was final, I got remarried. I was in love with Bill and felt very fortunate that he was willing to help support me and my two daughters. For a while, everything was fine. But as we got to know each other better, I realized this was the wrong relationship for me. Out of fear and loneliness I jumped too fast and now I'm facing those issues after a second divorce.

Here is a father who finds the change in life style worth it:

Yes, I have financial problems; however, they seem more manageable than when I was in an unhappy marriage because I'm more content with myself. Although I have less money than if I and a wife were working full time, I like the freedom my singleness gives me. My daughter, Hilary, and I survive on a much more modest income now.

Economic needs and parenting are inextricably intertwined. Single parents who have the skills and are able to get and manage paid employment may not be able to secure jobs that are flexible enough so they can spend time with their children. When they must work full time, they often can't find and afford the child care they require. They don't have the energy left at the end of the day to be sufficiently attentive to both their own needs and those of their children. If single parents choose to work at home or work part time so that they can be with their children, they have a hard time coping with the reality that most kinds of self-employment and most part-time work don't pay well or provide benefits, such as health care, sick leave and vacation pay, that all parents sorely need. These are some of the problems that single parents must contend with; and when there are no answers, they live with the frustration and anger they feel.

Furthermore, when marriage battles continue to be played out around money, or when the amount provided by welfare or child support is inadequate for the family's survival, the feelings of panic and powerlessness can become overwhelming for single parents, usually mothers, who depend on former spouses for child support or on welfare to provide a subsistence income for them and their children. Women and children are often dependent on the court and on government agencies, institutions which are not organized to respond fully or fast enough to human need.

The economic problems single parents face are very real and can last long beyond the initial separation. Yet in time many single parents find ways to support themselves and their children that make them feel more secure. Often they return to school or train to acquire skills.* Here are several, more unusual examples:

Betsy: When I separated I had to find a job. But it had to be a part-time job with flexible hours, since I had two pre-school children. I had a professional degree in social work, so I thought it would take time but it would be possible. After several months of looking, an old friend moved into town. She was also searching for a part-time job, and so we decided to submit our résumés together for one full-time job. We were turned down in several places and some agencies wanted to hire one or the other of us. Still we kept looking and eventually found a job together in a new hospital programme. We were elated when they said yes to us.

Jane: I met Emma when we were both still married. Our daughters were in the same play group, then nursery school and then kindergarten. Within about six months of each other, we each got separated from our husbands. For a while we stayed in our separate houses and struggled to pay the bills. Eventually I got fed up with the economic pressures and was also ready for a change. So one day when we were walking home from school with our kids, I told her my situation and asked if she'd like to share an apartment with me. She thought for a moment, but soon got very excited. The next day we were out looking for apartments, and before the week was out, we found one.

Loren: I lived alone in several different apartments and with a variety of communal groups before I found this group of people that I now consider my family. The core group met at a psychology conference; we were each searching for other people who were doing similar work – therapy and teaching – to form a support group. Well, we did more than that. After knowing one another for a while we decided to rent a house together where we could live and work. Three of us were single parents who were forging both new work lives and new personal lives and came together at just the right moment. The arrangement of living and working together was a financial and emotional blessing for all of us.

---

*In the US about 45 per cent of all married mothers work, and about 80 per cent of all separated and divorced mothers work. The implication is that one of the major tasks is learning to be a breadwinner (Dorothy Burlage, op. cit., p. 160).

Positive Aspects of Single Parenting

When parents first experience the pangs of being alone or the threat of economic insecurity, it is hard to perceive the positive aspects of single parenting. In fact, there is a necessary period for healing – sometimes a long time, as this woman discovered:

I went into Dr Lacey's office expecting some kind of miracle cure for my misery, and what I received was very different. We talked about my marriage and allowing myself time for healing. He told me he believed it took just as long to get out of a marriage as the number of years a person had spent living in it. I was shocked and not at all relieved. I had been married seven years and I didn't think I would last seven years if I continued feeling the way I did at the moment. I resolved I just wouldn't take so long.

Well, with my resolve and the desire to deny the importance of my marriage and the extent of pain splitting up caused me, I can say now, several years later, there is no set time. Still, there was truth in what Dr Lacey said. It has taken a long time for me to get comfortable as a single parent and to know, yes, indeed, that I am living my own life separate from my marriage.

Some of the negative elements subside as parents are able to resolve issues such as work, child care and economic and emotional support. Gradually perceptions do change. Here are some notes from one mother's journal:

I am enjoying my life, being alone, being with the kids. We are always outside, almost always with nothing on. We give birthday parties to Sami, make colourful drawings all over our sidewalks, play hopscotch, eat ice cream pies, swim in the plastic pool . . . plant the garden, water the garden, get dirty, hear from friends . . . my shrink tells me I am too healthy for her. I write constantly. I teach from time to time. I get new jobs. I think of new ideas. I eat salad and fruit and yogurt and almost never cook. I talk to my women friends. I visit my friends with new babies and give them support. I am glad I went through this separation in mid-winter, when the pain was so available, when there was no way to escape the dark and cold and isolation like there is now. Next winter will not be as terrifying. My emotional state is much stronger. I am feeling so much less rejected. I know I can be alone. I know how good I am. I know my children will survive.

Other negative elements may remain or even become clearer. As the anger passes, there may be moments – particularly on birthdays or other special occasions like holiday times – of missing the other parent or wishing to be back together as that former family. Some single parents celebrate holidays with other single parents and their children:

As the holiday season approached – my first without my husband – I started to worry. How would we celebrate – Rachel and Adam and I? Then it became obvious that we could make Thanksgiving together with Amanda and Beth, another single mother and her daughter who were our friends.

We had fun planning and preparing a feast. We decided to invite a few other friends in and had a wonderful day – eating, playing, laughing, celebrating together. Aside from being a joyous time for us and our children, our all being together really affirmed each of our single-parent families for what they are (rather than for what they are not or were formerly). Families celebrate holidays together and we were doing just that. As Amanda and Beth walked out the door, they said 'We'll have another celebration at Chanukah!'

The single parents we interviewed spoke of several positive aspects of this kind of family. We present them here and hope that these few will suggest others to you.

'When my spouse left,' reported one woman, 'I stopped knocking my head against the wall. Much of the stress I had been living with went as he walked out the door.'

A man gives voice to the same feeling when he says:

For me, the quality of my life has improved since my divorce. I have more loving and caring relationships; and my work is providing me with a level of satisfaction that I had not known previously. I'm finding that friendship, love and support derive more from the quality of individual relationships than from the state of marriage or non-marriage.

For these two, life feels easier. They are no longer using their energy to continue old feuds, but instead can spend the time getting on with living.

Many single parents who played a more passive role in their marriages speak about the pleasure of becoming more active about their lives. When a person initiates a divorce, s/he may feel proud to have done something positive for her/himself. Even the parent who did not initiate the divorce has to start making decisions – for instance, about where and how to live. This change is painful but brings with it a sense of activity and accomplishment.

Single parents, by necessity, end up doing a good deal of what *both* parents had done before the split. This can open a new kind of parenting experience to mothers and fathers alike. If a mother used to leave certain parent responsibilities to her husband, she may find her relationship with her children opening into new areas as she repairs the car, plays more sports and so on. She can clearly say yes or no to her children. She has the power to make decisions such as what she'll spend her money on. If she goes to work for the first time she may discover the possibility of spending brief high-quality time with her children rather than the all-day endurance-test kind of time she had been used to. Single fathers have spoken with great joy of a new closeness with their children that comes when they can no longer slip out from the direct daily moment-to-moment re-sponsibilities. Zack says:

I used to spend time weekends working in the yard, watching TV, and maybe taking the kids for Laurie for a couple of hours here and there. Now on the weekends when I have Judah and Lisa there's no one else to get them through the day – I'm it! And even though there are some moments when I climb the walls with exasperation, I love the closeness it brings us. I'm angry when I think back to what I missed for those first seven years.

There are strengths and joys in single-parent family life that all parents might learn from. As a single parent you have a particular opportunity to discover yourself as a parent. There is no buffer; many times there is no one who can substitute for you. While single parents feel pressured and experience the burden of being sole parent, they also gain a sense of self-sufficiency as a parent. As you help your kids with fights with friends, or prepare a meal if you haven't cooked for your family before, or earn the money that pays the bills, or watch the kids grow from childhood to adolescence, you can feel a sense of accomplishment – not that you necessarily did everything alone or that your feelings are so different from any parent's, but that it really was *your* job and you did it.

Without another central adult around in a day-to-day way, single parents can discover a simplicity and directness with their children, as Grace, a mother of one daughter, reports:

I came home from work too tired to prepare supper and I told Jenny we'd go out for pizza. She was pleased. I didn't have to consult with or wait for another adult. And out the door we skipped.

With no other regularly present adults to intervene, parents also experience more directly their effect on their children and their children's effect on them. The impact children can have on single parents and vice versa is expressed by this mother:

I was feeling very sad. My ten-year-old son noticed the tears in my eyes. He suggested I go have a good cry ('like you tell me to do, Mommy'). I lay down on my bed and bawled for a long time. Periodically he'd get up from his TV programme, check that I was O.K., pat me on the head and return to the show he was watching. I was crying because I was sad, but also in response to what my son had said and done. His caring really moved me at a time when there was no one else giving me that.

As parents allow children to have impact on their lives, they also provide space for a deep intimacy to grow. Although this intimacy with children is not reserved for single parents, they have a special opportunity to experience it, since their children often are the people they live most closely with. One of the difficult aspects about single parenting is that sometimes you do want your child to be an adult partner and can get very frustrated, often inappropriately, when s/he acts like the child s/he is rather than the adult you need. For instance, Anna says:

I sometimes get furious at Patrick when he wants something from me as his parent – anything from attention to help with a homework problem to a request to visit a friend – because they are all reminders that he is my child and not my adult equal. I do recognize that the times I have a lover or important other friends I see frequently, I don't get angry with him in the same way.

Yet as long as this intimacy is not a substitute for intimacy with adults, single parents can nourish a depth of relationship with their children that is sustaining for both. Eileen shares a special experience:

We are having a powwow under the bedspread tent. I ask my three-year-old son why he threw the chair. I say he must have been really angry. He agrees. I try to narrow the source of his anger from the many crises of his life. I tell him stories about dumb things all of us do when we're angry. I tell him about the time I slammed a door, only my head was in the way. I tell him his father threw a chair because his sister had made a puddle of water in it. We both laugh in the dark and feel we have a secret sharing about our anger.

Eric Levenson

There can also be a direct and reciprocal encouraging of strengths between parents and children in single-parent families. Children get to see adults' strengths: the courage to leave an unhappy marriage, the ability to support the family, the willingness to learn new skills – for example, building shelves or repairing a broken window or listening to others' feelings or the openness to reach out to new people. Adults give children more responsibility around the house and for themselves. This grows out of the necessity of sharing the work, perhaps, but it has the advantage of allowing children to learn about their own capacities. They acquire a sense of independence, as this father of a seven-year-old girl tells us:

I am able to get a degree of privacy for myself when Emily is home. I do it by encouraging and supporting a manageable independent attitude on her part. The other day while I was shopping she baked cornbread and took pieces around to everyone in the building. On another occasion she reorganized her room, rearranging her art supplies, books and toys. Seeing me occupied increasingly encourages Emily to concentrate on her own activities. Though the temptation is there to interrupt, she is becoming increasingly aware that there are times (mutually agreed upon) for privacy and times for sharing.

The way decisions are sometimes made in a single-parent family, such as how money is to be spent, involve the children so that they learn about decision-making, which can lead to self-sufficiency later on. In a two-parent family these decisions are often restricted just to the two adults.

As we discussed in the chapter on Sharing Parenting, single parents need help from other adults. No parent can do everything alone. The necessity of asking for help can become an opportunity as a single parent approaches an unfamiliar parent in the park with his or her youngster and says 'Let's go to my house and have some tea and talk while the kids play.' Of course, there is real disappointment when people you approach or ask for something don't come through, but there is an incredible sense of interconnection when they do. 'In a paradoxical way,' as one mother put it, 'we single parents are potentially less isolated than parents in nuclear families. We have expanded the trusted adult role to others, to non-parents outside the family, and those other people have a lot to offer us and our kids.'

Step-parents

As more and more parents divorce and then remarry, a growing number of families now include step-parents and children who can be related to one another in a variety of ways: as biological or adoptive siblings, stepsiblings, and half siblings.

It can be exciting when two adults choose each other with the wisdom derived from having tried before, but this new family constellation raises some unique issues. While we are aware of the stories of mean step-parents and step-parents who never develop relationships with their stepchildren, all the step-parents we interviewed were basically positive about being step-parents.

Many step-parents know their stepchildren before they get married, and many have even lived with them. So the issue of who these adults are to these children commonly gets raised before parents decide to marry and officially become step-parents.

Even after marriage it's difficult to find names for one another, as this stepfather recounts:

I realize I practically never call Jeanne and Trude my stepchildren and I don't think of myself as a stepfather. In fact, I'm embarrassed when I have to introduce them to someone and account for their relationship to me. It's something like the awkwardness of describing someone you live with and love if they're not 'wife' or 'husband' as just 'friend'. There's a taint of illegitimate claim in its connotations.

This step-parent saw the question of names differently:

Marrying Paul was a turning point in my relationship with Jonathan. I knew we would have a connection for the rest of our lives. The morning of our wedding Jonathan climbed into bed with us and asked how he would be related to me and to each member of my family. Having words for our relationship, even as vague and inadequate as the terms 'stepmother' and 'stepson' are, has helped us to recognize that we are part of the same family. We are not just each separately attached to the man who is my lover and Jon's father.

Nancy Scanlan

A stepmother told a mother who is a single parent:

You think it's stressful for you raising Lynn alone. Well, at least you are the real parent. I care for Aaron full time and still have no legal rights as a parent. I get frightened when I think his biological mother could take him away from me at any time. My commitment to Aaron is as deep as that of any mother who has raised a child for five years. Still, I feel he could be snatched from me and I would be crushed.

No matter how much they love the children and take responsibility for them, step-parents have no legal status as parents. Even if they are the primary parent in their stepchild's life they are not guaranteed the rights of a biological or adoptive parent. In this situation step-parents have a lot of responsibility and little power. Some step-parents, when they are free to do so, choose to adopt their stepchildren to ensure legal connections and also to balance the scale of responsibility and power.

Before step-parents and their children can make a new family together, they must make some peace with the families that each has come from. Whether or not these families are actually present in the lives of the reconstituted unit, it sometimes feels as if they lurk in the shadows, as one stepmother expresses in this poem:

> My ghost is real
> she has a life
> with options
>   that should be mine.
>
> The mail box seems small
> to hold her awesome power.
> Yet I have seen her paper body
> with foreign stamps
>   that change my life.
>
> Her voice is loud
> rings in the night
> tearing through my sleep
> waking my fears
>   to an unsure reality
>
> When she could cross
> my threshold
>   if I don't obey.
>
>   – Jeri Bain, 'The Haunting'

The 'other parent' often continues to exert a powerful influence on the new family's life. Norma shows how negative feelings about an absent parent can become focused on a child:

No one ever likes any child all the time. There is a tendency on the part of everybody in our family to blame 'the estranged parent' for Annie's negative characteristics. Both her father and I see her competitive feelings, her need for attention, her unwillingness to help in group situations as very much like her mother. When Al and I struggle with these in her, we find ourselves taking out on her some of our hostility to her mother. Al gets especially upset because he put up with those traits in her mother for too long.

Alexander describes his feelings about his stepson's father:

My relationship with Jeffrey's father has always been stilted and difficult. In fact, we really don't have any relationship. Yet I feel resentful of ways I think he has abandoned Jeffrey. I am also threatened by the power his money represents. At other times I've felt compassion for his isolation and separation from the boy I love. I never have expressed that to him, though if our communication was better, Jeff would probably benefit.

Children who spend time with both sets of parents may still wish that their biological parents could be back together, or that the two reconstituted families could be closer. In an attempt to minimize the separation, this child offered a novel solution: 'Why can't Alexis [his half sister] come with me to Mom's house when you go away for the weekend? We'll take good care of her, I promise.' His father and stepmother laughed as they retold this story, and added:

David makes a lot of sense. It would be so simple to send Alexis to Peggy's. She feels like an ex-officio member of the family anyway. She might even be willing . . . but then all the effort we've expended to separate our families would go down the drain.

Dealing with an ex-spouse is a process often filled with loyalty pulls and feelings of rejection on all sides, as one stepfather reports:

Since Paula and Robert had joint custody of the children, I thought it would be easier if we could be friendly and thus minimize the animosities between us and Robert. However, while that fit with my values, it didn't take account of the intensity of my negative feelings for Robert.

A stepmother shares her feelings about her husband's ex-wife:

It's painful to keep realizing that their mother exerts dominant parenting influence in their lives regardless of how I love them or would like to influence them. It's really a power struggle between me and her over-mothering the children. It affects my relationship with Philip: who is he loyal to – me, as his wife? Or her, as the mother of his children? Cynthia calls up a lot, which aggravates me. One time on the phone when she sensed how uncomfortable I was to have her be so much a part of our new household, she remarked 'Well, after all, Phil and I are raising our children together.' I realized she was terribly right – that the children would continue to link her to us as long as the children were connected to all of us. It takes a lot of sorting out for me to try not to let the children become targets of my feelings about her.

Step-parents cannot duplicate or substitute for the original family. Once they have come to terms with that fact, they can go on to develop genuine relationships with their stepchildren which are supportive, friendly, mutually nurturing and fun, as a stepfather talking about his stepson tells us:

I have really grown to love him. He has a wonderful sense of humour which we share. At first I felt competitive with his father, but no longer. Joseph and I have something very special between us. We really enjoy spending time together. I sometimes help him with his homework, we go for long walks in the woods together with our dogs, we like to cook a meal together. I can also help both him and his mother, Elena, when they get into a fight. I have the distance of a friend and often can mediate between them just because I'm not emotionally attached to Joseph in the same way that Elena is.

A stepmother gives another picture of what it's been like to be with her stepchildren:

I started out trying to be a superstepmother, and it was like I was performing a role.

For example, one of the luxuries I had most regretfully given up 'for the children' was staying in bed late on Saturday or Sunday morning. When I gave that back to myself, the children started helping their father make breakfast and brought it to me in bed. It was a grand procession as they entered the room – they were proud of what they had done and I certainly was pleased.

I also had to learn to be able to set limits and let the children know what behaviour I could or couldn't accept – which might be different for their father or mother. That was hard – because not having any 'instinctive' love from child to natural parent to fall back on, I was afraid that if I disciplined them they wouldn't like me and all would be lost. Once, when I did speak to my stepson about why his behaviour was annoying me, he got very hurt and angrily answered 'I don't care if you are my stepmother – from now on I'm not going to care about you, I'll always think of you like the stepmother in Snow White!' That really hurt. But our relationship at that point was strong enough to recover, especially because we had been honest with each other.

Just as single parents face social stigma, step-parents also have to contend with the myths of the wicked and cruel stepmother or stepfather. Children who are familiar with these fairy stories have ammunition – it's not only that you're not my real parent, but you are an evil one at that. These myths don't endear people to each other. One stepmother describes another helping her to think about these myths:

My friend Ada once said to me 'I suspect we've got to accept the fact that there's some truth in those terrible stepmother stories – that lurking inside of us somewhere are feelings that you would as soon feed the kids to the wolves or give them poisoned apples and be done with it.' I was shocked to hear her say that. I had worked very hard, after all, at becoming a good person, always gentle and loving and kind, and was determined my stepchildren would get everything they needed! I definitely did not like being cast as the wicked stepmother. But somehow accepting that I would have those feelings sometimes, and hearing from 'natural' mothers that they sometimes felt the same way, helped me develop a very solid relationship with my stepchildren.

As step-parents move toward being 'real' parents, they must deal with the fact that their relationship with their stepchildren doesn't have a history of caring and being cared for from the beginning. A stepfather discusses this:

Whenever I get into a bad place with my stepdaughter – when she is doing something I disapprove of or when we are arguing – I don't have the backlog, that history of a very intimate essential relationship that her mother has. I never fed her as a baby or had the responsibility for whether she lived or died. I never changed her or powdered her bottom. I have to respond purely here and now and that puts me in a colder place with Becky. As a result I love Becky in a different way than Carla does. At the moment it's especially difficult being with Becky. She doesn't feel very lovable and doesn't invite love. Carla's love comes from knowing she is her blood and remembering her fragility as an infant. My positive feelings are harder to be in touch with.

Step-parents and stepchildren often experience a push and pull – wanting trust to develop fast and yet being scared of getting close too quickly. Time and patience are key factors for most step-parents. Here a lesbian mother speaks of the slow process of adjustment:

When we first got together, Stephen was about four. Ann moved in with me without thinking about the consequences – really that she was going to become Stephen's parent. It took her about a year to get used to that, and it took him about a year to get used to her. At first he felt she had moved in on his territory – he was very jealous, vindictive, hostile. And she protected herself by refusing to recognize that any of those things were going on. And I was in between – getting angry primarily at her because I thought, now, you are the grown-up, you're supposed to be more adult at this. And feeling like I was having to referee, to protect them from each other. We very actively discussed what she was doing and what I felt about it and what her role needed to be. She started to make an investment in him. As she got more involved with him she got to love him and he got to love her. Within a year Stephen was feeling she was his parent.

One stepfather pointed out that special circumstances can make up for the lack of a long history:

Very shortly after we got married, Dorothy had a terribly difficult pregnancy. She was in bed so much that I became her son's major active parent. The intensity of those months made our trusting and our loving grow much more swiftly than it might have otherwise.

Like many step-parents who haven't yet had children of their own, this father found that when his own baby arrived he began to understand the parenting bond more deeply and to take his stepson into his heart in a new way. 'I even began to appreciate differently my stepson's natural father's connection to his son,' he added.

Step-parents need a strong couple relationship to sustain them and their new family. Any two adults who parent together benefit when they can communicate clearly with each other. But this is especially important for step-parents, for the parenting bond between them is grounded not in the fact that they had a child together but in the mutual agreement that the step-parent is willing or wants to share parenting. This couple went into therapy together, as the wife describes, to resolve some of their differences:

Simon and his kids moved into my house to join me and my three kids, making it hell for both sides. I saw our familiar ways being changed, and they felt like strangers. For instance, I like having big informal family meals where everyone pitches in. But when Simon's kids come for a weekend, he wants to give them special treats. One morning Debby and I made pancakes for everyone, and when Simon's son Dick came down late, Simon said 'Oh, can I scramble you an egg?' I was furious. The question is, are his kids guests or are they family? He sees them so seldom that he wants them to be guests and I want them as family. We went into therapy over that, and they ended up as family.

Pamela, another stepmother, still has ambivalent feelings about her new family.

Sal and I have lived together for three years, during which Mike has always been at our house four days each week. But I still consider the days when he's not here normal, regular days and the days he's here irregular or special days. To Sal, the opposite is true. The days when Mike is here are normal and on the days he's not here, someone is missing who belongs here. The difference in our views causes a lot of misunderstanding between us.

Sometimes tension comes to the surface and explodes. Carol describes such an incident:

Ed wanted us to treat his kids as special, I think because he was always trying to prove something when they were with us, to make up to them that he had ended the marriage. And this put a strange pressure on the two sets of children to get along with each other. For some months everyone was quite polite. But then one summer evening there was a terrible fight between my daughter and his. We were letting them handle it themselves, having learned to stand back. As the two girls went out the door to go for a walk and try to deal with their controversy, my other daughter screamed after her stepsister 'You always were a selfish bitch!' Ed was stunned. 'I thought you liked Marion,' he said. 'I never liked her, but you've always made me pretend I liked her' was my daughter's passionate reply. After that we had a long talk.

Sometimes it's easier, as this mother says, to spend time in smaller units than with the whole family:

Ruben's daughter and I tend to get into competition for her father's approval, especially since he's critical of what I do with her. So she and I have nicer times alone together than with him right now.

There are so many positives to combining families. Children gain siblings. And they share all sorts of skills between them all. It's nice for them to have a big family on weekends and a quieter household on weekdays. It's a way of children meeting a lot of people through each other.

The number of step-parents are growing as the number of people who get divorced and remarried increases. One result is that there is more literature available.* Among the resources in the USA is an especially valuable newsletter called *Stepparents Forum*.† It contains a wealth of personal experiences, discussion of step-parent issues, current research and literature.

To conclude this discussion on step-parenting, here is one very positive view:

... stepparents are ... prepared to take chances ... They may indicate a ... readiness to experiment, to work ... at relationships, to dispense with old ideas, ancient stigmas.

---

*See the Bibliography below.
†*Stepparents Forum*, Westmount, PO Box 4002, Montreal, H3Z 2X3, Canada.

In a sense, stepparents have taken a step. Perhaps that's what we should take the term to mean. They have taken a step, and it can be an exciting step . . .*

Parents Who are Gay[†]

A number of parents who have spoken in this book are gay. They haven't always been identified, unless it was relevant, because they are, like all the other speakers, parents. This section will focus on gay parents and look at some of the special problems and possibilities of gay-parent families.

The gay parents we interviewed share with other parents their loving, their caring, their dedication, their perplexities and angers. As one lesbian mother asserted, 'I'm not different, I'm a mother!' But gay parents live.in a society which regards them with suspicion and mistrusts their ability to raise children well. It is that difference which brings loss and pain to parents and children alike – pain which is balanced, in many cases, by an increased openness and honesty within the family, and by the nourishment of adult love given and received.

Custody

Probably the main issue for gay parents is custody. A gay parent's right to keep her/his children can be challenged in the courts by the other parent, by neighbours, by her/his own parents and by state social agencies. Jean, a lesbian mother, speaks:

We're the only people who all the time face having our children taken away, just by the very fact of who we are, not for neglect or abuse. You can always try to deal with the father but you can't deal with the state at all. And if the husband or neighbours make a gripe they can get the state all stirred up.

Lesbian mothers report painful, exhausting custody struggles, often fought at the children's expense:

My kids were sent back and forth by the court from me to their father and finally to foster homes while he fought for custody. He finally won. Then after a year he sent them back. He didn't want them, he just didn't want me as a lesbian to get custody. Once he'd proved his point he sent them back. It's taken us months to get settled as a family again.

Social disapproval of gays, plus the custom of awarding custody to mothers, means that very few openly gay fathers have custody of their children; and many have to struggle even for visitation rights. Alex, a gay father who lives with his kids, reports:

---

*Gordon Bawker, 'Stepparenthood: Stigma or *Challenge?*', *Stepparents Forum*, November-December 1975, p. 3.

[†]This section was written by Wendy C. Sanford, with special thanks to the Lesbians with Children group of the Cambridge Women's Center. In the UK, lesbian mothers can find mutual support groups through Lesbian Line (telephone 01-837 8602).

I went to conference for gays a year ago, and of all the gay fathers there, not a single one was living with his children – except the ones who were still in the closet, living with their wives.

The custody struggle has many costs to parents and children. One cost is that, as Elaine exclaimed, 'To show I deserve to have my children I have to prove I'm *better* than a straight parent. I have to be a superparent! And my kids feel the strain of my not being able to relax.' A social worker in the film *In the Best Interests of the Children* * commented:

In and around court, lesbian mothers are put under such close scrutiny that they don't seem to have, as most other mothers do, the right to be a mediocre mother.

Another cost of the threat of custody battles is that gay parents live with constant uncertainty. When will someone decide to raise a fuss? Alex feels the worry even though his situation is good in many ways:

I am not the children's legal guardian. We agreed that they would stay with me, but we're not divorced. At one point I very much wanted to be divorced, so I came very close to filing, but I stopped that legal divorce because I was afraid she might change her mind about my having the children and that if it was pointed out to the court that I'm gay there wouldn't be much chance of my keeping the kids.

Marilyn has less to fear than most, yet –

I knew that my ex-husband didn't want custody, or he wouldn't have left us when our son was a year old. But I can't help feeling, what if and what if and what if?? I've worried about it for years, and when Ann and I made plans to move to another city, I steeled myself for the battle. I dressed up and went to dinner with Art and his new wife, took a deep breath and said 'Ann and I are moving away.' And they both said 'Isn't that great!' And I knew they really didn't want my son.

Coming Out

Perhaps the major distortion caused by the custody issue is that it keeps so many gay parents from 'coming out', that is, telling people about their gayness. Bonnie, who has two pre-schoolers, spoke with gratitude in a lesbian mothers' group:

I'm lucky in that I'm out to my children's father, and he's very accepting. He's one of my best friends; he gets along very well with my lover. I'll be able to come out to my kids when they get old enough to understand it, and I thank the goddess for that!

The strain was evident in Polly's voice as she spoke the opposite:

I haven't come out to my kids because I'm not sure they can handle it and mainly because the fear of losing custody is too great, should they let the word get out. And kids

---

*A 16-mm colour documentary film about lesbian mothers and child custody. IRIS Films, Box 5353, Berkeley, Calif. 94705, USA.

have subtle ways of letting people know things. Maybe they'd want their father to know because it's too much to hold inside of them, or because they are angry at me. You know, kids use things. It makes me kind of closed in lots of other ways and not just verbally – closed to them in certain subtle ways that I don't like at all.

Even without the fear of a custody battle, coming out to their children is for some gay parents a major hurdle, partly because of the social prejudice and partly because sexuality is hard for many of us to talk about. Ted describes the steps leading to his coming out to his four teenage children:

My wife's and my relationship to our children had always been open, with secrets at a minimum. 'Kids, look, you can ask us anything you want. And any literature in the house is yours to read. We hope this will teach you to be the same way.' But here I was masquerading for years and keeping a great big secret from my kids. It really came to a crunch when I was at a gay gathering and hadn't told the kids where I was for fear of exposure. I came home and there were fire engines all up and down the street. I was horrified at the idea that I had not let them know where I was. I began to think, I've got to find a way to do it, but I am afraid that they won't love me, that they won't accept this in me. I knew a few people whose children knew, but when I talked with them they said 'Well, I never told them. They figured.' What helped me was a seminar for gay parents and parents of gays. There I heard so many parents talk about what it was like to come out to their children, who almost universally, positively responded. Everyone who spoke said 'Hey, it went fine.' And the younger they know, the better. That had been the opposite of what I had thought: wait until they're old enough to understand all this. So I tried it in a group of friends, then found the right time, and I've got to say that it was one of the most beautiful and exciting experiences of my life. As one might expect, my oldest daughter said she'd known it for a couple of years. My oldest son said 'I was ready to hear it.'

For Donna it was easier: 'When Stuart was four I told him I slept with Nan because I loved her. I waited some years to go into the issue of prejudice.'

Bob had left his marriage a few years before he came out and his wife had custody, so telling his children was not such a big deal – but he did it carefully:

I started out showing them. They met the man I was living with. They saw that we were affectionate with each other, and that we slept in a double bed together. After a couple of years I started referring to him as my lover. Then in a while we started talking about homosexuality. I feel that they grew to know about my gayness in a natural, everyday way.

Yet there are consequences to take into account, as these comments from a lesbian mothers' group indicate:

It's difficult being out to them because then you have to instil in them that cautiousness, that fear. Now they have to think about how their friends are going to react before they let them know. If you tell a kid who has to keep it secret from his or her father or grandparents, that's a big burden, that piece of knowledge. It's a real tough challenge to balance, saying 'This thing is okay and makes me very happy, but there's a big part of society that thinks it's wrong.' If they have to hide it, they must wonder if it isn't bad. We have to help them see the prejudice, but at the same time see that our loving is a very positive thing.

Patricia reports:

One day Dave asked me if the police knew I was gay would they arrest me. So there was fear there. He knew there were people outside who were against his mother, and he wondered how powerful they were.

For every openly gay parent we spoke with the benefits of openness seem to outweigh the problems. Tina speaks for many:

I think for those of us who are lucky enough to be able to be out to our kids, there are great results. Because we make ourselves open to our kids in this one area we are open to them in a lot of ways. This is something we dare to do to be different, and sometimes it hurts to be different. That we share that with them creates a very special relationship. It also helps them understand prejudice. They begin to see that a kid who calls another kid some name about their religion or race is probably being as bigoted and narrow-minded and hateful as someone who calls their mother a dyke. They can make connections that many people are never able to make.

Marlene remembers:

I came out to my ten-year-old son in the context of a relationship with someone he really cared a lot about. And I kept wondering, is he really as cool about this as he seems? A few months later we were visiting my parents and he tried to intervene with them for me. He came out of the room throwing his hands up and saying 'I tried to talk with them, but they are totally unreasonable.'

Bart has been pleased:

What I have found since I came out to them is that they have been open to me, too. My oldest daughter came to me and talked to me about her sexual life. My youngest daughter began, haltingly, to speak with me about getting her period. And one of my sons told me some things that I feel would have taken longer to tell – not specifically sexual things, but revelations that would have felt more dangerous to him had I not taken that risk.

Alfred, however, cautions against thinking that children are always accepting of a parent's homosexuality:

My friend's sixteen-year-old daughter has been quite hostile to her father and says it's because he's gay. She's broken off relations with him for a year now, and he's letting it drift along. I'm not sure they ever got along terribly well, and I don't know also whether she isn't testing him the way teenagers often do. It seems to me that kids are going to choose some part of our life to separate themselves from in an emphatic way, and she's chosen his gayness.

The final word on the benefits of coming out as a gay parent can be left with a ten-year-old boy who was asked on a video-taped interview at a lesbian mothers' weekend 'What is it like when your mother has a woman lover?' He responded: 'It's like having two mothers.'

However, coming out to their children doesn't end the dilemma. According to Marilyn:

How to front our relationship to whatever institution that we interact with is the major issue Ann and I have as Stephen's parents. Because if the wrong people find out they can make him feel bad. Yet I don't think Ann should be deprived of the recognition of parenthood. We were out in his day care centre and no one batted an eyelash, but he's started public school this year and we're having to proceed more carefully.

Conrad adds:

I'm out to my kids but I can't come out to the neighbourhood. It's too dangerous. There are people on this block – not many but some – who would come down and punch me out, and ridicule my children. So to have gay guests here is risky. The first time I had a gay friend in for a drink, I shook so badly carrying a tray of glasses I nearly dropped them. I didn't realize until that moment how frightened I was of being exposed. For it would break up my close-knit relationship with this neighbourhood. And this place is my kids' home – I can't move away just so I can be openly gay.

Intimacy

It seems like a long time to Conrad before he can get the intimacy he needs:

I feel resentful when I make plans to be with my gay friends and something comes up with the children and I can't leave them. There's no way I can live with another man until they grow up, and I have to choose lovers who are willing to put up with taking a second place to my children. My resentment is: now that I've decided that being gay is O.K., why the hell is it going to take so long? I feel like there's a desert in my heart: there's water close by, but I can't put it in there yet.

On one occasion my lover was in great distress. As he came walking down the street when the neighbourhood was full of people, I knew he was very upset. I walked toward him and I had to say 'Get out of here, they're watching.' I had to be cruel to my friend. I couldn't even go with him or offer him comfort.

One of the recurring themes of this book has been that in order to be loving, nurturing parents, we need loving and nourishment ourselves. A gay parent who cannot come out, or whose intimate relationships suffer from the constrictions, misses a lot. A woman in the film *In the Best Interests of the Children* put it simply: 'I can be a so much better mother now that my needs for love are being met.'

The women in a lesbian mothers' group find that in their relationships with women they in fact feel less torn between lover and children than when they were involved with men:

My kids are more comfortable with Alice than they ever were with any of my male lovers. She allows them to get to know her as a person. The men would give them a present or have a two-minute conversation, but mainly they were there to see me. Alice never puts me into the corner of having to decide between my kids and her the way men used to. It has something to do with the way women relate to others, especially to children. There's more emotion involved.

Since storybook endings don't happen to gay couples any more than they do to straight ones, gay families have their share of separations. Beth feels for her ex-lover:

We have been like a family for five years, and now we're not going to be. Joan doesn't have her own children, and it's a big question how she's going to relate to mine. They love her and she loves them. But there are no guidelines because she's not their parent and we weren't married. She feels she has no protection. She says 'I feel like I face this tremendous risk, because I stand to lose you and I stand to lose these kids whom I really love.'

What gay parents can do for each other as they get together to talk about special issues of their lives is to explore what customs, rituals, practices and observances might give separating gay parents and their lovers who have taken on parenting roles some guidelines in a society that doesn't recognize their right to be together, much less their need for protection and comfort as parents when they split.

Role Models for Children of Gay Parents

A question put to many gay parents is 'How will your children have role models of the other sex?' This is a more pertinent question to lesbian mothers than to gay fathers: more gay mothers have children living with them, and young children have so much daily contact with women in school that a child of a gay father isn't likely to miss out on female role models. Bringing men into her son's life has been something Nadine has had to work at:

Dennis sees his father twice a month, and one of our best friends where we used to live is a man, and his basketball coach is real important to him. I have hopes for some of my gay male friends who have said they wanted to spend time with kids. I'm completely open to men being in Dennis's life.

Some lesbian mothers have found companions for their sons in a 'big brother' programme organized by their town or church. Others believe that a special effort isn't necessary.

Jennifer raises a concern of many lesbian mothers: as a feminist who is angry at certain male characteristics and at men's dominance in our culture, how do I let my son know my opinions without making him feel bad about himself?

I don't want the kids to feel bad about themselves but I don't want them to turn into bad people either. I want to let them know what my values are. For instance, being insensitive to feelings is what I think of as most offensively male. And that's something I think I can help them with. It's not a matter of telling them not to be strong. It's more a matter of fairness – that you don't make rules for women that you don't have for men. That you're not going to grow up and get married and expect your wife to do all the shitwork.

Joyce said of the mothers' group:

What I love about this group is that we have a commitment to loving women, but it isn't like you have to sign a paper saying you hate men, you're a radical separatist, et cetera. Maybe because we all have kids, there's more flexibility, more tolerance. Many of us have male children, and it's hard to be anti-male when you have a male child whom you love.

Looking at the popular myth that children of gay parents will grow up gay, the women in the mothers' group pointed to both sons and daughters who had let them know they planned to get married and have children. 'Our kids are more open-minded, though,' Dorothy observed:

I think the truth is, whatever they'll be they'll be without guilt. When they get married it will be after having made a reasoned decision, because they're in touch with who they are and who they want to be, and not because they think it's the only 'right' thing to do.

The Importance of Support Networks

Gay parents feel that they especially need help and support from other gay parents, because what they are doing and how they are living find so little acceptance in society at large. The women in the Lesbians with Children group at the Cambridge Women's Center help each other in many ways. Hannah gives an example:

I asked the people in this group to have a dinner for me and the kids so it would make it easier for me to come out to my kids.

Lorraine said 'Just coming to the group was asking for help. It is wonderful finding out how many lesbian mothers there are. I had thought there must be two or three in the whole city.' Here are a few things that other mothers had to say about their group:

What I've always wanted for my children is a wider network of caring adults, and we're making one in this group. This group is a place where neither we nor our kids have to hide any part of our lives. This group has a commitment to kids. It's not enough just to come in and talk about being lesbian mothers; we include our kids now, having parties for us all, going to the beach together, and we feel better about that . . . At our parties the kids don't sit around and talk about us and who our lovers are – they play! But they must at some point look around the room and say to themselves, all these kids have gay mothers, and feel less isolated. It's good for them and us both to be in a place where we don't feel different.

What are the special attributes of gay-parent families as these men and women have described them? Certain things are harder. The need for secrecy, especially when there are custody struggles and when neighbours and children's schoolmates are prejudiced against gays, leaves gay parents even more isolated and without support than other parents. Job discrimination against gay people makes it more difficult for parents to provide economically for the family. Yet the parents we interviewed expressed the positive factors as well, both in their words and in their spirit. Dealing openly with sexual differences and with the effects of prejudice seems to bring a closeness to family interactions. Tackling decisions for which there are no precedents or models can lead gay parents out of the traditional 'parent knows best' stance, and turn them to their children to discuss possibilities and dilemmas in a spirit of mutual respect. Reaching out to other gay parents for support and understanding can help to build a caring community for parents and children alike. And when parents find the loving they need, the whole family can benefit.

Nuclear Families

We generally think of the nuclear family as two parents living together with children. This definition can include remarried couples, step-parents, parents who are gay, and nuclear families who live in groups or in other cooperative arrangements.

Parents living in nuclear families where the marriage is strong or at least resilient generally speak about being glad to be there. But in spite of the myth that all nuclear families are supposed to be happy, they recognize that they have problems. In fact they find they have a lot to learn from other family forms.

Just as the stigma about being a single parent can interfere with the functioning of a single-parent family, the constellation of myths about the nuclear family can create obstacles to healthy functioning. As we've seen in the earlier section on family myths, the nuclear family especially may feel it has an 'ideal' to live up to. One mother states:

The world expects us to be 'happy and intact' and so we act that way. As couples in nuclear families we sometimes find ourselves disguising most of our problems because we don't want to hurt the image of the 'perfect' or 'correct' family.

As with single-parent families, nuclear-family couples and children find themselves caught in the image that the perfect family *should* be able to care for everyone and everything – but it really can't:

Things sometimes get very heavy and intense with the four of us. At our worst family moments when everyone's upset or we're in a stew with each other, there's a feeling of claustrophobia. That's when I feel that we'd do better with other people around, that the intensity would be dissipated.

Nuclear families, like other families, need other people to share the burdens and pleasures of parenting and to add role models. This father explains how he and his wife decided to break out of the isolation:

We started a play group for our daughter with several other families. We liked living in our small family, and yet we also found that our nuclear group by itself was a restrictive environment for all of us. With the play group we gained a new circle of friends. We had other parents to watch and she had other children and adults to learn from.

Because of the myths that the family should provide all, some nuclear families find outsiders very threatening. But Ronnie, the mother of an eight-year-old, ponders the way her nuclear family is isolated:

Phyllis Ewen

Recently I've been wanting to try cross-country skiing with Alyssa and Howard, my husband. But Howard doesn't want to. Since it wouldn't be fun for the whole family, we do something else we can all agree upon. Other families we know who ski don't ask me and my daughter to go with them because they assume the family is taken care of and we are doing our own thing as a group. I haven't gotten up my courage to just ask if Alyssa and I can join them or to try to go ourselves. But I know that's what I need to do.

Even as our society becomes more tolerant and affirming of alternative kinds of families, many will continue to choose the nuclear family because it can be a powerful and enduring unit for parents and children. Here are some of the advantages that parents have cited.

Susan speaks of the shared history of two parents and the children they are raising:

My greatest joy is the ongoing strong relationship I have with Wayne – our sharing of our past, our growth and changes. As parents we see our close relationship helping our children grow and develop their own relationships. We depend on each other. We do share all the responsibilities, joys and problems. It's been a 'team effort' for us, and I know if the team isn't working it can be hell.

We do have the flexibility as an intact nuclear group to move about as we wish. The strength of our shared history could allow us to settle in a different city or live communally with other families. It's not that we live separately that makes the difference but, rather, that we really like living with one another.

Sometimes even when everything is not 'perfect', the nuclear family provides a lot for its members. Vera says:

I have thought many times of leaving Carl. I wanted more excitement than I found in my marriage. I still am a more adventurous person than Carl, but I've come to appreciate his solidness and to accept life as it is. I'm finally content with the compromises I've made and feel freer to enjoy myself and my family.

Denise continues in the same vein:

I like raising Meredith and Christopher in a nuclear family because there's another adult's viewpoint available. I count on Fred to have as much input into their lives. And it's a relief that there is someone else to balance me, someone whose outlook I respect.

Of course at moments when I disagree with him I find it hard to accept his influence on them. For instance, when he watches football all weekend I get mad because Chris is starting to imitate him. However, after all the years we've been together, I trust that we'll eventually talk about our disagreements.

The shared history, the rituals that develop in any family – around birthdays, holidays, mealtimes, sickness – all contribute to a long-term commitment that binds family members together. Norma, a mother of four, emphasizes a connection she is now building:

These are people I will be concerned about all my life and they about me. Rich, my husband, occasionally jokes about my consciously planting family memories – which he and the children won't be able to resist. For instance, that at Christmas I bake special cookies and breads, and his and the children's craving for those delicacies will draw us all back together for a family Christmas event no matter how physically separated the children become as they get older.

There is comfort living in a complete nuclear family. No matter how novelly you might divide family roles, to the outside you usually don't have to explain your family structure. Still, times are changing. This family was amused by their son's request:

Erik came home from school one day and told Gina and me he wanted us to get divorced so he could have two homes like his friends Adam and Orie. He was quite serious. Of course we told him no and explained why. I found myself laughing to myself about how traditions were changing.

Nuclear family life has practical economic advantages that must not be overlooked. Most families have problems about money, but the economic benefits of needing only one house or one car, for example, are outstanding in the eyes of couples that split and require more money to survive than they did as a nuclear family.

In a nuclear family parents can share an emotional and physical closeness with their children. The parents together can experience both the pleasure and pain of caring for their children and watching them grow. Josh says:

All experiences seem to be nicer when they are shared. Raising Emily – my wife and I look at each other endless times, when she's walking around or doing an acrobatic trick, or when she uses a word in a certain way. To think that this child is ours, that she grew out of our loving each other, that we have so much to do with who she is – it's wonderful and amazing to us.

The negative aspects of nuclear family life are as troublesome as the positive elements are supportive. Nuclear families tend to become ingrown and insulated from other people and experiences. The family form protects but also isolates them so that they can easily get stuck in roles and patterns of behaviour that the family itself has created. These patterns often keep individuals from exploring new ways to grow and develop. Because they have each other, they don't seek out others. Some nuclear families understand the problem and perceive outsiders as adding to their family. As Wilma says:

We love to have friends share meals and especially holidays with us because our relatives are far away. We enjoy them and the sense of extended family they bring.

Because the nuclear family has been viewed as the traditional family form for many of us, it is perhaps easier for parents in nuclear groups to fall into traditional male-female roles, with woman as nurturer and man as breadwinner. Even if both parents work, the mother sometimes winds up cooking, cleaning, shopping and managing child care. For some this is comfortable; for others it is exhausting. Because the system seems to be working – particularly for the husband – it takes a great effort to change. Divorced or single women often have an easier time liberating themselves from stereotyped roles.

Some nuclear couples are beginning to realign family responsibilities according to their needs. This realignment, if it takes place after many years, can be painful but exhilarating. As with single parents, sometimes necessity breeds opportunity as it did for Phyllis and her family:

After being at home for fourteen years, I decided I wanted to return to school. When I first applied, I started to plan together with my family – John, my husband, and our two children, Abby and Noah (who were nine and eleven at the time) – how we were going to handle the changes. They were excited that I was doing something I wanted to do, though they were nervous about the changes, especially in household routines. Shopping, cooking, cleaning, for instance, which were primarily my responsibilities, were now going to be shared. Fortunately, with support from my women's group, I started to prepare everyone before I was in the midst of term papers.

Much to my amazement, our family drew closer than we had been before. We made lists of chores for everyone to try, and set aside times to discuss how the new arrangements were working. There have been serious fights between John and me, but we have arrived with much effort at new levels of understanding. All in all, our family is stronger for the changes that my return to school has brought.

Betsy Cole

As in all relationships, nuclear families can settle into comfortable routines and find themselves stagnating there. As one mother tells us:

I find that my husband and I don't really talk to each other any more. Or when we talk, it is only about the children or indirectly through the children. I know it is essential for us to be talking directly about ourselves and about more than the children's school grades or what to send our parents for holiday gifts, but it's hard to find the time, so we end up ignoring or delaying. Later, tomorrow, next week . . .

Some nuclear families – of the traditional kind, with father, mother and child – seem very self-satisfied, less tolerant and less open than other families that have had to seek out new people or to expose themselves to new situations for their survival. Nuclear families may thus unnecessarily limit their own life experiences. It is difficult for families to grow and change, as we discussed earlier in the section on family systems. The routines get set and there is little pressure for them to be different. Sometimes problems persist, whether of lack of communication or boredom or a child in trouble, because parents don't know how to reach out to others outside the family.

As discussed before, when one member of the family gets into trouble s/he is often simply the flag bearer for the rest of the family. S/he is perhaps doing the family a favour by exposing a problem and forcing the family to seek help. One father reports:

We uncovered some problems of our own as Carolyn and I talked about Vicky cutting classes and decided to join a couples group. The meetings haven't been easy, but we are talking to each other once a week. Our relationship has become more lively and that rubs off on our children.

When the nuclear family is functioning poorly, it can be an extremely restrictive place to be; when it is working well, it can be seen as a model for cooperation between adults and among adults and children over a long period of time. As many parents have indicated, the nuclear family need not be limited by its members. One way a nuclear unit can extend itself is by a variety of cooperative arrangements with other families and perhaps by a group of families living near one another, as in the section that follows.

Families Who Live Cooperatively

Cooperative family living is one way families have found to maintain a small family unit (whether of single parents, nuclear family, etc.) with private living space and at the same time to have access to a larger family experience in which some living space and certain daily and special activities are shared in common. For many people cooperative living arrangements seem to offer the best of two worlds – a small intimate family group that provides privacy and continuity as well as a larger family group that supports the need for community and sharing.* Eleanor, a mother who lives cooperatively in a house with three other families, explains:

There was a common theme among the three families that purchased this house. Our nuclear families were important and we wanted to maintain them, but we also saw the possibility of broader bases of support for us and our children – a sense of extended families, more adult models for the children, etc. We also thought about cooperative things like sharing newspapers, a washing machine and dryer – some economic and ecological advantages to our living together.

A cooperative living situation can be difficult to set up, because it's hard to find the necessary living space in close proximity at prices everyone can afford, but for the people that we interviewed the trouble was well worth it. In fact, most people we spoke to are happy about the experience.

Cooperative living falls in between entirely separate one-family living arrangements and communal living. The concept is not new; extended families

*Cooperative housing is a relatively new option in the UK. For legal information on setting up a cooperative, contact the Housing Corporation, 149 Tottenham Court Road, London W1P 0BN; better still, ask if you can be put in touch with some existing co-ops.

lived this way in the past. What is new is the intention to create families that function cooperatively. One father, Harry, told us:

In our cooperative we have a strong link to each other's parents. When our small family went travelling this summer we stopped in to see two of the parents of other folks in this cooperative. We had a lovely time with them and they really felt like alternative grandparents for our kids.

People arrive at cooperative living in different ways. Some families that used to live in houses with other families but without separate apartments find that cooperative arrangements are a good compromise between living as one small, isolated family unit and living in one large group. Some families build an 'extended family' by creating supportive arrangements with neighbours and friends. They may arrange a weekly play group, an exchange of several mornings of care for the children or weekly or biweekly cooperative meals, etc.

When parents discover how helpful they can be to one another, these relationships sometimes grow into cooperative living arrangements. In one instance, two couples had been friends for several years, and when they had babies about the same time they decided to exchange child care; not long after, one of the families bought a house and rented an apartment in it to the other couple and their child. Families who want to live in the country and not be isolated may purchase land in common and construct separate houses on the land. Still another example is that of a group of ten families that wanted to extend a spiritual community which developed at church and acquired an apartment building with individual living units. Daniel, a member of this last group, reports:

First, before the time we started to think about living cooperatively, there had been a rash of church meetings. Everyone was going to meetings all the time and seeing each other a lot. And our being together so much had produced, rather than a desire to escape from each other, a desire to somehow find a way to see each other more and also more informally. When you are going to visit someone a few towns away, it turns out to be a whole evening's production – with baby-sitter, driving and staying longer than perhaps you want to. So we were looking for ways to see each other for an hour and go back home. Also, many of us had been cooperating with child care and were tired of the driving back and forth with the kids.

This church organization affirmed its members' need to develop more community with one another. This mother, Jaime, discusses it:

This is one way of dealing with living in a city which makes sense and is an extension of some principles of our faith. I think other members of our group would not want it to go that far and make those kinds of theological statements, but would simply say in our church community that the support of each other and the nurturing of family-life networks for supports, celebration, and so on is a good thing.

A key issue for many families is how to work out the boundaries between common and private space and time. Families that live cooperatively have to find ways to communicate with other families about when they want to be social and when they want to be alone, and how they want the flow of children between units to be managed. Diana and Nick live with their four children in a cooperatively owned apartment building. Diana says:

Sometimes there is an incredible flow between the apartments with kids. We are on the bottom floor and sometimes feel a little overwhelmed when each of our four different kids invites a friend in. When I'm feeling more need for privacy than Nick or vice versa, then we accommodate one another. This living arrangement has made us be a lot clearer with the kids, especially at times when we want to just be with them.

Another mother, Mary, who, after several years of cooperative living, can't imagine having to hire baby-sitters, reflects back on the time she first moved into the building:

In the beginning I was the tightest person. I did not want anyone to assume that I was around here to be a baby-sitter at the drop of a hat. I wanted to be notified at least twenty-four hours in advance. I've relaxed a lot since then.

Over time people work out ways of communicating about their needs. George, a father who lives in a large cooperative house, explains:

We've worked out some signs – if people are really feeling sociable, they'll prop open the door to their apartment. And that's an invitation to come in if you want. If the door is closed, then they don't want visitors. If there is a sign 'Please come back later', you know to return later. If you know somebody's going through a difficult time or they are sick, the word spreads, too. It's very reassuring to me to know I can have privacy when I want it. I shut the door and people won't barge through it or send their kids in.

Karen, who lives in the same building, describes a vocabulary they have: 'We say to children, "This is not a good time." And that simply has worked.' June, another mother, interjects: 'As they get older, we use it less. They just become more sensitive. In fact, sometimes they will ask, "Is this a good time?"'

But even when there are clear rules and ways of communicating, problems do arise:

There are times when other people's children become more of a responsibility than I want. For instance, one child who lived next door would show up at the front door to play at seven-thirty in the morning. Then it became my responsibility to say yes or no, rather than his parent saying before he runs out the door 'This is not a good time to visit.' It's an extra element of hassle, of dealing with a child who may not be able to stand up to rejection because of coming ten mornings in a row at seven-thirty. I was more upset at the parent than at the child and had to find a way to talk to her.

This last story suggests another difficult area – different styles of parenting emerge and can cause conflict between and among some families. As Ginny says:

Opening myself to other people's comments about my parenting was the hardest for me. Somebody can confront me directly a lot more easily about me than they can confront me about my child. That's my area of greatest vulnerability.

One group that met together before they bought property in common had a discussion about parenting. Here Keith describes that gathering:

We were about evenly distributed between people who had kids and people who didn't have kids, either married without kids or single people. And the non-parents said 'We don't know how to treat your kids because we don't understand your principles, your rules for your kids. So we don't know whether your kids are allowed to walk on the back of the couch or whether they can eat candy before meals or whether it's O.K. to raise our voices or spank them or whatever.' And the parents responded 'Treat the kids the way you want to treat them. They need to learn that different people have different ways of doing things, and they need to learn to relate to you as whoever you are and not like a mimic of us.'

Then the parents said 'We're scared about all you non-parents because we assume you've chosen to be non-parents and that our kids would be a nuisance to you and that you don't want to take care of them, and that we burden you by needing a baby-sitter, by our kids making too much noise.' And they said to us 'We're grown-up people. And when we're tired of your kids we'll give them back to you.'

The basic statement that evolved – Be yourself and deal directly with the kids – is one we constantly fall back upon.

Of course there are worries when people feel that their parenting is under scrutiny. Katherine says:

I was a new parent and was nervous about my abilities as a mother. I was glad our friends were downstairs, yet I also got anxious about living in a fishbowl. I get angry at my daughter, Susannah, but they never seemed to yell at their kids. The pressure to be a superparent was very great.

The benefits of living cooperatively are many. We name some here and present some others in the section on communal living.

A greater number of people means more role models for children and adults. Laurel, a small child, found new people to talk with. Her father, Evan, describes:

Laurel has always tended to be a relatively shy child. She rarely ventured out, particularly not to meet other adults. Laurel was four when we moved, and at one point on the day after we were here, we couldn't find her. We discovered that she was up in Gloria's kitchen sitting on the stool talking to her about something while Gloria was making dinner. She had just wandered up there, walked in and sat up on a stool. Now over time she and the other kids have so many other adults they feel comfortable relating to and learning from – and that excites me. They understand different skills, different ways of reacting to similar kinds of events, and that is one of the real strengths of this kind of living.

The supports that many people yearn for but find hard to ask for become second nature to some families that live cooperatively. Judith's impressions are:

Part of what works so well for us as parents is the give and take — feeling free to give because I know I'm not keeping score but that it's coming out fairly. The times it doesn't work out are relatively rare and obvious — and quickly dealt with because we all count so much on the system working well.

Peter Simon

The shared celebrations that occur are wonderful and varied in different living situations. Some families share events like birthdays. Or have musical jam sessions once a week. Here Lee tells about one of their ritual holidays:

At Christmas time we have an advent calendar out in the common hall and have a Christmas tree with little balls on it with a number for the days of Advent. Under each ball is a picture of someone in our larger family. And every morning or evening, whenever we do it, the kids in turn get a chance to lift the ball for that day and show the picture.

There is pride in belonging to a large family, as Molly describes:

Nathan and Leslie felt really fierce, the first couple of years we lived on the land, about who was or wasn't in their family. Their family was our small nuclear family and that was it. Now they feel proud about the larger group and feel a special bond with the other kids and adults who live here. There is an ease in communication that has developed, as well as the usual difficult times between kids. Over the summer when different kids were away, they would regroup so naturally. And they would be very excited when somebody returned from vacation.

There can be opportunities for intense sharing among adults. Don talked proudly of the retreats that are planned twice a year:

These are times to get away from the city for a weekend and catch up with each other. Normally one evening is devoted to hearing individually from each adult – for fifteen or twenty minutes – about what's going on in their life right now, how they are feeling, etc. Some of those retreats have been the most incredible interpersonal group experiences I've ever had. Truly remarkable problem-solving, a sharing, supportive time.

According to Rachel:

Our community works so well because it is not overloaded. It's not an isolated community. We go outside of the group to work and to school. The distance we get allows us to come back and enjoy everyone much more.

When Beatrice asked her daughter what she thought she would think later on about having lived in this community, her daughter replied, 'Think about? Think about! I'll still be here!'

Families Who Live Communally*

There are many families, including nuclear families, single-parent families and non-parent adults, who have chosen to live together in one large house or on the same piece of land rather than in separate units. These groups often have a commitment to being in one another's lives over time and view their unit as a family. Members of the group provide the same daily caring and have the same hassles as people who live in any other family unit. They choose to live together

*See, for instance, Rosabeth M. Kanter, *Commitment and Community: Communes and Utopias in Sociological Perspective* (Cambridge, Mass., 1972; London: Harvard University Press, 1977); also, in the USA, *Communities, a Journal of Cooperative Living* (Rte 4, Louisa, Va 23093); New Community Projects, an organization in Boston concerned with community living; and *Green Revolution* (monthly, from School of Living, PO Box 3233, York, Pa 17102).

in a commune out of the same needs as parents who elect to live cooperatively in separate apartments.

These families want close daily relationships with more caring adults, for themselves and for their children. They believe when more people live together, they can share the tasks and expense of living – of child care and household maintenance. As adults they can have more companionship, and time to themselves as well. Many have a vision of a new kind of family – one with more resources and fewer constraints than the nuclear family or single-parent family they have been familiar with. A father, Dave, puts together many of the appeals of living under the same roof with other families:

Living communally means we can live more cheaply. We are able to share household tasks. We have other adults around with whom we can share not only care of children, but also our parenting concerns. The help and support and caring both for adults and for children, when they are going through a bad period, is available right at home. While formerly we turned outside to friends, our friends here are readily and more continually accessible. They can also observe what is going on, and not just hear hours or days later what happened.

Julia, a mother of two pre-school children, tells what it means to her to have other adults around:

I felt such joy the first night my husband and I went out alone and left Esther and Selma without having to make special arrangements a week in advance. An added bonus was that we weren't just leaving them with sitters, but with friends who cared about their well-being – not only for the moment but for the long run.

Some groups of people meet for months before moving in together and are able to name and sort out some of the issues that arise in living communally. Other people face similar issues with little or no preparation. Gabriel remembers back to the beginnings:

At the time many of us began living communally we had no awareness about family systems – how resistant to change they can be and how painful changes can be for other family members. We arrived at the communal doorstep filled with hope, energy and high ideals, often trying to create an entirely new living situation without clear rules, limits and expectations to guide us through the transition. Those of us who previously were in nuclear families were familiar with the problems of living with one other adult person and child, but we didn't anticipate just how complex our lives would become when we added more adults and children. The needs and conflicts often increased geometrically.

Like many families, some communes have turned for assistance to outside resources, such as counsellors, who can come to house meetings and mediate family struggles. Others have managed alone.

Some of the thorniest problems come up around the adults' relationships to each other's children. Some groups ask that all adults share child care, and yet all too often only parents or only mothers do. Nora, a single mother, talks about the difference between the ideal and reality in her communal family:

We all agreed to share cooking. We made a weekly schedule, but when it came to meals for the kids, I and the one other mother in the house did a majority of the cooking. We were the only ones who seemed to be aware that Louise and Heather were hungry and had to eat.

In other groups parents have primary care for their own children unless they ask another group member for baby-sitting help. Fran, a non-parent adult, explains:

In our group, after some hassling over child care, we made a schedule in which each night one adult is responsible for child care after five-thirty p.m. Responsibility includes meals, play, bedtime stories, bedtime fights, etc. This turned out to be a really nice arrangement for both parents and non-parents. At first this change was confusing for the children. So we posted a great big 'Parent for the Night' schedule and they got used to the arrangement quickly.

Even when child care is equally shared, styles of parenting often clash. Who is going to have the final say? Some communes are committed to having the children parented by the whole group. In the long run, however, parents often have special feelings about how to raise their children and also a special sense of ongoing responsibility for them. Some of the greatest joys and hottest conflicts in group life centre on shared parenting.

This father, Chuck, tells about mealtimes in his house:

I only had to cook one evening a week and that was fine. Yet the sheer logistics of eating with eight adults and four children often overwhelmed me. One way we handled the crowd was to institute special rules for the children. Since there were more adults than children, adults' needs usually dominated dinner conversation. For me this felt like we reverted back to the days when 'children should be seen and not heard'. So either I felt I wasn't relating to my kids or else I was reprimanding them for not following the rules. Even though I wasn't comfortable with this arrangement, I was a lone voice among eight, and this pattern never changed as long as I lived in the house.

Some groups have handled this by having separate mealtimes for adults and kids. Whether at meals or other times, children can have the chance to be kids without dealing with parents' needs for quiet time or for adult conversation.

Another advantage of group living is being able to have adequate space for both children's and adults' needs. Marcia says:

In our house we made the kids a huge play space all their own in the basement and we had a lovely large living room for adults upstairs. None of us could have afforded such nice space or such separate areas in our own much smaller homes.

In other groups there may be undue or inappropriate focus on children. As Linda, one mother, says:

We had endless house meetings where we discussed 'the children'. After a while it became clear to me that we used the children to avoid talking about ourselves or as an avenue to say things to one another that we didn't have the courage to bring up directly.

Other groups have been able to talk openly about the difficult issues – such as parenting and sexuality – and natural boundaries evolve that respect the needs of the individual people involved.

With all the problems, the excitement of communal living remains. For parents, being able to share parenting with others, providing an opportunity for children to know more adults who will love and care for them, is very appealing; for adults, being open enough even to attempt living intimately with a group of people and struggling with the confusion of doing it is praiseworthy.

Peter Simon

When adults are able to take responsibility for children other than their own, there are pleasures and problems both, which Janet here speaks of:

In our house every kid became really close to an adult who wasn't the parent – somebody who was just the right person to be friends with. Scott became my friend. We both enjoyed singing and making up songs and spent wonderful times around the fire doing that. He was a lovely child, and it was an incredible moment when he was able to turn to me for help and attention – because for six years of his life only his mother would do. For the weeks prior to my leaving the house, he was grumpy whenever I was around. Finally one day, when we both happened to be in the kitchen, he came out and asked me with sadness in his voice 'Why are you going away? Why are you leaving me? You don't have to go, I don't want you to go.' The next moment we both burst into tears and sat on the kitchen floor hugging each other and crying. I felt I was saying good-bye to living with a stepson, and that was so very painful. Yet as we grieved we had each other. In time my whole relationship with Scott, including our parting, felt like a gift to me.

We believe that community is something families – whatever their form – hunger for. Families used to find community in churches and synagogues and in extended families. Since these don't work for many of us, we are searching for new forms. Group living is part of that search.

8. Society's Impact on Families

Paula Brown Doress, *with UK material by*
Michèle Cohen and Tina Reid

Many books, especially how-to-parent books, assume that what happens to our children is a result of what goes on between us and our children and depends almost entirely on life within the family. Our view is that it is impossible to parent alone. We parent in a context of relationships with other people; our families exist within communities, and are part of a complex web of social institutions, each of which has an impact on our parenting experience.

In spite of the clear limits on parental power, books for parents often do not take into account the realities of providing for our families and caring for them in a society whose institutions of work, schooling and health care often serve to obstruct rather than help parents. Although it can be instructive when 'experts' on child raising tell us what they think is the *ideal* way to handle a particular situation, we think it would be *more* helpful if books for parents also suggested how to deal with less than ideal situations in institutions which put efficiency, profits, rules and the convenience of professionals before the needs of parents and children.

The society at large and child-development specialists in particular have a way of asking only 'What do children need?' and then assuming that parents can and will provide it. It is as if society shared the young child's fantasy of parents as all-powerful and able to cope with any contingency. By posing the question 'What do children *and* parents need?' instead of just 'What do children need?' we feel that we can push our society in the direction of more realistic social supports for parenting.

The purpose of this chapter is to raise our consciousness as parents, first by looking at the ways that social attitudes toward parents and children influence our parenting experience, and then by looking at several of the major social institutions in terms of how they facilitate or hinder parenting.

When values and attitudes become embedded in the social fabric, they are 'institutionalized', that is, their force is transferred to powerful social institutions, whose practices are more resistant to change than the attitudes of individuals. These institutionalized attitudes remain as a kind of implicit policy of our society, even though the circumstances that created them may have long disappeared, and because of the complex interconnections of institutions with our families, they have a powerful impact on our lives as parents.

Segregation of Children and Adults Who Look After Them

We live in a society that admires and indulges children as long as they remain in their proper place – meaning, apparently, the home, the school and the shopping centre. Our society seems to believe that both mother and child should be at home and not interfere with the 'important business' or relaxation of adults out in the 'real world'.

Infants and very young children are appealing to many adults, who treat them as objects or pets to be oohed and aahed at. Yet research shows the pre-school years to be the period of parenting with the least public support. Furthermore, as Jennifer notes, once our children are no longer cute, cuddly babies, we get a lot less public affirmation of our parenting:

When I first became a mother, I noticed that people were suddenly so friendly. Strangers would come over to talk to me just for the chance to coo at a baby. But now that Benjy is in his 'terrible twos', when I take him into a store or a doctor's office I'm more likely to get cold stares than coos.

Attitudes toward children in public places vary from society to society. Margo tells of her travels through Europe with her husband and a three-year-old daughter:

In France, the attitude was 'What do you mean, bringing a child into a restaurant? Eating is serious business!' In Italy, the waiters would take Rachel over completely, they'd get a high chair, put a bib on her and feed her so that we could relax and enjoy our meal. Everyone seemed to really enjoy her being there.

In our own country, most of us have experienced both these attitudes and the whole range between as we go into stores, laundromats, recreational or health facilities, public meetings, etc., with our kids. Many of the day-to-day situations that we meet as parents, even those which primarily serve parents and children, seem to disregard our needs for welcome, for cooperation, for support.

In today's society, residential patterns exaggerate the separation of children from adult life by confining paid work to industrial areas and professional buildings, while most children, when not in school, live in suburbs or urban neighbourhoods which have lost these producing and marketing functions. The presence of a child in 'adult space' may be startling indeed, as Stan recalls:

When I was taking courses at the university, once or twice I took Michael along, and he would read the children's books in the School of Education library while I gathered material for my term papers. You know it's a very urban area, just blocks and blocks of college buildings and dorms and practically everyone you see is eighteen to twenty-eight or so. When I'd bring Michael with me, I'm not kidding you, heads would turn, and sometimes people would look puzzled to see a small person on campus, even at the Ed. School.

Though they have come to expect separation of children from their daily work life, Americans have traditionally practised 'togetherness' in their recreational and vacation time. The tradition is heavily reinforced by the media, which, in the 1950s and led by influential women's magazines, began to promote positively 'family togetherness'. The notion crossed the Atlantic, and in the UK, newspapers, magazines and advertising daily present us with images of ideal family life: working, playing and spending together. So what help do we get in living up to the image? For example, what kind of support can parents expect when travelling with children? Miriam tells us about a brief flight with her two-year-old son:

As we fastened our seat belts and took off, Jamie began to squirm in my lap and shout 'Off! off!' Resisting his efforts to explore his new surroundings at that point, I held him tightly and whispered 'No! no!' while frantically trying to engage him in quiet play, which he resisted. When he began to cry at the top of his lungs, the elderly lady sitting next to us informed me that none of her nieces or nephews had ever cried in public.

The stewardess appeared with a bottle full of juice and, without speaking to me, poked it in Jamie's mouth. I quickly stopped her. She looked me straight in the eye and said 'You must do something about your son!' My tension was mounting, of course, as was Jamie's. I scanned the area for a sympathetic face, but found none.

Finally the seat belt sign was turned off, and Jamie and I were able to walk up and down the aisles a few times. That settled him down and then he played quietly at our seat. I wanted to cry out of relief at that point, but of course I didn't. An hour later, en route to the baggage area, I was joined by a pleasant-looking woman who spoke commiseratingly to me: 'What you must have just gone through. I have four children of my own. I was sitting behind you, but I didn't know what to do.' I smiled politely, but thought to myself, I wish you had had the courage to speak up when I needed you.

Clearly, the friendly but helpless woman sitting behind Miriam had fallen victim to the norm of 'minding our own business'. Children are regarded as the private property of the parents, and when a problem comes up it's nobody else's business, unless a complaint is in order.

Public attitudes toward parents and children who move out of their 'proper place' border on the hostile. Yet we have a mythology that every adult ought to have children. This mythology, recently given the name 'pronatalism', refers to the traditional pressures pushing all adults to become parents, irrespective of interest, aptitude or desire. (We discussed these pressures in the section above on Deciding.) It is important here to point out that our culture, until quite recently, has been distinctly pronatalist but not notably supportive of parents and children.

We also want to distinguish between antinatalism, which means discouraging the bearing of children, and policies which are punitive toward parents and children. Currently the threat of overpopulation, coupled with the need for women in the work force, supports the relatively new idea that not every adult must become a parent. Advances in productive technology are changing the nature of the work force, so that fewer workers are needed in production, while more and more are needed in clerical and service jobs. The result is that there are more opportunities opening up for women and a decreasing number of the blue-collar jobs traditionally held by men.*

The need for women in the work force has discouraged them from having large numbers of children at the same time that the sheer cost of bringing up children has made it necessary for mothers to work. The lack of planning for the needs of parents in the labour force, such as child care, flexible hours (see pp. 329–35), has been an anti-parenting force, and the lack of planning that has left many fathers and mothers unemployed reflects extreme indifference toward families.

We are concerned that our society's growing antinatalism will be transformed into an anti-child (and thereby anti-parent) ideology; '... will we ... value our children all the more, because they are wanted? Or will we value them less than we do now, because only some of us will be parents while many of us will not?'† Though a decrease in the birth rate may be desirable for population control, all our children need good care, education and a nurturing and healthy environment. If we care about the future, we can ill afford to equate antinatalism with devaluing of parents and children. Our challenge will be to create a supportive atmosphere for parenting in an antinatalist time.

But would pro-parent and child policies, as some policy makers worry, have the effect of encouraging the bearing of more children? We think not, because parents who work outside the home cannot manage a large number of children as easily as one or two. Many adults of childbearing age have expressed a commitment of remaining 'child-free', and in the absence of social pressures to bear children, there is no reason why they should not remain so. Simply lifting the pressures to reproduce should have the desired effect of reducing the birth rate. There is no need to discourage parenthood by imposing extra burdens on parents or by withholding support from parents.

We need realistic education about parenting in secondary schools, because no one who truly understands the level of work and commitment required would choose to be a parent in the mistaken belief that such supports for parents as day care or parenting leaves can make it possible to raise children in our spare time.

Toward a Pro-parent Society

How can we as a society 'find ways ... to transform the responsibilities of parenthood into [an] ... undertaking that can be accomplished with a degree of pleasure and self-respect by most of those who will choose to become parents?'‡ One important way is through struggling to take back control from bureaucratic institutions that have come to wield so much power over our lives and our

---

*Jessie Bernard, *The Future of Motherhood* (New York: Penguin, 1975), p. 142.
†Mary Howell, *Helping Ourselves: Families and the Human Network* (Boston: Beacon Press, 1975), p.140.
‡Howell, op. cit., p. 141.

children's lives. This is a very hard thing to do because the institutions we work for have tremendous power over us and many of us have little choice about where or how much we work. Even institutions that exist primarily to serve families or children – schools, clinics, day care centres – do not always make family needs their priority. Though we want support from institutions, we, as parents, want to remain the primary caretakers of our children and the primary teachers of values; therefore, we must have control over services that care for, educate and socialize our children.

As we work toward taking back control, we can provide a model for our children. For example, if we can re-educate health care professionals to share their skills and information, parents can take more responsibility and participate more in our own and our children's health care (see pp. 355–61). We need to rescue ourselves from the rescue fantasies of those professionals who view parents as barriers preventing professionals from caring for children.*

In our daily lives there are countless details that could be more pro-parent. For example, the waiter or waitress who assures us that it's O.K. that our child has spilled some milk or is crying and the salesperson who opens the forbidden door to the toilets are displaying a 'parently' consciousness (whether or not they are parents doesn't matter), an ability to put human needs above efficiency or arbitrary rules. Such a parently consciousness is supportive, and if adopted by organizations or employers, would make our society a more livable place for everyone.

Parents who are travelling or shopping with an infant or small child need a place to feed or change her/him, and sometimes just a place to sit and relax together. In the USA, some chain restaurants have begun to offer an infant-changing area, but this is often merely a shelf in the ladies' room (of course!) and frequently not even kept clean. In the UK, motorway service areas are the only places we've come across that begin to offer facilities for changing babies. These are invariably found in the ladies' toilets; presumably fathers travelling alone with their infants have to manage in the car park. In London, there are also three department stores that offer facilities for changing babies and breastfeeding. These are John Lewis, Selfridges and the Brent Cross shopping area. It can be done!

Supermarkets, department stores and laundromats are among the many kinds of businesses that get a lot of their income from parents, yet do little or nothing to improve conditions for parents and children. Many commercial establishments provide only chewing gum and 'prize' machines or mechanical horses that cost money to ride for three minutes. And in the UK these are usually placed outside the shops. In Britain also we are usually not allowed to bring prams into shops and supermarkets; mothers have no alternative but to leave their babies unattended outside, with the very real risk of accident or abduction. Super-markets and department stores could provide a play space and child-care

*Mary Howell, 'Attitudes of Pediatricians Towards Mothers', in John Ehrenreich (ed.). *The Cultural Crisis of Modern Medicine* (New York: Monthly Review Press, 1978).

workers while parents shop. This service would help parents shop more efficiently and more economically, which is perhaps why the idea has never caught on. Groups of parents in a neighbourhood could get together and negotiate with supermarkets to get rid of the gum and sweet machines to minimize temptation for kids and stress on parents, or perhaps groups of parents could demand child care while shopping.

Nancy Scanlan

There are many more examples of how the needs of parents and kids can be better met in public places. Revolving doors, heavy push doors and street kerbs present substantial obstacles to parents walking with pushchairs and prams as well as to the handicapped and elderly. Traffic lights are timed to keep traffic flowing efficiently rather than for the needs of pedestrians, especially those of us slowed down by the paraphernalia of early parenthood or the wandering of toddlers.

There is a real need for 'parently concern' at all levels of our society. Although we don't really know what prompts parently concern or what encourages its expression, one factor is, surely, having spent time caring for young children. Of the parents we interviewed who had taken a major role in making institutions more responsive to the needs of parents and children, all were mothers, and most were not working in paid employment during the time they did this work. With the growing trend toward both parents working, one question that is raised is where such expressions of parently concern will come from. Will children be increasingly 'on their own' while parents are busier with work and other concerns? This is yet another reason to press for more flexible work schedules and reduced hours. Being a parent is broader than what the parent does at work or within the family. Our children, and society in general, benefit when parents have time to express their social concerns through working for change.

Individualism versus Family and Community Values

One of the most formidable barriers to providing more supports for parents and children is our society's over-emphasis on individualism. Self-reliance is a primary value for many people in our society; each of us is expected to be able to 'go it alone', and each family is regarded as an independent unit with its members depending primarily on one another. Parents are viewed as having sole responsibility for their children, and the sense of collective social responsibility for children that is seen in many other cultures is largely missing. Urie Bronfenbrenner, a student of child-raising practices in the Soviet Union and the United States, has noted the two cultures' differing attitudes toward what he calls 'diffusion of maternal [sic] responsibility' – the readiness of other persons besides the child's own parent to step into a caretaking role. As an example, he reports his own experience in the streets of Moscow:

> Our youngest son – then four – was walking briskly a pace or two ahead of us when from the opposite direction came a company of teenage boys. The first one no sooner spied Stevie than he opened his arms wide and called 'Ai malysh!' (Hey little one!), scooped him up, hugged him, kissed him resoundingly, and passed him on to the rest of the company, who did likewise, and then began a merry children's dance, as they caressed him with words and gestures. Similar behavior on the part of any American adolescent male would surely prompt his parents to consult a psychiatrist.*

Social responsibility for children is such a departure from our usual ways of child raising that we may not know how to accept such help when we encounter it. Joanne, an anthropologist and mother of two children, describes finding herself in such a situation:

> Once early on in the women's movement, when I was with some of my new women's movement friends, my daughter threw up in the car. All the women started helping me clean up, and when I thanked them they told me 'You don't have to thank us, because a child isn't just the parents' responsibility.' That had never occurred to me.

To cope with the loss of support, parents turn to 'experts' for information that in former times was exchanged within families and communities. Traditional women's magazines outdo each other in recruiting big-name experts for their advice columns. But turning to experts may not always be necessary or desirable. The tremendous growth in recent years of 'parent education', both professional and parent-run, indicates the depth and breadth of parents' needs for support in parenting. Some of the ways that parents are finding to support one another are discussed in the next chapter.

Inequality

The belief in individualism is grounded in a belief in equality of opportunity – the belief that any individual who works hard can achieve and be successful.

*Two Worlds of Childhood: U.S. and U.S.S.R. (New York, 1972, p. 10; London: Penguin, 1974).

Today we look around us and see that far from eliminating barriers to individual accomplishment, we have maintained distinctions of age, sex, sexual preference, marital status, race and class. These barriers to equal opportunity interfere with our roles as parents in a variety of ways.

Sexism

Sexism is based on stereotyping people according to their gender and requiring them to behave according to society's preconceived notions of female and male behaviour. Sexism is reinforced through powerful social institutions, such as the family, workplaces, schools, etc., which prevent or seriously limit women and men who want to change the traditional role distinctions they are forced to live with. Our society's notions of how women and men are supposed to act affect us as parents in many different ways. One of these is sexism in employment practices which limits women as providers and limits the energy and time available to men for nurturing.

Twentieth-century technology has automated much of the work which formerly required physical strength. In addition, with more effective means to control reproduction,* women don't have to take so much time off for pregnancy and child care. Yet, in spite of the fact that gender is irrelevant, most women in paid employment are segregated into a few occupations which are so underpaid that a visitor from another planet would suppose that women were a separate caste. In spite of the widespread belief that women are 'catching up' as a result of the women's movement and affirmative action, in fact the opposite is true. Recent census figures show that as more women join the labour force, the unemployment rate of women also rises. In the UK between 1976 and 1978, the number of women registered as unemployed rose by 53 per cent, against 9 per cent for men – and of course many women do not register. Furthermore, while the UK average basic wage of women has risen in relation to men's in recent years (it is now 72 per cent of men's average earnings, though this figure takes no account of men's greater overtime earnings), we do not expect the gap to close much further, because of the difference in the types of work that men and women do. These figures show that we must redouble our efforts to see that women are given equal opportunity from childhood onward to take their aspirations seriously and prepare themselves for paid employment. At the same time, we must push institutions to provide equal opportunity so that women can *use* their preparation and be fairly compensated.

How does sexism in employment affect parents? Mothers generally win approval for wanting to spend time with their children, but at the cost of not being taken seriously as workers and providers. Fathers are also hurt by job discrimination against women, for it limits how much parenting can be shared.

---

*But many of the most dependable contraceptives have serious side effects and complications. See *Our Bodies, Ourselves* (London: Allen Lane and Penguin, 1978).

When women are paid substantially less, men in these families have to earn more and thus have less time to be with their kids.

Within the family the traditionally sexist division of labour operates to put an unfair share of the child care and housework on women's shoulders. Studies of couples who both work outside the home show that men do not do substantially more housework when their wives are employed. Eliminating sex discrimination in the work force is the first step toward greater equality in the home. When women do not have equal earning power outside the home, they lack the bargaining power within the home to demand an equal sharing of child care and housework.* So it's a vicious circle. Unless the home tasks are shared equally, women will not be free to put the same amount of energy and commitment into work and will not be as able to advance on an equal basis.

Though for women parenthood is sometimes a barrier to being hired or to subsequent advancement, men are sometimes given special consideration by employers who believe fathers to be more dependable workers than other men. But the persistent notion that a good father is merely a good provider, and that 'a real man' will always put his work outside the home before family needs, seriously limits fathers who want to be close to their children and take an active part in their care. Men are raised to believe that child care threatens their masculine image and that their lack of preparation for child raising makes their contribution to family life of dubious value anyway.† The socialization of male children de-emphasizes learning the skills of emotional give-and-take that are the very fabric of the nurturing aspects of parenting, to say nothing of other personal relationships, while the socialization of female children often undercuts their future role as providers by discouraging and disparaging achievement outside the home. Researchers have found a syndrome among academically talented women which they call 'fear of success'.‡ This is the analogue of men's fear of competence in nurturing.

The real tragedy of the way that both women and men are socialized is that we are taught a separate set of strengths and skills and subtly encouraged to believe that we have no need of the complementary skills being taught to the other sex. We are socialized as if we were two separate species (and then we are expected to get along!). As Jean Baker Miller has observed, women are not only given a socialization that is lopsided in over-emphasizing 'affiliation' over achievement, but what is worse, women and men are taught to devalue the skills that women have, to the detriment of society as a whole. Society emphasizes and disproportionately rewards competitiveness and aggression while devaluing caring, cooperation and interpersonal skills. Miller suggests that 'The characteristics

*Mary Jo Bane, Here to Stay: The American Family in the Twentieth Century (New York: Basic Books, 1976).

†See the chapter on Sharing Parenting for a fuller discussion of these issues.

‡See Matina S. Horner, 'Towards an Understanding of Achievement-Related Conflicts in Women', in Stacey, Bereaud and Daniels, ed., And Jill Came Tumbling After: Sexism in American Education (New York: Dell, 1974). See also Sue Sharpe, Just Like a Girl (London: Penguin, 1976), p. 137.

most highly developed in women and perhaps most essential to human beings are *the* very characteristics that are especially dysfunctional for success in the world as it is. That is obviously no accident. They may, however, be the important ones for making the world different.'*

Many of the seemingly insoluble problems in the world today have come about through over-emphasis on 'masculine' modes of dealing with social and environmental problems. A great benefit of breaking down sexism would be the creation of a more 'parently' society by recognizing and validating the traditional nurturing strengths of women, and freeing men to develop them and/or to use them without fear of loss of status.

Racism

Racism is the stereotyping and oppression of persons because of their colour. The damaging effects of racism on individuals, families and societies have been amply documented, and there is little that we could add to this discussion. However, we do want to highlight briefly how racism specifically affects parenting.

Discrimination in employment and housing are two major material ways that our society undermines the parenting of minority parents. Discrimination in employment severely limits the ability of non-white parents to provide for their families. In the US the median income of a two-parent black family in 1975 was $10,487 compared with $13,089 for a two-parent white family.† Unemployment among minorities is double that of whites. As a result, non-white Americans are four times as likely to be poor as white Americans.

In the UK too, racism is an ever-present factor in the lives of parents from the new Commonwealth countries of the Indian sub-continent and the West Indies. Apart from facing harassment on the streets and in the schools, these families are three times more likely to be living in hazardous sub-standard housing, lacking the basic amenities, and much less likely to have the information to take advantage of public services, such as council housing, welfare benefits and even the National Health Service.‡ Immigrants' wages are low and their hours long and unsocial compared with those of the indigenous population. Black school-leavers are four times less likely to find a job than their white peers. So post-war British society, which welcomed immigrants' labour to fill low-paid jobs and shore up our public services, notably the health service and transport, has failed their children when young and continues to fail them as teenagers. For an enlightening glimpse of life in Britain for some immigrants, see Amrit Wilson's book *Finding a Voice* (London: Virago, 1978).

---

*Jean Baker Miller, *Towards a New Psychology of Women* (London: Penguin, 1978)

†Advisory Committee on Child Development of the National Research Council, *Toward a National Policy for Children and Families* (National Academy of Sciences, Washington, DC, 1976), p. 29.

‡*Urban Deprivation, Racial Inequality and Social Policy*, a report by the Community Relations Commission for the Home Secretary, 1977, gives facts and figures.

Sexism compounds the economic injustice suffered by non-white families because mothers in these families are more likely to be in the labour force and their earnings constitute a higher percentage of family income. So if women were paid more equitably, minority families (and all families with employed mothers) would benefit. Non-white single-parent families suffer the most grinding poverty.

Parents naturally want to protect their children and provide a safe environment, but non-white parents often must struggle especially hard to do this because, as Joyce Ladner says of the black community, 'The community power base still lies outside its borders.'*

Despite the many obstacles encountered by minority parents, many develop remarkable adaptiveness and resiliency which enable their families to survive against almost impossible odds.† Here is Barbara speaking of her experience as a black parent:

One thing that has helped – and I don't think I did it consciously – but even when Kevin was really young I tried to build up his awareness of who his ancestors were, where they came from and that kind of thing. That was a major part of his informal education – to teach him to be proud of who he is. Part of being a black parent is realizing that there are some hurts in life that you cannot protect your child from experiencing, and even if you could, would it be good to shelter them from reality that much?

Just as breaking down sexism will allow society to incorporate more of the traditionally female strengths, breaking down racism will enable all of us to learn from the strengths of role flexibility and extended family sharing which have enabled minority families to survive in a racist society.

How Society's Institutions Affect Our Parenting

Because of our culture's deep reluctance to recognize how much the family is intertwined with and dependent upon the rest of society, both outside observers and family members themselves tend to blame the family for its troubles. Yet the family is part of a larger system of interdependent social institutions, each of which has an effect on the others.

Our economy, which determines the work that parents can get and how much they can earn, is the lynch-pin of these interrelated subsystems which make up our larger social system: the amount of money we parents earn determines the quality of our family's housing and the quality and quantity of our children's education, as well as of nearly all the goods and services that families need. Therefore let us look first at the institution that most powerfully affects our families – our workplaces and the economic system.

---

*Joyce A. Ladner, *Tomorrow's Tomorrow: The Black Women* (New York: Doubleday, 1971).
†Andrew Billingsley, *Black Families in White America* (Englewood Cliffs, NJ: Prentice-Hall, 1968).

Parents and Work

Parents need to work – for money and for personal satisfaction. Fathers have traditionally had their parenthood defined in terms of their ability to provide, yet, as we have seen, many fathers today wish to cut back on the time and energy demands of their paid work in order to participate more in daily parenting. Though for mothers it has been harder to gain recognition of their role as providers, the majority of mothers today must also juggle the nurturing and providing parts of parenting. In the UK, one-parent families have an income of half the average two-parent family income.* In 1976 the vast majority of one-parent families, 660,000, were headed by women who were the sole providers. By 1979 this figure is estimated to have risen to 750,000 women.† Therefore the provider role has become a crucial one for mothers as well as fathers.

Both fathers and mothers need time to be with their children, with others and by themselves as well as time to be free to do work other than parenting. As we have seen, many parents have begun to share parenting in an attempt to better balance their double needs to work and to love. But the organization of paid work in this society often hinders us from combining these two important aims. Most paid work is so rigidly structured it imposes major limitations on our parenting. These include the time and timing of work hours, the inflexibility of work schedules, the dehumanizing quality of much industrialized work, sexist attitudes toward mothers and fathers and the assumption of most employers that parents will leave their parent selves at the door. This section will look at some of these limitations and at changes that need to be made. It will raise indirectly, but not attempt to address, the underlying political question of whether such limitations are inevitable and irremediable in an economy devoted to profit making and dominated by large, powerful corporate interests.

Time and Timing of Work Hours

Our view is that we as parents need to be able to provide for our economically helpless kids in such a way that we are not left too exhausted to carry on the nurturing and socializing parts of parenting them while also caring for ourselves. When we choose to become parents, our hope is that we will build a special bond with our children through sharing experiences together. Yet, even when we feel reasonably secure economically, this is dependent on keeping the job we have and/or advancing, and the time we must spend on most jobs does not allow enough time for our families. A 1977 study done in the US found that half the children surveyed wished their fathers would spend more time with them, and over a third wished their mothers would spend more time with them.‡

---

*Day Care and One-Parent Families. A system of family support (Finer Joint Action Committee report).

†These figures were given by David Webb of the National Council for One-Parent Families (255 Kentish Town Road, London NW 5).

‡Nicholas Zill, Foundation for Child Development, 345 E. 46 St, New York, NY 10017, USA.

The sheer number of hours that many parents work makes time with children a near impossibility. Maureen, a mother of four in a work-training programme, told us this about her family life:

On weekdays I don't see my husband from five a.m. until ten o'clock at night. On weekends he is so exhausted from carrying two jobs that he can't do anything but sit in front of the TV. If the kids are too noisy he explodes at them. I have to keep telling them that their Dad loves them or he wouldn't work so hard to support them, but it's hard for them to understand because he just has no energy left to give them any attention.

From the parents' point of view, the transition time between work and home must be taken into account as crucially important time for themselves. For many of us making this transition from home to work and from work back home is very stressful, as Debby, a mother of two younger school-age children, tells us:

When I first started back to work I was constantly worried that something would happen to one of my kids, and I think that was my guilt about 'Was I doing the right thing?' So I'd get to work and not really feel altogether there for the first half-hour. And it would work the other way, too. I'd get home after fighting the rush-hour traffic for forty minutes and I'd be grouchy and tense with the kids. It took me some time, but I learned eventually to leave my family worries at home, and to leave my work tensions at the office.

Joni, a single mother of two school-age children, chose to work near her home so that she could be there quickly if an emergency arose. With practically no commuting time, she found the transition problem heightened:

A lot of times I'd work until two-fifteen and I'd have to be home at two-thirty for the kids. Sometimes I think it would have been better if I had worked farther away, because I never had enough time for a transition between work and home. I finally had to work something out with the kids that I had to first have a cup of tea and be absolutely alone for a while, or I'd tell them 'I'll talk to you for five minutes and then I have to have my alone time.'

Norm, who has two school-age children, arranged his work schedule so that he could pick them up from school three days a week:

I'm enjoying the extra time with my kids, but it was hard at first because I'd be preoccupied with all the unfinished stuff at work. Sometimes I'd rush to the phone and make a business call as soon as we got home. But the kids let me know that they didn't like that, because that was supposed to be our time together. So now I try to get the calls out of the way before I leave work, or if I have to, I say to the kids 'I have an important call to make when we get home, and then I'll be free', so they know what to expect. Also, I have bursts of energy between ten p.m. and two a.m., so that's when I do some of the work that doesn't get done earlier in the day.

One way that some of us have found to have more time for parenting has been to choose to work fewer hours (and accept earning less money) in exchange for the flexibility that permits spending more time with our children. This option also means letting go of some of our personal ambitions, as in this father's story:

My father took care of us a lot because my mother was sick. That meant I grew up knowing him – how he worked as a person, what he cared about, what made him do the work he did. Saturdays and after school I went to the print shop instead of to the football field. That's why I have made it my business to know my kids. It means I work part time. So I am no whizzkid professionally. That pulls on certain things inside me – like a daydream I used to have of going back to the print shop famous and having my father there.

Most of the parents we spoke with who chose to work fewer hours have above-average earning capacity and therefore could still earn enough money for their families' needs. But for the majority of families every pound earned is needed.

Even jobs with reasonable hours rarely provide the flexibility we need as parents, so that our free time rarely coincides with those of our children's activities that we'd like to be involved with. Most workplaces are not dedicated to the fullest development of workers and their families and, therefore, do not recognize the needs of parents in their employee policies. In the UK, under the Employment Protection Act employers must give time off for certain civic duties, including being on the governing body of any maintained (state) school. Ironically, we have no legal right to take time off to go to our own child's school open day. Taking an afternoon off to attend a school function is regarded as so frivolous by most employers that parents often prefer to concoct an excuse rather than confront an employer or co-workers about why the time was needed. Jeff, a father of two school-age children, told us this about the time he had taken off a couple of hours to help his son set up an exhibition he had built at school.

I'd been involved right along as Timmy brought home the books about the Hopi Indians, studied them and decided what to make for his project. He had his mind set on something that was structurally complicated, but with a little help from me he could carry it out. Then when it was finished he needed help carting all those pieces to school and getting them all put together again. Of course, I couldn't tell anyone at work where I'd been for those hours, so I just called and said my car was stalled and that I'd be there as soon as I could get it fixed.

Conflicts Between Work and Parenting

A major problem for many parents is that their overall career prospects conflict outright with child-raising needs. The time when we are expected to work the hardest building the foundation of our work lives is during our twenties and thirties, the time that most of us also start our families. So these are the most demanding years both for work outside the home and for child raising as well. Dan is a father of three and a lawyer who is trying to meet this conflict creatively:

At Legal Aid I started off with a four-fifths workload and four days' pay, but I eventually left because it got to be too much. I was trying to do five days' work in four. When it became obvious that I was covering as many cases as the other lawyers, they wanted to pay me for five days and let me continue to come in four days. But I recognized that as a trap – then I'd be obligated to really work on the fifth day when there was a 'need' or staff meeting or something on Friday.

Gail Bryan

Now I have a partnership with another lawyer. I could make a lot more money by myself, but the partnership makes my life style possible. I made it clear from the beginning that I would not be there Tuesday afternoons and all day Friday. We cover for each other. I just tell people I have another commitment on those days. I wouldn't lie, but no one asks what it is. They just assume it's another professional commitment. I take care of the kids two days a week after school. Jan comes home early one day a week and we have a baby-sitter twice a week. Friday mornings I have just for myself and that's great! I've become attached to keeping this kind of distance from my work. I don't think I'll be working a five-day week even when they're grown up.

Even when our jobs offer us the flexibility we need, we still have our personal conflicts between being workers and being parents. We want time with our kids, but we want to feel competent and responsible at our work and to be respected by our co-workers.

Children and Work

Much has been written on the supposed harmfulness of mothers working. We believe that it is not only *not* harmful but beneficial to children when mothers and fathers are employed in work that provides satisfaction and self-esteem.* Many parents that we spoke with have been pleased to see the ways that their children identify with and learn through their parents' work roles. Elaine, who teaches a course in sex-role stereotypes, was gratified to learn from her daughter's teacher:

Natalie defended a character in a story against the whole class. In the discussion everyone else was labelling this girl as a 'tomboy', but Natalie insisted she was not! She was a 'liberated woman'. I was especially pleased when her teacher said that she was a good role model for the other girls in the class because she stuck to her point of view in spite of being a minority of one.

Gail Bryan

Dan, a lawyer, told us about his daughter going to court to change her name:

She has been using the name Beth for a couple of years now and really prefers it to the name we gave her. So one day she decided that she wanted to change her name legally, and I took her to court with me and showed her how to do it. She really felt that this was something she should be able to change if she wanted to, and my being a lawyer made it easier for her to feel that she could do it.

For parents, sharing our work lives with our children is an important way to share our daily life experiences and our values in a society increasingly fragmented and separated one generation from another. Mel, a father of two grown children with two more still at home, talks about the importance of a mid-life career change in providing opportunities to share with his children:

*See Martin Hughes *et al.*, *Nurseries Now: A Fair Deal for Parents and Children* (London: Penguin, 1980).

One of the reasons that I even considered the possibility of education as an alternative career to science was because I had children in school. That career change had a lot of impact on my relationship with my children. I started doing kinds of work that the children could be involved in. I could talk to them about it in a way that I hadn't before. The older children had memories of coming to the lab and watching Daddy work. Otherwise I didn't think about trying to relate my work directly to the children. Now I started going to their school, which I had never done much before. I spent a day in my daughter's classes because I wanted to know what schools were like ... Also, I took them with me to work and got them involved in workshops for teachers where we were trying out new materials and new teaching methods. They got to know the staff and my workplace quite well. One of the reasons that I changed my work was that I felt a lot of separation between my family and the people I saw socially and the work I did. Now those parts of my life are more integrated. I like that, I like it for the children and for my relationship with them.

As we've discussed earlier in the book, children no longer share as much in the family work as they did in the past. In addition, most children never even see their parents at work and they have little idea of what it is their mothers and fathers actually do when they are at their jobs. It is as if, for eight or more hours per day, we go into an alien world of which they know nothing.

In addition to needing to participate in family work, children should learn about the other work of society, because they will work outside the home as well as inside. Their schoolwork often seems so removed from what goes on in the world of work or the family that it is hard for them to see the connection between what they do in school and their future work roles as adults. In the Soviet Union there is a practice of a shop, office or business enterprise 'adopting' a group of children. The workers visit the children's classroom, day care centre or hospital ward, and the children spend time at the workplace learning about adults and their work. 'The aim is not vocational education, but rather acquaintance with adults as participants in the world of work.'*

In an American adaptation of this approach,

... two groups of twelve-year-old children ... spent six to seven hours a day for three days in virtually every department of the [Detroit Free Press], not just observing but actively participating in the department's activities ... in the press room, the city room, the composing room, the advertising department and the dispatch department. The employees of the Free Press *entered into the experiment with serious misgivings. 'This is a busy place: we have a newspaper to get out every day. What are those kids going to do, just sit around?' ... The children were not bored, nor were the adults. And the paper did get out every day ...†*

We think parents, workplaces and schools have to get together and find more ways of exposing children to work and working adults, and vice versa. In the

*Bronfenbrenner, op. cit., introduction.
†ibid.

absence of such social mechanisms, many of us try to find ways to share our own and our friends' work with our children by taking them to work with us on occasion and by having them work along with us in social ways, such as in food co-ops or exchanges of services with friends and neighbours. Many of us have observed our children's enjoyment of real work, as opposed to the busywork that is frequently assigned to them. We should not forget housework in our definition of 'real' work.

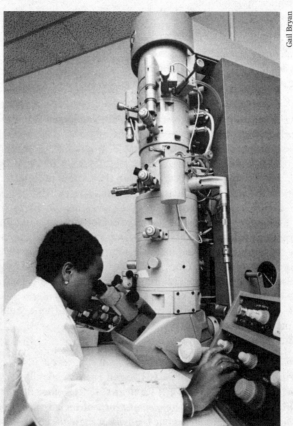

Gail Bryan

The 'Act as though' Principle

In spite of the growth of the female part of the work force, most paid work is still structured to fit the traditional life style of men, who could leave daily family responsibilities behind them when they went to work because the family was cared for through the unpaid labour of women at home. The man is enabled to act as though his job is his sole concern precisely because in many families an important part of the work of the wife and mother, whether she works in paid employment or not, is to arrange family activities and mealtimes around the husband/father's work schedule. Naturally, for the single female parent the problem is magnified.

While the man is at work the 'myth of separate worlds' is in force: the employer seems to admonish him: 'While you are here, you will *act as though* you have no other loyalties, no other life.'

Women who are professionals encounter the 'act as though' principle just as men do:

I was finishing up my training as a child therapist about the time my daughter was eight months old. When the placements were being given out, I asked for one that was near my home and where the hours would coincide with my husband's time at home. My supervisor was furious! Her voice was icy as she informed me that I was never to make such a request again. 'In fact, Mrs Wilson,' she went on to say, 'I would strongly suggest to you that you never again mention in this programme that you are a mother!' She made it clear that I was accepted into the programme in spite of being a mother, as if being a mother was a drawback instead of an asset in working with the emotional problems of children!

Women do not necessarily want to drop their parent consciousness at work. Unfortunately, employers assume that because women carry their family responsibilities with them they will not be as dedicated to their work as men are. This is one of the rationales that employers give for keeping women workers ghetto-ized in a small number of low-paying jobs and not considering them for promotion. Yet many studies show that on specific measures of performance, such as rates of absenteeism, for example, women and men are equally reliable.

We hope that as more and more women come into the work force, eventually the female norm of bringing family membership into the workplace will come to be recognized as a more sane way of living. Linda, who works with children in a day care centre where she finds her co-workers supportive of her as a parent, shares a fantasy of her husband demanding similar support at his workplace:

I am so aware of how unsupportive Bob's work environment is to his family and to his being a father. I keep saying to him 'Why don't you just march in there and say "I am a father!"' If people started insisting, maybe institutions and workplaces would start making some different kinds of arrangements for fathers.

What Do Working Parents Need?

There are a number of simple reforms that could considerably ease the stresses of the working parent without much cost to industry. Other changes would result in increased costs but would, we believe, be a good beginning toward a more equitable sharing by society of the costs of raising children. Some of these costs could be shared by the government through tax deductions or direct subsidies.

Sick Leave

Most American firms that provide sick leave typically allow between seven and fourteen days annually. For parents that may not be enough to cover both their own and their children's illnesses, and so we resort to a variety of compromises. Miriam is a computer programmer and single parent of a six-year-old son:

When Michael is ill and can't go to school, I just have to stay home with him. There's no other choice. When there is a school vacation or something I can plan ahead for, I

Peter Simon

make a trade with a friend and take their kids for a weekend, or I hire a sitter. But when a child wakes up with a fever, what can you do? So what happens is by the time I get a cold or something, usually I've used up my sick days with Michael, or if I haven't yet, I worry about needing them, so I just try to keep going. I sure don't work at peak efficiency on those days, but I show up, because I support myself and Michael on my salary and I can't afford to lose any of it.

In the UK employees have no statutory right to sick leave, paid or unpaid, although we can claim state sickness benefit if we have paid enough contributions, and we may win a case of 'unfair dismissal' at an industrial tribunal if sacked while away sick. Both the benefit and the unconditional likelihood of winning at a tribunal are meagre, so most of us rely on the entitlements won by trade union bargaining. By 1976, 78 per cent of employees were covered by employers' sick schemes – although for women manual workers the figure was only 58 per cent. In general, provision is still too low, hedged about with conditions and covers only the employee's own sickness; agreed leave to care for sick dependants is very rare. While some employers will allow a certain amount of leave 'on compassionate grounds', this is entirely discretionary and subject to management's prejudices. A father's obligation to look after his sick child would be beyond the imagination of most employers.

How do we manage when the children are ill? Very commonly we use up our annual holiday leave; we take days off, lose pay and risk dismissal; like Miriam we go to work when unwell ourselves so as not to lose too much time; sometimes we have no choice but to go through the anxiety of leaving the children unattended. Many of us give up the struggle to do paid work and settle for life at or on the poverty line, on supplementary benefit, if we are lone parents, or on one low wage.

If we can organize at our place of work, we may gain some of the conditions we need as parents. After representations by the local branch of NALGO, the London Borough of Islington has recently agreed in principle to allow leave for employees to care for sick dependants.

In this way we begin to create the climate for a national policy on sick leave. Sweden already has such a policy: in 1976 a law was passed authorizing sick leave for working parents whenever a child was ill, provided that half of the allotted leave time was taken by the father and half by the mother.

Leave for New Parents

The Employment Protection Act passed in the UK in 1975 gave pregnant workers the minimal right of six weeks' paid maternity leave, with the right to return to work up to twenty-nine weeks after confinement.* The provision is mean: pay is reckoned at 90 per cent of basic rate, leaving out the overtime, bonuses and tips that many women rely on to bring their wages up to an adequate sum; and the leave falls far short of the thirty weeks' paid leave recommended by the TUC, and of that provided by collective agreements already in operation. To be entitled you must have spent two years in the same job, which effectively excludes many women from the provision. The Act covers neither adoptive parents nor fathers. The social security benefits of maternity grant and

*For details and discussion of the law on both sick leave and maternity leave, see J. McMullen, *Rights at Work* (London: Pluto Press, 1978), and Anna Coote and Tess Gill, *Women's Rights: A Practical Guide* (London: Penguin, 1974 etc.).

allowance depend on the right number of contributions having been paid in the right contribution year, which means that many women, particularly young women, will not be able to receive them.

The law also takes little account of the facts of women's lives: that they must change jobs more frequently, commonly following a husband's transfer, miss 'contribution years' because of inadequate child-care provision, and still do not have complete control over their fertility – even were they willing to plan their familes to take advantage of the legal and social security systems.

As parents who work we can organize at our workplaces to improve on the bare legal rights. Much improved maternity rights have recently been agreed in principle with three London boroughs; in Lambeth these include forty weeks' paid leave (sixteen on full pay, twenty-four part-paid) and the right to return after a year. NALGO has also negotiated paternity leave of between five days and three weeks: little, but better than nothing.

The need for paternity leave is just beginning to receive recognition in the United States from some colleges and universities. So far, though, even when paternity leaves are available, the attitudes of employers and co-workers might make most fathers reluctant to use them. Carleton Dallery, a father of two and university teacher, made this comment:

Women have always taken risks professionally. They are subject to hostile comments and patronizing attitudes all the time in the academic world. All that happens now is that some men will have the opportunity to run the same kinds of risks ... There are plenty of academic leaders who still laugh at the guy who changes a diaper, but the laugh will be on them.

By way of contrast, in Sweden the government has been trying out a system of paid paternity leave since 1974. Parents are allowed seven months' leave after the birth of a child while receiving 95 per cent of their pay. If both parents work and both wish to use the leave they may split the seven months between them. Though only 7 per cent of new fathers in Sweden have taken time off through this leave, four times as many are in the programme now than at the beginning. In France, the Cabinet recently approved the extension of maternity leave from one to two years, with reinstatement guaranteed.

Bringing Kids to Work

There are a variety of reasons why parents might want to bring children to work on occasion. Sometimes we need to bring our kids because of school holidays, minor illnesses or medical appointments. Children, as we have noted, are usually interested in their parents' work and enjoy seeing the workplace and meeting co-workers. And for parents, bringing the kids in is a way to break down the 'act as though' principle and get recognition of ourselves as parents.

David is a physical education director at a university and a father of four. He is now sharing the daily care of their adopted two-year-old son with his wife:

When I bring Sam to work he will sit on the floor for hours with my huge box of athletic medals and throw them all over my office while I am making my calls or even seeing people. When he's done with that I just sweep the medals up and put them back into the box. I actually thought about taking a formal paternity leave and would have been prepared to do that, but I could see that it wasn't necessary because the place where I work is informal enough. I never would have thought of it in my earlier days, but now I can see that it is perfectly all right to have a new little child throwing medals around while I am doing some business.

Even for those few of us who have the option of bringing children to work, it is not always possible or desirable to work with our children present. Many parents want clearer boundaries between our work lives and our family lives. As Doreen puts it:

There are a lot of us who want that separation – who can't get anything else done when our kids are around. Let's make things more flexible. I need the option of staying home when they're sick or having someone else stay with them and going to work. I can't do both at the same time. Maybe an infant. After that they get too disruptive.

Ginny observes:

We were the first in our circle of friends to have children and, as they got pregnant, several of our friends have shared with us their plans for when they have kids. What they think is sort of like this: 'The third week after the baby is born, Lorna will go back to work and then I'll take the baby to work with me and put it on my desk.' Then I have to say 'Jim, you know what? It won't work. Babies don't just lie there like kittens only needing to be stroked a few times in a day.' People have no conception that taking care of kids is real work. When you make a choice to be a parent, you make a choice to take away some of the time you might put elsewhere. There isn't an infinitely expandable day where you can keep getting up earlier and earlier. Society needs to help people create some of those spaces and also to stop putting pressure on people to expect to do everything.

On-Site Day Care at the Workplace

One very direct way that companies can be supportive to parents is through providing on-site day care. This is a form of day care in which a company runs and/or partially subsidizes a day care centre on its premises for the children of employees. (Sometimes the centre may also have room for children of non-employees as well.) See the day care section below (pp. 398–408) for more discussion of the pros and cons of this and other types of child care.

Part-Time and Flexible Hours

Numerous studies of part-time workers in a variety of occupations consistently demonstrate they produce more and better in the time they work than do full-time workers. It stands to reason that people who work fewer hours give a better level of energy and attention to their work. But the choice of working part time too often means discrimination in salary and benefits and non-consideration for promotion as well. For women this is added to pervasive sex discrimination.

Although flexible time schedules are still the exception to the rule, it is estimated that about three hundred thousand employees in nearly one thousand companies and government agencies in the United States are on some form of flexible time schedule. In Europe there are more than five million flexible-time workers, though they are not evenly distributed: 40 per cent of workers in Switzerland, as compared to 6 per cent in Germany and less than 1 per cent in the UK. Increases in production, reduction of absenteeism, lateness and staff turnover, and improved morale were all noted.

Marilyn holds an unofficially 'flexitime' position in the financial office of a large university, which allows her to be more available for her teenage children's activities:

My job has grown more flexible as far as hours go. I can come in an hour or two earlier or later and leave an hour or two earlier or later, or I can expand or skip my lunch hour. This has been a real help – for example, when my son was involved in some special skating lessons early in the morning and I was driving him there. I just came in an hour later and either skipped my lunch hour or worked an hour later. That's a benefit I would hate to give up. I've had any number of offers to switch to other departments and earn more money, but for a working mother time flexibility outweighs a lot of other advantages.

Sacrificing promotion for flexibility has been one of the traditional options for employed mothers. Greater flexibility for all workers would make equal opportunities for women more of a reality.

But in pressing for more flexibility we must take care that we do not lose more than we gain. Experience in the UK has shown that, since the introduction of flexitime arrangements, time off for parental duties – visits to the antenatal clinic, for example – is often expected to be taken in 'own time' rather than 'firm's time'. Union representatives negotiating with management over the arrangements should make sure that practices already established to parents' advantage are written into new agreements. Flexitime should not mean the flexibility for parents who work to drive themselves into the ground: the day remains, inflexibly, twenty-four hours long.

The British TUC has also recommended that 'greater consideration should be given to enabling parents with young children to work on a part-time basis', provided that the pay and conditions of part-time workers are improved to at least pro rata with full-time workers.* Proper job-sharing or job-pairing seems to us a better way to do satisfying work which still allows us to spend enough, unrushed time with our children.

---

*TUC *Charter on Facilities for the Under-5's* (1978).

A Shorter Workday

Another possibility we might entertain here is that the eight-hour day is not sacrosanct. For parents a shorter day would relieve some of the pressures of balancing child care and paid work, and would allow them to be home when their children get out of school or soon after. In Sweden there has been a proposal to allow parents of young children to work six hours a day and be compensated for the other two hours out of the social security system. Interestingly enough, it was voted down, largely because the trades unions feared that passage of the bill would destroy their hope of establishing a six-hour day for everyone.*

Making Workplaces More Responsive to Family Needs

The attitudes and practices of employers reflect our lack of a national family policy. Though a pro-family programme may be initiated by a concerned company official in one organization or by pressure from workers in another, we need to take action at the national level to achieve broad-based change. The US government has been reviewing the notion of having 'family impact statements' attached to all federal legislation in much the same way as environmental impact statements are now required. Rosabeth Kanter proposes that we take a further step and have employing organizations file 'family responsibility statements' which would summarize how their policies affect the families of employees and what plans they have for improvement.† Obviously the usefulness and accuracy of such statements would be enhanced if working parents at every level of the organization participated in preparing them. Additionally, we think that workplaces should be pushed in the direction of adopting the kinds of changes we have been discussing through the use of tax incentives and other kinds of legislation.

The Economics of Work and Parenting

Many of the reforms which parents need at the workplace are blocked by a climate of economic insecurity and keen competition for scarce jobs. Because our society ranks people from childhood (through an educational system that is grossly unequal), many parents, particularly those in minorities, have an uphill struggle to gain access to the kinds of jobs that would provide a steady year-round adequate income for their families. When the economy tightens, parents at the bottom of the economic pyramid are pushed out of the paid-employment market altogether, and their families must subsist on unemployment and supplementary benefits, both of which are often administered in the most humiliating and inefficient manner possible.

*Urie Bronfenbrenner, 'Who Cares for America's Children?' (lecture presented 26 February 1976, at College of Human Ecology Alumni Association, Michigan State University), p. 15.

†Rosabeth Moss Kanter, Work and Family in the United States: A Critical Review and Agenda for Research and Policy, New York, Russell Sage Foundation, 1977.

Today, the threat of poverty is growing even for middle-class parents, who can no longer be sure that an education will insure against the spectre of material want. In recent years there have been unremittingly high rates of unemployment even among graduates and professionals. Some parents may worry about losing a job, or feel anxiety about finding one, but even if we feel reasonably secure about our work, there is anxiety about inflation that makes it ever harder to maintain our standard of living.

Though Reena and her husband both work, here is what she has to say about the difficulty of supporting themselves and their child:

It does a whole guilt trip on me, because in the first place, it's expensive to live in the city. That second income (and it's a good one) goes! In other words you don't see it coming in in a lump sum, you see it just kind of going out. So you say 'What the heck am I working for?' And 'There is my child that somebody else is taking care of.' What is this? It's as if we are in a rat trap we cannot get out of.

While many families can earn enough by having two wage earners, for most of these families, as with Reena's, it is still a struggle. Many families that could formerly live on one salary now need two salaries to get by. Higher wages create an illusion of prosperity while inflation reduces the purchasing power of the money we earn. Thus the corporate share of the pie is maintained and increased in spite of wage rises.

Parents are more likely than non-parents to experience the squeeze of inadequate income for family needs because in our society parents bear nearly all of the economic costs of having children. Families with children, especially those with young children, are at higher risk of being poor than families without children. In Britain the number of children living in poverty or on the margins of poverty rose from 2,250,000 in 1974 to 3,900,000 in 1976.* As we discussed in the Families chapter, separated parents, irrespective of education and skills, are at considerable risk of being or becoming poor. And when the custody parent is female, as is usually the case, pervasive sex discrimination further limits her chances of providing adequately.

We have children and value them for personal, psychological reasons, but economically children are a liability, for their economic value is only as future workers. That is why it seems fair that society should bear a greater share of the cost of raising them. Britain remains one of the few industrial nations where no comprehensive studies of the relative needs of adults and children have ever been conducted. Because there is nothing else, the supplementary benefit (SB) scales remain Britain's semi-official poverty line. But SB entitlement levels underestimate the needs and costs of children, especially older children.†

---

*Figures drawn from the House of Commons Hansard, Vols. 945 and 955; quoted by Ruth Lister in *A Budget for the Year of the Child*, *Poverty 4*, Child Poverty Action Group (CPAG).

†*Who Pays for the Children*, paper by the Outer Circle Policy Unit (4 Cambridge Terrace, London N1), 1978.

How Poverty and Unemployment Affect Families

The human suffering caused by poverty is broader in the case of parents than simply material deprivation. It is compounded by our guilt and anxiety over the effects of poverty on our children. Urie Bronfenbrenner found, after evaluating the results of a variety of US federally funded pre-school programmes designed to help 'disadvantaged' children (such as Head Start,* tutoring, home visits, etc.), that the most important indicators of success had to do not with the programmes themselves but with family living conditions:

When the breadwinner was unemployed, the family income below the poverty line, many children crowded into a small space, and only one parent present, without much schooling, no intervention program, whatever the strategy employed, was able to be very effective. Conversely, children from families that were not subject to these stresses were most likely to benefit from whatever opportunities were provided. The critical factor is the conditions under which the family lives. And these conditions are usually not in the family's power to control.†

Unemployment is a major barrier to effective parenting. It can interfere not only with the economic task of providing but also with the social and psychological tasks of parenting. When parents have work that is satisfying and adequately paid, they provide a positive role model, and their children are more likely to be motivated to learn and develop their potential. In order to make satisfying well-paid work a reality for all parents instead of being the prerogative of a small minority, we need fundamental changes in the organization of work and in our means of preparation and access to work.

As US Vice President Walter Mondale once observed, 'Family experts agree that if we want to place unbearable pressure on families, the most successful way to do it is to make sure that their breadwinners are unemployed.'‡

Lifting Economic Pressures on Families

'We subsidize farmers, railroads, shipbuilders, airlines and oil companies, provide grants for professors to do research, and permit investment tax credits for business . . . there seem to be few qualms about helping the affluent', observes the 1976 report of the US National Council of Family Relations, which recommended a national system of income maintenance for families.

Even with the best of employment markets there are situations when parents cannot work outside the home and they and their children still need support; for

---

*The Head Start programme in the US was designed for compensatory education of poor children to prevent learning problems which were attributed to a lack of the kind of pre-school experiences believed to stimulate interest in education.

†Report to the Office of Child Development of the US Department of Health, Education and Welfare, quoted in 'Who Cares for America's Children?' (lecture by Bronfenbrenner cited above), pp. 16–17.

‡US Senator Walter Mondale, 'Government Policy, Stress and the Family', *Journal of Home Economics*, November 1976, pp. 11–15.

example, there are parents who cannot work because of a disability, who cannot find adequate child care, or who prefer to be at home with a pre-school child or a sick family member.

Ironically, the closest thing in America to a child subsidy is foster-care payments. In many states, payment for foster care of children is already higher than welfare aid would be to the child's own family if the child stayed in her/his own family. This is particularly ironic because it is frequently the stresses of economic adversity that bring about conditions of abuse or neglect that cause children to be put into foster care, yet no provision is made to aid the family of origin.

The British welfare state pioneered support for parents, via the social security system and tax-free Child Benefit. These schemes may seem enviable compared with some countries, until actual figures are scrutinized.

Ruth Lister of the Child Poverty Action Group comments:

While the current child benefit ... may look impressive compared with the family allowance paid a few years ago, it does not compare well with the benefits paid by most of our EEC partners and does not even match the level of child support (in relation to average earnings) in many earlier years in this country.

Child Benefit, particularly since the abolition in 1979 of child tax allowances, is intended to place more tax-free income in the hands of parents, yet, over the past fifteen years, the burden of taxation has steadily shifted from the childless to those with children. Childless couples in 1978–9 retained 94 per cent of the tax-free income they enjoyed in 1963–4, while the share of a couple with two children had dwindled to 73 per cent. Moreover, low-paid parents pay proportionately more in tax and National Insurance than do well-paid parents.

Meanwhile, back on supplementary benefit (from which Child Benefit is deducted), the rates of payment for children consistently fall well below the sums needed to maintain them: in 1978, the weekly payment for children of 16 was £7.80 against the £14.10 that was the estimated actual cost of keeping them.* The amounts allowed by the state to foster parents are very much higher. We should like to see allowances for all our children brought up to the same standard.

The first thought that comes to people's minds when any such proposal is made is that higher allowances would encourage people to have more children when there is already concern about over-population. However, no correlation has ever been found between such subsidies (common in many countries) and the birth rate. In fact, in both France and the Soviet Union a subsidy introduced for the express purpose of encouraging women to have more children was found to be strikingly unsuccessful for this purpose.

---

*These figures were calculated by Margaret Wynn (*The Cost of Maintaining Children at Different Ages*, *Poverty Pamphlet 33*, CPAG) from family budget standards compiled in other countries. Interestingly no research is done in the UK on the actual cost of maintaining children of different ages.

Parents and the Decision-making Process

Despite the heritage of Beveridge on our left and the Tory claim to be 'the party of the family' on our right, British politicians have by no means been consistently committed to putting parents first.

In 1980 we are faced with massive cuts in public spending in areas which will hit parents hardest: health, education, social services, the benefits system. Whatever changes occur in government and policies, it seems likely that, for the next decade, we will be struggling to keep those services and entitlements we already have as much as pressing for improvements. We as parents need to let policy makers know what *our* criteria are for an economic policy that is supportive, not just as temporary relief but for continued economic security. We can act:

● at work, in our local union branch or professional body, to alert co-workers to our needs as parents, and to negotiate specific agreements in parents' interests. It is significant that progressive agreements, for example on maternity benefits, have been made where women have mobilized *within* a union. This impetus can raise men's consciousness as fathers who work; it can filter up to the national level of union activity and spread to the TUC, which is able to make reports and pass resolutions that are heard.

● in the community, by joining with others to improve and defend local services which may be threatened: the hospital, the schools, neighbourhood centres, playgrounds and nurseries.

● by participating in national organizations, such as Child Poverty Action Group, National Council for One-Parent Families, the National Children's Bureau, which research and lobby on behalf of children and parents.

● by approaching, on every issue, our elected representatives, MP or local councillor, as individual parents, or better still, as a group.

We feel that the context in which we parents choose to raise our children should be respected and encouraged by society. In Sweden, for example, the government is actively promoting recognition of the two-breadwinner family through its employment, social security and tax policies and through supporting trades unions and government commissions working toward the elimination of sexism in the work force. Why should our government, through its tax policies, for example, favour marriage, nuclear families or single-family suburban housing over other life styles? Though we say this out of an idealistic belief in freedom of choice, there is a pragmatic reason as well. We simply don't know at this time which of the new family forms will prove viable for the future, and we may even find a plurality of life styles as creative for society as a plurality of religions and cultures.

Child Care*

It is a rare mother who never looks for somewhere or someone to leave the children with on a regular basis before they reach five. Anyone who has spent even twenty-four hours looking after a couple of toddlers and tried simultaneously to do ordinary things like shop, cook or clean, will understand why. At present, more than a quarter of us with children aged under four must find such an arrangement, because we want or are forced to go out to work. It would be reasonable to expect nursery provision to be part and parcel of our welfare state, which after all makes school attendance compulsory for our over-fives. It comes as a shock to learn that there is no statutory obligation on government to provide anything of the sort.

Why Should the State Look After Our Children?

Society should help the parents of young children on the same principle that it aims to help other members when they are vulnerable, such as the sick and the old. The time when children are at their most dependent is the time when their parents are under the most strain, physical, emotional and financial. What is more, the conditions which nowadays make life more difficult, if not intolerable, for little children and their mothers have come about through the way we arrange society and not through any wish or fault of individual parents. Housing is developed where land is cheapest, not where it is convenient to shops or open space. Young families are imprisoned in high-rise blocks because they were cheap to build. Towns are planned around the fast transport of workers and goods. Settled communities are broken up as areas are redeveloped or people move to find work. Young couples can rarely depend on having relatives round the corner or long-standing neighbours down the street to provide a watchful eye and playmates for the kids or to give mothers the chance to have a break or a chat or even to work. Some of us have created informal networks, but many of us cannot or may prefer more formal child-care arrangements.

What is the National Policy on Pre-school Provision?

There is in the UK no coherent national policy on services for the under-fives. Over the last few decades any moves to increase or withdraw services have been inspired – quite openly – by political or economic crises, not, as one might expect, by any commitment to the interests of children or their parents. The changes have usually revolved around whether politicians do or do not want to include women in the work force. It's well-known that the government found the resources for day nurseries during the war, when women's labour was sought

*Much of the information on UK day care in this book comes from Martin Hughes *et al.*, op. cit. which offers a detailed examination of the nursery provision currently available, its shortcomings and the political issues involved. Recommended.

after. Similarly in the 1960s the government found enough money to provide nursery places for the children of particular women workers it wanted: ironically enough, nurses and teachers. But when women themselves take the decision to work, it is a different story: in 1974, when there were many more mothers of young children going out to work full-time than there were during the war, there were only a third the number of day nurseries available to look after their children. In the same year, mothers of all social classes throughout the country told the government what they wanted through its own official research organ, the Office of Population and Census Surveys. The women told interviewers that they wanted nursery places for 90 per cent of their over-three-year-olds and for nearly half of their even younger children. Lynda Chalker, a spokesperson for the Tories, who are now in power, has told mothers just what they can expect for the foreseeable future:

> The Tory Party has always concentrated more on the caring role of women than their industrial role ... If someone is going out to work and has taken a decision to have children as well, the financial responsibility for that child must, in toto, be theirs.*

Peggy Rothschild

Other countries have national policies on nursery provision which are not only clearly stated, but do not fluctuate with every political contingency. The government of Hungary, for example, pays mothers to stay at home to care for their children until they are three, if they so wish, whilst protecting their jobs. The allowance was introduced quite openly to help stimulate the flagging birth rate. But there is an equally explicit commitment to giving women as much choice as possible. So Hungary, with a fifth of the population of England and Wales, has twice as many nurseries to serve it. In Britain, politicians of all colours want women at home, looking after their children, alone, unless and until it suits the politicians otherwise.

*From an interview quoted by Martin Hughes *et al.*, op. cit.

How Do Mothers Manage?

Just as anti-abortion legislation has never stopped women in need from seeking out abortion, so the lack of official provision and approval has never stopped women from seeking out the child care they need. Since the turn of the century mothers have used any arrangement to mind their children that they could find, at times taking quite as great a risk as the back-street analogy suggests. Child-care provision in the UK is a jungle to which we attempt a more detailed guide in the next chapter. Three quarters of it is run commercially for profit or voluntarily by community or charitable organizations: either way the parents must pay for it. The State's contribution – the only free provision – takes the form of a scattering of council day nurseries, reserved for the most disadvantaged children, and, in some areas, places, usually part-time, in nursery schools or nursery classes for older pre-school children. It is a very small jungle, unevenly distributed: there are three and a quarter million children under the age of five in this country and a total of 650,000 places in all kinds of provision to cater for them. It is not surprising that an estimated 330,000 children must spend the day with minders who are not registered with the council as they are legally required to be, and who, whatever their aptitude, are almost certainly only doing this kind of work because it is all that is open to them. Whatever we manage to find in the way of child care, it is likely to fall short of what we want. We have little choice over what age a child can start nursery or the hours s/he attends: the vast majority of places are for three- and four-year-olds in short ($2\frac{1}{2}$-hour) sessions, and we usually have little say in how s/he spends the time there. For most parents and children the situation is bad enough; for a lone working parent and her child, it is desperate.

Campaigning for More and Better Nurseries

In 1979, with thousands of children already waiting on 'high-priority' lists for places in council nurseries, local authorities were ordered by the new Conservative government to make spending cuts which will probably mean the loss of some 12,000 nursery places. In defending the poor and scarce provision we already have, it is important not to lose sight of the provision we really want for ourselves and our children. We should demand:

- coherent national policy on and commitment to pre-school services.
- free full-time nursery places to be available to *all* our children aged 0–5.
- freedom of choice for parents over the age at which their children should start nursery and what hours they attend.
- parent involvement in the management of the nurseries they use.
- decent rates of pay, conditions and training opportunities for nursery workers.

There are several national organizations campaigning to defend and improve our nursery services and pressing for a committed national policy, but more immediate advances can be won by parents organizing together within their own communities, union branches or with nursery workers. The Children's Community Centre (20 Lawford Road, London NW5) is a full-time year-round nursery serving the local neighbourhood. It is funded by the local authority, but all decisions are made by parents and workers together. The Centre was won in 1972 by a group of women, many of them involved in the women's liberation movement, joining together to put pressure on the council. The Kingsway Nursery Centre in Holborn, London, is for working parents, but unlike other workplace nurseries, it is subsidized by several employers rather than controlled by one, and decisions are made together with parents and nursery workers. Finally the Thomas Coram Centre, also in London, which was initiated by a children's charity but is grant-aided by the local council, demonstrates the sort of local, flexible and comprehensive service that can be offered. As well as a full-time nursery to suit parents' working hours, there are extra services for the children, such as speech therapy, and for mothers, such as a launderette and mother-and-baby group.

Betsy Cole

Although it is clear that there is going to be very little public money available over the next decade, local authorities will still have a choice of priorities in spending their budgets and in what projects they recommend to central government for urban aid grants. By organizing together and by urging unions, community and voluntary groups to campaign on our behalf, parents must ensure that nursery provision gains or retains top priority. You will find addresses of some groups already campaigning for better nurseries in the list at the end of the book.

Afterword

Throughout this section we have referred to 'mothers' and 'women' more than to 'parents', and not at all to 'fathers'. This is because, however much we might wish it otherwise, the job of looking after the children, or of finding alternative arrangements, still overwhelmingly falls on mothers. If it were not so and our legislators, who are predominantly male, looked after their own children, this could have been a shorter and more cheerful section.

Care Facilities for the Over-Fives

Around 225,000 UK schoolchildren under the age of ten are left on their own for some time after school every day, and during the holidays 20 per cent of all schoolchildren fend for themselves. It's obvious that school does not magic away the need for extra child care for working parents. Some couples cope by working in shifts: the mother leaves for work as the father gets home, but this virtually abolishes any social life together and puts a great strain on relationships. If you are on your own with a child and you have a job, you must find someone else to baby-sit, and you are in no position to do this informally with swapping arrangements. Even when we don't work, we can't always be home at four on the dot and the holidays can be a headache for parents and one long yawn for the kids: older children don't want to be tied to apron-strings. Fortunately the problem is recognized. The 1944 Education Act instructs local authorities to secure 'adequate facilities for recreation' and specifically empowers them to do this by establishing or helping to establish after-school playcentres and holiday play schemes. Unfortunately many local authorities do not use these powers and it is common to see well-equipped school playgrounds standing empty while children play in dangerous streets outside the locked gates. The Act positively urges education committees to cooperate with any voluntary body – a PTA or community group, for example – taking the initiative. This should mean local authority grants for salaries and the loan of equipment and premises. It should be possible for a forceful lobby of parents to persuade an unwilling authority to take its duty, as defined in the Act, seriously, perhaps with the aid of local press, who are known to be fond of the occasional pious feature on 'latch-key kids'. Some parents, however, cannot afford to wait for the results of long-drawn-out campaigns. Single parents belonging to Gingerbread have set up their own after-school and holiday scheme in Croydon, even down to a mini-bus to pick up the children, and have largely financed it with a grant solicited from an EEC fund. But it is a scandal that some parents have to go to these lengths and other parents must live on their nerves, knowing the children are on their own, when sufficient legislation for out-of-school care exists, waiting to be used.

Parents and Schools

Parents want to feel good about the schools their children attend. We want our children to have a good educational experience, and we want to be able to go about our lives knowing that they are in a good place where they are being educated and treated respectfully and caringly.

Yet we have less control over our children's schooling than we'd like. Schooling is compulsory and so parents have limited choices about when and where to send our children. Only a minority of parents want to or can afford alternatives to state education. Most of us feel a commitment to the state schools but are often frustrated in our efforts to be involved or to change anything about them. How much we are allowed to be involved and put suggestions depends on the discretion of individual headteachers and their staff and, beyond them, the school governors and local education committee, who may be barely accessible, much less amenable, to parent consultation. The recent Taylor Report, *A New Partnership for our Schools*, which was sponsored by the Department of Education and Science, argues for more direct control of individual schools by parents and local people intimately connected with them. 'Every school is a special place, the school around somebody's corner', and Taylor recommends that each school should have a managing body responsible for running it which would be composed of four equally represented groups: the local education authority, the staff, the parents (and the pupils where possible), and members of the local community. The National Confederation of Parent Teacher Associations is delighted by the Report: for the first time parents would have a real voice in deciding what goes on in their children's schools. But the teachers' reaction has been hostile, fearing that such a way of running schools would somehow threaten their professional status. Fred Jarvis of the NUT went so far as to call the Report 'a busybodies' charter'. Politicians are currently considering the Taylor Report; if they accept its recommendations, schools could become not only less mysterious to parents but also a resource for the whole community.

If parents and concerned local people shared the responsibility for their local school we might begin to iron out the unjust differentials that undoubtedly exist between schools, at primary and at secondary level: everyone knows which are the 'better' schools in their area. Some of the differences stem from variables such as a head's particular philosophy, but others stem from things which should not be variable, such as the conditions and standards of equipment with which teachers and pupils are expected to work. These differentials may depend on the shape of local politics as much as on the relative wealth or poverty of an area. A richer local authority does not necessarily spend more on education. Our education is paid for out of the rates with additional grants from the Department of the Environment which bring the money available in poorer areas up to a national average – although the richer areas still stay better off. The local authority then has considerable discretion in allocating the grant; money negotiated on the basis of education estimates can be used for other needy services, such as housing or the social services, without legal sanction. Once its budget is allocated, the Education Committee has some choice on how it is spent. All these decisions are political; how much money is available for education services, and where exactly it goes, depends on the priorities and political colour of the controlling party on the local council and its committees. For example, one piece of research revealed that Barrow-in-Furness, with the lowest resources in the country, was spending more per head on its secondary school pupils than Eastbourne with three times as much money available.* By lobbying sympathetic councillors, or writing to the local press, it is possible for parents to make their demands heard, and sometimes even met, whether they be for better school meals, laboratory facilities or after-school programmes.

But even if our children's school is adequately funded, we as parents may not feel happy about their education. We may find that the values of the school are in conflict with our personal or family values. Though in our complex and varied society there is understandably a great diversity of values, the schools by and large tend to adhere to a traditional value system. Different parents will come into conflict with the schools over different issues ranging from modes of education (e.g., open classroom versus 'three Rs'); content of curriculum; attitudes toward authority within and outside the school; disclosure of personal information in the classroom; views expressed by teachers or in textbooks about racial minorities; life-style minorities; sexism; social-class differences – the list is endless. As a wider spectrum of values and life styles gains acceptance in our society, an increasing number of parents feel they are entitled to have their values recognized in the schools. How are parents doing this? Several parents we know brought books to the teacher's attention about single-parent families because the schoolbooks all featured nuclear families; another mother made a collage about women and work for her younger child's class and discussed women's history with her older child's class. These are small but good ways in which individual parents have participated.

We sometimes get the chance to get in on our children's education because teachers need our cooperation. Parents can learn a lot about children's lives at school by spending time there and helping out. But many of us want more control over our participation. Taking part in decision-making about our

---

*Quoted in Judith Stone and Felicity Taylor, *The Parents' Schoolbook* (London: Penguin, 1976), an excellent guide to the educational system in the UK.

children's education may bring us into conflict with teachers and officials who are jealous of their prerogatives as professionals. Generally, having an effect at this level means that parents have to get together as a group to make their wishes known and to have an impact on the educational system.

There are barriers to participation even at the level of contributing our time or suggesting materials, and one of these is the limits on our own time, as the following conversation indicates:

Elaine: I'd love to go on a class trip or help out in the classroom for an hour, but I can't. Most of the teachers are working parents, so they should understand. But they are upset because there are few parents around who have time to help in the ways that parents have traditionally helped out teachers. That creates tensions between parents and teachers – and between parents and kids, too. Your kid comes home with a note that says 'We need parents for our trip to the zoo', and they think it would be terrific if their parent could be the one to come. Sometimes they get the idea from the teacher that the parents who can come are the 'best' parents – the ones who 'really care'. Teachers should know that a lot of parents are working and need support for working.

Jennifer: The way I handle this problem for myself is by letting my kids' teachers know at the beginning of the school year what kinds of things I am willing to help out with, what my interests are, and what my time limitations are. I don't want them to assume that I can't do anything because I work, but obviously I can't do everything, either. And with advance notice of class trips, plays and projects I can be a lot more involved.

Another barrier to our participation in our children's school may be our discomfort at being there. The powerlessness we ourselves experienced as children in school can resurface and combine with our feelings of lack of control on behalf of our kids. We may not feel quite as grown-up as we do in other settings. Robbie, a mother who organized a parents' group within her son's school, speaks of this feeling:

We had to support one another to overcome the feelings that the school brought up in us. When you go into a school all your old socialization comes back. You start to feel, Can I walk here? Can we talk here? Can I get up and change my seat? And some teachers and principals have an uncanny knack of intuiting when a parent is feeling that way and just reinforcing it. When we talked about that in our group and laughed about it, that helped us the next time we had that experience to remember that we were adults and we didn't have to feel so powerless.

As this parent's experience shows, we can defuse our old childhood feelings of powerlessness and have more influence in our children's school if we get together with other parents. Yet we must not overlook the fact that part of our feeling of powerlessness stems from the very real power that the schools have over our children's present and future lives. Mary Howell describes the source of this power and her own reaction to it as a parent:

*Many parents (myself included) are anguished at a school report that focuses on a child's inadequacies and poor performance. There is a chilling awareness that recorded information has set a course for the child that may be inalterable. I know of few situations in which I personally feel so powerless in relation to another person as when I hear a teacher's report about one of my own children.**

Despite the many barriers, persistent parents working together have been able to make changes in schools. Robbie describes the success of the parents' group she was in in America:

I started a parents' group because I was insulted by the lack of a PTA in the school. It's a parent's right. After all, it's our kid . . . and we are the ones who know what they need and what they deserve.

I got started on this school issue when my son was throwing up in school. Now, this is something you don't want to tell anyone because it means that your child is neurotic and that you are a bad parent. But I found out that other kids were throwing up after lunch, too. It turned out that they had only fifteen minutes to eat their lunch and they weren't allowed to eat until everyone was quiet. Then they just had to gobble everything down really fast. So that was how our parents' group got together, around the lunch issue. You have to start with something like that because all the parents can relate to it. If you start out with some educational theory, not everyone will care about it or understand it.

There were so many different cultures in our neighbourhood, and because of that, so many different feelings about discipline, about structure or looseness in schools. We had to respect every parent's point of view – even if a parent said 'I want the teachers to beat the shit out of my kids if they don't behave', we had to believe that if a parent said that it was out of concern for her kids.

We learned a lot from each other. The black parents seemed to have more of an ingrained sense of their rights. The white parents had more political savvy and more clout. Some of us knew about organizing people. Others of us knew about education.

The main thing I learned was that you can't go to parents who have no choice about using the public [state] schools and say 'The schools here are rotten', because it just makes them feel like bad parents.

Eventually, as our kids moved up through the grades, our parents' group succeeded in winning alternative classes and, later, an alternative public school.

In Britain, the 1944 Education Act makes it more difficult to set up alternative schools or classes within schools, with or without funding from the local education authority (LEA). However, committed teachers and concerned parents have succeeded in setting up a number of free schools, sometimes with help from the LEA. In fact, section 56 of the Act, which empowers authorities to educate children 'otherwise than at school', could theoretically be used by an enlightened Education Committee to provide a variety of experimental facilities.

*Howell, *Helping Ourselves*, pp. 151–2.

A list of existing free schools is available from the Children's Rights Workshop, and White Lion Free School has copies of *How to set up a Free School – a Handbook of Alternative Education*, which explains what is involved, legally and practically (addresses in the list at the end of the book).

Some parent school-activists we spoke with felt that alternative classes and alternative schools separate the children of activists from other children and thereby abandon the rest of the community to inferior education; but other parents believe that alternative classes and schools can serve as models in pushing the system as a whole toward recognition of innovative ideas and methods, more democratic student-teacher relationships and greater opportunities for parent participation. The creation of an alternative is frequently less threatening to entrenched interests than attempts to overhaul existing schools, and may therefore be brought into being more rapidly. There is extra pressure on us as we try to work for change in schools because we want the changes to happen *now*, while our children are there.

Television

Television has become a major factor in the lives of parents and children – as recreation, as an aid in education and child care or, frequently, mainly as a bone of contention.

In the UK, 10 per cent of four-year-olds watch more than four hours a day, though they often watch schools programmes.* About 30 per cent of 7–10-year-olds watch up to twenty-one hours a week, and 27 per cent of 11–14-year-olds watch up to twenty-eight hours a week. About 10 per cent of 11–14-year-olds do their homework while watching television.[†]

Many a parent has despaired over the quality of what their kids are watching. In the USA a group of parents formed Action for Children's Television (ACT), a consumer activist group working toward improving the quality of children's television. In addition to tackling the TV industry, they believe it's also important to educate parents. Peggy Charren of ACT says:

We feel it's unrealistic and unhelpful to tell parents, as some books and articles do, 'Give away your television set because it's all bad; it's all destructive.' Instead, we want to suggest things that parents can do with the child to affect the television experience: limit hours of TV watching; select shows in advance, and encourage school-age children to select their own programmes, subject to the limitation of hours; watch some shows with your child, especially ones you object to – the most violent ones, the ones that are filled with stereotypes – and keep up a dialogue with your child about the images and values being projected and what you feel and believe about them.

*Guardian, 3 July 1979.

[†]*Children and Television*, a national survey among 7–17-year-olds, PYE Research, January-February 1978.

We think that parent intervention and comment makes a tremendous difference. In fact, research shows that the parent who intervenes with the child and the set has a tremendous effect on what the child internalizes from television. With violent programming, for example, when the parents say 'That's no way to behave' or 'Why would he draw the gun on somebody – why don't they just talk?' that kind of comment, annoying to the child as it might be, makes a tremendous difference. It probably doesn't have to happen every time your child sits down in front of the set. But whenever it does happen, it's very important.

In the UK there is also a Television Action Group, but its aims are very different from those of ACT. Television Action Group* was set up by Faith Hall, a speech therapist, and aims to point out the dangers of the medium *per se*, regardless of content. In her opinion, the mere act of watching television is injurious to healthy development. The success of the National Viewers' Association started by Mary Whitehouse also shows that it is possible to start a very vocal lobby about television. You may not agree with the views and aims of the above groups – why not consider starting one yourself?

Society's Influence on Family Health

All of us parents naturally want to protect and enhance our own and our children's health. Yet there are many powerful social and environmental influences affecting our health that are not within our control. We live in a society that has failed to take responsibility for caring for either its people or its environment. Protecting our children's health and our own becomes merely a holding action against enormous social and environmental forces that seem to be arrayed in opposition. What can we mean by health in a society that has allowed the poisoning of our rivers, streams, oceans, even the air we breathe and our food supply? The World Health Organization has estimated that some 85 to 95 per cent of cancers are environmentally caused, which is but one example of the link between environmental pollution and the health of individuals.

Health and Safety Regulation

Many people think that parents have an easier job caring for children today because of the many technological aids and conveniences we have. Yet the hazards that go along with urbanization and technology may outweigh the advantages. The family car is a boon to its owners but a threat to the health and safety of us all. A convenient electric fire can guard the baby against hypothermia, but we have to be ever watchful that the toddler doesn't electrocute herself. We are ultimately responsible for the protection of our own children, but we can only carry out that responsibility if there is adequate regulation of everyday health and safety hazards such as household appliances,

*Television Action Group, School House, Brookthorpe, Gloucester; send 3p and a s.a.e. for a leaflet.

medicines, traffic and food additives. For example, the accidental poisoning of children has decreased dramatically since the introduction of child-proof caps on medicine containers.

We might assume that we have enough watch-dog bodies to innovate safety measures and to check new developments for hazards. But industries are run for profit, and research and safety measures tend to reduce profit. A big business can form a powerful lobby to oppose outside controls in favour of voluntary controls, and to influence the form of any controls which are imposed by government. Our Ministry of Agriculture is responsible for the safety of our food, but 'there is a close relationship between the food processing firms and the government regulatory agencies ... In public, the companies hide behind government regulations, while in private they exert considerable influence in forming these regulations.'*

The business interests that put pressure on official agencies become all the more worrying as they expand and become more monopolistic. Increasingly huge corporations are taking over the farming as well as the processing of our food, so that the same people who are responsible for altering and adding to food in the factory are responsible for what goes into our vegetables and meat while they are still growing in the fields. In any case it is hard to have total confidence in the agents of a government which must collude in the building of 'butter mountains' or the deliberate destruction of tons of crops in order to keep prices up, and at the same time draws vast revenues from the sale of that well-known health hazard tobacco.

If more ordinary consumers, parents, were involved in decisions on health and safety regulations, or if more of the policy makers were intimately involved in domestic life and looking after children, we might have more confidence in legal safeguards and controls. We need to recognize that our interests are not being represented. We need parent and consumer representation in every regulatory agency, both national and local, that deals with the health and safety of families. Recognizing our lack of representation is an important step toward regaining control of the decision-making processes that affect family health.

Family-based Health Care

Most central to keeping ourselves and our families healthy are the preventive aspects of health care – the good health habits we practise within our own homes that we can carry out on our own without turning to medical professionals and institutions. Though we have more control over our own health practices, such as diet, exercise and sleep, than we have over the institutionalized aspects of our medical care, even here there are major environmental and social limitations we must struggle with.

---

*Food and Profit, Politics of Health Pamphlet 1, British Society for Social Responsibility in Science.

Food has many important symbolic meanings along with its central importance in maintaining life and preserving health. Our first memories are tied to
eating, and for many of us certain foods have the power to evoke feelings of
security. Therefore, it is really unfair to allow, much less encourage, the
distribution of questionable food to children who are too young to make a
reasoned judgement about what they do or do not want to risk ingesting into
their bodies. Food, especially snack food marketed primarily for children, should
be quality-controlled for purity, nutritive value and wholesomeness as well as
taste and general appeal. Kids have less experience and knowledge with which to
deal with deceptive advertising and social pressure. It is natural for us, as parents,
to want to protect them from threats to their health. We want to spare them the
pain of being overweight, of being harmed by chemical additives, of having acne
or bad teeth, but we are limited by a society which allows false and misleading
advertising to be directed even to children, which actively promotes unhealthy
food over wholesome food. Often even in schools and health care institutions,
vending machines offer only soft drinks and sweets! Inexpensive food available
away from home is often fatty meats like hot dogs and hamburgers – vegetables
and grains are about as scarce as caviar and truffles in your typical fast-food
restaurant.

In trying to change our own and our kids' food habits, we come up against a lot
of issues. For example, how 'different' do we want to make our kids feel? Most of
us have had to figure out some kind of compromise with ourselves about food and
it would be foolish to think that we can do a lot better with our kids. Are we as
adults willing to cut down on alcohol or give up smoking? The social pressures on
our kids to bring crisps and sweets to school may be equally great.

In addition to our worries about junk food and whether our kids are getting a
balanced diet, many of us are concerned about dangerous chemicals and
additives in our food supply. We are frightened by reports of carcinogens in
common foods, but we are reluctant to frighten our children because we don't
really know. We don't want to have to agonize over the chemical or caloric
content of every morsel that we or our children eat. Here are two parents
discussing their experiences of teaching their children about food additives:

*Naomi: My daughter wrote a report for school on additives in food. She also makes a
point of not eating hot dogs and packaged desserts. But one day she asked me plaintively
'Mom, what can we eat? Almost everything's got something bad in it.'*

*Matilde: I stopped buying red-dyed fruit juice and told my kids why. One day we were
at a friend's house and she served it. The kids were questioning whether they should
drink it, and I told them 'Once in a while is O.K.' Later on, though, Nina, my youngest,
kept complaining that she thought she had a stomach ache and I knew she was nervous
about having had the juice, so I really felt bad. How can you warn kids about stuff like
that without frightening them unduly?*

We need to offer alternatives to fill in for the foods we are discouraging our kids
from eating. And finally, we need to be sure our children understand *why* we feel

the way we do about certain foods and how we feel about certain kinds of advertising while giving them space to learn to decide for themselves.

Food can indeed be an emotion-laden issue, especially if one parent has the major responsibility for preparing it. Children, quite naturally, want to be able to decide what they eat. Yet if we have spent time preparing a meal, their refusing to eat it can feel like a personal rejection. In families where the work of meal preparation is shared, the emotional loading of this issue can be defused – especially once children are recruited into the choosing of menus, helping with and eventually cooking meals themselves.

Time and money are two objective limits in preparing family meals. In the UK, medical research suggests that the amount of money from supplementary benefit is not enough to feed children adequately. Yet, in 1977, 1.1 million children were being raised on SB, and a further half a million children were living in families whose incomes were less than that provided by SB.*

In families where there is enough money to buy the food, time can still be a big problem. Now that the majority of mothers work, the traditional women's magazines are full of articles suggesting how women can cook at weekends, in advance and so on, but the fact is there is just less time for mothers to cook. In families where the father and others take on part of the cooking, there is also a net gain of another imagination and another repertoire of menus.

Exercise is another important way for parents to spend time together with children, and one that is equally crucial for family health. Yet many communities lack even the simplest and least costly of recreational facilities and activities. Frequently such amenities as do exist fail to meet the needs of parents and children. For example, activities for parents, any adult activity, should offer child care for those who need it. Parents of infants and young children often miss out on opportunities to exercise because of lack of child care or baby-sitting at recreational facilities. While such parents get a lot of exercise carrying infants and chasing after toddlers, it is not the invigorating renewing exercise that tennis or swimming might be. Working parents are, of course, even more limited by time restrictions. As our kids get older we gain opportunities to exercise more when we make time to be involved in athletic or recreational activities with them, but eventually, as kids spend more time with friends we must once again make a point of setting time aside for exercise just for ourselves or with other adults.

Another need of families is for recreational activities for parents and children to participate in together. Often activities are geared to adults only or children only, but parents and children frequently enjoy participating together in low-key non-competitive community sports activities. For parents who have been working at a sedentary job all day, for children who have been in day care or school all day, such activities can occasionally be a nice way to let off steam and spend time together.

*Fact of Life sheet, Child Poverty Action Group (CPAG).

Since there are many ways to exercise without the use of expensive equipment, parents can come up with creative solutions among themselves, as these parents did:

Sam: Our pool used to not admit children under five, so those of us with young kids pushed to get the policy changed. Now we have several parents-and-toddlers sessions.

Liz: We are part of a group of three or four families who have picnic suppers together every other week or so, followed by a soccer or ball game. Everyone plays, even the youngest kids – and no one gets too serious about it. We don't get that much exercise here in the winter though because it gets dark so early and the gym is mostly being used by the high school.

Debby: My friends and I started a basketball team for women one night a week at the school. Those of us who have small children bring our kids and let them play on the climbing apparatus at the other end of the gym.

In areas in the UK where recreational facilities are few, they tend to be geared towards more traditional competitive team sports and dominated by the more ambitious local teams or schools, so that the exercise needs of adults and less athletically talented children are neglected. But local authorities are statutorily obliged to provide adequate facilities for recreation and 'social and physical training'. Local councillors should be reminded of this duty and encouraged to spend their budget more imaginatively than on the usual football pitches, and to open up their school gyms to more of the community. The National Sports Council had £15½ million to allocate in 1979 and while most of this money goes directly to local authorities, there is nothing to stop a small community group from applying for a share for particular projects.

Back in the schools, we should ensure that our children aren't discouraged from developing skills or barred from activities because of sexism. There are laws to back us up: the Department of Education and Science instructs local authorities to spend equally on sports that are traditionally for boys and those that are traditionally for girls, while the Sex Discrimination Act states that *all* sports facilities should be equally available to both sexes. Parents should be able to agree these principles with the school, although it may be more difficult to change the sexist attitudes of, say, the football coach or of the children themselves. Some schools are beginning to include more adventurous activities, such as rock-climbing, which are not only less inherently sex-divided and competitive than the traditional team sports, but are much more likely to develop as an interest that will continue to give enjoyment and exercise in adult life. We should like to see all school sports curricula developing in this direction.

Parents and the Health Care System

De-medicalizing Parenting

Often we call upon the services of the health care system when what we really want is information or support. Today professionals are more numerous and invested with greater legitimacy than in the past because their pronouncements, whether based on fact or opinion, have been endowed with the aura of science. Furthermore, many parents and children today live in isolated families where they are separated from the accumulated wisdom of other parents. This, too, deepens our dependence on experts. As one critic of the health system put it, much of the lore that was formerly passed down from woman to woman in families has been packaged by professionals and sold back to women.*

The 'medicalization of the first year of childrearing' is a concept propounded by Norma Swenson, a member of our collective whose years of experience in the childbirth movement have convinced her that the passive role thrust upon women in medically controlled childbirth has, as one implicit function, the teaching of women to be similarly dependent on doctors in their parenting. In her words:

> In other cultures, birth is just part of a woman's life in the community. In this country birth is placed in this strange medical world of the hospital and the male physician. This damages the confidence of women as individuals and as parents, gives us the notion that we're not capable of taking care of our own bodies and that body function is a deep and mysterious thing. So of course it carries over to caring for our babies.

How can we, mothers, fathers and even children, feel more capable of making judgements and taking charge of our day-to-day health care? We can learn and do a lot more if professionals will share their information. And we ourselves can learn some of the ways to take care of ourselves that have only recently been turned over to doctors.

Children can be taught in school to take their own temperature, care for scratches and cuts, to know what nutrients their bodies need, to carry out simple tests, such as those for TB, diabetes and high blood pressure. We all can learn to poison-proof spaces used by younger children. For adults, more free classes in family health and first aid could be given at neighbourhood centres or in schools or health institutions. We can also consult a few of the excellent books available on medical self-help and on pharmaceuticals (see the book list below).

Alternative Medicine

Monopoly of knowledge is a mainstay of the power of the medical profession, yet there are bodies of theory and traditions of practice of which most Western doctors are ignorant. Alternative therapies include acupuncture, homoeopathy,

*John McKnight, in Ivan Illich *et al.*, *Disabling Professions* (London: Marion Boyars, 1978).

naturopathy, osteopathy and herbalism, none of which are available on the NHS, apart from homoeopathy, which has enjoyed royal patronage. It is important to remember that the reason why our doctors do not offer these therapies is not that they don't work, but that they have never been taught how to use them. It is interesting to note that most of the drugs in the British Pharmacopoeia (BP) are synthetic versions of naturally found substances. The 'unorthodox' herbalist uses the originals. Some patients come to alternative medicine as a last resort when orthodox medicine has failed to help; many are vociferously pleased with the result. Such is the authority of the medical profession in our own minds, however, that we tend to think of such treatments as 'cranky' and are nervous of soliciting them for our children. While we would want to read more or discuss further with other knowledgeable people, we would not want automatically to dismiss treatment just because it is an alternative to mainstream medicine. Most branches of alternative medicine have professional bodies of whom you can make inquiries. You will find addresses in the reference sections of *OurBodies, Ourselves*.

The National Health Service

The National Health Service in Britain was founded to provide the best possible medical treatment for all, regardless of wealth and social class. It was introduced, however, with the hindrance rather than help of sections of a medical profession that was strictly hierarchical, upper-middle-class and profit-oriented. The change from totally private medicine was enormous, but the health service is still shot through with inequalities. Health workers are still grouped in a rigid hierarchy, dominated by male consultants drawn largely from the upper classes, and medicine, more than any other profession, is imbued with a jealously guarded and enormously powerful mystique. Because of the continuing coexistence of private medicine, doctors are attracted to the more privately lucrative specialisms, such as gynaecology, at the expense of others, such as orthopaedics. GPs want to live and work in pleasant surroundings, so industrial areas – where more illness occurs – are under-supplied. Spending on hospitals varies from region to region by as much as 50 per cent from the national average. Cuts in the services (when they are explained at all) are defended in terms of 'cost-effectiveness', a principle quite contrary to the intentions of the architects of the NHS.

It is not appropriate here to give a fuller history and critique of the health services (but see Chapter 17 of *Our Bodies, Ourselves*). It *is* appropriate to have a critical understanding of where our doctors and services come from. Parenthood is one of the periods of our lives when we come most into contact with the medical services; indeed it may be the first time in our adulthood that we are in real need of them. For those of us who have been lulled by the image of the NHS as 'the envy of the world' and for whom doctors have replaced the clergy as

founts of wisdom and comfort, it will come as a shock to realize that we may be
denied facilities freely available to friends in other parts of the country, or that our
GP doesn't appear to have heard a word that we've said. As parents we may be
lucky in finding good facilities and considerate staff, or we may have to make a
fuss and insist to get our children the care they need.

Doctor and Patient Relationships

What happens to us when we try on an individual level to get health
professionals to treat us respectfully and share the information we need in a form
we can understand? Betsy reports the condescending attitude she encountered
during antenatal visits.

*I had made a list of my questions beforehand. So, when the doctor asked 'Do you have
any questions?', I said 'I certainly do.' But when I pulled out my little list I could see that
he was affronted by it, even though I tried to be as nice as I could. I said 'I made this list
only because these questions leave my mind unless I write them down.' But I could tell
he was still annoyed. What he seemed to be saying was 'You'd better behave, you'd
better not ask too many questions, and do what I am telling you, and I know better than
you do, so there!'*

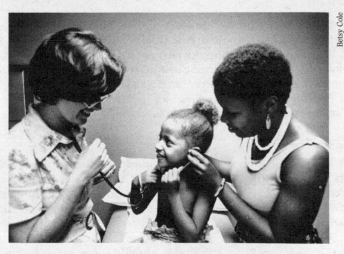

Betsy Cole

The authority and power that a doctor has in this society, and especially within a
health institution or within her/his own surgery dealing with a patient, can seem
overwhelming. Often when we are dealing with doctors we are vulnerable not
only because of illness or fear but because of our physical position while we are
being examined – lying down on a table. When, as parents, we must deal with
health professionals on behalf of our children, the feelings of vulnerability may be
heightened, as Tina reports:

It was hard to get the surgeon to answer all of my questions and I was afraid to push as hard as I usually do because I was feeling very keenly that my child's life was in his hands. At the same time I knew that if he couldn't be responsive to our concerns, then he wasn't the right doctor to be caring for Mark.

At times we may have to back up the actions of medical staff whose attitudes to children are very different from our own – and then have feelings of betrayal, our own and the child's reproaches, to deal with. An English mother of a much hospitalized seven-year-old describes such an incident:

When I arrived on the ward, a doctor had been trying for ages to persuade Sophie to accept an injection which she knew from experience to be particularly unpleasant. Instead of reminding her that it was necessary to show up her kidneys on X-ray, he kept insisting, untruthfully, that 'it won't hurt a bit'. Sophie, losing all patience, yelled at him 'All right, then, if it's so wonderful let's see you have the injection!' The doctor retired, hurt. Sophie received the injection and X-ray some hours later, having been tranquillized by a shot of Valium, administered with brute force, but still fighting. She has to have a lot of treatment and will cooperate if approached kindly and honestly. It's horrible to watch the technically excellent treatment your child urgently needs given in such an untherapeutic way, and to feel helpless to change the entrenched attitudes behind it all.

Not only must we handle our fears and anxieties for ourselves and our children, we may have to acquire new skills in assertiveness – skills in dealing with institutions and authorities – which our society has not taught us. These anecdotes describe the more extreme and stereotyped attitudes you are likely to encounter, but it's as well to be prepared for them. C. and G. Stimson's *Health Rights Handbook* (London: Prism Press, 1978) is a helpful, critical guide to the NHS and its doctors and how to handle them.

General Practitioners

In the UK, your GP is responsible for the primary health care of you and your children, and for referring you to specialists and other services. A caring, reliable GP with whom you have a mutually respectful and trusting relationship will be a great ally during your child's growing up. S/he may be hard to find. There is a shortage of GPs and they are unevenly distributed: 38 per cent of the country is officially under-supplied.

Most GPs now work in group practices or health centres, so that overheads are shared and government grants may be available. These savings to the doctors should show in improved patient facilities and supplies. The system may also mean that the usual doctors share weekend and night duties, so that you should see someone you know rather than a locum. Extra staff such as district nurses or midwives may also be available at a health centre.

On the other hand, group working can mean a more impersonal service in which you see a different doctor each time. It is obviously better for a child to see the same doctor consistently, both for the child's confidence and for continuous observation of her/his development.

Choosing a GP. The Family Practitioner Committee compiles lists of local doctors, with brief details, which are available at main post offices; but friends and neighbours will have more useful opinions and advice. In the end you must use your own observation and judgement. A trial visit to the surgery is perfectly reasonable and will help you choose. Questions to bear in mind are: is there an

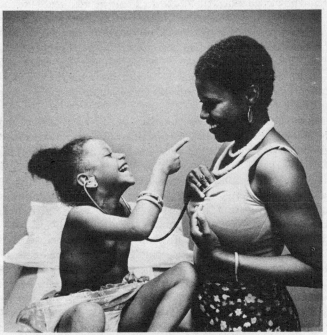

Betsy Cole

appointment system, and does it work? Are there evening surgeries (important if you have a job)? Can you see the same doctor each time? Or a different one if you choose? What are the doctor's special interests? Will s/he trust your judgement and come out on a home call if you think it necessary? Can *you* work with her/his attitudes?

Once we have children, GPs figure much larger in our lives; if possible, don't rush into choosing one and don't be afraid to change if you are unhappy with the service. It is quite easy to change doctors provided that you have found a new one that you prefer and who has agreed to take you on his/her list. The *Health Rights Handbook* and *Our Bodies, Ourselves* both give details of how to change and also offer useful suggestions on how to look critically for the service you want.

In the Hospital

Perhaps the ultimate in bending the needs of people to fit the requirements of institutions and the convenience of professionals is the modern hospital. Until fairly recently hospitals have not recognized family ties and patients' emotional needs as sufficient reason to change hospital policies and procedures. Patients, including infants and young children, have been and continue to be ruthlessly separated from their accustomed sources of emotional support and security. Parents still have to content themselves with visits, and occasionally with the comforting knowledge that some of the staff may express real human feelings towards their very young patients and will show affection towards them. Nurses and other health workers are typically so overworked, however, that frequently they can't give the quality or amount of caring that they want to give.

Many of us now insist on staying with our children at the hospital if we possibly can, because we or our friends have had experiences that show us we can't always depend on the supportiveness and comfort of staff members either for us or for our children.

James Robertson's film *A Two-Year-Old Goes to Hospital* was shown on television in Britain in 1961. This film emphasizes that 'The greatest single cause of distress for the young child in hospital is not illness or pain but separation from mother'. In a series of newspaper articles, Robertson then urged community pressure to bring about changes in the welfare of children in hospitals. A group of young mothers in Battersea took up the challenge, and formed the National Association for the Welfare of Children in Hospital (NAWCH). In the last decade, partly as a result of NAWCH's work, mothers have become more involved in the care of their children on hospital wards; most hospitals have extended visiting hours for children, and some offer sleeping-in facilities for parents, although expenditure on these does not have a high priority in hospital budgets. NAWCH groups also help parents choose hospitals where visiting is really free, and offer practical help to both parents and staff – by giving toys and clothes to the wards, organizing play schemes, speaking in the community, publishing leaflets and books. Some NAWCH groups have also set up sibling crèches; some organize child-minders to look after the other children of mothers with a child in hospital.*

In the US, a similar group, Children in Hospitals, discovered a way to politicize their efforts and make changes in hospital practices stick. Elizabeth Hormann told us:

Almost by accident we discovered a terrific tool to make change. When we would negotiate for rooming-in, or parents being present for anaesthesia, for instance, we found we had to negotiate over and over again for the same things. We thought it would be handy for parents to have a list of what hospitals have what policies, so we could just say 'If you want this or that, here is where to go.' We sent a bunch of questions to all sixty-eight of the paediatric units in the state, and even after follow-up letters hardly

*From the NAWCH pamphlet, available from 7 Exton Street, London SE1 8UE.

anybody responded to us. Then we sent a prepublication draft of the list to hospital administrators. For the ones that hadn't responded we just wrote 'No response'. After that, all came back with answers to basic questions, like visiting hours, rooming-in, specific policies for out-patients ... We noticed in doing that first questionnaire, that there were a number of policy changes made with a stroke of a pen ... After six years, we're still very fledgling, because we are seven or eight people, and we work out of kitchens, around having babies, around having kids in hospitals.

As the experiences of the women in this organization suggest, good health care for ourselves and our children is not merely a commodity that we can take for granted, but a process that can only result from the concern of involved parents and others.

Another way in which parents in Britain can work for change is to become involved in the Community Health Councils. The CHCs were set up to give the 'consumer' a voice in the health service. They have virtually no real power, but can lobby the health authority in the community's interests – if necessary with a blaze of publicity. Their role is to help individuals to bring complaints, though they do not themselves investigate; to comment on and criticize new developments, including closures; to identify priorities and to argue them with the relevant administrators. One third of the members are from voluntary organizations (half are appointed by the local authority and the rest by the Regional Health Authority), so that parents' groups, PTAs, women's groups and tenants' groups can be represented.

CHCs vary: some will merely 'rubber-stamp' decisions, others are highly critical and active. In the current climate of cuts, closures and job losses, the CHCs' voice could be crucial.

The unprecedented proliferation of baby and child-care books and the emergence of parent education courses over the last few years attest to the needs, anxieties and isolation of parents, but it is also testimony to our growing consciousness that we *can* find ways to help ourselves and one another. The experience of the parents we spoke with clearly points to the possibility and the effectiveness of parents getting together for support and to change institutions that undermine our beliefs and feelings as parents.

To accomplish this, we need to break through our individualistic notions of the self-sufficient nuclear family and work toward building a more parently consciousness in society based on our belief that we can be helpful to one another and to one another's children. If we educate professionals to be responsive to parents, we can get special kinds of help and support from them, but we must also insist on building connections with other parents in our schools, our communities, our health institutions, our workplaces. Whether we choose to work within or outside of institutions, we must build our networks with the needs of our children *and* ourselves in mind. When institutions can be made to serve parents and children, the whole society is strengthened.

9. Helping Ourselves and Finding Help

Jane Kates Pincus and Peggy Nelson Wegman,
with UK material by Michèle Cohen and Tina Reid

There comes a time when, after a brief period of preparation – pregnancy, waiting for adoption arrangements to be concluded, getting to know our future stepchildren – we become parents. Though we are parents in fact, it will take weeks, months and even years to become parents in our thoughts, feelings and abilities. Very often we will need help for both ourselves and our children.

Our needing help comes from the simple fact that *being parents is hard work and nobody is born knowing how to do it.* We want information, encouragement and companionship. There are certain skills we'll want to develop. Sometimes we need professional advice. If we're always feeling low, if our baby wakes constantly during the night, if our ten-year-old gets stomach aches every day before school, if our daughter runs away from home, it is absolutely natural for us to need and to seek help.

Yet often we don't even think to ask for help. We don't feel natural asking. We have been brought up to believe that what happens in our home is a private matter. Rarely in our families or schools do we learn how to ask for help. Often we judge our problems to be too trivial: our crisis-oriented helping systems – medical, psychological, social service agencies – don't have the time, interest or means to reach out to us in our daily lives. So we keep our problems to ourselves and isolate ourselves, not realizing that other parents are in the same predicament.

In this chapter we want to encourage each other to step out of our private worlds, to reach out to other people, especially when our lives are relatively calm, for it's then that we have more time and energy. Everywhere, in cities, suburbs and rural towns, resources for help exist, to be discovered, explored and, in the case of established institutions, changed if necessary to meet our needs. Sometimes we will have to create our own organizations.

Informal resources consist of the community of parents around us, men and women whom we meet at our workplaces, the market, laundromat, post office and library, at child welfare clinics, parties, church and club meetings and at women's centres. Living in the same area, other parents' questions parallel our own, their answers and solutions may be helpful to us, their experiences could be ours.

How do we ask others for help? By talking to that woman in the park who we've noticed and like instinctively; calling a single father we know; asking our downstairs neighbours to stay with our children an hour and finding out how we can be helpful to them; bringing up a worry at work; putting up a notice on a board: 'Would be interested in joining with other parents to discuss being parents – our problems, solutions, etc.'

With a family member, a friend, two friends or a group we can create small or large mutual 'networks' of help. The advantages of such networks are many: we talk over day-to-day parenting situations and resolve them, perhaps in an instant of clarity, perhaps over time. Knowing about each other's home lives, we teach each other to prevent crises by defusing tense situations. We draw out unexplored strengths in each other. Together we create *preventive* care and caring for ourselves. We can form baby-sitting pools, play groups, youth clubs or centres in which parents can meet.

If problems become too much for us and our friends to handle, we can help each other to recognize the kind of difficulty and direct each other to existing formal resources – therapists, doctors, hospitals, social service agencies, special-problems organizations. We can evaluate and use these many and valuable resources much more effectively together than if we deal with them alone in moments of tension and crisis.

It would be wonderful if, when in need, we could simply ask a friend, relative or group for help, and as simply, receive. It happens:

I phoned Amanda: 'Take my child! Calm him down! We're fighting again! Help!' Ten minutes later she's at my door, pulls John into her car (he seems relieved to be 'rescued'). At dinnertime he came home. We kind of looked at each other. Then we laughed and laughed and talked about our fight and how great Amanda is.

But the issues involved in helping each other and getting help are usually more complicated. The purpose of this chapter is to combine our vision and awareness of what effective help can be with a description of some of the dynamics and difficulties of asking for help. Learning to ask for help, perhaps one of the most important skills we can develop as parents, enables us to lean on each other, to use each other as sounding-boards. The informal resources we then create (pp. 370–78) may be sufficient to meet our needs. Or we may find formal resources (pp. 384–431) necessary and more effective.

Asking for Help

A first step in asking for help is *naming or identifying our problems*, standing back from our situation. One woman remembers when her children were young:

The three of us would spend the day crowded in one room. I'd yell at Hank when he came home each night and be really bitchy. I resented his freedom to come and go, and craved more of his attention for myself and my children. Looking back at myself then, I see a typical isolated young mother, cranky, hysterical sometimes, just drifting along, lonely, not even knowing I was depressed. I wish I'd had a wise friend to pop in with a loving, knowing grin and say: 'Why, Anne, you do look beat! It's clear you need (1) help with the housework, (2) an hour to yourself, (3) a big hug, (4) someone to talk to, (5) a way for you and Hank to communicate, (6) someone to tell you that your kids are beautiful and you're doing a good job!' These days if I'm feeling awful, I can usually figure out why. In those days, I couldn't.

Sometimes just naming our problems can ease tensions and enable us to look at our lives more clearly.

Parents in particular have many kinds of needs. Caring for our children, and caring for ourselves as well, require knowledge, skill, practice and support from others. Let's name some circumstances that call for help:

New situations, tense situations. We need help in dealing with new situations, which surprise or stun us – a sister's anger and jealousy, for instance:

She came running downstairs, crying hysterically 'I'm going crazy, I'm going crazy!' I ran upstairs to see what had happened. During a game they'd been playing in the dark (about murderers!) she had got so angry at him she had begun to strangle him. It scared her, it scared him and it scared me. Something so extreme had never happened before.

Other kinds of situations come up, which can drag on and on, such as the constant demands of a child before bedtime:

Every night he wants ten things – toys, food, more stories – before he'll go to sleep. Then the next night he wants the same and more. Now he won't go to sleep unless I stay with him.

Meeting a teacher may leave us feeling that our son is the worst troublemaker in class. Our thirteen-year-old begins to shut herself in her room every afternoon.

It's vital to keep in mind that ordinary situations can feel as difficult to cope with as more acute and serious problems. There will be no clear dividing line, no bell ringing to signal the beginning of a chronic problem from what looks at first like just another episode. For instance, your child waking constantly during the night, wanting you near, might at first be just an annoyance. But as time goes on, you realize that you are getting less and less sleep, and as a matter of fact, you are so exhausted every day that you are angry at her, frustrated at not having control, anxious because you don't know why it's happening, and you're on the verge of hysteria. Something needs to be done for both of you in order to change the situation.

Most of our child-rearing experience will consist of a kind of mid-ground area that is neither minor nor drastic – the ordinary minute-to-minute, hour-to-hour process of parenting. It is in this 'everyday' area that we need the most *continuous* help as parents – companionship, advice, psychological insight – and often we don't know whom to ask, or how. Perhaps we don't feel justified in asking for help at all: after all, there's no *real* crisis, is there?

Acquiring skills. We need to learn certain *practical* skills, like feeding, bathing and clothing a baby, tending a sick child. Because our family is often an isolated unit, and many of us have not yet had much experience with children, we may need guidance to do very simple things:

I learned in Joanne's class (she's a dynamite nurse) that I'd been preparing Joey's cereal all wrong. What did I know? I'd mix the whole box up with milk and put it in a bowl in the refrigerator. Then at breakfast I'd warm up a lump in a pan. Can you believe I didn't even think of mixing up a little at a time and adding some fresh fruit for flavour? Now it seems so obvious. Joey's glad I'm getting some education.

Jim Ritscher/Stock, Boston

We must learn *emotional skills* too. We have to learn to mediate between fighting children, to help our kids when they are upset, to know when to leave them alone. Crying, whining, anger, jealousy, sexuality – all these powerful emotions we have spent decades learning to understand in ourselves reappear in our children. We may need help in monitoring our own reactions to our children, understanding and controlling them, and working out ways to change destructive situations:

When my daughter used to cry and have tantrums I would think, Cry! Life is tough and unhappy, so cry like I did! And I'd let her cry. Once I walked out on her when she was having a tantrum. I slammed the door in her face, left her alone in the house (she was two) and went to pick up the laundry, when one of my greatest fears as a child was being left alone. Then, over three years of therapy with a woman therapist, I received a nurturance I never had before. I learned to fetch my daughter away from her lonely crying, to gather her into my arms and my loving. In order to know how to nurture my child, I had to be nurtured myself.

A kind of skill especially important for parents can be called *organizational* or *managing skill.* We need to learn to use our time well, organize tasks in the home, decide who does what most efficiently and, we hope, most happily.

Health problems come up in every family – we may discover our two-year-old is having seizures or our daughter has a hearing disability; our teenager develops allergies; we ourselves have recurrent severe backaches. Each specific problem generates its own series of questions and needs: how will it affect our child's life, our lives? What kind of help do we seek? Where? How do we evaluate the help available?

Accidents happen, too, to parents and children – burns, broken limbs, car or workplace accidents – each comes as a shock, a literal break in the continuity of our lives:

Just after the twins were born, Neil fell off a ladder twenty feet high and broke his hip. He was in the hospital six weeks.

Everything must stop until we find adequate medical care for ourselves and care for our children at home. Adjustments must be made as a family gets used to a schedule which enables parents, brothers and sisters to visit the hospital or to care for a family member at home. When such sudden things happen, we are always in need of practical support – food prepared for us by friends and neighbours, child care, housework and transport – as well as emotional support, and usually professional help.

Stress. All of our needs are intensified at times of financial and emotional upheaval. Job insecurity, long working hours, pressures to keep up or to succeed and advance in our work, changing towns to follow a job, unemployment, poverty and poor health, separation and divorce – stresses generated by our society put enormous pressures on parents and children alike.

When my husband Eric lost his job with a big engineering firm, he'd be home all day, depressed, just sitting around. I was already juggling part-time work at the phone company with taking care of Nellie, my three-year-old. Bart (my older son) was having serious trouble with his schoolwork. We started to fight all the time. Eric's inertia got on all our nerves and, anyway, where were we going to get money from now? We'd always been a peaceful family, I thought we'd start cracking into pieces.

In these cases, though such stress makes it easy to *name* our needs, our tensions are not so easily resolved, caused as they are by conditions often beyond our control. And for many of us there exist different levels and layers of need, which for all sorts of reasons we are unable to plumb adequately.

I used to beat my daughter. I did. I could not admit it to myself, to anybody. Do you know, I took her twenty times in one year to the same casualty department for her complaints and injuries. This was my only way then of asking for help, my only way. It took a year of this before they realized what was happening. Finally, they directed me to Parents Anonymous.

Naming our needs is a crucial first step in asking for help. Sometimes we can do it ourselves. We can make lists; we may already know someone willing to listen.

After we can say fairly clearly why we need help, a second step is *to push past our difficulty in asking for it.* Why is asking for help so hard? It may seem too risky, too frightening. It means allowing ourselves to be vulnerable, exposing our needs to others, as one parent fears:

I'm just sure if I started to say what I need, all my needs, from more money to more living, would start pouring out like rain, like a flood, and never stop. What would you think of me then? Would you still want to be my friend? Would you still think of me as competent?

Many of us are afraid we will be judged and found wanting. The more intimate and complicated our needs, the harder it is to ask for help. If our self-image is involved, asking is especially hard. For instance, when our children have problems, we often find ourselves so identified with them that to acknowledge something is wrong with them would be the same as saying something is wrong with us. Our pride and lack of confidence prevent us from asking for help.

Some of us cannot face admitting that we are at a point where we need help; such an admission means we will have to work at changing what is wrong, and such work will be difficult. Not only *our* changing but changes in other members of our family may also be involved. It will take time and energy when we are too busy or too tired.

When I'm most in need of help, I run from those people I know can help me most, because these are the times I am really, really low, and don't have any left-over spirit at all. When I am depressed, I don't reach out.

To ask for help can be troublesome because we must step out of our accustomed roles. A nurse and mother of seven says:

I am used to helping others, caring for them. If one of my children needs help, I find it right away for them. But when it comes to my needs, I can't ask. I've thought it over and figured it out: because then I'd have to change from a helper to someone needing help. I'd have to become someone else than whom I'm used to being. I can't do it. At least, I haven't been able to do it yet.

Women as carers are not 'supposed' to ask for help. Neither are men, themselves 'supposed' to be strong, self-sufficient, self-reliant. Often we feel tremendously isolated:

When I went to visit two friends this weekend, Janet told me that she was having incredible fights with her kids. She'd feel trapped, and think none of them would get out whole and was certain that nobody else's home was wracked with such strong emotions. Upset and alone, on Saturday Don at his house told me just about the same story about his family. He, too, felt he needed help, but was ashamed and thought no one else had troubles like his!

We isolate ourselves: sometimes we believe we can cope alone with whatever comes up. When this belief derives from positive inner strength, then acting upon it increases our capability. If we feel, however, that we *should* cope by ourselves, if we are being self-punitive and feel undeserving, then we can become worn down and depressed. We may turn inward, blaming ourselves. Pressures may accumulate until a crisis occurs, some sort of explosion which shakes up our lives – an injury, an illness, an emotional breakdown, which may happen either to us or to another member of the family. We have allowed the situation to become as extreme, dramatic and visible as possible, in order to give ourselves permission to ask for help.

A third stage in asking for help is *learning to recognize whom to ask*. Often people are much too busy to help, or have too many problems of their own to deal with. Sometimes they don't respond because they cannot cope with our problem, never having had a similar event happen in their lives. Or they identify so strongly with us that they become even more upset. They might not want to get too involved: women and men who are constantly moving from one place to another learn never to put down roots, never to get deeply involved with neighbours because they have had to part so often from so many people that leave-takings become too painful. They develop a certain detachment to protect themselves.

When we ask for help, we may be surprised by the responses we receive. We might be let down by the people we most expect help from, and aided beyond our expectations by a chance acquaintance or a chance occurrence.

I broke my leg last summer. In a cast, on crutches, I knew I'd be alone with my children for four days. I needed help in carrying things and cooking. Friends I'd expected to rush to my side had other obligations. One friend came to help and brought her whole family, which flabbergasted me at first, I felt too tired to have so many people around. Yet their presence unexpectedly gave me peace. Our children played quietly together. When she watered the plants and straightened up the kitchen, I felt she was nourishing and soothing me too. After she left, over the next few days I kept phoning people. Laura, an old friend, brought dinner one night, and Henry, my neighbour, drove me to the doctor's. My kids did the laundry. When I'd originally thought of asking for help, I'd unrealistically imagined friends racing to my rescue, though it was no crisis. The reality, the actual way help presented itself, was more piecemeal, yet adequate, as it turned out.

Something else to learn about asking for help is to realize *we are involved in a continuing process*. This process we create may or may not immediately hook in to a helping system (person or people) outside of our own lives. We cannot assume that the minute we ask we'll find the help we're looking for. We might find no one, we might not get the *kind* of help we need. If after asking, we feel angry, then we have to either simply ask again, or reshape and clarify our needs before we ask again. Our persistence in asking can teach us, give us practice in asking and strengthen us. It can also be negative, disappointing and difficult. We may become desperate: an older child who is beaten by her parent and courageously asks for help might find her story not believed by anyone to whom she turns.

Asking as a process may involve a combination of moves as we alternate in turning from people we know – informal help – to professionals – formal help.

My child has a chronic blood problem. Once I took him to a doctor who diagnosed the situation as a crisis and proposed an extreme 'aggressive' treatment, which upset me immensely. I talked with my friends, and they counselled me not to do anything drastic immediately and to get another medical opinion. I did so, and found that Doctor A had not investigated all of Jamie's records and had misinterpreted the records he did have. Doctor B checked Jamie out completely, found he was doing fine, and told me to watch for signs which would signal the beginning of any more acute problem. I told my friends, to alert them, too.

As a further step, we must realize that *each of us has a different style of asking for help:* some of us ask in indirect ways, and others ask more directly:

My mother phoned to tell me she had to have an eye operation. In a light, unconcerned tone she said it was nothing serious. I asked if she wanted me to come and stay with her. 'Don't bother' was her answer. But after the operation she was furious with me and my brothers for not calling immediately to see how she was. I finally realized that she had been incredibly worried, and either she hadn't known how worried she was or she hadn't been able to say 'Help! I need you near.'

A neighbour I had never seen before came breathlessly into my house having seen my children playing outside. 'Do you know any baby-sitters?' she cried. 'I have to go to work in a few hours and my baby-sitter is sick.'

It is possible that when we ask for help as directly as possible, others will respond more quickly. In the story above, the woman offered the baby-sitting services of her eldest daughter, and the two families have become friends.

Finally, we have to ask ourselves some questions: are we able to receive and accept help when it is offered to us? How do *we* respond when people ask us for help? If we have needed or received help, we may have a difficult time noticing and responding to others' needs. If we are asked directly, we may become caught in an odd inertia and think of many reasons for not extending ourselves. If we are not asked directly but want to help out, we may fear rebuff. Yet once we make the decision to do something useful – make a meal, care for others' children, step in after work to take them where they have to go, listen to their stories, provide clothes when a house has burned down – we have freed ourselves from our own isolation and stepped into a world of shared needs, humour, caring and exchange.

During difficult times, even when we are receiving help from friends or professionals, there are moments when we feel alone. Many of us seek advice from priests, rabbis or ministers, from our spiritual teachers. Some of us are strengthened by going into a forest or to the sea, letting ourselves experience both our solitude and the amazing continuity of nature. We can be nourished by combining all kinds of help with whatever form of prayer or meditation is natural to us. We can find ways to comfort ourselves.

Informal Help

Friends, families, acquaintances, people we haven't even met yet – these are the people we can draw on and help in return. One consequence of being parents is that we become more woven into the fabric of a community, especially when we allow our needs for companionship, support and practical help to connect us to others. As a start, we want to be open, able to ask for and receive help:

Ben Achtenberg

Those first three months with Cassie, I felt shocked by the intenseness of her demands. I never left the house, it was winter and cold out. All this time there were friends wanting to help me care for this beautiful baby, but I focused only on myself and her. One day Ruth, a neighbour, came by. We went to the park. Some enormous weight eased itself in me when she'd hold Cassie and sing to her. We laughed a lot. From then on Cassie and I began to visit and have people over. It was like being underwater for a long time and then popping into sunlight.

Little by little we make connections. Our contacts take many forms: light, momentarily helpful, they can be quickly over; develop into deep lasting friendships; or remain somewhere in between:

When my daughter was little, she'd just been to the doctor and had an injection. On our way home she was whiny and feverish. I met an acquaintance on the street. He said

'Poor thing. I remember how I felt in the Army after getting those shots.' I was amazed by his quick understanding of a tiny baby's discomfort, and by the gentle way he held her. She became quiet, and fell asleep.

I met Sarah in a childbirth class twelve years ago. We found we lived four blocks from each other. Our daughters were born a month apart and became fast friends, as did Sarah and I. We had monumental ups and downs, and have remained good friends. When my son was burned she sat with me at the hospital, and she gave me support when my life and marriage were most chaotic. I stayed near her when she lost her baby. We are still encouraging each other to explore and develop our strengths.

Families

If our families live nearby and we get along with them, they can be of tremendous help in caring for our children and sharing the ongoing process of grandparent-parent-child family living. Sometimes living near our families can be complex if we want to be close to them and yet maintain our independence.

In this town there are families where three generations live in one house. Cousins, aunts and uncles live down the road. I moved here with my husband, and his parents live a few houses away. I feel mixed about their being so close: I care about them and want Cal, our son, to know them. Sometimes I leave Cal with them. But they are such hectic, noisy people, always on the edge of some crisis. Usually when I go to work at the grocery I bring Cal with me. Mrs Olsen there has fixed up a playpen in the back room, and we call her Grandma Olsen. So I have my husband's family – I know his mom would love to keep Cal with her more often – and Mrs Olsen, who seems like family too, a quieter, more restful place.

Neighbourhoods

Neighbourhoods can be strong places of support:

After Walt was born I was sick as a dog, had to stay in bed for two weeks straight. The ladies from the church cooked me meals every one of those days, and did my housework. I never ate such good food in my life.

Three of us lived in a row of apartments connected by a fire escape. Our kids would run back and forth from one place to the other. I got Kyra's breakfast for two months running. She would come over in her pyjamas in the morning. Her parents would have Nela over a lot. Sometimes the guy who lived right under me would come up and knock and say 'I can tell it's really a bad day up there – why don't you just send the kids downstairs for a few hours?'

I think neighbourhood is especially important for parents who work. Your job is not always something you enjoy one-hundred-per-cent. Then when you come home you are with your children, and that's another demanding situation. People who work need

Peter Simon

quiet and time for ourselves. It's helpful if you have a neighbourhood where your kids can go out and play and you know they are safe. We are lucky – even though there's no park, the kids play fairly safely. I really feel our children are watched by all the people who live on the street, whether they have children or not.

In our neighbourhood we are always asking each other mundane questions like 'Do you wait up for them at night? What do you do if she doesn't come home on time? What should we do about the drugs around school? Did you let him have the car? What discipline works, what doesn't work?' Some parents put you off, saying, 'She's perfect, I have no problems', and that's no help. But most often we exchange 'war' stories, and that leads into our 'What do you do when?' questions.

We do end up with a network. Other adults spend time with my children. I also like to keep my house open and we encourage kids to hang around, play ping-pong and cards downstairs. We talk when anyone feels like talking.

Workplaces

Workplaces, too, can be places where we talk about ourselves, share experiences and get support:

My mother works at an office. She's been there seven years, so have the other women. They're all in their forties and fifties. They bring lunches, share recipes and food, and talk about their children, which is one way of talking about themselves. They discuss what their kids are doing and how they feel about it. It's an enormous relief just to talk out their problems. One woman's daughter was heavily into drugs and very self-destructive. Sometimes they give each other advice, or help each other outside of work, driving someone to a doctor's appointment so she doesn't have to go alone.

Me and my girlfriend work at the checkout counter of the supermarket. I didn't know her before I worked there. When it's not busy we're always talking to each other about our lives, our kids, our families. It's good to have her there.

Working at the same place means that we experience a day-to-day continuity with other people. We come to know each other as adults, out of our family contexts. By talking together we express ourselves, get relief and companionship, and yet we don't have to ask for help explicitly.

'Structured' Informal Help

As our children grow, we can help each other in more structured ways. Particular attention/care for the mother of a newborn, play groups, baby-sitting pools, child care, centres for teenagers and adults or more general support groups are some of the forms which organized, regular help can take.

Help during the First Three Months: Symbolic Mother, or 'Doula'

Many mothers can imagine how wonderful it would be to be cared for during their first three months of motherhood. Some cultures assume that a new mother before and especially after giving birth has specific needs, and assign to her a symbolic mother, who might be her own mother but more likely is a relative or friend, usually a woman, and one who has had children. In *The Tender Gift*,* Dana Raphael gives the name Doula to this role. The Doula may prepare the birthing place, cradle the new mother's head in her lap during delivery, soothe her, bake ceremonial cakes and give her little gifts. She may brush and arrange her hair, bathe and tend to the baby, cook meals and transmit to the mother some of the information and lore of the culture. She nurtures, advises and helps with this transition into a new role.

How can modern women (and men) be Doulas for each other?

Though I felt happy as a new mother, there were a million things I didn't know. It all came to a head one day when my baby, only a few months old, was very fussy. My husband was in hospital for surgery; I was alone with the baby, worried and exhausted. I worried that I didn't have enough milk. When I called my doctor, he was brusque with me, told me to bottle-feed as well as breast-feed, said I was not adequately nourishing my baby. He said 'It is my job to make sure that this baby doesn't suffer brain damage!' I was trembling when I hung up the phone. By some miracle (my baby was crying, I could hardly think straight), I had the presence of mind to call my friend Barbara. She

*Published by Schocken, New York, 1976. See also Sheila Kitzinger, *Women as Mothers* (London: Fontana, 1978).

told me 'Your doctor is ridiculous. Look, your husband is in the hospital, you're exhausted and worried, and this often makes the milk supply decrease for a time. The baby is fine. Offer him water or juice if he gets fussy, but mostly you need to take care of yourself. Lie down right now, drink a tall glass of milk, relax, and tell the baby everything is O.K. I want you to come here in half an hour and have dinner with me.' Even though I didn't know Barbara well, I sobbed throughout the whole dinner. I felt as if a twenty-ton weight had been lifted from my shoulders. I let the baby suck a lot, rested and drank as much as I could, and by the next day my milk was back. I felt that I had narrowly escaped a destructive experience! From then on, I called Barbara more and more frequently. We'd talk about general things, being a mother. She'd listen to me, give me helpful hints. She heard my craziest fears without being thrown by them, and reassured me many times that she and her children had gone through what we were going through, it was part of growing up. Sometimes she'd give me clothes her children had outgrown, a high chair, a toy. I felt enormously taken care of by her.

Gradually things settled down. I met other people with young children. Then, when my son was almost a year old, I got a phone call from a woman I had just met. She had just had a baby, didn't know anyone else with children, and felt lonely. As I reassured her and shared some of my experiences, I could hear the relief come into her voice, and at some point during the conversation I realized I had come full circle: I was doing for her what Barbara had done for me! We kept in contact over the next few months. Once I remember she said to me 'Nancy, I could never have survived this period without your help and support. How can I thank you?' I answered 'Pass it on!' The following year she told me that a woman she knew had recently had a baby, and this time my friend was in the giving role.

Informal Play Groups

One way in which parents of young children are getting together to help each other, which is also a way to get free time or work at a part-time job and be sure our children are well cared for, is to become part of an informal play group, where parents take it in turns to look after the children.

When our children are of pre-school age, we may not have money for day care, or may not like the available day care. We may want our children to be cared for by friends. We can contact other parents of small children by putting up a card in a shop, at church, in the post office or the laundromat, or at school, and talk about starting a play group. We can begin play groups with just one, two or three other friends, and meet for however long parents decide they want or need to have time for themselves and think is good for the children. Three to five children is a good number for a play group, though if enough parents and helpers are available, a larger group would be manageable.

My son began in a play group when he was one year old. With my downstairs neighbour's son and two other girls, all the same age, we had four babies to play with and put down for naps, four nappies to change. The four of them literally grew up together. Over the years a few other children came in and out, but the nucleus remained steady. We'd provide toys and crayons for them, give them lunch and snacks, watch them play, stop fights, take them to parks or museums. Some days would be tough, others like a dream. Sometimes there'd be conflicts between parents, or one child would be too disruptive. But basically, it worked satisfactorily for all of us. We were all attentive parents. I knew when I left Ben with his play group he'd be well cared for and among friends.

When Jack and I separated and I needed to move, I found an apartment in a building with two play-group families. It was a ready home for me. Andy could be with the kids he'd known since he was one year old. It made more difference than I can say.

Baby-Sitting Pools

In some communities parents take turns staying with each other's children, keeping track of the number of hours so that each person gives about the same amount of time. In this way we can enjoy evenings away from home without having to pay a baby-sitter.

Child Care – Child Minding

Sometimes we will need an arrangement even more structured and dependable than a play group, especially if we have a nine-to-five job. A friend might know of someone who can help. If we rely on advertisements, we have to be careful.

I once went to meet a woman as a baby-sitter for Jimmie. She had the TV going and her house was too spotless. She kept obsessively talking. I didn't like her one bit, reacted intuitively and got out of there fast.

On the other hand, many of us find 'second homes' for our children:

While I was teaching, Denise went to Mrs Jans' home every day and had such a fine time she'd sometimes stay overnight. She and 'Apple', Mrs Jans' daughter, became as close as sisters, playing and fighting as though they'd known each other for ever.

We can advertise for someone to look after our children in a local newspaper or by putting up signs in appropriate places:

When we lived in a university city, I'd advertise every September in an 'underground' paper I liked. My ad went: 'Wanted: a TERRIFIC CAPABLE *person to sit for my two children, aged. . .' Sometimes I would get twenty phone calls. I'd listen to their voices, and if they sounded warm, friendly and capable (you can tell a lot over the phone!) I asked them to come over. When they arrived I interviewed them, which wasn't always comfortable for either of us. We would talk, I'd ask them about themselves and their experience with children. Then I'd watch to see if they would go to the children. Each time, one person would stand out, go right into the children's room, talk and play with them; and I would choose her (it was usually a female! Men called, too, but I felt more comfortable with women). My friends were amazed that this system worked. It did, because the people who became our sitters were at a point in their lives between regular jobs, they needed money and liked children. They'd usually stay for a year, and then go on to other things.*

We live in the country high up on a hill, and we advertise for someone to live here in the house with us, because my husband has to be away often and I like having another adult nearby. For the past two years two women have shared housework and child care in exchange for room and board, and this year a young man lives with us. There are hitches: the people who live here are not always as responsible as I'd wish when I'm around – though they are fantastic if I have to be away! And I felt the two women on some deep level were seeking Family, when I didn't want to be a 'mother' to them but a peer. Still, we have remained good friends, and they are wonderful people for my children to continue friendships with as they grow up.

In the UK any person looking after children for pay must be registered with the local council. For details, look in the practical guide to Child Care which follows.

Community Centres for Parents and Children

We, along with our children, may want to create a centre in which we could meet in various combinations – children, parents and children or, at times, just parents. Perhaps our teenagers want a place for themselves alone. With cooperative effort and publicity, soliciting some charitable or local authority or urban aid funds and finding an unused building or flat, we can set up such a centre.

Support Groups

Support groups are another form of self-help where we can meet other people on issues vital to us at all stages of our own and our children's growth, and be comforted and surprised by the resulting give-and-take. We meet perhaps weekly, with three or more people, to talk about our common problems and get support from others. We discover how we are alike and where we are different; we get to see ourselves through other people's eyes. We hear what other people's children go through at different stages, how other parents handle different phases in their own and their children's lives. We learn about the resources they develop, or find and use. We may get emotional and practical support for making changes in our lives. Friendships flourish.

It can be useful for pregnant women to spend time with other pregnant women, to discuss and share their hopes, fears and questions about labour, childbirth, infant and child care. One father talks about his group:

We are four fathers. Three of us work full time. We began to meet before our children were born, and have stayed together to find out what the others had to say. We talk over lots of things, from how much time we like to spend with our children to what we feel our roles as fathers should be, to how our wives don't seem to be too interested in sex during these first months of parenthood (to our distress!). Now I'm finding that I really love to spend time with Jake and watch him change, and yet sometimes I get very bored. It's good to have this group to bring my home tales and troubles to.

Intentional Family

Another example of a support group is an 'intentional family':

When we moved to Denver we felt really uprooted. First thing we did was join the church. We discovered that it gathers together people of all different ages who don't know each other at all, and groups them together to form families. We decided to do it to see what it was like. It has taken us a while to get to know one another. We each live in separate homes and have our own friends. But we are committed to act as family to each other. We help if someone needs a floor sanded or house painted, take care of each other's children, celebrate holidays together, and get together a lot in between. Funny, but when you think of someone else as family – that is, the kind of family we'd all like to have had: most of us came from families that weren't half as positive as this one – well then, you feel more comfortable telling your troubles because you know people are there to help. You've heard about their troubles. Sometimes we sit down and help someone figure out what they need to do. Let me tell you, it has become a focal point for my own family. We have grown connected to everyone, though I feel closer to some than to others. There are sixteen of us now. The hard thing is when someone we are getting to know and trust has to move away.

One of the strengths of this kind of group is that by joining such a family we declare outright our need for community and support. We can work at creating for ourselves over time a consciously caring network. It's important that each of us make as clear as possible what we want from such a group. We each may expect different kinds of support and have varied ideas about what the family can and should do for us as well as about what we ourselves are able to contribute.

Getting Help from Formal Resources

We have talked so far about some of the kinds of help we may want during the course of our parenting and about the informal networks to which we may turn. Sometimes, however, because of the particular needs we have or the situation we are in, we cannot get from these informal, natural networks the kind, or amount, of help that we need. And so we will turn to what may be called 'formal resources'.* By this term we mean such resources as voluntary agencies, institutions, governmental provisions, social services and so on, ranging from those using a wide variety of trained professionals to those using few or no professionals at all.

Whichever resources you use, it is possible to get a great deal of help from them. There are some general points we would like to make which it may help you to keep in mind as you use them.

Informal resources should not be forgotten. Helpful as professionals, agencies or institutions may be, their usefulness is invariably increased when we simultaneously get help from the informal networks which have been discussed earlier in this chapter. This helps us not to become over-dependent on formal resources for things which they cannot really provide. For example, a therapist can be enormously supportive and caring, but is not a substitute for a friend; a doctor may know a lot about stages in child development, but is not an appropriate person with whom to discuss our day-to-day questions about parenting. Working to establish and maintain informal networks of support also enables us to see a fuller picture of ourselves; we can be at times the giver and the helper, not just the taker and the one being helped. A further important point is that in our contact with professionals we will occasionally run into problems in the relationships which are difficult for us to sort out. Often a friend who knows us, our family and our child can help us clarify what is going wrong, and provide us with an alternative view of the situation to that being offered by the professional.

No one kind of resource is best. People often wonder what kind of resource is 'best'. Sweeping generalizations are sometimes made about which kinds of resources are useful or not. For example, 'Day nurseries are cold, inhuman places where children do not get enough attention.' Or 'If you want a good therapist to help you with emotional problems, you have to pay a small fortune.' In fact, such generalizations are rarely helpful. There are excellent, warm day nurseries

*The addresses of the organizations referred to in this section can be found at the end of the book.

where children get lots of good attention, and it's often possible to get help from a competent therapist without paying immense sums. The best resource is the one which works best for you, and this will depend on the quality of a particular resource, the kind of person you are, the needs you have, and on what is available in your area.

For example, one parent whose child is seriously ill may find great solace in talking with someone in the clergy, while another might prefer to become immersed in the building of an organization to do research on the disease from which the child suffers. A parent might become involved in a parent-support group with other parents of similarly afflicted children, or might choose to work individually with a therapist. All of these are totally reasonable and valid ways of dealing with the same problem.

The mystique of professionalism. There is a mystique called 'professionalism' in which the true nature and importance of the professionals' knowledge and skills become inflated, so that they are seen as more powerful, more expert, more broadly knowledgeable than they either are or should be. Both professionals and lay people contribute to this problem, and it creates a syndrome in which the client's own strengths and intelligence are downplayed, and the power imbalance between professional and client is increased. A self-perpetuating cycle is created, in which professional help is seen as the only kind of help with any value, and the professional's view of a situation the only valid one.

The social responsibility of agencies and institutions. It is a sad fact that some agencies, professionals and institutions consistently fail to perceive the larger social issues underlying the individual problems which are presented to them. The result is that we often emerge from our contacts with these bodies feeling weaker, more isolated, more different from other people, rather than having been helped to understand the true and complex nature of many of the issues with which families struggle today; rather than having been helped to see the shared, social base for many of these 'personal' problems; rather than having been assisted in building networks with others in our community who are in the same situation. This failure actually reflects a fundamental problem in the society at large, and the majority of institutions will change only as we change the society in which we exist. This is perhaps the central issue in the discussion of social responsibility: that all of us must work to educate ourselves to understand the nature of our society and the problems facing it, and we must work to improve the ways in which society relates to and supports its members. The women's movement is a good example of how this sort of social awareness can benefit society. Through it many people (women and men alike) have been helped to understand more clearly the relationship between their own personal problems and larger social issues, such as sex-role stereotyping, economic discrimination and so on. This understanding has led to personal change, social activism and social change in many instances.

Deficiencies and biases. There are many areas in which the services available to parents are deficient, or are difficult to use. Fathers, for example, are often made to feel distinctly out of place when they try to act as parents to their young children and get some needed help. Poor people and minority-group members often feel the sting of scorn or outright exclusion in contacts with institutions. Resources for fathers, for single-parent families, for parents of children in the middle years and for full-time working parents are often poor or lacking. Perhaps the most glaring omission, and one which affects all of us, is that relatively little energy and money go into preventive and educational resources for parents, both at the level of government and in smaller ways. Parents who are not experiencing serious problems, but who want and would benefit from some helpful contact, may wind up having to wait until there is a real problem before they can find an appropriate source of help to which they can turn.

Skills for Using Formal Resources

While most of us have a lot of contact with institutions and professionals, few of us have ever been taught how to deal effectively with them. Here are some suggestions which you may find helpful. Some may seem relevant to your situation, and others will be less so. Certainly you will think of other ideas. Remember, the fundamental aim of all of these techniques is to *equip yourself*, so that you can get the very best help for yourself, your child, your family.

Identify the problem. The first step in resolving a problem is acknowledging that there is one. Perhaps it is something we need to find, such as child care. Or perhaps we say to ourselves: I am upset and worried a lot of the time, or my child keeps getting into trouble, or I feel like I can't cope with this.

Once we have said to ourselves, I need some help, then we can begin some of the specifics. Does it have mostly to do with the child, or mostly with you? What makes it feel worse, or better? What kind of help is useful to you, what kind is not useful? Are you in a crisis or not? How much help do you want?

If it is hard for you to answer these questions, try talking with two or three friends. Tell them that you are not asking them to come up with solutions, but only to be a sounding board for you to think out loud. You can even ask them to tell you in their own words what you say back to you. From this may come an initial formulation of what the problem or need is. Remember that this formulation may change with time; it is only a way to help you get started. You may come to a more complete understanding of what the issues are in your future contacts with professionals, but it helps to start with some concrete ideas. Remember, you are at the *beginning of a process*.

Start with what you already have. Think of whom you know and trust to ask first for help. A friend? A child's teacher? A co-worker? A health visitor? Ask them to sit and talk with you or ask what sources of help they have used with good

results. Do you know anyone who is an 'information gatherer'? Some people have a knack for remembering things they hear about all sorts of services, and like to pass the information on to others who can use it. Or ask other parents in a similar situation. For example, you can ask people you meet in the park or the laundromat whether they know of any good local play groups, or you can ask co-workers about what child-care arrangements they use. And don't forget to look in the telephone book: you may just find listed there the very organization you need.

Look for allies. Several people with related needs may get more action than one parent alone. For example, three parents with young children can start a play group. Neighbours can join together to set up a recreation centre for their teenagers. If a large number of male employees request the introduction of paid paternity leave in their company or via their union, they have a better chance than if each alone tried to work something out. In fact, many of the resources described in the following pages were started by parents banding together with other parents, because they all had similar needs and couldn't find any agency that could help them.

Write it down. Often, when we are looking for help, we feel needy, confused and overwhelmed. We keep forgetting parts of what we wanted to say, we forget to ask questions that matter to us, we only half-hear suggestions that are made to us which may prove useful later on. Tell yourself that it may take a while to get what you are looking for: in the meantime it will help to keep a small notebook. Write everything down that is pertinent: the name of each organization, its phone number and who referred you there. Write down when you phoned, whom you spoke to, and what they said. This will accomplish several things: (1) it will help you reconstruct what actually was said to you, when time or confusion has dulled your memory; (2) it will equip you more fully to speak with professionals and to tell them what you know; (3) it will help you to remember what you wanted to ask; (4) it will help you not to lose important bits of information, and to organize and increase your knowledge about what is available; and (5) your organization will impress the people to whom you speak, encouraging them to deal with you more respectfully and to be more specific in what they say to you.

Make contact. Phoning or going to places is not always easy and it takes some practice to learn the most effective methods. You may have to break through two walls; one is your own – the one that prevents you from asking for help easily – and the other is that which surrounds many institutions, which pushes people away rather than inviting them in. Some agencies are aware of how critically important the first contact is, and they make sure that it is a welcoming one. Other times, however, you may have to deal with people who are themselves overwhelmed with work, or who have a minimal commitment to and interest in the people whom they are supposed to help. Keep trying. Don't assume there is nothing for you behind that wall, or that there are not others in the organization with a genuine commitment to help.

Be persistent. It is often difficult to know who is the best person or what is the best place to call at first. Assume that you may not find the best one at first try; assume you will have to make several calls. This is very hard, because often you feel so bad when you call that all you want to do is dump your load in someone's welcoming lap, and all you may get is an answering machine that says 'At the

sound of the tone, please leave your name and number and a brief message . . .'
Even after you find the right place to go to, you may get the feeling that your
presence is not really wanted at all – for example, if you are trying to stay with
your sick child at the hospital, or if you are trying to talk to the staff of the youth
club which your child frequents. Fathers, especially, are often made to feel
unwelcome at places which exist presumably to serve parents. But keep going
anyway.

Be open to new sources of information. Help can come from places you don't expect
it. The Department of Health and Social Security, for example, though it sounds
like a reasonable place to call, may give you only a list of clinics and their
telephone numbers, while a worker at the local community centre may be able to
tell you just which bodies work especially well with parents of teenagers in
trouble – just what you wanted to know. Local newspapers, libraries, notice
boards, hospital social service departments, churches, schools, local health
centres, telephone 'helplines', can all be good starting places in helping to steer
you in a good direction. If your area has a neighbourhood advice centre or youth
counselling service, either of these is an excellent place to start. And don't
overlook the local politicians. In some situations a local councillor can be of great
service to you in cutting through the endless red tape surrounding some
institutions and organizations. What you hope for is someone who will take a
personal interest in you and act as your advocate. Do not feel that this is an
imposition. It is precisely what they are elected to do, and many are quite eager to
do it.

Let your friends help. Ask a friend or relative to help you when you feel stuck.
Someone can sit with you while you make phone calls, to cheer you on, to watch
the children for you so you can concentrate, or to help you look up agencies and
so on. And when you go to places, ask someone to come along with you, if you
feel it would help. You can take a friend to a doctor's surgery, to a child guidance
clinic, to a parent-teacher meeting or to the local social services office. It may help
you to feel stronger and more assertive, and to get a clearer picture of what is
happening.

Ask for referrals. No matter how unhelpful the place you call may be, try not to
just crumple and hang up despondently. Always ask them to suggest three other
places that they think might be able to help you. You can say 'Oh, you were one
of my last possibilities. Who else could you suggest I ring? I'd very much
appreciate any ideas you could give me.' They will almost certainly be able to
make suggestions, and you will not then be left with nowhere else to turn.

Keep your perspective. Be aware that professionals are people, subject to their own
personal needs and conflicts. Sometimes, for any variety of reasons, you will find
that you do not feel comfortable with someone to whom you have come for help.

You may be made to feel that there is something wrong with you, that your feelings and perceptions are invalid, that you do not 'deserve' help. You may feel the power imbalance between you and the professional is unreasonably great. Or you may find that you are running up against personal or institutional biases, or that you are being dealt with rudely or incompetently.

Try not to give up at this point. Keep asking for explanations of what you don't understand, and keep trying to re-explain how you see things and to restate your wishes until you know you have been heard. If you cannot make headway with a particular person, request an interview with someone else. This may feel awkward, but it is a common and perfectly reasonable thing to do, and it may make a big difference in the kind of help you receive. Many times difficulties in professional-client relationships can be worked through. Remember, it takes time to build a good working relationship.

Don't be intimidated. Remember that it can be a sign of strength to reach out for help, just as it is a sign of strength to give help. But knowledge and skill are very powerful. They are meant to be used as tools, not as weapons. A good helping relationship should not diminish either the giver or the receiver, nor should it create excessive dependence of one on the other. While getting help may at times be difficult and upsetting, its ultimate aim is to make you *feel* more able, and *be* more able, to handle your life.

The following sections are meant to be used as sources *of help* when the need for them arises. You may want to flip through them now to see what topics we have covered.

Pregnancy, Childbirth and the First Few Months

Pregnancy is a time of changes – of preparations, of unknowns, of questions. What will childbirth be like? Will the baby be O.K.? How will our lives change? We have many needs for real information, knowledge and preparation. For men and women alike, it is also a time of surprisingly intense feelings. We may feel joy and love and pride more strongly than we have ever felt them in our lives. And mixed in with these glowing feelings there are often negative ones we may not have expected, and which we may think we are not supposed to have.

Where can we turn to get some understanding of these physical and emotional aspects of the childbirth experience? If you have friends who have children, they are usually the best place to start. Talking with them about what you are thinking, and spending time with their babies or young children, often help to crystallize your questions and ease the sense of unpreparedness. But sometimes this sort of help isn't available, or doesn't fully meet our needs. And so we turn to more formal resources.

Medical Professionals. In Britain, most of us will experience birth in a hospital and may expect to get all our questions answered and all our fears assuaged at the antenatal clinic. While most hospital consultants may be wonderful obstetricians, few have the time, training or inclination to relate to expectant parents in a way that is really helpful. If you are a woman, you may find that you are rushed through the clinic, given patronizing platitudes when you ask questions, and generally treated as a not-too-bright, over-anxious intruder into a medical process which only vaguely concerns you. If you are a man, you may feel as if you have ventured into alien territory. If you are attending a large teaching hospital, you may never see the same consultant two clinics running.

Rather than letting your questions and needs go unanswered, this is a good time to begin to learn how to use formal resources in a way that can really help you. Look at the list of skills on p. 380, and apply some of them to this situation. Here are some things you could do:

● Do some research. Find out as much as you can about the hospital, its policies and the attitudes of the staff on different styles of childbirth, pain relief, intervention (induction, episiotomy), involving fathers and friends, practices after the birth, e.g. breast-feeding. Ask your friends, the local branch of the National Childbirth Trust,* a women's centre. Consult *The Good Birth Guide*.† You are checking the hospital's policies against its practices in other parents' experience.
● Be clear. Clear your own head and write down questions before you go to the clinic. And be clear with the doctor. When a question hasn't been answered, or you are worried about something s/he has said, say so.
● Stand up for yourself. For example, when the time comes to discuss your wishes and the consultants' procedures for delivery, don't let her/him rattle off a string of medical terms while you lie submissively spreadeagled on the examining table. Say that you want to wait until you are dressed and sitting up, with your partner or a friend present.
● Be realistic. Don't expect the consultant to fulfil all your needs. Turn to other medical personnel: the sister in charge of the antenatal clinic, other specialists (on nutrition or breast-feeding, for example) who may be on the staff. Some hospitals will arrange for you to visit and talk to staff in the delivery rooms and lying-in wards. Use your GP, friends, good books: you will find some recommended in the Bibliography below and more in *Our Bodies, Ourselves*.

What you are trying to establish is a good, cooperative working relationship, in which you and the medical staff looking after you respect and trust each other. When a disagreement arises in an uneasy relationship, it is generally the patient who loses.

Alternatives. It is most doctors' belief that British babies should be born in hospital, and by 1976, 95 per cent of them were. Although this figure was

---

*Write to the NCT at 9 Queensborough Terrace, London W2 3TB, for the address of a local teacher.
†Sheila Kitzinger, *The Good Birth Guide* (London: Fontana, 1979), a compilation of reports by mothers on hospitals and maternity facilities all over the UK. Recommended.

achieved with the help of the deliberate running down of other maternity facilities, alternatives do still exist in the UK, and there are also variations, in degree and kind, of hospital care. Possibilities to investigate are:

● Home confinement. Antenatal care is undertaken by a GP, working with local midwives; they deliver you at home and look after you and the baby for a minimum of ten days after the birth. An interested GP/midwife team is likely to have the understanding and to make the time to answer questions, and the regular antenatal contact enables you to build a good relationship well before the baby is born. If your own GP doesn't assist home deliveries, you can find one who will from the 'obstetric list', kept at the local post office, though you should ask around to find out what experience s/he has and what her/his ideas are. It isn't necessary to change GPs; you can retain one whilst going to the other for this special purpose.

● GP units. It's hard to arrange for a home delivery if there is no general hospital nearby to deal with unexpected complications and no 'flying squad' to take you there. A good alternative is to have the baby delivered in a GP unit attached to a hospital. They are usually less clinical in atmosphere and run by midwives, with a GP in charge of each mother; you see the same GP and midwife throughout pregnancy and at the birth. You can be home again within a few hours of the birth.

● Maternity hospitals, community hospitals. These are small, local hospitals in the charge of GPs and midwives, with consultants on call if necessary. They are likely to be more homely in atmosphere, though not necessarily – check it out.

● General/teaching hospitals. Most of these provide a uniformly high level of technology and specialist care in dealing with complicated pregnancies and births, but routine procedures for straightforward births vary enormously. For example, in some hospitals, induction and episiotomy (cutting your perineum to aid the baby's head to crown) are the rule rather than the exception; in others they are only done out of strict necessity. Likewise the approach of the staff varies. To some, childbirth is a medical procedure controlled by professionals, in which you are only one, sometimes tiresome, factor. For others, childbirth is your experience to which they are sympathetic, watchful assistants. If you don't like what you see at the hospital you are first referred to, it may be possible to find a preferable one in your area.

Choosing. The first consideration in choosing where and how to have a baby is you, your feelings and the course of your pregnancy. Some of us want a home delivery above all, some of us would feel safer or more comfortable in hospital. For help in clarifying your feelings, read the 'Childbirth' chapter in *Our Bodies, Ourselves.* This section gives an idea of other parents' experiences, describes the alternatives and how to organize them and goes deeper into the issues around provision for childbirth. See also *The Place of Birth* by Sheila Kitzinger (London: OUP, 1978). The second consideration lies in what facilities are easily available in your area. *The Good Birth Guide* may include descriptions of your local hospitals, but friends and the local NCT teacher may have more recent experience and information about hospitals and alternatives.

It is important to remember that you have the right to a choice, however discouraging the initial response to inquiries may be. 'If domiciliary (home) facilities are inadequate the Area Health Authority is responsible for making them so and would possibly be actionable if anything happened to the mother or her baby as a result of ... wilful refusal to provide facilities', says Margaret Whyte, founder of the Society to Support Home Confinements. SSHC is one of a number of organizations working to improve maternity services and to preserve real choice. Others include the NCT, the Association for Improvements in the Maternity Services, and the Association of Radical Midwives. If you have difficulties in exercising a choice, get in touch with these groups (their addresses are in the list at the end of the book) and enlist the support of family and friends. Don't enter an exhausting battle for your rights alone.

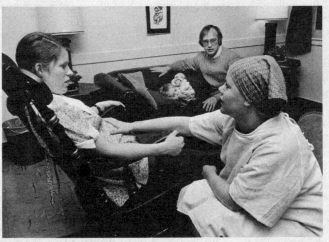

Abigail Heyman/Magnum

Books. If the pregnancy and childbirth handouts that you get at the doctor's seem to gloss over or trivialize the feelings you have, don't assume that there is something wrong with you – there is something wrong with the literature! Read one of the books described in the Bibliography. Having someone else describe private feelings which seem upsetting to you often helps to make them less so, and helps you to see the humour and the joy that go along with some of the worries.

Childbirth Classes. One way to get the benefits of contact with other parents-to-be, medical knowledge, exposure to good literature, and a family-centred approach is to participate in a childbirth class. We can't emphasize too strongly how helpful, supportive and enjoyable such a course can be. Perhaps you feel embarrassed, or think you should 'know it already'. Or perhaps you fear that you will be pressured into having natural childbirth, which sounds frightening to you. Many people today *are* urging expectant parents to learn about 'prepared childbirth' (the accurate term), but there is nothing mystical or superhuman about giving birth in this way. It involves changing some of the unnecessary and even harmful beliefs and practices that have collected around childbirth over the last several decades. And it also involves teaching the pregnant woman and her husband or a supportive friend about the process of labour and delivery and about certain useful techniques to use during labour, to help it proceed more easily and to help you remain awake and participating. With the benefit of such a course, you will not need to go through labour and delivery confused and perhaps frightened as things are 'done to you'. Instead, you will be able to play an active and joyful part in the process as well, often with fewer drugs. Even if you are fairly sure that you will want medication to eliminate all pain, or if your husband or a friend is unable to come with you, the knowledge and support you can gain in a childbirth class will still make childbirth a fuller and more positive experience.

In the UK, childbirth classes usually start two or three months before the expected date of delivery, and broadly fall into two categories: those run by the National Childbirth Trust (see p. 385) and those run by hospitals and local authorities. The NCT classes aim to prepare you not only physically but also emotionally. The classes are a mixture of teaching, group discussions and physical preparation. Most classes have a maximum of eight couples or twelve women at any one time. You do not have to be married to attend. The teacher is trained by the NCT and teaches in her own home. Because the NCT is not funded publicly, a fee is charged for these classes, but if you have little money or are unable to pay, the teacher will charge less or not at all. Hospitals and local authorities run free classes, often called relaxation classes. The quality and attitudes of these classes vary widely, some even urging you to accept drugs and instruments as a necessary part of childbirth, others just telling you to relax and let your mind wander. Some hospitals use the Lamaze or the Leboyer methods. To find out about these yourself, call the National Childbirth Trust, or consult *The Good Birth Guide*.

Subjects covered in childbirth classes should include such things as the physical and emotional aspects of pregnancy, labour and delivery; training in breathing and other techniques for handling labour and delivery; medications and their uses and effects; Caesarean delivery and other emergencies. There may also be discussions on other topics, such as breast-feeding, care of the newborn and what to expect after the birth. One of the most important benefits of such a class is meeting other people who are also expecting a baby and sharing questions, concerns and excitement with them. Many lasting friendships have begun in just such a setting.

There can be problems with childbirth classes. They may be too brief and superficial or too crowded. You may think that your class spends too much time on a certain subject, or too little. One not so obvious but sometimes difficult problem arises when your doctor or hospital feels irritated by the knowledge and the competence that such training can give to expectant parents. If you think this may be the case, you may want to consider changing both doctor and hospital.

Emotional Support. You may find that, helpful as childbirth classes are, you are still left wishing for more: more contact with other expectant parents, more opportunity to talk about what is going on for you, or perhaps more long-term involvement that will continue after the baby is born. A number of communities now offer such opportunities. Not all of them exist in any given area, but we will describe several to give you some idea of what exists and where you might find it.

Parent support groups. Such groups (described on p. 395) can give you loving attention and sympathy when you need it, as well as important information and ideas. And there's a lot of good company and laughter as well. Bear in mind that such groups are not intended to deal with major or very serious emotional problems. This kind of resource gets its strength from being a group of equals with things in common, though a good leader can add much in the early stages.

Family support schemes. You may prefer a group which stresses professionals over friends. A few organizations have begun to set up such groups, which are designed to help people with the normal, inevitable needs that are part of pregnancy, delivery and parenting (see Everyday Issues of Parenting [p.237] and under specific sections).

These schemes give you access to professional expertise at a time when you may really want it. But sometimes the staff seem more interested in conducting research than in actually helping the participants. Be cautious of groups which make you feel like an object of study, or which don't help you to respect and develop your own strengths.

Single and pregnant. If you are single and pregnant, and particularly if you are young, you may find it difficult to live the same life you did before. It is not necessary to isolate yourself or to feel ashamed. You will be needing lots of attention and help, and now is the time to get it. Try to find local groups and helping organizations specially for single expectant women, for this will get you off to a better start in caring for your baby and yourself. (They will be helpful even if you decide not to keep the baby.)

You might need advice on claiming social security rights and benefits or on housing for both before and after the baby is born. You might want someone sympathetic to talk to or the emotional support of a group of people in a similar situation. Even if you've planned quite intentionally to have a baby on your own, it's possible that you will feel very isolated once the baby is born – most new mothers do – and you will certainly face practical and financial difficulties, since our society is organized as though everyone lived in two-parent families with at least one breadwinner. There are a lot of formal organizations offering practical help: the local social services department, for example, or the Salvation Army, which aren't nearly as formidable as they sound; and there are self-help groups like Gingerbread which organize all sorts of workshops, practical schemes and social events. The best people to contact in the first instance are probably the National Council for One-Parent Families. Staff there are very friendly and can put you in touch with the other organizations we've mentioned; they also run a telephone helpline. Addresses for NCOPF and Gingerbread are in the list at the end of the book.

The First Few Months

Having a new baby can be one of the most exciting, beautiful times in your life. It is also stressful both physically and psychologically. The stress can seem unmanageable if you do not get sufficient help and support. (See Chapter 2 for a detailed discussion of this period.) Try to realize that becoming parents is one of the biggest life changes that you will ever make. Your daily work, your family system and your self-image are all changing, and if you take good care of *yourselves* during this period, it will have a direct, positive effect both on the baby and on your whole family. Try to arrange with friends or relatives or a paid sitter to get *regular* relief in caring for the baby, even if all you do at first is to stay home and nap. These arrangements are even better if made before the baby comes. It's harder to do anything when you feel overwhelmed.

Parents do not have to be with their baby all the time. In fact, it will be great for the baby as well as for you if you get some time off. (See the Sharing chapter for discussion.) Ideally, in the first few weeks someone should help you perform routine tasks like cooking, shopping and washing, so that you are free to care for the baby, establish breast-feeding, if that is your intention, and spend some time with your partner and by yourself.

Such help is not easy to find, but the social services departments of local authorities run a home help service for new mothers, especially if you have the baby at home, and they should be able to help you out for a few hours a week at least. Friends and neighbours are usually happy to do some shopping; don't be too shy to ask. The responsibility of a new baby, particularly if it is your first, together with the upheaval in your body and feelings, can make this a very exhausting time. It can be worthwhile hiring someone to help you with the housework, however distasteful you may find the idea beforehand. Ask neighbours if they know of anyone or look in the small ads section of the local paper. In London there are agencies such as 'Gentle Ghost' which will know of people looking for just this sort of short-term work. Be careful whom you choose, though. If isolation is your problem, you will find that your health visitor can be very companionable and understanding. She should be happy to chat about the baby, and supportive if you begin to feel panicky or depressed. She should visit you automatically soon after the birth. Don't be afraid to let her know you want someone to talk to, if she looks a sympathetic person.

As in pregnancy, some of the best help will come from other parents who understand what you are going through. You may find that your old friendships with people who do not have children no longer fill your needs, while sitting in the park or the laundromat and talking to a perfect stranger who has a child can be enormously comforting. A wonderful plan is to get together regularly with a friend who also has a baby, or to join a support group for new parents (see p. 395). There is almost no way to describe the difference that contacts with other parents will make to you during this period. To find a support group, get in touch with the NCT, your local baby clinic, a women's centre, or ask people you know. If you are looking for somewhere to spend time during the day, the local clinic may have a mother-and-baby club, or your local branch of the NCT, a community centre or Gingerbread group may run a drop-in centre or coffee morning. Unfortunately, many of these ways to meet other new parents are difficult to use if you are working during the day.

If you have had special complications, there are some other organizations you may want to call. Some are listed below; others may be found in the section on Parenting a Child with Special Needs (pp. 412–17).

Twins. Having twins is, at a conservative estimate, about four times as much work as having a single baby. You should expect that the first six months will be quite difficult, and that you will need constant and considerable help. One family called the first year of having twins Operation Survival! Arrange for regular, daily help, even if it strains your budget. Try contacting the social services department and any other source of help you can think of. Ask for extra time off from work in the beginning. Gradually things will become easier, and the good times will increase.

In the UK there is a National Association of Twins Clubs (of which there are twenty-two separate local associations). This group helps to provide practical and moral support, such as advice on managing the breast-feeding of two babies, and they make recommendations to manufacturers on twins' special needs. The National Childbirth Trust also publishes a leaflet about twins.

Caesarean Delivery. Some people find themselves beginning their lives as parents with what can be a sudden, major crisis – a Caesarean delivery. It is usually undertaken as a last-minute measure to save your life or the baby's; but rates are rising, and they vary from area to area, possibly as a result of the increase in obstetric interventions which interfere with the normal course of labour. Breech presentation and premature labour are two of the situations in which Caesareans are being increasingly used.

Although this procedure can save lives and prevent tragic complications at birth, it can, at the same time, leave emotional scars and make the post-partum period even more complicated than it normally is. You may feel grateful that the baby is all right and suffer only a brief sense of shock and disappointment that you were not able to deliver your baby vaginally. But particularly if it came unexpectedly, or was handled insensitively, you may have strong and conflicting feelings about a Caesarean delivery. Particularly if you had wanted to have an active 'prepared childbirth' with the minimum of drugs, you may feel robbed of a precious experience. And you may feel angry: at the doctors and hospital staff for how you were treated; at your partner or your friends for their responses to your disappointment; and also, perhaps, at the baby, for making all this happen. Sometimes women feel a sense of shame that their bodies did not 'perform' as they should have, and there may be guilt and apprehension that this 'failure' means that something is wrong with the baby. Sometimes, following a Caesarean delivery the parents are so full of shock and a sense of loss that it is difficult for them even to relate to their baby for several days. As new parents, you deserve help with these feelings.

We know of no self-help organization in the UK for mothers who have been delivered by Caesarean section, but the National Childbirth Trust can be a great help. They publish an understanding booklet, *How to Cope with a Caesarean Section*, and also run 200 or so postnatal support groups throughout the country where you can talk out your experience, possibly with parents who share it, in a sympathetic atmosphere. Even if your Caesarean is a planned one, the Trust's childbirth classes will still be relevant and valuable. With advance preparation, you may be able to go through at least part of your labour and, in some cases, avert the need for a Caesarean. And if a Caesarean delivery is ultimately necessary, you then will have the great advantage of knowing that it was necessary, and of understanding what was happening and why.

Breast-feeding. Breast-feeding and bottle-feeding both have advantages. Breast-feeding can feel very nice, it is convenient and always available, and some babies may have less trouble digesting human milk than manufactured milk.

Bottle feeding is much less demanding on the mother's timetable, makes it easier for her to return to work, and has the particular advantage of allowing the father, or another adult, to participate fully in the care and feeding of a young baby. And holding and cuddling can provide physical closeness just as breast-feeding does. Babies can thrive equally well either way; what is important is that you have a real choice.

In our culture, where bottle-feeding is common and ignorance and prejudice about breast-feeding are widespread, some aspects of women's lives work directly against their having success with breast-feeding, or even wanting to try: for example, public discomfort at seeing a mother feeding her child, the lack of workplace day care for most working mothers, women's clothing designs which make feeding awkward.

It is important to understand that breast-feeding requires coordination of our physical, mental and emotional resources. The exhaustion and worry that may be present during the newborn period can, if a woman gets no help and support, contribute to failure in breast-feeding. Very few women are actually physically incapable of breast-feeding: small breasts, inverted nipples, a full-time job outside the home or a premature baby need not be obstacles. Yet if you are surrounded by people who are misinformed or unsupportive, it may be difficult to establish or to continue breast-feeding your baby. (Occasionally, even with all possible help, various problems prevent a woman from breast-feeding.)

If you want to breast-feed your baby, or if you have tried and encountered problems, there are a number of things you can do:

● Talk to a woman who has breast-fed her baby who will spend time with you, help you learn what you need to know, give you support and encouragement. This may be all the help you need.
● Talk to a health visitor, district nurse, midwife, doctor, obstetrician or other professional who actively supports breast-feeding.
● Read the section on Feeding Your Baby in *Our Bodies, Ourselves* and one or two of the books that the authors describe and recommend in their Bibliography.
● Contact La Leche League (LLL), which was begun in 1956 by several mothers, 'just plain parents', in response to a need they themselves felt but could get no help with. The League is staffed by women who have successfully nursed their babies and who are dedicated to giving you the best information and help they can. There are seventy leaders throughout the UK who organize meetings and support groups and who are available on the other end of the telephone to give assistance at any time. To find a local leader, write to the national address, given in the list at the end of this book.

The National Childbirth Trust also have counsellors in many areas who have themselves experienced the difficulties and pleasures of breast-feeding. They counsel on a mother-to-mother basis and are available at any time to any woman. The NCT also produce helpful literature on feeding.

There has been and continues to be enormous pressure on mothers to bottle-feed their babies, not least from the lucrative baby-milk business. It's not surprising, therefore, that, in attempting to match this propaganda, literature on breast-feeding can appear moralistic and judgemental and that counsellors may seem overwhelmingly evangelical. If you dislike breast-feeding, or find it puts too much of a strain on you, or wish to stop for any reason, you should not be pressured to continue. Most of the resources mentioned above should be able to give you equally good advice on the best way to bottle-feed.

Don't hesitate to use any of these resources before the baby is born. Try making use of both informal and formal resources so that you can decide which method of feeding best suits your needs and your family's.

Everyday Issues of Parenting

Parenthood is not a series of constant problems and worries which leave our foreheads creased and our shoulders stooped, but there will be times for all parents when some reflection about what we are doing can make our lives happier and fuller, when a thoughtful conversation can alter our understanding of a situation, when some new information can help us solve a problem.

It is important to remember that parenting is not automatic or instinctive but, rather, that it is knowledge and experience and skill which are *learned* over time. Much of that learning takes place as a natural part of being parents, in talking with friends, with a partner, in being with our children. But in these times, when many of our fundamental beliefs are being challenged, and when the shapes of families and the roles of men and women are changing, we may need help in thinking and experimenting to find the ways of being parents that feel right to us.

And there will be times when the wish to learn more, or to be understood more clearly, comes from difficulties we are having as parents. Perhaps a child's demands have made us feel worried, resentful or inadequate. Perhaps we feel trapped by parenthood, but hesitate to admit it because we chose to be parents or because we think it's not 'right' to feel that way. Perhaps we often feel angry at our children, sometimes even wondering whether we really love them as we should, and feel not only guilty but also, at times, a bit crazy, because no one we know ever admits to feeling that way. Or perhaps we simply do not understand clearly how children develop, or what being a 'parent' really means.

There are a variety of resources to which parents can turn with these everyday needs. Parents who work both inside and outside the home from the time they get up till they go to bed have little private time left, and they may not want to use that time for activities that have anything to do with children. But the time spent learning about ourselves and about our parenting may ultimately *create* time, rather than take it away from us, by helping us to make choices which lead to our being happier and more effective as people and as parents.

Learning about Parenthood

Many of us have very little contact with babies or children before we have our own, and we start parenthood feeling we know next to nothing about them or how to look after them. Formal education courses are beginning to substitute for the learning by experience people used to acquire in the days of large families and close communities. Some young adults leave school having been taught child care or parentcraft to CSE, GCE O-level or even A-level (we wonder how many of these students are boys). The Open University offers two relevant courses: 'The First Year of Life' and 'The Preschool Years'; the Scottish Health Education Unit is planning a *Book of the Child* based on these courses, to be distributed free to all expectant mothers in Scotland in 1980. Antenatal courses offered at hospitals or by the National Childbirth Trust usually include some practical child-care training, and infant welfare clinics or health centres often offer parentcraft classes. Look for courses too at the adult education institutes; some run courses specifically for parents, but you may find other related courses, under Psychology, for example. There may be more experimental schemes in your area, like the Home Link project in Liverpool which is based on the idea of taking education to mothers of young children in their own homes, helping them to gain confidence in themselves, and recruiting mothers to visit and help others.

Ask about courses and projects locally, at the library, welfare and health centres and education institutes, or consult the National Children's Bureau. The Bureau publishes *Preparation for Parenthood: Some Current Initiatives and Thinking*, by Gillian Pugh, which gives a good idea of the range of possibilities. We want to warn parents, however, to look at any courses with a critical eye. Thinking about child development and child care is subject to fashion and fads which can be undermining or even damaging. Many of us suffered as babies in the 1940s because our mothers were persuaded by the Truby King idea that babies should only be fed at rigid four-hourly intervals. Our mothers suffered too, and King's ideas have now been largely rejected.

Parent Support Groups

The courses we have been describing may be good ways to learn about parenthood, about children and about ourselves. But they are not designed to provide long-term contact, or to help us work through those deeper personal issues which may affect our parenting.

Anyone who has cared for children knows that there are certain situations which we simply cannot handle, certain times when buttons get pushed and we get furious, or worried or withdrawn, or when we just feel terribly unsure of what to do. Many parents think that they should not look for help with parenting issués unless there is a crisis, as when a child is using hard drugs, or is doing badly at school or gets arrested.

If we try to put up a front to show that everything is fine, we wind up standing isolated behind the walls we have built, imagining that things are going just fine for everyone else but us. This fear that we are somehow different from other people, that we alone find parenting difficult, is very painful and disabling. It results from the great isolation in which most of us raise our children, and, in fact, conduct our lives. There are small, personal ways to begin to cut through this isolation, but you can also make yourself part of a network of other people who want a chance to talk about issues in their lives as parents, and come together specially for that purpose. Some self-help groups have been initiated by individual parents, although this takes some bravery since the times when you are most moved to look for support are likely to be the times when you are under most stress. Others have grown out of antenatal classes, such as those run by the National Childbirth Trust, who now have some 200 small postnatal support groups meeting regularly. More formal agencies also help to establish groups. The London Council of Voluntary Service initiates family discussion groups led by women from the neighbourhood who have received some training. Many mothers have gained a lot from talking in a women's liberation group – and a few fathers have received rare and valuable support from other men through the small, but growing, men's movement. If you would like to form a group yourself, consider asking the parents in your child's school or play group, or other parents in your workplace, or at your clinic, in your childbirth class, or even in the playground. However they form, whether they have a leader or not, if an atmosphere of openness, caring and support is maintained, support groups can offer one of the most valuable experiences you will ever have.

Community Centres for Parents of Young Children

Have you ever found yourself staring at a pile of unfinished work, dirty dishes, or unsorted washing, with a young child fussing and hanging on to you, and wished you could be anywhere but where you are? Your fantasized place to go might provide child care so you could do something else for a while. You would be able to meet other parents of young children, to share the pleasures of companionship, and to exchange ideas, information, joys and frustrations about the job of being a parent. It might have interesting activities for you or for your child, and, you hope, it would be free.

There are places that approach this fantasy, though they are few and far between. It can be upsetting to read about an exciting service which you cannot use because it is miles away from where you live. We offer these descriptions as models which may give you some ideas of what is possible. You may be able to find a similar centre near you, or you may even have the energy and determination to try to start your own.

One major disadvantage of such centres is that they have fairly large operating costs. But we believe that the basic ideas could be simplified, and adjusted to existing community resources, both for space and for staff.

Family Focus, in Chicago, calls itself 'a getaway spot and drop-in center for parents-to-be and parents with children three years old and younger.' It began in 1976, and already has two centres and several hundred regular users. Parents come with their children to participate in structured parent discussion groups, to relax by reading or working at a craft (for which the centre provides materials), or just to sit and enjoy the company of other parents. Children can either stay with their parents or play in the gymnasium-playroom under the care of trained staff members. Both centres are privately financed, and neither charges a fee. There are no income limitations or other requirements for users. Parents who use the centre describe it as 'a way to end the isolation I was feeling', 'a place to get the support and information I desperately needed about raising children', and 'a sort of replacement family'.

The staff of Family Focus believe that their work is preventive. In the words of the mother of four who developed the centres: 'We try to reach people at the very beginning of parenthood and help them learn to cope with all the problems that bedevil a young parent raising children in a city atmosphere. We'd have no trouble finding money to continue if we could prove the costs we'll save society later.'

In England, the Allfarthing Institute, in the London Borough of Wandsworth, has pioneered a scheme to cater to both women and children – while the children are involved in play activities under the supervision of play-group leaders, mothers can engage in various types of craft in the workshops or join in discussion groups where they can talk about common problems. There are now seven such workshops in the Borough.

There are also community centres and projects throughout the UK which have grown out of the frustrations and energy of local people. They aren't usually set up specifically for parents; they may not even have a building they can call their own; but they are a direct response to community needs and probably include your own. An outstanding example is the Craigmillar Festival Society in a vast, impoverished and depressing council estate in Edinburgh. 'The Festival' began largely through the anger and efforts of a local mother whose child wanted to learn the violin, but could find no tuition or facilities locally, while the lavishly budgeted International Edinburgh Arts Festival could happen down the road for a different set of folk. Craigmillar's Festival was intended partly as a local celebration and to supply some of the missing amenities, partly to cock a snook at the 'straight' Festival. It touched not only a great well of need, social and cultural, but also a great fountain of local energy. The Festival Society now organizes a huge range of clubs, activities and events all the year round, runs transport and equipment, has won a community building and an enormous operating budget from EEC funds. It employs some ninety people, almost all of them from the estate itself: control is absolutely in local hands. Almost everyone on the estate is involved with the Festival Society one way or another. There may not be such a project in your area – but there certainly could be. A few years ago Craigmillar looked the most unlikely place to spawn such a large-scale grass-roots success story.

Finding Out about Services for Children

There is no one easy way of finding out what is available for children and their parents in a particular area except to explore every avenue and not be discouraged if it turns out to be a dead end. This is time-consuming and can be nerve-wracking. It would be worthwhile getting together with a group of friends in a similar position to share out the work of investigating. If you are in an upsetting situation – looking for help with a handicapped child, for example – try to get another trusted person to take on some of the work; if necessary, a professional social worker. They can be very comforting as well as capable people.

There are obvious places to look for information that you can think of for yourself: the list of suggestions in the Child Care section below will help to jog your memory. In this section we make less obvious suggestions.

Neighbourhood Advice Centres have quietly mushroomed in many inner city areas. They have usually been set up by local people for local people, with some help from the council under urban aid programmes, but are managed quite independently, to give local information and general advice such as welfare or tenants' rights. They are more varied and reflective of the local community than the Citizens' Advice Bureaux (CABs) and, if there's room on their premises, they are quite likely to run a drop-in centre that mothers and children can use. In any case, they are good places to begin looking for other local facilities. If there's one in your area, you are likely to find it in a shop-front in a busy shopping area, but if you have trouble, you could contact the Consumers' Association for addresses.

There are several national organizations that concern themselves with children and parents: for example, Gingerbread, which is a federation of groups of lone parents. To find out about them try inquiring from the National Children's Bureau, which calls itself 'an organization of organizations'. Its main aims are to make available information about children, to improve liaison between people dealing with children, to evaluate and improve services and practice for children. It also runs an information service, collects and disseminates information and supports voluntary groups throughout the country. It publishes its own journal, *Concern*.

WIRES, a national information service for the women's liberation movement, could put you in touch with local women's centres and groups, who will almost certainly have a lot of information about the neighbourhood. WIRES is at 32a Parliament Street, York, and runs a newsletter and a telephone inquiry service. Both the main content and the small ads section of *Spare Rib*, the monthly magazine of the women's movement, are funds of information. If local newsagents and libraries don't already stock *Spare Rib*, ask them to. Two other publications which might help are *The Directory of Social Change: Women*, by Collins, Friedman and Pivot, published by Wildwood House, and *The Women's Directory*, by Faulder, Jackson and Lewis, from Virago Press. Finally, look out for small community alternative newspapers, which are more likely to have up-to-date information than any book.

Possibly a last resort, but a potentially powerful source of help for parents, are the local councillors, who often run regular 'surgeries' available to the people whom they represent. You can get the address and times of surgeries from your Town Hall. Regardless of whether you like their politics, they are there to serve you, and you may find that after spending several frustrating months trying to get some help, a call to your local representative will quickly get you what you need. While this is not the best route to many services, remember that it *is* your right, and it is a perfectly appropriate reason to call on an elected official.

Child Care

Every family with children faces sooner or later the need for child care. For a fortunate few, the job of finding good child care is easy, but for most of us, it is hard and discouraging work. Once we have worked through the complicated feelings that most of us have about whether, what kind and how much child care is all right, we find that even larger obstacles remain; most of us have to settle for less in terms of both time and kind than we would prefer. As a general guide to facilities in the UK:

● If your child is *under three* you are only likely to get her or him a nursery place if s/he is judged to be 'high-priority' (e.g. if your housing is appalling, if you are a lone parent with a job, if you or your child are disabled, or if you 'can't cope', then you may get a free place at the discretion of the council); or if your employer provides a nursery; or if you can afford private nursery fees. Usually you will have to look for a child-minder.

● If you are looking for *full-time care* for a child of any age – such as would allow you to work a full day – the same conditions apply, and again you will more than likely end up with a child-minder.

● If you are looking for a *full school-day* (six hours) for a child over three, you may find a place in a nursery school/class, although most of the places are split into half-day sessions for two children. A rising five-year-old should be assured of a full school-day.

● If you are looking for only *short sessions* (2½ hours) for an over-three, you should be able to find them.

In the Society chapter we discussed some of the attitudes and politics behind the overall lack of provision and the muddle of services which do exist. In this chapter we aim to give a practical guide.

Some Things to Know about Using Child Care

There are certain basic principles stressed elsewhere in this book which may help you to think about the child care you want.

● Child care is an important resource for *all* families with children. For single-parent families, or those with two parents who work outside the home, child care is critical for their daily functioning. For families with a parent at home, child care provides many benefits for both parents and children.

● In families that have two parents, child care should be seen as the shared responsibility of both mother and father.

● Children, as much as adults, need to spend time alone; they should have quiet time away from other children and away from institutions. They need regular time with their families in order to learn how to live in intimate relationships with other people.

● No one type of child care is best. What is most useful for you will depend on what you need, the age and personality of your child, and on what is available in your area.

It is difficult and time-consuming to find and to evaluate child care, particularly when you are struggling to start or keep a job, or have other children. Employers are usually extremely unsympathetic to parents' requests for time off for this purpose. It is nonetheless a task of crucial importance. Child-care situations vary from excellent to awful, and it matters a good deal that your child is safe, secure and happy while you are gone, not least for your own peace of mind.

Where to Look

The only strategy to discover what is available in your area is to ask everyone and to look in every place you can think of – and then ask and look again. Individuals to ask are friends and neighbours (even if you don't know them yet), other parents at work, any likely person looking after a child at the playground, shops, or launderette, your health visitor and GP. The first places to try are the social services and education departments of your local council. They are not only responsible for council-run provision, but should also know of all other legally endorsed provision. If you think your case is urgent enough to get you a council nursery place, ask to see a social worker, who can organize it on your behalf. However, you can't rely on council employees to know about or immediately bring to mind everything that's available. So other places to look are the local community centre, neighbourhood advice centre, Citizens' Advice Bureau, churches (who often provide space for play groups), health centre, women's centre, infant welfare clinic, tenants' associations down to notices in the public library or in shop windows.

Child-minders

Child-minders are responsible for a substantial part of the child-care provision in the UK. Some 92,000 of our children are cared for by registered child-minders, and between 100,000 and 330,000 by unregistered child-minders: estimates are hard to verify because unregistered child-minding is illegal although widespread. You are quite likely to find that a child-minder is the only choice of day-care open to you.

The local authority regulates the maximum number of children the minder can care for and checks that the home meets health and safety regulations. It is also supposed to ensure that the minder is a 'fit' and 'adequate' person, but these criteria are undefined and virtually impossible to apply. While few child-minders are deliberately cruel or neglectful out of ignorance, it is important to remember that many women who do not particularly enjoy minding children may be forced to do so simply because it is the only work open to them. The law doesn't stipulate any kind of contract or scale of fees between you and the child-minder. Charges in Inner London in 1979 range between £10 and £14 a week. The minder may refuse babies and control the hours, though usually they are long, say from 8 a.m. to 6 p.m. The minder may stop minding your child at any point, leaving you in the lurch. On the other hand, you may remove your child at any point: she has no job security. A few local authorities are now supporting child-minders in small ways: providing short training courses, or places and opportunities for minders and 'their' children to get together. However, very little money finds its way directly to minders for toys, equipment, home improvements and the like. A recent study in London found generally inadequate premises: e.g. a third had no outdoor play space.

But the nature of the child-minder herself is probably more crucial to you than the standard of the premises (so long as they are safe) or fancy play equipment; and there is no evidence to suggest that a 'legal' child-minder is any more likely to be a kindly, imaginative person than an 'illegal' one.

The pros of using child-minding are that it is a homelier, more informal 'back-street' system; it's local and there are usually other local children for yours to befriend and play with; the child-minder is likely to work more flexible hours than a nursery; if you're compatible, a firm and lasting friendship can flourish.

The social services department keeps the list of registered child-minders and can be quite helpful if you ring them. A better way of finding someone is probably to ask around among your friends (and co-workers, if you work already), or to approach other obvious parents at the launderette or local shops. There are many of us with the same problem and need.

There is no doubt that child-minders are scandalously exploited. They have no job security, work long and arduous hours, commonly ten or eleven hours a day, and for terrible pay: a recent BBC programme estimated it at 10 pence an hour after the expenses were paid! They have none of the other benefits like paid holidays, sick leave or pension schemes that most of us assume as automatic rights.

You may feel uncomfortable at contributing to this exploitation, while having no choice but to do so. In this case you could consider supporting one of the campaigns for more state day-care provision, or the move proposed by the TUC to turn child-minders into local authority employees, which should benefit minders and parents alike.

How to Choose a Child-minder

You will need to check out for yourself any person you leave your child with. Talking on the phone can give you a sense of a person, but be sure also to arrange for an interview. In addition to discussing such details as money, hours, responsibilities, you will want to get a feeling of what the person will be like with your child. What does the house look like? Do you feel comfortable there? Does it look like a house where a child would be safe, and welcome, where disruptions and messes would be tolerated, where there would be lots of things for a child to do? Observe how the person relates to his/her own child. Does the parent seem to enjoy the child? Is the interaction one that makes you feel comfortable or uneasy? Talk directly about such things as discipline, toilet training, activities. But you will learn more about what the person is like by watching how s/he relates to your child, and by engaging in conversation about home life, family, activities and previous work experience. You may feel awkward, prying into someone's personal life, but it is crucial that you get a sense of what this person is really like. You need to know whether this is someone who genuinely enjoys being with children, or whether s/he regards it as a job of last resort.

If you are interviewing an older person, try to judge whether s/he has enough stamina to keep up with an active child. If the person is young, does s/he have enough experience? Does s/he understand the seriousness of the responsibility? If your child is very young, be sure to look for someone who likes physical contact, who will hold and hug and comfort your baby, for this is how young children relate.

Having found a minder, it is best (if you are able) to start with a few hours at a time and gradually increase the time. And it is important not to slip into just taking everything for granted. Keep aware of how things are going – for example, ask 'What did s/he do today?', not simply 'Was everything O.K.?' If you think there might be a problem, drop in unexpectedly, if this can be done without antagonizing the minder. Be sensitive to warning signs, such as a child who sleeps *much* longer with a minder than when s/he is with you, or a child who is described as 'very clinging' or 'very aggressive' when s/he is not that way at home. Although it is common for children at various ages to cry when their parents leave and when they come back, if your child is unhappy most of the time you are gone, something is wrong and needs attention.

Council Day Nurseries

These are intended to provide substitute care where children or parents are thought to be in special need. Despite the fact that all working mothers, and any mother and small child in extreme isolation in the country, or beleaguered by trunk roads and high-rise housing in our inner cities will be in desperate need of nursery places, your circumstances will probably have to be very pressing indeed to win your child a place. The level of public spending is low and likely to sink lower; in 1976 there were 12,000 children waiting for places, while seventeen local authorities provided no places at all. Other disadvantages of this type of nursery are the effects of dividing children up at such an early age on the grounds of relative deprivation and the orientation towards welfare: looking after rather than teaching and stimulating the children as a matter of course. Advantages are that children are taken from as young as birth (although not many children under twelve months are placed) to five years, and they are open for a full working day and all year round, so they are most suitable for working parents. Fees are means-tested but minimal, premises and equipment adequate to good, and there are enough staff, trained nursery nurses, who usually look after the children in family groups (i.e. mixed ages). Apply through the social services department of the local authority, but get anyone you can think of – social worker, health visitor, GP, for example – to support your application.

Nursery Schools or Classes

Nursery schools or nursery classes within primary schools are run by the local education authority. Parents first starting on the trail of finding nursery places often confuse them with the council-run day nurseries – but they offer a very different kind of provision. They focus on educational experience and are staffed by nursery teachers, usually assisted by nursery nurses. Like all state schools, they are free, and standards of premises are usually high. The drawbacks for parents are the age range admitted (usually only three- and four-year-olds) and the hours (most places are shared by two children, so that each child gets a half-day session of about $2\frac{1}{2}$ hours). This is owing to the demand for places and not because it is thought that children of this age cannot cope with a full school-day. In any case, nursery schools are open only for the normal school-day, six hours, and the usual school terms, about forty weeks a year. Parents who work have to make a patchwork of arrangements to cope with after-school hours and the school holidays. But it is worth checking out which schools are available in your area and making sure your child will be eligible for a place when the time comes. It may be the best provision you can find. By the time your child is coming up to five, s/he will most likely be able to go to school for a full day in the reception class of the primary school.

Play Groups

Play groups have blossomed all over the place since the 1960s, largely because mothers, desperate for some kind of social life for their kids and any kind of break for themselves, have got together to organize them. About half are run by parent committees, which means you are more likely to have a say in what goes on than in any of the other provisions we have described. The rest are run by charities such as the Save the Children Fund and community organizations, such as a tenants' association. Local authorities run 1 per cent of play groups, but, quick to recognize a good, cheap (to the council) thing when they see one, give minimal grant-aid to others. They also used up, in 1976, nearly four and a half thousand of the available places for children from their high-priority waiting lists. It is impossible to give you any general picture of what play groups are like: they vary enormously. Because they operate on a shoestring, premises and equipment can be dauntingly poor. On the other hand the staff, who are paid also on a shoestring, are often so dedicated and enthusiastic as to make up for that. You may be asked to help out at play group on a rota with other parents and welcome the contact; but if your time without kids is very precious, or if you're very depressed, or if you're feeling frantic, parent involvement and a roomful of under-fives may be the last things you want. Play group fees vary – 33 pence per session was the average in 1977. The usual age-group is three to four; sessions are usually short, two or three hours in the mornings, and not for every day of the week: some 68 per cent of children in one survey attended only for one or two sessions a week. Play groups are thus no use to working mothers and of limited use to mothers with more than one child under five: the fees may be prohibitive for more than one child even if all ages were to be admitted. Many mothers are put off by the brevity of the sessions: with going to and fro, settling the child and chatting to staff and mothers, the free time gained may be hardly worth the effort.

Whatever their shortcomings, the grass-roots nature and the proliferation of play groups testify to the vast need they attempt to meet. Given that organizing by mothers themselves is the only immediate prospect of improvement in nursery services, we feel that centres such as the Children's Community Centre (described in the last chapter, p. 343) are a better model to press for rather than more play groups: i.e. full-time day care for all ages, fully funded by the council and managed and controlled by parents and workers. This particular example was set up by a group of women who organized and campaigned together.

Voluntary or Private Nurseries

Voluntary nurseries are run by a variety of agencies: by colleges for children of their students, by charities such as Barnardo's, by community groups, for example. Many nurseries, however, are run by private enterprise for profit. Orientation varies in terms of care or education, as do standards of premises, toys and equipment and staffing. You will have to investigate and judge for yourself. The advantages are that they offer full-time care all the year round and are thus an alternative for working parents to council nurseries and child-minding. Some will take children of all ages, but there are fewer places for the under-twos. The major drawback is the cost, which can be prohibitively high, since most of these establishments are unsubsidized. In 1976, local authorities placed 1,600 children from their 'high-priority' waiting lists in private nurseries, so if you think you have a case, it would be worth pressing it. To find where the voluntary and private nurseries are will probably take a lot of asking around. Always try the social services and education departments first, then likely charitable bodies (find addresses at the library), then the other people and places suggested at the start of this section.

Workplace Nurseries

Workplace nurseries are almost invariably run by employers for the sole purpose of recruiting female labour and are found in industries or services traditionally using female employees, such as textiles, electrical engineering, hospitals. The rare exceptions have been won by employees uniting on behalf of themselves and their children: for example, the local branch of NALGO has recently negotiated agreement to a workplace nursery with the London Borough of Camden.* Workplace nurseries are sometimes run directly by the firm's management, sometimes by a hired firm of specialists. Premises and equipment are generally adequate, though there is often no outdoor space. The staff are usually trained nursery nurses, but there may be fewer of them than the recommended one to five children. The hours coincide with work times and most take children from two to five years: only a minority cater for the under-twos. Some firms also run

Workplace Nurseries, a negotiating kit is available from NALGO, 1 Mabledon Place, London WC1H 9AJ.

after-school play schemes for over-fives. Fees are usually subsidized, but the employee's contribution can still be high; it averaged £5 a week in 1976. The drawbacks are much the same as those of tied housing and perhaps just as pernicious. Losing your job means losing the nursery place. If there is little alternative day care in your area, this will make you think twice before changing your job voluntarily or before speaking up about conditions either in the nursery or at work if you think you might risk dismissal. There is nothing to stop the employer withdrawing the provision if he no longer needs it to attract labour and, inevitably, the children of male employees are rarely, if ever, admitted. If you are thinking of taking a job with this kind of nursery provision, it's obviously a good idea to find and talk to other women already doing it, or better still, women who have tried it and have now moved on.

How to Look at a Nursery, Nursery School or Play Group

Parents have very little choice over what nursery provision they use; there is often only one option and the only choice to be made is whether to use it at all. In general, too, we have very little say in what goes on in the nursery. Nonetheless, it's essential to know what goes on, to understand how our children are feeling when they come home, and to make sure that nursery-time is complemented by home-time. It is possible to make small changes by clear, tactful suggestions to the staff, and you shouldn't be deterred from making them by fear of jeopardizing your child's place. Even though it may be difficult to find the time (take the day off work 'sick') or to overcome staff suspicion (smile, be polite, be firm), try to size up the place for yourself, and more than once. Here are some suggestions of what to bear in mind:

General Atmosphere. Is it warm and inviting and active? Are the children relating to one another, as well as to the adults? Is it pleasantly noisy, with varied activities going on? Is it bedlam, with children running, unsupervised, through the rooms? Or are the children too quiet, too controlled? Are the spaces cold and empty and lifeless?

If your child is young, look at the infant room. Is it clean? Does it have colours and mobiles and music? Are there safe, open spaces and objects for babies to explore? Is there a lot of holding and cuddling evident?

Physical Aspects. What is the physical layout like for older children? Is there safe, ample room for them to move about? Are the rooms colourful and interesting to be in? Are there a reasonable number of good, basic toys? It is not necessary to have great numbers of elaborate toys, but there should be adequate supplies, such as bricks, books, drawing materials, playhouse materials, things to build with, make music with, climb on and so on. Are these supplies easily accessible to the children? Are things which children should *not* have access to (cleaning supplies, sharp tools, electrical sockets, etc.) safely out of reach?

If you find it difficult to answer these questions, pick a child who reminds you of your own, and watch how s/he goes through the day.

Staff. How do they relate to the children? Do you feel comfortable with the way they handle fights, crying, toilet training, feeding? What do they do when a child breaks something or makes a mess? Are they physically affectionate, particularly when a child is upset? Do they seem to listen to and respect the children's feelings and ideas? Do they show respect and affection for one another? What values are they teaching the children in the way they handle various situations? What is the ratio of adults to children? One adult to five children is fine for four-year-olds, but that would be a poor ratio for an infant room.

Karen Kahn

Children. It is probably best if specific infants are assigned to specific staff members, so that somebody clearly considers your very young child his or her charge. Infants do not do well if they cannot form a strong bond with the person who cares for them, and if there are three or four shifting nurses, a very quiet baby or a very fussy one may not get the loving attention s/he needs.

Do the older children look involved, happy, relaxed, and engaged in some activity? Or do they seem restless and bored, or uncertain and timid? Do they look reasonably healthy? Beware of a nursery where low pay and/or low morale result in a high staff turnover, as this prevents strong emotional bonds from developing, and leads to chaos and insecurity for the children. Ask staff members how long they've been in the job and how long they're thinking of staying.

Philosophy and Parent Participation. Who runs the nursery? Try to see how this affects its quality. For example, in nurseries which are run as profit-making businesses, decisions are based on what is good for business, rather than on what is good for the children. Find out how much parent participation is encouraged at the nursery. Are there parents on the management committee? Do they help decide how money is to be spent? Who will be hired? How will the nursery be structured? Clearly the more parent involvement, the better.

After you have begun to use a nursery, you will still need to keep in touch to ensure that it is working out well. Be sure to keep the staff posted on events at home which will affect a child's day, such as illness, allergies, stress, family upheavals and so on. When you talk with the staff, encourage them to tell you how your child spends his or her day, not simply that 'he was a good boy' or 'she didn't cause us any trouble.' You could drop in unexpectedly several times. Remember, particularly if your child spends a good deal of time there, that the day-care workers must function as surrogate parents, not simply as custodians. It is often difficult, when you are working full time, to be involved with your child's day care, but a moderate amount of effort could make a substantial improvement in the quality of care.

The Over-fives

The school day is only six or seven hours long, the school year only forty weeks. Schoolchildren still need plenty of care, attention and entertainment out of school. Working parents must find extra provision and all parents welcome it. Local education authorities (LEAs) are empowered under the 1944 Education Act to set up after-school play centres and holiday play schemes or to assist voluntary groups to set them up. Your authority may be doing so: go to the education offices (address in the telephone directory) to find out what is available. If your area is under-supplied, you could campaign, preferably with other parents, to persuade the education committee to change its priorities and spend some money on out-of-school services. A strategy which might bring quicker results would be to approach an existing community group, such as a tenants' association or women's group, or possibly a charitable organization, and ask members to initiate a scheme in cooperation with the LEA. If you're working and juggling finely balanced arrangements with neighbours or child-minders, it's hard to find the time and energy to campaign for better provision. Don't be too shy to seek reinforcements from groups whose members may be only too willing to help and might have more time free to do it.

Other Possibilities

We have concentrated on describing the most common and widely distributed forms of child care, and if it makes depressing reading, that is because the general situation *is* depressing. Unless you are lucky, it's very likely that you will have to make compromises about the sort of child care you'd ideally like, and search hard to find the best compromise. But you may be lucky: you may come across one of the exceptional experiments that are being made within the usual forms of child care, or outside them, in entirely new frameworks. Some Save the Children Fund play groups, for example, are trying out four-hour sessions, including a lunch. This means a new dimension to play group for the children, more child-free time for their parents, and possibly more job satisfaction for staff. Extended sessions (until 6 in the evening) are also being tried in some ordinary ILEA nursery classes in Islington.

Examples of new approaches to child care are the Children's Community Centre, the Kingsway Nursery, and the Thomas Coram Children's Centre, all in London. Turn to the previous chapter (p. 343) for more detailed descriptions: we feel these examples belong with social commentary because we think them better models to aim and campaign for than little changes in the existing services. What they all have in common is that they were set up with the needs of parents in mind as much as those of the children; parents have a voice in their management; and they are open for full-time care, with some choice for parents as to what hours they use them. Finally, explore the local community centre, if you have one. It could have a slightly different name ('Community Arts Centre' or 'Neighbourhood Centre', for example), and it won't be specifically organized around child care, but it may already have a range of services which suit you, and it certainly will offer the possibility of establishing more. Community centres vary as they must if they truly reflect local needs, wants and character, but the sort of facilities you might find are: a play group, mother-and-toddler group, adult education classes, welfare, housing or legal advice sessions, workshops and clubs for children, teenagers, adults and pensioners, a swap shop, snack bar, tools and equipment to use, maybe a theatre, even a nursery. The appeal of this setting is that the under-fives aren't hived off from the rest of the community and could join in or progress to activities not easily accessible to the child who is always with her or his peer group in separate nursery facilities. At the minimum a community centre should offer a building and money for salaries, equipment and events which are in your – the community's – control.

Parenting Teenagers

One of the hallmarks of adolescence is change: physical changes, change in the child's role in society and change in the relationships between child and parents. As parents we are accustomed to being responsible for our children, to having a degree of influence over how they conduct their lives. But the adolescent years are the period when the struggle between holding on and letting go reaches its peak. Old ways of relating may not work any more, and communication may be strained as parents and teenagers try to figure out a mutually acceptable way to relate to one another.

Parents may worry that their children are in trouble, or simply may wonder what is going on in their now very private lives. But teenagers care intensely about their privacy, their standing with their friends, and their emerging independence. They may regard every attempt at conversation as 'meddling', 'treating me like a baby' or being 'hopelessly old-fashioned'.

Added to this is the complicating factor that teenagers are often at the cutting edge of social change: they tend to act out in a dramatic way what is going on under the surface in the society at large. They may behave in ways which are unfamiliar and alarming to their parents, yet which are common in their peer group. And it is often difficult for parents to judge whether this behaviour is symptomatic of some serious problem, or whether it is a reasonable and harmless part of growing up. We may end up trying to use standards of our own adolescence, which are inevitably out-of-date and often misleading. As we have discussed in the chapter on teenagers, parents themselves undergo a great many important changes during the years when their children are adolescents, in such areas as sexual identity, job changes and having to adjust emotionally to this new phase of parenthood. These changes can affect how we see our children, and what kinds of help we need.

Where can we turn, then, when we want some help in parenting our teenagers? What are the most useful forms of help we can get? As with any area of parenting, it depends to a large extent on what kind of person you are, and on what works for you. But it seems that, by and large, parents of teenagers tend *not* to use specialist organizations and professional resources unless there is a specific and fairly serious problem.

This is not to say that if you need help it is not available. You may not be able to talk directly with your teenagers about certain subjects, but is there a teacher or a youth club leader whom your child particularly likes and trusts? Or perhaps there is a neighbour, a relative or family friend to whom your teenager feels especially close. Sometimes another person can talk very openly with your child when you cannot, for the present, even make contact. Or you may be able to talk directly with such a person about your concerns and get a sense of how your child seems from another point of view. Teenagers need to be consulted, however, and it is important to conduct your dealings in such a way that your child does not feel betrayed, or as if you have gone behind his/her back.

You may find in these conversations that your child is seen quite differently by other people, and you may learn of strengths in your child which are difficult for you as parents to see clearly.

Certainly there is excellent information and wisdom that can be gained through talking with other parents of teenagers in your community. But some parents find that feelings of competition, and the strong wish to feel that they have 'succeeded' as parents, have prevented them from being part of such a helping network. If you find that this is the case for you, that it is difficult to be open with other parents of teenagers in casual social contacts, you may want to take advantage of a structured situation by enrolling in a course on parenting teenagers or in a parent discussion group. You may find courses and groups by phoning your child's school, a local college, a community centre, a child guidance clinic or youth counselling service. If you want to join such a group and none exists, an announcement at the next parents' meeting at school or a notice in the parent newsletter may turn up other interested parents.

There are other places in your community where you might find good opportunities to examine your role as a parent of teenagers. Some family service agencies may run courses on family life which are designed particularly for families with older children, and which give parents a chance to explore some of the issues of parenting teenagers.

Phyllis Ewen

Many local authorities offer a youth counselling service. This is primarily for the teenagers themselves, but counsellors are often extremely helpful to parents and, where appropriate, the whole family. Other authorities employ 'detached youth workers', who stay in their assigned areas long enough to become familiar to both the teenagers and parents of that community. Families often call on these workers for various kinds of help, including social services, court work and family crises. Your local authority may have such youth workers, but there is one caution: the very quality of street workers which makes them so effective with teenagers at times can also be a significant handicap. That is, they are often young, idealistic people who care intensely about the work they do, but may not always have the experience to separate their own issues from those of their clients. Parents of teenagers working with such an agency sometimes feel that the young workers are so biased toward the child's position that they are unable to be supportive of the parent or helpful to the family as a whole. This is not a reason to stay away from such forms of help, for young workers may be much more effective at working with your teenager than an older person might be; it is only something to keep in mind.

Sometimes the problems faced by teenagers and their families are not simply 'growing pains', but are serious, dangerous and very difficult to deal with. We cannot cover here all the very complex issues these problems raise. But we would like to mention briefly a few of the resources parents may find helpful in getting started.

If your teenager is confronting a serious problem, you may want to use a resource which has been set up to deal specifically with that problem. Most people have heard of Alcoholics Anonymous, a nationwide agency that runs self-help groups for alcoholics and is widely respected for its effectiveness. AA also sponsors Youth Groups in many places for teenagers who have a drinking problem. Al-Anon is another national group, similar to AA, but it serves the families of alcoholics rather than the alcoholics themselves. Alateen, which is a part of Al-Anon, is designed specifically for teenagers with alcoholic parents.

If drug abuse is the problem, there should be some sort of treatment and counselling within reach of your area. In the UK it is probably best to get the help of your GP if you can. If you think s/he may be unhelpful, a youth counsellor employed by the local authority (look in the phone book) will probably be experienced and helpful. Or you can write to RELEASE, 1 Elgin Avenue, London W9, a help organization that is likely to know of resources in your area and will treat your inquiry confidentially. (Unless the drug problem is serious and incapacitating, it may be best to avoid involving the school, as this may result in your child acquiring a label that is hard to shed.) There is no way to generalize about the quality of drug counselling; it varies considerably. If the problem is serious – real addiction to hard drugs – it can be treated in one of twenty or so special clinics. But remember, the doctor in charge must notify the Home Office of any such patient. This is purely a policing device. The Standing Conference on Drug Abuse (SCODA) is a sympathetic independent organization which can advise on clinics. Drug abuse is, of course, a problem with many social as well as personal components. You may have to try several approaches before finding the one which works best for you.

If you are the parents of a teenager who is pregnant (or whose girlfriend is), there are a number of resources to which you both can turn for help. If she wants an abortion, or thinks she might, and you have a good, sympathetic doctor, consult her or him straight away. Otherwise, help her to get a pregnancy test done at a Family Planning Association, British Pregnancy Advisory Service (FPA and BPAS) or Brook Advisory Centre, where she will have a chance to talk things through without being pushed into anything she is unsure about. Brook, in particular, are known for their caring counselling for young people in all sexual and relationship matters. All these agencies (addresses in the list at the end of the book) will also give information about the operation and the different options in arranging it (NHS or low-cost at a non-profit making clinic). It is important to remember that the emotional aspects of the procedure are as important as the physical ones, a fact which may be overlooked in such situations. (For information on services for young, single mothers, see pp. 389–90.)

There is always the question of how much you as a parent should be involved in such a situation. No simple answer exists. Obviously, the more support you can give to your child, the better. But not infrequently your child will not want you to be involved, and may not even tell you what is happening. It is important to respect this choice, and to see yourself as there to help if requested, not there to direct or control the resolution of the problem. This can be an extremely difficult and painful task, particularly when we are anxious for our child's welfare, and when their choices may go against our sense of what is best.

Don't overlook local social service agencies, youth counselling services, your doctor, a properly trained minister or vicar, or any other possible source of help which you feel might be useful to you or your teenager. Some areas have facilities that are specifically designed to work with young people. And you may find that your community has specific kinds of services which are not mentioned here; for example, some communities run temporary substitute homes for teenagers who cannot remain in their own homes, but wish to remain in the community in order to continue in school. Both teenagers and their families may receive counselling and attend group meetings.

Legal problems that may be encountered by families of teenagers are discussed on pp. 423–5.

An American resource worth mentioning as a useful model is a self-help group called Families Anonymous, which exists for parents whose teenagers have been in fairly serious and repeated trouble, including drug use, destructive behaviour and criminal offences. The organization was begun in Los Angeles in 1971, and has since spread to more than thirty states. Groups are made up entirely of parents, with no social workers or psychologists to lead the discussions. 'We all know what it's like, we've been there,' says one member. 'We don't give advice or make each other feel guilty. We just talk about what's worked for us.' One of the principal beliefs of the organization is that while there are better and worse ways to deal with very rebellious and disruptive children, no one, ultimately, can force another person to change his/her behaviour. Members learn to respect the separateness and individuality of their child, and at the same time to put the responsibility for the child's life on the child's own shoulders. They call this 'tough love' – the ability to let go of someone without ceasing to love and care about them. Some of the children of FA members have begun to build better lives for themselves; others have not. But most of the parents who are members of FA say that they have found more serenity and understanding, and feel better about themselves now than they have in a long time.

Parenting a Child with Special Needs

The term 'special needs' is used to indicate a whole range of problems, from mild to severe. It includes such things as vision or hearing loss, retardation and perceptual and learning difficulties. If you have a child with such needs, regardless of the nature or severity of the problem, you may at first feel overwhelmed with shock at seeing your image of an ordered and ordinary life so abruptly shattered. Mixed in with the sorrow, worry and love for your child are other, more confusing feelings. You may feel guilty, wondering what you did, or didn't do, to cause this to happen. You may worry whether you will be able to be a good enough parent to this 'hurt' child. Some parents of handicapped children say that, at first, anger permeated every part of their lives: anger at a partner for having 'produced' such a child, anger at the doctors for being unable to cure what's wrong, anger at the world for being so thoughtless, so unhelpful, so lacking in understanding. Perhaps most difficult to deal with is the pain, not just for oneself but for the child, for the hurts and frustrations that s/he may be forced to endure. These and other feelings are a normal and inevitable part of parenting a child with special needs; they are healthy reactions to this stressful situation. Knowing that these feelings are legitimate is a crucial step in getting the best help for both your child and yourself.

It is important, also, to understand that these very difficult feelings are not permanent, though at first they may seem so. Parenting a child with special needs is a long process, during which many changes will occur. There is a great deal of knowledge, skill and strength which, as they are acquired, will make positive changes in the way you deal with, and feel about, your situation.

Your Needs Are as Important as Those of the Child

The feelings you will experience, and the needs you will have, will depend to a great extent on what type of problem your child has. But whatever your situation, try to keep in mind that just as you need direct services for your child, you will need support for yourselves, as separate people, not just as accessories to your child. As one mother of a seriously handicapped child has written:

It is important to remember that as big and overwhelming a problem as it may seem, as deeply committed as you may always be to caring for your child, caring about yourself and being separate from 'the problem' is a goal you should have from the very beginning. You need to shed the totality of your identity as 'the parents of a hurt child' in order to break through the isolation, fear and loneliness that can otherwise surround you.

Equip Yourselves

In addition to getting support, it is very important to learn the skills of 'equipping' yourselves. Some of these have been described on p. 380. Here are some ways you can apply these skills to parenting a child with special needs. Certainly you will think of others.

If you suspect there is something wrong with your child, start to write down what you are thinking and observing. This does not have to be elaborate, just some notes about developmental milestones, things that seem odd or troublesome to you, how the child makes you feel. What worries you may in fact be perfectly normal, but if it troubles you over a long period of time, it may need some attention. Your next step should be to tell your family doctor what you've noticed, or, if you're close to your health visitor, talk it over with her. If the child is already at school, you can also consult the school nurse and doctor, class teacher and head teacher. They may reassure you that they can see nothing wrong. However, you do see more of your child than they do, and if you are still worried, persist in seeking more specialized help. You can ask your GP to refer you to a paediatrician at the local hospital or to the NHS District Assessment Centre. Ask for a full examination. If your child is handicapped in any way, it is very important that s/he is seen and the condition diagnosed as early as possible.

A full assessment of your child's special needs now and for the future might involve not only medical people, but also teachers, educational psychologists, therapists and social workers. It may be difficult to extract a detailed written report each time from these professionals, but try asking for one. In any case, it's a good idea for you to write down everything you learn from each interview or examination.

You, more than most parents, will need to understand how agencies and bureaucracies work, and how the power imbalance between professionals and lay people can work against your getting the help you need and deserve. Most professionals do not deliberately intend to mystify. A common problem is that specialists who are expert in their field can be genuinely amateurish in communicating with lay persons. Another is that a doctor's interest may be confined to the clinical diagnosis and prognosis of your child's disorder, whereas your interest encompasses the management of it, its social dimensions. Unless you, at least, perceive this difference, questions and answers can be at confusing cross purposes.

When you go to visit a professional, you may find that taking a partner or a trusted friend along will give you the courage to say what is on your mind, and will lead to a better outcome. It is always your right to do this. And don't let yourself be confused by technical jargon. When a word or idea is used that you don't understand, ask for clarification. Don't accept, 'It's too complicated for you to understand.' There is nothing of this nature that cannot be explained to someone who wants to understand it. You need this information to separate which decisions are technical ones from those which depend on your feelings, opinions and needs as parents. Keeping records, describing your own observations and asking for explanations will lead to your greater understanding. This understanding can help you to become knowledgeable, effective members of the team caring for your child, rather than feeling like confused, ineffective outsiders. (See the Society chapter.)

Where to Look for Help in the UK

Begin with people who already have, or could easily develop, an interest in your child. Talk with her/his GP, teachers, any specialists or therapists you see regularly for treatment. They may be able to give you moral support as well as practical suggestions. A good health visitor can be a great emotional support to the whole family, and through her links with the local community and the health services, she can help in innumerable practical ways, from finding nursery places to getting needed equipment and supplies. One health visitor we know of visited a distressed mother every day for the first six months of her baby's life.

There are local mutual-help parent groups grouped around almost every kind of disability throughout the UK. They've come together to share information and resources and, most importantly, although it might not be explicit, the experience and feelings of parenting children with special needs. Your health visitor, GP or area Community Health Council should know of local groups. If they can't help, try writing to a national organization which deals with your child's problem (the Down's Children's Association, for example) and may be able to put you in touch with a group. Parents of children with a rare handicap should write to the Social Work Department at Great Ormond Street Hospital, London WC1.

If there is no local group you might want to start one. Certainly this is not easy, particularly if you are feeling overwhelmed. But staff at any of the health services you use can probably put you in touch with other parents who are feeling isolated and overwhelmed too. Just talking on the phone can be enormously helpful and comforting.

Another important source of help is the social services department of the local council. Many of us are a little afraid of social workers, thinking of them as 'the council' and more interfering than helpful; or we may confuse them with officious DHSS staff we've met when claiming benefits. In fact these departments are responsible for many useful facilities, and an understanding social worker can be a real friend in need, informing you and speaking up for you about all manner of aids and allowances. The social workers attached to a hospital can be equally helpful.

Finally, you can look to the vast number of voluntary organizations which offer services and help to people with special needs. Some are local and you find out about them at the library, a Citizens' Advice Bureau or the Community Health Council; most are national and too numerous to list. Two are well worth contacting to find out about the others: the Voluntary Council for Handicapped Children, which is an umbrella organization for all societies dealing with disabled children, and the Disablement Income Group Charitable Trust, which collects information, promotes research and operates an advisory service for all disabled people and their families. This group produces an invaluable handbook, frequently updated, *An ABC of Services and Information for Disabled People*. Addresses and phone numbers are in the list at the end of the book.

Services for Children with Special Needs

There is a vast amount of services, practical aids, financial allowances and legal entitlements available for children with special needs. The difficulty is to find them. There is no central body set up to tell parents where to go for assistance. Explore all the resources described above and be very very persistent: help is there to be found. Here is a short indication of some of the areas in which you can ask for and expect to get help:

● Supplies and small-scale equipment. Essential supplies, incontinence clothing, for example, should be offered automatically through the health services; other items, such as remedial toys from a toy library, may also be available. Ask for whatever you need from the health visitor or social worker.

● Financial help and major equipment. Several DHSS allowances are available; some are means-tested, some are not; some are tax-free, some not. DHSS leaflet HB1 (*Help for Handicapped People*) gives details. Major ones to ask about are the attendance allowance, invalid care allowance, and additions to supplementary benefit, if you are claiming it. Other benefits include free milk for school-age children not in school, help with fares to hospital, and supplementary grants for extended education. Go to a local DHSS office for information and application forms (address in the phone book).

Local authorities are empowered to pay all or part of the cost of needed house adaptations and of special equipment and furniture.

The Family Fund (part of the Rowntree Trust) offers financial help with all sorts of expenses to the families of severely handicapped children.

● Holidays, leisure, 'time off'. Social service departments can arrange for children to be cared for in special holiday homes and foster homes, though sometimes only hospital places can be found. Voluntary agencies too can often provide for caring, stimulating holidays. Remember you need a break and a rest as much as your child does. The range of possible recreational activities, clubs and hobbies can be very wide, depending on where you live. Ask in the usual places, and contact the British Sports Association for the Disabled.

● Pre-school and education. Local education authorities are empowered to provide pre-school education for handicapped children from the age of two, though they do not always use these powers. In some areas children may be able to start school at two or three, but in any case education must be provided from the age of five in an ordinary school, a special unit, or a special school.

Some 'special' schools are lovely places to be for any child; others may not be quite right for your child or, at worst, they can be frankly awful. You must look around. Some local authorities can be persuaded to pay the child's fees at a voluntary school if you think it's the right one for her/him.

If you think your child might do better at a special school you can ask for an assessment. Parents can also be asked by the local education authority to allow their child to be assessed. Many find this and the procedure worrying: quite understandably, since you cannot legally refuse an assessment and you cannot withdraw a child from a special school, once registered there, without the local education authority's permission. However, you have a right to be present at any examination and to see the report on which the child's future depends. Read and use the DES Circular (2/75) to local authorities on *The Discovery of Children Requiring Special Education and the Assessment of their Needs*.

If at any time you feel unconsulted and caught up in some inexorable machine from which you cannot extricate yourself and your child, seek allies and help: from local councillors, your MP, the local ombudsperson.

These are only a few of the possibilities (and their snags) open to children and parents. There may be many more in your area, including help we haven't begun to cover, such as counselling for parents under stress. Soliciting help can be time-consuming and emotionally draining. Some of us find it hard to ask for things for ourselves and even for our children. It is really worthwhile trying to find a trusted

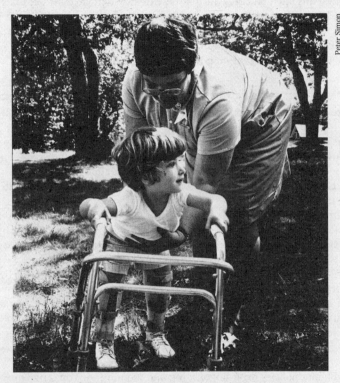

Peter Simon

ally to help with the inquiries and to speak for you and the child, over a particular issue, or for a longer period. Look for help from a family friend, a social worker, neighbourhood adviser, a church worker, a local women's centre. Don't be afraid to ask: people can be unstintingly generous.

An organization called 'Advocacy Services' was recently formed in New York, 'to accompany, advise, support and educate those interested in seeking appropriate services for children with special needs'. It is a personal service offered by two women, both teachers and parents of handicapped children, who have developed a particular expertise over the years and now wish to share it. We know of nothing similar outside of New York, but it's an example of a simple resource that could be started anywhere.

Hospitalization, Battering, Legal Problems and Other Crises

During our lives as parents there are many types of crisis that we may experience. Illness, violence, divorce, death, legal problems – all can befall a family with suddenness and leave chaos in their wake. How can we deal with these troubles? What resources are there to which we can turn? In this section we will mention a few types of crisis and some of the available resources. But it is important to realize that it is often precisely during these times when we most need help that we ourselves most resist it. We may feel we are rising to meet the challenge, yet in so doing we sometimes manage to convince ourselves and others that we do not need any help. Or our behaviour may become frantic and ineffective, and we see the problem as so large that no one could possibly help us with it.

Here are some ideas to bear in mind if your child has to go into hospital:

1. *Trust your instincts.*
You know your child better than anyone else does. If you feel s/he needs you, stay with her or him as much time as you can. You have the right to stay with your child whatever hours you wish to stay no matter what hours are stated for visiting by the hospital.

Children become fearful of even routine tests and examinations without the reassuring presence of a parent. Often they withdraw and become silent and 'good'. Hospital staff often interpret this as adjusting, but medical literature tells us this is a sign of emotional upset, when children need their parents.

You are experienced in the care of your child and can help in her care. Usually you can continue the routine things you do at home. She will react well to familiar handling. The nurses will tell you of special precautions that may be necessary. Medical sources report that children recover faster and with fewer complications when cared for by parents.

2. *Shop for a hospital.*
Find out about policies regarding visiting and rooming-in. Your child may need you full time, especially if she is too young to understand explanations, or is in pain, or is upset by being separated from you. A breast-fed baby will also need you beyond regular visiting hours so as not to interrupt the normal feeding routines.

3. *Prepare yourself.*
Find out in advance about tests, procedures, surgery, future treatment and special care so you can explain these simply to your child in language she will understand. Read, ask questions, talk with other parents about their experiences. If your child is an infant, your preparation will help you cope with the experience and be calm and reassuring.

Whatever your situation, times of crisis are times in which *everyone* needs help. The following suggestions may help you get started.

Hospitalization

Suppose your child becomes ill or is hurt and needs to go into hospital. Should you try to stay with her/him? How should you explain to the child what is going on? What are the hospital's policies? What are your rights as parents?

The answers to these questions have changed a lot since most of us were children. If your child needs hospitalization, you may find that you are quite uncertain about what is best for you to do, or you may know what you want but run into opposition from doctors and hospitals. In order to deal with this situation, several years ago a group of parents and health care professionals

---

4. *Prepare your child.*

Be honest with her. If she is old enough, tell her the reason for the hospitalization in terms she will understand. Assure her that you know these doctors and nurses have helped other children and will also be able to help her. Be sure to tell her there may be pain or discomfort for a short time, but that each day she will feel better and be getting ready to come home.

Sometimes a child will ask no questions or will refuse to talk about a planned hospital stay, but continue to mention the subject in the days before she is admitted.

Be honest about how much time you will spend with her. Always tell her when you are leaving. Let the nurses know when you are going so they can offer some comfort to the child. It may seem easier to slip away when she is playing happily, but when she finds you gone she will feel more confused than if she had seen you go. Children are often afraid you won't come back or that they won't go home again.

After a stay in hospital, parents often notice signs of upset that continue for days or weeks. Some children wake at night, cling more by day, fear doctor's visits, and wet their beds. Some try hard to behave perfectly, fearing a return to the hospital as a punishment.

5. *Work for changes.*

Write to the hospital and to particular staff after a hospitalization to let them know what you liked and disliked about your child's hospital experience. Request any policy changes that you would like to see made.

6. *Try to be there.*

Try to be there full time, but if you can't, get another family member or friend to cover for you. Especially when you know tests or other procedures are planned, be on hand.

banded together to form the National Association for the Welfare of Children in Hospital (described more fully on p. 360 of the Society chapter) which is an important resource to which parents may turn.

Find out what services *your* hospital has. They may have preparatory visits, in which you and your child can become familiar with areas of the hospital and some of its procedures. Or there may be a 'play person' who visits children during their stay to help them understand and talk about some of their experiences and fears. The hospital social work department may be able to send a staff member with whom you or your child can talk. As with all resources, the more you ask, the more you try to change what you don't like, the more you *get involved*, the better help you will usually get. (NAWCH has a number of useful publications, including recommended books and articles, which can give you some ideas of how to do this.)

If a parent goes into hospital, these same points are still important to keep in mind. Keeping in contact with your child while you are gone if you are able to, helping her/him to understand what is going on and telling her/him when you will come back, will make your hospital stay easier on the family.

You may also find that you need considerable help at home when one parent is ill or in hospital for a prolonged time. Most communities have some resources for parents to turn to. Social services (ask about home helps), hospital social worker, health visitor, all are appropriate resources to call on.

It is a sad fact, however, and one which deserves our attention as a society, that state help available for domestic crises is inadequate for most families' needs.

Death

While most people can imagine how deep their own sadness and loss would be if a member of the family were to die, often we are quite unprepared for how long it takes for these feelings to be resolved, and how many different forms grief can take. Increased fears, withdrawal, anger, denial, extreme changes in behaviour, strong feelings of dependence and regression are just some of the many faces of grief which a family may confront in children and in adults. Because it falls to the parents to try to help the family through this difficult time, it is important to know that there is help available. Certainly, friends, extended family and neighbours are important sources of support. A child's school, and particularly a favourite teacher, may also be of considerable help. There may be emergency services and funds to help out when a parent dies, which you can learn about by calling the resources listed in the previous section on Hospitalization. If either a parent or a child continues to experience serious difficulties after the initial phase of grief, you may find it very helpful to arrange for a few appointments with a mental health professional. Go to your GP for advice, or to the child guidance clinic, which usually helps both parents and children. Young children often have secret fears about the death of a parent or sibling, which can be very damaging in later years if not worked out.

Child Battering

There are difficult periods of parenting for all of us, when we feel as if we simply cannot make things go right. We may feel as if we are in a battle with our children, that we cannot make them behave as we want them to, no matter what methods we try. Perhaps we scream at them, hit them or find other ways to punish them severely. It seems as if they are asking for harsh treatment by their behaviour, and yet some part of us knows that something is wrong, that we are not acting as rational adults. We may sense that anger or frustration at other things in our life is getting mixed up with anger at our child, and that the child becomes the target for it. .

All of us who care for children have times like this. But sometimes your common sense may tell you that something is really wrong, that you are hitting your children too often or too hard. When your children tend to bear the brunt of your anger, when you often feel confused, guilty and out of control in your handling of children, when you feel as if you are repeating your own past, when you were treated cruelly or neglectfully, then you know that you need and deserve to get help.

There are many misconceptions about parents who beat their children: that they are poor and uneducated, that they are unpredictably violent and 'mad', that they don't love their children. None of these is true. Child battering occurs in all social classes and income brackets; it occurs in predictable circumstances which can come to be understood; and the parents involved often love their children profoundly. Child battering is part of a larger system of family and personal stress and may involve people who are still struggling with issues from their own childhood which interfere with the job of parenting.

Parents who batter their children have feelings very much like those of other parents, but they are unable to step back and get any distance on the situation they are in with their children. Often they find the following conditions in their lives:

- They are isolated from others, have no close, supportive relationships, no one to talk to.
- They were beaten or treated cruelly or neglectfully as children themselves.
- They feel guilty and ashamed about their behaviour with their children.
- When they get reassurance, it doesn't help but, rather, makes them feel worse, as if they are being told not to ask for help.

There are no official figures for child battering in the UK because, although the NSPCC has undertaken some research in this area, there is no government body carrying out adequate observation of non-accidental injury to children. But it was estimated that in one year over 7,000 children aged under fifteen were hurt in this way. Child battering remains one of the most difficult things for us to talk about. Parents find it very hard to acknowledge the problem, and professionals are often unsure of how to help. Nonetheless, people who are battering their children frequently ask for help, but they are not often heard. They go, sometimes again and again, to professionals like doctors and to hospital casualty departments, and they may either be ignored or be given false reassurances. These parents have come even more than most of us to mistrust professionals, and this adds to the difficulty of asking for help. And so they, who are often under tremendous stress, must identify their own needs and somehow reach past the barriers to getting help.

There is real help available if you are battering your children or are afraid you might. The cycle of violence, frightening as it is, can be stopped, but it is necessary to reach out of your isolation and make contact. Parents Anonymous is a mutual help group begun in 1978. Parents meet regularly to talk openly with others in the same difficulty and to give each other support, in a similar way to Alcoholics Anonymous groups. There are now a dozen local groups in operation. There is a crisis telephone service for parents in distress, 01-669 8900, where you can call between 6 p.m. and 6 a.m., seven nights a week, to talk to a sympathetic listener – usually a parent who has been in similar straits. They hope eventually to provide hostel-type accommodation for children, or child and parent, or even whole families where they can be helped.

It may seem as if contact with such groups would itself do little good, as far as the actual problem of battering is concerned, yet independent observers in the US report that physical abuse usually stops within the first month of a parent's involvement in the sister organization there. And parents who continue to have contact with PA find that their group can become the supportive community which has so far been lacking in their lives. It can aid them in finding other resources within the community to help improve their lives as parents as well as the lives of their children.

A mutual-help group like PA is not the only place you can turn to. The NSPCC, as a result of their study of the battered child syndrome, have established the National Advisory Centre on the Battered Child in London, which provides medical, psychological and psychiatric services. Special NSPCC units to help parents who injure their children are also being set up around the country. Each unit is manned twenty-four hours a day by a team of qualified and experienced workers. Ring 01-361 1181 if you need help.

You may be able to arrange for your child to be in day care for part of the day so that you get some time and space for yourself. Talking to a therapist, even for an hour or two a week, can provide a release valve for the pressure you feel, and help you understand more clearly where it comes from and how to handle it.

There are two more drastic solutions which occasionally may be necessary. Either you or your child may have to be hospitalized for a period of time, for either physical or emotional reasons. Alternatively, or in addition, you may need to have your child placed in foster care for a period of time, until the situation at home is under control. Both of these solutions are fraught with problems: you generally will have little control over where your child is placed, and you may feel lost in the legal and bureaucratic red tape. But if the situation at home is completely out of hand, any way you reach out can only improve it.

Wife Battering

All parents argue at times over certain situations they must face together. Job and financial difficulties, sexual problems and the demands of parenting can create stresses which weigh heavily on people. Sometimes, however, a man will habitually express his anger, frustration and sense of powerlessness by beating up his wife.

The most common reason why a woman may continue to tolerate such abuse is the very realistic fear of having nowhere to go and no way to support her family alone. In addition, she may keep hoping that things will improve or be afraid to anger her husband further by speaking up, or she may be reluctant to break up her family or leave the man she loves. Sometimes women imagine that the beatings have no effect on their children, believing that what children don't see can't hurt them, or that they are too young to understand. But in a home where violence is common, everyone is being damaged, even though only one member of the family is being physically hurt. Even a tiny baby suffers under such circumstances.

If this situation exists in your home, it is imperative that you get help immediately, to protect yourself as well as your children. Many areas throughout the country now have emergency shelters, or refuges, where you can go with your children while you work out what to do. The shelters, usually endorsed by local social services departments, are normally run by the National Women's Aid Federation (NWAF). This organization currently has ninety-eight women's aid groups, eighty-eight of which have at least one house. The NWAF refuges are managed by sympathetic women, usually feminists, and can provide you with immediate protection and shelter, some for short-term stays, others for longer. Workers will also give you guidance about housing, legal and welfare rights, as well as emotional support. In order to find a refuge in your area, ring the local social services department. You can refer yourself either by going to a refuge you know of, or by contacting NWAF (address in the list at the end of the book).

Legal Problems

Youngsters may brush with the law for all sorts of reasons from possession of marijuana to taking and driving cars, vandalism, drinking, stealing, and even more serious crimes. We ourselves may have had no more contact with policemen than an argument over parking, yet, particularly when our children are teenagers, we may find ourselves suddenly 'on the other side'. Then we have to deal not only with the very serious practical problems but also with our own feelings – that our children have humiliated us or put us or themselves in danger. We may find that we are torn between wanting to protect our kids and wanting to join the authorities in punishing them. We may feel publicly shamed, yet frightened for our children and angry at those who are 'after us'. Parents who've been in this situation say that it is a time when they have had to summon all their own resources to remain calm. It is also an important time to get outside help.

If your child is in trouble with the law, you should get good legal advice – as early in the process as possible. The difficulty, as in selecting other professionals, will be to find a good person to represent you. This is particularly difficult under these circumstances when you are under the special stress of problems with police and the courts.

This is what you should do:

● If the situation is urgent and seems serious, for example, if you discover your teenager is being held at a police station late at night and you are too frightened and bewildered to understand what has happened, much less what to do about it, ring RELEASE on 01-289 1123. RELEASE operates a twenty-four-hour and nationwide service to people, particularly young people, in trouble with the law. They will give you immediate advice and, if the situation warrants it, will arrange for someone to go with you to the police station to mediate with the police.

● If the situation can wait till office hours, you can ring RELEASE then and ask for a solicitor in your area known to specialize in the sort of case your child is involved in. All solicitors recommended by RELEASE will work on legal aid. A Citizens' Advice Bureau should also be able to offer sound advice about local lawyers. Best of all would be to go to a community law centre if there is one. These are centres where lawyers who know the neighbourhood, the local issues and, often, the local police make a positive effort to be available to the community for free advice. Find the address of the CAB in the local phone book. RELEASE will know of law centres.

It is always advisable to have a solicitor in court. You must not rely on your child's innocence to protect her or him. If you have no time to find one before the case comes up, tell the magistrate you want a solicitor and legal aid and ask to have the case adjourned.

Legal aid is state money paid to cover the cost of having a solicitor to represent you. Unless you're rich enough not to worry about the bill, you should always apply for it. The aid is means-tested but in general it is easier to get free legal aid for criminal cases than the official requirements suggest. You apply for it on a form obtainable from the court offices or a CAB, and it's best to do it on the spot. If there isn't time before the child goes to court, the magistrate should be told as soon as possible. S/he will either consider the application straightaway or adjourn the case.

There are of course special rules and procedures for children under seventeen in trouble with the law. For example, Judges' Rules state: 'As far as practicable children (whether suspected of crime or not) should only be interviewed (by the police) in the presence of a parent or guardian, or, in their absence, some person who is not a police officer...' We would be naïve to imagine that such rules are always followed. Nan Berger's *Rights Handbook for People Under Age* (Penguin, 1974) explains children's special rights. *Civil Liberty: the NCCL Guide* (Penguin, 1972) explains citizens' rights and procedures on arrest, bail, the courts and legal aid. *Trouble with the Law* (Release Publications and Pluto Press, 1979) explains not only 'rights' but also what can happen in practice, including the abuse of those rights.

When the worst happens, we're unlikely to have these books handy; we don't expect *our* children to get into trouble. Yet in inner city areas, it is becoming increasingly common for young people to be picked up and questioned by the police simply because they are young. Under a nineteenth-century Vagrancy Act,* the highly criticized 'sus' law, anyone can be stopped, arrested and charged because the police say they were acting 'suspiciously'. The 'sus' law is often used without any very obvious justification. If your child is black and male, some community leaders regard it as inevitable that he will be picked up for questioning at some time.

Even if you don't expect your child to have a brush with the law, it would be worthwhile reading a book such as *Trouble with the Law* in order to understand the difficult social world that our urban teenagers must navigate.

Therapy

What is Therapy For?

In an evaluation of formal resources, psychological therapy is probably the most difficult to write about. The issues with which it deals are complex, and raise questions that are sociological, political and ethical, as well as personal in nature. Many people have very strong opinions about whether or not therapy is of value or can actually help us to change in the ways we want. Then, we often wind up turning to mental health resources at those times in our lives when we are most needy, vulnerable and off balance. Even as we are struggling to let ourselves trust strangers with the intimate details of our lives, we must at the same time be alert, aware consumers, watching out for our own best interests. Finally, it is hard sometimes to decide when we actually want or need to use therapy, since the situations and problems with which it deals are on a continuum with those we encounter every day of our lives.

We believe that *good* therapy is an invaluable resource, and that the skills it can teach are an important part of living.

Here are some examples of common situations that families encounter, for which they might or might not want professional help.

A bright twelve-year-old boy had begun having difficulty going to sleep, and vomited many mornings before school, following his promotion to a special class for gifted children. Yet he had been bored in the ordinary classroom. His parents were unsure of what to do.

---

*As a result of much public agitation, this Act is to be repealed. But police representatives are pressing for even wider powers of detention to replace it.

A woman who had tried for many years to have a child finally succeeded in adopting a little girl. Her great joy at becoming a mother was marred by a continuing feeling of emptiness because she had never been able to become pregnant. She sometimes felt angry at her adopted daughter, and then felt overwhelmed with guilt for not appreciating what she had waited so long to have. She feared that her anger meant that she must not truly love her child, and was therefore not a fit mother.

Each of these situations was greatly improved when the parents gave it their careful attention, together with some help and advice from friends, teachers, support groups and organizations. When the twelve-year-old boy was given encouragement to talk about his feelings, it became clear that he felt under a great deal of pressure in the new class. He was given the option to go back to his former class, which he did. With the support of his parents and teachers, he then enrolled in the chess club, the maths club and the debating team. He enjoyed the extra challenges, without feeling pressure, and his symptoms promptly stopped.

The adoptive mother mentioned her fears to a friend who had herself adopted several children. The friend had experienced precisely the same sense of loss and feelings of anger and suggested that the mother attend several sessions of a group for adoptive parents. In doing so, the mother was greatly relieved to hear that her feelings were in fact quite common and natural. Her sense of grief began to lessen, as did her fear of being angry with her child. And the group became a source of new and valued friends.

Sometimes, simply paying attention to a problem, talking with others in a similar situation, trying to change what you think might be causing the problem, as well as patiently waiting a bit, are all that is needed to find a resolution. In the following instances, however, the attempts the parents made to solve the problem were unsatisfactory, and so they turned for help to mental health professionals:

A mother who had had a severe and prolonged postnatal depression following the birth of her first baby was pregnant again. She was terribly frightened that her depression would repeat itself.

In a family with five children, four had done well, but one had always been difficult for the parents to deal with. She was moody and sullen, and now had begun shoplifting and, her parents feared, drinking excessively. The whole family had always seen her as the 'black sheep', and were united in their rejection of her.

A bright, affectionate seven-year-old boy had been alternately angry and depressed for several months, and was having trouble concentrating and learning to read in class. His parents were separated, and were in the process of getting divorced.

In talking with a therapist once a week over a period of several months, the mother who had felt overwhelmed after the birth of her first child began to understand what had contributed to her feelings. She was able to anticipate what would make the next postnatal period easier, and she made work and child-care arrangements which, together with her new-found knowledge of herself, averted a second depression and enabled her to enjoy what she had once dreaded.

The second family, after an evaluation at a local mental health clinic, was encouraged to be seen as a family, rather than singling out the one child for treatment. The parents and all five of the children agreed, and with the help of two therapists (a man and a woman), they were able to understand how one child had become the scapegoat for general difficulties within the family. As they worked on some of these problems, the 'black sheep's' destructive behaviour lessened and her position within the family improved considerably.

The parents of the seven-year-old boy went to see a therapist to ask how they could help their son. After meeting with the boy, the therapist suggested that his behaviour was a reaction to the stress surrounding the divorce. He saw the parents several times, during which he helped them to work out ways of handling the situation so that pressure was taken off their son. Things improved somewhat, but when, several months later, the boy was still experiencing difficulties, the therapist recommended that the boy go into treatment with a child therapist. He went, and the parents immediately experienced great relief: they saw their son's therapist as a helpful ally. After one year, the child was considerably better, but he continued for the next several years to drop in on his therapist on those occasions when he felt the need to talk.

Things to Know about Using Therapy

What does therapy do? Simply put, good therapy can ideally help us do four things:

● *To put us in touch with our feelings* – to experience, in a 'safe' place, troublesome feelings that we have pushed away because they are too painful, confusing or scary, so that we can recognize them and begin to come to terms with them.

● *To understand 'what is'* – to understand ourselves and others better, to learn who we are, what we value, why we do what we do, how we relate to others, what we get from them and give to them.

● *To decide what we want* – to consider the possibilities, to imagine how we would like things to be, to see what parts of our lives we would like to keep, and what parts we would like to change.

● *To learn how to get there* – to develop the skills and confidence we need to cope with problems, and to change our lives so that they will be happier, more fulfilling, less isolated and more meaningful.

Being in therapy is not the only or even always the best way to learn these things. There are many other ways: through conversations with friends, through mutual-support groups, through joining a spiritual community, through meditation or through self-exploration. Each of these routes, including that of therapy, has its own strengths and weaknesses. Following are some of the qualities which distinguish *good* therapy from help we can get in other contexts:

● A therapist has training and knowledge about the emotional development and problems of both individuals and families, and can use this knowledge to help us understand our situation better.

● While a therapist cares what happens to us, s/he is not personally involved in our lives, and can be more objective than a friend or family member. We also have the benefit of privacy in working out our difficulties.

● A therapist is being paid to spend time working with us, so that we can feel free to ask for nurturance and attention without feeling the need to nurture back, or to help the therapist work on his or her problems. This can be important at a time when we are feeling stressed and depleted.

● A therapist may know of other resources in the community, and can help us to get in touch with them for help with such things as physical problems, financial stresses and occupational problems. Therapists also have access to back-up services available to a person or a family in crisis.

● In knowing we will have regular time to work with a therapist, we may be able to step back from the situation a bit and begin to get an overview, so that we can work not only to resolve the immediate problem, but also to build strengths and to learn skills that will help us deal with future situations.

Self-help Therapy

Some mutual-help groups have been working out ways of using therapy techniques in a leaderless setting – partly out of a wish to deprofessionalize therapy, partly because, in some people's experience, ideological differences with professional therapists have run counter to useful therapy. One group in the UK has written of their experience in *Red Therapy*, available from some bookshops or 52 Josephine Avenue, London SW2. Re-evaluation co-counselling is another method of self-help therapy where two people take the role of therapist and client in turn. *In Our Own Hands: A Guide to Self-Help Therapy* by Sheila Ernst and Lucy Goodison (London: Women's Press, 1981) includes self-help therapy and contact addresses for groups in its comprehensive and helpful exploration of all kinds of therapy available in Britain now.

What It Means to Need or Want Therapy

Sometimes people hesitate to go to a therapist, even when they think it might help. They worry that it means they are 'mad', or that they have failed as parents. Or they fear that it means their child is really 'mixed up', or a 'problem child'. Sometimes people believe that the very fact of wanting help means that their problems are different from and far more serious than those which most people experience. It is important to remember that life is a process during which each of us moves into and out of the space of needing help. Seeking help when we need it is not a sign of inadequacy but, rather, it is a mature first step towards finding a solution to what is troubling us.

How to Evaluate a Problem

There is no precise line which divides problems that require professional help from problems that don't. But here are some questions you can ask yourself if you are contemplating therapy, and trying to sort out what is going on.

● Does the problem have an obvious cause? For example, the birth of a sibling, the loss of a parent's job, a death in the family? Or does it seem related to more than a specific incident or stage?

● Have you tried other solutions and yet still feel there is a problem?

● How long has the problem gone on? Has it been brief and limited in scope, or has it persisted for a long time and perhaps taken a variety of forms?

● Has the same difficulty cropped up repeatedly at different times in your life and in different situations?

● How severe and unusual does it seem to you? Are your friends with similar-aged children describing similar problems, or do yours seem quite different and more extreme?

● By far the most important question: how much distress is the problem causing you, your child or your family, regardless of its apparent severity? For example, something that seems like a minor difficulty to you may be very upsetting to a child, and may wind up affecting his/her relationships with friends or school performance and self-image. On the other hand, your child may be going through a very common and normal stage, which doesn't bother most of your friends, but it may bother you a great deal. In either case, getting help makes sense.

Finding Therapy

First ask friends who may have been in the same need. After that, your GP should know of some local resources, their quality and the length of their waiting lists. Be cautious of hospital psychiatric departments – some will offer only drug or behavioural therapy. Local authority youth counselling services sometimes offer family therapy as well as advice for adolescents. There are child guidance clinics everywhere, sometimes run by the health authority, sometimes by the education authority. They can be very good sources of all kinds of therapy for parents and children (but if the schools' educational psychologist gets involved, make sure that your child doesn't acquire a 'label' that will accompany her/him through-out school). The Marriage Guidance Council is also helpful in directing you to therapy: don't be put off by the name – you don't have to be married to ask them. Finally, the Women's Therapy Centre and the Tavistock Centre are both in London but are sympathetic to inquiries from anywhere and will direct you to what resources they know of. Addresses in the list at the end of the chapter. *In Our Own Hands: A Guide to Self-Help Therapy* has been written by two women with wide experience of self-help therapy, therapy workshops and one-to-one therapy, both as 'therapists' and 'clients'. The book is a practical guide to what therapy is like and where it's available; it looks critically at the issues behind it and suggests ways to help you make up your mind about your own needs and how best to meet them.

Evaluating a Therapist

What is available? There are many different kinds of therapy and counselling. Some types involve mostly talking, while others use a variety of other techniques. You can go for a long time and deal with a number of issues, or you can go for a few sessions and stick to one specific topic. A child or a parent can go alone, two parents can go together, or any combination of children and parents can go. It is not necessary to work out beforehand exactly how long you want to go for, or even which *type* of therapist you want to see. The issue is to find someone you trust and with whom you feel comfortable.

How to judge quality. What we are looking for in a therapist is someone who will listen to us, who will reflect back what s/he hears or sees and help us clarify, understand, see patterns in our life and, ultimately, have some control over it. But therapists, like all professionals, vary considerably in quality. Here are some basic points to keep in mind.

The reputation of a therapist or an agency is important. Ask friends whom they have worked with, and how they feel about that person. When you are first looking for a therapist, you may have to 'shop around', that is, talk with several people before you find someone you feel comfortable with. Ask whether the therapist sticks to certain techniques (the best therapists are flexible in their use of techniques). While you are working in therapy with someone, observe the relationship s/he develops with you and your family. Does the therapist see your problems in a way that makes sense to you? Does s/he offer insights into the problem that have not yet occurred to you, but which seem to fit?

You should begin to feel like a member of a team working toward a goal, not like a passive object of treatment or study. Pay attention to your own reactions. You should have a sense of trusting the therapist, of understanding what is happening. Your questions and concerns should be treated with respect and dignity. And while therapy is not an instant or magical solution to difficult problems, you should begin after a while to see results. You should begin to feel better about yourself, and gradually be less dependent on the therapist.

Consider the following issues in choosing a therapist:

Individual competence. This is perhaps the single most important factor. There are a variety of ways in which a therapist can be incompetent, or simply not be right for you. Beware for example:

● If you feel judged, accused, labelled, ignored, investigated or otherwise disrespected.

● If you feel you're being made to conform to a traditional mould (particularly a problem for women in therapy) or to adjust to an unacceptable life situation.

• If you often feel pressured to go a great deal faster or deeper than feels safe to you; or, on the other hand, if you are being given patronizing reassurances or simplistic advice.

Perhaps the therapist you are seeing (or could see) is all right, but not great, and you wonder if you should bother to go at all. Certainly, if you can find a better therapist, do so. But remember that a little help is better than none at all, for it can get you *started* on the *process* of taking care of yourself.

Choosing the right person. Because basically anyone can call himself or herself a therapist, there are some people doing therapy who shouldn't be. They may be good at some other work but inadequate, or even damaging, as therapists. For example, some people consult a member of the clergy in times of emotional stress. This may work out very well or very badly. While priests are traditionally expected to assume the role of comforter, guide and adviser in times of need, many of them do not have the training to do therapy with people who are deeply troubled. A further example of an inappropriate choice would be asking an obstetrician to treat a severe postnatal depression. These may be the people to whom we first turn, since they are the most easily accessible, but they may not always be good choices.

The larger perspective. It is important to recognize that some things which we view as emotional problems actually may have more to do with the context of our lives than with our inner selves. Many have been discussed in the chapters throughout this book, particularly the Society chapter. Two examples of personal problems with a substantial social component may be the social isolation and stress felt by many young mothers, and teenage drug abuse. There are many others.

While it is not the fault of therapists that these larger issues exist, it *is* their responsibility to maintain a view of their clients within a social context, and to help them to gain an awareness of the social as well as individual sources of disturbing emotions and problems, and the strength that exists in making connections with other people through whatever means.

Whatever option you are considering, remember that at the time most of us first think about going to see a therapist, we may be feeling very distressed or bad about ourselves or our children, or as if we had neither the time nor the energy to do all the things we must do. Finding someone we will feel good about working with, trusting that it will make a positive difference, working through the initial resistance we naturally feel – these things can take great effort. We may think the whole thing is not worth it. But it is important to realize that the very *process* of saying to ourselves that we need help, the *process* of defining what is not the way we want it to be, the *process* of reaching out, finding, choosing a therapist, is in itself a central part of therapy. In a sense, it is the most important aspect, for it is the energy we bring to looking honestly at how we live, and the willingness to change what we do not like, that largely determine what we will get out of it.

Useful Addresses

A list of the helping and campaigning organizations mentioned in Chapters 8 and 9, with a few extra suggestions.

Al-Anon
61 Great Dover Street, London SE1 4YF. Telephone 01-403 0888.

Alcoholics Anonymous
11 Redcliffe Gardens, London SW10 9BG. Telephone 01-352 9669; or look in your local phone directory.

Association for Improvements in the Maternity Services (AIMS)
19 Broomfield Crescent, Leeds 6. Telephone 0532 751911.

Association of Radical Midwives (ARM)
12a John Street, Cambridge.

A Woman's Place
48 William IV Street, London WC1. Can put you in touch with other women's centres and groups in and out of London.

British Pregnancy Advisory Service (BPAS)
Main office: Guildhall Buildings, Navigation Street, Birmingham B2 4BT. Telephone 021-643 1461.

British Sports Association for the Disabled
Stoke Mandeville Stadium, Harvey Road, Aylesbury, Bucks., HP21 8PP.

Brook Advisory Centres
Main office: 233 Tottenham Court Road, London W1P 9AE. Telephone 01-323 1522 or 01-580 2991. Counselling for young people on sexual and relationship problems.

Child Poverty Action Group (CPAG)
1 Macklin Street, London WC2B 5NH. Campaigning and research organization. Also runs *Citizens' Rights Office* to help people claim welfare rights and help at tribunals. Telephone 01-405 4517.

Children's Rights Workshop
73 Balfour Street, London SE17. Telephone 01-703 7217. Research and useful publications.

Claimants' Union
East London branch: Dame Colet House, Ben Jonson Road, London E1. Telephone 01-790 3867. Will put you in touch with other CUs to get help in claiming benefits.

Consumers' Association
14 Buckingham Street, London WC2N 6DS. Telephone 01-839 1222.

Disablement Income Group
Attlee House, Toynbee Hall, 28 Commercial Street, London E1 6LR. Telephone 01-247 2128. Campaigns for better financial provision for all disabled people. The DIG Charitable Trust runs a comprehensive advisory service.

Family Fund
PO Box 50, York YO3 6RB. Financial help for handicapped children or parents.

Family Planning Association (FPA)
Main office: 27–35 Mortimer Street, London W1N 7RJ. Telephone 01-636 7866.

Gingerbread
9 Poland Street, London W1. Telephone 01-734 9014. Will put you in touch with local groups.

La Leche League
BM 3424, London WC1V 6XX.

Lesbian Line
Telephone helpline: 01-837 8602. Counselling and referral.

MAMA
26a Cumnor Hill, Oxford OX2 9HA. A mutual help organization for mothers experiencing post-natal depression.

Men's Centre
Bread and Roses Bookshop, 316 Upper Street, London N1. Will put you in touch with men's groups elsewhere.

National Association of Twins Clubs
c/o Woodstock, Heathdown Road, Pyrford, Surrey.

National Association for the Welfare of Children in Hospital (NAWCH)
7 Exton Street, London SE1 8UE. Telephone 01-261 1738.

National Childbirth Trust
9 Queensborough Terrace, London W2 3TB. Telephone 01-229 9319.

National Children's Bureau
8 Wakely Street, London EC1V 7QE. Telephone 01-278 9441.

National Council for One-Parent Families
255 Kentish Town Road, London NW5 2LX. Telephone 01-267 1361.

National Society for the Prevention of Cruelty to Children (NSPCC)
1 Riding House Street, London W1P 8AA. Parents' helpline: 01-361 1181.

National Women's Aid Federation (NWAF)
374 Gray's Inn Road, London WC1. Telephone 01-837 9316.

Nursery campaigns
A few of the organizations already informing and campaigning about nurseries (we anticipate that more will be formed as the government's new spending cuts begin to hurt):

The Finer Joint Action Committee (FJAC), c/o 255 Kentish Town Road, London NW5 2LX. Has been going since 1974; demands that national and local government act now to improve the provision of day care for the children of one-parent families. See the Bibliography for pamphlet.

The London Nursery Campaign, c/o Hackney Under Fives, 136 Kingsland High Street, London E8. Fighting for small integrated neighbourhood-based or workplace centres with flexible hours to suit the needs of children and parents. Will send lists of under-fives groups, nursery campaigns and interested individuals. Meets bi-monthly at the Kingsway Children's Centre, Kingsway Hall, Kingsway, Holborn, London WC2.

The NALGO Campaign, 1 Mabledon Place, London WC1H 9AJ. NALGO sees child care as a key issue, and is fighting for a comprehensive state-provided service of care and education for under-fives. They see negotiations for workplace provision as complementary to the campaign for a comprehensive state scheme. See the Bibliography for pamphlet.

The National Campaign for Nursery Education, 33 Hugh Street, London SW1. A collective organization for all under-fives groups and nursery campaigns. They encourage local groups, hold meetings, do surveys.

Parents Anonymous
Helpline: 01-669 8900.

Pre-school Playgroups Association
Alford House, Aveline Street, London SE11 5DJ. Telephone 01-582 8871. Will advise on how to set up a play group.

Release
1 Elgin Avenue, London W9 3PR. Telephone 01-289 1123. Advice for young people (and their parents) in trouble: abortion, drugs, the law. Twenty-four hour emergency phone service.

Society to Support Home Confinements (SSHC)
17 Laburnum Avenue, Durham City, Durham. Telephone 0385 61325.

Standing Conference on Drug Abuse (SCODA)
3 Blackburn Road, London NW6. Telephone 01-328 6556. Independent and helpful on addiction problems.

Tavistock Centre
120 Belsize Lane, London NW3. Telephone 01-435 7111. Therapy for children, adults, family groups. Can probably advise you on therapy elsewhere.

Television Action Group
School House, Brookthorpe, Gloucester. Telephone 0452 812503.

Voluntary Council for Handicapped Children
at the National Children's Bureau (above). Information, advice, umbrella organization.

White Lion Free School
White Lion Street, London N1.

WIRES
32a Parliament Street, York. Telephone 0904 35471. National information network of the women's liberation movement.

Women's Research and Resources Centre
190 Upper Street, London N1. Telephone 01-359 5773. Reference and research.

Women's Therapy Centre
6 Manor Gardens, London N7. Telephone 01-263 6200. Workshops and individual therapy for women by feminists. Can also inform you about therapy elsewhere. A Women's Therapy Centre is about to open in Bristol.

Bibliography

General

These books were particularly important to us in defining our point of view for the book as a whole.

Ariès, Philippe. *Centuries of Childhood: A Social History of Family Life*. New York: Vintage, 1962; London: Penguin, 1979. Suggests that our notion of childhood is a fairly recent social invention.

Bernard, Jessie. *The Future of Motherhood*. New York: Penguin, 1975; published in the UK as *The Future of Parenthood*, London: Calder, 1975. Highly readable sociological analysis with a deep awareness of the feminist issues.

Boston Women's Health Book Collective. *Our Bodies, Ourselves: A Book By and For Women*. New York: Simon & Schuster, 1976; London: Allen Lane and Penguin, 1978. Writing this book reinforced our belief that people are the best experts on themselves and moved us toward writing this book out of our experience as parents. It is useful to parents for couple issues, for early parenting issues and as a helpful aid in discussing sexuality and health issues with pre-adolescent and adolescent daughters. The British edition (edited by Angela Phillips and Jill Rakusen) is a mine of information, references and addresses useful to UK readers.

Bronfenbrenner, Urie. 'Nobody Home: The Erosion of the American Family', *Psychology Today*, Vol. 10, No. 12 (May 1977). A conversation based on a lecture at the College of Human Ecology Alumni Association, Michigan State University, 26 February, 1976. Humanistic expression of concern about how current changes in the family affect the socialization of children. Points to some solutions.

Callahan, Sidney Cornelia. *Parenting: Principles and Politics of Parenthood*. New York: Doubleday, 1973. Original analysis of the experience of being a parent at home and in society.

Collins, W., Friedman, E., and Pivot, A. *The Directory of Social Change: Women*. London: Wildwood House, 1978.

Curtis, Jean. *Working Mothers*. New York: Doubleday, 1976. Focuses largely on professional women in fairly traditional relationships and how they manage work and parenting. Especially helpful in setting out the issues at each stage of parenting.

Faulder, C., Jackson, C., and Lewis, M. *The Women's Directory*. London: Virago, 1976.

Filene, Peter G. *Him/Her/Self, Sex Roles in Modern America*. New York: New American Library, 1976. Historical view of our socialization into sex roles from the late nineteenth century to the present, with excellent material on how socialization influences our parenting.

Group for the Advancement of Psychiatry. *Joys and Sorrows of Parenthood*. New York: Scribner, 1975. Mental-health professionals focus on parents.

Howell, Mary C. *Helping Ourselves: Families and the Human Network*. Boston: Beacon Press, 1975. This is a warm, constructive, energizing book, which should be read by everyone.

Illich, Ivan. *Medical Nemesis*. New York: Pantheon, 1976; London: Penguin, 1976. Illich's healthy scepticism about professionals underscored our commitment to write a book by and for parents.

Klein, Carole. *The Myth of the Happy Child*. New York: Harper & Row, 1975. This book frees parents of a lot of unnecessary guilt by pointing out that childhood can't be, nor should be, an all-sunny experience.

Lazarre, Jane. *The Mother Knot*. New York: McGraw-Hill, 1976. Funny, passionate, human, uncompromisingly honest account of the author's early years of motherhood. Must reading for new parents.

LeMasters, E. E. *Parents In Modern America*. Homewood, Ill.: Dorsey Press, 1970. Good sociological study of parents as people who have needs of their own.

LeShan, Eda J. *How to Survive Parenthood*. New York: Random House, 1965. Easy-to-read, commonsense approach to parenthood and family life.

Levine, James A. *Who Will Raise the Children? New Options for Fathers (and Mothers)*. Philadelphia: Lippincott, 1976. Looks at fathers who have chosen child care and householding as at least half their work.

McBride, Angela Barron. *The Growth and Development of Mothers*. New York: Harper & Row, 1973. A pioneering book which encourages mothers to pay attention to their own continuing evolution.

McCrindle, J., and Rowbotham, S. (eds.). *Dutiful Daughters*. London: Penguin, 1979.

Mead, Margaret. *Culture and Commitment*. London: Panther, 1972. How rapid technological and social change affect parenting.

Miller, Jean Baker. *Towards a New Psychology of Women*. Boston: Beacon Press, 1976; London: Penguin, 1976. A vital new look at traditional women's strengths and their value for individual women and men for society as a whole.

Pleck, Joseph H., and Sawyer, Jack. *Men and Masculinity*. Englewood Cliffs, NJ: Prentice-Hall, 1974. This fine book contains four good articles about fathering.

Radl, Shirley. *Mother's Day Is Over*. New York: Warner, 1974. Harrowing personal account makes the point that we are not prepared for parenthood.

Rapaport, Rhona and Robert, and Strelitz, Ziona. *Fathers, Mothers and Society*. New York: Basic Books, 1977. Surveys the research in a wide variety of academic disciplines toward a new understanding of parenthood in modern society. Excellent discussions of some of the more controversial parenting issues.

Rich, Adrienne. *Of Woman Born – Motherhood as Experience and Institution*. New York: Norton, 1976; London: Virago, 1977. Written with passion and insight, this is a basic feminist book on motherhood. Focuses very little on men.

Sharpe, Sue. *Just Like a Girl*. London: Penguin, 1976.

Sheehy, Gail. *Passages: Predictable Crises of Adult Life*. New York: Dutton, 1976; London: Corgi, 1978. This imaginative book has helped countless people better understand their adult stages of development. Primarily upper-middle-class/professionally oriented.

Spinner, Stephanie (ed.). *Motherlove: Stories by Women about Motherhood*. New York: Dell, 1978. Fiction. A pleasure to read.

Wandor, M. (ed.). *The Body Politic*. London: Stage I Press, 1972, 1978.

Zaretsky, Eli. *Capitalism, the Family and Personal Life*. New York: Harper & Row, 1976;

London: Pluto Press, 1976. Historical evolution and politics of the separation between work and family life.

Considering Parenthood

Fallaci, Oriana. *Letters to a Child Never Born.* New York: Doubleday, 1976; London: Arlington Books, 1976. A sensitive autobiographical account of how being pregnant changes you.

Hanson, Gordon. 'Learning Parenthood: Tending Raw Eggs', *Sacramento Bee*, 11 January 1977. Story of a high school teacher who taught about the twenty-four-hour-a-day responsibility of early parenthood by requiring her students to carry a raw egg wherever they went.

Hawke, Sharryl, and Knox, David. *One Child by Choice.* Englewood Cliffs, NJ: Prentice-Hall, 1977.

Lankin, Patricia. 'Marriage Without Children Becoming a Chosen Lifestyle'. *Boston Sunday Globe, New England Magazine*, 10 April 1977.

McCauley, Carole Spearin. *Pregnancy After 35.* New York: Dutton, 1976.

Menning, Barbara Eck. *Infertility – A Guide for the Childless Couple.* Englewood Cliffs, NJ: Prentice-Hall, 1977.

Peck, Ellen. *The Baby Trap.* New York: Bernard Geis, 1971. Stresses the material advantages of non-parenthood.

Peck, Ellen, and Senderowitz, Judith. *Pronatalism: The Myth of Mom and Apple Pie.* New York: Crowell, 1974; London: Chartham Robert, 1977. A discussion of pronatalist influences in our society, and of non-parenthood as an option.

Whelan, Elizabeth M., Sc.D. *A Baby? ... Maybe.* New York: Bobbs-Merrill, 1976. Well-researched and helpful guide to deciding about parenthood.

Adoption

Anderson, David C. *Children of Special Value: Interracial Adoption in America.* New York: St Martin's Press, 1971.

Klibanoff, Susan and Elton. *Let's Talk about Adoption.* Boston: Little, Brown, 1973.

Kopecky, Gini. 'What It's Like for Singles Who Adopt: Four Family Stories', *MS.* magazine.

Ladner, Joyce. *Mixed Families.* New York: Anchor, 1977. On inter-racial adoption.

The Beginning Years of Parenting

A comprehensive bibliography on pregnancy, childbirth and the postnatal period can be found in *Our Bodies, Ourselves* (cited in the General list above). The following are primarily books that have come out since 1976. For books on adoption, see the preceding bibliography for Considering Parenthood.

Entering Parenthood

Bean, Constance. *Labor and Delivery: An Observer's Diary.* New York: Doubleday, 1977.

Bing, Elizabeth, and Coleman, Libby. *Making Love during Pregnancy.* New York: Bantam, 1977.

Coleman, Arthur and Libby. *Pregnancy: The psychological experience.* New York: Seabury Press, 1973.

Hausknecht, Richard, M.D., and Heilman, Joan Rattner. *Having a Caesarian Baby*. New York: Dutton, 1978. One of the best on the subject.

Kitzinger, Sheila. *The Good Birth Guide*. London: Fontana, 1979.

Kitzinger, Sheila. *The Place of Birth*. London: Oxford University Press, 1978.

McLaughlin, Clara J. *The Black Parents' Handbook: A Guide to the Facts of a Healthy Pregnancy, Childhood, and Childcare*. New York: Harcourt Brace Jovanovich, 1976.

Ward, Charlotte and Fred. *Home Birth Book*. New York: Doubleday, 1977.

The Beginning Years

We have found these books particularly helpful, though some of the authors make stereotypic assumptions about parents and take dogmatic positions. (For books and information about day care, see the bibliography for Helping Ourselves.)

Barber, Virginia, and Skaggs, Merrill M. *The Mother Person*. New York: Schocken, 1975; London: Severn House, 1977. Mothers of young children speak about their lives.

Berends, Polly Berrien. *Whole Parent/Whole Child*. New York: Harper's Magazine Press, 1975. A mother discusses the parent-child relationship during the first four years.

Brazelton, T. Berry. *Infants and Mothers: Differences in Development*. New York: Dell, 1969; London: Hutchinson, 1970.

——————. *Toddlers and Parents: A Declaration of Independence*. New York: Delacorte, 1974; London: Macmillan, 1976. The emphasis is on the differences between children and the way this can influence parental response. We caution parents to read these books with the understanding that their own child or response may differ.

Bushall, Agnes, *et al. The Balancing Act*. Portland, Me.: Littoral Books, 1975. Fine book on work and parenting.

Carmichael, Carrie. *Non-Sexist Childrearing*. London: Harper & Row, 1977.

Drabble, Margaret. *The Needle's Eye*. London: Penguin, 1972. A novel about a woman with children.

Fraiberg, Selma. *Every Child's Birthright*. New York: Basic Books, 1977. A clinical psychologist affirms the significance of mothering but does not give adequate attention to sharing parenthood.

——————. *The Magic Years*. New York: Charles Scribner and Sons, 1959; London: Methuen, 1977. A clinical psychologist talks about some emotional and behavioural problems that perplex parents in the early years.

Gesell, Arnold. *The First Five Years of Life*. New York: Harper & Row, 1940; London: Methuen, 1971.

Halpern, Howard. *Cutting Loose: An Adult Guide to Coming to Terms with Your Parents*. New York: Simon & Schuster, 1977.

Holstrom, Linda Lytle. *The Two-Career Family*. Cambridge, Mass.: Schenkman, 1973.

Kelly, Marguerite, and Parsons, Elia. *The Mother's Almanac*. New York: Doubleday, 1975.

Leach, Penelope. *Babyhood*. London: Penguin, 1974.

Lessing, Doris. *A Man and Two Women*. New York: Popular Library, 1963; London: Panther, 1968. The title story focuses on the behaviour of a new mother.

Marzollo, Jean. *9 Months, 1 Day, 1 Year: A Guide to Pregnancy, Birth and Babycare*. New York: Harper & Row, 1976. Personal experiences of a group of parents.

Newton, Niles. *The Family Book of Childcare*. New York: Harper & Row, 1957. Deals with both creative and practical concerns about parenting in the beginning years. Assumes a traditional family setting.

Pryor, Karen. *Nursing Your Baby*. New York: Harper & Row, 1973.

Raphael, Dana. *The Tender Gift*. New York: Schocken, 1976. Anthropological work on breast-feeding.

Rozdilsky, Mary Lou, and Banet, Barbara. *What Now?* Boston Association for Childbirth Education, PO Box 29, Newton, Mass. 32060, USA. Good practical guide for the first three post-natal months.

Schaffer, Rudolph. *Mothering*. Cambridge, Mass.: Harvard University Press, 1977; London: Fontana, 1978. Psychological research on the influences of mothering on children.

Spock, Benjamin. *Baby and Child Care*. London: New English Library, 1969.

Stern, Daniel. *The First Relationship*. Cambridge, Mass.: Harvard University Press, 1976; London: Fontana, 1977. One psychologist's view of how the relationship between child and caregiver builds up.

Winn, Marie. *The Baby Reader*. New York: Simon & Schuster, 1973. Excerpts from literature describing new parents' reactions to childbirth and their babies.

Winnicott, D. P. *The Child, the Family and the Outside World*. London: Penguin, 1969. A psychiatrist talks about the family as an emotional unit.

The Middle Years

During this period books of the parent-education movement may be helpful. See the bibliography for Helping Ourselves under 'Parent Education'.

Cohen, Dorothy H. *The Learning Child*. New York: Pantheon, 1972; London: Wildwood House, 1973. An educator and mother describes child development integrating the cognitive and emotional aspects. Emphasizes need for cooperation between parents and teachers.

Comer, James P., and Poussaint, Alvin F. *Black Child Care*. New York: Simon & Schuster, 1975.

Erikson, Erik H. *Childhood and Society*. New York: Norton, 1963; London: Penguin, 1974. Child development from a sociopsychological point of view.

Ginsburg, Herbert, and Opper, Sylvia. *Piaget's Theory of Intellectual Development: An Introduction*. Englewood Cliffs, NJ: Prentice-Hall, 1969. Excellent presentation of Piaget's theories.

Harrison-Ross, Phyllis, and Wyden, Barbara. *The Black Child – A Parent's Guide*. New York: McKay, 1973.

————, *The Black Child*. New York: Berkley, 1974.

Holt, John. *How Children Learn*. New York: Pitman, 1969; London: Penguin, 1973.

————. *How Children Fail*. New York: Delta, 1964; London: Penguin, 1969. The failure of schools to help children learn.

Salk, Lee. *What Every Child Would Like His Parents to Know*. New York: McKay, 1972; London: Hale, 1973.

Some Good Books for Kids

An important job that parents have is helping their kids interpret their experience in society. Here is a sampling of the kinds of books that parents and kids have found useful.

Burns, Marilyn. *I Am Not a Short Adult!* Boston: Little, Brown, 1977. A child's compendium of information and common sense about school, money, legal rights, child abuse, TV, children and adults, etc.

Mayle, Peter. *What's Happening to Me?* Secaucus, NJ: Lyle Stuart, 1975. Discusses the changes of puberty in words and drawings.

Widerberg, Siv. *The Kids' Own XYZ of Love.* New York: Stein & Day, 1973. Straightforward answers to most commonly asked questions about sexuality.

For a list of non-sexist books for children, write to the Children's Rights Workshop (book project), c/o 73 Balfour Road, London SE17, or to CISSY, c/o Pam Isherwood, Village Books, Shrubbery Road, London SW16.

Other Resources

How to set up a Free School: a handbook of alternative education. White Lion Free School, London N1.

Parenting Teenagers

Berger, Nan. *Rights Handbook for People Under Age.* London: Penguin, 1974.

Boston Women's Health Book Collective. *Our Bodies, Ourselves* (cited in the General list above).

Chew, Peter. *The Inner World of the Middle-Aged Man.* New York: Macmillan, 1976.

Davitz, Joel, and Davitz, Lois, *Making It from 40 to 50.* New York: Random House, 1976.

Erikson, Erik H. *Identity – Youth and Crisis.* New York: Norton, 1968; London: Faber, 1971.

Friedenberg, Edgar Z. *The Dignity of Youth and Other Atavisms.* Boston: Beacon Press, 1965. An educator takes a critical look at public education and its effects on teenagers.

————. *The Vanishing Adolescent.* New York: Dell, 1959. An exploration of the needs of adolescents.

Guest, Judith. *Ordinary People.* New York: Viking, 1976; London: Collins, 1977. A novel about a teenage son and his parents.

Harris, Janet. *The Prime of Ms. America: The American Woman at 40.* New York: Signet, 1976. A feminist approach to ageing.

Le Shan, Eda J. *The Wonderful Crisis of Middle Age: Some Personal Reflections.* New York: Warner, 1974.

Lessing, Doris. *The Summer Before the Dark.* London: Penguin, 1975. A novel about a forty-year-old woman.

Mitchell, Joyce S. *Other Choices for Becoming a Woman: A Handbook to Help High School Women Make Decisions.* New York: Dell, 1975.

National Council for Civil Liberties. *Civil Liberty: the NCCL Guide.* London: Penguin, 1972.

Release Collective. *Trouble with the Law.* London: Release Publications and Pluto Press, 1979.

Ruddick, Sara, and Daniels, Pamela (eds.). *Working It Out.* New York: Pantheon, 1977. Twenty-three women writers, artists, scientists and scholars in mid-life write about the problems and rewards of working.

Sorensen, R. C. *Adolescent Sexuality in Contemporary America: The Sorensen Report.* New ed. New York: World Publishing Co., 1973. Survey based on numerous interviews.

Watters, Pat. *The Angry Middle-Aged Man: The Crisis of America's Last Minority.* New York: Grossman, 1976. An out-of-work journalist explores his feelings about being middle-aged and jobless.

Parents of Grown-ups

Beauvoir, Simone de. *Memoirs of a Dutiful Daughter*. London: Penguin, 1970. The pain of watching a hated mother die.

Friday, Nancy. *My Mother/My Self*. New York: Delacorte, 1977; London: Fontana, 1978.

Ginandes, Shepard. *Coming Home*. New York: Delacorte, 1976. Explores the relationships between late adolescents and their parents which spill over into the early adult years.

Goode, Ruth. *A Book for Grandmothers*. New York: McGraw-Hill, 1978.

Hammer, Signe. *Daughters and Mothers: Mothers and Daughters*. New York: Quadrangle, 1975; London: Hutchinson, 1976.

Lukas, J. Anthony. *Don't Shoot! We are Your Children*. Interviews with ten young radicals who may be acting out covert parental attitudes.

Neugarten, Bernice L. (ed.). *Middle Age and Aging*. Chicago: University of Chicago Press, 1968.

Olsen, Tillie. *Tell Me a Riddle*. New York: Dell, 1976. The title story is about an elderly couple growing more and more unwillingly dependent on their adult children.

Paley, Grace. *Enormous Changes at the Last Minute*. New York: Farrar, Straus, Giroux, 1960; London: Virago, 1979. The title story tells about the relationship between a woman and her old father.

Phelps, Robert (ed.). *Earthly Paradise: An Autobiography of Colette*. New York: Farrar, Straus, Giroux, 1966. Includes many excerpts from Colette's writings about her mother.

Wharton, Edith. *The House of Mirth*. London: Penguin, 1979. A mother whose daughter's divorce is accepted by her peers. Recalls how her divorce caused her to become an outcast because of the standards of the time (1905).

Sharing

Bernard, Jessie. *The Future of Marriage*. London: Souvenir Press, 1973.

Biller, Henry, and Meredith, Dennis. *Father Power*. New York: Anchor, 1975.

Daley, Eliot A. *Father Feelings*. New York: Morrow, 1978.

DeFrain, John. 'A Father's Guide to Parent Guides: Review and Assessment of the Paternal Role as Conceived in the Popular Literature'. Paper presented at the National Council on Family Relations, American Association of Marriages and Family Counselors Annual Meeting, St Louis, Mo., 1974. Available at MIT library.

————. 'New Meaning for Parenting'. Paper presented at the Sixth Banff International Conference on Behavior Modification, 1974. Available at MIT library.

Demeter, Anna. *Legal Kidnapping*. Boston: Little, Brown, 1977.

Family Coordinator: Journal of Education, Counseling and Services. Special Issue, *Fatherhood*, Vol. 25, No. 4 (October 1976).

Fein, Robert A. 'Men's Experiences Before and After the Birth of a First Child'. Ph.D. dissertation, Harvard University, 1974. Included in *Journal* issue cited above.

Goldsmith, Mark. 'Part-time Jobs Liberate Both Parents'. *Christian Science Monitor*, 9 October 1974.

Greenwald, Carol S. 'Working Mothers – The Need for More Part-time Jobs'. *New England Economic Review*, September–October 1972.

Keshet, Harry Finkelstein, and Rosenthal, Kristine. 'Father as Caretaker After Marital Separation'. *Social Work*, Vol. 23, No. 1 (January 1978).

Kotelchuck, Milton. 'The Nature of the Child's Tie to His Father'. Unpublished Ph.D. dissertation. Department of Social Relations, Harvard University, 1972.

Levine, James. *Who Will Raise the Children: New Options for Fathers (and Mothers)* (cited in the General list above).

McBride, Angela Barron. *Living with Contradictions: A Married Feminist*. New York: Harper & Row, 1977.

Pleck, Joseph H. *Men's New Roles in the Family: Housework and Child Care*. Ann Arbor, Mich.: Institute for Social Research, December 1976.

Rapaport, Rhona and Robert. *Dual Career Families*. Baltimore, Md: Penguin, 1971.

Wortis, Rochelle P. *Childrearing and Women's Liberation*. In Wandor, M. (ed.), *The Body Politic* (cited in the General list above).

————. 'The Acceptance of the Concept of the Maternal Role of Behavioral Scientists: Its Effects on Women'. *American Journal of Orthopsychiatry*, Vol. 41, No. 5, (October 1971).

The Massachusetts Institute of Technology has a fine collection on men's liberation and fathering in its Humanities Library.

Families

Some Approaches to the Family

Bernard, Jessie. *The Future of Motherhood* (cited in the General list above).

Goode, William. *The Family*. Englewood Cliffs, NJ: Prentice-Hall, 1964.

Howell, Mary C. *Helping Ourselves: Families and the Human Network* (cited in the General list above).

Skolnick, Arlene S., and Jerome S. *Family in Transition*. Boston: Little, Brown, 1971.

Marital, Couple and Sexual Issues

(See also Sharing bibliography.)

Bach, George, and Wyden, Peter. *The Intimate Enemy*. New York: Avon, 1970. A couple's guide to fighting constructively.

Kaplan, Helen Singer. *The Illustrated Manual of Sex Therapy*. London: Souvenir Press, 1976.

Paul, Norman, and Paul, Betty. *A Marital Puzzle*. New York: Norton, 1975.

Rogers, Carl. *Becoming Partners*. London: Constable, 1973.

Seidenberg, Robert. *Corporate Wives – Corporate Casualties?* New York: Anchor, 1975.

Marital Separation

Adult Issues

Baguedor, Eve. *Separation, Journal of a Marriage*. New York: Simon & Schuster, 1972.

Bequaert, Lucia H. *Single Women: Alone and Together*. Boston: Beacon Press, 1976.

Bohannan, Paul. 'The Six Stations of Divorce'. In Paul Bohannan (ed.), *Divorce and After*. New York: Doubleday, 1976.

Brandwein, R., Brown, C., and Fox, E. 'Women and Children Last: The Social Situation of Divorced Mothers and Their Families'. *Journal of Marriage and the Family*, vol. 36 (1974), pp. 498–514.

Forman, Lynn. *The Divorced Mother's Guide: Getting It Together*. New York: Berkley, 1974.

Gettleman, S., and Markovitz, J. *The Courage to Divorce*. New York: Simon & Schuster, 1974.

Hetherington, E. M., Cox, M., and Cox, R. 'Divorced Fathers'. *Psychology Today* (April 1977), pp. 42–6.

Hunt, M. *The World of the Formerly Married*. New York: McGraw-Hill, 1966.

Krantzler, Mel. *Creative Divorce*. New York: Evans, 1973.

Weiss, Robert S. *Marital Separation*. New York: Basic Books, 1975.

Parent-Child Issues

Despert, J. L. *Children of Divorce*. Garden City, NY: Doubleday/Dolphin, 1953.

Gardner, Richard. *The Boys and Girls Book about Divorce*. New York: Bantam, 1971. For ages five and up.

Goldstein, J., Freud, Anna, and Solnit, A. *Beyond the Best Interests of the Child*. New York: Free Press, 1973. Legal and emotional aspects of custody issues.

Grollman, E. G. *Explaining Divorce to Children*. Boston: Beacon Press, 1969.

Hetherington, E. M. 'Effects of Father Absence on Personality Development in Adolescent Daughters'. *Developmental Psychology*, Vol. 7, No. 3 (1972), pp. 313–26.

Landis, Judson T. 'A Comparison of Children from Divorced and Non-divorced Unhappy Marriages'. *Family Coordinator*, Vol. 2 (1962), pp. 61–5.

Wallerstein, Judith, and Kelly, Joan. 'The Effects of Parental Divorce: Experiences of the Preschool Child'. *Journal of American Academy of Child Psychiatry*, Vol. 14, No. 4 (Autumn 1975), pp. 600–616.

————. 'The Effects of Parental Divorce: Experiences of the Child in Later Latency'. *American Journal of Orthopsychiatry*, Vol. 46, No. 2 (April 1976).

Single Parenting

Ashdown-Sharp, Patricia. *Guide to Pregnancy and Parenthood for Women on Their Own*. London: Penguin, 1975.

Bart, Pauline B. 'Divorced Men and Their Children: A Study of Emerging Roles'. Paper presented at the meeting of the American Sociological Association, Washington, DC, 1970.

Bel Geddes, Joan. *How to Parent Alone*. New York: Seabury Press, 1974.

Burlage, Dorothy. *Divorced and Separated Mothers: Combining the Responsibilities of Breadwinning and Childrearing*. Unpublished dissertation, Harvard University, 1978, and HEW Women's Action Program's publication.

Galper, Miriam. *Co-Parenting: A Source Book for the Separated or Divorced Family*. Philadelphia: Running Press, 1978. A guide to shared custody.

Hallett, Kathryn. *A Guide for Single Parents: Transactional Analysis for People in Crisis*. Millbrae, Calif.: Celestial Arts, 1974.

Hope, Karol, and Young, Nancy. *Momma: The Sourcebook for Single Mothers*. New York: New American Library, 1976.

Klein, Carole. *The Single Parent Experience*. New York: Avon, 1973.

Economic Consequences of Divorce

Coote, Anna, and Gill, Tess. *Women's Rights: A Practical Guide*. (London: Penguin, 1974, 2nd ed. 1977).

Step-parents

Baer, Jean. *The Second Wife*. New York: Doubleday, 1972.

Duberman, Lucille. *The Reconstructed Family: A Study of Remarried Couples and Their Children*. Chicago: Nelson Hall, 1975.

Lowe, Patricia Tracy. *The Cruel Stepmother*. Englewood Cliffs, NJ: Prentice-Hall, 1970.

Maddox, Brenda. *The Half Parent*. London: Deutsch, 1975.

McCormick, Mona. *Stepfathers: What the Literature Reveals*. La Jolla, Calif.: Western Behavioral Sciences Institute, 1975.

Reingold, Carmel Berman. *Remarriage*. New York: Harper & Row, 1976.

Roosevelt, Ruth, and Lofas, Jeannette. *Living in Step*. New York: Stein & Day, 1976.

Thomson, Helen. *The Successful Stepparent*. New York: Funk & Wagnalls, 1966.

Gay Parents

Galana, Laurel, and Covina, Gina. *The New Lesbians*. Berkeley, Calif.: Moon Books, 1977. Wide range of lesbians interviewed include some mothers.

Jay, Karla, and Young, Allen (eds.). *After You're Out: Personal Experiences of Gay Men and Lesbian Women*. New York: Music Sales, 1975. See especially the article 'Faggot Fathers'.

Riley, Marlyn. 'The Avowed Lesbian Mother and Her Right to Child Custody: A Constitutional Challenge That Can No Longer Be Denied'. *San Diego Law Review* Vol. 12 (1975), p. 779.

Silverstein, Charles. *A Family Matter*. New York: McGraw-Hill, 1977. Aimed primarily to be helpful to parents of gays, this book can aid gay parents as well.

Vida, Ginny (ed.). *Our Rights to Love: A Lesbian Resource Book*. Englewood Cliffs, NJ: Prentice-Hall, 1978. The most comprehensive resource for lesbians yet. See, especially, 'Lesbian Mothers and Transition' and 'Sharing Your Lesbian Identity with Your Children'.

Group Living (thanks to Rosabeth Moss Kanter for suggesting these books)

Dragon-Wagon, Crescent. *The Commune Cookbook*. New York: Simon & Schuster, 1978.

French, David and Elena. *Working Communally: Patterns and Possibilities*. New York: Russell Sage Foundation, 1975.

Houriet, Robert. *Getting Back Together*. New York: Avon, 1971; London: Abacus, 1973.

Kanter, Rosabeth Moss. *Communes: Creating and Managing the Collective Life*. New York: Harper & Row, 1973.

————. *Community and Commitment*. Cambridge, Mass.: Harvard University Press, 1972; London: Harvard University Press, 1977. Historical study of communal societies in the United States.

Kincaid, Kathleen. *A Walden II Experiment*. New York: Morrow, 1973.

Families of Different Cultures

Billingsley, Andrew. *Black Families in White America*. Englewood Cliffs, NJ: Prentice-Hall, 1968. Systems approach applied to family and society.

Community Relations Commission. *Urban Deprivation, Racial Inequality and Social Policy*. London: 1977.

Jackson, Harrisene. *There's Nothing I Own That I Want*. Englewood Cliffs, NJ: Prentice-Hall, 1974. Life on the bottom, told by a black woman who won't learn to quit.

Kingston, Maxine Hong. *The Woman Warrior: Memoirs of a Childhood Among Ghosts*. London: Allen Lane and Penguin, 1977. Stories based on a Chinese-American woman's growing up.

Kitzinger, Sheila. *Women as Mothers*. London: Fontana, 1978.

Ladner, Joyce A. *Tomorrow's Tomorrow: The Black Woman*. New York: Doubleday, 1971.

Careful and caring study of the lives of young women in a black neighbourhood of a Midwestern city.

Lewis, Oscar. *La Vida*. New York: Random House, 1961; London: Penguin, 1970. Anthropological study of Puerto Rican families in New York.

Rubin, Lillian Breslow. *Worlds of Pain: Life in the Working-Class Family*. New York: Basic Books, 1976. Interview-based study of white working-class families in California.

Sidel, Ruth. *Women and Childcare in China*. London: Penguin, 1972.

Wilson, Amrit. *Finding a Voice*. London, Virago, 1978.

Zborowsky, Mark, and Herzog, Elizabeth. *Life Is with People*. New York: Schocken, 1971. Retrospective study of Jewish life in the villages of Eastern Europe.

Family Systems and Family Therapy

Attneave, Carolyn, and Speck, Ross. *Family Networks*. New York: Random House, 1974.

Kanter, David, and Lehr, William. *Inside the Family*. New York: Harper & Row, 1975.

Ferber, Andrew, and Mendelsohn, Marilyn. *The Book of Family Therapy*. Boston: Houghton Mifflin, 1973.

Satir, Virginia. *Peoplemaking*. Palo Alto, Calif.: Science and Behavior Books, 1972.

Parents and Society

For books and articles on day care, see the bibliography for Helping Ourselves.

Bane, Mary Jo. *Here to Stay: The American Family in the Twentieth Century*. New York: Basic Books, 1976. Changes in family forms with implications for family policy.

BPW Foundation. *Hours of Work When Workers Can Choose: The Experience of 59 Organizations with Employee-Chosen Staggered Hours and Flextime*. 2012 Massachusetts Ave., NW, Washington, DC 20036.

Bronfenbrenner, Urie. *Two Worlds of Childhood: U.S. and U.S.S.R.* New York: Simon & Schuster, 1972; London: Penguin, 1974. Comparative study of attitudes toward children and socialization practices.

Cade, Toni (ed.). *The Black Woman*. New York: New American Library, 1974. Anthology presenting issues concerning black women and feminism.

Community Sex Education Programs for Parents: A Training Manual for Organizers. Institute for Family Research and Education, 760 Ostrom Ave., Syracuse, NY 13210.

Dapper, Gloria, and Murphy, Judith. *Part-time Teachers and How They Work: A Study of Five School Systems*. New York: Catalyst, December 1968.

Doron, Abraham, and Kramer, Ralph M. 'Ideology, Programme and Organizational Factors in Public Assistance: The Case of Israel'. *Journal of Social Policy*, Vol. 5, Part 2 (April 1971), pp. 131–49. Compares income maintenance systems in the United States, the USSR and Israel.

Gil, David G. *Unravelling Social Policy: Theory, Analysis and Political Action Toward Social Equality*. Cambridge, Mass.: Schenkman, 1973.

Howell, Mary C., M.D., Ph.D. 'Employed Mothers and Their Families'. *Pediatrics*, Vol. 52, No. 2 (August 1973) and No. 3 (September 1973). Myth-shattering article on the effects on children of mothers working.

Illich, Ivan. *De-Schooling Society*. New York: Harper & Row, 1971; London: Penguin, 1971. Radical re-examination of the role of schools as the arbiters of learning.

Kanter, Rosabeth Moss. *Work and Family in the United States: A Critical Review and Agenda for Research and Policy*. New York: Russell Sage Foundation, 1977. Survey of the literature on families and workplaces.

Keniston, Kenneth, and the Carnegie Council on Children. *All Our Children: The American Family Under Pressure*. New York: Harcourt Brace Jovanovich, 1977. The detrimental effects of growing up in poverty.

Korsch, Barbara M., and Negrette, V. F. 'Doctor-Patient Communication'. *Scientific American*, Vol. 227, No. 13 (August 1972), pp. 66–74. Technical study on how physicians tend to ignore women.

Lister, Ruth. *A Budget for the Year of the Child: Poverty No. 41*. London: Child Poverty Action Group, 1979.

Outer Circle Policy Unit. *Who Pays for the Children?* London: Outer Circle Policy Unit, 1978.

Stone, Judith, and Taylor, Felicity. *The Parents' Schoolbook*. London: Penguin, 1976.

Talbot, Nathan B., M.D. (ed.). *Raising Children in Modern America: Problems and Prospective Solutions*. Boston: Little, Brown, 1976. An anthology providing an overview of issues concerning children's needs. (There is a companion volume with the same title but a different subtitle that is not particularly useful.)

Tutko, Thomas, and Burns, William, *Winning Is Everything and Other American Myths*. New York: Macmillan, 1976. The authors show how over-emphasis on winning has virtually destroyed access to organized sports for the majority of American children.

Winn, Marie. *The Plug-In Drug: Television, Children, and the Family*. New York: Viking, 1977.

Wynn, A. and M. *The Cost of Maintaining Children at Different Ages: Poverty No. 33*. London: Child Poverty Action Group, 1978.

Helping Ourselves and Finding Help

General Approaches

Caplan, L., and Killilea, M. (eds.). *Support Systems and Mutual Help, A Multi-Disciplinary Exploration*. New York: Grune & Stratton, 1976.

Howell, Mary C. *Helping Ourselves: Families and the Human Network* (cited in the General list above).

Illich, Ivan, *et al*. *Disabling Professions*. London: Marian Boyars, 1978. Essays on how professions have weakened people's initiative and competence.

Rock, Maxine A. (with photographs by Nadler, Ronald D.). 'Gorilla Mothers Who Mistreat Their Young in Isolation But Not in Groups May Provide a Lesson for Humans'. *Smithsonian* (July 1978), pp. 58–63.

Pregnancy, Childbirth and Post-Partum

See *Our Bodies, Ourselves* and the bibliography for the Beginning Parenting chapter above.

Everyday Issues of Parenting

Children's Hospital Medical Center and Feinbloom, Richard, M.D. *Child Health Encyclopedia*. New York: Delacorte, 1975.

Jones, Sandy. *Good Things for Babies*. New York: Houghton Mifflin, 1976.

McMullen, J. *Rights at Work*. London: Pluto Press, 1978.

National Childbirth Trust. *Growing up with Good Food*. London.

Politics of Health group. *Food and Profit*. British Society for Social Responsibility in Science, 9 Poland Street, London W1.

Stimson, C. and G. *Health Rights Handbook*. London: Prism Press, 1978.

Parent Education

The following books illustrate some of the different kinds of material taught in parent education courses:

Dreikurs, Rudolf, and Soltz, Vicki. *Children: The Challenge*. New York: Hawthorne, 1964; published in the UK as *Happy Children: A Challenge for Parents*. London: Fontana, 1972.

Faber, Adele, and Mazlish, Elaine. *Liberated Parents: Liberated Children*. New York: Avon, 1974. Two parents share their interpretation of the theories of Haim Ginott.

Gordon, Thomas. *The PET Manual*. New York: Wyden, 1970.

Pugh, Gillian (ed.). *Preparation for Parenthood: Some Current Initiatives and Thinking*. London: National Children's Bureau, 1980.

Day Care

Breitbart, Vicki. *The Day Care Book*. New York: Knopf, 1974. Articles on different approaches to day care.

Collins, Alice H., and Watson, Eunice L. *Family Day Care: A Practical Guide for Parents, Caregivers and Professionals*. Boston: Beacon Press, 1976.

Evans, E. Belle, and Saia, George E. *Day Care for Infants*. Boston: Beacon Press, 1972.

Hughes, M., Mayall, B., Moss, P., Perry, J., Petrie, P., and Pinkerton, G. *Nurseries Now: A Fair Deal for Parents and Children*. London: Penguin, 1980.

Keyserling, Mary Dublin. *Windows on Day Care: A Report Based on Findings of the National Council of Jewish Women*, 1972.

Steinfels, Margaret O'Brien. *Who's Minding the Children: The History and Politics of Day Care in America*. New York: Simon & Schuster, 1973. Excellent.

Tizard, J., Moss, P., and Perry, J. *All our Children*. London: Temple Smith, 1976.

Trades Union Congress. *TUC Charter on Facilities for the Under-Fives*. London: Trades Union Congress, 1978.

Other Resources

Pamphlets

The Children's Community Centre Pamphlet. Children's Community Centre, 20 Lawford Road, London NW5. Describes how a group of women started London's first community centre, their aims and their experiences in the first years of running the centre.

Do-It-Yourself-Nurseries. London Nursery Campaign; send 50p to 33 Mundania Road, London SE22. Discusses staff, children, parents, premises, finance, activities, equipment.

I Want To Work but What About the Kids? Day care for young children and opportunities for working parents. Available free from the Equal Opportunities Commission, Overseas House, Quay Street, Manchester M3 3HN. Discusses present provision and demands. Excellent.

Not so Much a Nursery ... Available from Market Nursery, 65 Broke Road, London E8; 20p plus postage. A good short description of the campaign that won a community nursery in Hackney, East London.

Starting a Mothers' and Toddlers' Club. Available from 7 Royal Terrace, Glasgow G3 7NT; 10p.

Workplace Nurseries, a negotiating kit. Available free from NALGO, 1 Mabledon Place, London WC1H 9AJ. NALGO's campaign aims, the arguments for workplace nurseries, standards of accommodation and care in nurseries, Equal Opportunities — not just nurseries.

Exhibitions

We Need College Nurseries. Photographic exhibition compiled by NAFTHE. No hire charges; pay carriage only. Book at least one month in advance. Contact Paula Lanning, NAFTHE, Hamilton House, Mabledon Place, London WC1. Telephone 01-387 6806.

Who's Holding the Baby? Exhibition of cartoons, photos and montages on child care. Available for hire (minimum charge £10 plus carriage) from Hackney Flashers Collective, 152 Upper Street, London N1. Book well in advance.

Who's Looking after the Children? Photographic exhibition prepared by Southwark Trades Council's Nursery Campaign (emphasis on workplace provision). £5 plus carriage. Contact Linda Smith, 8 Halfort Road, London SE5.

Films

One, Two, Three. An 18-mm, 32-minute colour film about setting up and running a parent-controlled nursery in North London, the Children's Community Centre. Available from Liberation Films, £8. Book over the phone (01-450 7855) and confirm in writing to 2 Chichele Road, London NW2 3DA.

Who Needs Nurseries? We Do. A 16-mm, 11-minute colour cartoon film, giving facts about nursery provision from a child's point of view. Fact sheets and leaflets and a speaker from the group of women who made the film are available. £6 hire charge, plus postage; £1 for each additional day, £2 cancellation fee. Speaker £5 plus travelling expenses. Send s.a.e. for a booking form (giving at least one month's notice) to Leeds Animation Workshop, 20 Westminster Buildings, 31 New York Street, Leeds 2. Telephone 0532 460171.

Video

Colville Nursery Centre. A 25-minute video tape about setting up the Colville Nursery Centre. Hire from West London Media Workshop (Ken Lynham), telephone 01-969 1020. £5 plus postage for the video tape, or £10 plus travelling expenses for the tape, video equipment and a person.

Parenting a Child with Special Needs

Disablement Income Group. *An ABC of Services and Information for Disabled People.* DIG Charitable Trust, Attlee House, Toynbee Hall, Commercial Street, London E1 6LR.

Greenfeld, Josh. *A Child Called Noah: A Family Journey.* New York: Holt, Rinehart & Winston, 1972. On one special-needs child.

Kaufman, Barry N. *To Love Is To Be Happy With.* London: Souvenir Press, 1976. Parents, with the help of family and friends, create a special programme for a child who appears to be autistic.

Masse, Robert and Suzanne. *Journey.* New York: Knopf, 1975. The feelings and experiences involved in parenting a special-needs child.

Battered Wives

National Women's Aid Federation Report. *Battered Women, Refuges and Woman's Aid.* 374 Gray's Inn Road, London WC1.

Therapy

Avila, D. L., Combs, A. W., and Purkey, W. W. *The Helping Relationship Sourcebook.* Boston: Allyn & Bacon, 1972.

Ernst, Sheila and Goodison, Lucy. *In Our Own Hands: A Guide to Self-Help Therapy.*. London: Women's Press, 1981.

Red Therapy Collective. *Red Therapy.* 1978; from 52 Josephine Avenue, London SW2.

About the Authors

RUTH DAVIDSON BELL

As a child, not only was I taken care of by two loving and supportive, if a little disorganized, parents but I always felt that I could turn to grandparents, aunts, uncles, family friends, cousins and, later, teachers, for parenting when needed. Yet, with all that, eight years ago at age twenty-six, living three thousand miles from this vast cushion of support, my husband busy with new professorhood, I felt alone and overwhelmed when my son Zachary was born. Luckily, my pregnancy coincided with the first *Our Bodies, Ourselves* meetings, where I found a group of women who over time became my new support system – women who knew what I was experiencing because they had been there themselves. We worked closely together during the following years – writing together, teaching, growing, sharing the pain of personal tragedies and the pleasure of personal successes. Recently my son and I returned to Los Angeles and rejoined our family network. In my new project, an *Our Bodies, Ourselves* for teenagers, I feel I am carrying on the group's work in new territory. I deeply miss the collective, but daily feel the strength, independence and energy that grew in me through my eight years of working with them.

JOAN SHEINGOLD DITZION

I grew up in an extended child-centred family in New York City. My parents, Harry and Helen Sheingold, are both public school teachers with a deep sense of social conscience that I both respect and feel shaped by. As a young woman, I trained to create and teach art, married my husband Bruce, worked as an art educator in several different school and college settings, and began, in women's groups, seriously to think about feminist issues. I joined the *Our Bodies, Ourselves* group in its early days. I am not sure if it is totally coincidental that I gave birth to my first son, Robbie, while working on our first book, *Our Bodies, Ourselves*, and to my second son, Sam, while working on our second book, *Ourselves and Our Children*. Needless to say, I have had my hands full! There is a certain pleasure that having kids has given me that's like nothing else in my life. I feel a lot of love and energy in me for both my family and my work, and the daily challenge of my life is to balance these as creatively as I can.

PAULA BROWN DORESS

Growing up in a lively extended-family household with four adults who were new to this country, I had constant opportunity to compare differing attitudes and ways of living. The unique combination of tradition and scepticism provided the soil for a lifelong interest in how society shapes personal life. My husband, Irvin, and I have been married for fifteen years, and we are parents of two children, Hannah (twelve) and Benjamin (nine), who bring much warmth and joy into our lives. As our children get older I welcome the way that the balancing of work and family roles feels easier. Having been a community organizer, a teacher of women's studies, a writer and educator within the *Our Bodies, Ourselves* collective, I am moving into a new dimension of my work life by pursuing graduate studies in social psychology.

NANCY PRESS HAWLEY

The people and experiences that make up my life right now are: Joshua (twelve) and Gina (nine), my children – two people who have taught me to listen carefully and to love through harder times. Jeffrey, the man I've loved for five years and recently married – with whom I've learned that developing a relationship takes energy, humour, trust, disagreement, and playfulness. The women of *Our Bodies, Ourselves*, who have helped shape my vision of what is possible between people and have seen me through many changes. Flowers blooming in my backyard. Jogging city streets. Walking by the ocean. Delicious food. Laughing with friends. Savouring each emotion. I bring to this book a history of living in many different family forms and growing from each; five years of working with alcoholics and their families; and the experience of being in therapy myself and working as a therapist in private practice.

JANE KATES PINCUS

After fourteen years of living in the city, I moved to the country with Ed, my husband of eighteen years, my daughter, Sami, and my son, Ben. I left behind a caringly created support network – the *Our Bodies, Ourselves* group and many good friends. As I worked on the 'Informal Help' section of this book, I saw that I still reached back to the city for support, that I hadn't yet been able to move away. Finally, writing it focused my attention on people here. Especially from our neighbours, and from new friends, I learned to receive even when I can't give back in kind, and to appreciate the strange, unexpected forms help can take. Here in the country I learn farming skills, chase cows, and fall off horses. I batik and play my flute and work on women's health issues whenever I can. My family thrives.

ALICE JUDSON RYERSON

I am now living outside of Chicago in an old house which belonged to my family, where I manage Ragdale, a small retreat for working writers and artists. For many years I was a counselling psychologist in a new Quaker elementary school in Cambridge, Massachusetts. I also studied archaeology and worked on excavations in the Mediterranean, Iran, and – equally interesting – in New Hampshire, Martha's Vineyard, and Illinois. I have written poetry all my life, and have had a number of poems in little magazines. I was married for a long time, had been a mother four times, to Susan, Francie, Nora and Mitch, and a grandmother twice, to Noah and Sandy. Even though my children and grandchildren live far away from me, they continue willy-nilly to be of central interest in my life.

WENDY COPPEDGE SANFORD

I have done most of my growing up since I became a parent – and it continues! The facts about me are these: I am mother to a baseball-loving son named Matthew (who gave me a fielder's glove for my birthday), writer, editor, sex educator, Quaker, and seminary student. Although sometimes I don't play enough, when I do it's wonderful: I dance at every opportunity, and love to play music with friends on my new recorder. In the *Our Bodies, Ourselves* group, in my Friends Meeting, in the caring community of people known as the Northfield religious conference, in my apartment building full of children and cooperative adults, I am learning the richness of being interconnected with others. I bring this consciousness to the book, as I bring to it both the pain and the growing that come with divorce and single parenthood, the hope for mutuality in my relationships, and the effort to live my life with clarity, openness, and love.

JEANNE JACOBS SPEIZER

Calmly I entered the hospital on a beautiful spring day in May 1965 as the mother of an almost five-year-old, a three-year-old, and a baby on the way. I left the hospital three days later as the mother of four children under five! Now those children – Howie, eighteen; Linda, sixteen; Ilene, thirteen; and Sharlene, thirteen – are all teenagers, and during the time I was working on the teenager chapter I felt very qualified – sometimes overqualified – to talk about what it feels like to be an adult living in a household with adolescents.

As part of the apathetic generation of the fifties, I started my parenting experience intent on following all aspects of the feminine mystique. Luckily for me the women's movement came along, and I began to ask myself and my family hard questions. With the help of a couples group Frank and I began to explore new ways to live together as equals. We have made many changes in our relationship which have allowed us both to grow and change and to continue to like living together. For me the outward changes were returning to school to get a doctorate and joining the work world as a professional. The inward changes were an increased sense of pride about those things that I can do well and a decreased sense of guilt about only doing one sixth of the household jobs!

PEGGY NELSON WEGMAN

I grew up in a large, warm, boisterous family in New York. My early personal struggles left me with a strong desire to know what went on inside other people as well as myself, and to understand how personal change happens. I decided to become a therapist. A summer spent a dozen years ago as an awkward outsider, doing community organizing with migrant Appalachian families in Cleveland, left a stark, indelible imprint on my consciousness. For years afterwards I did therapy in many different settings and ways, working to find a mesh between the personal and the political. My image of my life is that of a patchwork quilt – not weaving a preplanned, predictable fabric but putting together related, sometimes clashing, pieces to create a harmonious whole. My husband, David, and our children – Jesse (five) and Marya (two) – are the joyous centre of this life. Energy that comes from living with them, from talking and sharing with friends, from my two enduring women's groups, and from work such as this book is leading me slowly but steadily toward a sense of who I am and what work I want to do.

DENNIE PALMER WOLF

I grew up in what most people would call a 'traditional nuclear family' – except that my father was as much a 'tinker' as a doctor and my mother was more 'firebrand' than housewife. Their out-of-the-ordinaryness, energy, and caring are probably the root of my own beliefs about juggling thinking and caring, work and family.

After two years of college, I married Tom Wolf and went to teach in a two-room school off the coast of Maine. Working with parents and children in a small traditional community gave me an intense interest in how anyone – child or adult – changes. I returned to school for degrees, went to Iowa to work on a farm-school with adolescents, ran a rural day care project, worked on a child-development curriculum for teenagers working in child-care settings, helped make films about the importance of play and art in the lives of children. Most recently I've settled down to a long-term study in which parents and observers work together to map out the course of early development. This research, my continuing relationship with my original family, and the experience of having two children, Lea and Alexi, have taught me to think about the imprint children leave on the lives of parents.

Index